The Jefferson-Hemings
Controversy

The Jefferson-Hemings Controversy

Report of the Scholars Commission

Edited by

Robert F. Turner

CAROLINA ACADEMIC PRESS
Durham, North Carolina

Library of Congress Cataloging-in-Publication Data

Scholars Commission on the Jefferson-Hemings Matter.
  The Jefferson-Hemings controversy : report of the Scholars Commission / edited by
Robert F. Turner.
    p. cm.
  ISBN 978-0-89089-085-1 (alk. paper)
  1. Jefferson, Thomas, 1743–1826--Relations with women. 2. Hemings, Sally. 3. Jefferson, Thomas, 1743–1826--Relations with slaves. 4. Jefferson, Thomas, 1743–1826--Family. I. Turner, Robert F. II. Title.
  E332.2.S35 2010
  973.4'6092--dc22   2010031551

Carolina Academic Press
700 Kent Street
Durham, NC 27701
Telephone (919) 489-7486
Fax (919) 493-5668
www.cap-press.com

This book is dedicated to the memory of our beloved colleagues

Professor Lance Banning
Hallam Professor of History
University of Kentucky
(January 24, 1942–January 31, 2006)

and

Professor Alf J. Mapp, Jr.
Eminent Scholar, Emeritus and Louis I. Jaffe Professor of History, Emeritus
Old Dominion University
(February 17, 1925–January 23, 2011)

Contents

Preface

For more than two centuries there have been rumors and allegations that Thomas Jefferson had a long-term sexual relationship with an enslaved woman named Sally Hemings. They originated from the pen of a disreputable journalist named James Thomson Callender in October 1802 and were picked up by Federalist editors and abolitionists in the United States and abroad. Most serious Jefferson scholars and many of Jefferson's political enemies dismissed them, in part because the notorious Callender lacked credibility and in part because the charge seemed so out of character for Jefferson. But the story resurfaced with the 1974 publication of Fawn Brodie's *Thomas Jefferson: An Intimate Biography* and became more believable in the 1997 book by Annette Gordon-Reed, *Thomas Jefferson and Sally Hemings*.

Perhaps the most decisive development in the case was the publication in the prestigious British science journal *Nature* in November 1998 of results of a DNA study linking Sally Hemings' youngest son to a Jefferson father. In January 2000 the Thomas Jefferson Memorial Foundation — owner of Jefferson's home at Monticello and long a protector of the former president's reputation — issued its own report concluding that President Jefferson fathered at least one and perhaps all of Sally Hemings' children.

Still, not everyone was convinced, and a group of doubters came together and established the Thomas Jefferson Heritage Society. Their first act was to seek a blue-ribbon reexamination of all of the evidence for and against Thomas Jefferson's paternity of one or more of Sally Hemings' children. They approached a diverse group of senior scholars with a simple request: carefully examine all of the evidence, draw your own conclusions, and issue a public report. The Heritage Society played no role in the actual investigation, and no member of the Scholars Commission was compensated in any way for his or her efforts in this process. This volume is the final product of that "Scholars Commission" inquiry.

After a year-long investigation involving individual research and group meetings in a hotel near Dulles Airport outside of Washington, D.C., summary majority and minority reports were drafted and approved by group members. In addition, members of the Commission were invited to express their personal views with individual statements concurring or dissenting from the majority report. In the pages that follow, the official Majority Report — adhered to by twelve of the thirteen members of the Commission — appears first, followed by the Minority Report. It should be emphasized that the statements of individual views that follow the official summary report are attributable only to the members whose names appear at the front of each such statement.

In an effort to provide some historical context to the reception given the report and relevant subsequent developments, the editor has attached a Postscript at the end of the volume. The views expressed therein are his alone, and the Postscript is not a part of the official Report of the Scholars Commission. Members of the Scholars Commission are listed with their academic institutions for purposes of identification only, and the views expressed herein are those of the individuals involved and should not be attributed to any university, organization, or other entity.

Copies of the majority and minority reports and supplemental statements of individual views were distributed at the National Press Club in Washington, D.C., on April 12, 2001. Members were then given additional time to expand and revise their individual statements, with the expectation that a book version of the Scholars Commission Report would appear the following year. Regrettably, publication was delayed because the professional duties of the chairman of the commission and editor of this volume involved the study of international terrorism and other aspects of national security law. As might be imagined, the demands on his time following the September 11, 2001, terrorist attacks left little time for extracurricular endeavors.

We are pleased finally to make this volume available. It does not pretend to be the final answer to the controversy, but we hope it will be useful in assisting interested readers to understand the relevant facts and issues and to identify points of disagreement between experts.

Robert F. Turner
Charlottesville, Virginia
February 14, 2011

Acknowledgments

Being asked to chair the Scholars Commission (SC), and to work with such a distinguished group of scholars, was among my most memorable and cherished professional activities. I want to thank the Thomas Jefferson Heritage Society (TJHS) and its members for giving me this opportunity, and all of my distinguished colleagues on the SC for their outstanding work in our shared search for the truth. I also owe each of them my profound apology for the long delay in finally getting this volume in print.

Sadly, because of my delay in getting the final manuscript ready for publication, two of the most active and distinguished members of the Scholars Commission passed away before the book was published. Professors Lance Banning and Alf Mapp attended all of our meetings and took an active part in bringing this work to fruition. Both were extraordinary human beings and superb Jefferson scholars. We have dedicated this volume to them, but I wanted to add a personal note to emphasize my own deep indebtedness to both of them. I like to think that although they are no longer among us, their contributions will live on for years to come through their writings and the work of their students. May they rest in peace with the knowledge that the world was a better place for their presence here.

I would be remiss if I did not thank several individuals who contributed to bringing this volume to fruition. Marilyn Yurk provided the guidance of a professional editor, as did Becky Gildersleeve. Carolyn Andersen provided valuable research assistance at a critical time.

I am also most grateful to Dr. Keith Sipe, Linda Lacy, Tim Colton, and their colleagues at Carolina Academic Press—who provided encouragement and a variety of other assistance in transforming the manuscript into a finished book. They patiently tolerated the numerous delays in the process caused by the post-9/11 increased demands on my time. I have worked with them on several other volumes over more than two decades, and they have never failed to exceed all reasonable expectations.

Additional acknowledgments for assistance with my own personal contributions to this volume appear at the end of the Introduction to my Individual Views.[1]

RFT

---

1. *See* pages 50–53.

Members of the Scholars Commission

Lance Banning
Hallam Professor of History
University of Kentucky
Professor Banning held the John Adams Chair in American History at the University of Groningen in the Netherlands and served as Leverhulme Visiting Professor at the University of Edinburgh. Two of his award-winning books (*The Jeffersonian Persuasion* and *Jefferson and Madison*) were nominated for the Pulitzer Prize in History.

James Ceaser
Professor of Government and Foreign Affairs
University of Virginia
Professor Ceaser is the author of *Reconstructing America* and has taught at Harvard University, the University of Montesquieu, the University of Basel, and Marquette University.

Robert H. Ferrell
Distinguished Professor of History, Emeritus
Indiana University
Professor Ferrell was educated and has also taught at Yale University. He is the author or editor of more than forty books, and was described as "the dean of American presidential historians" by the *Chicago Sun-Times.*

Charles R. Kesler
Dengler-Dykema Distinguished Professor of Government
Claremont McKenna College
Professor Kesler is Director of the Henry Salvatori Center at Claremont McKenna College and former chairman of its Department of Government. He has written extensively on the American founding and American political thought, and is co-editor of a widely-used edition of *The Federalist Papers*. He is the editor of *The Claremont Review* of *Books.*

Alf J. Mapp, Jr.
Eminent Scholar, Emeritus and Louis I. Jaffe Professor of History, Emeritus
Old Dominion University
Professor Mapp is the author of *Thomas Jefferson: A Strange Case of Mistaken Identity* (a Book-of-the-Month Club featured selection), *Thomas Jefferson: Passionate Pilgrim,* and has authored or edited more than another dozen books. A reference source for *Encyclopedia Britannica* and *World Book,* his numerous awards include Commonwealth of Vir-

ginia Cultural Laureate and a medal from the Republic of France's *Comite Francais du Bicentenaire de l'Independence des Etats-Unis.*

Harvey C. Mansfield
William R. Kenan, Jr. Professor of Government
Harvard University
Professor Mansfield has taught at Harvard for nearly four decades, chaired the Department of Government for several years, and is the author or editor of a dozen books, several of which address the era of the Founding Fathers. A former Guggenheim Fellow and National Endowment for the Humanities Fellow, he served as President of the New England Political Science Association and on the Council of the American Political Science Association.

David N. Mayer
Professor of Law and History
Capital University
Professor Mayer holds both a law degree and a Ph.D. in History, and is the author of *The Constitutional Thought of Thomas Jefferson* and numerous book chapters and articles concerning Thomas Jefferson. He earned his Ph.D. under the supervision of Professor Merrill Peterson.

Forrest McDonald
Distinguished Research Professor of History, Emeritus
University of Alabama
Professor McDonald has also taught at Brown University and was the James Pinckney Harrison Professor of History at the College of William & Mary. A former Guggenheim Fellow, he is the author of *The Presidency of Thomas Jefferson* and numerous other books, and his many awards and prizes include Thomas Jefferson Lecturer with the National Endowment for the Humanities.

Paul A. Rahe
Charles O. Lee and Louise K. Lee Professor in Western Heritage
Hillsdale College
Professor Rahe was educated at Yale and Oxford, where he was a Rhodes Scholar. He served as Chair of the University of Tulsa Department of History for several years, has also taught at Yale and Cornell, and is the author of the highly-acclaimed, three-volume set, *Republics Ancient and Modern: Classical Republicanism and the American Revolution.* He has received numerous academic prizes and held fellowships from the National Endowment for the Humanities, the Woodrow Wilson International Center for Scholars, the Center for the History of Freedom, and the Institute of Current World Affairs.

Thomas Traut
Professor of Biochemistry & Biophysics
School of Medicine
University of North Carolina
Professor Traut is Director of Graduate Studies and a former Ford Foundation and National Institute of Health Fellow. He is the author or coauthor of more than seventy publications, and shares his interest in Jefferson with his playwright wife, Karyn, who researched the Jefferson-Hemings relationship for seven years in preparation for her play *Saturday's Children.*

Robert F. Turner (Chairman)
Cofounder (1981), Center for National Security Law
University of Virginia School of Law
Professor Turner holds both professional and academic doctorates from the University of Virginia School of Law, and is a former Charles H. Stockton Professor of International Law at the U.S. Naval War College and a Distinguished Lecturer at West Point. He has taught both in Virginia's Department of Government and Foreign Affairs and the Law School, and is the author or editor of more than a dozen books. A former president of the congressionally established U.S. Institute of Peace, he has had a strong professional interest in Jefferson for more than four decades.

Walter E. Williams
John M. Olin Distinguished Professor of Economics
George Mason University
Professor Williams is Chairman of the Department of Economics at George Mason University and the author of six books. He is a nationally syndicated columnist.

Jean Yarbrough
Gary M. Pendy Professor of Social Sciences
Chair, Department of Government
Bowdoin College
Professor Yarbrough is a former National Endowment for the Humanities Bicentennial Fellow. She has lectured at the International Center for Jefferson Studies, is a consultant to the *Jefferson Papers* project, and serves on the editorial board of both the *Review of Politics* and *Polity*. Her numerous publications include *American Virtues: Thomas Jefferson on the Character of a Free People* and "Race and the Moral Foundation of the American Republic: Another Look at the Declaration."

The Jefferson-Hemings
Controversy

Scholars Commission on The Jefferson-Hemings Matter

Report
12 April 2001

Summary

The question of whether Thomas Jefferson fathered one or more children by his slave Sally Hemings is an issue about which honorable people can and do disagree. After a careful review of all of the evidence, the commission agrees unanimously that the allegation is by no means proven; and we find it regrettable that public confusion about the 1998 DNA testing and other evidence has misled many people. With the exception of one member, whose views are set forth both below and in his more detailed appended dissent, our individual conclusions range from serious skepticism about the charge to a conviction that it is almost certainly false.

In an effort to provide further clarification of our thinking about these issues, several members have written statements of individual views, which are appended to this report. They are the views of the scholars whose names appear thereon, and do not necessarily reflect the opinions of other members of the group. Although academic or other affiliations of members are listed for purposes of identification, nothing in this report is intended to reflect the opinion of any college, university, foundation, or other entity with which members of the group may currently or in the past have been associated.

Our dissenting member believes that there is not sufficient evidence to state conclusively one way or the other whether Thomas Jefferson fathered any children by Sally Hemings. Based upon the totality of the evidence that does exist, he finds the argument for Jefferson's paternity in the case of Eston Hemings somewhat more persuasive than the case against. He regards the question of the paternity of Sally Hemings' other children as unsettled.

Report of the Scholars Commission
on the Jefferson-Hemings Matter

Introduction

The release in November, 1998, of DNA evidence tying one of Sally Hemings' children to a Jefferson father, and the subsequent report by the Thomas Jefferson Memorial Foundation, have led to a widespread perception both within the academic community and among the public that science has conclusively proven that Thomas Jefferson had a sexual relationship with one of his slaves that produced one or more children. About a year ago, a number of Jefferson admirers formed the Thomas Jefferson Heritage Society (TJHS), and one of their first acts was to ask a group of Jefferson scholars to reexamine the issue carefully and issue a public report. This report is the result of that inquiry.

Background to the Controversy

On September 1, 1802, the Richmond *Recorder* published an article alleging that President Thomas Jefferson had fathered several children by his slave Sally Hemings. Its author was James Thomson Callender, a journalist who had fled Scotland for alleged sedition against the Crown and had briefly received financial support from Thomas Jefferson while Callender was supporting the Republican cause by attacking the incumbent Federalists. Callender was a talented writer with a proclivity for attacking those in power, and during his brief decade in America he vehemently attacked, among others, the first five men to serve as President of the United States. His skill with words exceeded his concern for the truth, and many of his allegations proved patently false. As President Jefferson learned more about the man's character, he rejected Callender's efforts to build a friendship and discouraged him from moving to the Charlottesville area, rebuffs which clearly stung the mercurial Callender. Callender's attack on Jefferson was prompted in part by President Jefferson's refusal to name him to the position of Postmaster for Richmond, Virginia, and was the fulfillment of a threat Callender had made to publish articles that would embarrass the President if the appointment was not forthcoming.

Callender had never visited Monticello, and he admitted that his charges were based upon conversations with people in the Charlottesville area who had noted the existence of light-skinned "mulatto" slaves on Jefferson's mountain. The story was picked up by the opposition Federalist press, but even some prominent Federalists dismissed it as untrue, recalling some of the falsehoods Callender had written about their own party leaders. Nevertheless, the story resurfaced from time to time over the decades and in 1873 was reinforced by allegations attributed to one of Sally Hemings' children and another former Monticello slave. Historians continued to discount it, but in 1974 Professor Fawn Brodie published *Thomas Jefferson: An Intimate History,* that gave the story new life and—while not well received by many historians—was a commercial success.

The story achieved attention again in 1997, with the publication by the University Press of Virginia of Professor Annette Gordon-Reed's *Thomas Jefferson and Sally Hemings.* Then, on November 5, 1998, *Nature* magazine published the results of DNA tests that strongly suggested that Sally Hemings' youngest son, Eston, had been fathered by someone with the same Y chromosome as Thomas Jefferson. This was not the same kind of precise "99.99 percent accurate" DNA testing that Americans learned of during the 1994 murder trial of O.J. Simpson, but rather was designed primarily to disprove paternity. The test could not distinguish between the offspring of male-line ancestors, and thus pointed the finger at Thomas Jefferson no more than it did at any of the other roughly two dozen known male descendants of Jefferson's grandfather present in Virginia at the time. Because of the general nature of the test, although no DNA from Thomas Jefferson was available, it was possible to use DNA extracted from the blood of descendants of Jefferson's paternal cousins. The resulting match did not prove Thomas Jefferson fathered Eston Hemings, but it did place him within a group of approximately twenty-five known Virginia men believed to carry the Jefferson family Y chromosome.

Nevertheless, the story was presented in much of the press as a conclusive confirmation of Thomas Jefferson's paternity of Eston and presumably other children born to Sally Hemings as well. The issue seemed conclusively resolved in January, 2000, when the Thomas Jefferson Memorial Foundation (TJMF) — the organization that maintains Thomas Jefferson's home at Monticello and has long been a champion of his legacy — issued a research report concluding there was a "strong likelihood that Thomas Jefferson and Sally Hemings had a relationship over time that led to the birth of one, and perhaps all, of the known children of Sally Hemings."

The Scholars Commission

Not everyone was convinced, however, and shortly after the TJMF report was released a group of Jefferson admirers, led by a former President of the Jefferson family's Monticello Association (MA), decided to establish the Thomas Jefferson Heritage Society (TJHS) in order to promote public education and understanding about the man. Convinced that Jefferson had not received a fair hearing, they decided to assemble a "blue ribbon commission" of prominent scholars for the purpose of reexamining the entire issue. This report is the result of that initiative.

The ground rules of our inquiry were simple: We were to have complete intellectual freedom to pursue the truth, including authority to establish our own procedures, to add new members, and to carry on our work independent of the influence of the TJHS or any other group. To help assure our independence, a private citizen who favored the idea of such an inquiry, but was not associated with the TJHS, generously contributed $20,000 to fund the work of the Scholars Commission — with the explicit understanding that she was funding scholarly research and would have neither influence on the outcome nor advanced knowledge of our conclusions prior to the public release of our report. Those funds have been used for travel, lodging, and publications costs. No member of the Scholars Commission has received compensation of any kind for their work on this project, and several have insisted on paying their own expenses to emphasize the independent nature of their involvement.

The Scholars Commission includes some of the nation's leading authorities on Thomas Jefferson and his era. Several members have written one or more books about Jefferson, and every member — even the lawyers in the group — holds a Ph.D. or other earned academic doctorate. Most of the members have either chaired their departments or held chaired professorships, and several serve or have served as "Eminent" or "Distinguished" professors. While our membership has fluctuated slightly over the months, the thirteen scholars who have persevered to the end come from prominent universities spread from southern California to Maine and then south as far as Alabama. They are trained in such diverse disciplines as history, political science, law, economics, and biochemistry. Most of us have studied Thomas Jefferson and his era for at least two decades, and we have held teaching or research appointments at Harvard, Yale, Stanford, Brown, Virginia, North Carolina, Kentucky, Indiana, Bowdoin, and many other respected institutions of higher learning.

We began this inquiry with diverse opinions on various aspects of the issue. Some members of the commission were avid admirers of Thomas Jefferson, others were not. At least one of us had for decades assumed the allegations of a Jefferson-Hemings relationship were true, many held serious doubts. But we each approached this inquiry as a scholarly search for the truth. Our initial work was done individually, with extensive communications by e-mail, letter, and telephone. After we had each had an opportunity to review all of the basic evidence and to pursue additional avenues of research we felt might prove fruitful, we gathered for approximately fifteen hours of face-to-face meetings at a hotel near Dulles Airport. Not surprisingly, our views in the end are not identical; but we have all reached general agreement on the conclusions which follow (with the exceptions noted). In addition, each of us was invited to submit additional views without restriction on any aspect of the issue we wished. It should be emphasized that the individual views which follow this report are only those of the members whose names appear thereon and should not be attributed to the Scholars Commission as a whole. Several of us have also elected to add our names to the individual views of other members; however this reflects a general agreement with their analysis and conclusions only, and responsibility for specific arguments and accuracy of facts belongs in each case to the primary author.

Before turning to the substance of our inquiry and our conclusions, we would be remiss if we did not acknowledge the cooperation of both John Works and the Thomas Jefferson Heritage Society, Daniel Jordan and Lucia Stanton of the Thomas Jefferson [formerly Memorial] Foundation, and James J. Truscott of the Monticello Association. None of these organizations has taken part formally in our deliberations, but all three have provided encouragement and have been fully responsive to any requests we have made of them for information. All three organizations received advance copies of our draft report as soon as it was completed earlier this month, and we are grateful for the feedback we have received. None of them, obviously, is responsible for any of our views.

We are also grateful to Ms. Karyn Traut—the playwright spouse of one of our members who researched this issue carefully for seven years more than a decade ago in preparation for writing *Saturday's Children,* who joined us at our Dulles meeting—and to Dr. Michael Moffitt of the Thomas Jefferson Heritage Society who has handled our finances and provided other administrative support.

Assessing the Evidence

The Almost Total Absence of Information about Sally Hemings

This has been in many respects a very frustrating issue to investigate, because there is so little information about Sally Hemings from which to work. One could probably write everything that we really know about her on an index card. Excluding Jefferson's various listings of slaves he owned and distribution lists for blankets and other supplies (on which she was treated like all of her relatives at Monticello), a few brief references from others about Sally being "mighty near white" and "very handsome" or "decidedly good looking," and notations about spending money for clothes and a smallpox vaccination while Sally was in Paris, Thomas Jefferson appears to have made reference to Sally Hemings in but four of his tens of thousands of letters. There is no evidence that he ever wrote to her directly or received mail from her (nor that she could have read them had he written), and the references that do exist consist of a note that "Maria's maid" (which might not even have been Sally) had a baby, two letters suggesting that "If Bet or Sally's children" came down with the measles they should be sent off the mountain, and finally a "d.o. Sally" notation in the margin of a letter saying that Jefferson was sending the bedding of Sally's older brother James Hemings back to America.

Indeed, the only credible surviving descriptions of Sally Hemings' talents or abilities are found in two 1787 letters from the remarkable Abigail Adams, wife of U.S. Minister to Great Britain John Adams, who kept the fourteen-year-old Sally and Jefferson's daughter Polly for two weeks when they arrived from Virginia on the way to join Jefferson in Paris. She described Sally as being "quite a child" and said that she "wants more care than the child [Jefferson's eight-year-old Polly], and is wholly incapable of looking properly after her, without some superiour to direct her." Based upon the surviving records, Sally Hemings appears to have been a very minor figure in Thomas Jefferson's life.

Assessing the Arguments

We began our inquiry by trying to identify all of the arguments and evidence in support of the proposition that Thomas Jefferson fathered one or more of Sally Hemings' children. We then looked carefully at the facts surrounding each of these allegations, and reached general conclusions on each. We then looked at evidence suggesting that Thomas Jefferson was not the father of any of Sally's children, and, after a careful review of the totality of the known evidence, we drew our individual conclusions and took a vote.

The DNA Tests

We are in full accord that much of the public has been misled about the significance of the DNA tests performed by Dr. Eugene Foster and his colleagues and first reported in the journal *Nature* in November 1998. While the tests were professionally done by distinguished experts, they were never designed to prove, and in fact could not have proven, that Thomas Jefferson was the father of any of Sally Hemings' children. The tests merely establish a strong probability that Sally Hemings' youngest son, Eston, was fathered by one of the more than two dozen Jefferson men in Virginia at the time, seven of whom there is documentary evidence to believe may well have been at Monticello when Eston was conceived.

Dr. Foster has cooperated fully in our inquiry and has readily acknowledged that the DNA tests do not suggest that Thomas Jefferson was Eston's father as opposed to someone like his younger brother Randolph or one of Randolph's sons. Indeed, every knowledgeable authority we have consulted, including other scientists who conducted the tests, has denied that these tests could possibly have distinguished among the male members of the Jefferson family in determining the paternity of Eston Hemings. These tests compared nineteen markers on the Y chromosomes of fourteen individuals: five living male-line descendants of two sons of Thomas Jefferson's paternal uncle, who was assumed to have the same Y chromosome as Jefferson's father and thus of Jefferson himself; three male-line descendants of three sons of the paternal grandfather of Peter and Samuel Carr;[1] five male-line descendants of two sons of Thomas Woodson; and one male-line descendant of Eston Hemings. The results showed a match between the haplotypes of the Jefferson descendants and the Eston Hemings descendant, but no other matches. In plain words, they showed that a descendant of one of Sally Hemings' children carries Jefferson genetic markers, not those of the Carr brothers, which effectively rules out the possible paternity of Sally Hemings' youngest child by any of the Carr brothers and points to some male Jefferson as his likely father. As we discuss below, the circumstantial case against some of Thomas Jefferson's relatives appears significantly stronger than the case against him.

The most important results from the DNA testing may well have been the determination that Thomas Woodson, long thought by many to be the "Tom" referred to by James Callender in 1802 as having been conceived by Sally Hemings in Paris and having a strong physical resemblance to the President, could *not* have been the son of Thomas Jefferson. Subsequent DNA testing of descendants of a third Woodson son confirmed the earlier results. Most of us believe this goes far towards undermining any remaining credibility of the original Callender allegations.

Madison Hemings' 1873 Statement

Nearly half a century after Thomas Jefferson's death a highly partisan newspaper editor in Pike County, Ohio, published an article alleged to be based upon an interview with Sally Hemings' second-youngest son, Madison. In the story, Madison is said to have claimed that Thomas Jefferson fathered all of his mother's children. This was followed shortly thereafter by an interview attributed to Israel Jefferson, another former Monticello slave, who corroborated Madison Hemings' story. There is no record that Sally Hemings or any of her other children ever alleged that Thomas Jefferson was their father.

There are many problems with Madison's story. He alleged that Thomas Jefferson became sexually involved with Sally Hemings in Paris, and when she refused to return to Virginia with him he promised to grant her special privileges and to free all of her children when they reached the age of twenty-one. Madison could not personally have known this information, and he provides no source for his alleged statements. Some sentences in his

1. Jefferson's sister, Martha, married his best friend, Dabney Carr, and they had three sons. Two of these, Peter and Samuel Carr, were alleged to have confessed to paternity of some of Sally's children, and were assumed by many to have been the father of all of her children.

account pertain to aspects of Jefferson's background that occurred long before Madison was born and that had been mentioned in published biographies of Jefferson. Several unusual words can be traced directly back to the 1802 Callender attacks on Jefferson, including the identical misspelling of a name.

Madison was also reported as saying that Dolley Madison was present at the time of his birth, and numerous reliable documents strongly suggest that this statement is false. Much of the information in the subsequent article attributed to Israel Jefferson is clearly false, and indeed he alleges recalling events that occurred before he was born. Thomas Jefferson's detailed records do not support Israel's claim to have held a position of great trust at Monticello, and Israel's allegation that his job included kindling Jefferson's fire each morning is expressly refuted by reliable sources published prior to his statement. On balance, the two alleged statements are clearly seriously flawed and do not outweigh the contradictory eyewitness accounts of others that exist on many of these issues.

The Correlation Between Thomas Jefferson's Visits to Monticello and Sally Hemings' Conceptions

Although Thomas Jefferson was absent from Monticello roughly half the time when Sally Hemings was having children, he appears to have been there when most and perhaps all of her children were conceived. (He was absent for most of the conception window for her son Beverly.) Several of us found this to be the most compelling evidence of a sexual relationship between Thomas Jefferson and Sally Hemings, and thus it received extensive consideration during our deliberations.

We believe that the simplest explanation for the long-known coincidence of Thomas Jefferson's return to Monticello and Sally Hemings' pregnancies is that Monticello was normally kept locked during Jefferson's absence, and thus his return would prompt visits to the mountain by numerous friends and relatives—including other candidates for the paternity of Sally Hemings' children such as the President's brother, nephews and cousins.

The Visitation-Conception Issue and the Monte Carlo Study

None of us was impressed by the "Monte Carlo" statistical study published in the *William & Mary Quarterly* and appended to the Monticello report, which for inexplicable reasons postulated both that there could only be a single father for all of Sally Hemings' children and that rival candidates to Thomas Jefferson would have had to arrive and depart on the exact same days as did the President. The assumption of random behavior by Jefferson's friends and relatives also makes little sense to us, as they would certainly have been far more likely to visit after he had returned from extended absences in Washington or elsewhere. Some of the data used in this study for the days Thomas Jefferson was at Monticello during the weeks before and after the conception of Eston Hemings were also inaccurate.

Our inquiry suggests not only that there is no serious evidence that Sally Hemings was monogamous, but there is very credible eyewitness testimony that she was often sexually involved with a man other than Thomas Jefferson. The Monte Carlo study and many other arguments on this issue are premised on the assumption that one man must have fathered all of Sally Hemings' children. There is reasonably credible evidence based upon eyewitness testimony that Jefferson's nephews Samuel and Peter Carr admitted paternity of at least some of Sally Hemings' children, and the DNA tests show only that they could not have been the father of Eston. Even without considering Thomas Jefferson's advanced age (sixty-four) and health, if the question is changed from trying to place a single suspect at Monticello nine months prior the birth of all of Sally's children to simply trying to identify the Jefferson men who were likely to have been in the Monticello area when Eston Hemings was conceived, the statistical case for Thomas Jefferson's paternity of Eston, based upon DNA evidence alone, falls below fifteen percent.

The Allegation that Sally Hemings and Her Children Received "Special Treatment" at Monticello

At first glance, one of the most powerful arguments in favor of Jefferson's paternity is the claim that Sally and her children received "special treatment" from Thomas Jefferson at Monticello. This claim overlooks the fact that virtually all of the children and grandchildren of Betty Hemings (Sally's mother) received special treatment at Monticello; and, within that family, Sally and her children appear to have received less favorable treatment than many. The widespread belief that Thomas Jefferson freed all of Sally's children when they reached the age of twenty-one is also simply not true.

Indeed, other than appearing upon various lists of Monticello slaves recording such things as clothing and blanket distribution (where Sally was treated exactly like her siblings), Sally and her children receive less frequent mention in Jefferson's records than most of her siblings. Princeton University Press recently published two volumes totaling more than 1,400 pages of Jefferson's *Memorandum Books,* containing thousands of entries documenting his financial transactions and the like. Sally's sons Madison and Eston share a single listing, indicating that on December 11, 1824, they sold 100 cabbages to Thomas Jefferson for two dollars—the same rate he paid other members of the Hemings family at that time.

Except for a brief period in Paris, when Sally's two dollars a month salary was far less than her brother or any of Jefferson's other servants were receiving, neither Sally Hemings nor any of her children received either a salary or recorded gifts from Thomas Jefferson—unlike many of her relatives. One of the clear reasons for Madison Hemings' obvious bitterness in the 1873 story in the *Pike County Republican* was that his alleged "father" (Thomas Jefferson) had never given him or his siblings any special attention—in sharp contrast to the loving attention Jefferson displayed towards his grandchildren by his daughters.

Even had Jefferson given special consideration to Sally's children, this would not have been proof that he was their father. First of all, by blood they were legally "white" (and, along with Sally, appeared as free whites in the 1830 Albemarle County census following Jefferson's death), and they were also quite possibly Thomas Jefferson's relatives. Sally was alleged by some to be the half-sister of Jefferson's wife Martha, and her children would also have been President Jefferson's nieces and nephews if their fathers had been either one of the Carr brothers or a member of Randolph Jefferson's family.

One of the greatest myths of this controversy is the allegation that Jefferson freed Sally Hemings and all of her children in his will or when they reached the age of 21. In reality, Sally's first child to reach that age was Beverly Hemings, who finally ran away from

Monticello at age twenty-four. Her only daughter to reach twenty-one ran away that year, but reportedly returned and was later given money and put on a stage for Philadelphia by Jefferson's overseer at Thomas Jefferson's request. We have no evidence of how old Harriet was at the time, or why this was done, but she was probably well past her twenty-first birthday; and the explanation for facilitating her departure may well have been Jefferson's well-documented human compassion rather than fulfillment of a promise allegedly made in Paris to Sally Hemings.

It is true that Sally's two youngest children, Madison and Eston, were freed in Jefferson's will. But according to the alleged "treaty" negotiated in Paris, Madison should have been freed when he turned twenty-one, well before Jefferson even wrote his will. He was twenty-two before he was actually given his freedom. More importantly, three other male members of the Hemings family (most of the brothers and nephews of Sally Hemings remaining at Monticello when Jefferson died) were freed in that will, and each of them received far more favorable treatment (including such things as money, tools, and homes on Jefferson's land) than did Sally's sons—who received no additional benefits and were required to work for Sally's brother, John Hemings, for a year before receiving their freedom. Two of Betty Hemings' sons were legally manumitted by Thomas Jefferson in the 1790s. Of her seven male descendants known to have been at Monticello at the time of Jefferson's death, all but two of them were freed in his will and a sixth (Sally's brother Peter) turned up as a free citizen of Albemarle county shortly after apparently being purchased by a relative for one dollar. We don't know why Sally's nephew Wormley Hughes, brother to Jefferson's most trusted (and most rewarded in his will) slave, was not freed, but he remained a trusted slave in the family of Jefferson's daughter and was eventually freed by her. Sally Hemings was not freed by Thomas Jefferson; and we are skeptical both that Sally Hemings would not have bothered to demand her own eventual freedom while negotiating the freedom of children she would not start having for more than five years, and that Thomas Jefferson would have made no provision for her freedom had they really been lovers for decades. The freedom granted to Sally Hemings' sons in Jefferson's will is consistent with his treatment of most other male descendants of Betty Hemings, and might also be warranted by the fact that, once freed, they were probably legally white under existing Virginia law.

The Physical Resemblance of Some of Sally Hemings' Children to Thomas Jefferson

There are at least ten possible fathers for Sally Hemings' children who could have passed down genetic material that might produce children physically resembling Thomas Jefferson and who are thought to have visited Monticello regularly during the years Sally Hemings was having children. Historically, the most common suspects were Peter and Samuel Carr, sons of Thomas Jefferson's sister Martha and his best friend Dabney Carr. Subsequent to the DNA tests, the most probable candidate for paternity of Eston Hemings was likely Randolph Jefferson, Thomas Jefferson's much younger brother, or perhaps one of at least four of Randolph's five sons. A little more than two weeks before Sally is estimated to have conceived Eston, Thomas Jefferson wrote to Randolph and informed him that his twin sister, Anna Scott Marks, had just arrived for a visit and that "we shall be happy to see you also." It is reasonable to assume that Randolph, a widower, would have brought his five sons (four and perhaps five of whom were 17–27 years of age) for the visit, and any of them could have also passed along Jefferson DNA that would have been consistent with Dr. Foster's DNA study and could have produced children resembling Thomas Jefferson.

The Original Accusations of James Thomson Callender

The 1802 allegations of a Jefferson-Hemings sexual relationship are highly unpersuasive. Callender was notorious for taking a small truth and multiplying it into a large falsehood. In this case, his "truth" was the existence of several light-skinned slaves at Monticello. This fact had been observed by European visitors as early as 1796, when Sally Hemings' first known child was an infant; and Sally and her siblings were presumably the basis of the stories. Callender was correct in noting that Sally had given birth to several light-skinned children, but his primary focus was on a ten- to twelve-year-old boy named "Tom," who was said to bear a "striking resemblance" to President Jefferson. For nearly two centuries, scholars who gave any credence at all to Callender's allegations assumed that "Tom" was Thomas Woodson, whose descendants have long asserted that this was the case. We have reached no conclusions on whether Thomas Woodson was the son of Sally Hemings. It would seem strange, if there was no "Tom" at Monticello fitting this description in 1802, that one of Jefferson's defenders would not have made the point—and at least one of them admitted there was such a child. There is no evidence of any other "Tom" who might fit this description, nor is there any evidence other than Woodson family oral history that Tom Woodson was ever at Monticello. The DNA tests have shown conclusively that Thomas Woodson could not have been Thomas Jefferson's child, but did not address his possible biological relationship with Sally Hemings.

The Oral History of Sally Hemings' Descendants

Part of the case for Thomas Jefferson's paternity of Sally Hemings' children is based upon oral history passed through many generations of three families. While oral history can be a useful, and is often a neglected, source of historical knowledge, in this case some of the family traditions are in conflict both with the DNA evidence and with each other.

For example, the assertion in the Research Committee report of the Thomas Jefferson Memorial Foundation that "The family history of Sally Hemings's descendants, transmitted orally over many generations, states that Hemings and Thomas Jefferson are their ancestors," is only partly accurate. In fact, these statements are believed to have been passed down by one known line of Sally's children, the descendants of Madison Hemings. Since we already know that Madison is alleged to have made this claim in 1873, we need not rely on oral history as authority. However, since Madison did not provide a source for his claim, it is difficult to establish whether it is true or not; and the fact that he presumably told his children as well as a newspaper editor obviously adds nothing to the credibility of his basic account.

Similarly, Thomas Woodson's descendants passed down this history, but since the recent DNA tests have ruled out Thomas Jefferson as Thomas Woodson's father, this oral history would seem clearly to be in error. We express no view on whether Thomas Woodson was Sally Hemings' son, although some members of our group believe that is not an unreasonable conclusion. No descendants of Harriet or Beverly Hemings have been located.

Most interestingly, until they were persuaded by Professor Fawn Brodie in the mid-1970s that Thomas Jefferson was their ancestor, the oral history of the descendants of Eston

Hemings was that his father was not Thomas Jefferson but an "uncle"—or perhaps a cousin. This would seem to be stronger evidence than most oral history, as it is essentially an "admission against interest." Presumably, because of Thomas Jefferson's great fame, most people would be honored to claim they were his descendants.

More importantly, this history is consistent with the theory that Thomas Jefferson's younger brother, Randolph, was Eston's father. This is consistent with the DNA tests. Thomas Jefferson's last surviving uncle died three decades before Eston Hemings was born, but brother Randolph was often referred to as "Uncle Randolph" because of his relationship to Thomas Jefferson's daughters, the eldest of whom was in general charge of Monticello during the entire period that Eston Hemings would have remembered.

Other Arguments

We considered as well a number of arguments that have been raised by supporters of the theory that Thomas Jefferson fathered children by Sally Hemings. For example, they quote several people who said they believed the story. But as we examined each of these, we found them unpersuasive. Georgia Federalist Thomas Gibbons did allege in an 1802 letter that the story was "as correct as truth itself," but there is no evidence he ever went near Monticello (he admitted he had never seen any of Sally's children) and he was a bitter political enemy of the President's. Among other things, Gibbons was one of the famous "midnight judges" appointed by the outgoing President John Adams, and he was denied his life-tenure job by Thomas Jefferson.

We discovered that another of these "sources," Vermont schoolteacher Elijah P. Fletcher, who claimed that while traveling through Charlottesville he encountered numerous people who confirmed the truth of the story, had shared a stagecoach from Washington, D.C., to Charlottesville with one of Thomas Jefferson's bitterest enemies, John Kelly, who gave Fletcher the guided tour of Charlottesville that produced these anti-Jefferson remarks. Kelly had owned the land on which Jefferson originally hoped to build the University of Virginia; but when he learned the offer to purchase was indirectly for the benefit of Thomas Jefferson he remarked "I will see him at the devil before he shall have it at any price." With Kelly as his tour guide, it is not surprising that Fletcher was exposed to many critics of the President.

We felt that the advocates of Thomas Jefferson's paternity have dealt too summarily with a variety of pieces of evidence that warrant more serious consideration. For example, the only eyewitness account pertaining to Sally Hemings' sexual behavior was made by Monticello overseer Edmund Bacon, who noted the rumors that Harriet Hemings was Thomas Jefferson's child and remarked: "She was not his daughter; she was _____'s daughter. I know that. I have seen him come out of her mother's room many a morning when I went up to Monticello very early." Bacon appears to be a credible witness, and unlike both the Hemings and Jefferson descendants, does not have an obvious interest in the outcome. But the Thomas Jefferson Memorial Foundation report dismisses his statement as having "problems of chronology" and moves on—without the slightest evidence beyond her son's assertion—to conclude that Sally must have been monogamous.

It is true that Harriet Hemings was conceived in 1800, and Bacon did not begin his service as overseer until six years later (although he worked at least some at Monticello prior to that). But if he saw another man repeatedly leaving Sally's room in the early morning hours, that strongly refutes the assumption that Sally Hemings was involved in a monogamous sexual relationship with Thomas Jefferson; and if his observations occurred after he became overseer they become tremendously more important in our search for the father of Eston Hemings, who was conceived around August 1807. Indeed, Bacon's statement may be the single most important piece of evidence in the case, given the general lack of reliable information.

We have as well a variety of surviving statements by, or attributed to, Jefferson's descendants, including his daughter Martha, grandson Thomas Jefferson Randolph, and granddaughter Ellen Randolph Coolidge. Some of these statements seem credible, either because the witness was writing in confidence to a loved one or because they included "admissions against interest" that one would not normally expect to find in a "coverup." Several of them also reinforce each other on various points, suggesting that if the information was not believed to be accurate there must have been a conspiracy to conceal the truth. There are various accounts attributed to Thomas Jefferson Randolph, for example, asserting that he claimed to have overheard Samuel and Peter Carr admitting paternity for at least some of Sally's children.

Ellen Randolph Coolidge's letters seem particularly credible, in part because she seems to have been willing to make public embarrassing family secrets (including the erratic behavior of a father she dearly loved). We discovered that a key sentence in one of her most important letters about this issue had been mistranscribed so as to reverse her clear meaning in the appendix to one scholar's book on this controversy, and the transcription error has unfortunately clearly influenced the scholarship of others.

We also looked at the fact that certain types of evidence that one would normally expect to find had this relationship existed do not appear to exist. Both in Paris and at Monticello, Thomas Jefferson was surrounded by visitors, with as many as fifty unannounced guests showing up at one time at his home. His children, grandchildren, and overseer allegedly had regular access to his room day or night, and no one could have entered without being subject to observation by others. And yet, throughout all the years with hundreds and hundreds of visitors, there is not a single record of anyone ever observing the slightest hint of behavior linking Thomas Jefferson and Sally Hemings romantically. No one reported seeing so much as a glance between them that suggested Callender may have been right.

Nor is there any clear evidence that Sally Hemings or any of her children ever alleged that Thomas Jefferson was her lover or their father, save for the statement attributed to an aging and clearly bitter Madison Hemings nearly five decades after Thomas Jefferson's death. Surely, if they believed the famous President to be their father, they would have found it to their benefit to make this fact known to others before 1873.

Among the strongest arguments against Thomas Jefferson's paternity of any of Sally's children are the things that one must accept as true to believe the story. Whatever one thinks of Thomas Jefferson's actual character, there can be little doubt that he was deeply concerned about his reputation. Nowhere was this more clear than in his desire for the love and respect of his daughters and other family members. While Jefferson presumably could have had his pick of a large number of beautiful and talented women in Paris, and he wrote flirtatious letters to several women after the death of his wife, it is not clear that any of these well-documented flirtations led to sexual "affairs." Yet we are asked to believe that Jefferson would have entrusted his reputation to the discretion of a fifteen- or sixteen-year-old child, who in the judgment of the respected Abigail Adams required more "care" than Jefferson's eight-year-old daughter, and who was presumably in daily contact with his young daughters.

Had Thomas Jefferson had such a sexual relationship, we find it very difficult to believe that he would have selected as his companion the teenaged maid to his young daughters. Many scholars who believe the allegations acknowledge that it would have been very difficult to keep the relationship secret from his daughters. We share that view, and we think it highly unlikely that Thomas Jefferson would have placed at risk the love and respect of his young children in this manner. Further, a prominent scholar who now embraces the story of a Jefferson-Hemings sexual liaison—and who has also studied the unpublished papers of Jefferson's daughter Martha—concluded that she must have been "in denial," as there is no indication that she was intentionally covering up her father's relationship with Sally Hemings. We believe a simpler explanation is that she honestly did not believe the relationship existed.

To accept the allegations, we must believe that Thomas Jefferson—whose deep love and open displays of affection for his daughters and grandchildren was so evident—totally rejected the sons born to him by a woman some would have us believe he dearly loved. We must believe as well that, in his final days, as he prepared his will, he freed the two sons he had always ignored—presumably knowing that freeing Sally's remaining children would be viewed by his critics as evidence of his guilt—yet made absolutely no provision for Sally Hemings' future.

Only a single one of Thomas Jefferson's known friends, University of Virginia cofounder John Hartwell Cocke, has been identified as believing the Callender allegations; but General Cocke did not become close to Jefferson until long after all of Sally Hemings' children were born. Nor does he provide any hint that his belief was based upon more than speculation and rumors. Other disparaging comments that he made about Thomas Jefferson suggest that his feelings about his famous associate in the founding of the University of Virginia may have been a bit cooler than believed by some, and indeed may have been affected by a measure of jealousy. In contrast to this single voice (one can not even characterize him as a "witness," since his observations of Thomas Jefferson occurred long after the events at issue occurred), the people who lived with Thomas Jefferson and worked with him most closely uniformly rejected the allegations, as did many of his most bitter political enemies.

And finally, to accept the allegation that Thomas Jefferson was the father of Eston Hemings, we must accept the allegations of Jefferson's personal enemies like scandalmonger James Callender and Georgia Federalist Thomas Gibbons—neither of whom had apparently ever even been to Monticello, and both of whom wrote about Sally Hemings in the most racist and defamatory manner—over the family traditions of Eston Hemings' own descendants, who passed down the oral history that he was *not* Thomas Jefferson's child but rather the son of an "uncle." (Could this have been "Uncle Randolph?") Since this account is essentially an "admission against interest" (assuming that most Americans would take pride in being descendants of the famous President), surely it warrants more respect than this.

Other Candidates for the Paternity of Eston Hemings

If Thomas Jefferson was not the father of Eston Hemings, the obvious question arises: "Who was?" Jefferson scholars for nearly two centuries have until very recently dismissed the Callender allegations, and without a great deal of apparent thought simply accepted the various reports that Thomas Jefferson Randolph had overheard Peter and Samuel Carr confessing to the paternity of Sally Hemings' children. But the 1998 DNA tests clearly ruled out any member of the Carr family as a possible father of Eston Hemings.

Candidly, we don't know who fathered Eston Hemings. The DNA tests narrowed the possible fathers down to a group of about two dozen known Jefferson males in Virginia at the time, and there is at least a theoretical possibility that there may have been illegitimate sons carrying the Jefferson Y chromosome among the slaves passed down from Thomas Jefferson's grandfather, through his father, to the President. But when we consider things like the geographic location of many of these Jefferson men, the list of "most likely suspects" narrows quickly to Thomas Jefferson and perhaps a half dozen of his relatives. We know almost nothing about many of them.

Emphasizing again that we are not reaching a finding that Randolph Jefferson was Eston's father, it does appear that the circumstantial case that Eston Hemings was fathered by the President's younger brother is many times stronger than the case against the President himself. Among the considerations which might point to Randolph are:

- In *Memoirs of a Monticello Slave,* former slave Isaac Jefferson asserts that when Randolph Jefferson visited Monticello, he "used to come out among black people, play the fiddle and dance half the night...." In contrast, we have not a single account of Thomas Jefferson spending his nights socializing with the slaves in such a manner.

- As already noted, we have Jefferson's letter inviting Randolph (and presumably his sons as well) to come to Monticello shortly before Sally became pregnant with Eston. It was common for such visits to last for weeks.

- Pearl Graham, who did original research among the Hemings descendants in the 1940s and believed the story that Thomas Jefferson fathered Sally Hemings' children, wrote in a 1958 letter to a leading Jefferson scholar at Princeton University that a granddaughter of one of Sally Hemings' children had told her that Randolph Jefferson "had colored children" of his own.

- Until Professor Fawn Brodie persuaded the descendants of Eston Hemings that President Jefferson was his father, their family oral history had passed down that Eston was fathered by "Thomas Jefferson's uncle." That is not possible, as both of his paternal uncles died decades before Eston was conceived. But to Martha Jefferson Randolph, who was generally in charge of Monticello during Eston Hemings' entire memory there, her father's younger brother was "Uncle Randolph" — and he was referred to as such in family letters.

- We don't know exactly when Randolph's first wife died, but we do know that he remarried — to a very controlling woman — shortly after Eston Hemings was born. About the same time, Thomas Jefferson retired from public office and spent the rest of his life at Monticello, where he could presumably have had access to Sally Hemings any night he wished. But Sally, although only in her mid-thirties, gave birth to no known children after Eston was born in 1808. Even the Thomas Jefferson Memorial Foundation report acknowledges that Sally's childbearing years may have corresponded to the years in which Randolph Jefferson was a widower.

Randolph Jefferson had at least four sons between the ages of seventeen and twenty-seven when Eston was conceived, and if one accepts the data relied upon in the Monticello report the number was five. One might expect the sex drives of young men in this age bracket to be greater than that of the sixty-four-year-old President, and with their father's reported example there is no reason to assume they were under strong social pressure at home to refrain from sexual relations with female slaves. Again, we have not the slightest bit of direct evidence that any of them ever fathered a child by Sally Hemings; but that puts them in essentially the same category as Thomas Jefferson as possible suspects.

A review of Thomas Jefferson's visitation patterns to Monticello does, indeed, show a remarkable correlation between his arrivals and Sally Hemings' pregnancies—some of the time. Indeed, she seems to have become pregnant remarkably quickly (in less than a month for three of her children) after he returned home; with the caveat, again, of *some* of the time. But between the years of her first conception and the birth of her last child, Thomas Jefferson came to Monticello more than twenty times, and Sally Hemings is believed to have become pregnant only about five or six times. Why did she become pregnant within days of his arrival on some occasions, and not become pregnant when on other occasions he returned and stayed months at a time? Why, if the alleged relationship began in Paris, did it take her more than five years to conceive a second child? Why did Sally stop having children when Thomas Jefferson returned permanently to Monticello?

The answer to all of these questions is *we don't know;* but it is not difficult to realize that there may have been another variable in the equation. When Thomas Jefferson returned home, his friends and relatives often came to Monticello to welcome him home; and some of those times Sally Hemings very quickly became pregnant. (Recent scientific studies strongly suggest that fecundity—a man's ability to father a child within a given period of time—decreases significantly as he ages.) Could the explanation for Sally getting pregnant in a matter of days on some of Thomas Jefferson's visits, and her not becoming pregnant on numerous other occasions when he remained at Monticello for many months at a time, be that her lover was one of his relatives who did not make it to Monticello every time the President returned home? We don't know, but it is among the simpler explanations—and it has the further virtue of being consistent with the eyewitness testimony of Edmund Bacon that while arriving for work early in the morning he often saw a man who was not Thomas Jefferson leaving Sally Hemings' room.

We were not tasked with the job of identifying the father(s) of Sally Hemings' children, and that has not been a primary focus of our inquiry. Our mandate was to examine the case against Thomas Jefferson. Trying to prove a negative is usually difficult. But we have found most of the arguments used to point suspicion toward Thomas Jefferson to be unpersuasive and often factually erroneous. Not a single member of our group, after an investigation lasting roughly one year, finds the case against Thomas Jefferson to be highly compelling, and the overwhelming majority of us believe it is very unlikely that he fathered any children by Sally Hemings. Certainly, there were far more likely suspects, including brother Randolph and his sons, for the paternity of Eston and perhaps other Hemings children. The evidence that the Carr brothers might have fathered some of Sally's older children remains unchallenged by the DNA tests, and may be true. Given Edmund Bacon's eyewitness account, making an assumption that Sally Hemings could not have had more than one father to her children makes no sense unless one is prepared to exclude Thomas Jefferson as a possible father. We make no finding that Sally was not monogamous (with someone other than Thomas Jefferson), because the evidence is simply not there to resolve that issue either way. Madison asserts that Sally's mother had at least four different fathers to her children, and the Bacon testimony makes it very illogical to assume that Sally was both monogamous and sexually involved with Thomas Jefferson.

Conclusions

We do not pretend that this is the final word on the issue, and it is possible that future developments in science or newly discovered evidence will warrant a reconsideration of our conclusions. We understand that DNA might be obtained from the grave of William Beverly Hemings, son of Madison Hemings, which could provide new information of relevance to this inquiry. If his Y chromosome did not match that of Eston Hemings and the descendants of Field Jefferson, that would confirm that Sally Hemings could not have been monogamous. A match with the Carr family would also be significant. A match with Eston might strengthen the case for Sally's monogamy, but would not conclusively establish even which Jefferson male was the father of either child. Our thoughts here are further tempered by our concerns about the ethical propriety of disturbing the remains of the dead in the interest of historical curiosity. It may also prove useful to search for evidence concerning the whereabouts of Sally Hemings over the years. This could prove decisive, but we are not optimistic about the existence of additional records of this nature at this point in history.

In the end, after roughly one year of examining the issues, we find the question of whether Thomas Jefferson fathered one or more children by his slave Sally Hemings to be one about which honorable people can and do disagree. However, it is our unanimous view that the allegation is by no means proven; and we find it regrettable that public confusion about the 1998 DNA testing and other evidence has misled many people into believing that the issue is closed. With the exception of one member, whose views are set forth both below and in the more detailed appended dissent, our individual conclusions range from serious skepticism about the charge to a conviction that it is almost certainly untrue.

For the Majority

Lance Banning

Professor of History
University of Kentucky

Professor Banning formerly held the John Adams Chair in American History at the University of Groningen in the Netherlands and this fall will serve as Leverhulme Visiting Professor at the University of Edinburgh. Two of his award-winning books (*The Jeffersonian Persuasion* and *Jefferson and Madison*) were nominated for the Pulitzer Prize in History.

James Ceaser

Professor of Government and Foreign Affairs
University of Virginia

Professor Ceaser is the author of *Reconstructing America* and has taught at Harvard University, the University of Montesquieu, the University of Basel, and Marquette University.

Robert H. Ferrell

Distinguished Professor of History, Emeritus
Indiana University

Professor Ferrell was educated and has also taught at Yale University. He is the author or editor of more than forty books and was described as "the dean of American presidential historians" by the *Chicago Sun-Times.*

Charles R. Kesler

Dengler-Dykema Distinguished Professor of Government
Claremont McKenna College

Professor Kesler is Director of the Henry Salvatori Center at Claremont McKenna College and former chairman of its Department of Government. He has written extensively on the American founding and American political thought, and is co-editor of a widely-used edition of *The Federalist Papers*. He is the editor of *The Claremont Review of Books*.

Harvey C. Mansfield

William R. Kenan, Jr. Professor of Government
Harvard University

Professor Mansfield has taught at Harvard for nearly four decades, chaired the Department of Government for several years, and is the author or editor of a dozen books, several of which address the era of the Founding Fathers. A former Guggenheim Fellow and National Endowment for the Humanities Fellow, he served as President of the New England Political Science Association and on the Council of the American Political Science Association.

Alf J. Mapp, Jr.

Eminent Scholar, Emeritus and Louis I. Jaffe Professor of History, Emeritus
Old Dominion University

Professor Mapp is the author of *Thomas Jefferson: A Strange Case of Mistaken Identity* (a Book-of-the-Month Club featured selection), *Thomas Jefferson: Passionate Pilgrim*, and has authored or edited more than another dozen books. A reference source for *Encyclopedia Britannica* and *World Book*, his numerous awards include Commonwealth of Virginia Cultural Laureate and a medal from the Republic of France's *Comite Francais du Bicentenaire de l'Independence des Etats-Unis*.

David N. Mayer

Professor of Law and History
Capital University

Professor Mayer holds both a law degree and a Ph.D. in History, and is the author of *The Constitutional Thought of Thomas Jefferson* and numerous book chapters and articles concerning Thomas Jefferson. He earned his Ph.D. under the supervision of Professor Merrill Peterson.

Forrest McDonald

Distinguished Research Professor of History, Emeritus
University of Alabama

Professor McDonald has also taught at Brown and was the James Pinckney Harrison Professor of History at the College of William & Mary. A former Guggenheim Fellow, he is the author of *The Presidency of Thomas Jefferson* and numerous other books, and his many awards and prizes include Thomas Jefferson Lecturer with the National Endowment for the Humanities.

Thomas Traut

Professor of Biochemistry & Biophysics
School of Medicine
University of North Carolina

Professor Traut is Director of Graduate Studies and a former Ford Foundation and National Institute of Health Fellow. He is the author or coauthor of more than seventy publications, and shares his interest in Jefferson with his playwright wife, Karyn, who researched the Jefferson-Hemings relationship for seven years in preparation for her play *Saturday's Children*.

Robert F. Turner (Chairman)

University of Virginia

Professor Turner holds both professional and academic doctorates from the University of Virginia School of Law, and is a former Charles H. Stockton Professor of International Law at the U.S. Naval War College and a Distinguished Lecturer at West Point. He has taught both in Virginia's Department of Government and Foreign Affairs and the Law School, and is the author or editor of more than a dozen books. A former president of the congressionally established U.S. Institute of Peace, he has had a strong professional interest in Jefferson for nearly four decades.

Walter E. Williams

John M. Olin Distinguished Professor of Economics
George Mason University

Professor Williams is Chairman of the Department of Economics at George Mason University and the author of six books. He is a nationally syndicated columnist.

Jean Yarbrough

Gary M. Pendy Professor of Social Sciences
Chair, Department of Government
Bowdoin College

Professor Yarbrough is a former National Endowment for the Humanities Bicentennial Fellow. She has lectured at the International Center for Jefferson Studies, is a consultant to the *Jefferson Papers* project, and serves on the editorial board of both the *Review of Politics* and *Polity*. Her numerous publications include *American Virtues: Thomas Jefferson on the Character of a Free People* and "Race and the Moral Foundation of the American Republic: Another Look at the Declaration and the *Notes on Virginia*," in the *Journal of Politics*.

Minority Report

With the report of the majority, I am in general agreement. I dissent only in believing it somewhat more likely than not that Thomas Jefferson was the father of Eston Hemings.

I am particularly impressed by two pieces of evidence—the DNA tests showing that Eston Hemings is very likely to have been a direct lineal male descendant of Thomas Jefferson's grandfather, and the fact that all of Sally Hemings's known children were conceived at a time when Thomas Jefferson was in the place where she almost certainly was as well. This suggests the possibility that Thomas Jefferson fathered all of her known children, but it does not prove that he fathered even one. What it does establish is a strong probability that her pregnancies during the period when she appears to have resided at Monticello were occasioned by his sojourns there.

It is, this fact notwithstanding, a mistake to jump to the conclusion that Jefferson must have been the father of Sally Hemings's children—for there were other events that normally coincided with his visits to Monticello, and among these one is pertinent to this inquiry: the presence of visitors whose offspring are tolerably likely to have looked like Thomas Jefferson—visitors such as Thomas Jefferson's younger brother Randolph, Randolph's four or five sons, and Peter and Samuel Carr, sons of his sister.

As is made clear in the majority report, Randolph or any one of his sons could have been the father of Eston Hemings, and there is reason to believe that Randolph and quite possibly his entire family were at Monticello on the occasion of a visit by his twin sister at the very time when Sally Hemings became pregnant with her son Eston. On the available evidence, it is impossible to be certain which Jefferson fathered Eston Hemings. Randolph Jefferson's known pattern of behavior makes him a likely suspect, but Thomas Jefferson is known to have been present and, in Randolph's case, his presence is only a likelihood.

I am also impressed by the testimony of Thomas Jefferson's grandchildren, by that of Edmund Bacon, and by that of Madison Hemings. It is obvious that someone lied but it is by no means clear who did so. I am not especially impressed by the argument that it would have been out of character for Thomas Jefferson to have abused his position as a slaveholder, for, in my judgment, in his public life he was a highly devious man. On the available evidence, I think the case open. Only with regard to Eston Hemings do I think it more likely than not that Thomas Jefferson was the father. I remain agnostic as to the paternity of Sally Hemings's other children.

There is, however, one thing that we do know, and it is damning enough. Despite the distaste that he expressed for the propensity of slaveholders and their relatives to abuse their power, Jefferson either engaged in such abuse himself or tolerated it on the part of one or more members of his extended family. In his private, as in his public, life, there was, for all his brilliance and sagacity, something dishonest, something self-serving and self indulgent about the man.

For the Minority

Paul A. Rahe

Charles O. Lee and Louise K. Lee Professor in Western Heritage
Hillsdale College

Professor Rahe was educated at Yale and Oxford, where he was a Rhodes Scholar. He served as Chair of the University of Tulsa Department of History for several years, has also taught at Yale and Cornell, and is the author of the highly acclaimed three-volume set, *Republics Ancient and Modern: Classical Republicanism and the American Revolution.* He has received numerous academic prizes and held fellowships from the National Endowment for the Humanities, the Woodrow Wilson International Center for Scholars, the Center for the History of Freedom, and the Institute of Current World Affairs.

Individual Views of
Scholars Commission Members

Individual Views of
Professor Robert F. Turner
joined by
Professor Alf J. Mapp, Jr.
Professor David N. Mayer
Professor Forrest McDonald
and
Professor Thomas Traut

Introduction

The Sally Hemings Scandal and
the Origins of the Scholars Commission

On September 1, 1802, one of the most disreputable scandal-mongers in the history of American journalism, James Thomson Callender, published an article in the Richmond, Virginia, *Recorder* alleging that, while Thomas Jefferson was America's Minister to France, he had begun a sexual relationship with a young[1] slave girl named Sally Hemings. Callender claimed that this affair had produced a ten- to twelve-year-old son named "Tom" whose features bore a striking resemblance to those of the President.

Callender's motive in writing the story is clear: He felt he had helped elect the third President by his vehement attacks on Jefferson's Federalist opponents, including George Washington, Alexander Hamilton, and especially President John Adams, whom Jefferson had defeated in the election of 1800. Callender demanded compensation for his services in the form of appointment as postmaster for Richmond. When Jefferson sent word the appointment was not going to happen, Callender responded that if the appointment were not forthcoming he would turn his pen on the new President and publish articles that would cause him great embarrassment. The Callender allegations, which will be discussed in greater detail in Chapter Three, were written by an angry and unprincipled drunkard for the purpose of fulfilling a blackmail threat. As Callender himself explained his behavior, he was seeking to extract "ten thousand fold vengeance"[2] against Thomas Jefferson.

In an (unrelated) 1819 letter to John Adams, Jefferson observed, "the proof of a negative can only be presumptive."[3] But few people who knew Thomas Jefferson well, even among his bitterest political enemies, took the Callender charges seriously. Despite Callender's gloating that he had destroyed the President's reputation, Jefferson and his Republican allies won decisively in the congressional elections of 1802 and Jefferson won reelection two years later by a nearly twelve-to-one landslide. But Callender's allegations were reprinted widely by some Federalist editors, and anti-American writers in Great Britain delighted in giving the story life across the Atlantic as well. Decades later, the story was reborn within the abolitionist movement to illustrate the terrible evils of the institution of slavery.[4] Miscegenation between master and slave was common enough on south-

---

1. Jefferson's *Farm Book* indicates at various points that Sally was born in 1773. We don't know the date. She arrived in Paris around the middle of 1787, so there would seem to be about an equal chance that she was thirteen years old as opposed to fourteen. *See, e.g.,* THOMAS JEFFERSON: THE GARDEN AND FARM BOOKS 244 (Robert C. Baron ed., 1987).

2. *See* Chapter Three.

3. *Jefferson to Adams*, July 9, 1819, in 15 WRITINGS OF THOMAS JEFFERSON 206 (Mem. ed. 1904).

4. LUCIA STANTON, FREE SOME DAY 107 (2000).

ern plantations to make such a charge credible, especially to those Americans who had also been led to believe that Thomas Jefferson was an atheistic tool of French radicals who were plotting to destroy the new Constitution.[5] But until the 1970s, prominent Jefferson scholars who even bothered to take note of the story consistently rejected it as being without foundation and totally inconsistent with Jefferson's reputation.[6]

The modern rebirth of the story can be attributed in the first instance to Professor Fawn Brodie, whose 1974 *Thomas Jefferson: An Intimate History* was a commercial success, despite being sharply criticized by scholars.[7] Dr. Brodie relied heavily upon an 1873 newspaper article purporting to record the testimony of Sally's son Madison Hemings, who reportedly claimed that Thomas Jefferson was the father of all of his mother's children and had (as Callender had charged more than seventy years earlier) commenced the relationship in Paris. Given the absence of hard evidence of the relationship, Professor Brodie sought to apply the tools of psychoanalysis to the issue by a careful study of Jefferson's letters and records.

The first evidence she finds of a Jefferson-Hemings romance was that, while traveling through Europe in the spring of 1788, Jefferson used the term "mulatto" several times in a journal to describe soil color—which Brodie saw as evidence that he was longing for the arms of his mulatto mistress back in Paris. As will be discussed in Chapter Nine, among the problems with this theory is that "mulatto" was an eighteenth-century term-of-art used by geologists to describe soil color—a term Jefferson had also used during previous travels before Sally Hemings arrived in Paris. In a review of Brodie's book, historian Garry Wills observed that during his 1788 trip Jefferson used "red" or "reddish" nearly five-times more frequently than he used "mulatto," and wondered why Brodie did not interpret this as a subliminal expression of his lust for his red-headed, nine-year-old daughter, Polly.[8]

Professor Brodie explained the absence of any significant references to Sally in Jefferson's letters and records by suggesting that someone probably destroyed the incriminating documents; or, alternatively, she saw it as proof that Jefferson was covering up his affair. She interpreted ambiguous notes in Jefferson's memorandum books about giving small sums to "charity," or leaving money in his dresser, as recording secret payments to Sally, despite the fact that similar notations appeared in Jefferson's records *years* before Sally arrived in Paris.

---

5. For a first-hand account of Federalist attitudes towards Jefferson, see Margaret Bayard Smith, *Reminiscences of President Jefferson, reprinted in* JEFFERSON READER 57–59 (Francis Coleman Rosenberger, ed. 1953). Ms. Smith was the daughter of Federalist Colonel John Bayard, and writes of believing that Jefferson was "a violent demagogue, coarse and vulgar in his manners, awkward and rude in his appearance, for such had the public journals and private conversations of the federal party represented him to be." *Id.* at 57. She writes of her subsequent shock after meeting Jefferson and "discovering the stranger whose deportment was so dignified and gentlemanly, whose language was so refined, whose voice was so gentle, whose countenance was so benignant, to be no other than Thomas Jefferson." *Id.* at 58.

6. This point does not appear to be in controversy between the factions in the current debate, and it is readily admitted by some of the most ardent advocates of Thomas Jefferson's paternity of Sally's children. *See, e.g.,* ANNETTE GORDON-REED, THOMAS JEFFERSON AND SALLY HEMINGS 3 (1997); and JOSEPH J. ELLIS, AMERICAN SPHINX 260, 365 (1996).

7. *See, e.g.,* Michael Kammen, *Jefferson: Farmer, Architect, Rebel, Statesman & Etc.,* WASH. POST, 7 July 1974 at D1 ("Mrs. Brodie does not so much humanize Jefferson as trivialize him. She is a historical gossip, incapable of distinguishing between cause and effect."). Historian Garry Wills characterized Brodie's scholarship as "sub-freshman absurdity," adding: "Error on this scale, and in this detail, does not come easily. There is a skill involved." Garry Wills, *Uncle Thomas's Cabin,* NEW YORK REVIEW OF BOOKS, Apr. 18, 1974 at 27.

8. Garry Wills, *Uncle Thomas's Cabin,* NEW YORK REVIEW OF BOOKS, Apr. 18, 1974 at 27.

Almost all serious scholars remained highly skeptical, but the story was kept alive in the public mind by a series of novels and Hollywood productions. For every reader who waded through Dumas Malone's masterful six-volume, Pulitzer Prize-winning series *Jefferson and His Time*, a thousand or more learned about Jefferson on the silver screen or their television sets. There, they viewed seemingly realistic video of the dashing Thomas Jefferson waltzing the beautiful young slave girl across the ballrooms of Paris. The story was titillating, and more and more visitors to Monticello began asking to see the "pictures" of Sally or the nonexistent "secret staircase" or the "hidden chamber" above Jefferson's bed where they had been taught the illicit romance had been consummated.[9] Many assumed the story in the movies and novels *had* to be true, for how could a work of pure fiction use the names of real people in such a scandalous way without being sued if the charges were false?

Yet another development contributing to the credibility of the "Sally" story has been the growth of investigative journalism during the past four decades and the resulting public disclosure of numerous scandals involving sexual misconduct by elected leaders who have often initially proclaimed their innocence. Scholars have entered the fray as well, accusing Presidents throughout history of similar misconduct. Sometimes their case is clear, but at other times they appear to have begun from a presumption of guilt, repeating partisan accusations or unsupported allegations as fact.[10] When Americans see a popular elected political leader such as President William *Jefferson* Clinton impeached by the House of Representatives for lying about sexual encounters with a woman thirty years his junior, and senior legislators forced to resign over sexual misconduct, perhaps it is not surprising that they are cynical when told Thomas Jefferson had absolute control over a handsome young slave girl and remained a gentleman.

Professor Gordon-Reed and "Transcription Errors"

The verdict among historians on "Tom and Sally" really began to shift with the 1997 publication of *Thomas Jefferson and Sally Hemings*, written by Annette Gordon-Reed, at the time an assistant professor at New York Law School (not to be confused with the more prestigious New York University School of Law). After acknowledging some of Professor Brodie's shortcomings, Professor Gordon-Reed, an African-American, proceeded to draw from Brodie's work in producing a far more believable account of how Thomas Jefferson *could* have had an affair with Sally Hemings.

As the final revisions are being made to my Individual Views in 2010, Professor Gordon-Reed has become perhaps the hottest property in the entire field of American his-

---

9. Like so many myths, this one has an historical predicate. Although there was no "staircase" during Jefferson's lifetime, one was installed by Jefferson M. Levy after he became the owner of Monticello in order to provide access to a bathtub he installed above the small (two-and-a-half-foot-wide) alcove above Jefferson's bed (which had been built and used by Jefferson as a clothes closet). This staircase was later removed as part of an effort to restore the property to its original plan. *See, e.g.,* Thomas Jefferson Memorial Foundation Research Committee, *Report on Thomas Jefferson and Sally Hemings* (Jan. 2000), Appendix H at 3 (hereinafter referred to as *Monticello Report*). This report is available on line at: http://www.monticello.org/plantation/hemingscontro/hemings_report.html.

10. On this point, see the Individual Views of Professor Robert Ferrell, Distinguished Professor of History, Emeritus, at Indiana University and widely regarded as among America's foremost presidential historians, beginning on page 281.

tory. Her latest book, *The Hemingses of Monticello*,[11] has pretty much swept the field of literary recognition in categories where she was eligible:

- On November 19, 2008, she won the National Book Award for non-fiction;

- On April 9, 2009, she received a Guggenheim Fellowship;[12]

- On April 20, 2009, she won the Pulitzer Prize for History;

- On May 28, 2009, she won the $50,000 George Washington Book Prize, awarded annually for the "most important new book about America's founding era";[13]

- On July 14, 2009, she was named Rutgers Board of Governors Professor of History by the State University of New Jersey;[14]

- On July 18, 2009, she won the SHEAR Book Award from the Society of Historians of the Early American Republic;

- On September 10, 2009, she received an Anisfield-Wolf Book Award;

- On September 30, 2009, it was announced that she had won the 2009 Frederick Douglass Book Prize given by the Gilder Lehrman Center for the Study of Slavery, Resistance and Abolition, the Gilder Lehrman Institute of American History, and Yale University. The prize was awarded at a dinner in New York in February 2010.

- On February 25, 2010, President Barack Obama honored Professor Gordon-Reed with the National Humanities Medal – America's "highest medal for achievement" in her field.[15]

- On April 30, 2010, Harvard Law School announced that she would join the Harvard faculty in July as a Professor of Law, Professor of History, and as the Carol K. Pforzheimer Professor at the Radcilffe Institute for Advanced Study;[16] and

- On September 28, 2010, she received a five-year, unrestricted $500,000 fellowship (widely known as a "genius grant") from the John D. and Catherine T. MacArthur Foundation.[17]

Indeed, her growing fame was such that the retirement of Supreme Court Justice John Paul Stevens led the head of the American Civil Liberties Union to recommend Professor Gordon-Reed as a possible replacement.[18]

---

11. Annette Gordon-Reed, The Hemingses of Monticello: An American Family (2008).

12. Mary L. Dudziak, *Goluboff and Gordon-Reed win Guggenheim Fellowships*, Legal History Blog, April 9, 2009, available at *http://legalhistoryblog.blogspot.com/2009/04/goluboff-and-gordon-reed-win-guggenheim.html*.

13. Neely Tucker, *Add Washington Book Prize to the 'Hemingses' Haul*, Wash. Post, May 29, 2009.

14. Annette Gordon-Reed Named Rutgers Board of Governors Professor of History, Rutgers Media Relations Press Release, July 14, 2009, available at *http://news.rugters.edu/medrel/news-releases/2009/07/annette-gordon-reed-20090714*.

15. Jacquelin Trescott, *Obama honors winners of National Medal of the Arts, National Humanities Medal*, Wash. Post, Feb. 26, 2010.

16. *Annette Gordon-Reed '84 to join the Harvard faculty*, Harvard Law School News & Events, April 30, 2010, available at *http://www.law.harvard.edu/news/2010/04/30_annette.html*.

17. Felicia R. Lee, *MacArthur Foundation Honors 23*, N.Y. Times, Sept. 28, 2010, available at *http://www.nytimes.com/2010/09/28/arts/28macarthur.html*.

18. Marcia Coyle, *An alternative short list for the high court*, National Law Journal, May 18, 2009, *available at*: http://www.law.com/jsp/nlj/PubArticleNLJ.jsp?id=1202430756479&slreturn= 1&hbxlogin=1. (The story began: "Is New York Law School's Annette Gordon-Reed, the Pulitzer Prize-winning law professor/historian, on President Obama's Supreme Court 'short list?'")

Interestingly, although serious problems involving altered historical documents in her first book (*Thomas Jefferson and Sally Hemings*) were made public in our 2001 report and have been identified elsewhere[19] as well, the prestigious committees charged with evaluating her work have apparently not found them troubling. This is all the more curious, given the reaction in recent years to charges of apparently less serious misconduct by other scholars.

As will be discussed in greater length in the Postscript to this volume,[20] when it was revealed in 2001 that Pulitzer Prize recipient Professor Joseph Ellis—at the time the preeminent scholar in the paternity-belief camp—had fabricated aspects of his own personal history (e.g., claiming to have served in combat in Vietnam when he spent his entire active duty service in the Army as a history professor at West Point), he was suspended for one year without pay, deprived indefinitely of his chaired professorship (it was restored in 2005), and permanently banned from teaching a popular seminar on the Vietnam War. Several prestigious lecture invitations were reportedly withdrawn as well.

Early the following year, historian Stephen Ambrose was widely criticized for what turned out to be multiple acts of apparent plagiarism,[21] and additional charges of plagiarism led Pulitzer Prize recipient Professor Doris Kearns Goodwin to take a "leave of absence" from the PBS *News Hour with Jim Lehrer* show and to resign from the Pulitzer Prize Board at Columbia University. Unsold copies of the book in question were withdrawn.[22]

In 2005, the University of Georgia Press revoked the 2004 Flannery O'Connor Award given to Professor Brad Vice when it was revealed he had drawn heavily upon and used passages without citation from a previously published short story by another author, and all remaining copies of his book were destroyed by his publisher.

Plagiarism, of course, is the use of another writer's words without attribution—taking credit for another's work. It is justly considered a serious offense, but it is not the worst possible misconduct by an historian. For it does not normally mislead the reader in a search for historical truth.

A far more serious offense was revealed in 2002, when an independent committee appointed by the Dean of Emory College to review accusations that Professor Michael A. Bellesiles had fabricated historical records in preparing his Bancroft Prize-winning volume, *Arming America: The Origins of a National Gun Culture*, concluded his "unprofessional and misleading work" entered "the realm of falsification."[23] Professor Bellesiles resigned his faculty position, and the Trustees of Columbia University voted to rescind the Bancroft Prize and requested that the accompanying $4,000 award be returned.[24]

In sharp contrast, Professor Gordon-Reed has apparently paid no price for what appear to be equally if not more serious transgressions against accepted standards of professional behavior. Professor Bellesiles' greatest offense appears to have been "making up"

---

19. The first person to my knowledge to discover material errors in the Gordon-Reed book was Eyler Coates in 2000. The following year, he included the Coolidge letter with changes identified in an appendix to THE JEFFERSON-HEMINGS MYTH 193–96 (Eyler Robert Coates, Sr., ed. 2001).

20. *See* pages 373–75.

21. History News Network provides a useful summary of "How the Ambrose Story Developed" at: http://hnn.us/articles/504.html.

22. Mark Lewis, *Plagiarism Controversy: Doris Kearns Goodwin And the Credibility Gap*, FORBES, Feb. 27, 2002, *available at*: http://www.forbes.com/2002/02/27/0227goodwin.html.

23. Robert F. Worth, *Prize for Book Is Taken Back From Historian*, N.Y. TIMES, Dec. 14, 2002, *available at* http://www.nytimes.com/2002/12/14/business/media/14BOOK.html.

24. *Id.*

historical evidence, whereas Professor Gordon-Reed appears to have repeatedly and materially altered important but not at the time readily available historical documents to make her case that Thomas Jefferson fathered children by Sally Hemings more credible. A few examples may illustrate the problem.

In Chapter Four we will discuss the already mentioned newspaper story that appeared in the *Pike County Republican* in 1873 and was presented as the statement of an elderly Madison Hemings—a son of Monticello slave Sally Hemings. When the Gordon-Reed volume was first published, copies of the original article were not easy to find (although a transcription had appeared as an appendix to Fawn Brodie's *Thomas Jefferson: An Intimate History*). I ultimately paid a researcher in the area to visit the Ohio Historical Society and make me a photocopy of the original article.

This newspaper article at first glance appears to be powerful evidence that Thomas Jefferson fathered all of Sally Hemings' children. But as will be discussed in greater detail in Chapter Four, it has some rather serious credibility problems. Several important factual statements attributed to Madison Hemings are plainly wrong—and to at least some extent they undermine the credibility of the article. Some were things that Madison Hemings clearly knew about, so the errors might suggest either that this was not really the account of Madison Hemings or that his memory had deteriorated in his old age (he was sixty-eight at the time) to the point that his entire statement might be suspect. For example, although it is well known that Madison's grandmother was Betty Hemings—the daughter of a white English ship captain and an African slave woman—the 1873 newspaper article reports Madison as declaring: "My grandmother was a fullblooded African...."

When Professor Fawn Brodie recognized this obvious error, she quite appropriately corrected it in her transcription by inserting the word "[great-]" before "grandmother" in brackets to disclose that she had altered the original document. But that served to emphasize the rather obvious factual error in the story, in the process casting doubt about either the legitimacy of the entire story or Madison Hemings' memory at the time—neither of which is helpful for the purpose of using the article as key evidence in this dispute. So Professor Gordon-Reed merely altered the original in her transcript (see **Figure 1** on the next page) to read "My great-grandmother was a fullblooded African...." Credibility problem solved.[25]

One might like to be charitable and attribute such alterations to ignorance of fundamental rules of scholarly writing. But that is not easy, as Professor Gordon-Reed was a member of the prestigious *Harvard Law Review* while a law student at Harvard. The standard reference on legal writing and citations is *The Bluebook*,[26] which was originated decades ago at Harvard by the editors of that same journal. Every law school with which I am familiar makes certain that its students are fully versed in the requirements to iden-

---

25. If the aged Madison Hemings confused his grandmother with his great-grandmother (whom he knew), how credible are his rather bizarre assertions about events in Paris that occurred years before his birth? If, on the other hand, the error was injected by *Pike County Republican* editor Samuel Wetmore—a strong critic of Thomas Jefferson—the accuracy of the rest of the article is similarly brought into question. There is also at least some evidence that Professor Gordon-Reed's transcription of the *Pike County Republican* article was copied from Professor Fawn Brodie's book, as both versions transcribe the date of Madison Hemings' marriage as "1834" rather than "1831" (which is clear on the microfilm I examined). However, Professor Brodie transcribed Madison's age at the time of Jefferson's death as "21," while Professor Gordon-Reed correctly transcribes "21 1/2"—evidence both that she can be a careful scholar and that she (or someone on her behalf) checked her work against the original.

26. THE BLUEBOOK: A UNIFORM SYSTEM OF CITATIONS (18th ed. 2005).

Figure 1. Altering Historical Documents #1: Changing "Grandmother" to "Great-Grandmother"*

In the 1873 *Pike County Republican* article reprinted in Professor Annette Gordon-Reed's 1997 book *Thomas Jefferson and Sally Hemings*, Sally Hemings' son Madison is reported to have said that his "grandmother" was a "fullblooded African." In reality, it is well established that Sally's mother Betty Hemings was the child of a white English ship captain and an African slave woman. If this was in fact what Madison said, he presumably confused his grandmother with his great-grandmother, whom he also knew—perhaps suggesting that his memory was faulty at the age of sixty-eight or that these were not his words. The original is clear:

> I never knew of but one white man who bore the name of Hemings; he was an Englishman and my greatgrandfather. He was captain of an English trading vessel which sailed between England and Williamsburg, Va., then quite a port. My grandmother was a fullblooded African, and possibly a native of that country. She was the property of

In her transcription, on page 245, Professor Gordon-Reed corrects the factual inaccuracy by simply inserting "great-" before "grandmother" without the use of brackets to disclose her alteration:

> I never knew of but one white man who bore the name of Hemings; he was an Englishman and my great grandfather. He was captain of an English trading vessel which sailed between England and Williamsburg, Va., then quite a port. My great-grandmother was a fullblooded African, and possibly a native of that country. She

As a former member of the *Harvard Law Review*, Professor Gordon-Reed cannot credibly claim to be unaware of this important requirement of scholarly writing. By omitting the brackets, she has increased the credibility of her evidence. This is far from the worst of her alterations.

---

* Passages reproduced in facsimile in this volume have been electronically scanned from the originals or photographs of the original documents.

tify alterations in documents, as in certain courtroom settings an intentional failure to do so could lead to disbarment or other serious disciplinary action.

Like other major style manuals,[27] *The Bluebook* is clear on the need to identify changes in original texts, and lawyers are trained to be meticulous in such matters. *The Bluebook* explains:

> When a letter must be changed from upper to lower case, or vice versa, enclose it in brackets. Substituted words or letters and other inserted material should

---

27. *See, e.g.,* THE CHICAGO MANUAL OF STYLE: THE ESSENTIAL GUIDE FOR WRITERS, EDITORS, AND PUBLISHERS 357–58 (15th ed. 2003).

also be bracketed.... Significant mistakes in the original should be followed by "[*sic*]" and otherwise left as they appear in the original.... [28]

For those familiar with the Jefferson family, an arguably greater problem with the 1873 newspaper story attributed to Madison Hemings arises when Madison reportedly discusses his mother's 1787 voyage to Europe with Jefferson's youngest daughter Maria.[29] The original article (see **Figure 2** on the next page) states:

> When Mr. Jefferson went to France Martha was a young woman grown, my mother was about her age, and Maria was just budding into womanhood.

The problem here is that Maria (born as "Mary" and also known as "Polly") Jefferson was born on August 1, 1778. Thus, when Thomas Jefferson arrived in France in July 1784 with eleven-year-old eldest daughter Martha, Maria (who remained in Virginia with relatives) was but five years old—hardly likely to have been "budding into womanhood."

How does Professor Gordon-Reed remedy this glaring factual inaccuracy in the story attributed to Madison Hemings? She merely deletes a few words—well, a *dozen* words—from the original and transcribes it as:

> When Mr. Jefferson went to France Martha was just budding into womanhood.

Had she inserted an ellipsis (...) between "Martha" and "was," the resulting alteration would be technically correct but terribly misleading and dishonest. But that might have flagged for readers that Professor Gordon-Reed had left something out of the sentence. Whatever the explanation, as **Figure 2** on the next page illustrates, Professor Gordon-Reed has materially altered historical evidence in such a manner as to make her document more credible. If intentional, that is a *very* serious violation of the rules of professional writing, and as a former member of the *Harvard Law Review* she cannot credibly pretend ignorance of the rules.

Sadly, this is hardly the only example of Professor Gordon-Reed's apparent tampering with evidence to strengthen her case. She includes in the book a transcription of an obscure 1858 letter written by one of Thomas Jefferson's granddaughters that clearly has been materially altered to totally change the clear intent of the original. In the very legible original, Ellen Randolph Coolidge wrote:

> He [Thomas Jefferson] lived, whenever he was at Monticello, and entirely for the last seventeen years of his life, in the midst of these young people [eight grandchildren when Madison was born], surrounded by them, his intercourse with them of the freest and most affectionate kind. How comes it that his immoralities were never suspected by his own family—that his daughter and her children rejected with horror and contempt the charges brought against him. That my brother, then a young man certain to know all that was going on behind the scenes, positively declares his indignant disbelief in the imputations and solemnly affirms that he never saw or heard the smallest thing which could lead him to suspect that his grandfather's life was other than perfectly pure.[30]

---

28. THE BLUEBOOK 69 § 5.2.

29. One might argue that this error is understandable, since the events in question occurred years before Madison's birth. But virtually all of the relevant statements attributed to Madison in this story fall in that same category.

30. The original (or more likely a copy made at the same time in her own handwriting) of this letter is in the Coolidge Family Papers, Special Collections Department, University of Virginia Library, Acc. No. 9090.

Figure 2. Altering Historical Documents #2: A Five-Year-Old Girl "Budding into Womanhood"

When Thomas Jefferson went to France in 1784, he was accompanied by his nearly twelve-year-old daughter Martha but left five-year-old Maria with relatives in Virginia. Sally Hemings was later chosen by those relatives to accompany Maria to Paris in 1787. In the 1873 *Pike County Republican* story (that is presented as the statement of Sally's son Madison), a serious factual error asserts that Maria was "just budding into womanhood" at the age of five. Such errors do not enhance the credibility of the document.

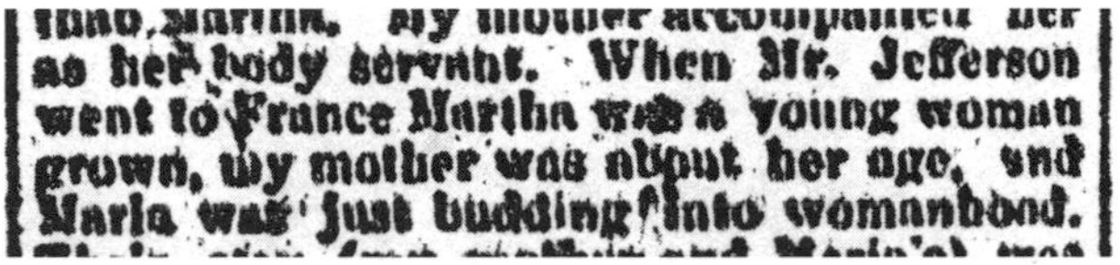

> 1873, Martha. My mother accompanied her as her body servant. When Mr. Jefferson went to France Martha was a young woman grown, my mother was about her age, and Maria was just budding into womanhood.

In her transcription of this document, Professor Gordon-Reed eliminates the credibility problem by deleting a dozen words to make it appear (incorrectly) that Madison was describing the almost twelve year old Martha rather than five-year-old Maria:

> My mother accompanied her as a body servant. When Mr. Jefferson went to France Martha was just budding into womanhood. Their stay (my mother's and

In fairness, Madison was here discussing events that occurred years before his own birth. But that is the case with virtually all of the comments attributed to him in this article of relevance to this inquiry. By materially altering her "evidence," Professor Gordon-Reed has misled her readers and violated a fundamental rule of ethical scholarship.

In Professor Gordon-Reed's *Thomas Jefferson and Sally Hemings,* however, the word "disbelief" in the final sentence above has been transcribed as "belief." (See **Figure 3** on the next page)[31] While it only involves the omission of three letters, it obviously at minimum confuses the meaning of the sentence.

Even more troubling is a far more elaborate alteration to this important letter that occurs just a few lines later. The original clearly reads:

> No female domestic ever entered his chambers except at hours when he was known not to be there and none could have entered without being exposed to the public gaze.

Professor Gordon-Reed transcribes this sentence instead as:

> No female domestic ever entered his chambers except at hours when he was known not to be in the public gaze.

(See **Figure 4** on page 37.)

---

31. The original Gordon-Reed transcription of this letter was still on the PBS Frontline "Jefferson's Blood" website in late 2009. See: http://www.pbs.org/wgbh/pages/frontline/shows/jefferson/cron/1858ellenlett.html (last checked August 25, 2009).

Figure 3. Altering Historical Documents #3: Changing "Disbelief" to "Belief"

In a private addendum to an 1858 letter to her husband Joseph, Thomas Jefferson's granddaughter Ellen Randolph Coolidge explained why the allegations of a sexual relationship between Thomas Jefferson and Sally Hemings could not be true. She noted in the process the indignant "disbelief" of her brother, Thomas Jefferson Randolph (who was especially close to the President at Monticello) in the story:

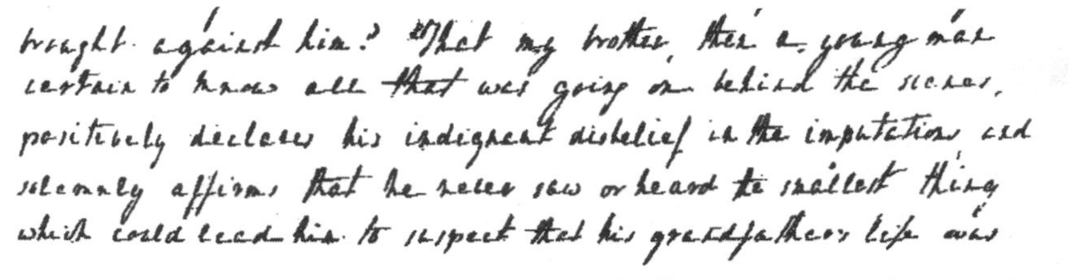
brought against him? That my brother, then a young man certain to know all that was going on behind the scenes, positively declares his indignant disbelief in the imputation and solemnly affirms that he never saw or heard the smallest thing which could lead him to suspect that his grandfather's life was

Courtesy Special Collections, University of Virginia Library.

However, in her transcription of this important letter (the original of which is kept safely secured with other valuable historical documents in a library at the University of Virginia), Professor Gordon-Reed transcribed the word "disbelief" as "belief."

comes it that his immoralities were never suspected by his own family—that his daughter and her children rejected with horror and contempt the charges brought against him. That my brother, then a young man certain to know all that was going on behind the scenes, positively declares his indignant belief in the imputa-

By deleting ten words and adding another (none attributable to merely having "skipped a line" or other carelessness), Professor Gordon-Reed has quite conveniently transformed a sentence that strongly undermines her premise into a grammatically coherent piece of evidence for her case.[32] Without this alteration, including this letter in her book would make no sense—as it otherwise does not support her position. With the alteration, Ellen appears to be admitting that Sally could have visited Jefferson's chambers when he was not "in the public gaze."

Also troubling is Professor Gordon-Reed's omission from both her analysis and her genealogical chart of five of the most likely suspects for the paternity of some of Sally's children. Professor Gordon-Reed qualifies her genealogical chart of "The Jeffersons and Randolphs" by adding "(Relevant Connections Only)"[33] and she then omits potentially highly

32. As already noted, even minor corrections in punctuation or spelling are supposed to be indicated in scholarly writings by the use of brackets, ellipses, or other standard markings. However, occasional "errors" are not uncommon. (There will no doubt be several in this volume, despite efforts to avoid them.) Attorney Richard Dixon pointed out to me that, in his 1966 edition of *The Federalist Papers,* Professor Benjamin F. Wright observed that an 1864 edition edited by Alexander Hamilton's son included more than a thousand departures from the original texts. Wright adds, however, that "[I]n no instance is the subject of an argument or interpretation changed" by the alterations. THE FEDERALIST PAPERS 11 (Benjamin F. Wright ed., 1966). What is especially alarming about the Gordon-Reed alterations is that most of them involve changing factual assertions to make her evidence more credible or her case stronger.

33. GORDON-REED, THOMAS JEFFERSON AND SALLY HEMINGS unnumbered page following preface.

Figure 4. Altering Historical Documents #4: Allowing Sally Hemings into Jefferson's Chambers When He Was Present

In the same 1858 letter discussed in **Figure 3**, Ellen Coolidge clearly asserts that Sally Hemings was not allowed in Thomas Jefferson's chambers when he was there:

> other than perfectly pure. His apartments had no private entrance not perfectly accessible and visible to all the household. No female domestic ever entered his chambers except at hours when he was known not to be there and none could have entered without being exposed to the public gaze.

Courtesy Special Collections, University of Virginia Library.

By deleting ten words from the original and adding another, Professor Gordon-Reed's transcription suggests instead that Sally was only allowed to be with Jefferson in his chambers "at hours when he was known not to be in the public gaze."

> the household. No female domestic ever entered his chambers except at hours when he was known not to be in the public gaze. But again I put it to any fair mind to decide if a man so admirable to his domestic character as Mr Jefferson,

This "mistake" (unlike those in **Figures 1–3**) was noted in the 2001 version of our report and has been corrected in the latest edition of *Thomas Jefferson and Sally Hemings* (below). The issue—particularly in the light of the other alterations to her "evidence"—is whether such dramatic changes by an obviously able scholar can be explained as mere "mistakes."

> the household. No female domestic ever entered his chambers except at hours when he was known not to be there and none could have entered without being exposed to the public gaze. But again I put it to any fair mind to decide if a man so

relevant people. Similarly, the index to her book does not even mention President Jefferson's younger brother Randolph or any of Randolph's five sons.[34] While one would again wish to be charitable and assume that perhaps—like many scholars who have written about Thomas Jefferson—she was simply unaware of these obscure relatives, her bibliography includes both a volume that provides a contemporary slave account of Randolph's habit of spending his evenings at Monticello playing his fiddle among the slaves and dancing "half the night,"[35] and Bernard Mayo's *Thomas Jefferson and His Unknown Brother*.[36] The Mayo book documents Randolph's apparent drinking problem and includes a letter

34. *Id.* at 285 (the index entries go from "Jefferson, Peter" to "Jefferson, Thomas," with no mention of Randolph). In addition, at least four of Randolph's five sons were clearly old enough to have fathered Eston. While the *Monticello Report* suggests that James Lilburne Jefferson, Randolph's youngest son, was born *circa* 1789 (and thus would have been seventeen or eighteen when Eston was conceived), I have some doubts about whether he was this old, which will be addressed in Chapter Ten.

35. James A Bear, Jr., Jefferson at Monticello 275 (1967).

36. The full text of this volume is available at http://www.archive.org/stream/thomasjeffersonh00jeff/thomasjeffersonh00jeff_djvu.txt.

from Thomas Jefferson indicating that he expected to welcome Randolph (and, one might assume, Randolph's five sons) to Monticello about the time Sally Hemings became pregnant with Eston—her only child later shown by DNA tests to have probably been fathered by a Jefferson.[37]

There is yet another problem with Professor Gordon-Reed's book. Despite her impressive legal training, she has written the brief for the wrong side—proceeding in the manner of a *defense* lawyer. Like Professor Brodie and novelist Barbara Chase-Riboud,[38] Professor Gordon-Reed's approach is not to try to prove that Thomas Jefferson *was* the father of any of Sally Hemings' children, but merely to argue that it was *possible* that such a relationship *could* have existed. *Thomas Jefferson and Sally Hemings* is replete with assertions that Sally "might have been Thomas Jefferson's lover,"[39] that "Thomas Jefferson and Sally Hemings could have been involved in a relationship,"[40] and that this or that factual allegation "could have" or "might have" been true.[41] And since, as will be discussed in Chapter Two, we have almost no reliable information about Sally Hemings, this possibility is of course true. But such statements, even if technically accurate, are probative of very little. (One might argue with similar logic that Sally "might" have been a wizard at Newtonian mathematics and perhaps the actual inventor of the mold-board plough for which Jefferson received so much acclaim—as disproving a negative is difficult.)

In the legal profession, these are the arguments of a *defense* brief; whereas, to win a paternity case against Thomas Jefferson, Professor Gordon-Reed would have to clear the much higher hurdle of proof of the alleged facts by "clear and convincing evidence." If she were the defense counsel for Peter Carr or Randolph Jefferson, and wished merely to raise sufficient doubt that her client was the father of one of Sally Hemings' children, it could be very effective to point out that Sally "might" have been seeing Thomas Jefferson or another man at the time of conception. Noting that Sally was reported to be physically attractive (motive), that she and Thomas Jefferson were living in reasonable proximity to each other much of the time (opportunity), and that other circumstances showed that they "could have" or "might have" had a relationship, a defense lawyer for another suspect might well succeed in introducing enough doubt about the guilt of his or her client to avoid an unfavorable verdict. But such arguments seldom even attempt to establish that the other suspect is guilty, or even that he or she is more likely to be guilty than the accused client. The goal of the defense lawyer is merely to convince the court that there is sufficient uncertainty about the *client's* guilt to avoid a finding of paternity.

All Professor Gordon-Reed attempts to do in *Thomas Jefferson and Sally Hemings* is to demonstrate, given the almost total absence of reliable factual information, that Thomas Jefferson and Sally Hemings *could* have had a relationship. But she doesn't even *allege* that the story of their romance is true, much less present clear and convincing evidence to support it. To be sure, she has constructed what at times is a very clever and creative argument; but it is an argument for the wrong brief.

For most Americans, scholars and public alike, by far the most convincing evidence that Thomas Jefferson fathered children by Sally Hemings came after Professor Gordon-Reed

37. *Id.* at 278.

38. *See, e.g.,* BARBARA CHASE-RIBOUD, SALLY HEMINGS (1992); and BARBARA CHASE-RIBOUD, THE PRESIDENT'S DAUGHTER (1994).

39. GORDON-REED, THOMAS JEFFERSON AND SALLY HEMINGS 158.

40. *Id.* at 162.

41. After admitting that "very little is known about" Sally (*id.* at 158), Professor Gordon-Reed peppers her chapter on Sally with speculations about what "may have" or "might have" been true or been thought or felt by various actors.

had published her book. In November 1998 it was reported in the press that scientists had used DNA tests to establish a genetic link between Thomas Jefferson and one of Sally's sons. In reality, as will be discussed in Chapter One, many of the press reports were factually wrong. The DNA tests had not linked any of Sally Hemings' children with *Thomas* Jefferson, whose DNA is not known to exist today. The tested DNA was extracted from the blood of several modern descendants of some of Thomas Jefferson's cousins. The scientific tests, which were professionally done and unexceptional in their methodology, supported two broad conclusions of relevance to our inquiry:

- Thomas Woodson, long thought to have been the child allegedly conceived in Paris and born to Sally Hemings in 1790 (even by many who were convinced that his father was not Thomas Jefferson), whose existence was the central focus of James Callender's 1802 allegations about a Jefferson-Hemings sexual relationship, could not have been the son of Thomas Jefferson; and

- Eston Hemings, the youngest son of Sally Hemings, almost certainly was fathered by one of more than two dozen Jefferson men (including the sixty-four-year-old President) who are known to have lived in Virginia at the time of Eston's conception.

A big part of the public misunderstanding of the DNA testing resulted from the fact that the tests involved were quite different from the highly precise "DNA fingerprints" Americans learned about during the O.J. Simpson trial. Instead of trying to link two individuals with 99.99 percent or greater reliability, the DNA tests performed in the Jefferson-Hemings study were designed primarily to *eliminate* paternity suspects. In this case, they showed that neither Peter nor Samuel Carr was the father of Eston Hemings and that some male Jefferson probably was. To most people, including some historians and the scientists who conducted the tests (who did not even know that Thomas Jefferson had a brother and five nephews living a few miles from Monticello), Thomas Jefferson was the only suspect once the Carr brothers had been eliminated. In fact, as will be discussed in Chapter Ten, that is not true. But the common perception was that DNA tests had proven Thomas Jefferson fathered Sally Hemings' children, and that certainly remained the "conventional wisdom" until the original version of this report was released in April 2001.

Jefferson's fate seemed further sealed in January 2000, when the respected Thomas Jefferson Memorial Foundation, keeper of Monticello and long dedicated to promoting scholarship and education about America's third President, issued a staff report following an investigation of the DNA evidence and other available information. In announcing this report to the press, Foundation President Daniel Jordan said that there was "a strong likelihood that Thomas Jefferson and Sally Hemings had a relationship over time that led to the birth of one, and perhaps all, of the known children of Sally Hemings."[42]

Feeding Frenzy

For a variety of reasons, for a brief period the Jefferson-Hemings controversy seemed finally resolved. Scholars and commentators rushed forward to embrace the new conven-

---

42. Daniel P. Jordan, Statement on the Monticello Research Committee Report (Jan. 26, 2000), *in Monticello Report* at 1.

tional wisdom, many of them proudly announcing they had always known Jefferson was guilty. For example, on November 8, 1998, the late historian Stephen Ambrose (discussed earlier in connection with a 2002 plagiarism charge[43]) appeared on the CNN program, "Both Sides with Jesse Jackson," and announced: "For my own part, I never doubted that he had a liaison with Sally. Whether there were children out of it or not was, you know, the hardest part, there's no doubt about it. What the hell do you think slavery was?"[44]

Ambrose went on to say: "This man has given us more than anyone except Washington and here he is a hypocrite, a liar, a misogynist, which he denounced very vehemently." Perhaps a bit more of the exchange will capture the spirit of the program:

JACKSON: Do you think the same people who would want to impeach William Jefferson Clinton would want to impeach Thomas Jefferson?

AMBROSE: We don't have *ex post facto* impeachment in this country.

JACKSON: Why do you think so many historians have denied this Jefferson-Sally Hemings relationship and why have they just denied it, lied about it, covered it up?

AMBROSE: Well, Jefferson was the first one to lie about it and the first one to cover it up and they've taken their lead from him.... [E]verything about it stinks. I think the worst thing, he didn't educate his own children. This is Thomas Jefferson. This is the founder of the University of Virginia. He did not teach his own children how to read and write. And that's, it seems to me ...

JACKSON: Which makes ... [Jefferson] a dead-beat dad.

AMBROSE: That's, you have a way with words and you picked it up there. That's right.

JACKSON: It's in common parlance. Give us some historical perspective on how this 200 year Jefferson-Hemings story, it just surfaced and just kept staying alive. It just kind of wouldn't go away.

AMBROSE: It wouldn't go away because it was true. The first to break it was a newspaperman named Callender, who was pretty disreputable. He would be called an investigative reporter today. And he started making the charges when Jefferson was living in the White House. And he continued to make 'em and Jefferson continued to deny them and at one point Jefferson tried to buy his silence, tried to bribe him. Now, the Jefferson people deny that, but anybody else looking at it, this was a straight out attempt to bribe Callender.... [O]ne of the aspects that I'd like to comment on [in] this business is the use of Sally as a sex slave is deplorable and we could use a lot worse words than that....

JACKSON:.... I suppose that would mean in the end it would be we'll judge William Jefferson Clinton by what he has been as a leader and not just by this present crisis which is so current and on TV by day and by night.

AMBROSE: Yeah, that's right.[45]

At times, the response seemed almost like a feeding frenzy, with the scholarly sharks circling the gravesite lusting after a piece of the fallen dead white male. Even Jefferson's own University of Virginia seemed anxious to embrace the new-found truth. Professor Ellis notes

---

43. *See* page 31.
44. *Both Sides with Jesse Jackson: Verdict Is Issued on Relationship Between Thomas Jefferson and Sally Hemings* (CNN television broadcast), Nov. 8, 1998.
45. *Id.*

that shortly after the DNA results were released, a "hastily convened scholarly conference" took place at the University of Virginia in May 1999. According to Professor Ellis, the conference "made its major focus the complicity of the historical profession in rejecting the existence of the sexual relationship prior to the DNA findings, suggesting that those who had found the circumstantial evidence unconvincing were harboring racist prejudices that now required purging."[46]

In fairness, the DNA evidence was but additional fuel for an assault on Jefferson that began more than a decade earlier.[47] In 1989, Dr. Peter S. Onuf was named the Thomas Jefferson Memorial Foundation Professor of History at the University of Virginia, bringing to the chair some very different perspectives than previous chair-holders Dumas Malone and Merrill Peterson—each of whom was widely recognized as the world's preeminent Jefferson scholar of his era.[48] But Professor Onuf matured in a more radical academic environment, and in 1993 he published an influential article in the prestigious *William & Mary Quarterly*. Writing in the same journal seven years later, Professor Ellis gave this account of the growing assault on Thomas Jefferson:

> Matters became even worse soon after Onuf's article appeared. In the volume [co-edited by Onuf] on Jefferson's legacy published to recognize the 250th anniversary of his birth, Paul Finkelman declared in prosecutorial tones that Jefferson should be banished from the American pantheon as a slave-owning racist. Michael Lind and Connor Cruise O'Brien wrote books actually calling for the dismantling of the Jefferson Memorial and the removal of his face from Mount Rushmore.[49]

The DNA evidence thus found a very receptive audience among many revisionist historians. Professor Onuf worked closely with the staff research committee that prepared the *Monticello Report* (discussed below), and according to two individuals who served on the committee, when asked whether he had "proof" for a factual assertion he had made about Jefferson, Professor Onuf replied: "We don't need proof. We are historians, we write history the way we want to."[50]

---

46. To his credit, in an accompanying footnote Professor Ellis added: "Unlike Professors Lewis and Onuf, I am unpersuaded that previous scholars who rejected or doubted the liaison were covert racists or blind defenders of Jefferson." Joseph J. Ellis, *Jefferson: Post-DNA*, 57 WILLIAM & MARY QUARTERLY 136 (Jan. 2000).

47. Some would date the modern, more critical, trend in Jefferson scholarship to the 1963 publication of Professor Leonard W. Levy's *Jefferson and Civil Liberties: The Darker Side*. But, despite his criticism, Professor Levy was an admirer of Thomas Jefferson. For example, he wrote: "I would strongly agree with anyone who contended that much of Jefferson was the best of his day and that the best of Jefferson was often the best of America." Professor Levy argues that Jefferson "cannot be held responsible for having been born a white man in eighteenth century Virginia." LEONARD W. LEVY, JEFFERSON AND CIVIL LIBERTIES viii–x (1989). As Professor Levy notes with obvious displeasure in the Preface to the paperback edition of his book, his criticisms of Jefferson were not widely embraced by his reviewers. *Id.* at xi–xxvi.

48. *See, e.g.*, ELLIS, AMERICAN SPHINX 15 (acknowledging Merrill Peterson as being "the best Jefferson biographer alive...."). Malone, who died a decade before Professor Ellis' book was published— was widely recognized as the world's preeminent Jefferson scholar even before publication of most of his six-volume biography, which won the 1975 Pulitzer Prize for History based upon the volumes published to that point. For example, in a 1956 introduction to a collection of letters between two nineteenth century historians, one scholar remarked that Henry S. Randall's work "will probably remain unsurpassed as a biography of the third president until the completion of *Jefferson and His Time* by Dumas Malone." George Green Shackelford (ed.), *New Letters between Hugh Blair Grigsby and Henry Stephens Randall, 1858–1861*, VIRGINIA MAGAZINE OF HISTORY AND BIOGRAPHY, July 1956 at 327.

49. Ellis, *Jefferson: Post-DNA* at 129–30.

50. My primary source for this alarming statement was Dr. Wallenborn, but another member of the Monticello committee who did not want to be identified recalled it as well. Professor Onuf has more

Published accounts suggest that Professor Onuf takes seriously this freedom from the constraints of historical facts. At a February 1999 forum on "Thomas Jefferson and Sally Hemings: The Facts and Their Significance," he reportedly asserted that the DNA revelations provided a "wonderful opportunity for rethinking and reconstructing Jefferson," and alleged that the only slaves Jefferson ever freed "were Hemings' children." Professor Onuf added that "Jefferson's days as an icon" were "limited."[51]

Even the Thomas Jefferson Memorial Foundation, for decades perhaps the greatest champion of the legacy of America's third President, seemed to get with the new program. It formally changed its name to "Thomas Jefferson Foundation"—deleting "Memorial" from its title—and subsequently a Monticello guide was reportedly chastised for being a bit too enthusiastic in his praise of Jefferson during a house tour. The guide asserts that he or she was cautioned that "we are not in the business of memorializing Thomas Jefferson any longer."[52]

The Thomas Jefferson Heritage Society

Still, not *everyone* was convinced. Several people with strong interests in Thomas Jefferson looked beyond the headlines and realized that the public had been misled about the nature of the DNA "proof." One was a retired University of Virginia Medical School Professor, Dr. White McKenzie Wallenborn, who as a Monticello guide had been a part of the Monticello Research Committee and had resigned in protest when he learned that his minority report had been concealed from others on the committee for eight months and was not released when the majority report was given to the press.[53]

Several skeptics joined together to form the "Thomas Jefferson Heritage Society (TJHS)," including lawyers, doctors, a consultant with a Ph.D. in environmental science, a retired Library of Congress expert whose extensive database of Thomas Jefferson quotations is featured on the University of Virginia website, an immigrant from Iran who became a highly successful building contractor, a retired Air Force veteran with a strong interest in genealogy, and some rather extraordinary[54] "ordinary people" with the common bond of a strong admiration for Thomas Jefferson and a sense that he had been "convicted" without receiving a fair trial. They asked a Jefferson descendant named John Works—an attorney

---

recently written: "If further evidence was needed to banish Jefferson from the national pantheon, the recent confirmation of his relationship with his slave Sally Hemings provides it...." PETER S. ONUF, JEFFERSON'S EMPIRE 3 (2000).

51. LuAnn Bishop, *Untangling "Historical Jumble" About Jefferson No Easy Feat, Say Scholars: The Portrait That Historians Have Traditionally Painted of Founding Father Thomas Jefferson is Long Overdue for a Major Overhaul*, YALE BULLETIN & CALENDAR, Feb. 22–Mar. 1, 1999, vol. 27, no. 22.

52. This account was provided to me by a Monticello guide who values her or his job under an assurance that I would not identify my source.

53. Two months after release of the *Monticello Report*, Dr. Wallenborn's minority report was posted on the Monticello website. *See: http://www.monticello.org/plantation/minority_report.html.*

54. I knew none of these people prior to being invited (along with some very distinguished local Jefferson scholars) to attend a March 7, 2000, luncheon at the Boar's Head Inn in Charlottesville to discuss the *Monticello Report*. I had never set eyes on or spoken to Mr. Works until he telephoned me after receiving our final report. With the exception of Dr. Michael Moffitt (who has been wonderfully helpful in managing the Scholars Commission's financial account—making hotel reservations, reimbursing members for air travel, assisting with mailings, and the like), I did not to my knowledge personally meet with anyone in the group between that luncheon and the release of our report on April 12, 2001.

working at the time as a petroleum company executive in Romania, who had once served as president of the Monticello Association (the family organization of descendants of Thomas Jefferson that owns the small family graveyard at Monticello)—to serve as their president.

One of the first decisions of the new TJHS was to establish a blue-ribbon panel of Thomas Jefferson scholars to reexamine all of the evidence and issue a public report. Thus was conceived the Scholars Commission on the Jefferson-Hemings Matter.

About the Scholars Commission

Between the spring of 2000 and April 2001, a number of American scholars who have long had a professional interest in Thomas Jefferson and/or his era engaged in a reexamination of all of the available evidence and arguments concerning Thomas Jefferson's alleged paternity of one or more children by his slave Sally Hemings. While our membership fluctuated slightly over the months, the thirteen scholars who persevered to the end come from prominent universities spread from southern California to Maine and south to Alabama. They are trained in such diverse disciplines as history, political science, law, economics, and biochemistry. Collectively, our professional careers span well over three centuries and include teaching or research appointments at Harvard, Yale, Stanford, Smith, Virginia, and many other respected institutions of higher learning.

Most of the scholars have risen to national prominence in their field. Several hold or have held such titles as "distinguished" or "eminent" professor, and most have held at least one chaired professorship or have served as chairman of their department or its graduate studies program. Every member of the group, even the lawyers, holds an academic doctorate, and among us we have authored or edited more than one hundred books, many of them dealing specifically with Thomas Jefferson.

None of this, of course, guarantees that we have reached the correct conclusions. We invite readers to consider our conclusions and the supporting arguments on the merits, to compare them to the conclusions of others, and to draw their own conclusions about where the truth may lie.

After decades of study, it would be remarkable if there was a single member of the Scholars Commission who did not enter the project with opinions both about Thomas Jefferson and about the allegation that he was sexually involved with Sally Hemings. Most, but not all, of us consider ourselves admirers of Thomas Jefferson; and most, but not all, of us had over the years been skeptical about the Sally Hemings story prior to the release of the DNA tests and the *Monticello Report*.

Our mission appeared at first to be a simple one. In the finest Jeffersonian tradition, we were asked to "pursue the truth, wherever it might lead," examining all of the known evidence and any new evidence we could find, considering all of the arguments on both sides of the issue, and then to issue a public report giving our best professional judgments about the likelihood that Thomas Jefferson fathered one or more children by Sally Hemings. We have done so to the best of our abilities. But it was not an easy task given the paucity of reliable information and the passage of roughly two centuries of time.

There is a reason that my Individual Views are the most extensive. When we began our inquiry, there were several existing summaries of what might be termed "the case against Thomas Jefferson."[55] Each of us began by carefully reading the Thomas Jefferson Memorial Foundation Research Committee's *Report on Thomas Jefferson and Sally Hemings* (a ten-page report supplemented by forty-three pages of appendices, also referred to herein as the *Monticello Report*), and most of us also read at least substantial portions of Professor Annette Gordon-Reed's *Thomas Jefferson and Sally Hemings*. In an effort both to identify the various major arguments in favor of Thomas Jefferson's paternity of one or more of Sally Hemings' children and to identify arguments in Jefferson's defense, with the encouragement of other members of the Scholars Commission I agreed to prepare a "working document" that would try to identify the arguments on both sides. In the end, this came down to identifying six major arguments in favor of Jefferson's paternity, critiquing each of them, and then looking at "evidence" acknowledged by Jefferson's critics which I felt they had dismissed too quickly and another series of relevant issues they had largely ignored. The plan was that others in the group would then identify points I had overlooked or omitted and provide their own critique of the arguments on both sides. When we gathered at a hotel near Dulles Airport for three days of lengthy discussions in December 2000, with the encouragement of others, I decided to use this "working document" as the basis of my own Individual Views—at which time I added this introduction and a new chapter about how little we actually know about Sally Hemings. My final Postscript was added years later to provide some additional thoughts and assess the initial impact of our efforts. Since 2001, I have also revised and made additions to these earlier chapters to reflect new thoughts or available information. So if my views read like the "counter-brief" to the arguments of revisionist scholars and the *Monticello Report*, that is because they were originally prepared to serve precisely that purpose.

I want to emphasize that, while several of my colleagues have agreed to add their names to this statement, and in preparing it I have benefited from the able counsel not only of many members of the Scholars Commission but also from a number of other individuals on both sides of the debate (some of whom are identified below), the words are mine and *responsibility for the specific arguments and the accuracy of facts is mine alone*. It is important to emphasize this point because I have continued to make additions and changes to the manuscript even after others had agreed to "sign on" or "concur" in my earlier draft; please do not assume that the scholars whose names appear alongside my own on the cover page to these Individual Views have even *read* every sentence of the final version.

Yet another caveat is in order. While one year may seem like a lot of time for such an inquiry, in fact most of us also have full-time jobs and we have had to do our work on this issue as an "extracurricular activity" in addition to the work for which we get paid. This document remains, in essence, a "working document" that I hope will assist others in understanding how I reached my own conclusions in this inquiry. It does not pretend to be the final word on the topic, and it leaves several issues unresolved. There is no doubt in my mind that careful research by scholars in the future will produce informa-

---

55. Some may ask why Thomas Jefferson would need to be "defended" for having a sexual relationship with an African-American woman following the death of his wife; were that the issue I would respond, "I hope they both found love and happiness" and continue my work on more serious matters. But, like many Americans, I have serious moral problems with the idea of a forty-five-year-old man "seducing" (or permitting himself to be "seduced" by) a thirteen-to-fifteen-year-old child (who, in this case, Abigail Adams tells us, lacked the maturity of Jefferson's own eight-year-old daughter). Far more importantly, while the common-law "age of consent" during Jefferson's lifetime ranged from ten to twelve, I find the concept of *consent* in the master-slave relationship very difficult to comprehend. In my view, if the relationship began in Paris as alleged, Thomas Jefferson was both a child molester and a rapist. Neither role is easy for me to accept based upon my understanding of the man following more than three decades of study.

tion relevant to this inquiry; however, in my judgment, the avenues that were not pursued further were unlikely to produce evidence that would have changed my basic conclusions.

To me, this is not as close a decision as it was for a few of my colleagues, and were I on a jury in this matter, I would have no difficulty finding Thomas Jefferson "not guilty." That is certainly true were the advocates of his alleged paternity obligated to meet the legal standard of establishing his guilt by "clear and convincing evidence" or even by "a preponderance of the evidence"; but I would go so far as to say that my research in connection with this project has persuaded me that he is "*innocent* beyond reasonable doubt." And perhaps I should add that, despite my long admiration for our third President, when first approached about this inquiry I had assumed—on the basis of press reports on both the DNA tests and the subsequent *Monticello Report*—that Thomas Jefferson's paternity of Eston Hemings had been scientifically established.

The first nine chapters of my Individual Views will examine the arguments that have been raised to support the conclusion that Thomas Jefferson fathered one or more children by Sally Hemings. Chapter Ten will then turn to a series of issues that I believe have been too quickly glossed over by Jefferson's critics, such as the eyewitness testimony of Thomas Jefferson's overseer that he often witnessed another man leaving Sally Hemings' room early in the morning while he was arriving at Monticello for work.

Chapter Eleven will look at some of the "evidence" that has received little consideration—in part because much of it apparently does not exist. That is to say, had a Jefferson-Hemings romance gone on in Paris and at Monticello for decades as alleged, there ought to be some direct evidence to support it. Someone should have seen or heard *something* and left a record. Like the dog that did not bark in Sherlock Holmes' short story, *Silver Blaze*, some of the strongest evidence in this case may be the fact that not one of the hundreds if not thousands of visitors who swarmed over Monticello while this relationship was supposedly going on left a shred of evidence of having observed any sign of the alleged affair. No one left a record of seeing a suggestive glance, a passing caress, or even the President and Sally Hemings walking or talking together. For seventy years[56] after the scandal broke, neither Sally Hemings—who for nearly a decade after Thomas Jefferson's death lived as a free white woman in Charlottesville—nor any of her children left any record of having asserted that her relationship with Thomas Jefferson went beyond that of master-slave. With but two exceptions that will be discussed in Chapter Four, none of the hundreds of slaves who lived at Monticello during this period left any record that they believed the story.

Then there is the issue of Thomas Jefferson's extraordinary investment in his own reputation, and his obvious devotion to his young daughters. Was he reckless enough to entrust his cherished reputation to the discretion of a child whom Abigail Adams had just described as wanting more care than his eight-year-old daughter? As a widower and a popular figure in Parisian diplomatic and social circles, where he could have had his pick among numerous beautiful and talented women, would Thomas Jefferson have jeopardized his daughters' respect by seeking passion in the arms of their young servant girl? These and other questions have in my view been given *far* too little consideration thus far in this debate.

---

56. This is meant to exclude the 1873 *Pike County Republican* article alleging that Madison Hemings made such a charge. There is a notation in an 1870 census record alleging that Madison was Thomas Jefferson's son, which could reasonably be interpreted as indicating that Madison made such a claim, so perhaps it would be more accurate to say "sixty-nine" years.

Methodology, Admissible Evidence, and Burdens of Proof

Perhaps a few words should be said at this point about the methodology of this inquiry and such things as the quality of acceptable evidence and burdens of proof. When the passage of centuries prevents us from examining witnesses, reliable documentary evidence is scarce, and recorded statements attributed to various individuals are in conflict, what are we to believe? Our task is to "search for the truth," but just where do we find that truth among the conflicting accounts and almost total lack of serious information about one of the alleged key participants?

Addressing the Jefferson-Hemings issues, the late historian Professor Douglass Adair— former editor of the *William & Mary Quarterly*, who was recently acknowledged by revisionist historian Professor Peter Onuf as "one of the most important early American historians of his generation"[57]—once observed: "The professional historian is taught to be extremely skeptical of any purported episode in a man's career that completely contradicts the whole tenor of his life and that requires belief in a total reversal of character."[58] Many of the most prominent "new believers" in the story that Thomas Jefferson fathered children by Sally Hemings have acknowledged that such behavior would have been totally out of character for him; and there is widespread agreement that journalist James Callender had neither credibility nor actual knowledge of events at Monticello. I continue to believe that the allegations of a long-term "affair" must be established by credible evidence before we can conclude the story is more likely than not the truth. Idle speculation and "could-have-been" hypotheses, reinforced by triple-hearsay accounts from unknown sources, are not sufficient.

On the other hand, it has been suggested that it is well established throughout the United States that paternity cannot be established without "clear and convincing" proof based upon evidence that would be admissible in court. That is, indeed, the legal standard; but we are not engaged in a legal dispute designed to affect the property or liberty rights of individuals. One might argue that Thomas Jefferson's reputation ought to be of sufficient interest to society that nothing short of legally sufficient proof should be permitted to tarnish it; but that ignores the realities of historical research. If we are in pursuit of the truth, we must be willing to consider not only "hearsay" evidence, but also second- and third-degree hearsay.

While not controlling, legal rules of evidence are also not irrelevant to our inquiry. There is a *reason* courts do not like to entertain hearsay accounts: experience over many centuries has confirmed that such statements tend to be less reliable and thus less probative of the truth than direct testimony of those who actually took part in a dispute or observed it first-hand. Each time a story is retold to a new person, additional risks of either intentional or inadvertent error enter the picture.

In Chapter Four, we will examine a classic evidentiary problem. A story is written by one man (an anti-Jefferson journalist), alleging to contain statements made by a second man (Sally Hemings' son Madison) about the truth of factual matters that occurred before Madison's birth and for which he provides no explanation or "source" for his reported beliefs. The issue is complicated further by the fact that Madison waited nearly half a century after receiving his freedom to tell his story, and thus his recollections may

---

57. Peter Onuf, *Adair, The Intellectual Origins of Jeffersonian Democracy*, 63 WM. & MARY Q. 1035, 1038 (2001).

58. DOUGLASS ADAIR, FAME AND THE FOUNDING FATHERS 181 (Trevor Colbourn ed., 1974).

not have been fresh. When we realize that he held clear feelings of resentment toward one of the subjects of his account, and he stood to gain personally in terms of his status and prestige from his account, the document becomes even more problematic. And when we consider that his views were set to paper, without the use of quotation marks to capture his actual words, by a highly partisan journalist who had an anti-Jefferson "agenda" of his own, the document's utility in our search for truth is yet further compromised.[59]

Yet another example of the problems of hearsay surfaces in Chapter Nine and involves a statement by a Vermont schoolteacher named Elijah Fletcher, who traveled through Charlottesville and, after meeting with local citizens, reported that the Sally Hemings story was a "sacred truth." This, too, is among the "evidence" relied upon by various advocates of Jefferson's paternity of Sally Hemings' children. It begins as weak evidence — a prejudiced source reporting local gossip — and falls completely apart when one realizes the rest of the story. It turns out that Mr. Fletcher happened to have shared a stagecoach from Washington, D.C., to Charlottesville, with one of Thomas Jefferson's most vocal local critics. With John Kelly as his "tour guide" in Charlottesville, it is not surprising that Elijah Fletcher was introduced to others with a low opinion of the President.

In these cases, we have found enough contextual evidence to realize that the testimony has been influenced by enough biased sources to leave it little probative value. But here we were fortunate; how do we assess similar statements where we have no knowledge of the background or context? It is a serious problem for the historian.

From a legal perspective, the burden of going forward with the evidence properly falls upon the party advocating a particular fact. This is one of the many alarming features of the way the Jefferson-Hemings issue has recently been handled. In a setting where virtually no information is known, the absence of knowledge is not "proof" of anything (other, perhaps, than of the fact that there is no reliable evidence). To argue that an alleged fact should be presumed to be true because there is no evidence that it did not occur is not sound scholarship. Without other evidence, we cannot fairly conclude that Mr. Jones is a murderer simply because there is no proof someone else committed the crime. Similarly, suggesting that Sally Hemings must have been monogamous[60] because scholars did not accuse her of being otherwise (in a setting where there is little indication many scholars gave serious thought to the matter, or for that matter that evidence existed to permit an intelligent judgment on the issue) contributes nothing to the search for the truth. But this has been a common practice in the current debate.

One cannot prove with absolute certainty that Thomas Jefferson and George Washington were not both secret agents of the British Government during the American Revolution. To be sure, they both played leading roles in the revolution against Great Britain; but one might argue that a good spy would want such "cover" to have access to all of the best secrets.[61] As far as I can tell, neither Washington nor Jefferson ever "publicly denied"

---

59. Many of the statements by Jefferson's descendants are, of course, subject to similar risks of bias.

60. Not only do we have the eye-witness statement by Edmund Bacon that he frequently observed another man leaving Sally's room early in the morning, but two of the sources relied upon by advocates of Jefferson's paternity (Callender and Gibbons) specifically referred to Sally as being a "slut" or a "prostitute." Since there is no reason to believe that either "source" had any reliable information on the matter, and both had clear motives to portray Sally Hemings in an unfavorable light, their statements are entitled to very little weight. As will be discussed in Chapter Ten, Edmund Bacon's statement is perhaps the most valuable bit of evidence existent on this issue.

61. It is not surprising that several of the top Soviet spies discovered in recent years were employed by the CIA, the FBI, or a military intelligence agency. See, *e.g.*, TIM WEINER, BETRAYAL: THE

serving the British, and few if any of their leading biographers have addressed the issue. These facts are not evidence that either is guilty of the charge, and yet they are precisely the kind of "evidence" that is being offered by some to establish Thomas Jefferson's paternity of Sally Hemings' children.

Indeed, one of the many frustrating aspects of reading the books of Fawn Brodie, Annette Gordon-Reed, and some of the other advocates of a Jefferson-Hemings sexual relationship is how they pretend to find evidence from the lack of any information. For example, Professor Gordon-Reed tells her readers "[t]here is no indication that Jefferson discouraged free movement on James's part while in France."[62] From that, we are asked to accept, it follows that "It is likely that James would show Paris to his sister...."[63] Of course, one could just as easily argue that there is no evidence that James, or anyone else, ever showed his sister around Paris, and from that pretend that we have "evidence" that she spent almost all of her time sitting in a room alone at the Abbaye.[64] Both arguments are equally flawed. The point is not that James might not have taken his sister to see the big city, but that our almost complete lack of information about her stay in Paris does not constitute "evidence" that makes either interpretation "likely."

This problem also infects the Research Report of the Thomas Jefferson Memorial Foundation, which in concluding that Thomas Jefferson likely fathered all of Sally's children argued: "convincing evidence does not exist for the hypothesis that another male Jefferson was the father of Sally Hemings's children."[65] Obviously, the same reasoning could be used to point the blame at *any* male Jefferson. As will be shown in this report, there is no "convincing evidence" of the paternity of any of Sally Hemings' children. But it does not follow logically that our inability to pin responsibility on suspects B through X *ipso facto* makes suspect A guilty.

On another occasion, Professor Gordon-Reed seems to be arguing that the burden of proof in establishing paternity falls on counsel for the defense:

> Because Jefferson defenders have not been able to remove him from the list of possible fathers of Sally Hemings's children and because they have not presented a convincing case for another man's paternity, they must rely on particular characterizations of Jefferson and Sally Hemings that render him incapable of such a response.[66]

Surely the concept of "innocent until proven guilty" survives. One can only imagine how frequently many wealthy male celebrities would be defending themselves in paternity suits if the standard of proof really were that an individual was guilty unless he could prove another man to be the father.

Since the results of the DNA tests were released, it has become common for historians to suggest that the "burden has shifted" to Jefferson's defenders. Professors Lander

---

STORY OF ALDRICH AMES (1995); ADRIAN HAVILL, THE SPY WHO STAYED OUT IN THE COLD: THE SECRET LIFE OF FBI DOUBLE AGENT ROBERT HANSSEN (2001).

62. GORDON-REED, THOMAS JEFFERSON AND SALLY HEMINGS 163.

63. *Id.*

64. There are situations, of course, where observable consequences are so likely to follow an event that the absence of those consequences may be valuable evidence that the event did not occur. Thus, if we are asked to believe that the accused murdered his lover in a crowded hotel by shooting her with a twelve-gauge shotgun while she stood on a white carpet moments before the police arrived, the lack of bloodstains on the carpet or walls, and testimony by occupants of adjacent rooms that they heard no noise, might be powerful evidence for the defense.

65. *Monticello Report* at 9.

66. GORDON-REED, THOMAS JEFFERSON AND SALLY HEMINGS 184.

and Ellis wrote in the essay accompanying the release of the DNA data in *Nature* that the new evidence had "sealed the case" against Jefferson *vis-à-vis* Eston's paternity, and added: "The jury remains out with respect to Sally's other children, but the burden of proof has clearly shifted."[67] Writing later in *Sally Hemings and Thomas Jefferson*, Pulitzer-Prize recipient Gordon Wood added: "clearly the burden of proof has shifted: until otherwise disproved, Jefferson is now presumed to have fathered one or more of Sally Hemings's children.... So accepting of the sexual relationship are most historians now that it will be difficult for any future scholarly cautionary notes to get heard."[68]

As a practical matter this may well be true. But as a matter of science and logic, the DNA tests did no more than establish that Eston Hemings' father was almost certainly a Jefferson. Once it is established that more than one Jefferson male was likely present at Monticello when Eston was conceived, the DNA tests create no presumptions between competing candidates for paternity. At that point, we must return to the study of history and the analysis of other potential evidence.

By what standard do we assess competing interpretative arguments from the available evidence? The fourteenth-century logician William of Occam is credited with the Latin maxim *pluralitas non est ponenda sine necesitate*, which roughly translates, "Entities should not be unnecessarily multiplied," or more colloquially, "Don't make more assumptions than are necessary to explain what is observed." This is often also identified as the "principle of parsimony," the "principle of simplicity," or merely "Occam's Razor," and it is at the heart of most scientific inquiry.[69]

There are, without doubt, conspiracies and cover-ups in life. But there are also wrongful accusations. Professors Brodie and Gordon-Reed have shown that, with a bit of creativity and some flexibility in handling the facts, it is possible to make an argument that Thomas Jefferson and Sally Hemings *might* have had a sexual relationship. That point is conceded. The issue before us is whether there is serious evidence suggesting that such a relationship was likely, and whether after evaluating all of the evidence there is a simpler explanation that is equally consistent with the known facts.

Finally, there is another logical fallacy at play in this debate. The fact that we have no information about where Thomas Jefferson was at a given hour on a particular night leaves open the possibility that he was in the arms of Sally Hemings or some other woman. But it does not constitute "evidence" of that relationship, nor is it correct to assume that the odds he was with Sally are "fifty-fifty." There is a temptation to think: "Well, either he was or he wasn't. With only two alternatives, the probability of one or the other is fifty percent. It's a toss-up question."

To illustrate the fallacy of this reasoning, let us consider another hypothesis. Let us assume that on a particular day in his professional life, no record exists of whether or not George Bush (either of them, or Bill Clinton if you prefer) wore socks. If someone without knowledge of the facts alleged that he wore orange socks on that day, we would not assume the odds were fifty-fifty in favor of such a proposition—and even if stated

---

67. Eric S. Lander & Joseph J. Ellis, *Founding Father*, Nature, Nov. 5, 1998, at 13.

68. Gordon S. Wood, *The Ghosts of Monticello*, in Sally Hemings & Thomas Jefferson 27 (Jan Ellen Lewis & Peter S. Onuf, eds., 1999).

69. I first encountered the concept from my father when I was a young student. He told me of an incident during his medical residency in which a colleague had listened to the symptoms of a patient—symptoms of a rather common disorder—and suggested a diagnosis of a very rare illness having similar symptoms. The presiding physician looked at him and said: "Mr. Jones. When you hear hoof beats, think of horses, not unicorns."

in the alternative that he either wore orange socks or did not wear orange socks, the odds would not change. Nor are the odds fifty-fifty that he wore no socks that day, as we can reasonably predict from things we do know about their behavior that these men have worn socks most of the days of their adult lives. Thus, we should resist the temptation to think: "Well, we can't conclusively prove that Thomas Jefferson had an affair with Sally Hemings or that he did not. Thus, the odds are fifty-fifty, and the issue is a 'toss up.'"

Acknowledgments

I am particularly grateful for the opportunity to work with the exceptional group of senior scholars who made up the Scholars Commission. I knew most of them from their Jefferson writings or by reputation, but before this inquiry few were even casual acquaintances, much less friends. Among the many sources of satisfaction during this inquiry have been the warm friendships I have made with a group of scholars I deeply admire. I am indebted to them for their cooperative spirits, their helpful comments on my own work, and their patience as our final product has been delayed through no fault of their own.

One of my first official steps after accepting the invitation to chair the Scholars Commission was to contact Dr. Daniel Jordan, the highly regarded president (1986–2008) of the Thomas Jefferson Memorial Foundation (renamed "Thomas Jefferson Foundation" in 2000) to seek his help. Consistent with his reputation as a gentleman, he invited me to join him for lunch at Monticello and offered whatever assistance we needed. He was fully cooperative. I am indebted as well to Ms. Lucia Stanton, the Shannon Senior Research Historian at Monticello, who has responded promptly and candidly to all of my questions. These are emotional issues for many, and there has been a tendency by some on both sides to view those who take a different view as being either "traitors" or "racists." I understand the passions, but I see few obvious villains on either side of the debate.

During our lunch, Dr. Jordan urged me to resist the temptation to focus our investigation on the *Monticello Report* itself, and suggested in the alternative that we gather together a large group of student assistants and search for new evidence of relevance to the issue. I had already struck out in an effort to interest members of the Jefferson Literary and Debating Society at the University of Virginia in the issue, which surprised me given their traditional devotion to their University's founder and enthusiasm for a good quarrel.[70] Indeed, I sensed that this issue was viewed by many at the University as being so politically sensitive that I went to unusual steps to try to disassociate my work on the inquiry from my employment by the University of Virginia. During our inquiry I made no use of law student research assistants, and even opened a new e-mail account at home to minimize the necessity of using my University of Virginia account in connection with my work as a member of the Scholars Commission. Anyone who is displeased with my work

---

70. I am pleased to report that, when this comment came to the attention of members of the Society after our report was released in April 2001, I was invited to address the group (of which I had been an active member as a law student many years earlier) on the work of the Scholars Commission, and several members of the group volunteered to help if further research was necessary.

ought therefore direct his or her anger at me rather than my employer. No reasonable person can accuse the University of Virginia of trying to "protect" the reputation of its founder in this matter.[71]

There was one very notable exception, and a tremendous one at that, as it came from the most senior official at the University. University of Virginia Rector[72] John "Jack" P. Ackerly III, came to see me after reading a summary of our report in the *Wall Street Journal*[73] in 2001 and provided deeply appreciated encouragement and support. Jack Ackerly—and based upon his comments, I believe a majority of the other members of the University of Virginia Board of Visitors at the time—recognized that Thomas Jefferson was not receiving a fair hearing and tried to be supportive without in the process interfering with the academic freedom of members of the faculty.

My research brought me into contact with a number of very able private citizens who possessed both a remarkable knowledge about Thomas Jefferson and a willingness to do the serious business of scholarly research outside the limelight and (like the members of the Scholars Commission) without compensation. The list of those who helped is a long one, but I would be unforgivably remiss if I failed to acknowledge the tremendous help I received from Cynthia Harris Burton,[74] Eyler Coates, Sr.,[75] former Monticello guides Dr. White McKenzie Wallenborn (who also served on the Monticello research committee), and Dr. Michael Moffitt. They have been critically important to my efforts in this inquiry, and each of them deserves a large measure of the credit for any good I may have accomplished. Obviously, they are not responsible for my errors.

As our work progressed, it became clear that there were three organizations with a particular interest in our inquiry: the Thomas Jefferson Heritage Society (TJHS, which had asked us to undertake the inquiry), the Thomas Jefferson Memorial Foundation (TJMF, or TJF now that it has dropped the word "Memorial" from its name), and the Monticello Association (MA), which, as noted, is the family association of descendants of Thomas Jefferson. We tried to deal fairly with all three groups, and solicited new evidence and arguments from each of them. When our Final Report was completed just six

---

71. Even after Professor Joseph Ellis had admitted to repeated falsehoods and been suspended without pay by his college (a development discussed in the Postscript to this volume), and our report had pointed out at least one major alteration of an historical document in Professor Annette Gordon-Reed's documentation, both were hired by the University of Virginia to join other Jefferson critics in a June 2002 program on Jefferson. Responding to public pressures, two members of the Scholars Commission were added to the program at the last minute to provide balance.

72. The title "Rector" was held by University of Virginia founder Thomas Jefferson from the University's establishment in 1819 until his death in 1826, at which time James Madison became the second Rector. The University was run by the "Rector and Board of Visitors" (still the corporate board) until 1904, when Edwin Alderman became its first President.

73. Robert F. Turner, *The Truth About Jefferson*, Wall Street Journal, July 3, 2001.

74. After thirty-five years as a historical researcher in the Charlottesville area, Ms. Burton is certainly among the nation's leading genealogist specializing in the Jefferson family. In 2005 she published an excellent book entitled *Jefferson Vindicated: Fallacies, Omissions, and Contradictions in the Hemings Genealogical Search*, featuring a Foreword by former Thomas Jefferson Memorial Foundation Curator and Resident Director, Emeritus, James A. Bear, Jr., that is available for sale through the Monticello Gift Shop or on amazon.com.

75. Sadly, Eyler Robert Coates, Sr., passed away on January 10, 2002. He was a truly remarkable human being, a man of strong character and conviction, and one of the finest "natural scholars" it has been my pleasure to encounter during my professional life. He served the cause of truth admirably, and he will be missed.

days before it was released to the public, copies were e-mailed simultaneously to the heads of each of the three organizations.

By far the most responsive group was the TJHS, perhaps understandably given the fact that they had initiated our inquiry. During our year-long inquiry, I received numerous e-mails, faxes, research papers, articles, and even an advance copy of a book that members of the group had coauthored.[76]

Many others have provided helpful assistance or encouragement.[77] I have also benefited from the generous cooperation I received from some of the major participants in this dispute, including Dr. Eugene Foster and Professor Joseph Ellis.[78] Dr. Terry Turner,[79] of the University of Virginia Medical School, also provided very helpful assistance—sometimes by pointing out weaknesses in arguments that had been suggested (such as that the fact Thomas Jefferson fathered mostly girls and his brother Randolph only boys might be scientifically significant for our inquiry). That may have been a more valuable contribution than suggesting a new positive argument on one side or the other of this issue.

---

76. The Jefferson-Hemings Myth: An American Travesty (Eyler Robert Coates, Sr., ed. 2001). Particularly helpful, in addition to those already mentioned, have been (in alphabetical order): Mr. Herbert Barger; Mr. Bahman Batmanghelidj; Ms. Pamela Buell; Richard Dixon, Esq.; James F. McMurry, M.D.; and Ms. Rebecca L. McMurry. (I understand that not all of these people are formally associated with the TJHS, but I trust they will not object to being grouped together since they have all been associated in the same effort.)

77. Particularly helpful was Christopher Posteraro, at the time a student at Harvard Law School (and editor of the *Harvard Journal of Law & Public Policy*, to which I have occasionally contributed articles), who volunteered to do some research for me in a Harvard library and located an important issue of the *Virginia Federalist* that contained perhaps the first published reference to the possibility that Jefferson had fathered children by a slave. Other new-found friends, including Donais Lee and Barbara Frank, have provided helpful comments on drafts.

78. Despite his later difficulties and my own frustration at trying to reconcile his reputation as an excellent scholar with what seemed to be obvious errors in his post-DNA writings on the Hemings issue, I must note that Dr. Ellis' letter to me of October 31, 2000, could not have been more gracious. I had written to him (along with several others who had embraced the view that Thomas Jefferson probably fathered children by Sally Hemings) to ask whether he had found new information or come up with new arguments that might assist us in our inquiry. To quote a portion of his hand-written letter, Professor Ellis replied:

I'm not sure we will end up in the same camp, but I do respect and admire the integrity of your motives and the depth of your inquiry.

I think you're right—that you are pretty much in the same position I was pre-DNA. And you do a better job than I did (in the appendix of *Sphinx*) in assembling the dog-that-didn't-bark evidence. The civility of your dialogue with and about the evidence truly impresses me.

Such civility was not possible in the immediate aftermath of the DNA announcement. I was dismayed by the racial politics surrounding all discussions, the Gordon-Reed innuendo about those who "got it wrong" being racists, the preference of black oral history over other forms of evidence. But I was also struck by the filiopietistic motives of the Jefferson defenders, who seemed like trial lawyers defending a client.

My still current position: that before the DNA the judgment of a liaison was impossible to render clearly or authoritatively, but the preponderance of evidence was against. And that after the DNA the balance has shifted in favor of the liaison, though certainty is not in the cards.

There was not a sentence here that struck me as unreasonable. But it did not explain to me why he repeatedly said to *other* audiences that the case against Jefferson had been established "beyond reasonable doubt" or had failed to discuss other possible Jeffersons as Eston's father. Nevertheless, I was deeply impressed by his candor and graciousness, and therefore in many ways saddened over his subsequent difficulties.

79. Despite our common last name, I have no reason to believe Dr. Turner and I are related.

During the subsequent nearly nine years in which, as time permitted, I made some final corrections and additions to my Individual Views, I have been particularly fortunate to have the assistance of Steven Corneliussen—a professional science writer at the Jefferson Laboratories in Newport News, Virginia. Steve remains an agnostic on the Jefferson-Hemings issue, but was outraged over what he perceived as the "abuse of science" by some who believed that Thomas Jefferson had fathered one or more children by Sally Hemings. He not only agreed to personally read and comment on each of my chapters, but also recruited some outstanding professional scientists to help review one particularly disappointing "scientific" contribution to the debate. (See Chapter Five.)

Last, but certainly not least, I am indebted to my now seventeen-year-old son, Thomas, for his many months of tolerance in 2000–2001 while I spent night after night reading and then working at my computer until the early hours of the morning. Living with a single parent as a seven-year-old child is not always easy; and when "Dad" sometimes seems preoccupied with other priorities, it can be all the more difficult.

Disclaimer

I should again emphasize that my work on this project has been personal and not on behalf of the University of Virginia, its School of Law, the Center for National Security Law, or any other organization or entity with which I am currently or in the past have been affiliated. I have undoubtedly made errors, and I am confident they will be identified by others.[80] I suspect I may well be accused of making some errors on points I will continue to believe are valid, and in those cases I will submit the verdict to the reader. As Thomas Jefferson said in his First Inaugural Address:

> When right, I shall often be thought wrong by those whose positions will not command a view of the whole ground. I ask your indulgence for my own errors, which will never be intentional, and your support against the errors of others, who may condemn what they would not if seen in all its parts.

Weigh the evidence on all sides and draw your own conclusions, for on this issue it is clear that some very able scholars—on one side or the other—have reached the wrong conclusions. As Jefferson reminded us, we are in the end answerable not for the right-ness but only the *uprightness* of our decisions.[81]

Ultimately, our goal must be a search for the truth. That, I am persuaded, can best be attained by vigorous and open public debate. As my University's founder, Thomas Jefferson, wrote in 1820:

> This institution [the University of Virginia] will be based on the illimitable freedom of the human mind. For here we are not afraid to follow truth wherever it may lead, nor to tolerate any error so long as reason is left free to combat it.[82]

We must never abandon that principle.

---

80. See my Postscript at the back of this volume.

81. "Your own reason is the only oracle given you by heaven, and you are answerable, not for the rightness, but uprightness of the decision." *Jefferson to Peter Carr*, August 10, 1787, in 6 WRITINGS OF THOMAS JEFFERSON 261 (Mem. ed. 1904).

82. *Jefferson to William Roscoe*, Dec. 27, 1820, in 15 *id.* 302.

As will be discussed in my Postscript—which, I emphasize, reflects my own personal views only and has not even been seen by some members of the Scholars Commission—the sad reality has been that, in the aftermath of our April 2001 report, not one of the leading scholars in the revisionist camp has been willing to engage in public debate with us on this issue. To mention just one example, a debate being planned for the 2002 annual meeting of the American Political Science Association had to be cancelled when no one could be found to defend the position that Thomas Jefferson fathered children by Sally Hemings.

The most common response, I am told, was that scholars had "moved on" to other issues. That was also the explanation given by Dr. Daniel Jordan, President of the Thomas Jefferson Foundation, in explaining why the foundation did not think it would be useful to comment in detail on the Scholars Commission report.[83] I will leave to the reader the question of whether the strength of this report may have been a factor in such decisions to "move on" and reluctance to defend their positions on the Jefferson-Hemings controversy. In the absence of public debates, we are left with the alternative, as lawyers say, of submitting the case to the jury of public opinion "on the briefs."

---

83. I had earlier expressed a desire to Dr. Jordan for their comments and for them to identify any errors they perceived in our report so that we could consider and perhaps correct them before the book version was published.

1

Understanding the DNA Evidence Linking Eston Hemings to Thomas Jefferson's Cousins

One of the most influential pieces of evidence in this controversy was the 1998 DNA study, performed by eight scientists led by Dr. Eugene Foster and reported in the November 5, 1998, issue of the journal *Nature*,[1] showing that someone with the male Jefferson Y chromosome was probably the father of Eston, the youngest son of Sally Hemings. Sadly, it is also perhaps the most misunderstood piece of evidence—in part because the scientific protocol was arguably flawed,[2] but far more importantly because of the unprofessional manner in which the research results were sensationalized by the prestigious, London-based international science journal.

For example, while the Foster article acknowledged that their study showed Thomas Jefferson *might* have fathered one of Hemings' children, *Nature* entitled the article: "Jefferson fathered slave's last child."[3] An accompanying commentary by Professors Eric S. Lander and

---

1. E. A. Foster et al., *Scientific Correspondence: Jefferson fathered slave's last child*, Nature, Nov. 5, 1998, at 27. This article is reprinted in Thomas Jefferson Memorial Foundation Research Committee, *Report on Thomas Jefferson and Sally Hemings*, Jan. 2000, Appendix A (hereinafter "*Monticello Report*").

2. When our report was initially released I saw no problems with the DNA testing. However, to the extent that the purpose of the testing was to determine the paternity of Eston Hemings, the tests used obviously could not do that. A team of eleven scientists, lawyers, and historians writing about biohistory ethics in a 2004 issue of *Science* magazine observed: "Often, investigators fail to pose an investigative question capable of resolution by genetic testing. For example, Eugene Foster's 1998 comparative Y-chromosome study of the descendants of Thomas Jefferson and his slave Sally Hemings was intended to establish whether the President had fathered Hemings' children. Yet the study protocol was inappropriate for determining the paternity of Hemings' children—the only possible conclusion was that some Jefferson and Hemings male-line descendants had common relatives." Lori B. Andrews, et al., *Ethics: Constructing Ethical Guidelines for Biohistory*, Science, 9 Apr. 2004 vol. 304, at 215, 216. Even accepting that the protocol could not have scientifically established the paternity of Eston Hemings, it is not my personal view that the tests should not have been undertaken. They did contribute to our understanding of this issue by establishing that Thomas Woodson could not have been the son of Thomas Jefferson, and it could have ruled out Thomas Jefferson as the father of Eston Hemings as well had Eston's descendants not carried the Y-chromosome found in the Jefferson family. Thus, while I don't dispute the observation by Andrews, et al., that Foster's protocol could not have determined Eston's paternity, I believe the tests might have contributed to our understanding of these issues had they not been inaccurately sensationalized by *Nature* and the popular press. Dr. Foster was very candid in acknowledging this inherent shotcoming in any test in the absence of a sample of Thomas Jefferson's DNA, so I cannot fault him for doing a useful if imperfect study.

3. One might try to be charitable and assume they were just asserting that *some* "Jefferson" was Eston's father, but the title is so likely to be perceived as referring to the former President as to be irresponsible even without the less ambiguous references discussed below.

Joseph J. Ellis was prefaced by a bold-type summary which proclaimed that the "DNA analysis confirms that Jefferson was indeed the father of at least one of Hemings' children."[4]

Professor Ellis, the Ford Foundation Professor of History at Mount Holyoke College, was a very important participant in the controversy. In 1996, he won the prestigious National Book Award for his Jefferson biography, *American Sphinx*. In that volume, Ellis had dismissed the likelihood of a sexual relationship between Jefferson and Sally Hemings as being "remote" and based upon "flimsy and wholly circumstantial" evidence.[5] When such a respected historian who was known to be critical of the allegation announced that the 1998 DNA evidence had forced him to not just reconsider but completely *reverse* his position, many assumed the debate was over and did not bother to look closely at the evidence. Professor Ellis' prestige increased early the following year with publication of his *Founding Brothers*,[6] which won the 2001 Pulitzer Prize in History.

The Clinton Impeachment Factor

The story also may have been influenced by the fact that President William Jefferson Clinton was facing impeachment in the Congress on grounds related to sexual misconduct when the *Nature* story was rushed into print[7] only days before the 1998 congressional elections.[8] At least one of the contributing authors, Professor Ellis, was an outspoken critic of those proceedings,[9] and the *Nature* article he coauthored emphasized the "striking" parallels of the two cases.[10] He wrote that the "dominant effect of this news" would be "to make Clinton's sins less aberrant and more palatable."[11]

Four months after the *Nature* stories were published, an editorial in *Natural Science* magazine cautioned:

> Both the media and the public at large should be skeptical about all scientific claims until they have been evaluated, not only by peer-reviewed journals, but also in the open forum of scientific and public discussion. In particular, the pub-

---

4. Eric S. Lander & Joseph J. Ellis, *Founding Father*, NATURE, Nov. 5, 1998, vol. 396, issue no. 6706 at 13.

5. JOSEPH J. ELLIS, AMERICAN SPHINX 366 (1996).

6. JOSEPH J. ELLIS, FOUNDING BROTHERS: THE REVOLUTIONARY GENERATION (2000).

7. *See, e.g.*, Eliot Marshall, *Genetics: Which Jefferson Was the Father?* SCIENCE, Jan. 8, 1999 at 153–54 ("Foster agrees that the headlines were 'misleading' because they suggested that the data were conclusive. He attributes this 'unfortunate' slipup to the haste with which his article and the Lander-Ellis essay went to press.... *Nature* staffer Rosalind Cotter agrees that 'the whole thing really was rushed through.'") *See also*, Andrew Cain, *Journal backs off on Jefferson Report: Says there is no way to prove he had child with slave*, WASH. TIMES, Jan. 7, 1999 at A1. In his discussions with me, Dr. Foster asserted that the rush to publish the articles was unrelated to the upcoming congressional election but rather was necessary because Professor Ellis had given the story to *U.S. News & World Report*, which was about to make it public.

8. The issue was scheduled for release on Tuesday, November 3, which was Election Day in the United States, but was released instead on Friday, October 30.

9. For example, Professor Ellis was one of "four hundred professional historians" who signed an advertisement in the *New York Times* on Oct. 30, 1998, denouncing the impeachment effort.

10. "Politically, the Thomas Jefferson verdict is likely to figure in upcoming impeachment hearings on William Jefferson Clinton's sexual indiscretions, in which DNA testing has also played a role. The parallels are hardly perfect, but some are striking." Lander & Ellis 13.

11. *Quoted in* Sean Wilentz, *What Tom and Sally Teach Us*, NEW REPUBLIC, Nov. 30, 1998, at 14.

lic should be skeptical about scientific claims that support political interests. When such claims lack intrinsic scientific significance (as in the case of those made in the Foster paper), their publication in a scientific journal should be recognized for what it is: an abuse of the scientific press.[12]

The DNA Tests

A more important contributing factor than the *Nature* articles to the misunderstanding may have been the widespread confusion about the nature of the Jefferson-Hemings DNA tests. Most Americans learned about DNA testing during the period leading up to and during the 1995 murder trial of O.J. Simpson, and they read in *USA Today* and other major papers that DNA "genetic fingerprints" are "99.9% accurate,"[13] or even "99.99 percent accurate."[14] When the Jefferson-Hemings DNA story broke four years later, it was not surprising that many people assumed scientists had matched Thomas Jefferson's DNA with that of one of Sally Hemings' children, and conclusively established Jefferson's paternity by this remarkable new technology. But that is clearly not the case.

First, there exists no known DNA from *Thomas* Jefferson to analyze. And since the only Jefferson children to have children of their own were daughters, there exists no unbroken male line of Thomas Jefferson's known descendants to test. So Dr. Foster used DNA taken from the blood of descendants of two of Thomas Jefferson's cousins.[15] For the testing that was done, this should not have been a problem. The tests were not designed to place Thomas Jefferson at a crime scene beyond reasonable doubt, but rather simply to ascertain whether one of Sally Hemings' children was likely fathered by *any* "male Jefferson." Since, in the absence of illegitimate birth at some stage, Thomas Jefferson should have had the same male Y chromosome as his paternal male ancestors and their direct-line male descendants—and, very important, his brother and his brother's sons as well—Dr. Foster's approach in using descendants of Thomas Jefferson's cousins was scientifically sound and unobjectionable.[16] The problem has been the widespread confusion by scholars, press, and public alike of this more general test—designed merely to ascertain whether

---

12. *"Jefferson fathered slave's last child"—journal article raises a question of credibility,* Natural Science, Mar. 19, 1999, available on line at: http://naturalscience.com/ns/articles/edit/ns_ed05.html.

13. Kevin Maney, *DNA Test Basks in Simpson Spotlight,* USA Today, Dec. 2, 1994, at 2B.

14. Andy Soltis, *Evidence Bolsters Cops' Case,* Boston Herald, June 18, 1994, at 2.

15. It is of course equally correct to describe the sources of the DNA as descendants of Thomas Jefferson's paternal uncle (Field Jefferson, elder brother of Thomas Jefferson's father, Peter Jefferson), as Dr. Foster does, or as descendants of Thomas Jefferson's paternal grandfather, as Professors Lander and Ellis do in *Nature.* The key point, conceded by all involved when pressed, is that the data from the DNA study do not point towards *Thomas* Jefferson's paternity any more strongly than they do towards any of his male relatives. To be sure, there are other variables that should influence a reasonable judgment in this matter—including proximity and opportunity when Eston was conceived, age and health of the possible fathers, character, and the like—that will be discussed below.

16. Some questions have been raised about the failure to follow all of the sample control procedures required for DNA testing to be admissible in a court of law. I personally am not especially troubled by this. Realistically, while there may have been somewhat greater risk of samples being inadvertently mixed up, such an error would presumably be far more likely to produce a false negative than a false positive result. My strong sense is that Dr. Foster and his colleagues in this enterprise are highly professional individuals whose work warrants a strong presumption of validity.

some male Jefferson likely fathered a Hemings child—with the far more precise "genetic fingerprint" technique made famous by the Simpson trial.

Considered by itself, the results of the DNA tests in the Jefferson-Hemings controversy suggest that the statistical probability Thomas Jefferson was the father of Sally Hemings' youngest child range from as high as seventeen to as low as four percent[17]—or perhaps a bit lower if the possibility of a slave father carrying the Jefferson DNA is considered.[18] The DNA tests could not discriminate among the more than two dozen adult male Jeffersons in Virginia at the time Eston Hemings was conceived, and there is reasonable evidence to suggest that at least seven[19] of those men (including Thomas Jefferson) may well have been at Monticello when Sally became pregnant with Eston.[20] It should be obvious that these DNA tests say nothing about the paternity of any of Sally Hemings' children whose descendants were not tested.

When one considers such factors as Thomas Jefferson's advanced age (sixty-four at the time of Eston's conception), his reputation, his health, and the fact that—unlike Thomas Jefferson—at least one of the other key suspects had a propensity, documented in *Memoirs of a Monticello Slave*, "to come out among black people, play the fiddle and dance half the night"[21] when he visited Monticello, the odds that *Thomas* Jefferson was Eston's father would seem to decrease even further. But if that is true, why have so many people across the country and around the world been so misinformed?

Overstating the Results

The problem lies not only with a news media prone to over simplifying and sensationalizing complex stories.[22] Numerous prominent scholars have contributed to the mis-

---

17. The difference is based upon whether one considers all Jefferson males of sufficient age to father a child and believed to have been in Virginia around the time Eston was conceived, or narrows the field of suspects to only those likely to have been in the vicinity of Monticello at the time—such as brother Randolph Jefferson and his sons, who lived near Monticello and were invited to visit shortly before Eston's estimated conception.

18. Thomas Jefferson inherited at least two slaves from his father who were thought to have been fathered by a white man. If their father (or grandfather) was their owner (Thomas Jefferson's father or grandfather), or another visiting member of the Jefferson family, they would have carried the same Y chromosome as Thomas Jefferson. We do not give this possibility any weight in our analysis, but we also cannot absolutely rule out the possibility that older Monticello slaves carried the Jefferson chromosome.

19. When this chapter was written in 2000, I was working from the data provided in the *Monticello Report* about Randolph Jefferson's children. They estimated James Lilburne Jefferson's year of birth as *circa* 1789. (*Monticello Report*, Appendix J at 3.) I am now less confident that James was seventeen or eighteen years old; so elsewhere you will find me counting only the four of Randolph's children (all sons) we know were well past their eighteenth birthday—an age which certainly would make them eligible suspects for the paternity of Eston Hemings.

20. We know that Thomas Jefferson was at Monticello at least part of the period in which Sally Hemings probably conceived Eston, and we know that he had invited his younger brother, Randolph (a widower who had at least four sons old enough to father a child and lived only about twenty miles from Monticello) to visit during this same period. This issue will be addressed in greater detail in Chapters Five and Ten.

21. Memoirs of a Monticello Slave, *reprinted in* Jefferson at Monticello 22 (James A. Bear, Jr. ed., 1967.) The description by former slave Isaac Jefferson is of Thomas Jefferson's younger brother, Randolph, who will be discussed in Chapter Ten.

22. For an excellent summary of the numerous articles and columns that misreported the DNA evidence in the *Washington Post, see* E. R. Shipp, *Reporting on Jefferson*, Wash. Post, May 30, 1999,

understanding by characterizing the DNA study as "confirming"[23] or "clinching"[24] the case for Thomas Jefferson's paternity.

In the article accompanying the Foster DNA study in *Nature*, the respected Professor Ellis announced that, when considered with the circumstantial evidence, the DNA evidence "seems to seal the case that Jefferson was Eston Hemings' father."[25] Writing later in the *William & Mary Quarterly*, Ellis concluded that "Jefferson's paternity of several [*sic*] Hemings children is proven 'beyond a reasonable doubt' "[26] by the DNA study. This is an absurd statement.

In an introduction to this same issue of the *Quarterly*, Rutgers University Professor Jan Lewis added that "virtually all professional historians" now accept "that Jefferson was the father of at least one of Sally Hemings's children...."[27] I am aware of no reliable survey of opinion on this issue, but to the extent that it is true that professional historians accept the allegations, I suspect it has as much to do with misunderstanding the significance of the DNA tests and widespread respect for Professor Ellis as it does with the actual merits of the case for Jefferson's paternity. This is being written before most of the professional historians on the Scholars Commission have voiced their final conclusions; but I will be greatly surprised if—after spending nearly a year looking carefully at all of the evidence—anything like "virtually all" of them find it probable that Thomas Jefferson fathered Eston Hemings.

Writing in *The New Republic*, Princeton historian Professor Sean Wilentz began: "The DNA test proving that Thomas Jefferson fathered at least one child with his slave Sally Hemings was good news...."[28] Consider also the case of Dr. Daniel Jordan, the respected President (1985–2008) of the Thomas Jefferson Memorial Foundation (TJMF)[29] that runs Jefferson's home at Monticello and promotes scholarship about the famous President. Few if any organizations have done more over the decades to promote the legacy of Thomas Jefferson. When interviewed for the 1997 Ken Burns PBS video, *Thomas Jefferson*, Dr. Jordan asserted there was "no historical evidence that there was a relationship between Thomas Jefferson and Sally," noted that such a relationship would be "totally out of character," and concluded that it was "morally impossible for that relationship to have occurred."[30] And yet, in a press statement on November 1, 1998, Dr. Jordan asserted: "Dr. Foster's DNA evidence indicates a sexual relationship between Thomas Jefferson and Sally Hemings, an African-American woman who was one of his slaves."[31]

---

at B6. An even earlier critique of media coverage of the story in general was provided in the same newspaper by David Murray, *Paternity Hype Visits Monticello*, WASH. POST, Nov. 15, 1998 at C1.

23. Jan Ellen Lewis & Peter Onuf, *Introduction* to SALLY HEMINGS AND THOMAS JEFFERSON 11.

24. Rhys Isaac, *Monticello Stories Old and New*, in SALLY HEMINGS AND THOMAS JEFFERSON 119.

25. Eric S. Lander & Joseph J. Ellis, *Founding Father*, NATURE, Nov. 5, 1998, at 13, *reprinted in Monticello Report*, Appendix A.

26. Joseph J. Ellis, *Jefferson: Post-DNA*, 57 WILLIAM & MARY QUARTERLY 126 (2000).

27. Jan Lewis, *Thomas Jefferson and Sally Hemings Redux: Introduction*, in SALLY HEMINGS AND THOMAS JEFFERSON at 121. See also the assertion that Jefferson "almost certainly" fathered at least one of Sally Hemings' children by Yale University Professor David Brion Davis, in his *Preface* to LUCIA STANTON, FREE SOME DAY: THE AFRICAN-AMERICAN FAMILIES OF MONTICELLO 12 (2000).

28. Wilentz, *What Tom and Sally Teach Us* at 14.

29. In 2001 this organization was renamed "Thomas Jefferson Foundation," or TJF.

30. The full text of this insightful interview can be found on the PBS web page at *http://www.pbs.org/jefferson/archives/interviews/Jordan.htm*.

31. Statement of Daniel P. Jordan, Ph.D., president, Thomas Jefferson Memorial Foundation, DNA Press Conference at the International Center for Jefferson Scholars, November 1, 1998, reprinted in *Monticello Report*, Appendix D.

Dr. Foster deserves credit for his efforts to correct the misunderstanding. He published letters in both *Nature*[32] and *The New York Times*[33] noting that the headline had overstated the actual conclusions of his work.[34] But he also may bear some of the responsibility for the misunderstanding.[35] Rather than saying that his findings "provide evidence that he [Thomas Jefferson] *was* the biological father of Eston Hemings Jefferson"[36]—which is not inaccurate, but may have been subject to misinterpretation—a more precise phraseology might have been to report that Thomas Jefferson "*may have been*" Eston's biological father.

Distinguishing History from Science

Another problem with the scientists' historical interpretation of their DNA findings was the exclusion of any alternative candidates for Eston's paternity other than Thomas Jefferson or his nephews by his sister Martha, Peter and Samuel Carr. Thus, the *Nature* article concludes: "The simplest and most probable explanations for our molecular findings are that Thomas Jefferson, *rather than one of the Carr brothers*, was the father of Eston Hemings Jefferson. . . ."[37] No consideration was given to any of the two-dozen other Jefferson males in Virginia at the time, each of whom carried the same Y chromosome as Thomas Jefferson and Eston Hemings. But this distinction was not picked up in the press.

More admirable were some of the observations of prominent scientists contacted by the Thomas Jefferson Memorial Foundation and asked to comment on the *Nature* articles. Particularly impressive were the comments of Dr. Kenneth K. Kidd, Professor of Genetics at Yale University, who recognized some "controversy" over the "interpretation" of the data and wrote:

> I think Eric Lander and Joseph Ellis in their News and Views commentary over-interpreted the results as proving that Jefferson was the father of Eston. . . . How many other male-line relatives of Thomas Jefferson were alive at that time? . . . [A]s with modern day paternity testing, we can prove a man is/was not the father, but we cannot absolutely prove a man is/was the father.

> So the proof ultimately rests on demonstrating that Thomas Jefferson was present at the time Eston was conceived *and that no other male relative with the same*

---

32. Eugene A. Foster, *The Thomas Jefferson Paternity Case*, Nature, Jan. 7, 1999, vol. 397 at 32.

33. Eugene A. Foster, *In Jefferson-Hemings Tie, a Family's Pride; Tenable Conclusions*, letter to the editor, *N.Y. Times*, Nov. 9, 1998, at A24.

34. Indeed, all of the letters on this issue in the January 7, 1999, issue of *Nature* challenged the interpretation that the DNA study pointed to Thomas Jefferson as Eston's father. Professor David M. Abbey, of the University of Colorado Health Science Center, noted "the authors did not consider all the data at hand in interpreting their results. No mention was made of Thomas Jefferson's brother Randolph ... or of his five sons." Dr. Gary Davis, of Evanston Hospital, in Evanston, Illinois, added that "If the data of Foster et al. are accurate, then any male ancestor in Thomas Jefferson's line, white or black, could have fathered Eston Hemings." *The Thomas Jefferson paternity case*, Nature, vol. 397, Jan. 7, 1999 at 32.

35. I am not personally critical of Dr. Foster for his role in this controversy, but it may be worth noting that he did not enter into the project as a "neutral." In his discussions with me, Dr. Foster acknowledged that he originally undertook the project hoping to prove that Thomas Jefferson fathered Sally Hemings' children.

36. Foster et al., *Jefferson fathered slave's last child* at 27 (emphasis added).

37. *Id.* (emphasis added).

Y chromosome was hiding in the bushes. That is something I have no knowledge of.... [38]

Similarly, Dr. David Page, of the MIT Center for Genome Research, "felt that more thought and attention could be paid to the 'competing hypotheses' in interpreting the results."[39]

In an e-mail to this writer on October 1, 2000, Dr. Foster elaborated on his position at some length.[40] He wrote that "The DNA tests do tell us that Eston Hemings was very likely fathered by a member of the Jefferson family,"[41] and added: "The scientific evidence alone would have told us that it was *possible* that Thomas Jefferson was Eston Hemings' father.... [Y]ou are right that our DNA findings say nothing directly about the paternity of any of Sally Hemings' children other than Eston Hemings."[42]

Dr. Foster has repeatedly voiced the opinion that "it is very likely that Thomas Jefferson was Eston Hemings' father."[43] Such statements may have contributed to public misunderstandings of the results of his study—in spite of his clear efforts to clarify the record. It is important to understand that his "very likely" conclusion is largely an *historical* rather than a scientific judgment based upon Dr. Foster's understanding of a wide range of historical data that are addressed in the chapters that follow. Responding to inquiries posed by the current writer, Dr. Foster on October 3, 2000, emphasized that he was relying heavily on historical evidence and clarified:

> You are perfectly correct that my conclusion " ... it is 'very likely' Thomas Jefferson was the father is based not solely upon ... [our] scientific DNA inquiry but involves interpreting those data in the light of historical evidence...." It is also true that " ... *there is nothing in ... [our] DNA study that itself would lead ... [us] to suspect Thomas Jefferson as the father versus Randolph [Jefferson] or his sons.*"[44]

In fairness to Dr. Foster, he has followed this issue closely and it is certainly legitimate for him to voice conclusions based upon more than his scientific expertise.[45] One need not intend criticism of him to observe that some of his public comments may nevertheless have contributed to a broad misunderstanding of his scientific research.

Similarly, Dr. Eric S. Lander, of MIT, who co-authored the "Founding Fathers" interpretive essay in *Nature* with Professor Ellis, wrote in a December 27, 1998, e-mail: "The DNA evidence strongly indicates that Eston's father was *either* Thomas Jefferson *or another male-line relative of Thomas Jefferson....* The DNA evidence obviously *does not distinguish among male-line relatives.* I leave it to historians to weigh the evidence."[46]

---

38. *Excerpted in Monticello Report*, Appendix B (emphasis added).

39. *Id.*

40. E-mail from Dr. Eugene Foster to Professor Robert F. Turner, Subject: Jefferson-Hemings, Oct. 1, 2000, 9:02 PM, on file with author.

41. *Id.*

42. *Id.* (Emphasis added.)

43. *See, e.g., id.*

44. E-mail from Dr. Eugene Foster to Professor Robert F. Turner, Subject: More TJ-SH, Oct. 3, 2000, 11:59 AM, on file with author (emphasis added.).

45. No admirer of Thomas Jefferson could credibly argue that Dr. Foster's medical expertise should preclude him from participating in serious discourse involving other disciplines. What a price we would have paid if Thomas Jefferson's expertise in architecture or agriculture had kept him from offering us his thoughts on politics, diplomacy, or even meteorology.

46. E-mail from Eric Lander to Herbert Barger, 27 Dec. 1998 00:48:34, Subject: "RE: JEFFERSON/HEMINGS DNA STUDY," a copy of which is on file with author (emphasis added).

Excluding Thomas Woodson

One of the most important, but largely overlooked, findings of the Foster DNA study was that Thomas Woodson could not have been Thomas Jefferson's child. This finding undermines both the original 1802 James Callender story and the strongest oral history claim that Jefferson fathered children by Sally Hemings. As will be discussed in Chapter Three, Callender's allegation that President Jefferson was sexually involved with Sally Hemings was largely premised upon the alleged existence of a ten- to twelve-year-old light-skinned slave named "Tom" whose "features are said to bear a striking although sable resemblance to those of the President himself."[47] This child has long been presumed by many to be Thomas Woodson, and no evidence of any other "mulatto"[48] child named "Tom" at Monticello has been found.

When Professor Annette Gordon-Reed wrote her 1997 book, *Thomas Jefferson and Sally Hemings*, more than half of the chapter on James Callender was devoted to the question "Was There a Tom Hemings?" She notes that:

> The nonexistence of Tom serves two functions for opponents of the Jefferson-Hemings story. First, it suggests that Callender lied about an essential item of his story. If he was lying about that, he was lying about the Jefferson-Hemings liaison....

> The second reason it is important for Tom not to exist is that it would suggest that Sally Hemings was not pregnant when she came back from France.... The notion that Sally Hemings was not pregnant when she came back from France is crucial to Jefferson's defenders because it makes it much easier to argue that someone other than Jefferson fathered all of Hemings's children.[49]

She then notes the strong oral history of the descendants of Thomas Woodson, who assert that he was the "Tom" of Callender's stories:

> Additional confirmation that Tom may have existed comes from a family that claims descent from this individual. According to the oral history of the Woodson family, which has been accepted by the Thomas Jefferson Memorial Foundation as accurate — except for the part about Jefferson being Tom's dad — Tom was sent to live with a family called the Woodsons after the scandal broke. He dropped the name Hemings in favor of Woodson.... The family has been interested principally in establishing that Tom Woodson existed rather than proving that he was the son of Thomas Jefferson.

> After the publication of her biography of Jefferson, [Professor Fawn] Brodie did additional research based upon the oral history of the Woodson family and found that a number of the details the family had passed down about Tom Woodson could be verified.... [S]he was able to determine that he had been born in 1790, the year that the mysterious Tom Hemings would have been born.[50]

Professor Gordon-Reed considers arguments on both sides of the "Was there a Tom?" issue, arguing in the process that Callender would have been foolish to manufacture such an allegation:

---

47. *The President Again*, Richmond Recorder, Sept. 1, 1802, *reprinted in Monticello Report*, Appendix E. It is perhaps noteworthy that the term "sable" was also used to describe Thomas Woodson.

48. I apologize to any readers who find this term as offensive as I do, but it is the term used at the time.

49. Annette Gordon-Reed, Thomas Jefferson and Sally Hemings 67–68 (1997).

50. *Id.* at 69–70.

The point for Callender's story was that the existence of children who looked like Jefferson would tend to prove that he was having sex with Sally Hemings. A boy old enough to compare closely to Jefferson and one named after him, too, would strengthen Callender's case; "President Tom" was an effective device. But was it so effective that Callender would have employed it knowing that Jefferson's supporters could easily point out there was no such boy?

The defenders of Jefferson never offered this rebuttal to Callender's claim.... [T]he fact that there was no twelve-year-old child at Monticello named Tom would have been an innocuous enough bit of information to pass along to those who were defending him. This alleged child appeared as a prominent and regular feature of Callender's articles. What if there had been no Sally Hemings at Monticello? Would the supporters of Jefferson have mounted a defense against the allegation of an affair with her without mentioning that she did not exist?

Other newspapers were investigating the story. If Tom did not exist, it seems likely that someone among Jefferson's supporters or anyone who could be described as neutral would have stumbled upon the fact that Tom did not exist, if he did not.[51]

In her 1974 book, Professor Fawn Brodie adds that "[a]t least two other editors, after checking, corroborated the story" of Tom Hemings.[52] My own Jefferson collection includes an original copy of the October 1, 1802, issue of the *Philadelphia Aurora*, published by William Duane. A page two article defending President Jefferson against Callender's charges, reprinted from the *Richmond Examiner*, stated: "That this servant woman [Sally Hemings] has a child is very true. But that it is Mr. Jefferson's, or that the connection exists, which Callender mentions, is false. I call upon him for his evidence, I challenge him to bring it forward."[53]

Surely Jefferson's friends and supporters discussed Callender's attack, and how best to counter it, among themselves. Is it probable that William Duane—or, for that matter, Meriwether Jones, editor of the *Examiner* and another Jefferson ally—would have gratuitously confirmed the existence of "Tom" without reason? Possible, yes—but hardly probable. Nor does it seem likely that none of Jefferson's many friends would have bothered to challenge this key point in Callender's argument if there was in fact no "Tom."

There is no evidence of any other slave at Monticello named "Tom" who might have been the son of Sally Hemings,[54] and indeed no record either of Thomas Woodson. Jefferson did not maintain his *Farm Book* records between 1783 and 1794,[55] so the absence of a record of birth may not be dispositive. (However, most, if not all, births during that

---

51. *Id.* at 70–71.

52. Fawn M. Brodie, Thomas Jefferson: An Intimate History 248 (1974).

53. *Richmond Examiner*, Philadelphia Aurora, Oct. 1, 1802, at 2.

54. Thomas Jefferson's wife Martha did inherit a slave named "Tom Shackleford," who first appears on the 1774 slave roster at Bedford and passed away in 1801. He is often listed simply as "Tom," and thus could cause confusion. *See, e.g.,* The Garden and Farm Books of Thomas Jefferson 259, 267, 290, 296, 298, 301 (Robert C. Baron, ed. 1987). I am indebted to Cynthia Harris Burton for this observation. By 1810 there were no fewer than three "Toms" among Jefferson's slaves ("Tom," "Tom Buck," and "Tom Lee.") *Id.* at 406. A slave named Ursula had a "Thomas" on Oct. 1, 1813. *Id.* at 386, 399.

55. *Monticello Report*, Appendix K at 2. There are at least four pages from the *Farm Book* that have been removed and, in some cases, may be on deposit as separate documents in other libraries. For example, the list of "Negroes Alienated, 1784–1794, inclusive" on deposit at the American Philosophical Society may be page 25 of Jefferson's *Farm Book*.

period are presumably reflected in later lists in the *Farm Book*.) Of greater significance is the absence of any listing of a slave child named "Tom" between 1795 and well after Callender's 1802 allegations. Some have suggested that Jefferson might well have decided to conceal the birth of his own illegitimate child,[56] but he routinely recorded the births of all of Sally's other children.

We may never know whether there was ever a "Tom Hemings" at Monticello. Other than James Callender's allegations, the only meaningful evidence for such a child has been the strong oral history of the Woodson family. Whether one concludes that there was no "Tom," or that the Woodson family tradition is accurate and their ancestor was the young man repeatedly mentioned by Callender and Federalist critics, one thing is now clear beyond reasonable doubt: Based upon DNA testing of six descendants of three of Thomas Woodson's sons, Thomas Jefferson *could not have been* his father.[57] That may be the most significant finding of the DNA tests. Professor Gordon-Reed argued: "If he [Callender] was lying about that [Jefferson's paternity of a ten- to twelve-year-old Hemings child named "Tom"], he was lying about the Jefferson-Hemings liaison...."[58]

Finally, of course, it is clear that the DNA tests addressed only the issue of the paternity of Eston Hemings and Thomas Woodson. No continuous male-line descendants of any of Sally Hemings' other children had been identified when the tests were done, and thus the tests provide no scientific evidence concerning the paternity of Harriet I, Beverly, Harriet II, or Madison Hemings. Specifically, the Foster study does not rule out the possibility that one or more of these older children were fathered by Peter and/or Samuel Carr, who reportedly admitted having fathered children by Sally Hemings. This issue will be addressed in Chapter Ten.

Other Possible DNA Testing — William Hemings and Thomas Jefferson

It is worth noting that the grave of Madison Hemings' son, William Beverly Hemings, was recently discovered in the U.S. Military Cemetery at Ft. Leavenworth, Kansas. According to Herbert Barger, there are no known descendants of William; and other descendants of Madison Hemings reportedly have refused to cooperate in having the body exhumed to search for usable DNA that might shed further light on this issue. That is presumably their option, although in the absence of known direct descendants of the deceased, it may be that authority to make this decision rests within the government. In any event, our understanding about this issue might well be enhanced by such an effort. That said, before any steps are taken to exhume anyone, some serious thought needs to be given to the ethical implications of disturbing gravesites and human remains to satisfy historical curiosity.

I am told that some members of the Hemings family have suggested that they will consider the exhumation of William's remains only if the Jefferson descendants agree to dig

---

56. *See, e.g.*, Michael Durey, With the Hammer of Truth: James Thomson Callender and America's Early National Heroes 159–60 (1990).

57. It may still be theoretically possible that Jefferson was Woodson's father. But this would probably mean either that Thomas Jefferson was of illegitimate birth (a theory now being suggested by *A President in the Family* author Byron Woodson) or that the same man illegitimately fathered sons by the wives of three of Thomas Woodson's sons over a period of more than a decade.

58. Gordon-Reed, Thomas Jefferson and Sally Hemings 67.

up Thomas Jefferson. At first this may seem only equitable, but the proposal that Thomas Jefferson's remains also be exhumed misunderstands the science involved in Y-chromosome DNA testing. It is theoretically possible, of course, that Thomas Jefferson was of illegitimate birth and thus might not share the Y chromosome found in the descendants of his cousins. But no serious scholar has suggested such a possibility (which, if true, would exclude him as a candidate for Eston's paternity), and if usable DNA could still be extracted from Thomas Jefferson's remains, it would almost certainly possess the same Y chromosome as the other male Jeffersons. Those who argue that Thomas Jefferson was probably not the father of Sally Hemings' children do not deny that he was the legitimate son of Peter Jefferson and carried the same Y chromosome extracted from the blood of modern-day descendants of his cousins.

In contrast, I am told by experts that DNA testing of William Hemings' remains probably would provide enough information to establish that he (and thus Madison) was a descendant of: (1) a male Jefferson, (2) a male member of the Carr family, or (3) someone other than a Jefferson or a Carr. To be sure, the presence of a Jefferson Y chromosome in William's remains would not conclusively establish that Thomas Jefferson fathered Madison Hemings. It would presumably be interpreted by some as strengthening the case for that conclusion, but there were two dozen other potential fathers carrying the same Y chromosome. On the other hand, if William were shown to carry the Y chromosome of the Carr family or to be unrelated to both the Carrs and the Jeffersons, that would strongly suggest that Sally Hemings was not monogamous and thus would undermine much of the circumstantial case against Thomas Jefferson.

In fairness to the Hemings descendants, the suggestion that William's remains should be exhumed and examined may seem like a "no-win" proposition. It could undermine their claim to such illustrious ancestry if William did not carry the Jefferson Y chromosome; but, if he did, the doubters would simply note that Randolph Jefferson and two dozen other men remain possible fathers. But this is not a game of chance or a sporting contest; it is a search for truth involving the reputation of one of America's most beloved Founding Fathers. And ultimately, as a pragmatic matter, if the Hemings family is seen as blocking the search for truth by denying access to potentially important evidence, they may find it difficult to persuade others of the certainty of their conviction that they are, in fact, descendants of Thomas Jefferson.[59]

Conclusions

In summary, contrary to conventional wisdom, the DNA study conducted by Dr. Eugene Foster and colleagues and reported in *Nature* did not "prove" that Thomas Jefferson fathered any of Sally Hemings' children. Rather, it excluded the reasonable possibility that Thomas Woodson was the child of Thomas Jefferson or any other male member of the Jefferson family, and it established the very strong probability that Sally's youngest son, Eston, was fathered by one of the more than two dozen adult Jefferson men who

---

59. When I first wrote this in 2000, I believed that it would be useful to pursue DNA testing from William Hemings' grave. Candidly, I am now much less sure of that. As I have reflected on the issue, there are important ethical implications that my eagerness to get to the truth led me to overlook. At the same time, I'm not sure—given the paucity of the case for Thomas Jefferson's paternity as I see it now—that any results from such a test would make much difference.

were in Virginia at the time he was conceived. As will be discussed in Chapter Ten, there is documentary evidence to support the conclusion that at least seven Jefferson men may well have been present at Monticello when Eston was conceived; and apparently no evidence one way or the other concerning the whereabouts of the remaining theoretical suspects.[60] Because of his advanced age (sixty four), health, and character, Thomas Jefferson may arguably have been the *least* likely of the group to have fathered a child by Sally Hemings[61]—although some of the relatives lived sufficiently far away from Monticello to be less likely candidates on that basis alone. But the DNA tests clearly show that it is *possible* that Thomas Jefferson was Eston's father. Since the tests do not address the issue of the paternity of Sally's other children, they tell us nothing at all about that paternity.

---

60. In reality, a number of other Jefferson relatives might have been at Monticello when Eston was conceived. George Jefferson, for example, served as the President's agent in Richmond, and presumably visited Monticello often to discuss business or simply for a family visit. While the *Monticello Report* asserts there were no known visits by George Jefferson to Monticello, Cynthia Burton's research reveals that is not the case. *See Jefferson to Callender*, Sept. 6, 1799, in 9 THE WORKS OF THOMAS JEFFERSON 82 (Fed. Ed. 1905) ("Mr. Jefferson happens to be here …"—a clear reference to George Jefferson.) Another letter, ironically also involving Callender, places George Jefferson back at Monticello in April 1801. In a letter dated April 27, 1801, Callender informed James Madison that George Jefferson had hand-delivered a letter from him to Jefferson at Monticello earlier that month. *Quoted in* Worthington Chauncey Ford, *Thomas Jefferson and James Thomson Callender,* 51 NEW-ENGLAND HISTORICAL AND GENEALOGICAL REGISTER 153–54 (Apr. 1897). But it is correct that, in the absence of some other purpose, Thomas Jefferson did not normally make a record of the visits to Monticello by close friends and relatives.

61. *See* Chapter Eleven.

2

The Enigmatic Sally Hemings:
So Few Facts, So Much Fantasy
and Speculation

Several books have been written about Sally Hemings, and Hollywood has provided us with movies and a miniseries showing a beautiful young slave girl and the dashing American diplomat and President dancing across the social scenes of Paris and embracing in the White House. The miniseries portrays a powerful Sally Hemings ordering Monticello overseer Edmund Bacon to escort unwanted white visitors off the plantation.

Is this fact or fantasy? The truth is that we really do not know, but there is not the *slightest* bit of reliable historical evidence to support a finding that Thomas Jefferson and Sally Hemings ever so much as held hands in Paris or anywhere else, nor is there any evidence Sally Hemings ever got within fifty miles of Washington, D.C.

The 1998 DNA tests discussed in Chapter One have undermined the 1802 James Callender charge that there was a twelve-year-old slave child named "Tom" at Monticello, conceived by Thomas Jefferson and Sally Hemings in Paris in 1789 and closely resembling President Jefferson in physical appearance. There is not a single eyewitness account by anyone clearly linking Thomas Jefferson romantically to Sally Hemings, not from one of the hundreds of slaves who were owned by Jefferson over the years,[1] nor from any of the thousands of visitors who swarmed over Monticello when Thomas Jefferson was home. Both Thomas Jefferson and his family denied the allegations. No one has found any record in which any person claimed that Sally Hemings ever alleged that her relationship with Thomas Jefferson ever went beyond that of master-slave, even during the years after Jefferson's death, when she lived for nearly a decade as a free woman in Charlottesville; nor did any but one of her children leave a record of making such an assertion, and in that instance he waited until Jefferson had been dead nearly fifty years, and the statement attributed to him is clearly inaccurate on several key points.[2] Edmund Bacon, the Monticello overseer during most of Jefferson's presidency and retirement years, both denied the allegations of Jefferson's paternity and stated that he had often personally witnessed another man leaving Sally's room early in the morning while he was arriving for work.

---

1. The two arguable exceptions to this are 1873 articles in the *Pike County* [Ohio] *Republican* alleging to report the recollections of former Monticello slaves Madison Hemings and Israel Jefferson. As will be discussed in greater detail in Chapter Four, both statements are filled with factual inaccuracies, and were actually written by an anti-Jefferson journalist of minimal credibility. While Israel does claim that "Mr. Jefferson was on the most intimate terms with [Sally]," and seeks to confirm Sally's son Madison Hemings' assertion that Jefferson was his father, he adds that he "did not positively know" the truth of the situation. His statement does not allege that he ever personally witnessed any "intimacy" between them.

2. *See* Chapter Four.

But one could, of course, also argue a different conclusion from the same absence of material evidence. There is no clear proof that "Tom and Sally" did *not* dance in Paris or Washington. There is no proof she was not pregnant when she returned to Virginia in 1789. Other than the case of Thomas Woodson, the slave child alleged to have been born to Sally shortly after she returned from France (who has been positively excluded as the child of Thomas or any other Jefferson male by a half dozen DNA tests), there is no proof that Thomas Jefferson did not father all of Sally's children. We have almost no information about Sally Hemings, and this has permitted speculation to run rampant and to replace the normal tools of scholarly research.

Indeed, the most remarkable fact associated with this entire inquiry is probably how *little* we really know about Sally Hemings.[3] If we exclude the various lists of slaves in Jefferson's records — recording such things as the distribution of food, bedding, and clothing over the years (in which Sally and her children are treated exactly like other members of her family) — everything we reliably know about Sally Hemings can be printed on an index card (see **Figure 5** on the next page).

Sally's Birth and Arrival at Monticello

The most reliable evidence suggests that Sally Hemings was born on an unknown date in 1773[4] to Betty Hemings, a slave belonging to Thomas Jefferson's father-in-law John Wayles, and became Jefferson's property the next year following Wayles' death. These facts are recorded in Jefferson's *Farm Book*.[5]

It is commonly asserted today that Sally's father was John Wayles himself, which would have made her half-sister to Jefferson's wife Martha. There is nothing in the Jefferson records to document this,[6] but it is the type of delicate matter that might well not have been recorded on paper. The issue is not critical to our inquiry,[7] but if true it might pro-

---

3. Former Monticello resident director James A. Bear, Jr., correctly notes the irony that "less is known of the well-known Sally Hemings than of many of her brothers and sisters." James A. Bear, Jr., *The Hemings Family of Monticello*, VIRGINIA CAVALCADE, Autumn 1979 at 84.

4. Some use the year 1774, but since Jefferson's *Farm Book* includes an entry saying he received Sally on January 14, 1774, and giving her year of birth as 1773, the later date is almost certainly wrong. *Role of the slaves of John Wayles which were allotted to T.J. in right of his wife on a division of the estate. Jan. 14, 1774,* in THOMAS JEFFERSON: THE GARDEN AND FARM BOOKS 227 (Robert C. Baron, ed. 1987).

5. *Id.*

6. LUCIA STANTON, FREE SOME DAY: THE AFRICAN-AMERICAN FAMILIES OF MONTICELLO 103 (2000).

7. The first public reference to the allegation of which I am aware was by Jefferson's Georgia Federalist enemy Thomas Gibbons, who is discussed further in Chapter Nine. There is no reason to believe that Gibbons would have had any knowledge of the facts in this matter. In preparation for their book *Anatomy of a Scandal*, genealogists Rebecca and James McMurry spent several years researching John Wayles, and concluded: "We simply found no hints of John Wayles's being involved in such a relationship, and we found strong, though not incontrovertible, evidence against it." REBECCA L. MC-MURRY & JAMES F. MCMURRY, JR, ANATOMY OF A SCANDAL xviii (2002). Former Monticello guide White McKenzie Wallenborn asserts that Sally was born at Guinea Plantation in southeast Cumberland County, which was about three days' travel from Wayles' plantation, The Forest. Dr. Wallenborn notes that John Wayles was not in good health for the last few years of his life, and the trip to Guinea Plantation where Betty and Sally Hemings lived would have been too stressful for a man of his age and health. (E-mail from White McKenzie Wallenborn to Bob Turner, Mar. 31, 2002, 6:41 PM, Subject: TJ letter.) I not only remain an agnostic on the matter, but I do not see it as being at all critical to this issue and I have little interest in knowing the answer.

Daughter of Betty Hemings • born 1773, inherited by Jeffersons 1774 • arrived at Monticello c. 1775 • stayed with TJ's in-laws after TJ went to Paris until she accompanied Mary (Polly) to Paris in 1787 at age 13 or 14 • ship captain said she was immature, and Abigail Adams added Sally was "wholly incapable" of babysitting 8-year-old Mary without supervision and "wants more care than the child," but was "good natured" • TJ purchased clothes, a smallpox vaccination, and gave Sally a small salary while in France • spent 5 weeks boarding with Mrs. Dupré in 1789 • returned to Monticello with Jeffersons in 1789 to become house servant • often spoke of her trip to Paris • away from Monticello and said to have been ill in Sept. 1790 • had 5 known children (perhaps as many as 7), four lived to adulthood, youngest fathered by man with Jefferson family Y chromosome • TJ's distribution lists (for food, clothing, etc.) and other records show no "special treatment" as compared to other Hemingses and house servants • said to be "mighty near white," "decidedly good looking," and "very handsome" with "long straight hair" by two witnesses • alleged to be mistress of married man and "near relation of Mr. Jefferson's" • unidentified man other than TJ was reportedly witnessed leaving her room early many mornings • not freed in TJ's life or will, but listed as "free" person in 1833 and perhaps 1830 censuses • may have died around 1835. 1873 newspaper claimed Madison Hemings and a friend said TJ fathered all of her children.

Figure 5. What We Believe We Know about Sally Hemings. Virtually everything that we believe we know about Sally Hemings—from Thomas Jefferson's *Farm Book, Memorandum Books,* letters, and from surviving accounts of eyewitnesses like overseer Edmund Bacon, former slave Isaac Jefferson, and other members of the Monticello community—can be recorded on a 3×5 index card. I have excluded allegations from people like Callender and Gibbons (who had no direct knowledge when they labeled Sally a "slut" and a "prostitute"), as well as the 1873 assertions attributed by Samuel Wetmore to sixty-eight-year-old Madison Hemings about events that could only have occurred more than a decade before Hemings' birth. For reasons of credibility discussed in Chapter Four, I've also excluded Israel Jefferson's alleged statement to Wetmore that Sally was Thomas Jefferson's "chambermaid." But even if we included those and I've missed a few other references, they could easily be included on the reverse side of the index card. I've also excluded known information that tells us little of relevance to our inquiry, such as the names of Sally's children, siblings, and other known relatives.

vide additional reasons for Thomas Jefferson to give favorable treatment to Sally, her siblings, and presumably their children.[8]

We know essentially nothing else about Sally until 1787. Jefferson's wife Martha died four months after giving birth to their daughter Lucy in 1782, and, when Jefferson was

---

8. Until 1847, the only evidence of John Wayles' paternity of Sally seems to have come from Thomas Jefferson's political enemies Thomas Gibbons and Thomas Turner, probably reporting rumors or speculation. (A useful summary of this issue appears in *Monticello Report,* Appendix F at 6.) That year, in what may be the most important evidence in support of such a relationship, former slave Isaac Jefferson said "Folks said that these Hemingses was old Mr. Wayles's children." (JEFFERSON AT MONTICELLO 4 [James A. Bear, Jr., ed., 1967].) Then, in 1873, Sally's son Madison Hemings alleged that, after his wife died, John Wales [*sic*] took Betty Hemings as his "concubine" and fathered six of her children. This article is discussed in Chapter Four. While Sally Hemings may well have been John Wayles' daughter, these rumors and political attacks hardly constitute persuasive proof of that fact.

appointed U.S. Minister to France and set forth across the Atlantic in July 1784, he was accompanied by his eleven-year-old daughter Martha and a single slave (James Hemings, older brother to Sally).

One of the challenges when studying the Jefferson family is keeping track of the players. Martha, the President's eldest daughter, not only shared her mother's first name (also the name of one of Thomas Jefferson's sisters) but was also known as Patsy. Daughter number two went by Mary, Maria, and Polly at various times. From entries in the *Farm Book,* there appear to have been nearly a dozen different slaves named "Sally" or "Sal" over the years at Monticello[9]; and, in 1815, a slave identified as "Will's Sal" gave birth to a daughter named "Harriet"[10]—the same name Sally Hemings gave to two of her own daughters. Although none of them came close to fitting the description provided by James Callender in 1802, over the years there were several "Toms" among Jefferson's slaves.[11]

It is believed that Sally and her family moved to Monticello around 1775, and by 1787 she was living at "Eppington," the Chesterfield County home of Martha Jefferson's sister Elizabeth and her husband Francis Eppes. They had agreed to care for Jefferson's daughters Polly and Lucy while their father was serving as U.S. Minister to France. When Thomas Jefferson learned that two-year-old Lucy had died of whooping cough, he instructed the Eppes to send Polly to Paris in the company of someone like Isabel Herne, a much older slave than Sally Hemings, to care for his eight-year-old daughter on the five-week voyage across the Atlantic. However, Isabel was suffering from complications from childbirth at the time and the Eppes decided instead to send thirteen- or fourteen-year-old Sally Hemings to accompany Polly.

Abigail Adams' Observations about Sally Hemings

About the only credible information we have about Sally's maturity and talents comes from two letters written by Abigail Adams to Thomas Jefferson after Polly and Sally arrived in London en route to Paris in the summer of 1787. Polly and Sally lived with the Adams family for three weeks. Mrs. Adams, whose husband was serving as U.S. Minister to Great Britain and whose "sharp intellect" is acknowledged even by champions of the "Sally"

---

9. In addition to Sally Hemings, a quick perusal of the *Farm Book* reveals the following: In 1777 Will and Abby had a Sally at Shadwell and a Sal was born at Bedford. The following year Sue had a Sally at Elk Hill. In 1788 Kate gave birth to a Sally. A Sally was born on the Tufton farm and another to Molly at Bedford. Jenny and Lewis had a "Sally" in 1792, and in 1797 a "Sall" at Lego passed away who reportedly was born about 1735. In 1798 Jenny and Lewis had their Sally, and Hanna named her new baby Sally as well. We also have Aggy's Sally, born in 1812. This doesn't include the Sally who apparently accompanied Jefferson's sister, Anna Scott Marks, on a visit. *See* THOMAS JEFFERSON: THE GARDEN AND FARM BOOKS 240, 244–246, 248, 300, 383–84, 387, 389–90, 446, 465, 469, 471. This may not include every "Sally," nor am I certain that some of these entries do not refer to the same "Sally."

10. *Id.* at 390.

11. To add to the confusion, Thomas Jefferson's brother and favorite grandson were named, respectively, Randolph Jefferson and Jefferson Randolph. While the grandson went by the name "Jeff," his full name was Thomas Jefferson Randolph, which causes still more confusion because his father (daughter Martha's husband) was Thomas Mann Randolph, who had a half-brother also named Thomas Mann Randolph. Both Thomas Mann Randolph and Thomas Jefferson Randolph were occasionally referred to as "Col. Randolph."

story,[12] wrote Jefferson on June 26 that Polly had arrived safely and was accompanied by a "Girl" who was the sister of the servant (James Hemings) Jefferson had taken to Paris.[13]

The following day, Mrs. Adams wrote again, this time advising Thomas Jefferson that Andrew Ramsay, the ship captain who brought Polly from Virginia, had expressed the view that Sally was not a capable caregiver: "The Girl who is with her is quite a child, and Captain Rams[a]y is of opinion will be of so little Service that he had better carry her back with him. But of this you will be a judge. She seems fond of the child and appears good natured."[14] After having had ten days to observe the two children, on July 6 Abigail Adams added in another letter: "The Girl she has with her, wants more care than the child, and is wholly incapable of looking properly after her, without some superiour to direct her."[15]

The only surviving observation by someone who had been in a position to directly observe Sally Hemings' behavior (a qualification excluding the allegations of James Callender and Federalist activists who had apparently never even seen Sally) to comment upon her abilities was thus Abigail Adams—a woman of remarkable intelligence and judgment, who certainly had no sympathy for slavery—and she recorded that at the age of thirteen or fourteen Sally Hemings needed more care than an eight-year-old[16] who was so emotionally distraught she was clinging to all around her.[17] From her letters, it is clear

---

12. *See, e.g.,* Fawn M. Brodie, Thomas Jefferson: An Intimate History 238 (1974); Joseph J. Ellis, American Sphinx 85 (1996).

13. *Abigail Adams to Thomas Jefferson*, June 26, 1787, in 11 The Papers of Thomas Jefferson 502 (Julian P. Boyd, ed., 1955).

14. *Id.*, June 27, 1787, at 503. While Fawn Brodie attempts to dismiss Captain Ramsay's negative comments about Sally Hemings' talents by assuming he wished to ravish her on the trip back to America, an even more "creative" approach is found in E. M. Halliday's post-DNA volume *Understanding Thomas Jefferson* (which appropriately is dedicated to "the memory of Fawn Brodie"). He notes that Abigail Adams estimated that Sally was "about 15 or 16," and concludes:

> [T]he most sensible interpretation of Abigail's overestimate of Sally's age—for she was only fourteen   is that the girl was already physically a woman, with well developed breasts that must have been obvious despite her nondescript shipboard attire. It must have made Mrs. Adams nervous to think of this nubile creature living under the same roof in Paris with a master who, she was aware, loved attractive young women and had been without a sexual partner (as far as she knew) for a long time now.
>
> Being Abigail, she took action, or at least made a stab at it. She found a willing ally in Captain Ramsay.... After consulting with him, she sat down and wrote Jefferson to bring him up to date on Polly's state of mind.... [I]t is an index of Abigail's apparent apprehension about having Sally join the household in Paris that ... she was so ready to block a brother-sister reunion....

E. M. Halliday, Understanding Thomas Jefferson 86–87 (2001).

Professor Fawn Brodie would no doubt have loved the approach, which to its credit at least avoids the stereotyping of Captain Ramsay. But being one year off in estimating Sally's age hardly warrants such a complex explanation, and there is not the slightest bit of historical evidence to support it. There is certainly no reason to assume that Abigail Adams thought Thomas Jefferson had a special fondness for "young" (teenaged) women. The youngest women we do know he was attracted to during that period of his life were roughly *twice* the age of Sally Hemings. It may be worth noting that a Monticello slave who knew Sally at the time she left for Paris estimated her age to be "about eleven years old" at the time. *See* Memoirs of a Monticello Slave, *reprinted in* Jefferson at Monticello 4. As will be discussed, Monticello overseer Edmund Bacon described Sally as "a little girl" when she left for Paris.

15. *Abigail Adams to Thomas Jefferson*, July 6, 1787, in 11 The Papers of Thomas Jefferson 551 (1955).

16. Polly reached her ninth birthday shortly after arriving in Paris.

17. Ten days after arriving in the comfort of the Adams home in London, Polly was still so upset that Abigail Adams told her father: "[S]he last evening ... was thrown into all her former distresses, and bursting into Tears, told me it would be as hard to leave me as it was her Aunt Epps [*sic*]. She has

that Captain Ramsay—in whose judgment Thomas Jefferson also apparently placed confidence[18]—shared that view.

That's basically it. Other than listing her name among other slaves for the distribution of blankets, food, and the like, and a few passing references in letters or other documents, the only other known surviving accounts of Sally Hemings focus on her physical appearance.

In 1847, Charles W. Campbell took down the recollections of a former Monticello slave and blacksmith named Isaac, who provided the following account of Sally Hemings:

> Sally Hemings' mother Betty was a bright mulatto woman, and Sally mighty near white; she was the youngest child.... Sally was very handsome, long straight hair down her back. She was about eleven years old when Mr. Jefferson [*sic*] took her to France to wait on Miss Polly. She and Sally went out to France a year after Mr. Jefferson went. Patsy went with him at first, but she carried no maid with her. Harriet, one of Sally's daughters, was very handsome. Sally had a son named Madison, who learned to be a great fiddler.[19]

About fifteen years later, Monticello overseer Edmund Bacon recalled his memories of nearly two decades at Monticello and mentioned Sally Hemings. He wrote:

> Sally Hemings went to France with Maria Jefferson when she was a little girl. Mr. Jefferson was Minister to France, and he wanted to put her in school there. They crossed the ocean alone. I have often heard her tell about it. When they got to London, they stayed with Mr. Adams, who was Minister there, until Mr. Jefferson came or sent for them.[20]

It may (or may not) be significant that Bacon does not praise Sally for her competence or the quality of her work. When he writes of Martha Jefferson Randolph's slave nurse, Ursula, he speaks of how much Jefferson's grandchildren were attached to her, calling her "Mammy." Sally's brother John Hemings was praised as "a first-rate workman" who "could make anything that was wanted in woodwork."[21] Sally's nephews Joe Fossett and Burwell Colbert were, respectively, described as "a very fine workman"[22] and "a fine painter."[23] But Sally—who Hollywood and some scholars would have us believe was Thomas Jefferson's constant companion and closest confidant—is remembered only as someone who once traveled to Paris and later spoke about it.

The only other first-hand description we have of Sally Hemings is from President Jefferson's favorite grandson, Thomas Jefferson Randolph, who in 1852 reportedly commented to historian Henry Randall that Sally and one of her sisters[24] were both "light colored and decidedly good looking."[25]

Edmund Bacon's recollection that Sally liked to talk about her voyage to France is also the only surviving record that clearly recounts any statement ever made by Sally Hemings. Beyond knowing that Sally often mentioned Paris, there is not a single scrap of paper

---

been so often deceived that she will not quit me for a moment lest she should be carried away. Nor can I scarcely prevail upon her to see [Jefferson's servant] Petit." *Abigail Adams to Thomas Jefferson,* July 6, 1787, in 11 THE PAPERS OF THOMAS JEFFERSON 551.

18. *Jefferson to Elizabeth Wayles Eppes,* July 28, 1787, in *id.* at 634.

19. JEFFERSON AT MONTICELLO 4.

20. *Reprinted in id.* at 100.

21. *Id.* at 102.

22. *Id.*

23. *Id.*

24. The "sister" may have been Betsey Hemings, who belonged to the Eppes family.

25. *Quoted in* STANTON, FREE SOME DAY 114.

known to contain anything ever written by Sally Hemings (indeed, there is *serious* doubt about whether she was literate[26]), and there are "no accounts of any statements made by her."[27] It is reasonable to assume that Sally might[28] have been the source for some of the statements attributed to her son Madison in the 1873 story in the *Pike County Republican*, which is discussed in Chapter Four. But Madison does not attribute the information specifically to his mother, and both some of the vocabulary used and the identical misspelling of a name suggest that James Callender's or Thomas Turner's writings may directly or indirectly have been the source for some of the statements attributed to Madison Hemings.[29]

Historian Joseph Ellis, one of the preeminent scholars to embrace the belief that Thomas Jefferson fathered Sally's children, has acknowledged in a recent issue of the *William & Mary Quarterly* that—except for Madison's statement—the "historical record is almost completely blank" about Sally Hemings.[30] He writes that "nothing in the vast historical literature, sheds any light on the character of the relationship between Jefferson and Sally Hemings."[31] We do not know exactly when she was born or died, where her body was buried, or—as Professor Fawn Brodie has conceded—anything at all about her personal "feelings."[32] Yet most Americans would be shocked at this reality, as Hollywood and creative scholars have painted a far more detailed portrait based almost entirely on speculation and fantasy.

Sally Hemings in Paris

We know that Sally Hemings and Polly Jefferson arrived in Paris in the middle of July 1787.[33] We know that Sally returned to Virginia with Jefferson and his daughters when his diplomatic service came to an end, and that they arrived back at Monticello on December 23, 1789. Beyond that, with some very minor and often ambiguous exceptions, Professors Lander and Ellis were correct in noting, in their *Nature* commentary that accompanied the Foster DNA report, that "[t]here is no evidence of what transpired" in Paris involving Sally Hemings.[34]

Professor William Howard Adams, in his 1997 *The Paris Years of Thomas Jefferson*, provides this accurate summary of what is known about Sally Hemings during her stay in Paris:

---

26. In addition to having no surviving writings by Sally Hemings, her son Madison reportedly stated that he learned to read by persuading Jefferson's white grandchildren to teach him his letters. (*See* Chapter Four.) Had Sally been literate, one might have expected her to play some role in teaching her children to read and write.

27. *Monticello Report*, Appendix F at 2.

28. On the other hand, it may be significant that Madison is not quoted as attributing his stories to his mother. If he based them on Callender's allegations or derivative stories, or even made them up, he might have been reluctant to attribute them to his deceased mother. Then again, perhaps he did attribute them to Sally and this point did not make it into the Wetmore article. Once again, we simply do not know.

29. *See* Chapter Four.

30. Joseph J. Ellis, *Jefferson: Post-DNA*, 57 WILLIAM & MARY Q. 127 (Jan. 2000).

31. *Id.*

32. BRODIE, THOMAS JEFFERSON 467.

33. DUMAS MALONE, JEFFERSON AND THE RIGHTS OF MAN 136 (1951). Adams says she arrived on July 16. WILLIAM HOWARD ADAMS, THE PARIS YEARS OF THOMAS JEFFERSON 220 (1997).

34. Eric S. Lander & Joseph J. Ellis, *Founding Father*, NATURE Nov. 5, 1998, vol. 396, issue no. 6706 at 13.

[T]he evidence is meager. Apart from nine notations in Jefferson's Memorandum Book recording purchases of clothing, her servant's pay, and a fee for smallpox vaccination, Sally Hemings is completely absent from the Paris record. We know nothing of her living arrangements or duties at the rue de Berri.... She was known to at least one of Polly Jefferson's classmates at the convent, and there has been reasonable speculation that she acted as maid for the Jefferson girls while they were in school.[35]

There is indeed some logic in assuming that Sally spent most of her Paris experience at the Abbaye Royale de Panthemont on the rue de Grenelle, the convent school where Martha and Polly Jefferson resided ("except on special weekends"[36]) most of the time they were in Paris, along with daughters of other socially prominent Paris residents.[37] She was, scholars seem to agree, charged with serving as the children's maid; and Jefferson already had a full staff of servants at the Hôtel de Langeac, his cramped Paris residence on the Champs-Elysées, before Sally arrived. The problem with assuming Sally would remain near the daughters whom it was her purpose to serve as a ladies' maid is that this makes it difficult to sustain the "Tom and Sally" fantasy[38] of which many people seem to have grown so fond.

Professor Gordon-Reed almost appears to use the lack of any information to assume that Sally would have spent her days lounging around Jefferson's residence in a gown of fine French lace, nibbling on fine chocolates while waiting for the start of another night of passion (in the cramped, two-bedroom residence Jefferson shared with others). She asserts: "There probably was not much work for Sally Hemings to do during her stay in France. Martha and Mary were boarding at school. Jefferson had been in Paris for three years, and the residence already had a staff of servants."[39]

Similarly, in its January 2000 report, the Thomas Jefferson Memorial Foundation Research Committee asserted that, while in Paris, Sally "probably lived at Jefferson's residence on the Champs-Elysées, the Hôtel de Langeac," but notes "it is also possible that she may have lived with Jefferson's daughters at their convent school, the Abbaye de Panthemont."[40]

However, the official Monticello position both before and after the *Monticello Report* was more consistent with the actual evidence. In a short 1989 biography of Sally Hemings on the Monticello web page, updated in 1994, Lucia C. Stanton wrote: "It is not known whether Sally Hemings lived at Jefferson's residence, the Hotel de Langeac, or at the Abbaye de Panthemont, where Martha (Patsy) and Mary (Maria) Jefferson were boarding students." More recently, in her 2000 book, *Free Some Day*, Ms. Stanton wrote:

Escorted by Jefferson's French butler, the two girls [Polly and Sally] arrived in Paris on July 15, 1787. Polly Jefferson immediately joined her sister, Martha (Patsy), at the Abbaye de Panthemont, a fashionable convent school with a number of English as well as French students. It is not known whether Sally Hemings lived at the convent or at the Hôtel de Langeac, Jefferson's residence on the Champs-

---

35. Adams, The Paris Years of Thomas Jefferson 221.

36. Ellis, American Sphinx 82.

37. *See, e.g.*, Edward Dumbauld, Thomas Jefferson: American Tourist 63 (1946); George Green Shackelford, Thomas Jefferson's Travels in Europe 13 (1995).

38. The use of the term "fantasy" here is not intended to exclude the *possibility* that Thomas Jefferson and Sally Hemings found each other attractive or even produced children together, but rather refers to the romantic tale of "Sally" and "Tom" dancing across Paris and Washington that is so contrary to known evidence as to be almost certainly untrue. Surely, had such an "affair" been so indiscreet, *someone* would have made note of it for history.

39. Gordon-Reed, Thomas Jefferson and Sally Hemings 163.

40. Thomas Jefferson Memorial Foundation Research Committee, *Report on Thomas Jefferson and Sally Hemings*, Jan. 2000 (hereinafter referred to as *Monticello Report*) Appendix H at 2.

Elysées. It was not uncommon for the servants of boarding students to continue to attend their mistresses in the Abbaye and some of the Jefferson sisters' schoolmates knew Sally well enough to send her greetings in their correspondence.[41]

Given these circumstances, one has to wonder why the *Monticello Report* declared it "probable" that Sally did not accompany the daughters she was in Paris to serve when they went to the convent—all the more so since the revisionists seem to agree there would have been no work for her to do at Jefferson's residence and Sally was repeatedly mentioned in letters between Martha and her schoolmate Marie de Boridoux.[42]

Other assertions about Sally's life in Paris for which there does not appear to be the slightest serious evidence include Professor Brodie's claim that Sally was in "daily contact" with Thomas Jefferson[43] (which would only have been likely if she had not accompanied the daughters to the Abbaye, an issue that cannot be resolved with the available information); and that she received "formal education" while in Paris.[44] Consider this excerpt from Professor Gordon-Reed's book:

> Brodie stated that soon after Hemings came to Paris, a French teacher named Monsieur Perrault was engaged. It was apparently James Hemings who hired the tutor. There is no indication from documents from France that Sally Hemings was included in the lessons, although in later years one political enemy of Jefferson referred to Hemings as having had the "benefits of a French education." Though the presence of a tutor does not support Fawn Brodie's claim about Jefferson's feelings toward Hemings, it does illustrate the extraordinary things she was exposed to as a young woman.

> Sally Hemings, who had been entrusted with an assignment and had succeeded in carrying out that assignment, was now living in an opulent residence, learning a new language (either formally or informally) and a new set of customs.[45]

None of this is seriously supported by evidence. Sally did arrive safely in Paris with Polly, but if the evaluations of both Captain Andrew Ramsay and Abigail Adams are to be believed (and they are the *only* witnesses who we know observed and commented upon Sally's behavior at the time), she hardly distinguished herself in "carrying out that assignment." The un-contradicted testimony is that Captain Ramsay took care of Polly while at sea, and Abigail Adams did so while Polly and Sally stayed in London before Adrien Petit arrived to escort them to Paris. We have no reason to believe Sally lived in "an opulent residence" as opposed to the servants' quarters at the convent, although that may possibly have been true; and there is no credible[46] evidence Sally was learning French in any meaningful way. (James Hemings was learning to cook from French chefs, so his need to be able to communicate in French was obvious. It is well documented that James did receive tutoring in French, but Sally's name does not appear in any of those references.)

Of course, there is also no clear proof that Sally was *not* being tutored in French, and perhaps Italian and Chinese as well. Indeed, there is no proof Sally Hemings did not spend most of her days teaching English literature to the people of Paris. But the almost total ab-

---

41. Stanton, Free Some Day 109.

42. James A. Bear, Jr., *The Hemings Family of Monticello*, Virginia Cavalcade, (Autumn 1979), 85. *See also* 16 Papers of Thomas Jefferson xxxi (1961).

43. Brodie, Thomas Jefferson 228.

44. "There are indications that his [Madison's] mother Sally received some formal instruction while in France." Gordon-Reed, Thomas Jefferson and Sally Hemings 149.

45. *Id.* at 163.

46. *See* Chapter Four.

sence of information does not make such speculation true, or even "probable." The proper answer is, with very few exceptions, we simply *do not know* what Sally Hemings did in Paris.

In fairness, there is some evidence that Sally may have received some "formal training" during her stay in Paris. During the spring of 1789, Jefferson paid his launderer to board Sally for more than a month. Speculation about the purpose of this entry in Jefferson's *Memorandum Books* ranges from a quarantine period away from his daughters while Sally recovered from her smallpox vaccination to possibly training Sally at the laundry in the proper care of fine fabrics.[47] Since Martha was being presented to French society at the time, the utility of Sally's having such training may support the latter interpretation. But we will likely never know if that is, in fact, the explanation.

Much of the modern speculation that Sally Hemings may have been "educated" in Paris may come from a partisan letter written by a Georgia Federalist named Thomas Gibbons, who will be discussed further in Chapter Nine. In 1802, Gibbons responded to an inquiry by Federalist representative Jonathan Dayton, who was clearly searching for evidence with which to attack the Republican President. There is no evidence that Thomas Gibbons had ever seen Sally Hemings or even visited Monticello, but he did not hesitate to assert that Sally Hemings was "the most abandoned prostitute of her color — pampered into a lascivious course of life, with the benefits of a French education, she is more lecherous than the other beasts of the Monticellian Mountain."[48]

If so, the account may parallel the confusion caused by Fawn Brodie's ignorance that the expression "mulatto soil" was a geological term of art (also discussed in the Introduction and Chapter Nine). I am informed, although I have not had an opportunity (or, for that matter, sufficient interest) to research the issue, that having the benefit of a "French education" was a disparaging euphemism in the early nineteenth century, not for having engaged in advanced studies at the Sorbonne, but rather for a woman trained or skilled in the arts of sexual pleasure (e.g., a prostitute). The context of the Gibbons charge would more reasonably support such a meaning. Gibbons was not accusing Sally Hemings of being a highly educated, sophisticated woman, but rather clearly alleging she was "more lecherous than the other beasts" at Monticello *because of* her alleged "French education." Gibbons' letter was peppered with vicious racist stereotypes. While he admitted that he had never even seen any of Sally's children, he told Dayton: "That Jefferson lives in open defiance of all decent rule, with a mulatto slave, his property, named Sally, is as correct as truth itself, and that his children, to wit, Tom, Beverly & Harriot [*sic*] are flat nosed, thick lipped, and Tawny...."[49]

Gibbons' clear purpose was to make President Jefferson look bad. Presumably, Jefferson's alleged behavior might have been more forgivable to many people had Sally been perceived as a slightly darker version of the educated and accomplished Maria Cosway or Angelica Schuyler Church. It is unlikely that Gibbons knew anything beyond Callender's allegations about Sally's life in Paris, and he had no motive to portray her in any favorable light. Not only does the context strongly suggest an unusual meaning for "French education," but we know the word "French" was used during that era as a disparaging adjective in a number of other bawdy euphemisms. Yet, in the absence of almost any reliable information about Sally Hemings, some scholars who seek support for the Jefferson-Hem-

---

47. *Monticello Report*, Appendix H at 3. *See also*, BRODIE, THOMAS JEFFERSON 233 (suggesting this was to provide a chaperone for Sally while Jefferson was away from Paris).

48. *Thomas Gibbons to Jonathan Dayton*, Dec. 20, 1802. This portion of the letter is quoted by Professor Gordon-Reed. GORDON-REED, THOMAS JEFFERSON AND SALLY HEMINGS 171.

49. *Id*. (This portion of the letter, the original of which is located in the Clements Library at the University of Michigan, is quoted by neither Professor Gordon-Reed nor the *Monticello Report*.)

ings story find this sentence to be reliable evidence that Sally was formally "educated" in France.

Yet another assumption about Sally Hemings' life in Paris that is widely presented as fact is that she knew she had a legal right to freedom while in France. As will be discussed in Chapter Four, Thomas Jefferson himself was unaware of this unwritten customary practice of French law until well into his stay in Paris. And yet Professor Brodie writes: "Both Sally and James Hemings knew they were free if they chose to make an issue of it."[50] She attributes the statement to the 1873 Ohio newspaper article reporting on an alleged conversation with Sally's son Madison (discussed in Chapter Four), but the article gave no source for Madison's statement and he was not born until more than fifteen years after Sally returned from Paris.

Similarly, the *Monticello Report* asserts that Sally and James "would almost certainly have been aware of their right to freedom and the means to achieve it," because "there was a community of former slaves in Paris and freedom cases were brought and won in this period."[51] Implicit in this reasoning appears to be an assumption that Sally and James "hung out" with this "community of former slaves," or perhaps that free servants of Patsy's or Polly's friends at the convent would have known this and been willing to risk their own comfort by spreading dissension among the slaves of the powerful American Minister to France. Perhaps this is true. But, once again, the real answer is that we simply do not know.

The *Monticello Report* also clearly accepted as fact Madison Hemings' allegation that his mother confronted her powerful master in Paris and refused to return to Virginia (where all of her American family and friends lived) unless Jefferson would agree to enter into a "treaty" to free any children they might produce years in the future when the children reached the age of twenty-one. Several statements in Madison's article seem clearly false, and this one is totally out of character with what we know about the personality of Thomas Jefferson and what little we know about Sally Hemings. Yet Monticello research historian Lucia Stanton writes:

> Madison Hemings's allusions to the promises Jefferson made to his mother to persuade her to leave France evoke a woman who, although limited by her race and condition, exercised a measure of control over her own destiny. The several references to Jefferson's "promise," "treaty," and "solemn pledge" even suggest Sally Hemings's strength and agency at other times in her life, condensed for the sake of transmitting a story into the single negotiation over the return to Virginia. In Madison Hemings's account, his mother's actions were driven by concern for the welfare of her children.... [52]

Now, every word of this may be true. Perhaps Sally Hemings was this precocious, prescient, powerful feminist role model who confronted the American Minister to France and "negotiated" special privileges for the children she anticipated she might bear some years in the future. Otherwise, we are assured, she was going to demand her freedom and remain in France. And yet, in these remarkable "negotiations," Sally Hemings apparently did not bother to ask for her *own* freedom in the event of her alleged lover's death — when her value as a slave would presumably have been minimal and without which she might have been subjected to abusive treatment of various kinds by a new owner. Indeed, it seems more than a little strange — if Sally's desire to have her own freedom was so great she would abandon her home, family, and friends in Virginia to commence a new life in a for-

---

50. BRODIE, THOMAS JEFFERSON 234.
51. *Monticello Report*, Appendix H at 3.
52. STANTON, FREE SOME DAY 117.

eign land that was on the brink of a bloody revolution—that Sally would not have bothered to include any provision for her own eventual manumission in the "treaty" she allegedly compelled Jefferson to accept.

It is said that Madison's "treaty" story is confirmed by the fact that Thomas Jefferson freed all of Sally's children when they reached the age of twenty-one, but in Chapter Six we show that this widely believed assertion is clearly false. Indeed, as will be discussed, the only two of Sally's children to be legally manumitted by Thomas Jefferson in his will were treated less favorably than *all* of the other children and grandchildren of Sally's mother who were freed during his life or in his will. And, as will also be discussed in Chapter Six, all but two of Betty Hemings' sons and grandsons who remained Thomas Jefferson's property at the time of his death were given their freedom in his will, and the two exceptions gained freedom shortly thereafter.

Sally Hemings at Monticello

Our knowledge of Sally Hemings after she returned to Monticello is equally barren. Contrary to the Hollywood version of the story, there is not the slightest bit of evidence she ever lived in the Monticello big house.[53] Jefferson's grandson, Thomas Jefferson Randolph, reportedly showed historian Henry Randall "a smoke blackened and sooty room" away from the mansion and asserted it was Sally's room.[54] There is some speculation that she may have shared a small stone house with her sister Critta, and then lived in a twelve- by fourteen-foot log cabin on the plantation.[55]

There is no known document including a single quotation attributed to Sally Hemings, nor any document known to contain so much as one word written by her hand. Had she been literate, one might have thought she would have attempted to teach her children to read; yet Madison in 1873 reportedly stated "I learned to read by inducing the white children to teach me the letters...."[56] Still, the absence of serious information means we cannot *prove* that Sally was not literate in several languages. We just do not know.

Hollywood movies portray Sally dancing with the President at the White House. Thomas Jefferson took nearly a dozen Monticello slaves to the White House,[57] but there is not a bit of evidence that Sally was ever one of them. On the contrary, the Monticello overseer at the time asserted that Sally remained at Monticello during Jefferson's presidency.[58]

Then there is the issue of whether Sally served as Thomas Jefferson's "chambermaid" at Monticello. Without any citation, Professor Gordon-Reed asserts: "There is evidence that

---

53. *Monticello Report,* Appendix H at 3; Bear, *The Hemings Family of Monticello* 85.
54. *Monticello Report,* Appendix H at 3.
55. *Id.*
56. [Samuel E. Wetmore], *Life Among the Lowly, Number 1. Madison Hemings.,* Pike County Republican, Mar. 13, 1873, *reprinted in Monticello Report,* Appendix E at 27–28. Former Monticello slave Peter Fossett told a journalist in 1898 that "Mr. Jefferson allowed his grandson to teach any of his slaves who desired to learn, and Lewis Randolph first taught me how to read." *Once the Slave of Thomas Jefferson: The Rev. Mr. Fossett, of Cincinnati, Recalls the Sage of Monticello—Reminiscences of Jefferson, Lafayette, Madison and Monroe,* The World (New York), Jan. 30, 1898, at 33.
57. Jefferson at Monticello 104.
58. *Id.* at 100.

Hemings was Jefferson's chambermaid."[59] Similarly, the *Monticello Report* asserts that from the "1790s to 1827," Sally Hemings was employed as a "chambermaid and seamstress."[60] In response to an inquiry about the foundation for this statement, Lucia Stanton wrote: "Madison Hemings's and Israel Jefferson's [1873] statements are the only references to Sally Hemings as Jefferson's chambermaid. Ellen Coolidge in 1858 wrote that 'no female domestic ever entered [Jefferson's] chambers except at hours when he was known not to be in the public gaze.' ..."[61] Although not cited to any specific source, this quotation was obviously taken from the altered transcription of Ellen Randolph Coolidge's hand-written letter that appears as Appendix E of Professor Gordon-Reed's *Thomas Jefferson and Sally Hemings*.[62] As **Figure 3** on page 36 reveals, counting both words that were deleted and those moved within the sentence, the Gordon-Reed transcription of this sentence includes nearly a dozen alterations that have the effect of reversing the clear meaning of the original letter.

The numerous shortcomings of the 1873 statements attributed to Madison Hemings and Israel Jefferson are addressed in Chapter Four. As will be shown, there are enough problems with both statements to warrant serious skepticism about allegations that are not consistent with other evidence. Even Professor Brodie admits that Jefferson's "body servant" or "valet" was always a male: "Jupiter, who accompanied him to William & Mary; James Hemings, his valet in Paris; and Burwell, who attended him to his death...."[63]

Does this mean that Sally Hemings *could not have been* a "chambermaid" at Monticello? Of course not. We know so little about Sally's role at Monticello that it is theoretically possible that she was a *blacksmith*. Further, it seems clear that other slaves besides Burwell Colbert had at least occasional access to his bedroom. Jefferson's grandson refers to "the person who cleaned and made his bed,"[64] and perhaps *that* could have been Sally Hemings or one of her sisters. We will probably never know.

One might speculate that, given the Callender stories and the constant stream of strangers visiting Monticello most of the time Thomas Jefferson was at home, neither he, nor Martha, nor Burwell would have wanted to encourage further rumors by assigning Sally to make his bed. Even if the Sally story were true, and Thomas Jefferson was engaged in a long-term secret love affair with his slave, one might think he would have had enough discretion to assign a different servant the task of making his bed given the large numbers of relative strangers staying in the house at any given time. But all of this is mere speculation, and, unless new evidence surfaces, we may never know the truth.

Thomas Jefferson's Known Statements about Sally Hemings

Thomas Jefferson was a prolific writer with a refined sense of history. Long before the world had computers, photocopying machines, or even carbon paper, Thomas Jefferson

---

59. GORDON-REED, THOMAS JEFFERSON AND SALLY HEMINGS 178.
60. *Monticello Report*, Appendix H at 4.
61. Lucia Stanton, "Responses to Bob Turner's questions of 14 November 2000," attachment to e-mail from Dan Jordan to Robert Turner, Dec. 8, 2000, 4:22 PM, question 12.
62. GORDON-REED, THOMAS JEFFERSON AND SALLY HEMINGS 259.
63. BRODIE, THOMAS JEFFERSON 50.
64. *Monticello Report*, Appendix E.

painstakingly copied most of his letters in longhand to preserve a record for posterity (or, perhaps, for his own future reference). His burden was eased when he acquired a "poly-graph" machine that made simultaneous copies of his letters with a duplicate quill. When he died, he left behind some 65,000 documents, including approximately 50,000 letters he had written or received over the years.

In 1997, Princeton University Press published two volumes of Jefferson's *Memoran-dum Books* containing more than 1400 pages of notes made during the last six decades of his life. Some of the entries are so trivial as to be almost amusing—recording in-significant financial transactions of a dollar here or a quarter there. It is tempting to assume that Jefferson kept a record of every event in his life, but that is not close to being true. Some of his financial notes seem so trivial as to defy any rational attempt to explain his criteria for inclusion, but in general he presumably tended to record or write about things he found interesting or remarkable. He made copious notes in his *Garden Book* and *Farm Book*, and yet visits to Monticello by close friends and family members often went unrecorded—a situation we will address in more detail in Chap-ter Ten.

The Hemings family played an important role in Jefferson's life, and this is reflected in his numerous references to them in various documents. Sally's brother James Hem-ings, for example, is mentioned 175 times in the *Memorandum Books* and references to James take up 33 lines in the index.[65] Her brother Robert is included roughly half as often.[66]

In contrast, Sally Hemings is far less prominent in the Jefferson *Memorandum Books*. There are three references to Jefferson buying clothes for her in Paris,[67] a notation of two dollars spent on a midwife for Sally when Harriet was born,[68] a reference to a payment to a "Dr. Sutton" for inoculating Sally for smallpox after she arrived in Paris,[69] and a pay-ment in 1789 to a Mrs. Dupré for "5. weeks board of Sally."[70] (As noted, one can only speculate about the reason for this expense, but it may have been so Sally could be trained to care for fine French fabrics, as Martha Jefferson was becoming more active in French society and was acquiring a more sophisticated wardrobe.) In addition, Sally's name is included in five lists of Jefferson's Paris servants who received wages paid through Adrien Petit, the *maître d'hôtel* Jefferson had inherited from John and Abigail Adams; but it is note-worthy that Sally's wages were only half that of her brother James and one-fifth that of the average French servant.[71] But that is it, as far as the *Memorandum Books* go, and they ultimately tell us very little about Sally Hemings.[72]

Jefferson's *Farm Book* provides little additional insight. Sally Hemings and her chil-dren are included on many lists of Jefferson's slaves, ranging from records prepared for tax purposes to lists noting which slaves received blankets, clothing, or other supplies at a particular time. The only clear conclusion we can draw from this is that Sally was treated exactly like the other members of the Hemings family, which is to say she received significantly better treatment than most Monticello slaves.

---

65. 2 Jefferson's Memorandum Books 1502 (James A. Bear, Jr. & Lucia C. Stanton, eds. 1997).

66. *Id.*

67. 1 *id.* 729, 731.

68. 2 *id.* 1053.

69. 1 *id.* 685.

70. *Id.* 731.

71. *Id.* 690, 718, 721, 722, 725 (paid small wage in 1788–1789).

72. Sally Hemings is also mentioned by the editors of the published edition of the *Memorandum Books* in a half dozen footnotes. *See* 1 *id.* 285, 677, 686, 746; 2 *id.* 1299, 1408.

Nor do we learn about Sally Hemings from Thomas Jefferson's voluminous correspondence. In literally tens of thousands of letters, Jefferson made reference to Sally Hemings only four or five times. Professor Gordon-Reed mentions three of these. In 1799 Jefferson informed his son-in-law John Wayles Eppes that "Maria's maid" (*possibly* Sally Hemings, but I believe this unlikely[73]) had given birth to a child,[74] and three years later he wrote two letters during a measles epidemic saying that "if Bet or Sally's children" came down with the illness they should be sent to stay with their grandmother Betty Hemings further away from the big house.[75]

Professor Gordon-Reed missed at least[76] two other letters. Around November 1790, Jefferson wrote overseer Nicholas Lewis that his two daughters, and Martha's husband Thomas Mann Randolph, "are to be furnished with whatever the plantations will furnish...."[77] After a list of examples ("corn, fodder, wheat ... fire-wood," etc.), he adds: "They are to have also the use of the house-servants, to wit, Ursula, Critta, Sally, Bet, Wormeley and Joe. So also of Betty Hemings, should her services be necessary."[78] (See **Figure 6** on the next page.)

Several comments may be in order about this note. If Sally Hemings was Thomas Jefferson's true love who had recently given birth to his child, would he have included her in this list of servants to be assigned to wait on Thomas Mann Randolph and others? Would he not have at least listed her name first, if she were in some way special to him? From what we know about the house servants, Ursula was important.[79] The list is neither alphabetical nor chronological by birth, and may well reflect Jefferson's perception of the

---

73. *See* pages 91–93.

74. *Jefferson to Eppes*, Dec. 21, 1799, in 31 Papers of Thomas Jefferson 274 (2004).

75. Gordon-Reed, Thomas Jefferson and Sally Hemings 178–79. *See also*, The Family Letters of Thomas Jefferson 231–32 (Edwin Morris Betts & James Adam Bear, Jr. eds. 1966).

76. There is also a written "Memorandum" Jefferson gave to overseer Edmund Bacon before departing for Washington, in which he notes that "Mrs. Randolph [Jefferson's daughter Martha] always chooses the clothing for the house servants; that is to say, for Peter Hemings, Burwell, Edwin, Critta, and Sally." *Reprinted in* Jefferson at Monticello 54. It is unclear whether this list is in any special order; however, Peter and Burwell were both very important slaves and Sally was Betty Hemings' youngest child.

77. Thomas Jefferson, *Memorandum for Nicholas Lewis,* undated [ca. Nov. 7, 1790], in 18 Papers of Thomas Jefferson 29 (1971).

78. *Id.*

79. Before the Hemings arrived at Monticello, the two most privileged slaves were "King George" (aka "Great George") and "Queen Ursula," the parents of blacksmith Isaac whose story was taken down in *Memoirs of a Monticello Slave. See* Jefferson at Monticello 3. Bacon notes that Ursula was Martha Jefferson's nurse and "took charge of all the children that were not in school." *Id.* at 101. According to Isaac, when Governor Jefferson fled Richmond just ahead of the pursuing British in 1781, George stayed behind and hid Jefferson's silver. As a reward, Isaac says George was given his freedom, but "continued to sarve [*sic*] Mr. Jefferson" and both he and Ursula were thereafter paid a lifetime wage. *Id.* at 8. Former Monticello Resident Director James Bear adds: "I have seen no evidence to substantiate Isaac's claim concerning the freeing of his father, George. However, among TJ's 'taxable property in Albemarle' in 1782 were '129 slaves, 2 free.' (Account Book, April 15, 1782). Since the freed ones are not identified, perhaps George was one of them." *Id.* at 124 n.27. Professor Jack McLaughlin notes that Jefferson left no record of having formally freed George or Ursula and included them on his slave rolls in future years, but notes their special status at Monticello and speculates they may have been offered manumission and elected instead to continue serving Mr. Jefferson. He notes the remarkable independence given Great George as "an overseer at Monticello." Jack McLaughlin, Jefferson and Monticello: The Biography of a Builder 103–05 (1988). Professor Ellis adds: "Great George and his wife, Ursula, referred to as King George (a joke on George III) and Queen Ursula, were slaves in name only and effectively exercised control over management of the household." Ellis, American Sphinx 179. Indeed, according to Jefferson's records, George and Ursula often received more favorable treatment than even Betty Hemings and her family in the distribution of food and clothing. The Garden and Farm Books of Thomas Jefferson 264, 284, 286, 290.

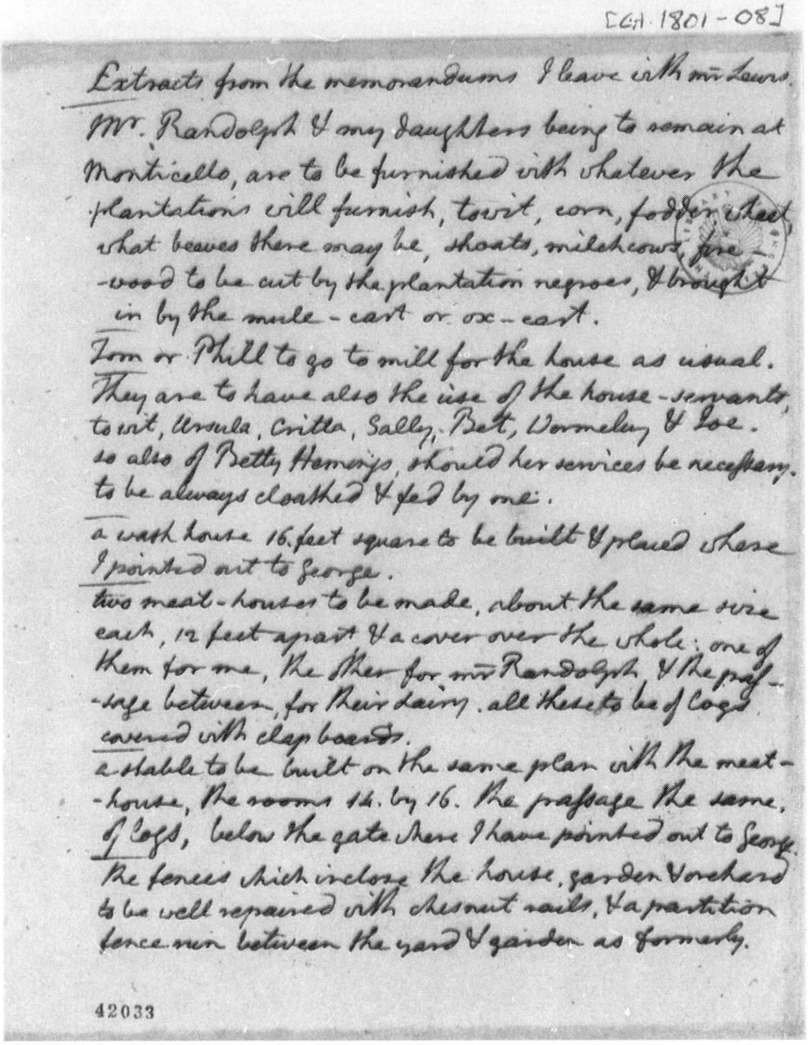
[CA. 1801-08]

Extracts from the memorandums I leave with mr Lewis.

Mr. Randolph & my daughters being to remain at Monticello, are to be furnished with whatever the plantations will furnish, towit, corn, fodder, wheat, what beaves there may be, shoats, milchcows, fire-wood to be cut by the plantation negroes, & brought in by the mule-cart or ox-cart.

Tom or Phill to go to mill for the house as usual.

They are to have also the use of the house-servants, to wit, Ursula, Critta, Sally, Bet, Wormeley & Joe. so also of Betty Hemings, should her services be necessary. to be always cloathed & fed by me.

a wash house 16. feet square to be built & placed where I pointed out to George.

two meat-houses to be made, about the same size each, 12 feet apart & a cover over the whole: one of them for me, the other for mr Randolph, & the passage between, for their dairy. all these to be of logs covered with clapboards.

a stable to be built on the same plan with the meat-house, the rooms 14. by 16. the passage the same, of logs, below the gate where I have pointed out to George.

the fences which inclose the house, garden & orchard to be well repaired with chesnut rails, & a partition fence run between the yard & garden as formerly.

42033

Figure 6. Instructions from Thomas Jefferson to Monticello Overseer Nicholas Lewis (undated). Library of Congress, The Thomas Jefferson Papers, Series 1, image 486.

importance of each slave. (Equally possible, he listed their names at random as they came to his mind, or perhaps listed the ones he thought might be of most use to his relatives first.) The one person on the list who is clearly given preference is not Sally Hemings but her mother, Betty, who is only to be made available "should her services be necessary." Again, if Sally Hemings was the love of his life, would Jefferson not at least have given her the distinction of being made available only if her services were "necessary?"

Finally, there is another letter in which Jefferson writes from Philadelphia to his daughter Martha that he had shipped James Hemings' bedding that had finally arrived from Paris back to Monticello, and in the margin he adds: "Sally's do [ditto]."[80] Not exactly the stuff of love letters.

---

80. *TJ to Martha Jefferson Randolph,* May 8, 1791, in 20 Papers of Thomas Jefferson 381 (1982).

While Jefferson corresponded extensively with some other members of the Hemings family, there is no record of any written (or oral, for that matter) communication by Thomas Jefferson to Sally Hemings. The reverse is implicit in the fact that no verbal or written communication by Sally Hemings to anyone has survived. As revisionist scholar Andrew Burstein observed in the *William & Mary Quarterly*, "Nothing he [Jefferson] wrote even remotely supports the existence of a physical connection with Sally Hemings."[81]

Sally Hemings' Known Statements about Thomas Jefferson

There are no known documents or statements clearly attributable to Sally Hemings about Thomas Jefferson or any other subject.[82]

Sally Hemings' Children

Other than the Callender charge and the oral history of the descendants of Thomas Woodson, there is no evidence that Sally gave birth to a son named "Tom" in 1790. There is also no clear proof that she was *not* the mother of Thomas Woodson, and the fact that at least one Jefferson defender at the time seemed to acknowledge the existence of the twelve-year-old "Tom," and none of his defenders appear to have denied there was such a child, may strengthen the Woodsons' claim. The decisive fact about Thomas Woodson is that six different DNA tests of descendants of three of Thomas Woodson's sons showed that he could not have been fathered by any member of Thomas Jefferson's immediate family.

From Thomas Jefferson's *Farm Book* and other records, we know that Sally gave birth to a daughter on October 5, 1795,[83] who was named "Harriet" or "Harriot." She died on October 5, 1797,[84] and is often referred to as "Harriet I" to distinguish her from a later child given the same name who lived to adulthood. On April 1, 1798, Sally gave birth to a son named Beverly[85]; and in early December 1799, she *may* have produced a daughter who did not survive infancy and may have been named "Thenia." I have serious doubts about this assertion that will be addressed at the end of this chapter.[86]

The *Farm Book* informs us that Sally gave birth to a second daughter named Harriet in May 1801.[87] Like Sally and her other children, there is very little in Jefferson's records about Harriet. Indeed, Jefferson made no reference to her in his extensive *Memorandum Books*.

---

81. Andrew Burstein, *Jefferson's Rationalizations*, 57 WM. & MARY Q. 183 (Jan. 2000).

82. *See, e.g., Monticello Report*, Appendix F at 2; and STANTON, FREE SOME DAY 114.

83. THOMAS JEFFERSON: THE GARDEN AND FARM BOOKS 248.

84. *Martha Jefferson Randolph to Thomas Jefferson*, Jan. 22, 1798, in THE FAMILY LETTERS OF THOMAS JEFFERSON 153–54 (Edwin Morris Betts & James Adam Bear, Jr., eds. 1966).

85. THOMAS JEFFERSON: THE GARDEN AND FARM BOOKS 382. *See also, id.* at 246, 301.

86. *See* pages 91–93.

87. THOMAS JEFFERSON: THE GARDEN AND FARM BOOKS 382.

Sally's sons Madison and Eston were born, respectively, on January 19,[88] 1805, and May 21, 1808. Sally Hemings is not believed to have had any more children after 1808, when she would have been about thirty-four years old.

An undated *Farm Book* "Roll of the Negroes according to their ages"—which includes an entry for August 1804, but may well have been maintained over a period of many years—includes this entry under slaves born in 1801: "Harriet. Sally's run. 22."[89] In addition, we have this apparently credible account by former Monticello overseer Edmund Bacon about Harriet Hemings: "When she was nearly grown, by Mr. Jefferson's direction I paid her stage fare to Philadelphia and gave her fifty dollars. I have never seen her since and don't know what became of her."[90] Among other possible interpretations of these data are: (1) Jefferson arranged for Harriet to be informally freed and sent to Philadelphia in 1822 (the year she would have turned twenty-one) and covered his action by falsely documenting that she had "run"; or (2) Harriet ran away in 1822, was returned, and Jefferson—perhaps fearing Harriet might face harm if she fled again—arranged for Bacon to put her on the stage. One might hypothesize another dozen or so explanations, but the reality is that we are unlikely to know the truth with any certainty.

The same list noting that Harriet had "run" in 1822 said next to Beverly Hemings' name: "run away 22."[91] This has led some to speculate that perhaps the siblings left Monticello together. While in the absence of more detailed records one cannot rule this out completely, it is not clearly[92] consistent with Edmund Bacon's account of Harriet's departure.

Whether they left together or separately, there is credible evidence that Thomas Jefferson allowed both Beverly and Harriet to leave Monticello. In an 1854 letter to her husband, Jefferson's granddaughter Ellen Randolph Coolidge wrote:

> It was his principle (I know that of my own knowledge) to allow such of his slaves as were sufficiently white to pass for white men, to withdraw quietly from the plantation; it was called running away, but they were never reclaimed. I remember four instances of this, three young men and one girl, who walked away and staid [*sic*] away. Their whereabouts was perfectly known but they were left to themselves—for they were white enough to pass for white.[93]

Later in the same letter, she makes it clear that these almost white slaves included children of Sally Hemings:

> One woman known to Mr. J. Q. Adams and others as "dusky Sally" was pretty notoriously the mistress of a married man, a near relation of Mr. Jefferson's, and there can be small question that her children were his. They were all fair and all set free at my grandfather's death, or had been suffered to absent themselves per-

---

88. Jefferson records Madison only as having been born during the month of January 1805, but the date of January 19 is provided in the account attributed to Madison Hemings by Samuel Wetmore discussed in Chapter Four.

89. THOMAS JEFFERSON: THE GARDEN AND FARM BOOKS 386. The number "22" may refer to the year in which Harriet left (1822).

90. JEFFERSON AT MONTICELLO 102.

91. THOMAS JEFFERSON: THE GARDEN AND FARM BOOKS 386.

92. Bacon does not say that he put *only* Harriet on the stage, and Lucia Stanton has suggested to me they may have left together because women did not travel alone in that era; but one might have thought Bacon would have added "with her brother" if both had been involved.

93. *Ellen Randolph Coolidge to Joseph Coolidge*, Oct. 24, 1858, *reprinted in Monticello Report*, Appendix E.

manently before he died. The mother, Sally Hemmings [*sic*], had accompanied Mr. Jefferson's youngest daughter to Paris and was lady's maid to both sisters.[94]

Unlike the children of some of Sally Hemings' siblings, Sally's own children received very little attention in Jefferson's extensive *Memorandum Books*. Beverly is mentioned once,[95] daughters Harriet I and Harriet II are not mentioned by Jefferson at all,[96] and sons Madison and Eston share a single entry noting they were paid two dollars for 100 cabbages on December 11, 1824.[97] This was the same sum he had paid another slave for the same number of cabbages about two years earlier.[98]

Substituting Speculation for Scholarship

In the absence of meaningful information about Sally Hemings, proponents of the "Sally story" have resorted to the most bizarre speculation and fantasizing. There is not the slightest evidence that Sally Hemings spoke more than a few words of French or had any formal training in the language,[99] yet Professor Brodie takes the established fact that brother James had a French tutor and asserts that "one could expect that Sally would likely have been included."[100] Having thus established this "fact," she goes on to write: "Jefferson had under his roof in Paris two slaves who were learning to speak French, who counted themselves free, and were thinking of becoming expatriates."[101] This would have been a reasonable statement had Dr. Brodie used "might have been" instead of "were"—but as written it is unsupportable nonsense. From what little we know, it is equally likely that Sally Hemings cried herself to sleep at night praying to be reunited with her mother and siblings.

Most historians would presumably examine the available records and conclude that Sally Hemings and her children were relatively minor figures within the important Hemings family at Monticello. But Professor Brodie recognizes a classic cover-up when she sees one:

> The necessity for secrecy concerning Jefferson's liaison with Sally Hemings pervaded every aspect of their relationship. Even in his *Farm Book* she remained surprisingly anonymous. Though he wrote Sally's name many times, on the slave inventories, the distribution lists for fish, beef, blankets, and linen, he never included her last name, as he did that of her mother and several of her brothers. He listed her often just below that of her sister Critta, and there is no indication in the *Farm Book* that she was singled out for special treatment.[102]

To be sure, Sally Hemings' absence from Monticello records *could* be the result of a cover-up. But Occam's Razor would guide us to consider first the more simple explanation—

---

94. *Id.*

95. 2 Jefferson's Memorandum Books 1299 (receiving twenty-five cents for expenses from Jefferson in April 1814).

96. The second child named Harriet is mentioned in a footnote by the editors explaining a two-dollar expenditure by Jefferson for a midwife for Sally when Harriet was born in 1801. *Id.* at 1053 n. 15.

97. 2 Jefferson's Memorandum Books 1408.

98. *Id.* at 1391 ("10. [November 1822] Pd. Israel for 100. Cabbages 2.D.")

99. *See, e.g.,* William Howard Adams, The Paris Years of Thomas Jefferson 323 n.32 (1997).

100. Brodie, Thomas Jefferson 233.

101. *Id.* at 235.

102. *Id.* at 291.

that Sally Hemings really *was* a minor figure at Monticello. Yes, as the Thomas Jefferson Foundation's Lucia Stanton has asserted, Sally Hemings did have an "enduring connection"[103] with Thomas Jefferson. But I am persuaded she is mistaken about its character: for more than fifty years, Sally Hemings was one of Thomas Jefferson's many slaves.

If one excludes Hollywood productions and writings openly identified as fiction, perhaps the most remarkable conclusions drawn by a scholar from the near total absence of information about Sally Hemings comes from David Brion Davis, Sterling Professor of History at Yale University. In his Preface to Lucia Stanton's *Free Some Day,* he asserts that "Sally Hemings ... knew Thomas Jefferson at least as well as did any of his white friends and relatives."[104] I find not the slightest bit of historical evidence to support such an assertion by such a distinguished scholar.

Was Sally Hemings Monogamous?

Ironically (since the original version of the allegation portrayed her as a "slut" and "prostitute" who had no fewer than fifteen lovers[105]), much of the circumstantial case against Thomas Jefferson is premised on the *assumption* that Sally Hemings had to be monogamous. Candidly, I personally place very little weight on anything James Callender wrote, and my strong sense is that Sally Hemings was but an innocent victim of his racism and his vendetta to harm Thomas Jefferson. The *irony* has less to do with Callender's veracity than with the fact that some revisionists seek to employ him as a reliable source to show the alleged sexual relationship occurred, but then conveniently ignore him in assuring us that no one ever suggested that Sally Hemings was not monogamous.

As discussed in Chapter One, the basic scientific conclusions from the DNA testing were that Eston Hemings was almost certainly fathered by a Jefferson male and Thomas Woodson was not. Based upon those findings, it would be fairly easy to identify half a dozen Jefferson males[106] who might well have been at Monticello when Eston was conceived and nearly another twenty[107] who arguably might have been there. But identifying other suspects who are likely to have been there when all five or six children were conceived is obviously more difficult, and since Thomas Jefferson lived at Monticello, he quickly becomes a prime suspect once one postulates that Sally had to have been monogamous.

The January 2000 *Monticello Report* summarized the argument thusly:

> The committee concludes that convincing evidence does not exist for the hypothesis that another male Jefferson was the father of [all of] Sally Hemings's children. In almost two hundred years since the issue first became public, no other Jefferson has ever been referred to as the father; denials of Thomas Jeffer-

---

103. STANTON, FREE SOME DAY 117.

104. David Brion Davis, *Preface,* in STANTON, FREE SOME DAY 11.

105. *See* Chapter Three.

106. For example, we know that Thomas Jefferson invited his widower brother, Randolph, to visit Monticello shortly before Eston was conceived, and we know that Randolph had five sons, at least four of whom were between the ages of 18 and 27 and thus presumably far more likely fathers of a child than the sixty-four-year-old President. (Since we only have years for the births of Randolph's children—and some of these are only estimates—there is no way to know their precise age on any given date.)

107. *See, e.g., Monticello Report* at 9 ("During these eighteen years at least twenty-five adult male descendants of Jefferson's grandfather Thomas Jefferson (1677–1731) lived in Virginia.").

son's paternity named the Carr nephews. Furthermore, evidence of the sort of sustained presence necessary to have resulted in the creation of a family of six children is entirely lacking, and even those who denied a relationship never suggested Sally Hemings's children had more than one father.[108]

It is creative advocacy, in a setting where there is almost a total absence of relevant information, to argue, in essence, that "I am right because there is no proof that my guess is wrong"; but this hardly *proves* the proffered fact. Let us look at some of the facts that we can establish by at least a preponderance of the evidence:

- Monogamy was certainly not an element in the original story of a Jefferson-Hemings sexual relationship published by James T. Callender and circulated by Jefferson's Federalist opponents. As Chapter Three will show, Callender described Sally Hemings as "a slut as common as the pavement,"[109] and Georgia Federalist Thomas Gibbons, who is relied upon by the *Monticello Report* on other points, called Sally "the most abandoned prostitute of her color."[110]

- It is not true that none of Sally Hemings' contemporaries alleged that she had more than one lover. An 1874 letter from Thomas Jefferson Randolph reprinted in the *Monticello Report* states, for example, that the paternity of Sally's children had been "admitted by others."[111] He used the plural "others," not "another." Presumably, he was referring to Peter *and* Samuel Carr, the sons of Thomas Jefferson's sister Martha.

- Professor Brodie tells us that Sally Hemings "had a model in her own mother,"[112] who Madison Hemings reportedly said "had seven children by white men and seven by colored men — fourteen in all."[113] The use of the plural "men" in both categories suggests that Betty Hemings had children by no fewer than four men.

- Ms. Helen Leary, former president of the "Board for Certification of Genealogists" and a self-proclaimed "leading authority on early families of the Upper South," adds that it is "a pattern observable in both historical and contemporary life that girls raised in a particular environment tend to grow up accepting that familiar lifestyle as both the norm and their fate."[114]

- Perhaps more importantly, the assumption that slave women had the *prerogative* to say "no" to sexual advances in colonial Virginia is not self-evident.

- One of the few apparently unbiased eye-witnesses to Monticello life during this period — in the sense that he was not related to either side and, having years earlier moved away from Virginia, was no longer subject to retribution from anyone for telling the truth — was Monticello overseer Edmund Bacon. Bacon not only asserted that young white men visiting Monticello were "intimate with the Negro women"[115]; but, far more importantly, he alleged that he had personally observed a man who was not Thomas Jefferson coming out of Sally Hemings' room "many a morning when I went up to Monticello very early."[116]

---

108. *Id.*
109. *Quoted in* Rothman, in Sally Hemings and Thomas Jefferson 95.
110. *See, e.g.,* Gordon-Reed, Thomas Jefferson and Sally Hemings 171.
111. *Monticello Report*, Appendix E at 43.
112. Brodie, Thomas Jefferson 229.
113. *Monticello Report*, Appendix E at 31. *See also,* Jefferson at Monticello 26 n.1.
114. Helen F. M. Leary, *Sally Hemings's Children*, 89(3) Jefferson-Hemings: a Special Issue of the National Genealogical Society Quarterly 197 (Sept. 2001).
115. Jefferson at Monticello 88.
116. *Id.* at 102.

It is possible that "Jeff" Randolph was lying to protect a grandfather he dearly loved. The account published by Henry Randall might be further suspect because of the possibility that Randall might have either misunderstood, forgotten, or intentionally altered what he was told. But the Jeff Randolph account published by Randall does not *read* like a cover-up. If that were his goal, why would Jefferson's grandson admit the remarkable similarity in physical appearance between Thomas Jefferson and some of Sally Hemings' sons? And if his motive were merely to defend his grandfather, why would Jeff Randolph extract a pledge from Randall *not to publish* his references to the Carr brothers? If Jeff Randolph made no such statement and instead the entire story is a Henry Randall fabrication, why would the famous historian confirm the physical similarities—and how do we explain the account by Jeff Randolph's sister, Ellen Coolidge, that Jeff had told *her* as well that the Carr brothers had admitted paternity and Jeff had extracted a similar promise of confidentiality from her?

Occam's Razor tells us that assuming several witnesses are lying about something in the absence of clear evidence to that effect is not the soundest approach in the search for the truth if there exist simpler explanations—such as that Sally Hemings was *not* monogamous. Rather than simply making assumptions on such a key issue, we should compare the evidence on all sides and see where it points. Against the evidence already discussed—which includes two eye-witness accounts and various admissions against interest—the advocates of Thomas Jefferson's paternity rely largely on the fact that Jefferson scholars, who over the years almost unanimously (at least until the Gordon-Reed book was published) rejected the Callender charges, have not denied that Sally was monogamous. One might counter by observing that they also have not expressly concluded that she *was* monogamous. Finding the Callender allegations without merit, most have simply accepted the Randolph family explanation that one or both of the Carr brothers likely bore responsibility for Sally's children.

To this they add Madison Hemings' alleged statement that Thomas Jefferson fathered all of his mother's children. Obviously, Madison Hemings could not have known the full scope of his mother's sexual behavior or the actual paternity of children conceived prior to his own birth (which would leave only Eston). In the absence of reason to believe otherwise, it seems normal for children to assume that their parents are good and honorable people—and implicit in that assumption may be a belief that they are sexually monogamous.

Nor is it likely that the Carr brothers, assuming they were sexually involved with Sally Hemings, would have been confident that her children were their own. Like Madison, they might have hoped that Sally was faithful (if they even cared), but sometimes not even the mother can be certain of the paternity of her child. At any rate, the case for the Carr brothers being the fathers of Sally's children would presumably be much stronger for the older children.[117]

What other "evidence" of Sally's monogamy are we offered? The *Monticello Report* informs us that "[f]ull-sibling relationships are further supported by the closeness of the family, as evidenced by documentation of siblings living together and naming children after each other."[118] At best, this statement is problematic. First, it presupposes that Sally Hemings' children would *know* the truth about their paternity. Second, it assumes that "full-sibling relationships" are inherently closer than those of half-siblings, which is at best a stereotype and—based upon my limited observations—may well be false. Most importantly, it is difficult to read the account attributed to Madison Hemings in the *Pike County Republican* and conclude that Sally Hemings' children were especially "close." For exam-

---

117. *See* Chapter Ten.
118. *Monticello Report* at 7.

ple, Madison said of his sister Harriet: "I have not heard from her for ten years, and do not know whether she is dead or alive." He apparently did not know when his younger brother died, and there is no indication he had been in recent contact with Beverly. This is hardly the kind of "evidence" that overcomes multiple eyewitness testimony to the contrary.

Sally Hemings' Life after Thomas Jefferson's Death

One of the many inconsistencies with the theory that Thomas Jefferson and Sally Hemings were "lovers" for decades and any concomitant assumption of rational behavior on the part of the former President is that Thomas Jefferson made no apparent provision for Sally's welfare at the time of his death. When he wrote his final will he must have known that Sally's monetary value to his estate was minimal (she was valued at fifty dollars in preparation for the slave auction). Some have argued that to list her in his will would confirm the Callender allegations in the minds of many Americans; but were that his concern, why did he include in his will both of his remaining alleged "sons" by this same slave woman? Surely he knew that would fuel similar speculation.

No one knows exactly what happened to Sally Hemings. Although she was not freed in Jefferson's will, she was not sold with other slaves in 1829, and by 1830 apparently was listed as a free white woman in the U.S. census for Charlottesville.[119] She is also listed as a free person living in Charlottesville in a special 1833 census.[120] Yet the following year, in her will, Martha Jefferson Randolph wrote that she wished her children to give "Betsy Hemmings [sic], Sally & Wormley … their time."[121] Giving slaves "their time" was an informal way of granting *de facto* freedom without running afoul of the Virginia statute requiring manumitted slaves to leave the state within one year.[122] But if Martha had not already given Sally "her time," how do we explain the fact that Sally was reported to be living in Charlottesville four years earlier as a free person? This provision was not included in Martha's 1836 will. Sally Hemings had died the previous year, having "spent her entire life in legal bondage."[123]

The *Monticello Report* states that the language in Martha's will about giving the three remaining Hemings "their time" was "probably a written reinforcement of a previous verbal arrangement."[124] This is somewhat ambiguous, as some have speculated that (on the assumption that Sally and Thomas Jefferson were lovers) such an "arrangement" must have been at the President's informal direction prior to his death. The *Monticello Report* notes that there is no evidence to support this theory,[125] and this language may simply mean that Martha had already given Sally "her time" and was merely reducing it to writing to avoid any question at the time of her death.

The one thing the will does seem to confirm is that after Thomas Jefferson's death, three members of the Hemings family, including Sally, wound up the property of Martha Jefferson Randolph. This by itself may be important for our inquiry, particularly given

---

119. Bear, *The Hemings Family of Monticello* 85. *Accord*, BRODIE, THOMAS JEFFERSON 468; GORDON-REED, THOMAS JEFFERSON AND SALLY HEMINGS 209.

120. *Monticello Report*, Appendix H at 5.

121. *Id.* Cynthia Burton asserts that this "Betsy Hemmings" was the wife of Peter Hemings.

122. "'Giving time' was an informal method of emancipation that avoided the effects of the 1806 removal law…." *Monticello Report*, Appendix H at 5.

123. STANTON, FREE SOME DAY 107.

124. *Monticello Report*, Appendix H at 5.

125. *Id.*

the lack of more significant evidence to guide us. For if Thomas Jefferson had commenced a sexual relationship with Sally Hemings while she was Martha's maid in Paris, and continued that affair for decades after they returned to Virginia, with Sally bearing him several children and producing the Callender scandal that did at least some damage to his reputation, it is difficult to believe that Martha would not have learned of the relationship. One might suspect that in such a situation, she would have resented this slave woman, either because of the scandal caused by the relationship or even because she saw Sally as a rival for her father's affections.

For that matter, would she likely have rushed home to Monticello with her own innocent children every time the President returned home, so her children could be exposed to this allegedly immoral environment? Would Jefferson have pleaded with her to bring the children to Monticello if his primary interest was being alone with the "handsome" Sally Hemings to produce still more illegitimate children? None of this makes the slightest sense unless most of what we know about the character of Thomas and Martha Jefferson Randolph is false.

Even if Jefferson's daughter did not resent Sally, there is strong evidence that one of Martha Randolph's strongest desires was to protect her deceased father's reputation. Indeed, this desire was so great that she reportedly called her children to her side on her deathbed and asked them to defend their grandfather's reputation. Had Sally in fact been Thomas Jefferson's lover, how likely is it that Martha Randolph would have rewarded her by sending her to live with her sons in Charlottesville, where she could tell her story to neighbors or anyone else who would listen?

How likely is it that Thomas Jefferson would have left Sally's future in the hands of his daughter had the affair actually existed? On the other hand, if Sally Hemings were nothing more than an average member of a favorite family of slaves—a loyal house servant who had been victimized by James Callender and the Federalists through no fault of her own—the few facts that we know about her final years make total sense.

Elizabeth Langhorne, in her 1987 book, *Monticello: A Family Story*, alleges that the reason Sally Hemings was not freed in Thomas Jefferson's will had something to do with the fact that she had not belonged to him for several years:

> First of all, Sally did not "belong" to Jefferson: she was considered in the family as the property of his granddaughter Ellen. This becomes clear at the time of Ellen's marriage. Sally, in fact, had been Ellen's maid for virtually the entire time of Jefferson's retirement. This, and Ellen's legal ownership, comes to light in a letter that Ellen wrote to her mother in 1825, while she and Joseph Coolidge were still on their wedding trip.[126]

Langhorne goes on to discuss lengthy negotiations to hire "Sally" out or sell her to various University of Virginia faculty members. Monticello's Lucia Stanton, who is certainly among the foremost modern authorities on slave life at Monticello, believes that Langhorne has confused Sally Hemings with a different Sally. Others who have looked closely at the issue disagree. Both arguments strike me as being possible, and the most interesting thing may be that we really do not *know* what happened to this woman we are now told was so important at Monticello.

The "conventional wisdom" is that Sally Hemings apparently lived with her sons Madison and Eston in Charlottesville until her death around 1835,[127] but Professor Gordon-

---

126. ELIZABETH LANGHORNE, MONTICELLO: A FAMILY STORY 258 (1987).
127. BRODIE, THOMAS JEFFERSON 209.

Reed observes that "No record of Sally Hemings's life during that period [the nine years she lived after Jefferson's death] survives."[128] Indeed, there is not even a record of when Sally Hemings died or where she was buried. The assumption that she lived with Madison and Eston in Charlottesville is based upon the 1873 statement attributed to her son Madison, supported by a notation in a census report that there was an older woman present in their home. I do not know which story to believe, but am inclined to believe that Ms. Stanton got this one right and that Elizabeth Langhorne may have confused two of the many Sallys at Monticello. Otherwise it is difficult to understand the statement in Martha Randolph's 1834 will referring to "Sally."

In summary, virtually everything we know about Sally Hemings can be printed on an index card (see **Figure 5** on page 69). There is no record of a single sentence that she uttered or wrote, and from what we know from Jefferson's surviving records, she was at best an average member of a very special family of Monticello slaves. Neither Sally Hemings, nor any of her children, nor any other eyewitness left any record to support the anti-Jefferson allegations of James Callender in 1802 for more than seventy years; and the heart of the Callender charge has been largely disproved by the DNA tests eliminating Thomas Woodson as a possible son of Thomas Jefferson.

The 1873 statements attributed to Madison Hemings and Israel Jefferson were both filtered through the pen of a highly partisan political journalist with a clear agenda of harming the reputation of Thomas Jefferson. As will be shown in Chapter Four, Israel's statement is so full of falsehoods as to lack credibility, and most of the relevant "facts" attributed to Madison Hemings occurred long before he was born and are not attributed to any original source. There is circumstantial evidence that at least some of his information came from the original James Callender and Thomas Turner articles published seven decades earlier, published statements by other Jefferson critics, and even books previously published about the famous President. These issues will be addressed in Chapter Four.

Sally's Alleged Child "Thenia"

It seems clear that a slave child was born at Monticello in early December 1799. In a letter to John Wayles Eppes, husband of his daughter Maria (Polly), Jefferson wrote:

> Those of your people who were unwell when you went away are still so & one who has been cured is ill again, Augustine, I believe it is. Maria's maid produced a daughter about a fortnight ago, & is doing well.

Quoting only the second sentence in this excerpt, the *Monticello Report* concludes: "The most likely candidate for 'Maria's maid' still living at Monticello, rather than with the Eppes, is Sally Hemings."[129] This child's lifespan is identified as "(1799–1800)." Since we know that Sally traveled to Paris with Maria (Polly), and we believe that she served as a lady's maid to both Maria and her older sister Martha at that time, it is *possible* that Sally continued in this role after returning to Monticello or that Jefferson used this description because of the Paris connection. But there is so little reliable information that it is also quite possible that a different slave served Maria after her return to Monticello and

---

128. GORDON-REED, THOMAS JEFFERSON AND SALLY HEMINGS 209.
129. *Monticello Report*, Appendix H at 10.

produced the child in question. Sally Hemings, it should be recalled, gave birth to Beverly less than a year before "Maria's maid" conceived the child in question, and may well have still been nursing.[130] Former Monticello slave Peter Fossett asserted that slave children at Monticello "were nursed until they were three years old."[131]

There are strong arguments against the assumption that Jefferson was referring to Sally Hemings. When Martha and Maria got married and left Monticello, neither took Sally Hemings with them. Instead, Jefferson gave Maria Betsy Hemings, the daughter of Sally's oldest sister Mary, as a wedding present on October 12, 1797, when Betsy was about fourteen years old—a little more than two years before the otherwise unidentified "Maria's maid" gave birth. Yet another candidate for "Maria's maid" was Critta Hemings, another of Sally's older sisters, whom Polly borrowed from Monticello in 1801 when Betsy was too ill to take care of Polly's child Francis.[132] After Paris, Thomas Jefferson obviously knew Sally Hemings' name—three months before writing of "Maria's maid" he identified Sally Hemings simply as "Sally"[133]—and this reference suggests he may well have not known the new mother's name. It takes less effort to write "Sally" than "Maria's maid."

Perhaps more importantly, the context seems to be a discussion of slaves belonging to John Eppes—"your people"—who were left in Thomas Jefferson's care because they were too "unwell" to travel when the Eppes left Monticello. Rather than traveling with ill servants, the Eppes may have entrusted their care to those at Monticello and returned home. In updating John Eppes on the status of his slaves, Jefferson adds a note that "Maria's maid" had a child. Obviously, from the context, "Maria's maid" was well along in her pregnancy when the Eppes returned home, and might well have been left behind to be cared for by relatives and to avoid the discomfort and perhaps risks of traveling in the final stages of her pregnancy.

This interpretation is also supported by the fact that Jefferson made no references in his own records either of Sally (or any other Monticello slave) giving birth to the child in question, nor to its assumed death the following year. Indeed, there appears to be nothing in the surviving records to suggest that this child did not live a long life—as the property of John Eppes. Since there are no references in Jefferson's records to this child beyond the letter to Eppes, Monticello scholars seem to have simply assumed it died shortly after birth. Since it was born in December 1799, they presumably assumed it might have died in 1800. Plausible, but hardly probable.

One reasonable explanation for Jefferson's note is that "Maria's maid" was left at Monticello to have her baby—perhaps because her mother or an experienced midwife lived there—giving Jefferson all the more reason to mention her status to her owner (John Eppes). The most logical candidate for "Maria's maid" is presumably Betsy Hemings.

---

130. A 1988 international conference on lactation infertility in Bellagio, Italy, concluded: "Demographic data indicate that in many developing countries, the protection from pregnancy provided by breastfeeding alone is greater than that given by all other reversible means of family planning combined." Kathy I. Kennedy, Roberto Rivera, & Alan S. McNeilly, *Consensus Statement on the Use of Breastfeeding As a Family Planning Method*, 39(5) Contraception 478, 485 (May 1989). I am indebted to Cynthia Burton both for suggesting this point and providing the source.

131. *Once the Slave of Thomas Jefferson: The Rev. Mr. Fossett, of Cincinnati, Recalls the Sage of Monticello"—Reminiscences of Jefferson, Lafayette, Madison and Monroe,* The World (New York), Jan. 30, 1898, at 33.

132. *Mary Jefferson Eppes to Thomas Jefferson,* Nov. 6, 1801, in The Family Letters of Thomas Jefferson 211 (Edwin Morris Betts & James Adam Bear, Jr., eds. 1966).

133. On September 27, 1801, Jefferson recorded spending $3.00 "for Mrs. Sneed for Sally," believed to have been a midwife fee for the birth of Harriet Hemings. 2 Jefferson's Memorandum Books 1053 (James A. Bear, Jr. & Lucia C. Stanton, eds. 1997).

Monticello scholars have attributed the child born to "Maria's maid" to Sally Hemings (and presumably Thomas Jefferson), but this seems based on the flimsiest of evidence and is likely a result of a careless misreading of Jefferson's *Farm Book* records. Page 54 of the *Farm Book* is entitled "Diary 1796." The following page is dated "1799.Oct." and constitutes a distribution list for beds, blankets, shoes, and other items for various slaves. On this list, under the name "Doll" are the indented names "Thenia .93." and "Dolly 94." On the same list, "Sally" is followed by an indented "Beverly 98"—a clear reference to Sally's first son who was born in 1798. Page 56 is entitled "Plantation" but is undated. It is a distribution list for fish and beef to various slaves. On this list, under "Sally" are listed "Beverly" and "Thenia" but Thenia's name is struck through. From this evidence, and the Jefferson-Eppes letter referring to "Maria's maid" having a baby, Monticello scholars have apparently concluded that Sally must have given birth to a child named "Thenia" whose name was struck-through because she died.

However, on this same undated list the child "Thenia" is not listed under "Doll." Page 58 of the *Farm Book* includes an unrelated list dated "1799, June 27." At the bottom of that page is another list dated "1800. July 15." The next page begins with a November 1800 list in which Thenia is back under Doll, and Beverly appears alone under Sally.

From this it is certainly possible to speculate that Doll's Thenia was absent for some reason on one list, that Sally gave birth to a separate Thenia about that time, and then Sally's Thenia died as Doll's Thenia returned home. It is also possible that Jefferson mistakenly listed Doll's Thenia as Sally's child, and then struck-through the name when he realized his error. But perhaps the simplest explanation is that for some reason Doll's Thenia was living for a brief period with Sally Hemings, and soon thereafter she returned home. (If we turn back to page 50 of the *Farm Book*, we find a "Bread List" for 1796 and under Sally's name is the name "Edy," although Monticello does not interpret that as evidence of another Hemings child.)

As the preceding paragraphs demonstrate, the *Farm Book* lists are not always in chronological order. The undated list that seems to shift the name "Thenia" from under the name of "Doll" to that of "Sally" is located between lists dated October 1799 and a list on the following page dated four months earlier. Perhaps the undated list was prepared following the December birth to "Maria's maid." We just do not know. But, given the many uncertainties and alternative scenarios, to assume that the child was born to Sally Hemings and that its name was "Thenia" is a bit of a stretch. To this one might add that including a child of six or seven (like Doll's Thenia) on a meat ration list would make a lot more sense than listing a new-born infant—all the more so if the infant was the child of a slave who was the maid to a woman who did not even reside at Monticello.

3

James Thomson Callender and the Origins of the 1802 Jefferson-Hemings Scandal

The allegation that Thomas Jefferson fathered children by his slave Sally Hemings first came to the attention of the American people in September, 1802, when a journalist named James Thomson Callender made the accusation as part of a series of vicious attacks on the President. These were quickly picked up and reprinted by Jefferson's enemies in the Federalist press, and publicized as well by Jefferson's enemies as far away as England. Assessing the probability of a sexual relationship between Thomas Jefferson and Sally Hemings becomes easier once one understands the origins of the allegation.

The report of the Thomas Jefferson Memorial Foundation Research Committee on this issue included only a single sentence of background on Callender and then provided copies and edited transcripts of some of his articles. That sentence reads:

> 1802. Journalist James T. Callender, although his account is obviously sensationalized, stated that he was repeating what he had heard from others; he included some details that can be verified, and others that cannot.[1]

Professor Annette Gordon-Reed, in her 1997 book, *Thomas Jefferson and Sally Hemings*, argues: "James Callender's statement in 1802 that Sally Hemings had five children is extrinsic evidence that corroborates Madison Hemings's claim that Sally Hemings had a child upon her return to the United States from France."[2]

Both accounts would seem to be a bit gentle with the author of this allegation, given what is known about James Thomson Callender. To begin with, if one is to believe Federalist newspaper accounts published only days before the allegation that Thomas Jefferson had a sexual relationship with Sally Hemings was first printed, James Callender was a self-confessed liar. An article printed on the front page of the *Columbian Centinel Massachusetts Federalist* on August 28, 1802, entitled "Origin of the dispute between Callender and the President," quotes Callender, who was angrily demanding a government job, as shouting out in front of the White House after having been turned away by a servant, "*Sir, you know that by* LYING *I made you President....*"[3]

---

1. Thomas Jefferson Memorial Foundation Research Committee, Report on Thomas Jefferson and Sally Hemings, January 2000 [hereinafter cited as "*Monticello Report*"], at 4.

2. ANNETTE GORDON-REED, THOMAS JEFFERSON AND SALLY HEMINGS 215 (1997).

3. *Origin of the dispute between* CALLENDER *and* THE PRESIDENT, COLUMBIAN CENTINEL MASSACHUSETTS FEDERALIST, Aug. 28, 1802 at 1 (italics and small caps in original) (identified as having been reprinted from the *New-York Commercial Advertiser,* n.d.). Original copy in author's personal library.

Writing in *The New-England Historical and Genealogical Register* in 1896, Worthington Chauncey Ford (brother of Paul Leicester Ford, who edited two multi-volume sets of Jefferson's *Writings*) began: "Of all the foreigners who were connected with journalism in the United States at the beginning of the century, James Thomson Callender was easily first in the worst qualities of mind and character."[4]

Pulitzer Prize-winning historian Dumas Malone refers to Callender as "one of the most notorious scandalmongers and character assassins in American history,"[5] and notes that one of his attacks on Jefferson alleged that it "would have been advantageous to his reputation if his head had been cut off five minutes before he began his inaugural speech."[6] (By most accounts, the address was a masterpiece.[7]) Professor Joseph J. Ellis, in *American Sphinx*, writes: "Callender's motives, all historians agree, were scurrilous and vengeful. He probably heard the rumors about miscegenation at Monticello while imprisoned in Richmond ... and felt no compunction about reporting the gossip as fact."[8]

Another recent scholar, who, like Professor Ellis, believes that Thomas Jefferson did father children by Sally Hemings, provides this account: "James Callender was an angry, bitter, and cynical man who made a career by specializing in invective and character assassination. He ruthlessly, viciously, and often crudely ravaged anyone unfortunate enough to be caught in his journalistic sights...."[9] He quotes historian John Chester Miller as writing: "Callender made his charges against Jefferson without fear and without research.... He never made the slightest effort to verify the 'facts' he so stridently proclaimed. It was 'journalism' at its most reckless, wildly irresponsible, and scurrilous. Callender was not an investigative journalist; he never bothered to investigate anything."[10]

Callender came to the United States in 1793 from Scotland, where he claimed to have played some role[11] in writing a controversial book, *The Political Progress of Britain*, and was vulnerable to arrest for sedition. He settled in Philadelphia, and soon set his pen to work by attacking George Washington, Alexander Hamilton, and John Adams,[12] the

---

4. Worthington Chauncey Ford, *Thomas Jefferson and James Thomson Callender,* 50 NEW-ENGLAND HISTORICAL AND GENEALOGICAL REGISTER (No. 199, July 1896) at 321.

5. DUMAS MALONE, JEFFERSON THE PRESIDENT: FIRST TERM, 1801–1805 at 212 (1970).

6. *Id.* at 211, citing RECORDER (Richmond), Sept. 15, 1802.

7. During a National Public Radio (NPR) interview on January 16, 2001, Professor Joseph Ellis referred to Jefferson's first inaugural address as "probably one of the two or three great inaugural addresses in American history." NPR Morning Edition with Bob Edwards, Jan. 16, 2001, 11:00–12:00 AM. In 1966, Daniel J. Boorstin edited *An American Primer*, pulling together in 900 pages the great speeches and documents that have survived through time as "a kind of American catechism," beginning with The Mayflower Compact (1620) through Lyndon Johnson's 1966 Address on Voting Rights. Two documents from Thomas Jefferson made the volume, The Declaration of Independence and his First Inaugural Address. AN AMERICAN PRIMER xiii, 65, 211 (Daniel J. Boorstin, ed. 1966).

8. JOSEPH J. ELLIS, AMERICAN SPHINX 364 (1998).

9. Joshua D. Rothman, *James Callender and Social Knowledge of Interracial Sex in Antebellum Virginia,* in SALLY HEMINGS AND THOMAS JEFFERSON 88 (Jan Ellen Lewis & Peter S. Onuf, eds. 1999).

10. *Quoted in id.* at 89.

11. Given the poorer quality of much of his later work, it is not unreasonable to raise questions about Callender's contribution to this earlier volume. It is unnecessary to examine that issue for present purposes. It is clear that Jefferson and most others involved believed that Callender was the primary author.

12. In an 1813 letter to Jefferson, John Adams accused Callender of "terrorism" for his unprincipled and libelous attacks. *Adams to Jefferson*, June 30, 1813, in 2 THE ADAMS-JEFFERSON LETTERS: THE COMPLETE CORRESPONDENCE BETWEEN THOMAS JEFFERSON AND ABIGAIL AND JOHN ADAMS 346, 347 (1959).

leaders of the Federalist Party.[13] Professor Ellis notes that, in a pamphlet entitled *The Prospect Before Us*, Callender described Adams as "a mentally unstable monarchist who, if re-elected, intended to declare himself king and his son, John Quincy, his royal successor."[14] Callender's work soon came to the attention of Thomas Jefferson, who viewed him as an able writer and political ally and on several occasions provided financial support for his work.

Jefferson's assistance to Callender particularly offended his once-close friends John and Abigail Adams. In a candid letter, Mrs. Adams charged:

> One of the first acts of your administration was to liberate a wretch who was suffering the just punishment of his crimes for publishing the basest libel, the lowest and vilest slander, which malice could invent or calumny exhibit, against the character and reputation of your predecessor; of him, for whom you professed a friendship and esteem, and whom you certainly knew incapable of such complicated baseness. The remission of Callender's fine was a public approbation of his conduct.[15]

Jefferson responded with a summary of his relationship with Callender:

> As early, I think, as 1796, I was told in Philadelphia that Callender, the author of the Political Progress of Britain, was in that city, a fugitive from persecution for having written that book, and in distress. I had read and approved the book; I considered him as a man of genius, unjustly persecuted. I knew nothing of his private character, and immediately expressed my readiness to contribute to his relief, and to serve him. It was a considerable time after, that, on application from a person who thought of him as I did, I contributed to his relief, and afterwards repeated the contribution. Himself I did not see till long after, nor ever more than two or three times. When he first began to write, he told some useful truths in his coarse way; but nobody sooner disapproved of his writing than I did, or wished more that he would be silent. My charities to him were no more meant as encouragements to his scurrilities, than those I give to the beggar at my door are meant as rewards for the vices of his life, and to make them chargeable to myself.[16]

Jefferson obviously benefited politically from Callender's attacks on Washington, Hamilton, and especially Adams, to whom Jefferson had lost the presidential election of 1796 and against whom he was expected to run in 1800. Callender also falsely accused Jefferson's rival Alexander Hamilton of forgery and treasury fraud; and, in order to defend his public behavior, Hamilton found it necessary to disclose that he had been romantically involved with a married woman. But while Jefferson may secretly have welcomed these attacks on his political rivals, it is clear that he also soon realized the sordid side of James Callender; and when Callender hinted that he would like to move to Albemarle County to join Jefferson's community of friends like Madison and Monroe, Jefferson ignored his letters. When Callender was jailed for violating the Alien and Sedition Laws, he blamed Jefferson for not coming quickly to his aid; and even after Jefferson won the election of 1800 and pardoned Callender and all other victims of the controversial laws, Callender blamed Jefferson for delays in the return of his fine and other alleged grievances.

---

13. ELLIS, AMERICAN SPHINX 282. *See also, id.* at 259.

14. Joseph J. Ellis, *The First Democrats,* U.S. NEWS & WORLD REP'T, Aug. 21, 2000, at 38.

15. *Abagail Adams to Jefferson,* July 1, 1804, in 10 WORKS OF THOMAS JEFFERSON 86–88 n.1 (Paul Leicester Ford, ed. 1905).

16. 11 THE WRITINGS OF THOMAS JEFFERSON 42–43 (Mem. ed. 1903).

According to Michael Durey, author of the Callender biography, *With the Hammer of Truth*, the mercurial journalist wrote of his attacks on Jefferson: "chastisement was promised, and the promise has been kept with the most rigid punctuality."[17] Alleging that Jefferson was behind the attacks on him by Republican editors, Callender characterized his response as "ten thousand fold vengeance" upon Jefferson.[18]

The primary basis for Callender's bitterness may well have been that he had realized that Jefferson and his Republican friends neither liked nor respected him.[19] Callender seems to have believed that his attacks on John Adams were responsible for Jefferson's electoral victory, and he was outraged at the ingratitude of Jefferson and his friends. At any rate, Callender sent word that an appropriate reward for his contribution to Jefferson's victory would be appointment as Postmaster of Richmond, a position worth $1,500 a year.[20] When Jefferson turned him down, Callender resorted to blackmail, sending word that if the appointment was not forthcoming he would publish a series of articles that would destroy the President. To his credit, Jefferson refused to give in.

In a letter dated May 29, 1801, Jefferson provided this account to James Monroe:

> Since mine of the 26th Callender is arrived here. He did not call on me; but understanding he was in distress I sent Captain Lewis to him with 50. D. to inform him we were making some inquiries as to his fine which would take a little time, and lest he should suffer in the meantime I had sent him &c. His language to Captain Lewis was very high-toned. He intimated that he was in possession of things which he could and would make use of in a certain case: that he received the 50. D. not as a charity but a due, in fact as hush money; that I knew what he expected, viz. a certain office, and more to this effect. Such a misconstruction of my charities puts an end to them forever. You will therefore be so good as to make no use of the order I enclosed you. He knows nothing of me which I am not willing to declare to the world myself. I knew him first as the author of the *Political Progress of Britain*, a work I had read with great satisfaction, and as a fugitive from persecution for this very work. I gave to him from time to time such aids as I could afford, merely as a man of genius suffering under persecution, and not as a writer in our politics. It is long since I wished he would cease writing on them, as doing more harm than good.[21]

More than a year later, but still well before Callender wrote about Sally Hemings, President Jefferson wrote again to Monroe, giving more details on his relationship with the controversial journalist:

> I am really mortified at the base ingratitude of Callender. It presents human nature in a hideous form. It gives me concern because I perceive that relief, which was afforded him on mere motives of charity, may be viewed under the aspect of employing him as a writer. When the *[P]olitical [P]rogress of Britain* first appeared in this country it was in a periodical publication called the *[B]ee*, where I saw it. I was speaking of it in terms of strong approbation to a friend in Philadel-

---

17. MICHAEL DUREY, "WITH THE HAMMER OF TRUTH" 159 (1990).

18. *Id.*

19. "Before this election year, Jefferson was pleased with Callender's writings and approvingly sent the ragged writer small sums of money. He did not, however, wish to become any closer to a man whom most readers would soon recognize as a bitter, ranting mercenary." ANDREW BURSTEIN, THE INNER JEFFERSON 227 (1995).

20. 3 HENRY S. RANDALL, THE LIFE OF THOMAS JEFFERSON 17–20 (1858).

21. *Jefferson to Monroe*, May 29, 1801, 9 WORKS OF THOMAS JEFFERSON 262–63.

phia, when he asked me if I knew that the author was then in the city, a fugitive from prosecution on account of that work, and in want of employ for his subsistence. This was the first of my learning that Callender was author of the work. I considered him as a man of science fled from persecution, and assured my friend of my readiness to do whatever could serve him. It was long after this before I saw him, probably not till 1798. He had in the mean time written a 2nd part of the *political progress* much inferior to the first, and his history of the U.S. In 1798, I think I was applied to by Mr. Leiper to contribute to his relief. I did so. In 1799, I think S. T. Mason applied for him, I contributed again.... But I discouraged his coming into my neighborhood. His first writings here had fallen far short of his original *[P]olitical [P]rogress* and the scurrilities of his subsequent ones began evidently to do mischief. As to myself no man wished more to see his pen stopped: but I considered him still as a proper object of benevolence. The succeeding year he again wanted money to buy paper for another volume. I made his letter, as before, the occasion of giving him another 50 D. He considers these as proofs of my approbation of his writings, when they were mere charities, yielded under a strong conviction that he was injuring us by his writing. It is known to many that the sums given to him were such and even smaller than I was in the habit of giving to others in distress of the federal as well as the republican party without attention to political principles.[22]

Jefferson then turned to the more immediate cause of Callender's anger towards him:

Soon after I was elected to the government, Callender came on here [Washington, D.C.] wishing to be made postmaster at Richmond. I knew him to be totally unfit for it: and however ready I was to aid him with my own charities (and I then gave him 50. D.) I did not think the public offices confided to me to give away as charities. He took it in mortal offence, and from that moment has been hauling off to his former enemies the federalists.... This is the true state of what has passed between him and me. I do not know that it can be used without committing me in controversy as it were with one too little respected by the public to merit that notice. I leave to your judgment what use can be made of these facts. Perhaps it will be better judged of when we see what use the tories will endeavour to make of their new friend.[23]

Upon being notified that Jefferson would not help him, Callender may have traveled to Albemarle County to search for information he could use in his vendetta.[24] He also may have obtained information while imprisoned in Richmond, where the U.S. Marshal, David Meade Randolph, was a Jefferson relative with a strong dislike for the new President.[25]

Fawn Brodie provides this account:

After his release from jail he was annoyed because of a delay in the repayment of the fine, but still more embittered by what seemed a growing hostility of Jef-

---

22. *Jefferson to Monroe*, July 15, 1802, in 9 WORKS OF THOMAS JEFFERSON 387–89 (1905).

23. *Id.* at 389–90.

24. It seems clear that Callender spoke with people from Albemarle County, but there is no clear evidence he personally traveled there. Cynthia Burton informs me that much of his information may have come from meeting with Albemarle Clerk John Nicholas in Richmond. The issue is not in my view critical to our discussion.

25. The most detailed discussion of the possible role of David Meade Randolph in this controversy I have seen is: REBECCA L. MCMURRY & JAMES F. MCMURRY, JR., ANATOMY OF A SCANDAL: THOMAS JEFFERSON AND THE SALLY STORY (2002).

ferson toward him. He would complain to Madison that Jefferson "had on various occasions, treated me with such ostentatious coolness and indifference, that I could hardly say that I was able to love or trust him." If his hero had feet of clay he must know it at all costs. Sometime before April 1801 he set out for Charlottesville to question Jefferson's neighbors, and it was here that he learned in surprisingly accurate detail a great deal about Sally Hemings.[26]

James Callender was not the first to raise questions about the presence of light-skinned slaves at Monticello—they predated the arrival of Sally Hemings' children. Nor was he even the first journalist to hint that Jefferson might be their father.

Brodie wrote that "As early as June 23, 1800, [Federalist editor W. A.] Rind had written that he had 'damning proofs' of Jefferson's 'depravity.'"[27] The article in question actually seems to have appeared on June 28 and was a reprint of an article from the Boston *Commercial Gazette*, and it made no specific reference to sexual impropriety.[28] However, on September 14, 1801—just under a year before Callender raised the "Black Sal" story—the *Washington Federalist* wrote:

> [I]t has long been currently reported, that a man very high in office, has a number of yellow children, and that he is addicted to golden affections. It is natural to suppose it possible that personal or political enemies of Mr. J. might raise such reports, when they were wholly unfounded—and on the other side it is observed that, what every body says must be true. Certainly such reports, and others of a more delicate nature, tho paler complexion, are current. If they are false and malicious they ought to be contradicted.[29]

This report may well have been premised simply upon the widespread knowledge that there were a number of light-skinned slaves at Monticello.

Although he never visited Monticello,[30] Callender may have visited Charlottesville (there seems to be no record of such a visit), apparently spoke with some of Jefferson's enemies, and heard about Sally Hemings. On September 1, 1802, he added the Hemings allegation to his campaign of "slanderous stories"[31] designed to destroy Thomas Jefferson:

THE PRESIDENT AGAIN

> It is well known that the man, *whom it delighteth the people to honor,* keeps and for many years has kept as his concubine, one of his own slaves. Her name is SALLY. The name of her eldest son is TOM. His features are said to bear a strik-

---

26. FAWN BRODIE, THOMAS JEFFERSON 323 (1974).

27. *Id.*

28. After praising John Adams and describing Jefferson as "a philosophical infidel" and a "heretick," later in the article the writer—using the pseudonym *Attilius Regulas*—asserted: "While those who have the damning proofs of human depravity, are too apt to indulge their fears that so black and foul and large a current cannot be turned." Attilius Regulus, *From Russell's Commercial Gazette to the PEOPLE of the United States,* VIRGINIA FEDERALIST, vol. II, no. 115, June 28, 1800. I am indebted to Christopher Posteraro for searching through old copies of the *Virginia Federalist* in the Harvard Library to find this article for me. This was apparently the basis for Callender's assertion that "[s]ome years ago this story had once or twice been hinted at in Rind's Federalist." [Callender,] *The President Again,* THE RECORDER (Richmond, VA), Sept. 1, 1802.

29. WASHINGTON FEDERALIST, Sept. 14, 1801.

30. DUMAS MALONE, JEFFERSON THE PRESIDENT: FIRST TERM 212 (1971). This point seems to be generally conceded even by revisionist scholars. *See, e.g.,* BURSTEIN, THE INNER JEFFERSON 228.

31. BURSTEIN, THE INNER JEFFERSON 228. Technically, of course, written defamation is classed as "libel" rather than "slander."

ing although sable resemblance to those of the president himself. The boy is ten or twelve years of age. His mother went to France in the same vessel with Mr. Jefferson and his two daughters. The delicacy of this arrangement must strike every person of common sensibility. What a sublime pattern for an American ambassador to place before the eyes of two young ladies![32]

Callender may well have selected this particular line of attack because of his own virulent racism. Joshua Rothman writes:

> Callender detested African Americans and found the notion of sex across the color line repulsive.... Once he reported the Jefferson-Hemings story, he described Hemings herself in the most racist terms, calling her a "wench" and "a slut as common as the pavement," accusing her of having "fifteen, or thirty" different lovers "*of all colours*," and referring to her children as a "yellow litter."[33]

In another article dated September 22, 1802, Callender made clear his objective of politically destroying Thomas Jefferson:

> Unless the republicans cast him overboard, the universal horror of mankind will sink their vessel. It is at present something more than two years till the next election for president.... The timely disruption of this unhappy secret gives room for the republicans to desert their chieftain, and to rally round the standard of a more decent leader.... I do not believe that at the next election of 1804 Jefferson could obtain two votes on the Eastern side of the Susquehanna; and, I think hardly four votes upon this side of it. He will, therefore, be laid aside.[34]

History shows that Callender's prediction was wrong. Although Callender drowned in the James River in a drunken stupor long before the election of 1804, Jefferson was reelected in a landslide electoral vote (162–14) and the Republicans gained in Congress as well. Callender's reputation was such that few who knew about him appear to have believed much that he wrote.[35] Indeed, Jefferson's biggest problem was explaining to people why he had ever given money to this despicable man.[36]

Looking back, what does the Callender story tell us about the likelihood that Thomas Jefferson fathered children by Sally Hemings? First, we know that the story originated as a part of a personal vendetta conducted by a vengeful and unprincipled man searching for allegations to injure President Jefferson. We know that Callender based his stories on rumors and gossip, which in turn were based not upon reliable evidence but merely upon the fact that there were light-skinned slaves at Monticello—a reality that predated Sally Hemings' years as a mother. Light-skinned slave children suggested that *someone* was having sex with the servants, and that someone *could* have been Thomas Jefferson. Not only did James Callender not have a scintilla of hard evidence that such a relationship between Jefferson and Sally Hemings actually existed, but nearly two centuries later there is *still* no persuasive evidence.[37]

---

32. THE RECORDER, Sept. 1, 1802.

33. Rothman, in SALLY HEMINGS AND THOMAS JEFFERSON 95 (emphasis in original).

34. THE RECORDER, Sept. 22, 1804.

35. *See* Chapter Ten.

36. Even Professor Brodie acknowledges this point. *See* FAWN BRODIE, THOMAS JEFFERSON: AN INTIMATE HISTORY 317 (1974).

37. As will be discussed in Chapter Eleven, one of the most significant facts in this inquiry is the total absence of any evidence that anyone ever observed Thomas Jefferson and/or Sally Hemings do anything that would lend credence to the Callender allegations. There is no record that any of the hundreds of visitors to Monticello ever saw Jefferson going to the slave quarters at unusual hours, or

Callender's allegations were based largely upon the reported existence of a ten- to twelve-year-old son of Sally Hemings, bearing a strong physical resemblance to Thomas Jefferson and named "Tom." The fact that none of Jefferson's defenders suggested, in their many counterattacks on Callender, that no "Tom Hemings" existed, is itself interesting. Callender's description might easily fit a young slave named Thomas Woodson, allegedly born around 1790, whose descendants have for nearly two centuries believed he was the son of Sally Hemings and Thomas Jefferson. There is no evidence of any other "Tom" at Monticello who comes close to fitting Callender's description.

This brings us to perhaps the most interesting results of Dr. Eugene Foster's DNA tests, reported in the journal *Nature* on November 5, 1998, and discussed in Chapter One, that "Thomas Woodson was *not* Thomas Jefferson's son."[38] The presence of a ten- to twelve-year-old slave child named "Tom" was at the heart of Callender's case. We don't know whether or not Thomas Woodson was that "Tom," but we do know that, if he was, Callender's allegation that "Tom" was the son of President Thomas Jefferson was false. Without the slightest indication that there was another "Tom" at Monticello in 1802 who came close to Callender's description, little is left of the allegation that started the entire controversy more than two centuries ago.

James Thomson Callender's allegations against Thomas Jefferson in 1802 lacked credibility and were uniformly rejected by major Jefferson scholars for more than 170 years. During the latter part of the twentieth century, Professors Fawn Brodie and Annette Gordon-Reed attempted to restore life to them. Their most credible argument was that Thomas Woodson was the child of Sally Hemings and Thomas Jefferson, conceived in Paris and born at Monticello in 1790. Thanks to the DNA tests, we now know that is not true. If there was ever any doubt about it, it should be clear now that Callender's allegations were clear fabrications based solely upon the kernel of truth that there were light-skinned slave children at Monticello.

Obviously, it is possible that Callender fabricated a story that happened to be true. It is also theoretically possible that, after having been subjected to Callender's scurrilous attacks in 1802, Thomas Jefferson for some strange reason might have decided to *begin* a sexual relationship with Sally Hemings that produced Eston Hemings in 1808—and perhaps other children. But in examining the totality of the evidence, it is useful to remember that the original charge was clearly a politically-motivated falsehood. The DNA tests have shown that Thomas Jefferson did not father a child by Sally Hemings in Paris named Tom as Callender alleged. The story passed down by generations of descendants of Thomas Woodson—presumably by honorable people acting in good faith at every repetition of the story—is clearly false.

---

ever saw Sally entering or leaving his chambers. There is not a single report of their walking off together, or even exchanging suggestive glances or the slightest caress or touch in passing during the normal routine of business at Monticello. Even after Jefferson's death and her own *de facto* freedom, there is no record that Sally Hemings ever told a single individual that Thomas Jefferson fathered any of her children or otherwise treated her as other than a slave. There is no record that more than one of Sally's known children ever alleged that Jefferson was their father, and the sole exception waited nearly fifty years after Jefferson's death, provided no source for his assertion of facts he could not have personally known, and accompanied the charge with a number of other highly dubious claims. (*See* Chapter Four.) What we have instead are Callender's charges supplemented by a newspaper story published more than seventy years later alleging that one of Sally's children confirmed the story and a great deal of speculation by clever scholars about how such a relationship was "possible."

38. *See* Chapter One (emphasis added).

Finally, if one takes the allegations of James T. Callender as serious evidence that Thomas Jefferson fathered children by Sally Hemings, and concludes that Callender "was not usually a liar"[39] and was "concerned with accuracy"[40]—or, as Professor Gordon-Reed puts it: "Exaggeration, rather than fabrication, was Callender's chief journalistic flaw"[41]— then what are we to make of Callender's allegations about Sally "[r]omping with half a dozen black fellows,"[42] and "[h]aving fifteen, or thirty gallants of all colours,"[43] or being "a slut as common as the pavement?"[44] Professor Gordon-Reed grossly misstates the reality when she alleges that Callendar would merely "exaggerate matters to make a better story."[45]

James Thomson Callender was in reality an unprincipled drunkard and a vile racist, who spent his decade in America defaming each of the first five men to become President of the United States. The problem, of course, is to distinguish between his many lies and the kernels of truth upon which they were sometimes based; and it is more than a little problematic for champions of the Sally story to rely upon Callender as a probative witness when he supports their case and then ignore his factual allegations that do not.

---

39. Rothman, *James Callender and Social Knowledge of Interracial Sex in Antebellum Virginia* 89.

40. *Id.* at 101.

41. GORDON-REED, THOMAS JEFFERSON AND SALLY HEMINGS 62.

42. [James T. Callender,] *Armory*, RICHMOND RECORDER, Sept. 15, 1802.

43. [James T. Callender,] *Advertisement Extraordinary: Voyage to France, or, the Progress of a Republican President*, RICHMOND RECORDER, Sep. 15, 1802. *See also,* Rothman, *James Callender and Social Knowledge of Interracial Sex in Antebellum Virginia* 95.

44. [Callender,] *More About Sally and the President*, RICHMOND RECORDER, Sep. 22, 1802. *See also,* Rothman, *James Callender and Social Knowledge of Interracial Sex in Antebellum Virginia* 95.

45. GORDON-REED, THOMAS JEFFERSON AND SALLY HEMINGS 76. Professor Ellis characterizes Callender's approach as a "truth-be-damned fashion...." ELLIS, AMERICAN SPHINX 259.

4

Madison Hemings' 1873 "Memoir" in the *Pike County Republican*

In their commentary article accompanying the publication in *Nature* of Dr. Eugene Foster's DNA study, Professors Eric S. Lander and Joseph J. Ellis argued that one of three pieces of evidence supporting a Jefferson-Hemings relationship[1] was that "Sally's fourth child, Madison, testified late in his life that Sally had identified Jefferson as the father of all her children."[2] Professor Annette Gordon-Reed asserts that Madison Hemings is "[t]he most important historical witness in this story...."[3]

In fact, most of the relevant statements attributed to Madison Hemings in the 1873 newspaper article to which the *Nature* commentary and Professor Gordon-Reed refer[4] have to do with events that occurred years before his birth and are asserted without any explanation of how Madison might have known them to be true.[5] Despite assertions by many scholars that Madison attributed his information to his mother, in fact the 1873 story makes no such claim. His "testimony"—in addition to other serious problems—was not that of a "witness" at all, but rather at best unsourced hearsay that is clearly at odds with the little relevant "eyewitness" testimony that is available.[6]

Nevertheless, this article is relied upon heavily by believers in a Jefferson-Hemings sexual relationship. Indeed, white historians who have refused to accept the truth of this ac-

---

1. Obviously there was a "Jefferson-Hemings *relationship*"—the issue is whether it was exclusively a master-slave relationship or also a sexual one.

2. Eric S. Lander & Joseph J. Ellis, *Founding Father*, 396 Nature 13 (Nov. 5, 1998).

3. Annette Gordon-Reed, *Why Jefferson Scholars Were the Last to Know*, N.Y. Times, Nov. 3, 1998 at A27.

4. The relevant text of the article reads: "Soon after their arrival [from Paris], she gave birth to a child, of whom Thomas Jefferson was the father. It lived but a short time. She gave birth to four others, and Jefferson was the father of all of them." Professor Ellis made the same error in *American Sphinx*. Joseph J. Ellis, American Sphinx 364 (1996). In fairness, the great Jefferson scholar Dumas Malone made the same error in reporting that Sally Hemings was Madison's source. *See* Dumas Malone, Jefferson the President: First Term 498 (1970). The Monticello research committee correctly noted that Madison "did not specifically mention when or how he learned the identity of his father." Thomas Jefferson Memorial Foundation Research Committee, *Report on Thomas Jefferson and Sally Hemings,* Jan. 2000 (hereinafter referred to as *Monticello Report*) Appendix F at 2.

5. Obviously Madison had no personal knowledge of his own conception or that of his elder siblings, and he would have only been two years old when Sally's last known child, Eston, was conceived.

6. I have in mind here not only the observation by Monticello overseer Edmund Bacon that as he arrived for work early in the morning he often saw a man who was not Thomas Jefferson leave Sally's room, but also the fact that not one of the hundreds if not thousands of visitors who were present at Monticello over the years left a known record of having witnessed anything that would suggest a sexual relationship existed between President Jefferson and Sally Hemings.

count have been accused of racism.[7] And now that six separate DNA tests have conclusively established that Thomas Woodson could not have been Thomas Jefferson's child, the 1873 statement attributed to Madison Hemings is probably the strongest piece of evidence remaining in support of the proposition that Thomas Jefferson fathered one or more children by Sally Hemings.

There are, however, many sound reasons for treating this account with skepticism — particularly where it is the only source for an allegation. Some of these pertain to Madison Hemings' credibility and that of his unidentified sources. Others are more objective in nature. None of them require the reader to assume that prominent Jefferson scholars like Merrill Peterson[8] were "racists."

Madison Could Not Have Known Whether
Key Parts of His Story Were True

To begin with, the most important pieces of information for our purposes in Madison's "memoir" — or, more accurately, a story written by Jefferson critic Samuel Wetmore, the editor of the *Pike County Republican*, claiming to represent the views of Madison Hemings — are statements about facts concerning which Madison could not *possibly* have possessed first-hand knowledge because they occurred before his birth. He is clearly repeating "hearsay," and the credibility of his statements, assuming they are even reported accurately, thus can be no greater than that of his undisclosed source(s) — minus any risks that he might have intentionally or otherwise altered the story. Assuming that his source was one of the two individuals who would have presumably known the truth — Thomas Jefferson or Sally Hemings — the passage of five and four decades, respectively, since their deaths would presumably increase the risks of error even if the witness's personal veracity could be established. Then we also must consider the additional risk that Samuel Wetmore might have intentionally altered the story to further his clear political agenda as a Republican Party activist. Indeed, the fact that his story does not state that Madison Hem-

---

7. *See, e.g.,* ANNETTE GORDON-REED, THOMAS JEFFERSON AND SALLY HEMINGS at 10–11, 224–28 (1997); Annette Gordon-Reed, *Why Jefferson Scholars Were the Last to Know,* N.Y. TIMES, Nov. 3, 1998 at A27; Annette Gordon-Reed, *"The Memories of a Few Negroes,"* in JAN ELLEN LEWIS & PETER S. ONUF, SALLY HEMINGS AND THOMAS JEFFERSON 236–52 (1999); and Annette Gordon-Reed, *When the Past Speaks to the Present: A Cautionary Tale about Evidence,* HISTORY NOW (Dec. 2004), *available at* http://www.historynow.org/12_2004/print/historian4.html ("[A] bias led historians to give more weight to the [Jefferson] grandchildren's accounts than to the account of Madison Hemings, despite the fact that the grandchildren's accounts were themselves contradictory. No doubt the high esteem in which Thomas Jefferson was held by the public and by the historians contributed to the acceptance of the grandchildren's claim that Jefferson did not father the Hemings children. But no doubt racism — sometimes conscious and sometimes unconscious — played a role in privileging the grandchildren's claims over the claims of Madison Hemings.").

8. Until his death on September 23, 2009, at the age of 88, Professor Merrill Peterson was almost certainly the world's leading Jefferson historian as the Thomas Jefferson Memorial Foundation Professor of History, Emeritus, at the University of Virginia. Suggestions that Professor Peterson might have been motivated by racism are particularly unwarranted. A *Washington Post* obituary observed: "Dr. Peterson was noted for recruiting African-American faculty members and made a memorable 1965 speech at the university's central building, the Rotunda, called 'Sympathy for Selma.' He saw the Rev. Martin Luther King Jr.'s civil rights marches in Selma, Ala., and across the South as a 'link in the heritage of American liberty.'" Matt Schudel, *Merrill Peterson, 88; wrote on role of Jefferson, Lincoln,* WASH. POST, Oct. 2, 2009, *available at* http://www.boston.com/bostonglobe/obituaries/articles/2009/10/02/merrill_peterson_88_wrote_on_role_of_jefferson_lincoln/.

ings specifically attributed the assertions about his paternity to his mother (who left no independent record of ever claiming such a relationship with Jefferson to anyone) may make it even more suspect.

Madison admits having read about Jefferson after leaving Monticello, and—as will be discussed—some of his terminology and the spelling in the article suggest he (or Wetmore, who actually wrote the article) was familiar with the original James Callender and Thomas Turner allegations published seven decades before Madison allegedly asserted that Thomas Jefferson was his father. Since Madison himself cannot possibly be a reliable source for this information, and we cannot tell which parts of his account may have come from his mother, from the writings of scandalmongers like Callender, from rumors, from poor recollection of statements he may have heard a half century or more earlier, or even from a fertile imagination, some caution on the part of the reader is prudent even if the story attributed to him seems initially compelling.

The Words of the Story Are Likely Those of an Anti-Jefferson Editor

The hearsay problem is further complicated by the fact that the article in question clearly seems to be in the words of Samuel F. Wetmore. Even Professor Gordon-Reed acknowledges both Wetmore's strong anti-Jefferson sentiments[9] and the fact that the story may well have been actually written by Wetmore,[10] a point conceded earlier by Professor Brodie.[11] Not only is the style consistent with several other articles written by Wetmore, but the vocabulary is nothing like that in other accounts of the era by self-educated former slaves.[12] For example, the story includes the following language:

> [A]n intimacy sprang up between them which ripened into love....[13]

> [S]lave masters ... had no compunctions of conscience which restrained them from parting mother and child of however tender age....[14]

and

> [A]s soon after her interment as he could attend to and arrange his domestic affairs in accordance with the changed circumstances of his family in consequence of this misfortune....[15]

Although the article about Madison Hemings was written in the first person, Professors Brodie and Gordon-Reed are almost certainly correct in noting that these are most likely the words of Samuel Wetmore; and, given his clear anti-Jefferson bias, this raises serious additional questions about the veracity of the entire account.

---

9. Gordon-Reed, Thomas Jefferson and Sally Hemings 13.

10. *Id.* at 149.

11. Fawn Brodie, Thomas Jefferson: An Intimate History 438 (1874). *See also,* Lucia Stanton, *The Other End of the Telescope,* 57 William & Mary Quarterly 142 (Jan. 2000).

12. *See, e.g.,* Memoirs of a Monticello Slave 10 (1951). ("Sally mighty near white," "Folks said that these Hemingses was old Mr. Wayles' children.")

13. [Samuel E. Wetmore], *Life Among the Lowly, Number 1. Madison Hemings,* Pike County Republican (Waverly, Ohio), Mar. 13, 1873 at 4, reprinted in *Monticello Report,* Appendix E at 27–28.

14. *Id.*

15. *Id.*

As Professor Gordon-Reed admits,[16] Samuel Wetmore was a Republican Party activist who moved to Waverly, Ohio, following the Civil War "in hopes to be useful to the Pike County Republicans" and revived the local party newspaper.[17] According to Professor Dumas Malone—perhaps the greatest Jefferson scholar to date—Wetmore was regarded by others as a "carpetbagger," and "quite clearly, the story was solicited and published for a propaganda purpose."[18] Wetmore obviously had no first-hand knowledge about Thomas Jefferson and Sally Hemings, and any alterations to Madison Hemings' own statement would further decrease its value as historical evidence. And it seems clear that Wetmore was not overly concerned with getting his "facts" correct, unless Madison Hemings grew nearly three inches in height between ages twenty-six and sixty-eight.[19]

Madison Was the Only Member of His Family to Claim that Thomas Jefferson Was Their Father

Even if one assumes that Samuel Wetmore captured every nuance uttered by the elderly Madison Hemings and recorded it perfectly, there is still the question of why, if the story was true, neither Madison's mother nor any of his siblings left any record of having made such an assertion. For that matter, why did Madison wait until nearly a half century after Thomas Jefferson's death to assert his claim? Professor Brodie suggests that this delay was because Madison only "came to sense the importance of the story of his mother and her children" after moving to Ohio,[20] but he lived in Ohio for more than thirty-five years before his story was recorded. Further, such speculation is hardly kind to a man of Madison Hemings' reported intelligence (his friend Israel admits that he saw the benefit as soon as he was freed), and there may be other explanations for why Madison Hemings waited until most of the people who might credibly contradict his account had passed from the scene.[21]

There is also the problem of Madison Hemings' clear *bitterness* towards Thomas Jefferson. Professor Brodie[22] acknowledges this, as does Professor Gordon-Reed, repeatedly.[23] Perhaps this bitterness was fully warranted; and if Thomas Jefferson *had* been his father and then ignored him, one could easily understand why, after quietly seething for half a century, an elderly Madison Hemings might have really "unloaded" his emotions to fellow Jefferson critic Samuel Wetmore. Whether or not this bitterness was justified, the question is whether Wetmore's summary of remarks allegedly made by an angry and el-

---

16. GORDON-REED, THOMAS JEFFERSON AND SALLY HEMINGS 8.

17. Dumas Malone & Steven H. Hochman, *A Note on Evidence: The Personal History of Madison Hemings,* JOURNAL OF SOUTHERN HISTORY, vol. 41, no. 4, Nov. 1975, at 525.

18. *Id.*

19. The Albemarle County Minute Book recorded Madison's height in 1831 as a precise "5:7 3/8 inches high," whereas Wetmore described him in 1873 as "five feet ten inches in height." *Monticello Report,* Appendix H at 12. Adding nearly three inches to Madison's height might be expected to increase the credibility of his assertion to be the natural child of the six-foot two-and-one-half-inch tall Thomas Jefferson.

20. BRODIE, THOMAS JEFFERSON 441.

21. One might draw a parallel with a war veteran who waits a half century before suddenly claiming great acts of personal heroism during the conflict. It is certainly possible that the accounts are truthful, but they should be viewed with greater skepticism because the "hero" waited until others who might confirm or deny the accounts had passed from the scene.

22. BRODIE, THOMAS JEFFERSON 358.

23. GORDON-REED, THOMAS JEFFERSON AND SALLY HEMINGS 17, 44, 150.

derly Madison Hemings is the most probative evidence we have as to the pertinent facts in this inquiry. For without Madison's 1873 account, and the confirmation by his friend Israel that will be discussed below, the case for Thomas Jefferson's paternity rests only on DNA tests placing him in a group of more than two dozen potential fathers and a lot of circumstantial speculation.

Even if one assumes Madison Hemings had the best intentions, finest memory, and highest integrity—all of which are possible, but none of which are clearly established—his story still has major problems because of our uncertainty about his sources. Several scholars have assumed that he was merely retelling facts he learned from his mother, Sally Hemings. This is possible, but it does not explain why he does not mention that, or why neither Sally nor any of her other children made such claims in the many years after they were freed and left Monticello. [24]

Even if Sally was Madison's source, there is no assurance that these factual assertions were true. His mother might have conveyed such a story with the hope that it would instill pride in her son and perhaps give him additional confidence as he headed out into the uncertainty of life on his own. Writing in *The Inner Jefferson*, Andrew Burstein—who after the release of the DNA test results would embrace the idea that Thomas Jefferson fathered children with Sally Hemings[25]—reasoned:

> The evidence against Jefferson is largely provided by the testimony of Madison Hemings, Sally's son who was born in 1805, when Jefferson was sixty-two. Madison told an Ohio newspaper in 1873 that his mother had informed him [*sic*] that Thomas Jefferson was his father, and that Sally first carried a child of Jefferson when she returned from France in 1789. Presumably, Madison believed these statements to be true. But it is also possible that his claim was contrived—by his mother or himself—to provide to an otherwise undistinguished biracial carpenter a measure of social respect. Would not his life have been made more charmed by being known as the son of Thomas Jefferson than the more obscure Peter or Samuel Carr?[26]

A contemporary newspaper in Waverly, Ohio, responded to the publication of Madison's "memoirs" with the assertion that "there are at least fifty negroes in this county who lay claim to illustrious parentage," and reasoning: "It sounds much better for the mother to tell her offspring that 'master' is their father than to acknowledge to them that some field hand, without a name, had raised her to the dignity of a mother."[27]

To be sure, the language is offensively insensitive, but the underlying argument must be taken seriously. Indeed, as will be discussed, Madison's fellow slave at Monticello, Israel Jefferson—who was the subject of a similar Wetmore article later that year—admitted that he had changed his surname from that of his known father (Gillette) to that of his master (Jefferson) after gaining his freedom because "it would give me more dignity to be called after so eminent a man."[28]

---

24. Obviously, we can't be *certain* they did not make such claims. But there is no record of any such claims, and the nature of the information is such that one would expect *someone* to have recorded it if it had been widely discussed.

25. See, e.g., Andrew Burstein, *Jefferson's Rationalizations*, 57(1) WILLIAM & MARY Q. 183 (Jan. 2000).

26. ANDREW BURSTEIN, THE INNER JEFFERSON 230–31 (1995).

27. WAVERLY WATCHMAN, *quoted in* Malone & Hochman, *A Note on Evidence* at 527.

28. [Wetmore,] *Life Among the Lowly, No. 3,* PIKE COUNTY [Ohio] REPUBLICAN, Dec. 25, 1873, at 4.

We can be fairly confident that Sally Hemings was not the source of all that was in Madison's story. First of all, he admits that "much" of his knowledge about Jefferson he learned not from personal observation but after Jefferson's death — apparently from books.[29] Indeed, some of the many errors in Madison's statement as reported by Wetmore can be found in books about Jefferson published prior to the 1873 interview. During the later part of his life Thomas Jefferson had a number of health problems.[30] Nevertheless, in 1862, Charles Scribner published the Reverend Hamilton W. Pierson's *Jefferson at Monticello*, based upon lengthy interviews with former overseer Edmund Bacon. On page 71 of that book, we find this statement about Thomas Jefferson:

> He always enjoyed the best of health. I don't think he was ever really sick until his last sickness.[31]

Eleven years later, Madison Hemings' story asserts:

> My father generally enjoyed excellent health. I never knew him to have but one spell of sickness, and that was caused by a visit to the Warm Springs in 1818. Till within three weeks of his death he was hale and hearty...."[32]

Similarly, overseer Bacon asserted that Thomas Jefferson did not have much interest in agriculture, and Madison Hemings asserted: "Unlike Washington he had but little taste or care for agricultural pursuits."[33] One must wonder how Madison Hemings would *know* about George Washington's agricultural interests, if not from books — as Washington died long before Madison was born. The similarity between the comments of Bacon and Madison Hemings on this issue was noted by Professor Ellis in *American Sphinx*.[34]

Some of Madison Hemings' story pertains to alleged facts that he would have been extremely unlikely to have personally known while at Monticello, but which appeared in published materials which Madison or Wetmore might well have seen. For example, Madison is reported to have said that Jefferson "practiced law at the bar of the general court of the Colony."[35] The statement is true enough, but Thomas Jefferson's practice before this court — which was composed of the governor and members of his council — ceased three decades before Madison Hemings was born, and the court itself had not existed for more than four decades before it was allegedly "recalled" by Madison Hemings in 1873.[36] Among other places, this fact about Jefferson appears on page 33 of B. L. Rayner's *Life of Jefferson*,[37] which was published nearly forty years before Madison's account, and on page 10 of William Linn's *The Life of Thomas Jefferson*,[38] also first published in 1834.[39]

---

29. *Id.* ("Of my father, Thomas Jefferson, I knew more of his domestic than his political life, during his lifetime. It is only since his death that I have learned much of the latter.... I learned to read by inducing the white children to teach me the letters and something more; what else I know of books I have picked up here and there....")

30. *See* Chapter Eleven.

31. *Reprinted in* JEFFERSON AT MONTICELLO 71.

32. [Wetmore,] *Life Among the Lowly No. 1.*

33. *Id.*

34. JOSEPH J. ELLIS, AMERICAN SPHINX 168 (1996).

35. [Wetmore,] *Life Among the Lowly No. 1.*

36. I am indebted to Richard Dixon for this observation.

37. B.L. RAYNER, LIFE OF THOMAS JEFFERSON 33 (1834).

38. WILLIAM LINN, THE LIFE OF THOMAS JEFFERSON 10 (2d. ed. 1839).

39. My copy is from the second edition, published in 1839, and I am assuming this fact appears as well in the earlier edition. However, since the second edition came out more than three decades before publication of the Madison/Wetmore article, the point is unimportant.

Even more troubling, several of the unusual words which appear in the story appear in the earlier writings of James Callender,[40] and a name misspelled in a published account by Jefferson critic Thomas Turner is misspelled in an identical manner in Madison's account.[41] It is quite possible that Madison had read a copy of Callender's 1802 allegations, perhaps along with other documents circulated by Jefferson's enemies, prior to his encounter with Samuel Wetmore. If so, such writings could have been the source for his belief that Thomas Jefferson was his father. It is even possible that—just as Professor Fawn Brodie, a century later, persuaded Eston Hemings' descendants that their ancestor was Thomas Jefferson's son[42]—Samuel Wetmore produced copies of the Callender articles and persuaded Madison that he was the famous president's child.[43] Since the article provides no source for this assertion, the only thing we can be certain about is that Madison Hemings could not personally have known that the key parts of the article (in terms of their relevance to our inquiry) attributed to him were true.

Portions of Madison's Story Are Inconsistent with Known Facts

Portions of Madison's story are almost certainly false, and others are so inconsistent with facts that we do know as to be very difficult to believe. Assuming for the moment that these articles contained Madison's statements unembellished by Samuel Wetmore, there is no reason to doubt that they were sincerely held beliefs and that Madison was recounting the truth as he understood it. After all, since the events occurred before his own birth, he could at best only be passing on statements he obtained from others. But if his source for the clearly erroneous information was the same source for his contention that Thomas Jefferson was his father, we need to view that allegation too with a cautious skepticism.

An example of one of the almost certainly *untrue* stories is Madison's account of how he was named. The article asserts:

> As to myself, I was named Madison by the wife of James Madison, who was afterwards President of the United States. Mrs. Madison happened to be at Monticello at the time of my birth, and begged the privilege of naming me, promising my mother a fine present for the honor. She consented, and Mrs. Madison dubbed me by the name I now acknowledge, but like many promises of white folks to the slaves she never gave my mother anything.[44]

---

40. *See* Chapter Three.

41. Like Thomas Turner, Madison (or, more likely, Wetmore, since Madison's information was likely provided in an oral interview) spelled Thomas Jefferson's father-in-law's name as *Wales* rather than *Wayles*.

42. *See* Chapter Eight.

43. My own belief is that Madison had heard the story before encountering Wetmore, as there is a notation in a census report a few years earlier identifying him with the famous president. Wetmore was a census taker that year, but not necessarily the census taker in Madison's area. He could have learned of the claim through a colleague. There has been some suggestion that the notation that Madison was the son of Thomas Jefferson seems to be in a different hand and pen than the other entries—suggesting that it may have been added later (perhaps by Wetmore?)—and I simply have not had the time or resources to follow up on this. The issue is not critical to our inquiry, but I mention it in case other scholars may wish to pursue it.

44. [Wetmore,] *Life Among the Lowly No. 1.*

There is not only no evidence that Dolley Madison was present at Monticello when Madison Hemings was born on January 19,[45] 1805; there is substantial circumstantial evidence that she was more than one hundred miles away in Washington, D.C. To begin with, we know that Dolley Madison did not like to be separated from her husband and lived with him in Washington during his service as secretary of state in the Jefferson administration. On the few occasions when they were separated, they wrote letters to each other regularly. We know that James Madison was in Washington, D.C., during January 1805, and there are no known letters between the two of them from this period.[46]

The Madisons always left Washington during the heat of August and September, and normally spent those months at Montpelier—often exchanging visits with Jefferson at Monticello lasting a week or more at a time. Jefferson normally also returned to Monticello for at least a few weeks around April, but the Madisons returned less frequently. Neither family normally attempted to make the trip during the cold winter months.[47]

In addition, the two people Dolley Madison might most likely have traveled all the way to Monticello to visit were *not present* at Monticello when Madison Hemings was born. On January 7—twelve days before Madison's birth at Monticello—President Jefferson wrote a letter to Martha Jefferson Randolph datelined "Washington" and noting that her husband, Thomas Mann Randolph, had written that he planned to bring Martha to Washington. But Jefferson warned against attempting the trip, citing "such a spell of severe weather we have not known for years."[48] (Thomas Jefferson hated cold weather and complained of it often.[49]) Two days after Madison's birth, again writing from Washington, Jefferson expresses concern that he has just received Martha's letter of 11 January containing "information of your illness."[50] A third letter, written from Washington one week later, makes it clear that Jefferson is writing to the ill Martha at her home at Edgehill, not at Monticello.

In the January 21 letter, Jefferson emphasizes the "dreadful spell of weather," of which he asserts he has seen nothing similar "since the last winter we were in Paris" more than fifteen years earlier. The third letter, dated January 28, reports that the ground had been covered with snow for twenty-four days (*i.e.,* from about the fourth of January), and the previous day they had received another six to eight inches of snow.[51] A review of Jeffer-

---

45. The only evidence we have that Madison was born on January 19 is from Madison's own statement. However, Jefferson's *Farm Book* confirms that Madison was born in January 1805. This issue is not significant for our inquiry, as the weather that January was so bad that neither Jefferson nor the Madisons would have ventured the long trip to Charlottesville from Washington.

46. *See, e.g.,* RALPH KETCHAM, JAMES MADISON 444 (1990). I am also indebted to David B. Mattern, Senior Associate Editor of the James Madison Papers Project at the University of Virginia, for his search of Madison's papers during this period.

47. *Id.* at 415, 426.

48. THE FAMILY LETTERS OF THOMAS JEFFERSON 265–66 (Edwin Morris Betts & James Adam Bear, Jr., eds. 1966). I am indebted to Cynthia Harris Burton for calling this letter to my attention.

49. In an 1801 letter to William Dunbar, Jefferson wrote: "I have no doubt but that cold is the source of more sufferance to all animal nature than hunger, thirst, sickness, & all the other pains of life & of death itself put together.... [W]hen I recollect on one hand all the sufferings I have had from cold, & on the other all my other pains, the former preponderate greatly." *Jefferson to Dunbar*, Jan. 12, 1801, 9 WORKS OF THOMAS JEFFERSON 170 (Fed. ed. 1905). Among many other references to cold weather, Jefferson wrote in an 1821 letter to John Adams: "During summer I enjoy it's [*sic*] temperature, but I shudder at the approach of winter, and wish I could sleep through it with the Dormouse, and only wake with him in spring, if ever." *Jefferson to Adams,* June 1, 1823, *reprinted in* 2 THE ADAMS-JEFFERSON LETTERS 578 (Lester J. Cappon, ed. 1959).

50. THE FAMILY LETTERS OF THOMAS JEFFERSON 266.

51. *Id.* at 267.

son's other correspondence indicates that he left Monticello between September 11 and October 9, 1804, and did not return until March 1805.[52] The Madisons returned to Washington from Montpelier in early October.[53]

There is also the question of whether, even had she been present, and given the social realities of the day, Dolley Madison would have "begged" any Monticello slave for the privilege of naming a slave child after her husband. Would she have perceived this as a great honor? Any answer would be pure speculation. But even if one accepts that as being likely, would it hold true for the notorious *Sally Hemings*—whom James Callender had libeled to the world as "a slut as common as the pavement,"[54] and Annette Gordon-Reed called "one of the most vilified women in American history"?[55] Surely Dolley Madison was aware of the harm done to Thomas Jefferson's reputation by the allegation that Sally Hemings had a mulatto child named "Tom." Why on earth would she "beg" this same woman to name her latest child "Madison"? There is no reason to assume that Dolley Madison wished to fuel new scandals for the benefit of the Federalists as her husband contemplated a presidential campaign of his own.

Even if for some reason Dolley Madison had wished her husband to be so "honored," might she not have been more likely to suggest the idea to Thomas or Martha Jefferson than to "beg" the new mother, a slave? (Professor Gordon-Reed argues that Sally probably did not name her own children in any event.[56]) Would Dolley Madison—a woman of illustrious reputation[57]—likely have made such a "bargain" and then failed to follow up with the promised gift? We obviously do not know the answer to any of these questions; but even had Dolley Madison been present at Monticello, Madison Hemings' story would seem unlikely. This comment is not intended as criticism of Madison, who obviously had no memory of conversations by others made hours after he was born; nor is it intended to be critical of Sally Hemings. Despite Callender's viciously racist rantings, there is no serious evidence that Sally Hemings was other than a fine and decent woman. But her image in the minds of the *public* came entirely from the pen of Callender, and anyone who "begged" her to name a child after a candidate for national political office would presumably not be trying to further that candidacy.

Like many of Madison's reported allegations, this one is contrary to both the known evidence and common sense. In fairness to Madison, he obviously had no first-hand knowledge of the alleged incident, and—assuming that neither he nor Samuel Wetmore simply fabricated the story to provide a flavor of detail while discrediting (because of the social realities of the day) two of Jefferson's closest friends with an allegation for which

---

52. 11 WRITINGS OF THOMAS JEFFERSON 49, 53, 62, 69 (Mem. ed. 1903).

53. Since the *Papers of James Madison* for this period have not yet been published, I am once again indebted to David B. Mattern for his assistance.

54. [James T. Callender,] *More about the President,* Richmond RECORDER, Sept. 22, 1802. The point here is not that Sally Hemings was in fact a bad person. There is not the slightest bit of serious evidence to support such a conclusion. As was discussed in Chapter Three, James Callender was a vicious racist who probably knew almost nothing about Sally Hemings and simply defamed her in his campaign to hurt Thomas Jefferson. The issue here is not about Sally's character, but rather that her public identification with an alleged scandal would make her an unlikely individual for the wife of a presidential aspirant to approach with such a request. It would be in some ways comparable to the wife of a potential presidential candidate "begging" Monica Lewinsky to name an illegitimate child after her husband. (I intend by this comparison no disrespect to Ms. Lewinsky—or to Sally Hemings—but merely remark about the perceptions of some in the public.)

55. GORDON-REED, THOMAS JEFFERSON AND SALLY HEMINGS 208.

56. *Id.* at 200.

57. Presumably it is unnecessary to document Dolley Madison's fine reputation.

there is no evidence—it appears that he was likely misled. Presumably Dolley Madison was not his source, which would make Sally Hemings the most likely one. If Sally misled Madison about this incident, how much can we rely upon his other assertions that may have come from her?

Other Parts of the Story Are Very Difficult to Believe

Also in the "highly incredible" category is Madison Hemings' account of the alleged "treaty" between Sally Hemings and Thomas Jefferson:

> Their stay (my mother and Maria's) [in Paris] was about eighteen [sic[58]] months. But during that time my mother became Mr. Jefferson's concubine, and when he was called back home she was *enciente* [French for "pregnant"] by him. He desired to bring my mother back to Virginia with him but she demurred. She was just beginning to understand the French language well, and in France she was free, while if she returned to Virginia she would be re-enslaved. So she refused to return with him. To induce her to do so he promised her extraordinary privileges, and made a solemn pledge that her children should be freed at the age of twenty-one years. In consequence of his promises, on which she implicitly relied, she returned with him to Virginia.[59]

One hardly knows where to start with this incredible statement. A few observations may be useful:

- The only first-hand commentary we have about Sally's personality at the time she traveled to Paris was from the captain of the ship that transported them from Virginia—who thought that Sally would be of no use to Thomas Jefferson and suggested he take her back to Virginia—and from Abigail Adams, who hosted Jefferson's daughter Polly and her maid Sally for three weeks in London while awaiting the arrival of another Jefferson servant to take them to Paris. Adams—whose character, judgment, and intelligence are well-documented—described the frightened slave girl as "quite a child"[60] and as wanting "more care"[61] than Jefferson's eight-year-old daughter Polly. Is it credible that Sally would so quickly have been transformed into a self-assured young woman with the courage and wit to confront her "master"—the United States Minister to France?[62]

- Would the proud Thomas Jefferson have tolerated such behavior and submitted to such a demand? If he found himself in the embarrassing circumstance of having impregnated a child servant, who was already blackmailing him into submitting to her demands, would Thomas Jefferson likely have gone to great lengths to make certain she returned to Monticello with him—where her presence might easily destroy his cherished reputation? Would he have made sure her room on the ship was near that of his daughters?

- As a technical matter, to obtain her freedom Sally would have had to retain a French lawyer and file an expensive lawsuit before a court that might, or might *not*, have

---

58. The stay was actually twenty-six months.
59. [Wetmore,] *Life Among the Lowly No. 1.*
60. 11 THE PAPERS OF THOMAS JEFFERSON 503 (Julian P. Boyd, ed. 1955).
61. *Id.* at 551.
62. VIRGINIUS DABNEY, THE JEFFERSON SCANDALS 103 (1981). ("The notion that a sixteen-year-old slave would defy her master and seek to drive a hard bargain with him is incredible on its face.")

interfered with the "property" claimed by the powerful American Minister to France—who, it should be recalled, was immune from the process of French Courts by the well-established international legal principle of diplomatic immunity.[63]

- Then there is the issue of how Sally Hemings, even if she were fluent in French, would have learned that she was allegedly "free" under French law.[64] Unlike Thomas Jefferson, Sally Hemings was not trained in jurisprudence. And we know that Jefferson himself was unaware of this law until he specifically *researched* the issue at the request of a constituent.[65] There is not the slightest bit of evidence, besides Madison's allegation (concerning facts about which he clearly had no personal knowledge), that Sally had any knowledge of French law at this time.[66]

- If we assume that, upon arriving in Paris, Sally suddenly blossomed into a brilliant and independent personality broadly cognizant of legal matters, must we not presume that she also realized that any agreement she negotiated with Thomas Jefferson in Paris would be absolutely unenforceable once she returned to Virginia? Surely such a sophisticated young woman would have known that, as a slave, she had no legal standing in Virginia courts to bring any action against a Caucasian? It might have been more credible if Madison had simply alleged that, while in Paris, Thomas Jefferson *promised* Sally he would free her children. The idea that the young slave compelled Thomas Jefferson to agree to a "treaty" is simply not credible. For that matter, nor does it fit with the story that "Tom and Sally" were madly in love with each other.

- Speaking of Sally Hemings' children, we must address as well the question of her remarkable *prescience* as an immature child in Paris. Now that the DNA studies have established that Thomas Woodson was not the son of Thomas Jefferson, there is little reason to believe[67] that Sally Hemings had a child before Harriet I was born in late 1795—whether by Thomas Jefferson or any other father.[68] Is it reasonable to assume that Sally Hemings would have bargained with Thomas Jefferson for the eventual freedom of children, the first of who would not be *conceived* for more than five years?

- There is serious question about whether the Sally Hemings who stayed with Abigail Adams would have *wanted* to be left behind in Paris when Thomas Jefferson and his entourage returned to Monticello—where Sally's mother and siblings awaited and where she knew she would be well treated, fed, clothed,

---

63. This issue is discussed in greater detail in Chapter Nine.

64. WILLIAM HOWARD ADAMS, THE PARIS YEARS OF THOMAS JEFFERSON 137 (1997).

65. *Jefferson to Paul Bentalou*, Aug. 25, 1786, in 10 THE PAPERS OF THOMAS JEFFERSON 296.

66. It is certainly possible that Sally could have learned from the servants of other students at the Abbaye about slaves who had gained their freedom in France by petitioning the court, but presumably the other servants were *not* slaves. Even if they were cognizant of these legal technicalities, there might well be risks to their own employment in providing such information to Sally if Martha and Polly's powerful father learned they were the reason he lost his slave. In the total absence of relevant information, we can only speculate; but the assumption that non-slave servants would both have this knowledge and willingly convey it to Sally is not that obvious.

67. It is certainly possible that Thomas Woodson was Sally's child. But he clearly was not Thomas Jefferson's. Thus, the real point here is that there is little reason to believe that Sally could have had a child by Thomas Jefferson until years after she allegedly compelled him to yield to her demands in Paris.

68. Indeed, the *only* source for a child other than Thomas Woodson born to Sally Hemings in 1790 is Madison Hemings' own statement. James Callender asserted that there was a ten- to twelve-year-old "Tom" at Monticello in 1802—which is consistent with a 1790 date of birth—but this obviously could not be the same child that Madison claims died shortly after being born.

and otherwise provided for as were all of the Hemings family members. France, it should be recalled, was at the time on the eve of a violent revolution. Other than Madison Hemings' account, there is no reason to believe that Sally had significant French language skills.[69] Indeed, Madison's account strongly suggests that Sally was not even literate in *English* two decades after returning from Paris.[70]

- There is also the issue of the "extraordinary privileges" Sally was allegedly promised as a part of this "treaty" arrangement. The available evidence, as will be discussed in Chapter Six, suggests that Sally received no special consideration from Thomas Jefferson when compared to other members of the Hemings family—indeed, she did not even receive her own freedom in his will. Surely, had the two been "lovers" for decades prior to his death, Thomas Jefferson would at least have given Sally her freedom rather than risk her being sold and abused by some future master. And if Sally were so anxious to claim her freedom in Paris, why did she not bargain at least to be freed upon the death of her famous lover? This version of events makes absolutely no sense.[71]

- Indeed, if Sally was nearly as clever and courageous as we are led to believe by the revisionists, why did she not simply say: "Sweetheart, I'll go back with you if you promise to manumit me as soon as we get to Virginia." He could then pay her a small "wage" as he had done in Paris, and her children who were seven-eighths white would have been born free under Virginia law. Callender had not even arrived in the United States, there was no hint of scandal, and Jefferson could easily have invented a story of some great "service" on Sally's part to explain the special treatment in case anyone noticed, e.g., "I was choking on a snail, when she grabbed me and hugged my chest, freeing my air passage and saving my life!"

- Nor, for that matter, were Sally's children "freed at the age of twenty-one years." Beverly, her oldest son, was probably twenty-four at the time he was recorded as having "run away" (perhaps with Jefferson's consent or acquiesence) from Monticello[72]; Madison was twenty-two when freed following Jefferson's death.[73] It is unclear whether Harriet was twenty-one or twenty-two when she reportedly was informally freed with Jefferson's consent.[74] Eston was released at nineteen pursuant to a decision by the administrators of Thomas Jefferson's will following the

---

69. We know that a tutor was hired to teach French to Sally's brother, James, but this was presumably because he had to converse in that language in order to be trained as a French chef.

70. "I learned to read by inducing the white children to teach me the letters and something more; what else I know of [from] books I have picked up here and there, till now I can read and write." [Wetmore,] *Life Among the Lowly No. 1.* Presumably, if Sally had been literate she would have taught her children herself.

71. As an economic matter, a twenty-one-year-old slave was *far* more valuable than a much older woman. Female slaves could produce more slaves for the master, while males could perform hard labor. If Jefferson were willing to free Sally's future children, promising to give Sally (who was valued at fifty dollars following Jefferson's death) her freedom in his will would have been of little consequence to his estate. The only "logic" to the treaty story is that it fits with some of the facts that Madison and Wetmore knew were publicly known in 1873.

72. THE GARDEN AND FARM BOOKS OF THOMAS JEFFERSON 386 (Robert C. Barron, ed. 1987). We really don't know whether Beverly was a few months short of his twenty-fourth birthday or had passed it; but he was clearly well beyond the age of twenty-one.

73. Lucia Stanton, *The Other End of the Telescope: Jefferson through the Eyes of His Slaves*, 57 WILLIAM & MARY QUARTERLY 141 (Jan. 2000).

74. *See* JEFFERSON AT MONTICELLO 102.

75. Jefferson's will is reprinted in JEFFERSON AT MONTICELLO 118.

former president's death.[75] Jefferson had instructed that Eston be required to work for his uncle, John Hemings, for another two years.[76]

In summary, the allegation of a "treaty" between Thomas Jefferson and Sally Hemings simply fails to pass the "straight-face" test. Other than Madison Hemings' unsourced allegations—reported second-hand by the anti-Jefferson Wetmore—there is not the *slightest* bit of evidence to support it. It is inconsistent with what little we know about the personality of Sally Hemings and the great deal we know about Thomas Jefferson. All things considered, it must be regarded as one of many parts of Madison's alleged "memoir" that call into question the veracity of the entire document.

Professor Gordon-Reed's efforts to legitimize and build her case around this document are at times almost amusing. Totally ignoring the fact that all of the crucial details occurred years before Madison was born, and that he thus could have had no first-hand knowledge of the veracity of his assertions—she writes: "Madison Hemings's memoirs must stand or fall on the basis of his credibility alone. To that end, it must be said that these memoirs are properly described as items of direct evidence that Thomas Jefferson and Sally Hemings were involved in a relationship."[77] She even attempts a little sleight-of-hand analysis in suggesting that Madison's story is corroborated by other evidence:

> Sometimes even without his realizing it, a number of details offered in Hemings's statement give rise to circumstantial evidence that supports his basic claim. For example, the notion that there was a promise of freedom for Sally Hemings's children when they reached the age of twenty-one is supported by the circumstances and timing of her children's departures from Monticello.[78]

As indicated above, it is simply not true that Sally's children were "freed" when they reached the age of twenty-one (or that they departed Monticello upon turning twenty-one). We know that Beverly Hemings was at least twenty-three (and more likely twenty-four) when he ran away from Monticello, apparently never to be heard from again by Thomas Jefferson. Madison did not obtain his freedom until he was twenty-two. We don't know how old Harriet was when she finally left (probably twenty-one), and Eston did not turn twenty-one until well after Thomas Jefferson's death.[79]

Even if each of Sally's children had been freed on their twenty-first birthday, that fact would not "corroborate" Madison's 1873 statement. This reasoning might make some sense if the children had been freed *after* Madison made his statement or if Madison was likely unaware of these details. But Madison presumably *knew* the facts more than four decades before he gave his statement. It is just as reasonable to conclude that he formulated his testimony to fit with the known facts as that the earlier events independently *corroborate* his claims. And since "the circumstances and timing of her children's departures from Monticello" do not in any serious way *support* the allegation that each of them was set free upon reaching the age of twenty-one, Professor Gordon-Reed's allegation makes even *less* sense.

There are other clear factual errors in the account attributed to Madison—facts that Madison himself should certainly have known, but which an Ohio journalist like Samuel Wetmore might not have known. For example, Wetmore claims that Madison

---

76. *Id.*

77. GORDON-REED, THOMAS JEFFERSON AND SALLY HEMINGS 212.

78. *Id.* at 213.

79. However, Jefferson's will did provide that Madison and Eston should be given their freedom at the age of twenty-one.

asserted that all four of Sally's children were freed by Thomas Jefferson's will,[80] whereas we know that, of Sally's children, only Madison and Eston were mentioned in the will. Are we to assume that Madison Hemings was knowingly overstating his case, or was his memory just failing him in his old age? Alternatively, was this erroneous assertion simply an effort by Samuel Wetmore to add credibility to the anti-Jefferson story he was writing? Does it matter, in terms of the document's historical value as a source for the truth?

The Gordon-Reed Alterations to the Wetmore Article

In the introduction I discussed the alarming alterations contained in Professor Gordon-Reed's transcription of the Wetmore article in the first edition of her *Thomas Jefferson and Sally Hemings*.[81]

For example, in the original Wetmore article, Madison is alleged to have said: "My grandmother was a fullblooded African...."[82] This statement is clearly erroneous, as Sally Hemings' mother, Betty Hemings, was half-white—a point acknowledged by Gordon-Reed on page one of her book and repeatedly thereafter.[83] This obvious factual error in the account attributed to Madison is not apparent to readers of the first edition of *Thomas Jefferson and Sally Hemings,* however, as her appendix has Madison saying "My *great*-grandmother was a fullblooded African...."[84] (See **Figure 1** on page 33.)

Then there is this sentence attributed by Wetmore to Madison: "When Mr. Jefferson went to France Martha was a young woman grown, my mother was about her age, and Maria was just budding into womanhood."[85] This might well have come from Madison Hemings, as he was not born until more than two decades after Jefferson went to France. But, in reality, when Jefferson went to France Martha was only eleven and younger sister Maria was only *five*—hardly likely to have been "budding into womanhood."

The errors are not material to our inquiry, except that they establish that Madison Hemings' knowledge of events prior to his birth was, at best, imperfect. Such obvious factual mistakes may call into question the reliability of other statements about that era attributed to Madison Hemings in the Wetmore article. So Professor Gordon-Reed solved the problem of her witness' credibility by simply altering the text of the Wetmore article once again, so in her appendix it reads: "When Mr. Jefferson went to France Martha was just budding into womanhood."[86] Unlike her alteration of the Coolidge letter, where, in addition to deleting words, others had to be moved around to produce a coherent sentence with the opposite meaning, in this case all she had to do was to delete a few words. (Well, a *dozen* words.) And as a comparison of the two documents demonstrates (see **Figure 2** on page 35), the deletions cannot be explained as merely "skipping a line" during the transcription.

---

80. [Wetmore,] *Life Among the Lowly No. 1.*
81. *See* Introduction, at 29–38.
82. [Wetmore,] *Life Among the Lowly, No. 3,* Pike County [Ohio] Republican, Dec. 25, 1873, at 4.
83. Gordon-Reed, Thomas Jefferson and Sally Hemings 1, 23, 128, 164.
84. *Id.* 245 (emphasis added).
85. [Wetmore,] *Life Among the Lowly, No. 3,* Pike County [Ohio] Republican, Dec. 25, 1873, at 4.
86. Gordon-Reed, Thomas Jefferson and Sally Hemings 246.

There are other errors in the Gordon-Reed transcription as well. Indeed, several of these are identical to errors that were made in transcribing the same document for the appendix of Fawn Brodie's volume, *Thomas Jefferson: An Intimate History*. For example, Brodie inexplicably transcribed the wrong date for Madison's marriage and his age at that time. Interestingly, Professor Gordon-Reed made precisely the same errors, substituting 1834 for 1831 and 28 for 23.[87]

However, in her substantive "correction," Professor Brodie properly used *brackets* to indicate her alteration of "grandmother" to "[great-] grandmother" in the original Wetmore article. That's what scholars who alter text are supposed to do, but it does not solve the problem that "flagging" the error in the statement attributed to Madison undermines its credibility. Surely Madison knew the difference between his grandmother and his great-grandmother, but perhaps Samuel Wetmore did not. The story becomes more credible if the brackets are deleted and Madison is portrayed as getting more of his facts right.

The Infinite Monkey Theorem asserts that an infinite number of monkeys given an infinite number of typewriters and an infinite amount of time would eventually type *Hamlet*. It is theoretically possible that Professor Gordon-Reed just inadvertently happened to delete the precise words necessary to correct Madison Hemings' error about a five-year-old girl "budding into womanhood" while maintaining a coherent sentence. If one is prepared to accept those convenient "errors" as innocent (keeping in mind that Professor Gordon-Reed was a member of the prestigious *Harvard Law Review*), then the rather dramatic alterations to the Coolidge letter (see **Figures** 3 and 4 on pages 36 and 37) are but another step down the ladder of credulity.

The Statement Attributed to Israel Jefferson

Nine months after the Madison Hemings story was published, Samuel Wetmore sought to corroborate it with an interview with another former Monticello slave, Israel Jefferson. It was clear—assuming for the moment once again that Wetmore reported accurately—that Israel shared Madison's bitterness,[88] and he made some of the same factual mistakes that appeared in the earlier piece.[89]

Shortly after Israel's story was published, a copy was apparently sent to Jefferson's grandson, Thomas Jefferson Randolph, who wrote a scathing six-page letter to the editor in response.[90] Citing Jefferson's handwritten records, he convincingly points out error after error in the article. Whereas Israel had written of witnessing the excitement as Jefferson "and other members of his family" prepared to leave for Washington to assume the duties of president of the United States,[91] the president's grandson responded:

---

87. *Id.* 248; BRODIE, THOMAS JEFFERSON 475. In this instance there may well be an honest explanation for the errors. Microfilm copies sometimes have imperfections (*e.g.*, small white blotches perhaps caused by lint or dust on the film) that make it difficult to read particular letters or numbers, and it might well be that a "4" could appear to be a "1" and an "8" confused as a "3." But the numerous other "errors" are more difficult to explain.

88. His delight at having returned to Albemarle County to find "the proud and haughty [Thomas Jefferson] Randolph in poverty" is particularly apparent. [Samuel Wetmore,] *Life Among the Lowly, No. 3*, PIKE COUNTY [Ohio] REPUBLICAN, Dec. 25, 1873, at 4. This article appears in the *Monticello Report*, Appendix E at 32. Hereinafter cited as "[Samuel Wetmore,] *Life Among the Lowly, No. 3*."

89. For example, Israel alleges that Jefferson "was hardly ever sick...." *Id.* For a discussion of Jefferson's health problems, see Chapter Eleven.

90. *Monticello Report*, Appendix E at 41.

91. [Samuel Wetmore,] *Life Among the Lowly, No. 3* at 32.

Israel is made to say that he recollects distinctly, the departure of Mr. J and family for Washington D.C. when he went to assume the duties of President. Mr. Jefferson left home alone, taking not even a servant with him Dec. 1st. 1800 to preside over the Senate as Vice President where he was March 3 1801. Israel, by the record was born Dec. 28 1800. He is thus made to recollect distinctly events occurring a month before his birth.

He is made to say that he commenced the duties of life as waiter at Monticello and attendant on Mr. J's person at the commencement of his second term March 1805. He was then at the mature age of four years and his whole family on the list of slaves on the farm leased to Mr. Craven 1801 to 1809.[92]

Israel (or Wetmore) appears to be the source of the popular myth that Thomas Jefferson freed Sally Hemings and her four children in his will. He writes:

Mr. Jefferson died on the 4th day of July, 1826, when I was upwards of 29 years of age. His death was an affair of great moment and uncertainty to us slaves, for Mr. Jefferson provided for the freedom of 7 servants only: Sally, his chambermaid, who took the name of Hemings, her four children — Beverly, Harriet, Madison and Eston — John Hemmings [sic], brother to Sally, and Burrell Colburn [sic], an old and faithful body servant.[93]

In reality, as will be discussed in Chapter Six, Sally Hemings was not freed in Thomas Jefferson's will; and of the five members of the Hemings family who were, only two were descendants of Sally Hemings — and they were treated far less favorably than Sally's brother John or the freed sons of her sisters Mary and Bett.[94]

Another difference concerns whether Israel had been responsible for kindling Thomas Jefferson's fire each morning and waiting on his person — which Israel presumably had mentioned to add credence to his claim to have "intimate" knowledge of Jefferson's relationship with Sally Hemings.[95] He is reported by Wetmore to have said:

The private life of Thomas Jefferson, from my earliest remembrances, in 1804, till the day of his death, was very familiar to me. For fourteen years I made the fire in his bedroom and private chamber, cleaned his office, dusted his books, run of errands and attended him about home.... I also know that his servant, Sally Hemmings [sic] ... was employed as his chamber-maid, and that Mr. Jefferson was on the most intimate terms with her, that, in fact, she was his concubine. This I know from my intimacy with both parties, and when Madison Hemmings [sic] declares that he is a natural son of Thomas Jefferson, the author of the Declaration of Independence, and that his brothers Beverly and Eston and sister Har-

---

92. *Monticello Report,* Appendix E at 41.

93. [Samuel Wetmore,] *Life Among the Lowly, No. 3* at 4.

94. As will be discussed in Chapter Six, the key to being freed was not being a child of Sally Hemings but being a male descendant of *Betty* Hemings, Sally's mother. Sally's brothers Robert and James were freed by Jefferson in the 1790s, and with but a single exception the remaining sons of Betty's daughters Mary, Bett, and Sally were freed in Jefferson's will — along with Sally's brother John. A useful annotated genealogical chart appears in JEFFERSON AT MONTICELLO, Table B, following page 24. I say that Sally's sons, Madison and Eston, were treated less favorably, because Burwell received immediate freedom and $300, John Hemings and Joe Fosset received their tools, freedom after one year, and (like Burwell) a "comfortable log-house" on Jefferson's land; while John Hemings also received "the service of his two apprentices, Madison and Eston Hemings, until their respective ages of twenty-one years, at which period respectively, I gave them their freedom." *Id.* at 121–22.

95. [Samuel Wetmore,] *Life Among the Lowly, No. 3* at 4.

riet are of the same parentage, I can as conscientiously confirm his statement as any other fact which I believe from circumstances but do not positively know.[96]

In response, Thomas Jefferson Randolph asserted that "Jefferson rose at dawn and always kindled his own fire," and alleged: "Israel was never employed in any post of trust or confidence about the house at Monticello."[97]

What is one to make of this "he said, she said" scenario? Can we ever really know the truth? In this controversy—that occurred nearly half-a-century after his death—Thomas Jefferson comes to our rescue by way of his remarkable record-keeping behavior. We can confirm with reasonable certainty—from records made in Thomas Jefferson's own hand decades before this dispute occurred—that Israel was wrong about his date of birth[98] and thus could not have witnessed Jefferson's departure for Washington. We know from numerous sources that Sally Hemings' nephew, Burwell Colbert, not Israel, was Thomas Jefferson's personal servant.[99] (Nor, for that matter, is there any evidence besides these two stories in the *Pike County Republican* that Sally Hemings was ever Thomas Jefferson's "chambermaid."[100]) There was one exception: for a brief period during 1819—long after Sally Hemings stopped having children—Burwell Colbert fell ill and Israel Gillette did temporarily serve as the chief waiter at Jefferson's Poplar Forest estate about 70 miles from Monticello.[101]

We can also confirm Thomas Jefferson Randolph's statement that Israel did not even live at Monticello until he was more than eight years old, which was long after Sally Hemings' last child was born.[102] This point is acknowledged by the senior historian at Monticello.[103]

What about Israel Jefferson's claim that he kindled Thomas Jefferson's fire? Fifteen years before that statement was made, historian Henry Randall included as an appendix to volume three of his *Life of Thomas Jefferson* a letter from Thomas Jefferson Randolph which stated "He always made his own fire."[104] Four years later, another book published this statement by former Monticello overseer Edmund Bacon: "He never had a servant make a fire in his room in the morning, or at any other time, when he was at home. He always had a box filled with nice dry wood in his room, and when he wanted fire he would open it and put on the wood."[105] There is, however, evidence that Israel Gillette was responsible for taking firewood to the Monticello kitchen.[106]

Two things might be offered in Israel Jefferson's defense. First, he was seventy-three years old when the interview was published, and he was recalling events that occurred, in at least one instance, even before he was born. More important, the record we have to examine is presumably not the statement of Israel Jefferson, but rather an article by an anti-Jef-

96. *Id.*

97. *Id.*

98. FARM BOOK 386.

99. *See, e.g.,* FARM BOOK 382 (listing "Burwell" first among "Roll of Negroes. 1810. Feb. in Albemarle. House etc."; and no reference on this list to any "Israel"). *See also id.* at 402, 403, 409, 412, 418.

100. As has already been discussed, based upon Thomas Jefferson's records, Sally Hemings appears to have been a relatively minor figure at Monticello.

101. LUCIA STANTON, FREE SOME DAY: THE AFRICAN-AMERICAN FAMILIES OF MONTICELLO 94, 123 (2000). The source cited by Ms. Stanton is a letter from one of Jefferson's granddaughters from Poplar Forest reporting that Israel was temporarily serving as "chief waiter."

102. FARM BOOK 128, 168–70. The Craven lease was written on August 22, 1800, prior to Israel's birth, and was to commence on the first day of the new year.

103. STANTON, FREE SOME DAY 87–88.

104. 3 HENRY S. RANDALL, THE LIFE OF THOMAS JEFFERSON 675 (1858).

105. JEFFERSON AT MONTICELLO 72.

106. STANTON, FREE SOME DAY 131.

ferson political activist who would have us believe that he is accurately conveying Israel Jefferson's recollections. We cannot with great confidence sort out the details of what may have happened more than a century ago. Perhaps Israel Jefferson embellished his background to help his friend, or perhaps his comments were reported inaccurately to support Wetmore's personal agenda. We *can* recognize that the statement attributed to Israel Jefferson is filled with errors—and probably falsehoods[107]—and give it no greater consideration than it deserves.

Conclusions

What can be concluded from the 1873 *Pike County Republican* "memoirs" of Madison Hemings? It is difficult to quarrel with the conclusion of Professor Gordon-Reed that "not every word in Hemings's statement is a lie."[108] Indeed, that may understate the case for his veracity. Perhaps Madison Hemings believed every word of his statement—if, in fact, the article reflected his views in the first place. There is really no need to question his character or truthfulness, as it is for our purposes unimportant whether the many errors in the article constitute intentional falsehoods on his part or instead reflect misinformation provided to him by others—perhaps compounded by the normal problems associated with attempting to recall details that occurred a half-century earlier.

It does not matter whether Madison Hemings was a bitter ex-slave who conspired with Samuel Wetmore or an innocent victim of Wetmore's clear anti-Jefferson political agenda. The end product is the same—an unreliable piece of political propaganda, largely founded at best on unsourced hearsay, and peppered with clear factual errors and incredible accounts about which Madison Hemings clearly had no personal knowledge. It was not racism, but sound professional judgment, that led past generations of historians to rely instead upon the eyewitness testimony of Edmund Bacon, Thomas Jefferson Randolph, and Ellen Randolph Coolidge.

It has been suggested[109] that the primary reason prominent Jefferson historians over the years have concluded that Edmund Bacon's eyewitness testimony was more credible than the statement attributed to Madison Hemings was that Madison was black and the historians were white. Ignoring for the moment the reality that all of Sally Hemings' children were apparently seven-eighths white, it is obvious that the tendency of many people to embellish their own histories transcends racial lines.

Indeed, the sad reality is that people of all colors and races occasionally find it desirable to falsify their background. This fact was recently brought into focus brilliantly in the book *Stolen Valor*,[110] which discusses hundreds of cases in which American men falsified claims involving alleged military service in Vietnam. Rich, poor, black, brown, and white, the perpetrators included judges, legislators, teachers, and convicted felons. Their only common feature was an apparent belief that pretending to be a combat vet-

---

107. One never makes such a conclusion casually. However, in this case, we are not just dealing with a faulty memory of early childhood events, but an elaborate portrayal of a role at Monticello that clearly had no basis in reality.

108. GORDON-REED, THOMAS JEFFERSON AND SALLY HEMINGS 174.

109. *See, e.g., id.* at 11, 224.

110. B.G. BURKETT & GLENNA WHITLEY, STOLEN VALOR: HOW THE VIETNAM GENERATION WAS ROBBED OF ITS HEROES AND ITS HISTORY (1998).

eran of the Vietnam War would benefit them. And for similar reasons, people of all colors and economic circumstances have been claiming famous ancestry throughout history.

Addendum:
The Ellis Revelations

As will be discussed in the Postscript at the end of this volume, a few weeks after our report was made public the history profession was shocked by the revelation by the *Boston Globe* that Professor Joseph Ellis—who played such a critical role in reversing the conventional wisdom about the Jefferson-Hemings controversy and had just won the 2001 Pulitzer Prize in History—had a long history of telling untruths to his students and others dating back decades. Among other falsehoods, he told his students he served in combat in Vietnam as a paratrooper, whereas the record shows he spent his entire military service teaching history at West Point. He told stories of catching the winning touchdown in a homecoming football game, whereas his high school yearbook showed his only foray onto the gridiron was as a member of the band. Claims of having been a civil rights activist in Alabama and an anti-war activist at Yale also proved to be false. Many of his supporters emphasized that there was no suggestion that his dishonesty influenced his professional writings, but a review of his repeated misstatement of the facts in the DNA story—at a time when Ellis was known to be involved in the effort to stop the impeachment of President Clinton for sexual improprieties—raises serious questions about that assumption.

This issue will be addressed in greater detail in the Postscript.

5

Thomas Jefferson's Visitation Patterns to Monticello and Their Correlation with Sally Hemings' Conceptions

In his prize-winning 1968 history *White Over Black*, Professor Winthrop D. Jordan appears to have been the first scholar to assert that Thomas Jefferson was home at Monticello "nine months prior to each birth"[1] by Sally Hemings. More recently, Dr. Fraser D. Neiman, the Director of Archaeology at Thomas Jefferson's home, Monticello, has published a computer-assisted quantitative analysis in the prestigious *William & Mary Quarterly*[2] which, if I understand it correctly, concludes that this correlation between Jefferson's presence and Hemings' conceptions establishes a 99 percent probability that Thomas Jefferson was the father of Sally's children.[3] Dr. Neiman's concludes that "[s]erious doubt about the existence and duration of the relationship and about Jefferson's paternity of Hemings's six children can no longer be reasonably sustained."[4] This statistical study has been hailed by believers in Jefferson's paternity as being likely to "quiet those who have resisted accepting Jefferson's paternity."[5]

Professor Annette Gordon-Reed had previously written that the "pattern of Sally Hemings's conceptions of children and Jefferson's presence at Monticello is perhaps *the most compelling evidence* of the existence of a relationship between the two."[6] This was also one

---

1. WINTHROP D. JORDAN, WHITE OVER BLACK 466 (1968). I have not researched this issue carefully enough to take a stand on whether Winthrop Jordan or Dumas Malone first noted this point. I know from a letter I received from Professor Forrest McDonald that Winthrop Jordan, as a Ph.D. candidate at Brown University in the 1960s, made the point to him. Other scholars have credited the discovery to Professor Malone. *See, e.g.,* JOSEPH J. ELLIS, AMERICAN SPHINX 365 (1996). For present purposes, it is not necessary to resolve the matter.

2. Fraser D. Neiman, *Coincidence or Causal Connection? The Relationship between Thomas Jefferson's Visits to Monticello and Sally Hemings's Conceptions,* 57 WILLIAM & MARY QUARTERLY 198 (Jan. 2000).

3. "The probability of getting six visit-conception coincidences ranges between 0.8 and 1.5 percent." *Id.* at 206. As discussed in Chapter Two, it is far from clearly established that Sally Hemings had more than five children.

4. *Id.* at 210.

5. Jan Lewis, *Thomas Jefferson and Sally Hemings Redux: Introduction,* 57 WILLIAM & MARY QUARTERLY 122 (Jan. 2000).

6. ANNETTE GORDON-REED, THOMAS JEFFERSON AND SALLY HEMINGS 195 (1997) (emphasis added.).

of the three arguments relied upon by Professors Lander and Ellis in *Nature* for the assertion that Thomas Jefferson was the father of one or more of Sally's children.[7]

"Junk Science"

Thomas Jefferson was a man of science, and he would expect us to respect both the results of DNA testing (a technology that surely would have fascinated him) and any serious logical analysis—especially one based upon mathematics. However, he would also expect us to be rigorous in our examination of the methodology used and the assumptions upon which scientific analysis is premised. This is where Dr. Neiman's study appears to have serious shortcomings.

Candidly, to borrow a term used by several of my colleagues during our Dulles sessions of the Scholars Commission, Neiman's "Monte Carlo"[8] study struck me as being "junk science" long before I became involved in a technical discussion with scientists who confirmed its fatal deficiencies.

Another term that was used during the Dulles meetings was "GIGO"—computerese for "Garbage In, Garbage Out," or "if your input is not reliable, your output from the computer will be no better." As our report reflects, *none* of us was impressed by it. Nor was I particularly surprised when a member of the Monticello Research Committee told me that, after Dr. Neiman completed his computer simulations, he entered their next meeting, slapped his papers on the table, and exclaimed with glee: "I've *got* him! I've *got* him!"[9]

To begin with, the paper includes some distracting factual errors. Neiman writes: "Molecular geneticists found the Jefferson-Y haplotype in recognized male-line descendants of Thomas Jefferson,"[10] when in fact there are no such descendants.[11] Jefferson's only children to reach maturity were both daughters, and the DNA samples used in the tests were from male-line descendants of Thomas Jefferson's cousins.

It is also inaccurate to say that Thomas Jefferson was at Monticello nine months before each of Sally's children was born—or even 267 days, to use Dr. Neiman's figure for the human gestation period.[12] Using Dr. Neiman's figures, for example, we find an estimate that Beverly Hemings was conceived on July 8, 1797 (a nine-month gestation would

---

7. Eric S. Lander & Joseph J. Ellis, *Founding Father*, NATURE, Nov. 5, 1998, at 13.

8. Five months after our report was released, one of the few public criticisms of our work took us to task for describing the Neiman study as "the Monte Carlo study" and asserted "'the Monte Carlo study' is a nickname that the Commission itself gave to the article in the course of its meeting." Thomas W. Jones, *The "Scholars Commission" Report on the Jefferson-Hemings Matter: An Evaluation by Genealogical Proof Standards*, NATIONAL GENEALOGICAL SOCIETY QUARTERLY 213 (Sept. 2001). In reality, Dr. Neiman himself described his methodology as "[t]he Monte Carlo study" on page 208 and used the term *Monte Carlo* more than two dozen times in just six pages to identify a major part of his work. I am told that Monte Carlo simulations are quite common in science.

9. Conversation with Dr. White McKenzie Wallenborn.

10. Neiman, *Coincidence or Causal Connection* 199.

11. Obviously, if Thomas Jefferson were the father of Sally Hemings' male children they would pass down his Y chromosome; but no serious scientist would try to establish paternity by simply *assuming* such a relationship and then doing a scientific comparison of Eston Hemings' DNA with Eston Hemings' DNA and announcing a match. This would be but a logical tautology.

12. Neiman, *Coincidence or Causal Connection* 198. Various sources give the average human gestation period as 266 or 267 days, but the difference is of no significant relevance for our purposes. This "average" can vary by weeks in individual cases of full-term birth.

have begun on July 1), and that Thomas Jefferson had not been at Monticello since May 5 and did not return until July 11. While it is certainly possible that Sally did not become pregnant until after the estimated conception date, it seems somewhat more likely statistically that she conceived *prior* to Jefferson's return.

Roughly ninety percent of mothers give birth within two weeks of their estimated due date, permitting us to identify a four-week conception window during which Beverly was likely conceived. For more than sixty percent of this conception window, Thomas Jefferson was not present at Monticello.

Thus, statistically, one would presumably have to conclude that it was somewhat *less* rather than more likely that Thomas Jefferson was present at Monticello when Beverly Hemings was conceived. This observation is hardly dispositive of the issue, as the data do suggest that Thomas Jefferson *could* have been present at Monticello when Sally conceived Beverly. But if, based solely on his visitation patterns, the odds are that Jefferson was not the father of Beverly Hemings, it follows *ipso facto* that there is less than a fifty-fifty chance that he was the father of *all* of Sally Hemings' children.[13]

The One-Father Assumption

Neither can science change the fact that any statistical study of the conception coincidences, whether or not it accounts for conception-window absences, must rely on numerous *assumptions* about circumstances two centuries ago. Some of these assumptions are far more than incidental. For example, the Neiman study simply *assumes* that all of Sally Hemings' children must have had the same father. There is not only no reliable evidence to support this assumption, there is credible eyewitness testimony that, if Sally Hemings was monogamous,[14] it was with someone other than Thomas Jefferson. And if either of these possibilities is true (that Sally was monogamous with someone else or had children by multiple fathers), then Dr. Neiman's (or anyone else's) statistical analysis based upon Jefferson's presence at Monticello becomes irrelevant to our inquiry.

Two arguments have been offered to support the conclusion that Sally Hemings was monogamous. In 1873, her son Madison Hemings reportedly told a journalist that Thomas Jefferson was the father of all of his mother's children.[15] But he gives no source for that information, and it is clear from the circumstances that he could not possibly have known the truth from his own observations. As harsh a thought as it may be to ponder, Monticello scholar Lucia Stanton quotes former slave Henry Bibb as writing in 1849: "It is almost impossible for slaves to give a correct account of their male parentage...."[16]

Madison Hemings was not present at his own conception or that of any Hemings child born in 1790[17] or those of Harriet I, Beverly, or Harriet II. He would have been but an

---

13. I am indebted to Dr. William C. Blackwelder, a Fellow of the American Statistical Association, for this observation.

14. In using the term *monogamous* I do not mean to imply that Sally Hemings necessarily had freedom to choose her sexual partner(s).

15. Thomas Jefferson Memorial Foundation Research Committee, *Report on Thomas Jefferson and Sally Hemings,* Jan. 2000 (hereinafter referred to as *Monticello Report*) Appendix E.

16. Lucia Stanton, Slavery At Monticello 21 (1996).

17. I refer here to his allegation that a child was born soon after Sally returned from Paris, without passing judgment on whether the "Tom" referred to by James Callender was Thomas Woodson, someone else, or a fabrication.

infant when Eston was conceived. One need not intend any disrespect for Madison Hemings, or doubt the sincerity of the statement attributed to him, to note that a statement that is either unsourced hearsay (possibly ultimately based upon his knowledge of the Callender charges) or supposition ought not be given greater weight than the eyewitness observations of Monticello overseer Edmund Bacon, who alleged that, early in the morning while arriving for work, he had *repeatedly* seen a man other than Thomas Jefferson leaving Sally Hemings' room.[18]

Nor is the fact that Jefferson historians have not alleged that Sally was *not* monogamous—assuming for the moment it is even an accurate statement[19]—serious evidence of anything beyond the fact that their interest in Sally ended when they concluded that she was not Thomas Jefferson's "concubine." From the surviving documentary evidence, Sally Hemings and her children were very minor figures at Monticello—far less important than many of her relatives. (*See* **Figure** 7 on page 141.) As the late Professor Merrill Peterson—formerly the Thomas Jefferson Memorial Foundation Professor of History at the University of Virginia, and widely regarded as the dean of living Jefferson scholars following the death of Dumas Malone—wrote in his classic study, *Thomas Jefferson and the New Nation*: "*It is of no historical importance*, but the best guess is that Sally's children were fathered by Peter Carr...."[20]

There is no evidence that *any* of the major Jefferson scholars who have consistently rejected the allegations about Sally Hemings reached serious conclusions about whether Sally had one or more sexual partners—their consensus conclusion was merely that Thomas Jefferson was not the father of her children. And again, obviously, if Sally was not monogamous, the factual foundation, such as it is, upon which the Neiman study is based collapses.

Stacking the Deck

Another problem with the Neiman study is its apparent assumption that any other candidate for paternity would have to have had "identical arrival and departure dates" as Thomas Jefferson at Monticello.[21] This certainly would decrease the probability of a statistical match, but it is an unnecessary complication of the problem and essentially irrelevant. Obviously, all that would be necessary for someone other than Thomas Jefferson to have fathered any or all of Sally's children would have been for that person to have been present (wherever Sally was) during the period of conception. To assume that he (or they) had to arrive on precisely the same day, remain the same amount of time, and then depart on the day Thomas Jefferson did, is to establish a condition that makes sense

---

18. JEFFERSON AT MONTICELLO 102 (James A. Bear, Jr., ed. 1967). This statement will be addressed at greater length in Chapter Ten.

19. Historians have certainly quoted Thomas Jefferson Randolph's assertion that Peter Carr said to his brother Samuel that "you and I" brought disgrace to Jefferson in the Hemings matter, as well as his letter to the *Pike County Republican* alleging that paternity of Sally's children had been "admitted by others (rather than another)." *See* Chapter Ten. While some historians have casually speculated about who the "father" of Sally's children might have been, I am unaware of any major Jefferson scholar before the 1990s actually concluding on the basis of scholarly research that Sally was monogamous.

20. MERRILL D. PETERSON, THOMAS JEFFERSON & THE NEW NATION 707 (1970) (emphasis added.).

21. Neiman, *Coincidence or Causal Connection* fn.12; see also p. 208 concerning the "pattern of Jefferson's visits to Monticello, a pattern that is unlikely to have been identical to the pattern of arrivals and departures for his male-line relatives." This requirement of an "identical pattern of presence" is also relied upon in the *Monticello Report* (at 7).

only if one is *trying* to increase the apparent probability that Thomas Jefferson was the father.

An even more serious flaw in the methodology is the assumption of "random"[22] behavior on the part of other potential fathers. It does not take a rocket scientist to understand that Thomas Jefferson's friends and relatives would generally[23] schedule their visits to Monticello to coincide with *his* presence there—their presumptive purpose being visiting with him, not taking part in a public tour of the plantation. Furthermore, they might be somewhat more likely to visit *immediately after* he returned home—to welcome him and perhaps receive the latest reports on events in Washington and the world—than during any other particular time of his visit. Depending upon the length of his visit, they might return again; but knowledge that he had arrived or was about to return would presumably precipitate a desire for a visit.

To illustrate the fallacy underlying Dr. Neiman's approach, let us consider a slightly different hypothesis. Suppose it is learned that, on six occasions over a period of seven years, visitors to Monticello suffer some similar harm (food poisoning, stolen property, beatings by unknown assailants—it does not matter greatly for our purposes). During these seven years, Thomas Jefferson is present at Monticello approximately half of the time. A comparison of the dates of the harmful incidents shows that Jefferson was at Monticello when each visitor suffered harm. If we were following Dr. Neiman's methodology, we would then simply *assume* that there had to be a single culprit, design a sophisticated statistical model, and learn that it is almost *certain* that Thomas Jefferson was poisoning, assaulting, or stealing the belongings of his visitors. This conclusion is supported by a scientific test simulating 400,000 possible scenarios, and figures do not lie. But then someone observes that the only time visitors came to Monticello was when Thomas Jefferson was present and there is no serious evidence the same individual committed every crime. Does that affect the reliability of our scientific study? Of course it does—and it would even if we identified a small number of exceptions when people did briefly stop in at Monticello when Jefferson was absent.

Cause and Effect

Discussing the assertion that Thomas Jefferson was at Monticello nine months before each of Sally's children was born, Professor Winthrop Jordan commented in *Sally Hemings and Thomas Jefferson* that this "obviously ... provided no firm proof of paternity. *His presence at Monticello* might well have resulted in rearrangements concerning who occupied what room and *most certainly would have altered the pattern of visits to the plantation* not only from distant admirers and acquaintances but also *from relatives* and friends from the neighborhood."[24]

Another contributor to this same volume—a book characterized by its contributors' widespread acceptance of the Jefferson-Hemings story—added that "It was his [Jefferson's]

---

22. "In the Monte Carlo approach, the probability of an observed outcome is estimated by comparing it to a very large number of random outcomes generated by a simulation model of the process responsible for the observation." Neiman, *Coincidence or Causal Connection,* at 203.

23. This is not to question that a relative or friend might not stop by briefly to pick up or drop off a document or for some other purpose while Jefferson was away.

24. Winthrop D. Jordan, *Hemings and Jefferson: Redux,* in SALLY HEMINGS AND THOMAS JEFFERSON 41 (Jan Ellen Lewis & Peter S. Onuf, eds. 1999) (emphasis added.).

wont throughout his life to entertain large numbers of guests, and a constant stream of visitors made its way to Albemarle County to call *whenever he was at Monticello*."[25] And yet Dr. Neiman premised his statistical analysis on the assumption that visitors to Monticello would behave *randomly*.

Nor, for that matter, are the data being relied upon in these assessments totally accurate. With respect to Jefferson's visits, the problems range from trivial to possibly significant. For example, in the calculations concerning the only Hemings child linked by DNA to a Jefferson male, my colleague in this inquiry, Professor Forrest McDonald, has observed both that the calculations ignored the fact that 1808 was a leap year; and, far more importantly, ignored the fact that Thomas Jefferson was *away from Monticello* for as much as nine days overlapping Sally's probable conception window.[26] Even a cursory review of the major collections of Jefferson's writings would have revealed that trip.

Where Was Sally?

If the revisionist scholars have been careless with Jefferson's visitation dates to Monticello, the lack of evidence in surviving records precludes anything more than guesswork on whether *Sally Hemings* may have been at Monticello on any given day. Indeed, it is remarkable how often the total absence of data is used as *evidence* to make an argument in the speculation about Thomas Jefferson and Sally Hemings. Thus, the *Monticello Report* asserts: "There is *no record* that Sally Hemings was anywhere but at Monticello from 1790 to 1826."[27] Given the apparent dearth of documentation on Sally's activities subsequent to her return from Paris, one might have argued with equal validity that "there is no record that Sally Hemings was clearly present at Monticello when Eston Hemings was conceived," or "there is no evidence Sally Hemings was not in New York for two years between 1790 and 1826." Thomas Jefferson both loaned and leased slaves to relatives, friends, and others,[28] and some of the more privileged members of the Hemings family were even allowed to hire themselves out during his absence and keep their earned income.[29] We know from surviving records that this occurred with respect to certain slaves, but we can not be sure it did not happen with others. There is no reason to be confident that a record of every such transaction would have survived after nearly two centuries.

The uncertainty about Sally's presence at Monticello is not mere idle speculation: Cynthia Burton has documented at least one period during 1790 when Sally was apparently

---

25. Joshua D. Rothman, *James Callender and Social Knowledge of Interracial Sex in Antebellum Virginia*, in SALLY HEMINGS AND THOMAS JEFFERSON 8 (emphasis added.).

26. Professor McDonald notes that Jefferson's letters indicate he left on 9 September for a nine-day trip to his Bedford property (Poplar Forest). I reached the same conclusion after examining several editions of Jefferson's papers. However, Cynthia Burton wrote me just as this book was going to press that, after carefully examining Jefferson's *Memorandum Books* for the period, she believes that Jefferson may have remained at Monticello until as late as September 10 and returned as early as the 17th.

27. *Monticello Report*, Appendix F at 1 (emphasis added.).

28. *See, e.g.,* THE GARDEN AND FARM BOOKS OF THOMAS JEFFERSON 304, 452 (Robert C. Baron, ed. 1987).

29. *See, e.g.,* 1 JEFFERSON'S MEMORANDUM BOOKS 263 n.11 ("During Jefferson's prolonged absences from Virginia after 1783, Martin [Hemings] apparently was at liberty to seek employment where he pleased, and at one point was in the service of James Monroe."); and *id*. 342 n.36.

away from Monticello.[30] There also exists a record of a death-bed statement attributed to Jefferson's eldest daughter, Martha—reportedly confirmed by her son, Thomas Jefferson Randolph—that Sally Hemings and Thomas Jefferson were "far distant from each other ... for fifteen months prior" to the birth of the child that most resembled the President.[31] Historian Henry S. Randall, whose three-volume *The Life of Thomas Jefferson* was published in 1858, wrote in a letter a decade later that, while reviewing "an old account book of the Jeffersons" he was able "to prove the fifteen months separation."[32] Perhaps everyone is lying to cover up Thomas Jefferson's indiscretions; or perhaps records that would document Sally Hemings' absence from Monticello at the time one of her children was conceived have been lost or misplaced over the years. The point is that, given these statements and the total absence of documents clearly establishing that Sally was at Monticello when each of her children was conceived, we simply do not know the truth.

Deathbed testimony is often made an exception to the judicial prohibition against "hearsay" evidence because it is thought to be unusually reliable,[33] and Martha Jefferson had a reputation for veracity and good character.[34] If Martha Jefferson did make the statement, it does not sound like an intentional falsehood—as she is reminding her children of a fact she asserts they already knew. If they did not know that Thomas Jefferson and Sally Hemings had been separated, she would presumably have worded her statement differently to make it more credible. There is also no evidence that historian Henry Randall was not telling the truth. But at the same time, we cannot say with certainty that any or all three sources were not simply trying to protect Thomas Jefferson's reputation.

Our obligation as students of history is to seek the truth on the basis of all of the available evidence—judging the veracity of each piece of evidence on the basis of the totality of the circumstances. But in this endeavor it is not clear that the absence of evidence (regarding Sally's whereabouts for years at a time) ought to be regarded as superior in probative value to the reported death-bed testimony of one witness who was in a position to know the facts, reportedly confirmed by a second witness (also in a position to know the facts) to a prominent historian, who subsequently stated that he had independently confirmed the facts.

Cause or Catalyst?

Why did Sally Hemings tend to get pregnant shortly after Thomas Jefferson returned to Monticello? Perhaps it was because Thomas Jefferson was her lover and they consummated

---

30. BURTON, JEFFERSON VINDICATED 106. Ms. Burton notes that in an October 1790 letter to her brother-in-law Thomas Mann Randolph, Mary (Polly) Jefferson wrote "we were at Cumberland when you sent for [S]ally but she was not well enough to have gone...." The letter is *available at* http://memory.loc.gov/master/mss/mtj/mtj1/012/1300/1351.jpg.

31. *Letter from Henry S. Randall to James Parton* on Jefferson and the "Dusky Sally Story," June 1, 1868, *reprinted in* MILTON E. FLOWER, JAMES PARTON: THE FATHER OF MODERN BIOGRAPHY 237 (1951), *reprinted in Monticello Report*, Appendix E at 25.

32. *Id.*

33. However, in this instance Martha Jefferson's statement would still be inadmissible hearsay, as it was recounted years later by Henry Randall with the assertion that he had been told the story by Martha's son. Even if Martha and Thomas Jefferson Randolph were known never to have told a lie, their credibility in this instance can be no greater than that of historian Henry Randall—who *could* have fabricated the entire matter.

34. *See* Chapter Ten.

their relationship each time he returned to Monticello—although this theory does not explain the many times he was present when Sally did not become pregnant. According to Dr. Neiman's calculations, Sally probably became pregnant with Beverly, Thenia,[35] Madison, and Eston on the average about twelve days after Thomas Jefferson's return to Monticello. This suggests that, if Jefferson's return to Monticello was a factor in her conceptions, Sally and her sexual partner(s) were remarkably fertile. Yet during the time Sally was producing known children, Thomas Jefferson visited Monticello more than twenty times, and during the period of their alleged romance, he was present for hundreds of months during which she does not appear to have become pregnant.[36] Some of these, to be sure, can be explained by the fact that she was already pregnant or had recently given birth when Jefferson returned. But for someone who routinely seems to have become pregnant within a few weeks after he returned home, what do we make of the numerous opportunities when they were both allegedly at Monticello and she did not conceive a child? And for that matter, why did it take her nearly a year to become pregnant in 1794–95, and nearly three months in 1800?

If we rephrase the inquiry, a simpler explanation may become evident. What if we ask: "Why did Sally Hemings *not* become pregnant when Thomas Jefferson was absent from Monticello?" If her sexual partner (or partners) was a relative of Thomas Jefferson's who did not normally reside at Monticello, his presence at Monticello would likely occur during the President's presence at Monticello.

Monticello Was "Shut Up" When Jefferson Was Away

Critically important in understanding the correlation between Jefferson's visits to Monticello and Sally Hemings' pregnancies is a fact not mentioned by the revisionist scholars: Thomas Jefferson's home at Monticello was normally kept shut up and locked during Jefferson's vice presidency (1797–1801) and presidency (1801–1809) when he was in Philadelphia and subsequently Washington, D.C. In a letter to W. H. Van Hasselt during the summer of 1797, for example, Jefferson wrote that "the office to which I have been called takes me from home all the winter during which time my daughters also go into the lower country to pass their winter, so that our house is shut up one half the year."[37] That this continued through his presidency has been confirmed to me by Lucia Stanton at Monticello and is apparent from other sources as well.

How can we account for the fact that most of Sally's pregnancies occurred within a month of Jefferson's return home? In the absence of birth-control medication or devices, if the flood of visiting friends and relatives resulted in Sally becoming pregnant shortly after Jefferson returned home, this would obviously preclude her getting pregnant during the ensuing year or so irrespective of the frequency of her sexual encounters or how long Thomas Jefferson remained at Monticello. Lacking firm evidence about the paternity of her children (and neither Sally nor any of her children except Madison, whose reported claims are problematic,[38] left any clear record of believing

---

35. As discussed in Chapter Two, there is serious question about whether Sally had a child in 1799.

36. However, in fairness, we have no information about whether Sally Hemings may have lost children due to miscarriage.

37. *Jefferson to Van Hasselt*, Aug. 27, 1797, *reprinted in* THE GARDEN BOOK 257 (Edwin Morris Betts, ed. 1974).

38. *See* Chapter Four.

Thomas Jefferson was their father), we have no alternative but to resort to speculation on this point. But since Thomas Jefferson's return to Monticello is well documented to have produced a flood of visiting friends and relatives, it does not seem that remarkable that Sally would often quickly become pregnant upon his return and would not — as far as we know — become pregnant when he or those who would come to visit him were not there.

Old Age and Fecundity

Thomas Jefferson would no doubt wish us to invoke the latest scientific findings in our quest to resolve this matter. Interestingly, modern scientific research does shed some light on our dilemma. A scientific paper published in the journal *Human Reproduction*[39] while our inquiry was in progress examined the effects of aging on fecundity and concluded that "[I]f the man's age was treated as a continuous variable there was a significant linear relationship" and his ability to father a child within twelve months decreases approximately three percent per year.[40]

This study did not include subjects nearly as old as the sixty-four-year-old Thomas Jefferson (his age at the time of Eston's conception), and we cannot say with certainty that the results would continue precisely as they were observed among younger men; but it is reasonable to suspect that biologically the elderly Thomas Jefferson would have been far less likely to have impregnated Sally Hemings within a few weeks[41] of his return to Monticello than any of his much younger male relatives who could have been present when she became pregnant with Eston Hemings.[42]

As our sole dissenting member correctly observes,[43] the correlation between Thomas Jefferson's presence at Monticello and Sally Hemings' conceptions of children is nevertheless a significant argument in favor of the proposition that Thomas Jefferson was the father of some and perhaps all of her children. But the significance of these data has been overstated. Correlation does not necessarily prove causation.[44] The evidentiary value of the correlation in this case is substantially lessened when one realizes that other potential fathers would not have behaved randomly, as Dr. Neiman postulates, but would likely have timed their own visits to Monticello to coincide with Thomas Jefferson's return home or at least his presence at Monticello.

There is credible, eyewitness evidence that a man other than Thomas Jefferson often spent the night in Sally's room. There are at least two reported confessions or admissions

---

39. W. C. L. Ford, et al., *Increasing paternal age is associated with delayed conception in a large population of fertile couples: evidence for declining fecundity in older men,* 15(8) HUMAN REPRODUCTION 1703–08 (Nov. 2000). This study received considerable attention in the popular media.

40. *Id.* at 1705.

41. Dr. Neiman asserts that "four out of five conceptions" by Sally Hemings occurred "within a month of Jefferson's arrival." Neiman, *Coincidence or Causal Connection* 209.

42. Again, we must be cautious about extrapolating these data to apply to a sixty-four-year-old man in the early nineteenth century, as this study involved modern men of a much younger age. Nor do the observed trends apply to every specific individual. But the general principle that fecundity decreases with advanced aging is nevertheless likely valid and significant.

43. *See* Minority Views of Professor Paul Rahe.

44. *See* Steven T. Corneliussen, *Have Scientific Data Proved Hemings-Jefferson Link?*, RICHMOND TIMES-DISPATCH, Jan. 14, 2007 at E1.

of paternity by Jefferson's nephews involving at least *some* of Sally's children.[45] It is not unreasonable to expect that Sally may have lived or been forced to live as did her mother, who, according to an account attributed to Sally's son Madison, produced children by at least four different men.[46]

On balance, there is clearly no reason to *assume* that Sally was monogamous. We simply do not know. As noted in Chapter Three, the originator of the allegation of a Jefferson-Hemings sexual relationship asserted that Sally Hemings was "a slut as common as the pavement."[47] Without the assumption of monogamy, the correlation between her pregnancies and Thomas Jefferson's visits to Monticello (which would obviously trigger visits by his friends and relatives) is of limited probative value in the search for the paternity of Eston Hemings or any of Sally's other children.

---

45. *See* Chapter Ten.

46. [Samuel F. Wetmore], *Life Among the Lowly, No. 1, Madison Hemings,* PIKE COUNTY REPUBLICAN, Mar. 13, 1873. "It is … a pattern observable in both historical and contemporary life that girls raised in a particular environment tend to grow up accepting that familiar lifestyle as both the norm and their fate." Helen F. M. Leary, *Sally Hemings's Children: A Genealogical Analysis of the Evidence,* JEFFERSON-HEMINGS: A SPECIAL ISSUE OF THE NATIONAL GENEALOGICAL SOCIETY QUARTERLY 197 (Sept. 2001). (Ms. Leary accepts the assertion that Thomas Jefferson fathered children by Sally Hemings, and identifies herself as a former four-term president of the Board for Certification of Genealogists. *Id.* at 165 n. Her article is discussed in the Postscript to this volume.)

47. [Callender,] *More About Sally and the President,* RICHMOND RECORDER, Sep. 22, 1802. *See also,* Rothman, *James Callender and Social Knowledge of Interracial Sex in Antebellum Virginia* 95.

6

"Extraordinary Privileges" for Sally Hemings and Her Children

One of the greatest myths of this entire controversy is that Sally Hemings and her children received "extraordinary privileges" at Monticello. As descendants of Betty Hemings they were indeed treated better than Monticello field slaves; but, as compared to Sally's ten siblings who lived to adulthood and their children, their treatment was at best average.

Yet, Professor Gordon-Reed contends the "strongest evidence for a relationship between [Thomas] Jefferson and [Sally] Hemings is what happened to Hemings's children."[1] In her widely praised volume, she repeatedly refers to "Jefferson's freeing of Hemings's children"[2] and asserts that "he freed them all."[3] The same claim is made by David Brion Davis, Sterling Professor of History, Emeritus, at Yale University.[4]

Similarly, in "A Review of the Documentary Evidence," attached to the January 2000 report of a research committee of the Thomas Jefferson Memorial Foundation, we find among the "UNQUESTIONED" evidence this statement:

> Thomas Jefferson freed Sally Hemings's children.
>
> The children of Sally Hemings that are known from Jefferson's records all became free by the age of twenty-one, the only case of an entire enslaved Monticello family achieving freedom.[5]

The first part of this statement is not only not "unquestioned"; it is demonstrably *false*. It is the 1873 allegation of Madison Hemings[6] and Israel Jefferson[7]—and the legend of

---

1. ANNETTE GORDON-REED, THOMAS JEFFERSON AND SALLY HEMINGS 218 (1997).

2. *Id.* at 50.

3. *Id.* at 201.

4. David Brion Davis, *Preface* in LUCIA STANTON, FREE SOME DAY: THE AFRICAN-AMERICAN FAMILIES OF MONTICELLO 12 (2000).

5. Thomas Jefferson Memorial Foundation Research Committee, *Report on Thomas Jefferson and Sally Hemings,* January 2000 [hereinafter referred to as *Monticello Report*] Appendix F at 2. At another point in their report, the Monticello Committee asserted: "One distinction accorded to Sally Hemings and to no other enslaved Monticello family was the freedom granted all of her children *after* the age of twenty-one." *Id.,* Appendix H at 5 (emphasis added). This is cute, and closer to being accurate (but Eston was only nineteen when freed). But Beverly Hemings did not leave Monticello until he was at least 23 and most likely 24 years old. *See* Chapter Four. Monticello's Shannon Senior Research Historian, Lucia Stanton, writes in a recent monograph that Beverly and Harriet Hemings left Monticello "soon after their twenty-first birthdays, possibly together." LUCIA STANTON, FREE SOME DAY 116 (2000). If we are to rely on Jefferson's records, this is clearly false with respect to Beverly.

6. *See* Chapter Four.

7. *Id.*

Hollywood fiction—but it is easily refuted by Thomas Jefferson's meticulous records, which show, for example, that Sally's oldest confirmed child, Beverly Hemings, was born on April 1, 1798,[8] and left Monticello in 1822.[9] These facts are admitted elsewhere in the *Monticello Report*[10] and by Professor Gordon-Reed.[11] The date of his departure in 1822 is not recorded, but it could not have been before January 1, at which time Beverly would have been three months short of his twenty-fourth birthday. The odds are three-to-one that he left after the first of April, which would have made him twenty-four, not twenty-one as is so commonly alleged and believed. When questioned about this point, Monticello's respected senior historian Lucia Stanton acknowledged that "Beverly Hemings would thus have been between twenty-three and twenty-four when he left," and confirms that the allegation in the *Monticello Report* that he left at age twenty-one "is not precisely accurate...."[12] (More correctly, he would have been *either* twenty-three or twenty-four.)

Nor, despite common allegations to the contrary, is it clear that Beverly left Monticello in 1822 "evidently with Jefferson's permission." When I raised this issue with Ms. Stanton, she explained that there were two reasons for the conclusion. First, they had found "no record of any attempt to bring Beverly Hemings back to Monticello," whereas in some other cases Jefferson had attempted to recover runaways.[13] But these were cases where Jefferson either was expressly aware of where a slave had gone (e.g., when Beverly's cousin Jamey, son of Critta, ran away after being punished by the overseer) or at least had a reasonable suspicion of where he might be found. If, as Madison alleged, Beverly left Virginia, the fact that Jefferson left no letters detailing efforts to locate and bring him back is hardly "proof" that Jefferson had approved his departure. Once again, the honest answer is that we really do not know.

Professor Gordon-Reed's other piece of evidence is a letter from Jefferson's granddaughter, Ellen Randolph Coolidge, who recounted that it was her grandfather's "principle" to permit slaves who were light enough to pass for white to "withdraw quietly" from Monticello, after which he made no effort to reclaim them. This is a bit ambiguous, and could mean that Jefferson encouraged them to "run away," or that if they did run and he thought they had a chance to make a new life he did not force them to return. At best, Beverly may have received the same treatment Jefferson gave to other light-skinned slaves who fled from Monticello, which is hardly convincing evidence that he was Thomas Jefferson's son.

The theory that Beverly may have run away on his own initiative may be reinforced at least somewhat by a letter alleging that in July 1820, Beverly was "missing" from the carpentry shop for several days.[14] The fact that he was reported missing without explanation does not prove that he had tried to run away, and in the absence of more details, its sig-

---

8. *See, e.g.,* THE GARDEN AND FARM BOOKS OF THOMAS JEFFERSON 386 (Robert C. Barron, ed. 1987).

9. *Id.*

10. *Monticello Report*, Appendix H at 8–9. In describing Beverly's departure, the Monticello Research Committee alleges: "He was not legally manumitted, but left Monticello in 1822, evidently with Jefferson's permission, and henceforth lived as a white man." *Id.* at 9.

11. GORDON-REED, THOMAS JEFFERSON AND SALLY HEMINGS 218. But even here Professor Gordon-Reed gets her facts wrong, asserting that Beverly left "two years after his twenty-first birthday...." *Id.* Since we do not know on what date in 1822 Beverly actually "ran away," we cannot tell whether Gordon-Reed's error is a matter of as few as nine or as many as twenty months.

12. Lucia Stanton, "Response to Bob Turner's Questions of 14 November 2000," question 3.

13. *Id.,* question 14.

14. *Letter from Edmund Bacon to Thomas Jefferson,* July 16, 1820 ("do you no [*sic*—know] that Beverly has been absent from the carpenters for about a week."), University of Virginia Library.

nificance should not be overstated. But it certainly is consistent with the idea that Beverly was not a happy slave just putting in his time until he knew Jefferson would set him free.

According to John Cook Wyllie, perhaps in the mid-1960s the leading expert on slavery at Monticello,[15] Sally's daughter Harriet II "ran away in 1822 and then [was] freed by TJ."[16] This is presumably based in part upon Jefferson's *Farm Book*, which contains a cryptic note next to Harriet's name: "run. 22."[17] Presumably, 1822 was the year in which she ran away (which was also the year in which she turned twenty-one). While Wyllie seems to suggest that there may have been two distinct events, with Harriet being "freed" at some point *after* having "run away" (and presumably having returned or been brought back), many scholars have assumed that Jefferson's "run" notation actually referred to his decision (which will be discussed in a moment) to facilitate her departure.

It seems clear that Harriet's final departure—when overseer Bacon says he gave her fifty dollars and put her on a stage to Philadelphia—was with Jefferson's approval.[18] Whether it was the same incident Jefferson recorded as Harriet having "run" in 1822, or thereafter, since Edmund Bacon ended his service as Monticello overseer on October 8, 1822,[19] it presumably had to have been prior to that date. Harriet was born during the month of May, so there would appear to be about a fifty-fifty chance that she left when she was twenty as opposed to when she was twenty-one years old. It is not unreasonable in this case to conclude that she probably left Monticello around the time she turned twenty-one—but she was the *only* one of Sally Hemings' children to gain freedom, *de facto* or *de jure*, anywhere near that close to their twenty-first birthday.

Even if we accept that Harriet Hemings was allowed to leave Monticello about the time she turned twenty-one, that still is not serious evidence of the alleged "treaty" that Madison Hemings reportedly alleged that Thomas Jefferson was compelled to conclude with Sally Hemings—promising to free all of their children when they turned twenty-one—as a condition of her agreement to return with him from Paris to Monticello. Putting someone on a stage out of town is hardly satisfaction of a solemn contractual agreement to grant her "freedom." The standard means of granting a slave legal "freedom" was manumission, which Jefferson used to free two of Sally's brothers long before Harriet turned twenty-one. It is true that some slaves were informally "given their time"—an informal process in which slaves were permitted to live as if they were free without being legally manumitted in order to permit them to remain in Virginia following enactment of the 1806 removal statute, which required manumitted slaves to leave Virginia within one year. That would not have been a consideration in the case of Harriet, who was reportedly put on a stage to Philadelphia. It would be very difficult to argue that simply facilitating the "running away" of a slave fully satisfied the terms of a "treaty" or other formal agreement in which her mother was promised her children would be "freed."[20]

It is also clear that Madison Hemings was not given his freedom when he turned twenty-one years of age. On the contrary, he was nearly six months past his twenty-first birthday when Thomas Jefferson died, and Madison did not actually receive his freedom for

---

15. Jefferson at Monticello 124 n.10.
16. *Id.*, Genealogical Chart B, after p. 24
17. The Garden and Farm Books of Thomas Jefferson 386.
18. Jefferson at Monticello 102.
19. *Id.* 40.
20. Obviously, Jefferson might have manumitted all of Sally's children. The added "cost" to Sally of such an "informal" compliance with the terms of the alleged "treaty" was that she would probably never see her child again—presumably a rather material difference.

another year—when he was roughly twenty-two and one-half.[21] Had Jefferson survived another few years, there is no reason to believe that Madison would have been freed even at age twenty-two (although we cannot be sure either way).

Presumably, if Madison Hemings was the President's own son whom Jefferson had pledged to free when Madison turned twenty-one, Jefferson would have realized when he wrote his will that Madison had already passed that landmark. If he had forgotten the age of his son, would not Sally or Madison have reminded him of his promise long before the will was written? Jefferson was a good enough lawyer to know that tacking on another year to Madison's slavery would violate any "treaty" with Sally. While we can rationalize that he was too honorable to totally ignore his alleged "son" and his "solemn word" to his lover, but too afraid that freeing Madison as allegedly promised would be seen as confirming the Callender allegations, a far simpler explanation is that there was no "treaty" and Madison and Eston Hemings were freed in the will along with all but two of the other remaining sons and grandsons of Betty Hemings.

Furthermore, Sally Hemings *herself* was neither freed during Thomas Jefferson's lifetime nor mentioned in his will. Nor, as the Thomas Jefferson Memorial Foundation has acknowledged, is there any known document suggesting that Sally's ultimate freedom was at Thomas Jefferson's request.[22]

Now it is true that the oral memoir[23] attributed to Madison Hemings by Samuel Wetmore in 1873 did not allege that Sally's "treaty" with Thomas Jefferson provided that she, too, would gain freedom. Madison reportedly said that in Paris Sally was only concerned about the freedom of any children they might produce. Since Sally was not freed by Thomas Jefferson, for Madison to have alleged more would have undercut his case. But by suggesting that Sally really was not concerned with obtaining her *own* freedom, do we not undercut the theory that the *reason* a "treaty" was negotiated in the first place was that Sally was willing to abandon her home, her family, and her alleged "lover" to secure her own immediate freedom as an expatriate in France?

In retrospect, the absence of any provision to look out for Sally makes the existence of the alleged "treaty" all the more difficult to accept. Assuming they were lovers, does it pass the "straight-face test" for either Sally Hemings *or Thomas Jefferson* to enter into such a "treaty" without any consideration at all for *Sally's* future?

Surely, if the allegations of a love affair were true, and if Sally were so prescient as to anticipate a need to provide for the future welfare of children she would not start conceiving until 1795,[24] she would have realized that her three-decades-older lover was likely to die before she did. Both of them certainly would have realized that if Sally became the property of someone else before Thomas Jefferson actually died at the age of 83, an event that could easily have occurred decades before it did given the life expectancy of the era, the handsome young slave woman might well have found herself in a horribly abusive environment of sexual exploitation. Surely, even if Sally had not raised the issue, had she been his true love, Thomas Jefferson would have wanted to provide for her eventual free-

---

21. Lucia Stanton, *The Other End of the Telescope: Jefferson through the Eyes of His Slaves*, 57 WILLIAM & MARY QUARTERLY 141 (Jan. 2000).

22. *Monticello Report*, Appendix H at 5.

23. *See* Chapter Four.

24. I am not here questioning that Thomas Woodson might have been Sally's child. But if he was, he clearly was not Thomas Jefferson's child; so Sally Hemings was clearly not producing children with Thomas Jefferson while in Paris.

dom as well as that of their children. We might add that if Thomas Jefferson was anxious to provide for the welfare of his children, why did he subsequently totally ignore them? The pieces simply do not fit together.

One might expect the alleged "lovers" to anticipate that Thomas Jefferson's daughters (and their future husbands, who might someday become the executors of Jefferson's estate) would learn of their relationship and might well *resent* Sally—particularly if the relationship became known to the general public and harmed their famous father's reputation. But by Madison's account we must assume that they were indifferent to the possibility of the beloved Sally being sold into sexual slavery, and—treaty or no treaty—in the end Thomas Jefferson made no provisions for Sally Hemings in his will and apparently left her future to the discretion of his daughter Martha. The questions we need to consider are: (1) whether it is believable that Sally would be so careful to provide for the future freedom of children that were not to be born for more than half a decade, but would have paid no attention to her own future; and (2) whether Thomas Jefferson, if Sally Hemings were really the secret love of his life and his life's companion for decades, as some would have us believe, would have totally ignored Sally at the time of his death?

There is not the *slightest* bit of evidence that Sally Hemings received "extraordinary privileges" of any kind upon returning to Virginia. She seems to have been largely ignored by Thomas Jefferson, and was apparently treated no more favorably than most of her sisters. If the language "freed at the age of twenty-one years" means that her children would be legally granted their freedom upon turning twenty-one, that clearly did not happen either—despite claims to the contrary by senior Monticello scholars and others.[25]

But even if Jefferson *had* freed Sally, and *had* legally manumitted each of her children on their twenty-first birthday,[26] that still would not come *close* to proving that Thomas Jefferson had a sexual relationship with Sally Hemings. There were other, much simpler, explanations for any special treatment they received—including the fact that they were legally white[27] and may have been blood relatives of both Thomas Jefferson[28] and his

---

25. *See, e.g.,* Stanton, *The Other End of the Telescope* 142.

26. Madison Hemings' 1873 allegations obviously are of little probative value in ascertaining the significance of the fact that two of Sally's children may have gained their freedom during their twenty-second year (between their twenty-first and twenty-second birthdays). Had Madison alleged the existence of a treaty providing for the freeing of Sally's children at twenty-one *before* he knew when the children were freed, it would have been far more significant.

27. Technically, as long as they remained slaves they were not classified as "white"; but had they not been slaves, any children Sally produced with white fathers would legally have qualified as "white" in Virginia at the time. *See, e.g.,* Lucia Stanton & Dianne Swann-Wright, *Bonds of Memory*, in SALLY HEMINGS AND THOMAS JEFFERSON 182 n.5 (1996) ("Until 1910 Virginia law declared that a free person with more than three-quarters white heritage was white.... Madison and Eston Hemings were listed as white in the 1830 Virginia census....") *See also,* Gordon S. Wood, *The Ghosts of Monticello*, in SALLY HEMINGS AND THOMAS JEFFERSON 23; JOSEPH J. ELLIS, AMERICAN SPHINX 179 (1996). However, so long as they remained legally slaves they would not have been classified as "white" even if they had only one or two percent African blood.

28. The two most common suspects for the paternity of Sally Hemings' children historically have been Peter and Samuel Carr, who allegedly admitted paternity in the presence of Jefferson's grandson. Their mother was Martha Jefferson Carr, Thomas Jefferson's sister and the wife of his best friend from childhood, Dabney Carr. After Dabney's death in 1773, Jefferson took a special interest in the welfare and education of the Carr children and they were frequent visitors to Monticello. It would be quite logical for Thomas Jefferson to show special consideration for the grandchildren of his sister or those of Dabney Carr. Other possible fathers include Thomas Jefferson's brother, Randolph Jefferson, or at least four of Randolph's five sons (Thomas Jefferson's nephews). *See* Chapter Ten.

beloved wife.[29] They were also more skilled[30] than other Monticello slaves, and thus more likely than most to be able to succeed on their own if freed. To allege in such a setting that the only possible reason Thomas Jefferson would show special consideration for Sally Hemings' children was because he was their father is silly. He gave far better treatment to several of Betty Hemings' other descendants who could not even arguably have been his children.

If anything, Jefferson's actual treatment of Sally's children is powerful circumstantial evidence for the fact that they *were not* his children. Madison was clearly bitter at having been totally ignored by the man he claimed to believe was his father, and noted in contrast Jefferson's great fondness and open displays of affection for what he termed Jefferson's "white" grandchildren.[31] But, based upon their racial mix (seven-eighths white), Madison and Eston were also "white"; and even if he felt a need to be discreet around visitors, there is no reason to assume Thomas Jefferson would not have been privately affectionate if Sally's boys had actually been his natural sons.

Alternatively, if one assumes they would have been sources of great embarrassment to him, how does one explain the fact that he did not simply send them away as young children (as he allegedly did with Tom Woodson as soon as the scandal broke). If he did not care about them and viewed them as sources of embarrassment, why did he free them in his will? The most likely answer is that we will never know the full truth, but the revisionist interpretation (linking Jefferson and Sally Hemings romantically) is very difficult to reconcile with the realities of his behavior. On the other hand, if we assume that Sally and her children were simply descendants of Betty Hemings, their treatment makes total sense.

In two volumes of more than 1400 pages of Jefferson's *Memorandum Books*, containing more than fifty years of brief notations and financial records—including numerous references to each of the more popular Hemings family members (see **Figure 7** on the next page)—there is but a *single* entry pertaining to Madison or Eston Hemings. On December 11, 1824, Jefferson made a notation that he "Pd. Madison and Eston for 100. Cabbages 2.D."[32] That was exactly the price he paid Israel Gillette (another Monticello slave who is seldom mentioned in Jefferson's records[33]) for the same quantity of cabbages on November 10, 1822; but less than a month later Israel was able to extract *three* cents per head of cabbage from the Monticello sage—a fifty percent increase over the two cents a head price Jefferson paid earlier to Israel and later to his alleged "sons," Madison and Eston.

---

29. *See, e.g.,* WINTHROP D. JORDAN, WHITE OVER BLACK 467 (1968). While there is no record in Jefferson's papers to support the charge, it was alleged by some that Sally Hemings and several of her siblings were the children of Martha Wayles Skelton Jefferson's father, who as a widower allegedly had a long-term affair with Sally's mother Betty. For our purposes it is unnecessary to examine this issue, beyond noting that the issue remains unsettled. A recent book concludes that John Wayles probably was not Sally's father. REBECCA L. MCMURRY & JAMES F. MCMURRY, JR., ANATOMY OF A SCANDAL xviii (2002).

30. Professor Gordon-Reed suggests that the only exception may have been Peter Hemings. GORDON-REED, THOMAS JEFFERSON AND SALLY HEMINGS 39.

31. *See* Chapter Four.

32. 2 JEFFERSON'S MEMORANDUM BOOKS 1408 (James A. Bear, Jr. & Lucia C. Stanton, eds. 1997).

33. In addition to twice buying cabbages from Israel, Jefferson records once paying him one dollar apparently to clean out a sewer and on another occasion giving him twenty-five cents for running an errand. *Id.* at 1311, 1381, 1391, 1414.

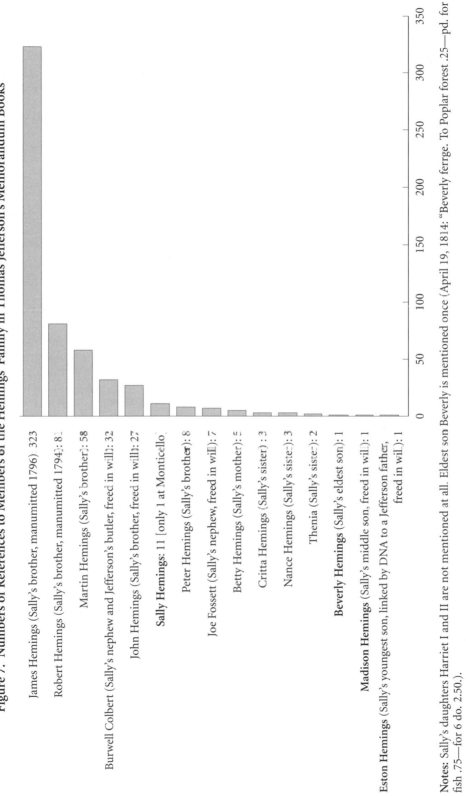

Figure 7. Numbers of References to Members of the Hemings' Family in Thomas Jefferson's Memorandum Books

James Hemings (Sally's brother, manumitted 1796) 323

Robert Hemings (Sally's brother, manumitted 1794): 81

Martin Hemings (Sally's brother): 58

Burwell Colbert (Sally's nephew and Jefferson's butler, freed in will): 32

John Hemings (Sally's brother, freed in will): 27

Sally Hemings: 11 [only 1 at Monticello]

Peter Hemings (Sally's brother): 8

Joe Fossett (Sally's nephew, freed in will): 7

Betty Hemings (Sally's mother): 5

Critta Hemings (Sally's sister): 3

Nance Hemings (Sally's sister): 3

Thenia (Sally's sister): 2

Beverly Hemings (Sally's eldest son): 1

Madison Hemings (Sally's middle son, freed in will): 1

Eston Hemings (Sally's youngest son, linked by DNA to a Jefferson father, freed in will): 1

Notes: Sally's daughters Harriet I and II are not mentioned at all. Eldest son Beverly is mentioned once (April 19, 1814: "Beverly ferrge. To Poplar forest .25—pd. for fish .75—for 6 do. 2.50.).

The Real Explanation for "Special Treatment"

The greatest fallacy in the "special treatment" argument is that it ignores the real connection that fully explains Jefferson's behavior. Long before Sally sailed for Paris or began producing children, Thomas Jefferson was showing favorable treatment to slaves at Monticello named Hemings. The reason Madison and Eston Hemings were freed in Thomas Jefferson's will is presumably the same reason Jefferson freed Sally's brother, John,[34] and sons of her sisters Mary[35] and Bett[36]—not to mention having freed Sally's brothers Robert and James nearly three decades earlier. He believed they could succeed on their own because of their skills and light skin tone.

It is worth noting that, of the five Hemings men freed pursuant to the March 27, 1826, codicil to Jefferson's will, Sally's sons received by far the *least favorable* treatment. The relevant provisions of the codicil stated:

> I give to my good, affectionate, and faithful servant Burwell his freedom, and the sum of three hundred Dollars to buy necessaries to commence his trade of painter and glazier, or to use otherwise as he pleases. I give also to my good servants John Hemings and Joe Fosset, their freedom at the end of one year after my death: and to each of them respectively all the tools of their respective shops or callings: and it is my will that a comfortable log-house be built for each of the three servants so emancipated on some part of my lands convenient to them with respect to the residence of their wives, and to Charlottesville and the University, where they will be mostly employed, and reasonably convenient also to the interests of the proprietor of the lands; of which houses I give the use of one, with a curtilage of an acre to each, during his life or personal occupation thereof.

> I give also to John Hemings the service of his two apprentices, Madison and Eston Hemings, until their respective ages of twenty one years, at which period respectively, I give them their freedom.[37]

It might be worth noting that the reason Jefferson did not free more of his slaves in his will is that Virginia law at the time would have effectively prevented it. Although Section 53 of the *Revised Code of Virginia of 1819* did expressly permit slaveholders to "emancipate and set free his or her slaves" in their last will and testament, Section 54 added "[t]hat all slaves so emancipated shall be liable to be taken by execution, to satisfy any debt contracted by the person emancipating them, before such emancipation is made."[38] Thomas Jefferson died with debts exceeding $100,000, and—while, out of respect for the great patriot, his creditors permitted the emancipation of the five men named in his will—had Jefferson attempted further to alienate this "chattel property" (as slaves sadly were considered at the time) they would certainly have protected their financial interests.

Professor Gordon-Reed—after noting that Beverly and Harriet Hemings had already "left Monticello," leaving behind Madison and Eston—asserts: "Both of these young men

---

34. For information on John Hemings, *see* Stanton, Free Some Day 135–40.

35. Mary's son Joe Fosset was freed in Jefferson's will. Some of his descendants have alleged that he was also fathered by President Jefferson (*see* Chapter Eight). For additional information on Joe Fosset, *see* Stanton, Free Some Day 131–33.

36. Bett, also known as "Betty Brown," was the mother of Jefferson's most trusted servant, Burwell Colbert.

37. *Reprinted in* Jefferson at Monticello 121–22 (1967).

38. Revised Code of Virginia of 1819, §§ 53 & 54 (1819).

were freed by Thomas Jefferson's will of March 1826, the only public example of Jefferson's preferential treatment of any of the Hemings children."[39] On the contrary, the facts clearly demonstrate that "preferential treatment" was the *norm* with the children and grandchildren of Betty Hemings at Monticello. Professor Winthrop Jordan, in his National Book Award-winning masterpiece, *White Over Black*, notes that the "entire [Betty] Hemings family seems to have received favorable treatment."[40]

In an appendix to the fourth volume of his Pulitzer Prize–winning biography of Jefferson, Dumas Malone — widely regarded as the preeminent Jefferson scholar of all times — addressed what he termed "The Miscegenation Legend":

> Any special favors the Master may have shown the artisans — including Betty's son John Hemings and her grandsons Joe Fosset and Burwell — may be attributed to their recognized merit; and when Jefferson provided in his will for their emancipation, he had reason to believe they could maintain themselves as freemen by their skills.
>
> More talk was occasioned by Jefferson's continuing solicitude for other descendants of Betty Hemings whose color was light enough to be remarked upon. The particular reference is to the six youngest of the children she brought to Monticello, of whom Sally was the last. Two of her sons in this group, Bob and James, were freed by their master in the 1790's, apparently without exciting any special comment. This action of Jefferson's met another test: he was confident at the time that as freedmen they could take care of themselves. Betty's daughter Thenia was sold to James Monroe, who could be expected to be kind to her. Two others, Critta and Sally, remained at Monticello as household servants and were apparently treated with indulgence, but this was the rule rather than the exception there.... In his will, Jefferson provided for the emancipation of Sally's sons Madison and Eston when they should reach the age of twenty-one.... This action, again, was in line with the policy Jefferson followed with respect to other men slaves he freed.
>
> A rational explanation can be given for his actions in all these cases, but his concern, in life and death, *for the descendants of Betty Hemings* could hardly have failed to excite some local comment and thus to have laid some foundation, albeit unsubstantial, for the legend that arose and grew.[41]

The fallacy that Sally Hemings' children were given preferential treatment in comparison to other descendants of Betty Hemings at Monticello becomes evident when one examines how her male descendants were treated at the time of Jefferson's death. Betty Hemings had five sons and sixteen known grandsons (including Madison and Eston) when Thomas Jefferson died in 1826. But only seven of these twenty-one males are believed to have still been Thomas Jefferson's property. (See **Figure 8** on the next page.) Five of those were formally freed in his will, and the remaining two are known to have achieved their freedom within a year or two:

---

39. GORDON-REED, THOMAS JEFFERSON AND SALLY HEMINGS 38.

40. JORDAN, WHITE OVER BLACK 465. More recently, Professor Jordan wrote: "He treated all members of the Hemings family as standing in a different category than all his other slaves...." Winthrop D. Jordan, *Hemings and Jefferson: Redux*, in SALLY HEMINGS AND THOMAS JEFFERSON 48 (Jan Ellen Lewis & Peter S. Onuf, eds. 1999).

41. DUMAS MALONE, JEFFERSON THE PRESIDENT — FIRST TERM, 1801–1805 at 495–97 (1970) (emphasis added). *See also,* James Bear's footnote explaining the Hemings family in JEFFERSON AT MONTICELLO 123 n.3 ("This remarkable family included a number of very able craftsmen and artisans. John Hemings is perhaps the best known, for he is believed to have made much of the furniture produced in the Monticello cabinet shop during TJ's lifetime. James was an excellent cook...." There is no mention here of Sally.)

Figure 8. Sons and Grandsons of Betty Hemings Manumitted by Thomas Jefferson or Known to Have Been at Monticello at the Time of His Death

Boldface type indicates those who were manumitted by Thomas Jefferson during his life or in his will.

First Generation

James Hemings	**Robert Hemings**	Peter Hemings	**John Hemings**
manumitted by Thomas Jefferson in 1796	manumitted by Thomas Jefferson in 1794	sold to his nephew Daniel for $1 at auction following Jefferson's death, then freed	freed in Jefferson's will

Second Generation

Joseph Fossett	**Burwell Colbert**	Wormley Hughes	**Eston Hemings**	**Madison Hemings**
(son of Mary Hemings Bell), freed in Jefferson's will	(son of Betty Brown), freed in Jefferson's will	(son of Betty Brown), freed shortly after Jefferson's death	(son of Sally Hemings), freed in Jefferson's will	(son of Sally Hemings), freed in Jefferson's will

- Sally's sister Mary gave birth to three boys, only one of whom, Joe Fossett, was known to have been present at Monticello at the time of Jefferson's death, and he was freed in Jefferson's will.[42]

- Sally's brother Martin had no known children and apparently died by 1807.[43]

- Sally's sister Bett (aka "Betty Brown") had two sons who were known to have lived at Monticello until 1826.[44] One of these was Burwell Colbert, Jefferson's most trusted servant,[45] who was born in 1783[46] and was to be immediately freed in Jefferson's will and given the most preferable treatment of the five Hemings males who

---

42. Joe Fosset had been allowed to retain a percentage of the profits from his work as a blacksmith before being manumitted.

43. There is some speculation that Martin may have died a decade before this. There were several "Martins" at Monticello over the years, and at least one of them died in 1807. The key point is that no one alleges Martin Hemings was still alive and the property of Thomas Jefferson when the 1826 will was prepared.

44. This does not count Edwin, who was given to Thomas Jefferson Randolph a decade before Jefferson's death.

45. JEFFERSON AT MONTICELLO 99; FAWN BRODIE, THOMAS JEFFERSON: AN INTIMATE HISTORY 459 (1974).

46. THE GARDEN AND FARM BOOKS OF THOMAS JEFFERSON 246.

were freed at that time. The other, Wormley Hughes, a gardener, was not freed in Jefferson's will—but was freed soon thereafter. He will be discussed below.[47]

- Sally's sister Nance had one son, Billy, who appears to have died in the 1790s.

- Sally's brother Robert was manumitted by Thomas Jefferson in 1794.[48]

- Sally's brother James was manumitted by Thomas Jefferson in 1796.[49]

- Sally's sister Thenia was sold to James Monroe in 1794.

- Sally's sister Critta had a son, Jamey, who ran away in 1804.

- Sally's brother Peter reportedly had a wife and five children, but no details (names, gender, etc.) are known. By 1830, he was listed as a free man living in Charlottesville. It appears that Peter Hemings was sold at auction following Thomas Jefferson's death for one dollar to his nephew, Mary Hemings' son Daniel, who then gave him his freedom.[50] Whether the Jeffersons knew this was going to happen is unknown.

- Sally's brother John was freed in Thomas Jefferson's will. There is no information in the surviving records about whether or not he had male children.

- Sally's sister Lucy died in 1786 at the age of nine.

Thus, of the seven sons and grandsons of Betty Hemings known to have been at Monticello at the time of Thomas Jefferson's death, five (more than seventy percent) were freed. In addition, two of Betty Hemings' other male descendants had been legally manumitted in the 1790s—bringing the total percentage freed to 78 percent. Being included within this group was thus not particularly remarkable, and it is even less "special" when we realize that of the seven Hemings males legally manumitted by Thomas Jefferson, Sally Hemings' sons Madison and Eston received by far the least favorable treatment.

Among Sally Hemings and her siblings, Thomas Jefferson freed all of Mary and Sally's male children and all but one of Bett's. Of the seven remaining male descendants of Betty Hemings still at Monticello when Jefferson died, Sally's sons ranked fourth and fifth—slightly *below average*—in terms of favorable treatment.

After this chapter was initially drafted, I submitted a series of questions to the Thomas Jefferson Foundation and received the very generous assistance of both President Daniel

---

47. For more information on Wormley Hughes, *see* STANTON, FREE SOME DAY 133–34.

48. Robert Hemings had hired himself out to Dr. George Stras of Richmond, who owned Robert's wife, Dolly. He was manumitted by Jefferson on Christmas Eve, 1794, in return for a payment of £60 advanced by Dr. Stras. *See, e.g.,* James A. Bear, Jr., *The Hemings Family of Monticello* 29 VIRGINIA CAVALCADE, Autumn, 1979 at 80; and STANTON, FREE SOME DAY 118.

49. Lucia Stanton suggests that James probably bargained for his freedom while in Paris. *Id.* at 126–27. There does not appear to be any serious evidence to support such speculation, and we know that in September 1793 Jefferson made an agreement to free James if James would first train another slave as a French cook. Part of this bargain may have been that James also compensate Jefferson for his investment in training James in Paris. Based on entries in Jefferson's *Memorandum Books*, James seems to have stopped receiving wages from Jefferson after January 1794, and it is possible that his wages were retained by Jefferson in repayment for educational expenses. But this is entirely speculation. (The specific details are of no importance to our present inquiry other than noting there is no serious evidence of any Jefferson-Hemings "treaty" in Paris.) Jefferson manumitted James on February 5, 1796, and three weeks later gave him thirty dollars for expenses to Philadelphia. But James apparently had difficulty adjusting to the outside world. Despite his extensive training as a French chef, he soon turned to drinking and committed suicide in 1801. *See* 1 JEFFERSON'S MEMORANDUM BOOKS 471; 2 *id.* 936, 1051 n.10. Martha Jefferson wrote that John Hemings also turned to alcohol after manumission: "His liberty poor fellow was no blessing to him." *Quoted in* STANTON, FREE SOME DAY 149.

50. Lucia Stanton, "Response to Bob Turner's Questions of 14 November 2000," question 18.

Jordan and Lucia Stanton, the former Monticello Research Director and currently Shannon Senior Research Historian at Monticello's International Center for Jefferson Studies. In response to a number of written questions, Ms. Stanton provided the following information:

> Of the males of Sally Hemings's generation, only Peter Hemings (not freed) and John Hemings (freed) are known to have been alive (Robert and James had died; Martin's fate is unknown, but he was definitely not at Monticello). Of the males of the next generation, those alive were Joseph Fossett (freed), Robert Bell (born free in Charlottesville), Wormley Hughes (not freed but "given his time"), Burwell Colbert (freed), Brown Colbert (sold in 1806, a slave in Lexington, VA in 1826), Edwin Colbert (given to Thomas Jefferson Randolph in 1816), Robert [Colbert?] (sold in 1820), Billy (son of Nance; fate not known, but not a Monticello slave), James Hemings (ran away in 1804; not recovered, but apparently returned to visit in 1815).[51]

Elsewhere in the same set of responses she added:

> [Peter Hemings] is no doubt the "Peter, Old man" sold for one dollar. His purchaser was Daniel Farley, a free black of Charlottesville who we think was Peter's nephew Daniel, the son of Mary Hemings.... Farley must have then freed Hemings, who is listed as a free black in the 1830 census.[52]

This confirmed my own initial findings that, of Betty Hemings' seventeen children (including Sally) and thirty-seven grandchildren (including Madison and Eston), only two males who remained the property of Thomas Jefferson at the time of his death were not freed in his will — and both of them apparently became free men almost immediately. The fact that two of Sally Hemings' sons were freed in the will is thus typical of the general treatment given Betty Hemings' male descendants who remained at Monticello when Jefferson died, and is hardly serious evidence that Thomas Jefferson was their father.

There is obviously no "pattern" here of preferential treatment for Sally Hemings' children over other members of the Hemings family. It does not matter why Peter and Wormley were not freed in Jefferson's will. Douglass Adair asserts that Jefferson made a decision in 1774 (when Sally Hemings was about one year old) "that the Hemings boys when they were grown and after they had learned a trade and could support themselves, would be given their freedom if they wished it."[53] One might speculate that Jefferson feared that Peter lacked the skills to make it on his own, but he once described Peter as a "servant of great intelligence and diligence,"[54] and Peter seems to have done well as a tailor after being freed.[55] However, for some reason, Peter was valued at only one dollar for the slave auction that followed Jefferson's death. We have so little information that we can do no more than speculate about why he was not freed in the will.

---

51. *Id.*, Question 16.

52. *Id.*, Question 18.

53. *Quoted in* GORDON-REED, THOMAS JEFFERSON AND SALLY HEMINGS 201.

54. James A. Bear, Jr., *The Hemings Family of Monticello*, VIRGINIA CAVALCADE, Autumn 1979 at 82.

55. "Peter Hemings continued his trade of tailor after Jefferson's death (there are references to clothing purchased of him in Randolph and Bankhead accounts until 1838)." Lucia Stanton, "Response to Bob Turner's Questions of 14 November 2000," question 18.

Wormley Hughes seems to have been a favorite with Thomas Jefferson,[56] and the nearly two dozen references to him in Jefferson's *Memorandum Books* suggest both that he was trusted and that he was very honest.[57] Unlike Sally's children, he was occasionally paid for his work.[58] There is some evidence in Jefferson's *Farm Book* that Wormley may have had less talent[59] than some of the other Monticello slaves, and that might explain why he was not freed in the will. Instead, he was apparently treated like Sally Hemings and entrusted to the care of Jefferson's daughter Martha. It is speculated that Jefferson may have told Martha orally that Wormley should be given his freedom if he desired it,[60] and in her 1834 will Martha asked her heirs to give Wormley and Sally[61] "their time."[62]

It is also possible that Wormley did not wish to be freed at the time of Jefferson's death. He seems to have been very fond of the Jefferson family, he was certainly not treated like most slaves, and perhaps he stayed on by choice, hoping to continue his role as family gardener rather than trying to fend for himself on his own. It really does not matter: the reality is that most of the remaining adult male descendants of Betty Hemings were freed in Thomas Jefferson's will, and Wormley was spared the fate of being sold on the auction block. And again, rather than being singled out for special benefits, Sally Hemings' sons received the *least favorable treatment* of any of the Hemings who were formally given their freedom by Thomas Jefferson and ranked *below average* in treatment among all remaining male descendants of Betty Hemings at Monticello upon Jefferson's death.

The first person to suggest in writing that Sally Hemings received special treatment, "above the level of his other servants," was the scandalmonger James Callender in 1802.[63] But the Monticello Research Committee admits: "Jefferson's records do not reveal any privileges accorded to Sally Hemings that distinguish her from others in her family."[64] Indeed, this may understate the case, as many of her relatives appear to have received far better treat-

---

56. *See, e.g.,* Stanton, *The Other End of the Telescope* 141, 150.

57. Thus, there are numerous entries showing that Wormley was given a dollar or so for travel expenses, and a few days later Jefferson would record receiving twenty-five cents or so back from Wormley. 2 MEMORANDUM BOOKS 1260, 1261, 1302.

58. *See, e.g., id.* at 1384.

59. For example, in 1794, when Wormley would have been about thirteen years of age, Jefferson recorded the "actual work" done by various slaves in his *Farm Book*. Burwell received a score of "19," while Wormley received the lowest number of "16.25." THE GARDEN AND FARM BOOKS OF THOMAS JEFFERSON n. 367. The following year, Jefferson made a diary notation that the "abler boys" should be assigned as "binders," while the "smallest boys" were to be "gatherers." Wormley was listed in this second group. *Id.* at 278. Consider also a memorandum from Jefferson to overseer Edmund Bacon, dated 1807 (when Wormley would have been about twenty-six), stating that "Wormley must be directed to weed the flower beds about the house, the nursery, the vineyards, and raspberry beds, when they want it." (JEFFERSON AT MONTICELLO 65.) This could suggest that Wormley lacked motivation, as a gardener might be expected to do such things without being "directed."

60. *See, e.g.,* STANTON, FREE SOME DAY 143.

61. I should note that, despite the common interpretation that this reference to "Sally" meant Sally Hemings, there were several other "Sallies" at Monticello and Edgehill and there is no clear evidence this referred to Sally Hemings. Indeed, since Sally was reportedly already living in Charlottesville as a free woman with her sons, a case might be made that this was a reference to a different Sally. We just do not really know.

62. STANTON, FREE SOME DAY 143.

63. *Monticello Report*, Appendix E.

64. *Id.*, Appendix H at 4.

ment than did Sally. For example, Jefferson wrote letters to her brothers James and John, but not to Sally;[65] and when returning from trips, Jefferson would often bring gifts for his family members and a few favored slaves—once bringing an almost new suit of clothes for Sally's brother Robert[66]—but there is no record of any such generosity to Sally.[67]

While part of the time she was in Paris Sally did receive a small monthly salary, it was half of what her brother James was paid and only twenty percent of the average wages paid to Jefferson's other servants.[68] There is no suggestion that it continued after she returned home, where Burwell and John Hemings received an annual gratuity and where Robert, James, and Martin were even permitted to hire themselves out to other masters when Jefferson was away and to keep their wages for themselves.[69]

Indeed, the lack of evidence of special consideration for Sally Hemings—who was never among the dozen or so slaves Jefferson took with him to the White House[70] (including three females who were paid salaries[71]) and was herself ignored in his will[72]—has led some advocates of the alleged relationship to go to bizarre lengths to find signs of the love they *know* he had to feel for Sally. Typical is this example from Professor Fawn Brodie's 1974 *Thomas Jefferson: An Intimate History*:

> There is also what one might call hard evidence as well as psychological evidence that Jefferson in Paris treated Sally Hemings with special consideration. On November 6, 1787, he paid 240 francs to a Dr. Sutton for Sally's smallpox inoculation, a very great sum.[73]

Unfortunately (for Professor Brodie), Jefferson's concern about the risk of exposing his daughters to smallpox predates the decision by the Eppes family to send Sally to France to serve as their maid, as he had specifically instructed that an older slave named Isabel accompany Polly *if* she had already had smallpox.[74] Sally was selected without Jefferson's knowledge for the trip, because Isabel was recovering from childbirth. Further, in 1778 Jefferson had paid for a smallpox vaccination for Sally's brothers James and Robert[75]— and no one (thus far) seems to have suggested this was evidence of a sexual liaison. Indeed, over the years Jefferson inoculated scores of his slaves against this dreaded disease.[76] Monticello's Lucia Stanton notes that "Jefferson took pains to arrange for slaves in regular contact with his family" to have smallpox inoculations.[77]

Then there is the thirty-two dollars Jefferson spent on new clothing for Sally in 1789. This has given Hollywood an excuse to portray the young slave girl as dancing across Paris in the arms of the dashing American minister, but the more likely explanation is more basic. As the *Monticello Report* explains: "Jefferson spent almost ten times as

---

65. GORDON-REED, THOMAS JEFFERSON AND SALLY HEMINGS 176.
66. FAWN M. BRODIE, THOMAS JEFFERSON 249.
67. One might argue that after the Callender allegations in 1801 Jefferson would not have wanted to record special gifts to Sally, but that would not explain the absence of such notations prior to that time.
68. *Monticello Report*, Appendix H at 3.
69. STANTON, FREE SOME DAY 104, 121.
70. JEFFERSON AT MONTICELLO 99–100.
71. STANTON, FREE SOME DAY 129.
72. The arguable exception would be the freeing of her two sons, along with most other Hemings males still at Monticello.
73. BRODIE, THOMAS JEFFERSON 233.
74. *See* Chapter Two.
75. 1 MEMORANDUM BOOKS 388 n.56, 408.
76. STANTON, FREE SOME DAY 91.
77. *Id.* at 110.

much on the clothing of his daughter Martha, who was just beginning to go out into society and to balls. Sally, as her lady's maid, would also have needed an improved wardrobe."[78]

Indeed, there is precedent for Jefferson spending money on clothing for slaves in such settings. Professor Ellis notes that in 1775, when Jefferson went to Philadelphia (where he would draft the Declaration of Independence the following year), "he had outfitted Jesse, Jupiter[79] and Richard, his black servants, in formal attire befitting the regalia of a proper Virginia gentleman...."[80]

Also relied upon is the fact that, in planning his return voyage to the United States, Jefferson instructed that Sally's room be "convenient to that of my daughters,"[81] leading Professor Brodie to assert: "So he insisted that on shipboard he be close to all three young females, from whom he would not—and could not—in the end be separated."[82] Acknowledging that Professor Brodie's interpretation might go a bit far, Professor Gordon-Reed tells her readers: "At a minimum this note indicates that Jefferson counted Sally Hemings among those who would have been offended if they were excluded from his company on the voyage home and that this concerned him to some degree."[83] In their eagerness to find evidence of romance, it apparently did not occur to either writer that Jefferson just might have wanted Sally's cabin to be near to that of his daughters because her *job* was to serve as their maid.

The paucity of references to Sally Hemings in Jefferson's voluminous records—in addition to being portrayed as obvious evidence of a "coverup"[84]—requires a certain amount of creative speculation by writers determined to find evidence of his generosity towards young Sally. If there are no records suggesting gifts, at least we can find ambiguities. When Jefferson records the purchase of a "locket" for 40 francs, Professor Brodie suggests that "perhaps" it was for *Sally*.[85]

After Jefferson and his entourage returned from Paris, and there was no longer a need to dress Sally to appear in French society as a ladies' maid to the daughters of the American minister, Sally was clothed like all of her relatives and appropriate notations were made in the *Farm Book*. But Professor Brodie put a slightly different "spin" on the story:

> With the return to America secrecy deepened. Jefferson's casual notations of expenditures for Sally's clothes disappeared altogether from his account books. Instead there were numerous small sums for "charity," always given upon his arrival at Monticello after an absence, and several curious references to leaving "small money in my drawer at Monticello," one of which amounted to the sizeable sum of twenty dollars.[86]

One can hardly wait for Oliver Stone to write the next screenplay, premised on the theory that any ambiguous expenses in Jefferson's records were obviously secret payments to Sally Hemings. (Callender, on the other hand, might have used this "evidence" as proof that Sally really was a "prostitute.")

---

78. *Monticello Report*, Appendix H at 3.
79. Jefferson's relationship with Jupiter was so close that he occasionally borrowed money from him. *See, e.g.,* 2 JEFFERSON'S MEMORANDUM BOOKS 1000.
80. ELLIS, AMERICAN SPHINX 28.
81. *Jefferson to James Maurice*, Sept. 16, 1789, in 15 PAPERS OF THOMAS JEFFERSON 433 (1958).
82. BRODIE, THOMAS JEFFERSON 243.
83. GORDON-REED, THOMAS JEFFERSON AND SALLY HEMINGS 180.
84. *See* Chapter Two.
85. BRODIE, THOMAS JEFFERSON 239.
86. *Id.* at 249.

Among the many problems with this approach—for anyone who is at all concerned about ascertaining the truth—is that "casual notations of expenditures for Sally's clothes" did not "disappear" after Jefferson returned from Paris. For example, in 1796 he recorded in his *Farm Book* that Sally was issued seven yards of linen, seven and three-quarters yards of woolen, one pair of stockings, and one pair of shoes.[87] However, essentially identical entries appear for *all* of the Hemingses at Monticello for that year.[88] Another problem with Brodie's creative speculation is that the ambiguous notations for "charities" and leaving sums of money in drawers appeared in Jefferson's records *years* before he could have become involved with Sally Hemings.[89]

Fawn Brodie notes that Jefferson recorded having once paid Madison and Eston for "100 cabbages"[90]—one of numerous such minor and insignificant transactions Jefferson had with slaves at Monticello that have already been mentioned in this chapter. But far more creative was Professor Gordon-Reed's explanation of the *absence* of any recorded sales between Sally Hemings and Thomas Jefferson:

> One could argue that it is useless to speculate about why Sally Hemings never sold anything to Jefferson and the Randolphs. However, it is important to consider this.... We may sell to our children to teach them the value of money or to parents, siblings, and friends to maintain the integrity of those relationships. We do not usually sell to our spouses or to those who are the equivalent of spouses, because that is like selling to oneself.[91]

Freud reminds us that "sometimes a cigar is just a cigar." In that spirit, is it just possible that Sally was never recorded as having sold cabbages to the Jeffersons because she did not *grow* any extra cabbages?

Despite the impressive creativity of scholars like Fawn Brodie and Annette Gordon-Reed, the reality is that neither Sally Hemings nor any of her children received any "special privileges" beyond those normally accorded to other descendants of Betty Hemings. Indeed, among the Hemings family, Sally and her children appear to have ranked no higher than "average." In terms of their importance at Monticello and their treatment by the President, they were far below such relatives as James and Robert[92] Hemings or Burwell Colbert.[93]

Madison Hemings is alleged to have made this very point in the *Pike County Republican* article discussed in Chapter Four. He said of his alleged "father" Thomas Jefferson: "He was not in the habit of showing partiality or fatherly affection to us children. We were the only children of his by a slave woman. He was affectionate toward his white grandchildren, of whom he had fourteen...."[94] Pulitzer Prize–winning historian Gordon Wood adds that Jefferson treated Sally's children "with remarkable coldness and detachment."[95]

One might respond that his behavior towards Sally's children was "remarkable" only if one *assumes* that they were, in fact, also *his* children. If they were not, one would not

---

87. The Garden and Farm Books of Thomas Jefferson 286.

88. *Id.*

89. Gordon-Reed, Thomas Jefferson and Sally Hemings 193.

90. Brodie, Thomas Jefferson 438.

91. Gordon-Reed, Thomas Jefferson and Sally Hemings 194.

92. Robert Hemings, who was manumitted by Jefferson on Christmas Eve, 1794, was so trusted by Jefferson that he was permitted to travel around on his own, and Jefferson often did not even know where he was. *See, e.g.,* 20 The Papers of Thomas Jefferson 330 n.

93. *See* **Figure 7** on page 141.

94. *See* Chapter Four.

95. Sally Hemings and Thomas Jefferson 24.

expect him to treat them differently than he did the children of his other house servants. Returning to the quotation from Professor Gordon-Reed at the start of this chapter — that the "strongest evidence for a relationship between [Thomas] Jefferson and [Sally] Hemings is what happened to Hemings' children"[96] — one might reasonably conclude, in contrast, that Jefferson's treatment of Sally's children is but further evidence for the *absence* of the alleged sexual relationship.

The reality is captured well by Lucia Stanton, who began her career at Monticello as secretary to Resident Director James Bear and, under his apprenticeship, became one of the most knowledgeable authorities on Thomas Jefferson in the world. In her 2000 monograph, *Free Some Day: The African-American Families of Monticello*, she writes: "Madison Hemings maintained that Jefferson 'induced' [Sally] to return with promises of 'extraordinary privileges' and freedom for her children when they reached the age of twenty-one. These 'extraordinary privileges' are not visible in the lists of Jefferson's Farm Book, almost the only source of her subsequent life at Monticello."[97]

---

96. ANNETTE GORDON-REED, THOMAS JEFFERSON AND SALLY HEMINGS 218 (1997).
97. STANTON, FREE SOME DAY 112.

7

The Physical Resemblance of Some of Sally Hemings' Children to Thomas Jefferson

In a commentary accompanying the *Nature* report that Eston Hemings was probably fathered by a Jefferson male, Professors Eric S. Lander and Joseph J. Ellis identified three pieces of historical evidence that they claim point to Thomas Jefferson as the most likely father. The first of these was that "several of the children bore a striking physical resemblance to Jefferson...."[1] This argument was repeatedly emphasized as well in the *Monticello Report*, which said of some of Sally's children: "It was evidently their very light skin and pronounced resemblance to Jefferson that led to local talk of Jefferson's paternity."[2]

In an era when sexual relations between master and slave were often revealed by the arrival of light-skinned offspring, such local gossip would not be surprising. But speculative neighborhood gossip is hardly compelling evidence that Thomas Jefferson was sexually involved with Sally Hemings—especially when one realizes that similar gossip about the presence of "white" slave children at Monticello dates back at least to 1796, at which time it was almost certainly referring to Sally and her siblings, who had been inherited by Jefferson from his father-in-law's estate, rather than to any children Thomas Jefferson might conceivably have fathered by Sally.

Joshua D. Rothman, at the time a doctoral candidate in the University of Virginia Department of History doing his dissertation on race relations in antebellum Virginia, observed in *Sally Hemings and Thomas Jefferson*:

> As early as 1796, a number of French visitors noted evidence of sex across the color line on Jefferson's resident plantation. The Duc de La Rochefoucauld-Liancourt mentioned particularly Mr. Jefferson's slaves who had "neither in their color nor features a single trace of the origin, but they are sons of slave mothers and consequently slaves." The Comte de Volney, also traveling during the summer of 1796, similarly noted slaves at Monticello "as white as I am."[3]

Presumably, the light-skinned slaves in question were the children of Betty Hemings inherited by Thomas Jefferson upon the 1773 death of his father-in-law—including Sally herself. Thus these accounts cannot reasonably be interpreted as evidence of a sexual relationship involving Thomas Jefferson. It is certainly possible that, if Thomas Woodson

---

1. Eric S. Lander & Joseph J. Ellis, "Founding Father," *Nature*, vol. 396, Nov. 5 1998, at 13.

2. Thomas Jefferson Memorial Foundation Research Committee, *Report on Thomas Jefferson and Sally Hemings* at 8 (hereinafter referred to as "*Monticello Report*"). *See also, id.* Appendix F at 1.

3. Joshua D. Rothman, *James Callender and Social Knowledge of Interracial Sex in Antebellum Virginia,* in Sally Hemings and Thomas Jefferson 87 (Jan Ellen Lewis & Peter S. Onuf, eds. 1999).

was, in fact, Sally Hemings' son, he was among those slaves being observed, as he would have been about six years old in 1796. But Dr. Foster's DNA study has ruled out Thomas Jefferson's paternity of Thomas Woodson.[4] Sally's first clearly documented child (Harriet I) was not born until October 5, 1795,[5] and thus was unlikely to have been seen by foreign visitors to Monticello the following year.

Later, Sally Hemings did have several children, some of whom were described as bearing a strong resemblance to Thomas Jefferson. There are no known drawings, paintings, photographs, or other likenesses of Sally Hemings or any of her children,[6] but there is enough descriptive evidence to establish that at least some of her children seemed to some observers to bear a physical resemblance to the President. Ironically, perhaps the strongest statement of this perceived likeness comes not from a revisionist critic but from Thomas Jefferson's own grandson, Thomas Jefferson Randolph, whose explanation of the original rumors was reported by historian Henry S. Randall:

> He [Jefferson's grandson] asked me if I knew how the story of Mr. Jefferson's connection with her [Sally] originated. I told him I did not. "There was a better excuse for it," said he, "than you might think: she had children which resembled Mr. Jefferson so closely that it was plain that they had his blood in their veins." He said in one case the resemblance was so close, that at some distance or in the dusk the slave, dressed in the same way, might have been mistaken for Mr. Jefferson.[7]

Note the qualifications "at some distance" or "in the dusk"—both circumstances that might obscure the ability of observers to see facial details and thus focus attention more on such features as size, build, posture, and perhaps skin tone. "Jeff" Randolph went on to explain that, in his view, the Jefferson "blood" in Sally's children came not from the President, but from Jefferson's nephews Peter and/or Samuel Carr.[8]

Unfortunately, we know little about the specific features of most of Sally Hemings' children, and thus we must rely upon the conclusions of others in this already highly speculative task of assessing resemblances that were perceived two centuries ago. The most commonly remarked upon feature seems to be that some (but not all) of Sally's children were very light skinned—almost white. That is consistent with the theory that Thomas Jefferson was their father, but no more so than if they were fathered by any other Caucasian. Sally Hemings, it should be remembered, was said to be "mighty near white" herself.[9]

The first published allegation that Sally Hemings had a child that resembled Thomas Jefferson came from the pen of James Thomson Callender, the disreputable and embittered journalist who engaged in a personal vendetta against Thomas Jefferson and was discussed in Chapter Three. In the Richmond *Recorder* of September 1, 1802, Callender wrote:

> It is well known that the man whom it delighteth the people to honor, keeps and for many years has kept as his concubine, one of his own slaves. Her name is SALLY. The name of her eldest son is TOM. His features are said to bear a striking although sable resemblance to those of the President himself.[10]

---

4. *See* Chapter One.

5. The Garden and Farm Books of Thomas Jefferson 31 (Robert C. Barron, ed. 1987).

6. James A. Bear, Jr., *The Hemings Family of Monticello*, Virginia Cavalcade, Autumn 1979 at 81.

7. *Letter from Henry S. Randall to James Parton on Jefferson and the "Dusky Sally" Story*, in Milton E. Flower, James Parton: The Father of Modern Biography 236 (1951), included at Appendix E of *Monticello Report*.

8. *Id.*

9. *See* Chapter Two.

10. *The President Again*, Richmond Recorder, Sept. 1, 1802, *reprinted in Monticello Report*, Appendix E.

It is perhaps noteworthy that various other sources, not clearly hostile to Thomas Jefferson, described Thomas Woodson in terms that might support the supposition that Thomas Jefferson could have been his father. One observer in 1840 proclaimed: "I have never found a more intelligent, enterprising, farming family [than Woodson's] in the State of Ohio,"[11] for example; and others noted his "intelligence" and the fact that he was "tall."[12] Such accounts were clearly found persuasive by Professor Fawn Brodie in her conclusion that Jefferson and Hemings conceived Thomas Woodson in Paris at the start of a lengthy love affair.[13] But, again, six separate DNA tests have conclusively ruled out any Jefferson male as the father of Thomas Woodson.[14]

Known Children of Sally Hemings

Sally Hemings' first clearly documented child was born in late 1795 and survived for just two years. No physical description of "Harriet" (sometimes identified as "Harriet I" to distinguish her from an 1801 child also given the name "Harriet") appears to have survived.

On April 1, 1798, Sally gave birth to a son named Beverly Hemings. The only known description of Beverly was that by Ellen Randolph Coolidge, Thomas Jefferson's granddaughter, who said he was "white enough to pass for white."[15] Again, since Sally herself was very light skinned and reportedly ultimately passed for white herself,[16] this description does not suggest that Thomas Jefferson, as opposed to any other Caucasian male, was Beverly's father.

In December 1799, Sally may[17] have had another daughter—possibly named Thenia—but the details are sketchy. This child may have died as an infant, and no physical description is known to have survived.[18]

In May 1801, Sally gave birth to "Harriet II," who lived to adulthood and left Monticello in 1822. The only surviving descriptions of Harriet asserted that she was "white enough to pass for white,"[19] "nearly as white as anybody,"[20] and "very beautiful."[21] Once again, the sketchy descriptions are of little value in establishing her paternity beyond suggesting that her father may well have been a Caucasian. (Neither of Jefferson's daughters by his wife who lived to adulthood was widely described as being physically "beautiful.")

On January 19, 1805, Sally gave birth to Madison—the only one of her children believed to have left behind any kind of written biographical statement.[22] Madison is the

---

11. *Monticello Report*, Appendix H at 6.

12. *Id.*

13. Fawn M. Brodie, Thomas Jefferson: An Intimate History 31 (1974).

14. *See* Chapter One.

15. *Quoted in Monticello Report*, Appendix H at 8.

16. The 1830 Charlottesville census appears to identify Sally Hemings as a white woman. Whether she personally identified herself as a Caucasian at that time is unknown.

17. There seems to be no clear evidence that this was Sally's child, or even that the child was named Thenia. *See* discussion on pages 91–93.

18. *Quoted in Monticello Report*, Appendix H at 10.

19. *Id.* (observation of Ellen Randolph Coolidge).

20. *Id.* (observation of former Monticello overseer Edmund Bacon).

21. *Id.*

22. The statement is attributed to Madison, but appears to have been written by journalist Samuel Wetmore. *See* Chapter Four.

only one of Sally Hemings' known children to have clearly claimed to be the son of Thomas Jefferson, so his case is particularly important. Unfortunately, Madison left behind no known photographs, sketches, or other detailed evidence of his physical appearance. He appears to have been darker in color than some of Sally's other children,[23] and was several inches shorter than his younger brother Eston. The issue of Madison's height illustrates the uncertainty of the evidence in this matter. While Thomas Jefferson was generally said to be 6 feet, 2½ inches tall,[24] the official Albemarle County records gives Madison's height at age twenty-six as 5 feet, 7⅜ inches,[25] a difference of greater than 7 inches. But Madison's biographer—an anti-Jefferson Republican Party activist who is the source of most of what we are told is true about Madison—alleges Madison Hemings was 5 feet, 10 inches tall at age sixty-eight.[26]

Sally Hemings' last known child was born on May 21, 1808, and was named Eston. He is her only child who has been linked by DNA testing to a male Jefferson father, and he may have had the closest physical resemblance to the President. Albemarle County records describe Eston in 1831 as "6 feet one inch high, Bright Mulatto."[27] Ohio journalists described him later as "very slightly colored, of large size"[28] and "of a light bronze color, a little over six feet tall, well proportioned, very erect and dignified"[29]—asserting that "his nearly straight hair showed a tint of auburn, and his face, indistinct suggestion of freckles." (Thomas Jefferson also had auburn hair and freckles.) Eston was also said to be "decidedly intelligent."

There is also a report that two residents of Eston's community in Ohio visited Washington, D.C., in the 1840s (approximated twenty years after Jefferson's death), and upon observing a statue of the late President (see **Figure 9** on the next page) remarked that it reminded them of Eston Hemings.[30] There is no suggestion that either man had ever actually seen Thomas Jefferson, and the *Monticello Report* asserts that "local rumors" in Ohio at the time alleged Eston was Jefferson's son.[31] The alleged observers may also have been influenced by the fact that the statue in question was made of bronze, which was the term used to describe the color of Eston Hemings' skin.

We do not have a specific date for this incident, but it was later reportedly mentioned to Eston—who had moved away from Ohio in 1852 at the age of forty-four—and the statue had been moved from the Capitol to in front of the White House five years earlier.

---

23. Official Albemarle County records described him in 1831 as having a "light complexion" (*Monticello Report*, Appendix H at 12). Unlike some of Sally's children, Madison appears not to have endeavored to live as a white person. Whether this was merely a consequence of personal preference or was influenced by his skin color is not known.

24. This was the description provided by his grandson in 3 HENRY S. RANDALL, THE LIFE OF THOMAS JEFFERSON 675 (1858).

25. Quoted in *Monticello Report*, Appendix H at 12.

26. *Id. See also* Chapter Four.

27. *Quoted in Monticello Report*, Appendix H at 13. Cynthia Burton informs me that, two years later, in an 1833 Special Census of Free Blacks in Charlottesville, "Eston Hemonds" was listed as "negro" and not "mulatto" as reported in the *Monticello Report* (*id.* at 16). I have not checked this, but mention it in case others wish to do so.

28. CHILLICOTHE LEADER, Jan. 26, 1887, *quoted in Monticello Report*, Appendix H at 15.

29. DAILY SCIOTO GAZETTE, Aug 1, 1902, *quoted in Monticello Report*, Appendix H at 15.

30. *Id., quoted in* ANNETTE GORDON-REED, THOMAS JEFFERSON AND SALLY HEMINGS: AN AMERICAN CONTROVERSY 15 (1997).

31. *Monticello Report*, Appendix F at 6.

Figure 9. Statue of Thomas Jefferson in Washington, D.C., said to resemble Eston Hemings.

Thus, they were presumably comparing the statue to an Eston Hemings in his late thirties or early forties.[32]

French sculptor Pierre-Jean David D'Anger had never personally seen Thomas Jefferson and made the statue in question entirely on the basis of a painting belonging to Lafayette that had been made in 1821 — shortly before Jefferson's seventy-eighth birthday.[33] Thus, the Ohio visitors to Washington, D.C., were drawing a comparison between Eston Hemings and a statue of a man nearly twice Eston's age made by a sculptor who had never set eyes on his subject.

Making an accurate, three-dimensional statue from a single, two-dimensional painting is no easy task, and several people who had known Thomas Jefferson complained that the statue was not a good likeness.[34] The statue had been commissioned six years after Jefferson's death by an independently wealthy American naval officer named Uriah Phillips Levy, who admired Jefferson greatly and offered the statue as a gift to Congress. Several

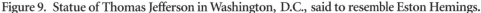

32. It is also possible that the observers saw the statue before it was moved to the more prominent location on Pennsylvania Avenue; but that would have made Eston even younger and a meaningful comparison all the more difficult.

33. THE LIFE PORTRAITS OF THOMAS JEFFERSON 76–77 (1987).

34. MELVIN I. UROFSKY, THE LEVY FAMILY AND MONTICELLO 1834–1923 at 54 (2001); and MARC LEEPSON, SAVING MONTICELLO 63 (2001).

legislators complained that it was not a good likeness of the former President, but Congress ultimately chose to accept the gift. Beginning in 1847, the statue stood in front of the White House, where it was presumably observed by the two Ohioans. At minimum, both Eston and the statue were tall and bronze.

There were other slaves at Monticello who were described as being tall and intelligent,[35] but who were not even arguably Thomas Jefferson's children. However, even Jefferson's grandson, while vigorously denying the President's paternity of any of Sally's children, reportedly admitted that it was clear that some of Sally's children had Jefferson blood in their veins.

Modern science has proven him right, as we now know from DNA testing that Eston Hemings was probably fathered by a member of the Jefferson family or by some other male carrying the Jefferson DNA marker. Whether that father was President Thomas Jefferson, or his brother Randolph, one of Randolph's sons, or perhaps even a paternal cousin, *any* of them would have passed on genetic material that could easily explain the perceived physical resemblance. Similarly, Thomas Jefferson's nephews Peter and Samuel Carr — sons of his sister Martha — would have carried sufficient "Jefferson" genetic material to possibly produce children bearing a likeness to the President; and they remain serious candidates for the paternity of any of Sally's older children.

Before closing this discussion, perhaps another comment is in order about the alarming practice of advocates of the Jefferson-Hemings story trying to present the lack of information on an issue as "evidence" of something beyond the reality that we simply *do not know* a great deal of information after the passage of nearly two centuries. On page 217 of *Thomas Jefferson and Sally Hemings*, Professor Gordon-Reed notes Thomas Jefferson Randolph's comment that Sally's children obviously had Thomas Jefferson's "blood" in their veins. From this, Professor Gordon-Reed asserts:

> A declaration from a close Jefferson relative saying that it was obvious that Jefferson's "blood ran in [the] veins" of Sally Hemings's children and that one child could be mistaken for Jefferson must be regarded as strong evidence indeed. Declarations against interest are regarded as having a high degree of credibility....

> Randolph's statements on the resemblance effectively narrowed the universe of white men who could have fathered Hemings's children from that of any white man who visited Monticello during the years that Sally Hemings was giving birth. Had Randolph never said that the children looked so much like Jefferson, those who wanted to absolve Jefferson of responsibility could say ... that the father could have been any one of hundreds of visitors to Monticello. *Randolph's assertions brought the possible fathers down to three men: Thomas Jefferson, Peter Carr, or Samuel Carr.*[36]

As a factual matter, Professor Gordon-Reed's conclusion that Jeff Randolph's comment brought "the possible fathers down to three" is simply not true. It entirely ignores the possibility, for example, that Randolph Jefferson or one of his five sons could have fathered one or more of Sally's children. Each of them would have carried "Jefferson's blood" in his veins. Indeed, one of the many serious shortcomings in Professor Gordon-Reed's highly praised volume is her *total disregard* of Randolph and his family in the first edition of her book. Although she lists in her bibliography Bernard Mayo's *Thomas Jefferson and His Unknown Brother Randolph*[37] — and thus was presumably aware of the existence

---

35. *See, e.g.*, Jefferson at Monticello 23.
36. Gordon-Reed, Thomas Jefferson and Sally Hemings 217 (1997) (emphasis added).
37. *Id.* at 278.

of Randolph Jefferson — she excludes Randolph and his family from her genealogical table of "The Jeffersons and Randolphs (Relevant Connections Only),"[38] as well as from the nearly fifty entries in *Appendix A* to her book, entitled "Key to Important Names."[39] Nor are Randolph Jefferson or any of his children referenced in her index.[40]

One does not like to speculate about the motives of others, and in this instance it really does not matter whether the exclusion of six key "suspects" from Professor Gordon-Reed's volume was an error of ignorance, over-enthusiastic advocacy, or oversight. In reality, the list of "possible" fathers who could have produced children with Sally Hemings who had "Jefferson's blood" in their veins numbered *at least twenty-five*,[41] not "three" as Professor Gordon-Reed asserts; and any list of "serious suspects" certainly must include at least five of the six males of the Randolph Jefferson family, who we know were invited to visit Monticello shortly before Sally Hemings conceived Eston — the only child who we know with reasonable certainty carried "Jefferson's blood" in his veins.

Nor do we have any information about the possibility that Thomas Jefferson's paternal grandfather, who matured sexually more than a century before Eston Hemings was conceived, might have produced unknown children in or out of wedlock whose descendants might be candidates for Eston's paternity. What we do know is that there were more than two dozen adult men in Virginia when Eston was conceived who carried the same DNA marker found in one of Eston's descendants, most of them much younger and in better health than the sixty-four-year-old President. There may have been more.

In summary, the reported perceptions of physical resemblance of some of Sally Hemings' children to Thomas Jefferson would seem probative of very little. Not enough information is known about most of her children to draw a serious comparison. Eston was tall (but not as tall as Thomas Jefferson), and the most commonly noted "likeness" of others appears to be their very light skin. Even in the case of Eston, a physical resemblance is readily explained if one assumes that he was the son of any Jefferson male, and that conclusion is strongly reinforced by the DNA tests. The physical resemblance does little to assist us in determining whether that Jefferson male was President Thomas Jefferson, his brother Randolph, one of Randolph's five sons — all of whom were quite likely at Monticello when Eston was conceived — or even President Jefferson's cousin George or one of more than a dozen other Jefferson men who might have paid an unrecorded visit to Monticello at that time.

---

38. *Id.* at xxii.

39. *Id.* at 239–44.

40. *Id.* at 285. Ironically, in one of her numerous attacks on the character of earlier Jefferson historians, Professor Gordon-Reed refers to the practice "of a historian rendering nonexistent some available evidence that hurt his position." *Id.* at 49.

41. *See, e.g., Monticello Report* at 9.

8

Reassessing the Oral Tradition of Sally Hemings' Descendants

The January 2000 report of a Research Committee of the Thomas Jefferson Memorial Foundation said that the "family history of Sally Hemings's descendants, transmitted orally over many generations, states that Hemings and Thomas Jefferson are their ancestors."[1]

Later, in talking with a United Press International journalist on the day in 2001 when the Scholars Commission report was originally released, Monticello President Daniel Jordan emphasized that the foundation "never said that DNA proved it. We said that the science and the history, *especially the oral history,* suggest a high probability that Thomas Jefferson fathered all of Sally Hemings' children."[2]

Before briefly discussing the importance of oral history—including its serious shortcomings as compared with some other sources of historical evidence—it is useful to clarify to what this statement is actually referring. A reader might mistakenly conclude that the foundation's highly acclaimed "Getting Word" project—which has reportedly interviewed more than 100 descendants of Monticello slaves since 1993—has spoken to descendants of all of Sally Hemings' children and consistently been told that they learned as children that they were descendants of President Thomas Jefferson. But that is not even *close* to being an accurate statement.

On the contrary—if one accepts the clear DNA evidence that Thomas Woodson was not Thomas Jefferson's child[3]—the Getting Word project has located descendants of only two of Sally Hemings' known children. They have no "oral history" from descendants of Beverly or Harriet Hemings. Indeed (again, excluding Thomas Woodson), only the descendants of a *single* child of Sally Hemings (Madison) have alleged that they were told that Thomas Jefferson was their direct ancestor prior to the publication of Professor Fawn Brodie's 1974 biography making that allegation.

Once again, it is not my view that Thomas Woodson was not Sally Hemings' child. I neither know nor greatly care about the answer to that question. Reportedly, the most powerful oral history seems to have come from statements by descendants of Thomas Woodson. One need not question the veracity of Thomas Woodson (who obviously had no firsthand knowledge of his own paternity) or any of his descendants to observe that seven or eight generations of very sincere oral tradition are less probative of the paternity issue than Dr. Foster's extensive DNA tests. Whether Thomas Woodson was, or was not, the son of

---

1. Thomas Jefferson Memorial Foundation Research Committee, *Report on Thomas Jefferson and Sally Hemings,* Appendix F, p. 3 (hereinafter cited as "*Monticello Report*").
2. Kurt Samson, *Slave's Children Not Jefferson's,* UPI wire service, COMTEX, Thurs., 12 Apr. 2001, 20:46 ET (emphasis added).
3. *See* Chapter One at pages 62–64.

Sally Hemings, the oral history that he was the son of Thomas Jefferson seems clearly to be in error and thus probative of nothing relative to the current inquiry. Its primary utility at this point may be to emphasize the shortcomings of oral tradition as an historical source.

That Thomas Woodson may honestly have believed and asserted that he was the child of Sally Hemings and Thomas Jefferson is deserving of consideration. But its value as "evidence" is not enhanced simply because numerous generations of descendants from several of his children have retold the story in good faith and embraced it as true. Assuming that they have not at any point intentionally or inadvertently distorted his testimony, the modern "oral history" can be no more probative of the truth than the credibility of his original account. This reality may well be frustrating to families who must rely largely upon such accounts for information about their ancestry, but surely its truth is self-evident.

The Eston Hemings Family Oral Tradition Asserted Thomas Jefferson Was *Not* Eston's Father

Most significantly, the oral history from the four interviewed descendants of Eston Hemings—the only child of Sally Hemings indicated by DNA testing to have almost certainly been fathered by someone carrying the Jefferson DNA marker—is more consistent with a conclusion that Eston was fathered by the President's younger brother Randolph or one of Randolph's five sons.

The oral traditions of Eston Hemings' descendants are explained in this quotation from Julia Westerinen in the book *Jefferson's Children*:

> I was told we were related to Jefferson's uncle; that's what was handed down in the family. I don't know who started that lie.... It was 1975, after Fawn Brodie's *Thomas Jefferson: An Intimate History* came out. My aunt recognized Eston's name from our family tree and she called the author. Fawn did the research, came east and interviewed us, and said, "You're directly descended from Thomas Jefferson, but through this woman named Sally Hemings, who was his slave." So that's when we first found out about it.[4]

Ms. Westerinen made the same point in an interview with *People* magazine in late 1998: "My parents told us we were related to Thomas Jefferson's uncle, which made us cousins removed several times."[5]

Now, it is clear that Eston could not have been fathered by either of Thomas Jefferson's paternal uncles, as both had been dead for several decades when Eston was conceived. But there was a frequent Jefferson visitor to Monticello who was known as "Uncle" and who thus would seem to be a prime suspect when one considers both the DNA tests and the oral history of Eston's family. For example, in a January 30, 1800, letter to her father, Martha Jefferson Randolph referred to the President's brother as "Uncle Randolph,"[6] and

---

4. SHANNON LANIER & JANE FELDMAN, JEFFERSON'S CHILDREN: THE STORY OF ONE AMERICAN FAMILY 56 (2000).

5. Patrick Rogers, Glenn Garelik & Amanda Crawford, *Out of the Past: All Tom's Children—A President's Presumed Affair With a Slave Gives New Meaning to the Term Jeffersonian*, PEOPLE, Nov. 23, 1998, at 77.

6. THE FAMILY LETTERS OF THOMAS JEFFERSON 182 (Edwin Morris Betts & James Adam Bear, Jr. eds. 1966).

about four months before Eston was conceived, Thomas Jefferson received a letter from his granddaughter, Ellen Randolph, written from her family's nearby home at Edgehill, which noted: "Uncle Randolph Jefferson is with us...."[7]

It thus appears that the oral history concerning Eston's paternity is in error. He was not fathered by an uncle of Thomas Jefferson. One of the few things that we know with reasonable certainty about Sally Hemings is that she spent at least part of her life serving Martha and Maria, Thomas Jefferson's two daughters who survived to adulthood. To Maria (who had passed away prior to Eston's birth) and to Martha, Thomas Jefferson's brother was "Uncle Randolph." Professor Brodie reminds us that Madison and Eston would "have remembered no years without Martha Randolph in total charge"[8] at Monticello.

Randolph was also known as "Uncle Randolph" by Thomas Jefferson's grandchildren, and it would seem reasonable that Sally Hemings would also have identified him by this relationship. The DNA tests tell us that Randolph Jefferson was one of at least two dozen men, in addition to President Thomas Jefferson, who were equally as likely (considering only the DNA evidence) to have fathered Eston Hemings.

We also have reliable testimony by former slave Isaac Jefferson that Randolph was fond of spending his evenings at Monticello playing his fiddle with the slaves and dancing "half the night."[9] We have the oral history of Eston's family asserting that his father was a Jefferson "uncle." We have a letter from Thomas Jefferson, dated August 12, 1807, inviting Randolph to visit Monticello—and this was about a week before the start of the three-week window during which it is estimated that Sally conceived Eston. None of this, of course, *proves* that Randolph was Eston's father; but, to the extent it is of value, the Eston Hemings family oral history obviously supports Randolph's paternity far more than it does Thomas Jefferson's. (It also shows, as discussed in other chapters, that Professor Gordon-Reed and others should have considered Randolph Jefferson in their studies.)

Of course, if one assumes that Professor Brodie was correct in her conclusion that Eston was, in fact, the son of Thomas Jefferson, then perhaps she performed a valuable service by so informing Eston's descendants. But in so doing, she obviously corrupted the oral history process. Descendants of Eston Hemings who now proudly tell their children they are related to President Jefferson are not passing on eight generations of family "oral tradition," but rather the far more recent conclusions of an unrelated Caucasian historian. This does not make their story *wrong*, but it should exclude it from consideration as legitimate Hemings family "oral history." If their "source" is Professor Brodie, we should focus our inquiry on her scholarship.

We are now told that the oral history of Eston Hemings' family was corrupted on a previous occasion, about a century ago, when white descendants decided to conceal their connection to a black slave woman. As recounted in the *Monticello Report*:

> For Eston Hemings Jefferson's descendants, the story of connection to Thomas Jefferson also remained alive, altered to protect their passing into the white world. They heard that they were descended from Jefferson's uncle, and Eston Hemings's name and the places the family had resided were changed, in order to sever their connection with Sally Hemings and African Americans.[10]

---

7. *Id.* at 343. As with so many other things, I am indebted to Cynthia Burton for bringing these letters to my attention.

8. BRODIE, THOMAS JEFFERSON 440.

9. *See* Chapter Ten.

10. *Monticello Report*, Appendix G.

Two questions about this story come readily to mind:

- First, one has to wonder why it was necessary to delete the name of the famous Thomas Jefferson in order to preserve a heritage of racial purity.[11] Thomas Jefferson was not black, and excluding his name would be a rather drastic approach to "purifying" family genealogy. A far simpler and less speculative explanation for the original oral history would be that the story was *true*—that Eston Hemings was the son of a Jefferson family "uncle" who visited Monticello. And that explanation is far easier to reconcile with what we know about Thomas and Randolph Jefferson.

- Second, and perhaps more important, one has to wonder how this century-old corruption of the family's oral history would suddenly come to light now? There is abundant testimony on the public record from Eston's descendants claiming the family history was "corrected" following a visit by Fawn Brodie in the mid-1970s. If the oral history prior to that time had included information about the earlier modification ("Honey, now that you are about to graduate from high school I want to tell you something important; you are the great, great granddaughter of Thomas Jefferson—except you are to tell your children it was his uncle ..."), they would not have *believed* the "uncle" story before Fawn Brodie came calling to "correct" the record. This new allegation about an earlier corruption seems clearly to be someone's creative speculation in an attempt to discredit the oral history of Eston's family in order to strengthen their post-DNA claim to be descendants of President Jefferson. It serves as an excellent example of the weakness of oral traditions, as at any time as the story is passed down to a new generation it can be altered as the storyteller wishes.

Later, in response to one of my questions, Monticello historian Lucia Stanton endeavored to clarify the belief that the Eston Hemings oral history was modified prior to Professor Brodie's involvement. In early December, 2000, she wrote:

> Subsequent to the Report, we have learned that the oral history of Eston Hemings's descendants was "altered" about sixty, rather than a hundred, years ago. Note that when Eston's son Beverly Jefferson died in 1908, he was described in a newspaper as the grandson of Thomas Jefferson. In the 1940s Eston Hemings's great-grandsons created a family tree that included descent from Thomas Jefferson's uncle and completely omitted the Ohio portion of their ancestors' lives. We think it is significant that this family passed on the story of descent from Thomas Jefferson for over a century, at probable risk to their lives as "passing" members of the white community (it would not have been hard for someone to learn that Jefferson had no surviving sons by his wife, Martha).

Candidly, the reason I had asked her to explain the basis of the allegation that the family history had been "altered" was that I suspected it might have been supposition based upon the fact that a friend of one of Eston's sons had written to a newspaper following his death that Eston was Thomas Jefferson's son. Is "oral history" regarded as so inherently suspect that a single letter to the editor, by an unknown writer who is not a family member and who provides not the slightest reason to explain the basis of his assertion, is automatically considered superior authority? One can only imagine the reaction of Hemings descendants

---

11. The argument on the other side would be that even a slight risk of being discovered to have African-American ancestry would be so upsetting to the white Hemings that they could not chance acknowledging their relationship to the famous President. While this strikes us as silly today, we cannot rule it out as a possibility. But it is in this instance clearly a supposition, in a setting where there are reasonable explanations that do not require such creative reasoning.

if someone sought to introduce a comparable document in opposition to their claim. Nor, for that matter, was it relevant to anything that someone might have learned that Martha Jefferson "had no surviving sons." Eston's descendants would have equally been Thomas Jefferson's descendants had they traced their lineage to Martha or Mary.

Might not this 1908 letter to the editor be equally explained in other ways? The allegation that Thomas Jefferson fathered children by Sally Hemings was hardly a great secret. Perhaps Beverly joked about it with one of his friends, or perhaps his friend knew of the rumors from other sources and elected to assert it at the time of Beverly's death to make his deceased friend seem more important. It might be noted that a Madison, Wisconsin, obituary was entitled "*Colonel* Beverly Jefferson, Veteran Hackman."[12] Hemings family genealogist Judith Justus, in her book *Down from the Mountain: The Oral History of the Hemings Family*, asserts that military records reveal that Beverly Jefferson spent only three months in the Army after enlisting during the Civil War.[13] Without explanation, she concludes that the word "Colonel" was likely a "courtesy" title; but in the absence of evidence to the contrary it might also suggest that Beverly Jefferson had embellished his background to impress his associates — perhaps telling some he was a former colonel in the Army and also the grandson of Thomas Jefferson.[14] We have no way of knowing whether this is true, or not. The point is, there are many very simple and credible explanations for the letter to the editor without having to dismiss the Eston Hemings / Jefferson family (pre-Brodie) oral history; but, of course, in this instance that history is an *impediment* to the claim that Eston was Thomas Jefferson's son.

One really need not resolve this dilemma, as alleged "oral history" that has clearly been corrupted once (by Professor Brodie), and possibly twice, is entitled to little weight. Further, the only way this history would be meaningful as evidence would be if Eston himself had been part of the chain. The fact that Eston does not appear to have ever clearly asserted[15] that Thomas Jefferson was his father increases the risk that, if Beverly Jefferson or his family really did believe he was Thomas Jefferson's grandson, the story might have entered the family traditions as an indirect result of someone having read the widely publicized articles of James T. Callender (or perhaps the account attributed to Madison Hemings[16]) and accepted them as true.

As already noted, Eston Hemings could not have been fathered by Thomas Jefferson's "uncle." Thomas Jefferson's only paternal uncles, Thomas and Field Jefferson, died re-

---

12. *Colonel Beverly Jefferson, Veteran Hackman,* MADISON DEMOCRAT, Nov. 12, 1908 (emphasis added).

13. JUDITH P. JUSTUS, DOWN FROM THE MOUNTAIN 93 (1991). *See also, id.* at 101.

14. One colleague who has examined this issue more thoroughly than I have has observed that Beverly's older brother served as a colonel during the Civil War (*Obituary of Col. John W. Jefferson,* MADISON DEMOCRAT, June 14, 1892) and his brother-in-law was a captain. She speculates that, "like his Uncle Madison," Beverly Jefferson "may have felt inferior to the rest of his family" and thus embellished his record. That is as plausible as much of the speculation circulating as fact in this dispute (although Beverly seems to have been genuinely successful in his life), but speculation is no substitute for facts. All we really seem to know here is that Beverly was not a colonel, but some people called him "Colonel" and at least one of his friends — of whose veracity we know absolutely nothing — claimed that Beverly was also the grandson of Thomas Jefferson. This is at best third- or fourth-degree hearsay involving sources of unknown veracity.

15. There is a great risk in suggesting that someone "never said" something. All we can reasonably say is that there does not appear to be any clear surviving record of such a statement, despite the fact that Eston was asked about the rumor and had decades in which to make such a claim.

16. This is discussed in Chapter Four. If the story came from Madison, that does not make it false; but it does mean that it is no more reliable that Madison's original story, despite the number of times it may have been repeated by Eston's descendants.

spectively in 1723 and 1765, and the DNA tests have ruled out paternity by a maternal uncle. Eston was not conceived until 1807. However, in keeping with the highly speculative spirit of this inquiry by advocates of Thomas Jefferson's paternity, it is easy to imagine ways in which such an oral history story *might* have been started. For example:

- President Jefferson's brother Randolph was the paternal uncle of daughters Martha and Maria Jefferson, and thus was referred to as "Uncle Randolph" when he visited Monticello. It is not difficult to conceive how Eston might have been told that "Uncle Randolph" was his father. As the story was passed from generation to generation, with many years sometimes passing between each retelling, it would not be surprising for someone to forget the name Randolph and to recount only that Eston was the son of "Thomas Jefferson's uncle."[17]

- Another possible explanation is that Eston was the son of Uncle Randolph's third son, Peter Field Jefferson,[18] who was sometimes known as "Field" and is thought to have been about 21 or 22 years old at the time of Eston's conception. He presumably would have accompanied the rest of his family to visit Monticello about the time Eston was conceived. (As already mentioned, we know Randolph was invited to visit about that time.[19]) This third son of Randolph shared the name *Field* with Thomas Jefferson's youngest uncle, who died decades before Eston was conceived. Over several generations, the word might have been passed down that "Field Jefferson" was Eston's father. At some point, a curious descendant may have decided to do some genealogical research and discovered that "Field Jefferson" was Thomas Jefferson's uncle, and may then have confused two individuals having the same name.

There is not the *slightest* bit of direct evidence to support either of these hypotheses, which places them in the same category with most of the other speculation that has driven "scholarship" on this topic in the absence of reliable historical data. The hypothetical examples *prove* nothing, but they do show how the oral history that Eston Hemings was a descendant of Thomas Jefferson's "uncle" *might* have developed. Similarly, the "or cousin" part of the story[20] might have emerged out of the confusion resulting from someone researching the family genealogy and realizing that both of Thomas Jefferson's uncles died decades before Eston Hemings was conceived—and thus the legend that he was fathered by Jefferson's "uncle" was clearly in error. If Eston's father was not an uncle, they might have speculated, perhaps he was a cousin. Whatever the real explanation, the fact that Eston Hemings' descendants passed down for generations the story that he was *not* the son of Thomas Jefferson is significant. Human nature suggests that people are far more likely to alter or embellish their "family tree" to claim descent from a distinguished individual than to conceal such a relationship.

---

17. Much of the writing of Fawn Brodie, Annette Gordon-Reed, and other revisionists is founded on just this sort of speculation. As with their other hypotheticals, the fact remains that there is no way to confirm that this is in fact an accurate account of what happened.

18. Peter Field Jefferson grew up to become a successful businessman in Scottsville, Virginia, and died in 1861. I vaguely recall seeing a reference somewhere, from a source of unknown reliability, to Randolph Jefferson's "third son" having fathered "colored children" by slaves, but have not been able to find my note. I mention this as a point other scholars may wish to pursue, and not as a fact to be accepted as true. I do not personally view Field as a particularly likely candidate for Eston's paternity.

19. *See also* Chapter Ten.

20. Some descendants of Eston Hemings claim the original family oral history was that Eston was the child of "an uncle or cousin" of President Jefferson.

Although it will not likely be a popular conclusion at Monticello, we might add that the oral history of the twenty-two descendants of Madison Hemings who were interviewed in the "Getting Word" project is also of little value to our inquiry. We know[21] that Madison Hemings claimed that Thomas Jefferson was his father, and thus—unless the oral history adds more details—no benefit is gained by showing that Madison also told his children, they told their children, and so on for generations. If Madison was mistaken about, or intentionally misrepresented, the truth, or if Samuel Wetmore intentionally or inadvertently altered Madison's account, the fact that others repeated this story for generations in good faith adds nothing to the probative value of his original account.

Shortcomings of Oral Traditions

A more general comment may be warranted about the inherent shortcomings of "oral history" (sometimes called "oral tradition" to distinguish it from verbal testimony later taken down from actual *witnesses* to historic events) as evidence—and this obviously applies equally to accounts passed down by white and black families. The reality was captured by Professor Jan Lewis, of Rutgers University   co editor of the volume *Sally Hemings and Thomas Jefferson*, and a true believer that Jefferson fathered Sally's children—in her introduction to a forum on this topic that appeared in the prestigious *William & Mary Quarterly*[22] in January 2000. Discussing a contribution by Monticello's Lucia Stanton, Professor Lewis writes: "Stanton reminds us that oral history is not intrinsically reliable but must be checked against other sources."[23]

The very popular genealogy software "Family Tree Maker," by Broderbund, provides this cautionary note to users evaluating stories passed down through the generations:

Tall Tales

Family tradition is another potential source of erroneous genealogical information. Frequently, such tradition holds that the family is descended from some particularly noteworthy or interesting ancestor, such as a high noble in England or a French Huguenot who fled persecution. In many of these cases, the relationship is fictitious, arising as the family history was passed down and embellished through the generations. In more extreme cases, the family may not have any roots in the supposed ancestor's home country. Similar inaccuracies may also surround the history of the family surname and the deeds of various ancestors.

Once again, using a variety of sources to piece together the family tree is crucial for ensuring accuracy. Although family traditions may serve as useful clues for directing your search, they should not be taken at face value.[24]

---

21. This may be an overstatement, as there is at least some chance that the Wetmore article alleging to represent the views of Madison Hemings did not, in fact, reflect those views. As was discussed in Chapter Four, Wetmore appears to have had a strong political agenda of his own. However, I am prepared to assume, for the moment, that the views represented in the article were based upon statements actually made by Madison Hemings.

22. Jan Lewis, *Thomas Jefferson and Sally Hemings Redux: Introduction*, in 57 WILLIAM & MARY QUARTERLY 121 (Jan. 2000, no. 1).

23. *Id.* at 122.

24. *Genealogical Research Tips, Other Danger Zones*, FAMILY TREE MAKER, (Broderbund software version 6.0, 1999).

In his own autobiography, Thomas Jefferson began by recounting that the "tradition of my father's family was, that their ancestor came to this country from Wales, and from near the mountain of Snowden, the highest in Great Britain." Then, noting that his father married into the Randolph family, he reports: "They trace their pedigree far back in England and Scotland, *to which let every one ascribe the faith and merit he chooses.*"[25]

Writing in *History Now* in 2004, Professor Gordon-Reed—while accusing white historians of racism for having given more weight to statements made to historians by Jefferson's grandchildren than to the 1873 account attributed to Madison Hemings (discussed in Chapter Four)—argued that it was necessary "to subject claims made by masters and those made by slaves or the children of slaves to the same rigorous standards of proof."[26] One cannot quarrel with that statement. But even Professor Gordon-Reed recognizes a difference between "modern-day forms of oral history interviews in which scholars pose questions and record the answers of eyewitnesses to historical events," and what she calls "oral history tradition" in which "stories are passed privately and informally from one generation to another." She adds: "Scholars have been slow to accept oral tradition as historical evidence, for they are aware that stories can be changed or embellished as they pass from one generation to another. This concern that a story told to many people across decades may produce error cannot be lightly dismissed."[27] Yet one of her three "lessons" to be learned from the Jefferson-Hemings story, she tells us, is that "we must not privilege one form of evidence over another."[28]

Does she mean that Madison Hemings' assertion that Thomas Jefferson "had but little taste or care for agricultural pursuits"[29] should be given equal weight to the hundreds of pages of contemporary records to the contrary in Jefferson's own handwriting, or that the "oral traditions" handed down in good faith by descendants of Thomas Woodson should be given equal weight with the six DNA tests of descendants of three of Woodson's sons showing no connection with the Jefferson DNA? To her credit, Professor Gordon-Reed is apparently willing to give the Woodson DNA test results more weight than the oral traditions of his descendants, as she writes:

> What we know of the Woodson link to Jefferson and Hemings comes exclusively from generations of Woodsons, who passionately asserted the truth of their own family tradition. Their claims could not be dismissed out of hand, however, for different branches of the family, who had no contact with one another, had preserved the same account of Woodson's paternity. Once again, DNA testing was determinate: The DNA results that bolstered the Hemings family tradition totally discounted the Woodsons' claim.[30]

In an effort to explain some obvious factual errors in James Callender's accounts of Thomas Jefferson and Sally Hemings, Joshua Rothman writes in *Sally Hemings & Thomas Jefferson:*

---

25. This document is reprinted in various sources, including S. N. RANDOLPH, THE DOMESTIC LIFE OF THOMAS JEFFERSON 18 (1871) (emphasis added).

26. Annette Gordon-Reed, *When the Past Speaks to the Present: A Cautionary Tale about Evidence*, HISTORY Now (Dec. 2004), *available at* http://www.historynow.org/12_2004/print/historian4.html.

27. *Id.*

28. *Id.*

29. [Samuel E. Wetmore], *Life Among the Lowly, Number 1. Madison Hemings,* PIKE COUNTY REPUBLICAN (Waverly, Ohio), Mar. 13, 1873 at 4, reprinted in *Monticello Report*, Appendix E at 27–28.

30. Annette Gordon-Reed, *When the Past Speaks to the Present: A Cautionary Tale about Evidence*, HISTORY Now (Dec. 2004), Appendix E at 27–28.

Most people who knew the story had probably heard it secondhand, at best. Callender's information came to him through at least one other person and more likely through two, three, or four. The more people the story passed through before it got to Callender, the less likely that all of the facts would be correct.[31]

Obviously, this is equally true of family "oral history" or "family tradition" — irrespective of the race of the storytellers. And when the stories are preserved in human memories for years at a time between retellings, the chances of errors obviously increase. Further, there is a natural temptation for each party to the exchange to embellish the family legacy to instill pride and confidence in the next generation.

Historians cannot be held to the same standards of evidence demanded of attorneys in a court of law where people's rights or liberties may hang in the balance, but the rules of evidence are nonetheless relevant to any factual inquiry. The reason "hearsay" evidence is normally excluded from court is that both experience and reason show that it is less reliable than first-person testimony. No attorney would ever consider offering fourth- or fifth-degree hearsay ("I overheard a fellow say that he heard from a guy that a friend of his knew a woman who said she heard ...") to a judge or jury, and yet the oral history we are asked to accept in the Hemings case is sixth- or seventh-degree hearsay at best. One of the many problems with hearsay is that one cannot be certain that one or more people along the chain did not forget, modify, embellish, or otherwise alter the original story.

Consider this account, also in *Sally Hemings & Thomas Jefferson*, from two champions of Hemings family oral history, Lucia Stanton and Dianne Swann-Wright, concerning the oral history of Madison Hemings' youngest daughter, Ellen Wayles Hemings, who married a man said to have "no white blood":

> Some of Ellen's descendants tell an interesting story about the origin of this union: Madison Hemings, old and infirm, arranged this marriage for his last unmarried daughter, joining her, possibly against her will, with a much older man he recognized as able to support her. Ellen and Andrew J. Roberts's marriage record, however, is dated a year after Madison Hemings's death and reveals Roberts to be only five years older than his wife.[32]

Or consider this question: What is one to make of the oral traditions of the descendants of Betty Hemings' eldest daughter, Mary, who allege such things as that Mary was "one of the three colored women by whom Jefferson had children,"[33] and that Jefferson was "unscrupulous in his sexual demands upon colored women?"[34]

In settings where "family tradition" is the only information available, it obviously warrants attention. At minimum, it may lead historians to other and more reliable leads. In some and perhaps many cases it may prove to be generally accurate, but it is seldom the most reliable of evidence.

In the current dispute, on balance, the Hemings family oral tradition supports the conclusion that "Uncle Randolph" Jefferson or one of his sons was the father of Eston Hemings — the only Hemings child shown by DNA testing to have probably been fa-

---

31. Joshua D. Rothman, *James Callender and Social Knowledge of Interracial Sex in Antebellum Virginia,* in SALLY HEMINGS AND THOMAS JEFFERSON 102 (Jan Ellen Lewis & Peter S. Onuf, eds. 1999).

32. Lucia Stanton & Dianne Swann-Wright, *Bonds of Memory,* in *id.* at 171.

33. *Quoted in* Lucia Stanton, *The Other End of the Telescope,* WILLIAM & MARY QUARTERLY 145 (Jan. 2000).

34. *Id.* This quotation is attributed to hearsay evidence provided by a "Charlottesville resident."

thered by a Jefferson. That, in turn, would undermine the theory that Sally Hemings was monogamous or else rule out Thomas Jefferson's paternity of any of her children. This oral tradition evidence is not highly probative, however, and obviously does not rule out the possibility that Thomas Jefferson fathered one or even all of Sally Hemings' children.

There is reportedly compelling oral history from the descendants of Madison Hemings identifying Thomas Jefferson as the father of all of Sally Hemings' children; but the existence of a similar account attributed to Madison himself in 1873 makes it unnecessary to rely upon subsequent family traditions. One might think that if the descendants of Madison Hemings were truly anxious to find the truth, they might cooperate in an effort to obtain DNA from the gravesite of Madison's son William. But, thus far, that is reportedly not the case. Candidly, there are ethical considerations that also ought to be taken into account before disturbing a gravesite to satisfy historical curiosity.

* * *

Months after this chapter was drafted, another bizarre twist surfaced regarding the Eston Hemings "oral history." According to an article in the March 3, 2001, *New York Times,* Julia Jefferson Westerinen is now asserting that her father and his brothers "met in the 40's and decided to kill the story" that they were descendants of Thomas Jefferson.[35] Perhaps this is true. But in November 1998 Julia Jefferson Westerinen repeatedly— including to the *New York Times*[36] and on the Oprah Winfrey Show[37]—alleged that, until Fawn Brodie[38] informed them they were direct descendants of the famous President, her family believed "we were distantly related" to Jefferson through a "nephew" or "uncle." According to Judith Justus' book *Down from the Mountain,* Ms. Westerinen's father, William McGill Jefferson, passed away in 1956 and his two brothers—Carl S. Jefferson, Jr., and Beverly Frederick Jefferson—by 1960.[39]

Presumably, some family member is now prepared to announce that he or she recalls one of these deceased relatives having decades ago disclosed a conspiracy to alter the family tree to conceal the reality of having African-American ancestors. And perhaps that is true.[40] But the simple reality is, it is also possible that this is but a new attempt to enhance the claim to famous ancestry—a claim that has reportedly earned Ms. Westerinen many thousands of dollars on the college lecture circuit. That is one of the most serious problems with having to rely upon oral history as a source of the truth: anyone, at any stage of the process, can embellish or otherwise alter the facts.

---

35. Madison J. Gray, *A Founding Father and His Family Ties,* N.Y. TIMES, Mar. 3, 2001.

36. Dinitia Smith & Nicholas Wade, *DNA Test Finds Evidence of Jefferson Child by Slave,* N.Y. TIMES, Nov. 1, 1998 at 24.

37. Oprah Winfrey Show, Transcript of Nov. 12, 1998, pp. 7, 10–11. (The statement "we thought we were distantly related" prior to the publication of Fawn Brodie's book was made by Ms. Westerinen's son, Art, but Julia Westerinen interjected "Yes" in response to the comment.)

38. For Professor Brodie's account of her role, *see* Fawn Brodie, *Jefferson's Unknown Grandchildren,* AMERICAN HERITAGE, Oct. 1976, at 94–95.

39. JUSTUS, DOWN FROM THE MOUNTAIN 93.

40. Let me stress that I am *not* accusing Ms. Westerinen or any of her relatives of dishonesty. I've never met them. I have absolutely no reason to believe she is not telling the truth to the best of her knowledge. My concern is not about *her* as an individual, but about the changing nature of the story that is being told. The reality is that, at any stage of the process, anyone involved can—honestly or otherwise—conclude that the story they were told was erroneous (or not impressive enough) and alter or embellish it, telling the next generation that the new story has been passed down through many generations.

Thomas Jefferson's "Other" Black Children

If one relies upon claims of oral traditions, the allegations that Thomas Jefferson fathered children by Monticello slaves go far beyond Sally Hemings. Although the 1873 *Pike County Republican* article discussed in Chapter Four attributed to Madison Hemings asserts Madison stated Sally's children "were the only children of his [Jefferson's] by a slave woman,"[41] a 1926 publication entitled *Cincinnati's Colored Citizens* asserts that "'Jos' Fossett was the son of America's President and remained with him at Monticello until he went above to join the great galaxy of other notables."[42]

An article in the *Washington Afro-American* asserted that:

> It was common knowledge that President Thomas Jefferson had a violent love affair with brown-skinned Sally Hemings. A considerable number of the Jefferson slaves were his own children born by various colored girls on his plantation.[43]

The November 1954 issue of *Ebony* magazine included two stories about Jefferson descendants. The primary story states:

> Many reputable historians concede that Jefferson fathered at least five Negro children and possibly more by several comely slave concubines who were great favorites at his Monticello home. Although the great bulk of material written on Jefferson is discreetly silent on this point, numerous authorities hold that the slaves Jefferson freed in his will were his own children. At least three and possibly all five of these slaves—Burwell, Joseph Fossett, John, Madison and Eston Hemings—were sons of the celebrated "Black Sal," a stunningly-attractive slave girl with long pretty hair and milk-white skin.
>
> Perhaps the best-known Negro descendants of Jefferson are the great grandchildren of one of these slaves, Joseph Fossett.... [44]

The second story, entitled "Family Tradition Kept Alive by Some of Descendants," identifies Peter Fossett as Thomas Jefferson's child and discusses the special privileges he received at Monticello.[45]

In July 1993, following Thomas Jefferson's two-hundred-fiftieth birthday, *Ebony* ran a story on the descendants of Jefferson's first alleged son by Sally Hemings, Thomas Woodson, whose oral history appears to be the strongest of any of his alleged slave children. The story recounts the oral history of Virginia attorney Robert H. Cooley III, who told a gathering of Jefferson scholars at the University of Virginia "his story—a story that he and hundreds of African-Americans across the country grew up hearing from their elders." According to *Ebony*:

> The story of the relationship between Jefferson and Sally Hemings ... Cooley informed them ... is fact—fact backed up by almost 200 years of oral history

---

41. [Samuel E. Wetmore], *Life Among the Lowly, Number 1. Madison Hemings,* PIKE COUNTY REPUBLICAN (Waverly, Ohio), Mar. 13, 1873 at 4, reprinted in *Monticello Report,* Appendix E at 27–28.

42. CINCINNATI'S COLORED CITIZENS: HISTORICAL, SOCIOLOGICAL AND BIOGRAPHICAL 180 (Wendell P. Dambey, ed. 1926).

43. *The Vice-President's Colored Wife,* WASHINGTON AFRO-AMERICAN, n.d. (I am in possession of a photocopy of this article that is not dated.)

44. Lerone Bennett, *Thomas Jefferson's Negro Grandchildren,* EBONY, vol. X, no. 1, Nov. 1954 at 78.

45. *Family Tradition Kept Alive by Some of Descendants,* EBONY, Nov. 1954 at 80.

passed down through generation after generation of Jefferson's and Hemings' first-born son, Thomas Woodson.[46]

Ebony provides this testament from another descendant of Thomas Woodson:

> "From the time I was a little boy my family insisted I know my heritage," said [John Q. T.] King, who can still remember his great-aunt Minerva opening the family Bible to the pages of the family tree and explaining that Thomas Woodson—"our family patriarch"—was the first-born son of Jefferson and Hemings.[47]

The Woodsons were featured again in *Ebony* in February 1999, in a story subtitled "Did Jefferson Also Father Children By Sally Hemings' Sister?"[48] Asserting that DNA tests had recently "provided virtual proof-positive that America's third President fathered at least one child by Hemings," the story quotes Woodson descendant John King as saying: "We have always had implicit faith and extreme confidence in the oral history of our family...."[49]

The story notes that "five lines of Thomas Woodson descendants who had been dispersed throughout the world for four generations and had no contact with one another maintained consistent oral accounts of their relationship to Jefferson," and quotes John Q. T. King as saying the oral accounts were not just consistent, "they were almost identical."[50]

Indeed, the Woodson family belief in this story was so strong that they readily volunteered for Dr. Eugene Foster's DNA study to establish their claim. According to *Ebony*: "While the test offers almost certain evidence that Jefferson is the father of Hemings' youngest son, Eston, it did not establish a definite Y chromosome match on Thomas...."[51]

In reality, of course, the Woodson tests not only "did not establish a definite Y chromosome match on Thomas," they established with reasonable certainty that Thomas Jefferson could not have been the father of Thomas Woodson. A subsequent sixth DNA test also revealed no link between descendants of any of three sons of Thomas Woodson and the Jefferson family.

No one questions the sincerity of the Woodson family belief in their illustrious heritage. For generations, the same story was passed down through Woodson families across the land. Similar stories were passed down by at least some lines of the Joe and Peter Fosset families and the family of Madison Hemings. (It is more than a little ironic that the oral history of Eston Hemings, the one Monticello slave who has been connected to a Jefferson father by DNA, apparently did *not* claim direct lineage from *Thomas* Jefferson.) The Woodson experience clearly demonstrates the risks inherent in relying upon "family tradition" or "oral history" as fact.

Other Monticello Slave Accounts Make No Reference to the Alleged Jefferson-Hemings Affair

Concerning the allegation that Thomas Jefferson fathered children by Sally Hemings, no discussion of the stories passed down by the descendants of former Monticello slaves

---

46. Laura B. Randolph, *Thomas Jefferson's Black and White descendants debate his lineage and legacy,* Ebony, July 1993 at 25–26.

47. *Id.* at 26.

48. Laura B. Randolph, *The Thomas Jefferson-Sally Hemings Controversy: Did Jefferson Also Father Children By Sally Hemings' Sister?,* Ebony, Feb. 1999 at 189.

49. *Id.* at 190.

50. *Id.*

51. *Id.*

would be complete without noting the apparent lack of confirmation of the allegation by other Monticello slaves (with the exception of Israel Jefferson, whose alleged statement has already been addressed in Chapter Four).

It is difficult to imagine that Sally Hemings could have carried on a sexual relationship with Thomas Jefferson for decades without the knowledge of others in the slave community. After two centuries, it is not possible to go back and interview slaves at Monticello to ascertain what they knew or believed. Nevertheless, it is of some significance that—with the exception of the 1873 accounts attributed to Madison Hemings and Israel Jefferson—none of the hundreds of slaves who lived at Monticello during all or part of this alleged relationship have left behind any hint of such knowledge. Surely this would have been recognized as significant news, and surely someone would have left a record if the accounts were at all widespread among those living at Monticello.

Isaac Jefferson

Indeed, it is noteworthy that former slave Isaac Jefferson, whose *Memoirs of a Monticello Slave* were taken down by Charles W. Campbell in 1847 and first published in 1951, gave no hint of any such relationship. While the Thomas Jefferson Memorial Foundation staff report attempts to downplay the importance of Isaac's observations by noting that he left Monticello in 1797 (when he was reportedly given to Jefferson's daughter Polly), Isaac claims to have left Monticello in 1822,[52] and former Thomas Jefferson Memorial Foundation Resident Director James A. Bear, Jr., notes that a year after being deeded to Polly, Isaac "apparently joined the family of her sister, Martha Randolph,"[53] who lived at Edgehill after 1800 but returned to Monticello in 1809.[54]

Isaac would have been fourteen years old when Thomas Jefferson and Sally Hemings returned from Paris, and twenty two or twenty three when Harriet I was born. Both during that period, and during the subsequent thirteen-year period beginning in 1809, he would presumably have been cognizant of the major gossip among the slaves and might well have been witness to signs of a decades-long love affair between Sally Hemings and Thomas Jefferson—had such a relationship actually existed. Isaac was the son of perhaps the second most important slave family at Monticello,[55] and his factual account seems far more accurate than either Madison Hemings' or Israel Jefferson's.[56] Although his *Memoirs* are not lengthy, Isaac specifically discusses Sally Hemings and others in her family; but he offers not the slightest corroboration of the allegations made by Madison Hemings and Israel Jefferson nearly a quarter-century later. Like Edmund Bacon, Isaac Jefferson's testimony is unusually credible in this matter, as he is providing, for the most part, eye-witness accounts, and he lacks the obvious bias that one might expect to be present with respect to both the Jefferson and the Hemings descendants. While one might argue that in 1847 an African-American man might be hesitant to even discuss rumors of a sexual

---

52. JEFFERSON AT MONTICELLO 22 (James A. Bear, Jr. ed. 1967).

53. *Id*. at 129 n.89.

54. *Id*. at 123 n.3.

55. *See* Chapter Six.

56. He was, for example, fully aware of Jefferson's love for agriculture and gardening, and of various health problems during his life. *See* JEFFERSON AT MONTICELLO 12, 18, 19, 128 n.73. This is not to say that Isaac made no errors. Several are pointed out by Bear in the footnotes. But his errors are almost always explained by Bear as matters of understandable confusion—such as mistaking wild dogs for wolves (*id*. at 128 n.85) and confusing the names of the children of Jefferson's father and father-in-law (*id*. at 128–29 n.86).

liaison between a white master and one of his slaves, that cannot be the case here because Isaac expressly mentioned the rumors that Sally herself might have been the child of Thomas Jefferson's father-in-law John Wayles.

Peter Fossett

There is also the account of Peter Fossett, the son of Betty Hemings' son Joe Fossett who was freed in Jefferson's will. As a prominent Baptist minister in 1898, Peter Fossett was interviewed by a New York *World* reporter and gave a highly laudatory account of Thomas Jefferson. He emphasized Jefferson's kindness towards his slaves, and since he was being interviewed by a predominantly African-American newspaper, presumably he could have presented Jefferson in an even more favorable light to many readers by asserting that Jefferson took a slave woman as his *de facto* wife after Martha's death. But Peter Fossett made not the slightest suggestion that Thomas Jefferson was sexually involved with Sally Hemings or any other Monticello slave.[57]

---

57. *Once the Slave of Thomas Jefferson: The Rev. Mr. Fossett, of Cincinnati, Recalls the Sage of Monticello — Reminiscences of Jefferson, Lafayette, Madison and Monroe*, THE WORLD (New York), Jan. 30, 1898, at 33.

Miscellaneous Arguments Said to Support Thomas Jefferson's Paternity of Sally Hemings' Children

There are a number of other arguments that have been voiced in support of the conclusion that Thomas Jefferson fathered one or more children by his slave Sally Hemings; and, while none of these are important enough to warrant an extended discussion, it may be useful to address them briefly here.

"Psychohistory" and Jefferson's Use of the Term *Mulatto*

Jefferson scholars had consistently rejected the Callender charges, and the subsequent 1873 allegations of Madison Hemings and Israel Jefferson, as without merit until 1974, when Professor Fawn Brodie published *Thomas Jefferson: An Intimate History*. In an apparent attempt to psychoanalyze Jefferson from a careful reading of his letters, she tells her readers:

> The first evidence that Sally Hemings had become for Jefferson a special preoccupation may be seen in one of the most subtly illuminating of all his writings, the daily journal he kept on a seven-week trip through eastern France, Germany, and Holland in March and April of 1788.... Not normally a diary keeper, he did write an almost daily account of his travels. Anyone who reads with care these twenty-five pages must find it singular that in describing the countryside between these cities he uses the word "mulatto" eight times.[1]

Professor Brodie then goes on to quote each of these usages, and we find that each of them involves the use of "mulatto" to describe the color of "plains" or "hills" or "clay" or "the valley."[2] It is unclear what credential Professor Brodie held in the field of psychiatry, but her background in geology was clearly incomplete. She apparently simply did not understand that "mulatto" was a term-of-art used in the description of soils.

Reviewing the Brodie volume in 1974 for the *New York Review of Books*, historian Garry Wills wrote:

> She [Brodie] offers as "evidence" of his "special preoccupation" with Sally the "singular" fact that he used the word "mulatto" eight times in twenty-five pages

---

1. Fawn Brodie, Thomas Jefferson 229 (1974).
2. *Id.*

of his travel account that spring. But all these references are to the color of the soil, and the OED [*Oxford English Dictionary*] gives that use of the word as peculiarly American and eighteenth-century.... Unfortunately for Ms. Brodie's thesis, he had used "mulatto" in exactly the same way during his tour of southern France, the spring before Sally arrived in Paris. The category already existed in his mind. Ms. Brodie tries to solve this difficulty by stressing, once again, the repetition. In the tour of France, she tells us, Jefferson used the word "mulatto" only once in forty-eight of Boyd's pages as opposed to eight times in the twenty-five pages of his Holland tour.

Well, as usual, Ms. Brodie has her facts wrong, even before she loads them with unsustainable surmise.... For instance: on the seven-week tour of Holland he used the word "red" only seven times; but on the nine-week tour of southern France he used it (or "reddish") *thirty-eight* times. Such a disparity must reflect "special preoccupation" of some sort, according to the Brodie method. Since his daughter had Jefferson's reddish hair and complexion, and he was arranging for her to come join him, the soil descriptions are really covert expressions of an incest drive. How on earth did Brodie miss that "curious" fact?[3]

Opinions of Jefferson's Friends and Neighbors

The January 2000 report of the Thomas Jefferson Memorial Foundation Research Committee asserts that "Several people close to Jefferson or the Monticello community believed he was the father of Sally Hemings's children."[4] The statement is broad enough to be almost certainly true, as far as it goes, but it is less clear that it has sufficient probative value to warrant consideration in a search for the truth. But the *Monticello Report* goes on to expand on this "research finding" by alleging: "Numerous sources document the *prevailing belief* in the neighborhood of Monticello that Jefferson had children by Sally Hemings."[5] As will be seen, there is not the slightest bit of credible evidence to suggest that the "prevailing belief" in the Monticello neighborhood was that Thomas Jefferson was the father of any of Sally Hemings' children.

Furthermore, there is no suggestion that *any* of the people mentioned in the *Monticello Report* claimed or had first-hand knowledge about the identity of the father(s) of Sally Hemings' children. None of them is said to have claimed that they observed Thomas Jefferson and Sally Hemings in any setting that might suggest an intimate relationship, or that either of the principals or anyone else with apparent first-hand knowledge of the truth ever alleged in their presence that Thomas Jefferson was the father. Those who said they "believed" the story were presumably either acknowledging the fact that some slave owners did father children by slaves, commenting more generally about their perception of Thomas Jefferson's character, or perhaps even venting their jealousy or dislike for the highly popular and successful preeminent citizen of the community.

More important, the fact is that most people who actually *knew* Thomas Jefferson, were in a position to evaluate his character from extended personal exposure, and left a

---

3. Garry Wills, *Uncle Thomas's Cabin*, NEW YORK REVIEW OF BOOKS, Apr. 18, 1974 at 27.
4. Thomas Jefferson Memorial Foundation Research Committee, *Report on Thomas Jefferson and Sally Hemings*, January 2000 [hereinafter referred to as *Monticello Report*] at 7.
5. *Id.* (Emphasis added.)

record of their views on the matter, *rejected* the Callender charges. Trying to ascertain whether a person accused of some wrongful or otherwise controversial behavior is guilty by asking people in the neighborhood who were not present and claim no first-hand knowledge of the facts is hardly the most useful technique in a serious search for the truth; but since it is being relied upon by Jefferson's critics it may be useful to emphasize that if this "jury" is limited to those who knew Thomas Jefferson well, their overwhelming verdict was a clear "not guilty." For example:

- All of Thomas Jefferson's relatives who left a record of opinion on the issue emphatically rejected the allegations.

- James Madison, Jefferson's closest friend for many decades, a man of impeccable integrity, and the man Professor Ellis admits "probably knew Jefferson as well as or better than anyone else alive,"[6] dismissed the allegations. Callender had approached Madison during his attempt to extort appointment as the postmaster of Richmond from the President, and he wrote that Madison responded to the Hemings charge by saying "that he had known Mr. Jefferson for the greater part of his life; and that he knew so much about the excellence of his heart, as to make this allegation incredible."[7] This language is unfortunately omitted from the portion of this article reprinted in the *Monticello Report*.[8]

- Edmund Bacon, who was at Monticello day after day for more than fifteen years as Jefferson's overseer and knew all of the participants in the alleged scandal well, dismissed the allegations as untrue.[9]

- David Humphreys, Jefferson's long-term friend and secretary during his service as U.S. minister to France, did not believe the story.[10]

- Jefferson's physician, Dr. Robley Dunglison, "did not believe the story."[11]

- Thomas Paine stayed with Jefferson at Monticello during the controversy and later denounced Callender's charges as falsehoods.[12]

- Jefferson's friend (but for many years, including the time of the Callender charges, a bitter political rival) John Adams, himself a repeated victim of James T. Callender's libels, rejected the story.[13]

- John Quincy Adams, son of John and Abigail and later to serve as America's sixth President, suggested that the Federalists had been compelled to resort to such scandal mongering because the voters had "completely and irrevocably, abandoned and rejected" their political program.[14]

---

6. ELLIS, AMERICAN SPHINX 180.
7. THE RECORDER (Richmond), Sept. 29, 1822.
8. *Monticello Report*, Appendix E at 4. *See also,* JOSEPH ELLIS, AMERICAN SPHINX 180 (1997).
9. JEFFERSON AT MONTICELLO 84, 102, 117 (James A. Bear, Jr., ed., 1967).
10. *Monticello Report*, Appendix F at 4.
11. *Id.*
12. FAWN M. BRODIE, THOMAS JEFFERSON 361 (1974).
13. ELLIS, AMERICAN SPHINX 366 (1997). The *Monticello Report* notes that historian Page Smith interprets Adams' statement as reflecting a belief that the allegations were true. (*Monticello Report*, Appendix F at 4.) This is because Adams added that "Callender and Sally will be remembered as long as Jefferson, as blots in his character. The story of the latter is a natural and almost unavoidable consequence of that foul Contagion in the human Character, Negro Slavery." But these comments pertain not to the truth of the accusations, but rather to Adams' expectation that the Callender charges would be believed by some because it was well known that some slave owners did sexually exploit their female slaves.
14. ELLIS, AMERICAN SPHINX 261.

- Jefferson's long-time political opponent Alexander Hamilton, another Federalist victim of Callender's pen, did not believe the story.[15]

- Even General Light-Horse Harry Lee, a Federalist and political adversary of President Jefferson's in Virginia, said there was "no foundation whatsoever for that story."[16]

Revisionist accounts have made various references to the story being widely accepted in Charlottesville and among Jefferson's friends, but they are short of specifics. Indeed, their "evidence" seems to come down to allegations by Jefferson's critics and recorded statements by three individuals.

John Hartwell Cocke

Indeed, among those individuals alleged to have been "close" to Thomas Jefferson, only a single one is cited in the *Monticello Report* as believing the Callender allegations: General John Hartwell Cocke, who served with Jefferson on the Board of Visitors of the University of Virginia. The *Monticello Report* notes that: "Decades after Jefferson's death, Cocke referred in his diary to the prevalence in Virginia of masters with slave families— 'nor is it to be wondered at, when Mr. Jefferson[']s notorious example is considered.'"[17]

Professor Annette Gordon-Reed similarly relies upon statements from Cocke's diary as evidence that Jefferson fathered children by Sally Hemings, noting that Cocke was "one of the founders and first board members of the University of Virginia," and "not an enemy of Jefferson."[18] This is an accurate statement, as far as it goes, but it does not provide enough information about the proffered "witness" for us to assess seriously the probative value of his testimony.

For example, Sally Hemings' last known child was conceived around August 1807. Thomas Jefferson's first mention of John Hartwell Cocke in his *Memorandum Books* occurred in 1811,[19] and Cocke's name does not even appear in the index to the twenty-volume Thomas Jefferson Memorial Association collection of *The Writings of Thomas Jefferson*.[20] Cocke went off to war in 1812, and resurfaces in the *Memorandum Books* on April 20, 1814, when he sold a horse to the former President.[21] Their collaboration on the University of Virginia did not commence for another three years,[22] nearly a decade after Sally Hemings' last child was conceived.

It is perhaps remotely conceivable[23] that Jefferson spoke openly during the early meetings of the Board of Visitors about a sexual relationship with Sally Hemings, or that he and Sally were openly affectionate or showed signs of some special relationship in the general's presence during gatherings at Monticello. But there is no evidence of this, and had any of it actually occurred, one would expect more specific evidence to exist. A far more likely explanation is that General Cocke heard the rumors and allegations and ei-

---

15. *Id.* at 366.
16. *Monticello Report*, Appendix F at 4.
17. *Id.* at 5.
18. Annette Gordon-Reed, Thomas Jefferson and Sally Hemings 215 (1997).
19. 2 Jefferson's Memorandum Books 1271 (James A. Bear, Jr. & Lucia C. Stanton, eds. 1997).
20. 20 The Writings of Thomas Jefferson 51 (Mem. ed. 1905).
21. 2 Jefferson's Memorandum Books 1299, 1304.
22. Dumas Malone, Jefferson and His Time: The Sage of Monticello 253 (1981).
23. This is no more difficult to accept than much of the "evidence" revisionist scholars ask us to accept, including that Jefferson would have carried on this relationship in settings where his daughters were likely to learn of it.

ther assumed they were true or felt it desirable to record them for some other reason we can only speculate about.

We do know that General Cocke's diary includes other rather negative references to Thomas Jefferson, possibly suggesting a bit of jealousy on his part that the former President had received too much of the credit for their shared enterprise, or just displeasure at Jefferson's greater fame and accomplishments in life. For example, when the Virginia House of Delegates resisted Jefferson's request for more money for his new University, General Cocke—to whom Jefferson had entrusted the business of approaching the legislature for the additional funding—wrote, "The temper of the House ought to be an admonition to the 'Old Sachem' that the State has had enough of his buildings."[24]

Similarly, on September 19, 1836, General Cocke wrote in his diary that he had "commenced taking off Roof of the House to be replaced by a new one to get rid of the evils of flat roofing and spouts and gutters, or in other words to supersede the Jeffersonian by the common sense plan."[25] (In 1820, Cocke had moved into his mansion that had been constructed following Jefferson's recommendations regarding the roof.[26]) While such entries do not suggest that Jefferson and Cocke were "enemies," they also do not suggest the warm friendship and admiration that would make it remarkable for General Cocke to embrace the rumors about Thomas Jefferson and Sally Hemings.

Other contemporary sources suggest that General Cocke's ultimate hostility toward Jefferson may have had political roots. In the spring of 1840, Cocke reportedly told Lucius Manlius Sargent that Jefferson deserved much of the blame for the injuries done to George Washington's reputation in the south.[27] Whatever the degree of his hostility toward Thomas Jefferson and the source or sources of his information, the important observation is that there is no reason to believe that John Hartwell Cocke had first-hand knowledge about any possible sexual relationship between Thomas Jefferson and Sally Hemings.

Furthermore, Cocke's knowledge of Jefferson or Monticello did not come close to that possessed by many of the people who *dismissed* the allegations (such as Madison, Bacon, or family members). General Cocke's cryptic diary entries provide not the slightest hint that these comments were based upon anything more than Callender's allegations or rumor. There is no suggestion that he ever witnessed or overhead anything at Monticello or elsewhere that might have given him some relevant and personal knowledge about the facts in this dispute. Under the circumstances, the probative value of his testimony is limited at best.

In addition to John Hartwell Cocke, the *Monticello Report* correctly notes that, "beyond the circle of family and acquaintances," there were people who believed the story. Thus, they note that, during and after the presidential campaign of 1800, "Federalist newspapers hinted at a relationship between President Jefferson and a slave."[28] If the partisan rantings of Federalist editors—most of whom had probably never come within fifty miles of Monticello—are to be accepted as "evidence" of the truth, then Thomas Jefferson must

24. S. Allen Chambers, Jr., *Of the Best Quality*, Virginia Cavalcade 38, 158–71 (1989). The "Old Sachem" appellation came from fellow University of Virginia board member Joseph Cabell. Malone, The Sage of Monticello 365.

25. Frank E. Grizzard, Jr., *A Young Scholar's Glimpses of the Charlottesville Academy and the University in August 1819*, Magazine of the Albemarle County Historical Society 54, 82 (1996).

26. 2 Jefferson's Memorandum Books 1271 n.96.

27. I am indebted to Ms. Pauli Abeles, who found this information in a manuscript written by Sargent she had borrowed from one of his relatives while she was doing genealogical research on an unrelated issue.

28. *Monticello Report*, Appendix F at 5.

also presumably be found guilty of being "an atheist" and a "French infidel,"[29] to mention but two of their frequent charges against him.

Thomas Gibbons

A similar response applies to the allegations of Jefferson's Federalist opponent Thomas Gibbons, who in an 1802 letter from his home in Georgia confirmed "as correct as truth itself" that Jefferson was the father of Sally Hemings' children (admitting he had never actually seen any of them). This is *almost* as persuasive as interviewing at random a resident of Georgia who had no knowledge of the facts beyond Callender's charges but who was *not* a known political enemy of Thomas Jefferson. Gibbons does not appear to have ever been *near* Monticello, but he had every reason to be resentful of Thomas Jefferson—who was not only the political leader of the Republicans who had thrown the Federalists out of power, but had personally blocked Gibbons' "midnight appointment" as a federal judge by John Adams in the constitutional dispute that led to the famous Supreme Court case of *Marbury v. Madison*.[30]

A reading of the entire Gibbons letter reveals it to be bigoted drivel. He spends several paragraphs denouncing all Virginians (who, *inter alia,* he alleged were "more ignorant of Government and finance than of Theology, if it be possible"), refers to the children of Sally Hemings (he admits he had never seen) as being "flat nosed, thick lipped and Tawney," and then attacked the governor of Virginia ("a Miserable creature").[31] Surely it tells us something that the revisionists are reduced to such authority in trying to make their case.

Elijah P. Fletcher

Next, as more of this alleged "evidence" that the paternity was widely accepted as factual by Jefferson's friends and neighbors, we are offered the testimony of Elijah P. Fletcher, a Vermont schoolteacher who rode through Charlottesville on his way to Lynchburg, Virginia, where he later became the mayor. In the words of the *Monticello Report*: "Passing through Charlottesville, Fletcher talked to members of both political parties, who told 'many anecdotes much to [Jefferson's] disgrace.' He gained the impression that 'the story of Black Sal is no farce—that he cohabits with her and has a number of children by her is a sacred truth.'"[32] Coming from New England, where, according to one source, "half the clergy"[33] engaged in anti-Jefferson attacks during the campaign of 1800, it is not sur-

---

29. S. N. RANDOLPH, THE DOMESTIC LIFE OF THOMAS JEFFERSON 268 (1871).

30. Interestingly, Thomas Gibbons later became the petitioner in another landmark Supreme Court opinion by John Marshall, *Gibbons v. Ogden*, 9 Wheat. (22 U.S.) 1 (1824), concerning the scope of the federal commerce power.

31. *Gibbons to Dayton*, Dec. 20, 1802. The original of this letter is located in the Jonathan Dayton Papers in the William L. Clements Library at the University of Michigan in Ann Arbor.

32. *Monticello Report* Appendix F at 5. *See also, Elijah Fletcher's Account of a Visit to Monticello,* [8 May 1810], 3 PAPERS OF THOMAS JEFFERSON (RETIREMENT SERIES) 610 (J. Jefferson Looney, ed., 2006).

33. RANDOLPH, THE DOMESTIC LIFE OF THOMAS JEFFERSON 269. Professor Dumas Malone quotes the Reverend Azel Bakus as giving a sermon a few days before the 1804 election in which he described Jefferson as "a liar, whoremaster, debaucher, drunkard, gambler" and a man who kept "a wench as his whore, and brings up in his family black females for that purpose." DUMAS MALONE, JEFFERSON THE PRESIDENT: SECOND TERM 378 (1974).

prising that when he entered Charlottesville, Fletcher would have been susceptible to accepting the local gossip as "sacred truth."

But there is, in fact, more to the story. To put this source in a bit more context, it needs to be understood that Fletcher happened to have shared the stage from Washington, D.C., to Charlottesville, with John Kelly—a strong Federalist and one of Thomas Jefferson's most bitter critics in Charlottesville.[34] When they arrived in Charlottesville, Kelly took Fletcher around to speak with other local critics of the former President. Kelly's personal hatred for Jefferson was so great that, upon learning Jefferson was involved in the project, he refused to sell the plot of land on which Jefferson originally wanted to build the University of Virginia, exclaiming, "I will see him at the devil before he shall have it at any price."[35] From Kelly and his anti-Jefferson friends, Fletcher divined his "sacred truth."[36]

Consider these excerpts from a letter Fletcher wrote on May 24, 1811:

> Thursday, May 2nd, I bade my scholars farewell at Ale[xandria] and on Friday morning 3d. entered the stage coach in company with 3 Virginia gentlemen.... We arrived ... at Char[lottesville], a village of about 400 houses, courthouse, and good taverns. Mr. Kelly, the only remaining fellow traveler, left me here, as he resided in town. Gave me a polite invitation to call [and?] spend some time with him....
>
> Wednesday 8th I started again for Monticello. Mr. Kelly, when I got to Char., went with me.... We rode up to the front gate of the door yard, a servant took our horses, Mr. Jefferson appeared at the door. I was introduced to him and shook hands with him very cordially.... [37]

Presumably, Thomas Jefferson did not spend the visit trying to persuade his guests of his own shortcomings. Although Fletcher does not provide the details (beyond disclosing that his tour guide in Charlottesville was "Mr. Kelly"), he does provide a summary of what he "learnt" while visiting Charlottesville:

> I learnt [Jefferson] was but little esteemed by his neighbors. Republicans as well as Federalists in his own County dislike him and tell many anecdotes much to his disgrace. I confess I never had a very exalted opinion of his moral conduct, but from the information I gained of his neighbors who must best know him, I have a much poorer one. The story of black Sal is no farce. That he cohabits with her and has a number of children by her is a sacred truth.... [38]

In context, this is not particularly powerful evidence of the Jefferson-Hemings relationship. Fletcher entered the scene with a low opinion of Jefferson based upon rumors he had accepted as fact in New England. His testimony seems to be little more that hearsay accounts based on the views of John Kelly and Kelly's anti-Jefferson friends. It is again a reflection of the paucity of their case that the revisionists have resorted to proffering such "evidence."

---

34. *Id.* at 34–35.

35. 1 Philip Alexander Bruce, History of the University of Virginia 1819–1919 at 168 (Centennial ed., 1920), available online at: http://etext.virginia.edu/toc/modeng/public/BruHist.html. *See also*, Malone, The Sage of Monticello 255; and Gene Crotty, Th. Jefferson Trivia: The Many Facets of a Fascinating Man 31 (2000).

36. I am indebted to former Monticello guide White McKenzie Wallenborn, who now owns part of the land John Kelly refused to sell for the construction of the university, for bringing this information to my attention.

37. The Letters of Elijah Fletcher 34–36 (Martha von Briesen, ed. 1965).

38. *Id.* at 36.

This is not to deny that Thomas Jefferson had critics in Charlottesville, even among his neighbors. Many highly successful people are resented by some of their neighbors. While the *Monticello Report* cites only John Hartwell Cocke and Israel Jefferson (whose problematic statement was addressed in Chapter Four) in support of its allegation that "[n]umerous sources document the prevailing belief in the neighborhood of Monticello that Jefferson had children by Sally Hemings,"[39] it is not to be doubted that others may have assumed the allegations to be true as well. It was, after all, well known that there were light-skinned slave children at Monticello, and it was also well known that miscegenation between master and slave was not uncommon on Virginia plantations. Add even a small measure of envy and it is easy to see how some in the community might have found much satisfaction in the belief that their more prominent neighbor up on the mountain was less perfect than he appeared.

In reality, Thomas Jefferson was so busy with national and international affairs that he barely *knew* many of his neighbors in Albemarle County. When his sister Anna Scott Jefferson married Hastings Marks in 1788, Jefferson wrote her from his post in Paris: "Though Mr. Marks was long my neighbor, eternal occupations in business prevented my having a particular acquaintance with him, as it prevented me from knowing more of my other neighbors...."[40] A sense of having been ignored by their famous neighbor might contribute further to the normal tendencies of human beings to be envious of those around them who have achieved great prominence, just as the lack of direct knowledge might make them more likely to assume critical facts alleged by others were true.

But it is important to keep such criticism in perspective. There is not the slightest evidence that all or even most of Thomas Jefferson's neighbors were hostile to him or believed the Federalist charges, and indeed his reputation for kindness and generosity to all around him is well established.[41] Professor Gordon-Reed notes that mid-nineteenth-century historian Henry Randall stated that Callender had received information from "Jefferson's neighbors,"[42] adding, "Because those who lived in the neighborhood of Monticello probably were not all members of the Federalist party, it is likely that some of the talk arose out of the human need to gossip...."[43] She seems to be implying that "all" of Jefferson's neighbors told Callender they believed Thomas Jefferson was the father of Sally Hemings' children—a suggestion for which there is not the slightest bit of evidence. Callender was not engaged in a search for the truth; he was looking for ammunition to use to attack Thomas Jefferson. All he needed was a single source to tell him of the existence of mulatto children at Monticello and provide a few details like names, and he was primed to go to work.

We have no public opinion polls from the era to rely upon in assessing the views of Thomas Jefferson's neighbors, and the passage of time precludes such research at this date. However, it is worth noting that when, after visiting Charlottesville and encountering some Jefferson critics, an Episcopal clergyman wrote in the *Episcopal Recorder* (Philadelphia) in 1840 that "Jefferson's character was held in aversion in the neighborhood in which he lived and died,"[44] the statement outraged even the editor of the Charlottesville Whig Party newspaper. (As a leading opponent of the political party Jefferson had founded, he may have wished to make it clear that he and his fellow Whigs were not responsible for the allegations against the popular local hero.[45]) This led to a public meeting on July 18, 1840,

---

39. *Monticello Report* at 7.
40. THE DOMESTIC LIFE OF THOMAS JEFFERSON 135.
41. *See, e.g.,* JEFFERSON AT MONTICELLO 76–76, 80, 97, 111, 113, 117.
42. GORDON-REED, THOMAS JEFFERSON AND SALLY HEMINGS 63.
43. *Id.*
44. *Quoted in* 3 HENRY S. RANDALL, THE LIFE OF THOMAS JEFFERSON 676 (1858).
45. *Id.*

at which the "citizens of Albemarle" adopted a resolution denouncing the article in the *Episcopal Recorder* and disavowing its charges against "their illustrious countryman."[46] In response, the author of the article that occasioned the meeting wrote a letter emphasizing that he was "convinced" that the allegations voiced against Mr. Jefferson "were not true."[47]

Were there people in Albemarle County who alleged that Thomas Jefferson fathered children by Sally Hemings? Of course there were; there were people as far away as Great Britain who alleged that Jefferson "was the father of children by almost all of his numerous gang of female slaves...."[48] Is this serious "evidence" of anything of relevance to this inquiry? Hardly. The fact that such information is even mentioned may primarily serve to remind us of the scarcity of serious evidence in support of Jefferson's paternity. And to allege, as the *Monticello Report* does, that there was a "prevailing belief" in the Monticello neighborhood that Thomas Jefferson fathered children by Sally Hemings is preposterous.

Verdict of the American People

It is sometimes said that we occasionally "miss the forest" by focusing on the trees. The Callender stories were not limited to Virginia, but were spread across America by Jefferson's Federalist political enemies. Callender believed that his efforts would destroy Thomas Jefferson politically, and had the American people believed him that might well have happened.

Indeed, as his first term came to an end, Thomas Jefferson gave serious consideration to retiring to the tranquility of his beautiful Monticello. Among the considerations that led him to run for a second term was his desire to submit his character to the judgment of his fellow citizens, thinking that in so doing he would effectively answer his critics in Europe and around the nation. On July 18, 1804, writing to his friend Philip Mazzei, President Jefferson explained:

> I should have retired at the end of the first four years, but that the immense load of Tory calumnies which have been manufactured respecting me, and have filled the European market, have obliged me to appeal once more to my country for justification. I have no fear but that I shall receive honorable testimony by their verdict on these calumnies. At the end of the next four years I shall certainly retire. Age, inclination, and principle all dictate this.[49]

Thomas Jefferson ran for President three times. In 1796 he lost by a narrow margin (68–71 electoral votes—the popular vote was not recorded) to John Adams. Four years later, Jefferson and Aaron Burr each received 73 electoral votes, Adams received 65, and after thirty-six ballots the House of Representatives broke the tie and elected Thomas Jefferson our third President. Two years later, James Callender unleashed his fury against the President, writing: "I do not believe that at the next election of 1804 Jefferson could obtain two votes on the Eastern side of the Susquehanna; and, I think hardly four votes

---

46. *Id.* at 677.
47. *Id.*
48. Dumas Malone, Jefferson the President: First Term 213 (1970).
49. 11 The Writings of Thomas Jefferson 40 (Mem. Ed. 1903). *Webster* defines "calumny" as "(1) a misrepresentation intended to blacken another's reputation, (2) the act of uttering false charges or misrepresentations maliciously calculated to damage another's reputation."

upon this side of it. He will, therefore, be laid aside."[50] In reality, in the election of 1804 Jefferson defeated Federalist Charles Pinckney by a margin of nearly twelve-to-one (162 electoral votes to 14).

The election of 1804 was not a public opinion poll on the credibility of the Sally Hemings story for American voters. But it was, in part, an opportunity for the American voters to pass judgment on the character and performance of Thomas Jefferson. Callender thought his attacks would finish Jefferson politically, and the election is certainly relevant in assessing the public reaction. If we cannot say with confidence that the landslide of 1804 constituted an explicit rejection of the Callender charges, it is at least clear that the voters did not respond to his attacks as he predicted and that Thomas Jefferson remained a very popular leader.

Why Jefferson Never Publicly Denied the Callender Charges

It is also argued that if Thomas Jefferson had not been sexually involved with Sally Hemings, he could easily have issued a public denial.[51] His silence thus serves to confirm for many revisionists the truth of the allegations. But this analysis overlooks a Jefferson practice of ignoring criticism that predated the Sally Hemings charges—a practice that Professor Ellis attributes to the fact that Jefferson "was by nature thin-skinned and took all criticism personally."[52]

Thomas Paine explained Jefferson's public silence on this and other Callender charges in a different way: "It is, perhaps, a bold sentiment but it is a true one, that a *just man, when attacked, should not defend himself.* His conduct will do it for him, and Time will put his detractors under his feet."[53]

Five years before Callender published his allegations about Jefferson and Sally Hemings, Jefferson wrote to Alexander White:

> So many persons have of late found an interest or a passion gratified by imputing to me sayings and writings which I never said or wrote, or by endeavoring to draw me into newspapers to harass me personally, that I have found it necessary for my quiet & my other pursuits to leave them in full possession of the field, and not to take the trouble of contradicting them in private conversation.[54]

In her 1871 book, *The Domestic Life of Thomas Jefferson,* Sarah N. Randolph (Jefferson's great-granddaughter) explained:

> During the political campaign of the summer of 1800, Jefferson was denounced by many divines—who thought it their duty to preach politics instead of Chris-

---

50. THE REPUBLICAN, Sept. 22, 1804.

51. *See, e.g.,* Fawn M. Brodie, *Of Jefferson and Sally,* Letter to the Editor, N.Y. TIMES, June 13, 1974 ("Jefferson never publicly denied the relationship.").

52. ELLIS, AMERICAN SPHINX 73. Professor Ellis' observation about Jefferson's sensitivity to criticism is certainly accurate. (*See, e.g., Jefferson to Francis Hopkins,* Mar. 13, 1789, *reprinted in* 14 PAPERS OF THOMAS JEFFERSON 651, Julian P. Boyd, ed. 1958.) ("I find the pain of a little censure, even when it is unfounded, is more acute than the pleasure of much praise.")

53. Thomas Paine, *Another Callender—Thomas Turner of Virginia,* 2 COMPLETE WRITINGS OF THOMAS PAINE 988 (Philip S. Foner, ed. 1945).

54. *Jefferson to White,* Sept. 10, 1797, in 8 WORKS OF THOMAS JEFFERSON 341 (Fed. Ed. 1904).

tian charity—as an atheist and a French infidel. These attacks were made upon him by half the clergy of New England, and by a few in other Northern States; in the former section, however, they were most virulent. The common people of the country were told that should he be elected their Bibles would be taken from them.[55]

Jefferson's reaction to these attacks was reflected in private letters he wrote to friends and supporters during the era. For example, in a May 26, 1800, letter to James Monroe, Jefferson stated:

> As to the calumny of Atheism, I am so broken to calumnies of every kind, from every department of government, Executive, Legislative, & Judiciary, & from every minion of theirs holding office or seeking it, that I entirely disregard it, and from Chace it will have less effect than from any other man in the United States. It has been so impossible to contradict all their lies, that I have determined to contradict none; for while I should be engaged with one, they would publish twenty new ones. Thirty years of public life have enabled most of those who read newspapers to judge of one for themselves.[56]

On August 13, 1800, Jefferson wrote to Uriah McGregory of Connecticut. Referring to "the fatherless calumnies ... which no man will affirm on his own knowledge, or ever saw one who would," Jefferson wrote:

> From the moment that a portion of my fellow-citizens looked towards me with a view to one of their highest offices, the floodgates of calumny have been opened upon me; not where I am personally known, where their slanders would be instantly judged and suppressed, from a general sense of their falsehood; but in the remote parts of the Union, where the means of detection are not at hand, and the trouble of an inquiry is greater than would suit the hearers to undertake. I know that I might have filled the courts of the United States with actions for these slanders, and have ruined, perhaps, many persons who are not innocent. But this would be no equivalent to the loss of character. I leave them, therefore, to the reproof of their own consciences. If these do not condemn them, there will yet come a day when the false witness will meet a Judge who had not slept over his slanders.[57]

However, with respect to the charges involving Sally Hemings, Jefferson *did* deny them privately, and most Jefferson scholars[58]—including some who now believe the allegations that he fathered children by Sally Hemings[59]—have acknowledged this.[60] The July 1804 letter to Philip Mazzei appears to be one such denial, but there was another the following year that was far less ambiguous.

Consider the facts. Professor Brodie tells us:

---

55. SARAH N. RANDOLPH, THE DOMESTIC LIFE OF THOMAS JEFFERSON 268–69.

56. *Jefferson to Monroe*, May 26, 1800, in 7 THE WRITINGS OF THOMAS JEFFERSON 447–48 (Paul Leicester Ford, ed. 1896). Ironically, Jefferson tells Monroe in the next line: "I think it essentially just and necessary that Callendar should be substantially defended." This was clearly premised upon his belief that the Alien and Sedition Laws were unconstitutional.

57. *Reprinted in* RANDOLPH, THE DOMESTIC LIFE OF THOMAS JEFFERSON 269; and 10 THE WRITINGS OF THOMAS JEFFERSON 171 (Mem. ed. 1904).

58. MALONE, JEFFERSON THE PRESIDENT: FIRST TERM 216.

59. *See, e.g.,* JOSEPH J. ELLIS, AMERICAN SPHINX 7 (1996).

60. This point is conceded by the report of the Thomas Jefferson Memorial Foundation. *Monticello Report* at 4 ("Most historians interpret Jefferson's statements ... as his denial of all Federalist allegations against him, except for improper advances made forty years earlier to John Walker's wife, Elizabeth. These allegations included the relationship with Sally Hemings.").

The publicity [over the Callender charges] Jefferson hoped was buried surfaced again in 1805, when the *New England Palladium* dragged up all the old charges, saying that Jefferson was "a coward, a calumniator, a plagiarist, a tame, spirit-less animal," a man who had "taken to his bosom a sable damsel," and had "as-saulted the domestic happiness of Mrs. W_____." ... A Virginian named Thomas Turner added to the fires by restating all the old charges in the *Boston Repertory* of May 31, 1805.[61]

There appears to be little information about this "Thomas Turner," the byline used when Callender's old charges were repeated in 1805. Thomas Paine then came to Jefferson's defense, in the process asking "if any body knows him" [Turner], and adding: "Who he is the Lord knows, for his name is not known in the list of patriots."[62]

On July 1, 1805, President Jefferson wrote Navy Secretary Robert Smith a cover letter (see **Figure 10** on the next page) attaching a longer letter sent to Attorney General Levi Lincoln. The Lincoln letter has not been found, but in the cover letter Jefferson wrote: "You will perceive that I plead guilty to one of their [Federalist] charges, that when young and single I offered love to a handsome lady [Elizabeth Walker]. I acknolege [*sic*] its incorrectness. *[I]t is the only one founded in truth among all their allegations against me.*"[63]

Professor Gordon-Reed provides this commentary on Jefferson's denial:

> It was Brodie's position that because Jefferson wrote the letter to Lincoln and Smith to provide satisfaction to John Walker, he would have had no reason to bring up the Sally Hemings charge, for it had nothing to do with that dispute. In addition because Walker and the other individuals who had taken up his cause had made multiple allegations of bad acts on the part of Jefferson in his dealings with the Walkers, Brodie believed that Jefferson's reference to "all their allegations against me" was not clearly a denial of a liaison with Hemings.... If Jefferson wrote the letter as a way of giving John Walker satisfaction, why would he take the opportunity to raise an issue beyond the scope of their dispute in a letter that already must have been galling for him to have to write?[64]

Had the Hemings issue not just resurfaced, there might be some merit to this reasoning. Jefferson was writing to provide satisfaction to the husband of a woman toward whom he had behaved poorly decades earlier, and there was certainly no obligation on his part to address the Callender charges. But he clearly elected to do so. Saying "the allegations that have been made against me are false" might have been ambiguous. In the wake of the revival of the Callender charges concerning Sally Hemings, saying that the Walker incident "is the only one founded in truth among *all their allegations* against me"[65] is not. Jefferson may, of course, have been lying. But he clearly was denying the charges concerning Sally Hemings. This point is conceded by Professor Ellis.[66]

---

61. BRODIE, THOMAS JEFFERSON 374.

62. *Another Callender—Thomas Turner of Virginia*, 2 THE COMPLETE WRITINGS OF THOMAS PAINE 980–81 (Philip S. Foner, ed. 1945).

63. This letter is also reprinted in *Monticello Report*, Appendix E at 6–8 (emphasis added).

64. GORDON REED, THOMAS JEFFERSON AND SALLY HEMINGS 143, 145. In a letter to the editor of the *New York Times*, Professor Brodie asserted: "Though the scandal broke in the Federalist press in 1802, Jefferson never publicly denied the relationship. The letter Malone believes to indicate a private denial actually refers only to charges regarding Mrs. Betsey Walker." Brodie, N.Y. TIMES, June 13, 1974.

65. Emphasis added.

66. ELLIS, AMERICAN SPHINX 7.

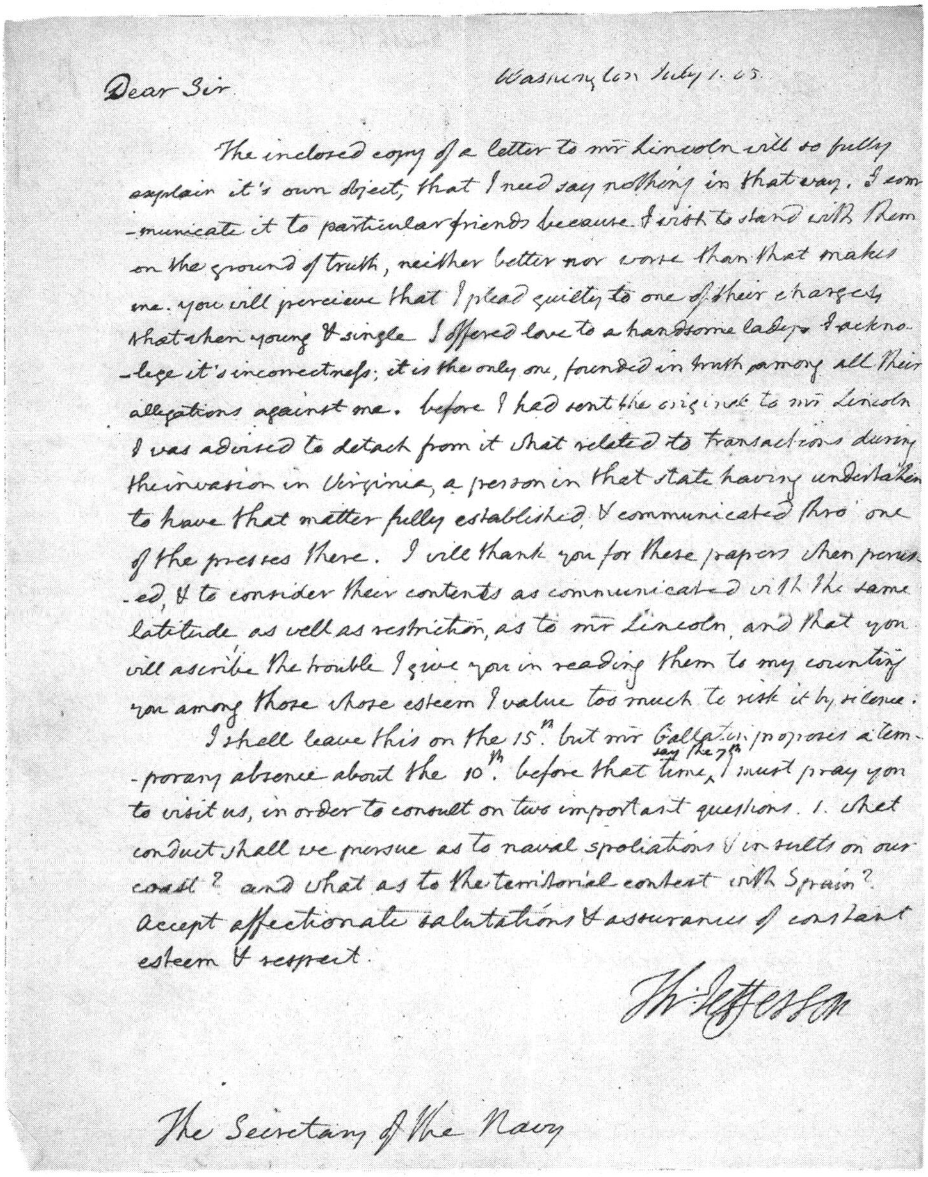

Washington July 1. 05.

Dear Sir

The inclosed copy of a letter to mr Lincoln will so fully explain it's own object, that I need say nothing in that way. I communicate it to particular friends because I wish to stand with them on the ground of truth, neither better nor worse than that makes me. you will percieve that I plead guilty to one of their charges, that when young & single I offered love to a handsome lady. I acknolege it's incorrectness; it is the only one, founded in truth among all their allegations against me. before I had sent the original to mr Lincoln I was advised to detach from it what related to transactions during the invasion in Virginia, a person in that state having undertaken to have that matter fully established, & communicated thro' one of the presses there. I will thank you for these papers when perused, & to consider their contents as communicated with the same latitude as well as restriction, as to mr Lincoln, and that you will ascribe the trouble I give you in reading them to my counting you among those whose esteem I value too much to risk it by silence.

I shall leave this on the 15th but mr Gallatin proposes a temporary absence about the 10th. before that time, say the 7th I must pray you to visit us, in order to consult on two important questions. 1. what conduct shall we pursue as to naval spoliations & insults on our coast? and what as to the territorial contest with Spain? Accept affectionate salutations & assurances of constant esteem & respect.

Th: Jefferson

The Secretary of the Navy

Figure 10. 1805 Letter from President Jefferson to Navy Secretary Robert Smith denying all but one of the Federalist charges against him. Reproduced by permission of The Huntington Library, San Marino, California.

Nor, for that matter, is this Jefferson's only denial of the Callender charges. Writing through the "safe channel"[67] of a hand-carried letter to Robert Livingston in Paris, Jefferson discussed the Callender charges a few weeks after they first surfaced in 1802:

> You will have seen by our newspapers, that with the aid of a lying renegade from republicanism, the federalists have opened all their sluices of calumny. They say we lied them out of power, and openly avow they will do the same by us. But it

---

67. *Jefferson to Robert Livingston*, Oct. 10, 1802, in 10 The Writings of Thomas Jefferson 335 (Mem. ed. 1904).

was not lies or arguments on our part which dethroned them, but their own foolish acts, sedition laws, alien laws, taxes, extravagances and heresies. Porcupine, their friend, wrote them down. Callendar [*sic*], their new recruit, will do the same. Every decent man among them revolts at his filth.... [68]

Two weeks later, Jefferson said of the Federalists in a letter to Attorney General Lincoln:

Their bitterness increases with their desperation. They are trying slanders now which nothing could prompt but a gall which blinds their judgments as well as their consciences. I shall take no other revenge, than, by a steady pursuit of economy and peace, and by the establishment of republican principles in substance and in form, to sink federalism into an abyss from which there shall be no resurrection for it.[69]

Perhaps the greatest of all Jefferson scholars, the late Dumas Malone, summed up Jefferson's response to the Callender charges and provided his own assessment of their veracity:

The obscenity and vulgarity of these extracts, from Callender and others, serve to illustrate the low taste of the journalism of the era, but in our time the pertinent question is whether there was any validity whatever in the tale he told. A trifold answer can be given to this. (1) The charges are suspect in the first place because they issued from the vengeful pen of an unscrupulous man and were promulgated in a spirit of bitter partisanship. (2) They cannot be proved and certain of the alleged facts were obviously erroneous. (3) They are distinctly out of character, being virtually unthinkable in a man of Jefferson's moral standards and habitual conduct. To say this is not to claim that he was a plaster saint and incapable of moral lapses. But his major weaknesses were not of this sort; and while he might have occasionally fallen from grace, as so many men have done so often, it is virtually inconceivable that this fastidious gentleman whose devotion to his dead wife's memory and to the happiness of his daughters and grandchildren bordered on the excessive could have carried on through a period of years a vulgar liaison which his own family could not have failed to detect. It would be as absurd as to charge this consistently temperate man with being, through a long period, a secret drunkard.

He himself said, after his retirement, that he never wished slanders of him by political enemies to be answered by anything but the tenor of his life. "I should have fancied myself half guilty," he said, "had I condescended to put pen to paper in refutation of their falsehoods, or drawn to them respect by any notice from myself." This was nearly always his policy with respect to attacks on his public conduct, and it appears to have been almost invariable in matters that he regarded as strictly private. He ignored attacks on his religion and morals, relying on the good sense of the public and believing that his assailants would defeat their ends by their own excesses.[70]

The internal quotation is from a letter to Dr. George Logan dated June 20, 1816, in which Jefferson also asserted that, "the man who fears no truths has nothing to fear from lies."[71]

---

68. *Id.* at 336.

69. *Jefferson to Levi Lincoln*, Oct. 25, 1802, in 10 THE WRITINGS OF THOMAS JEFFERSON 339. Both this and the Livingston letter are quoted by Brodie, but she dismisses them because Jefferson did not expressly say that Callender's comments about Sally Hemings were lies. BRODIE, THOMAS JEFFERSON 360.

70. MALONE, JEFFERSON THE PRESIDENT: FIRST TERM 214–15.

71. *Jefferson to George Logan*, June 20, 1816, reprinted in 11 Works of Thomas Jefferson 527 n.1 (Paul Leicester Ford ed., Fed. Ed. 1905).

During his own lifetime, Jefferson's strategy of letting his reputation respond to his critics seemed to work. As Professors Lander and Ellis note: "Nor did the scandal affect Jefferson's popularity. He won the 1804 election by a landslide...."[72]

Ohio Census, Rumors, and Newspaper Allegations

The *Monticello Report* also seeks to find "evidence" that Thomas Jefferson was the father of Madison and Eston Hemings (as well as Thomas Woodson) in a series of newspaper articles and a note by an Ohio census taker. Thus, on pages five and six of Appendix F to the *Monticello Report*, we read:

> 1840. Thomas C. Woodson was described in a newspaper as "the son of his master" (*The Colored American*, 31 Oct. 1840).

> 1870. Madison Hemings was described as Jefferson's son by an Ohio census taker (U.S. Census, Ross County, Ohio, 1870).

> 1887 and 1902 recollections. Citizens of Chillicothe, Ohio, recalled that Eston Hemings resembled Jefferson and was reported to be his son.

> 1908. A letter to the editor by a private citizen from Milwaukee on the death of Beverly Jefferson, son of Eston Hemings Jefferson, described him as "a grandson of President Thomas Jefferson" (*Chicago Tribune*, Nov. 1908).

> 1916. Thomas Wesley Woodson was described as the great-grandson of Thomas Jefferson in the *Centennial Encyclopedia of the African Methodist Episcopal Church* (1916).[73]

The probative value of any of this is not readily apparent. We know from Dr. Foster's extensive DNA testing of the Woodson family that Thomas Jefferson could not have been the father of Thomas Woodson (which in turn precludes his being the great-grandfather of any of Woodson's descendants).[74] The census taker was obviously not engaged in paternity testing, but presumably merely recorded the assertion of Madison Hemings, whose claim was voiced in greater detail three years later and has been addressed in Chapter Four. The Callender charges were well publicized, and could easily have accounted for both the "rumors" in Ohio and the reference to Thomas Jefferson in the 1908 letter to the editor. We can speculate at length about how each of these stories *might* have come about,[75] but the relevant point is that there is no suggestion that any of the statements were founded on a serious investigation of, or direct knowledge of, the facts. Such accounts are no more probative of the truth than would be a collection of names of people with no personal knowledge of the facts who, after reading James Callender's 1802

---

72. Eric S. Lander and Joseph J. Ellis, *Founding Father*, NATURE, Nov. 5, 1998 at 13.

73. *Monticello Report*, Appendix F at 5–6.

74. This is obviously technically not fully accurate, as Jefferson could have had a descendant who married into the Woodson family, but there is no reason to suspect such a coincidence.

75. For example, Eston might have told his son Beverly that he was fathered by "Uncle Randolph Jefferson," but—having learned of the Callender charges and Madison Hemings' assertion—Beverly may have, either seriously or as a joke, asserted to a friend that he was "Thomas Jefferson's grandson." Or the friend could have decided to add this "fact" *sua sponte*, to make his deceased friend seem more important. It is even possible that a copy editor at the *Tribune* had heard the story and decided to add the reference. There are numerous possible explanations for how this might have occurred, and it is unlikely we will ever know the correct one.

allegations, reported that they "believed" Thomas Jefferson had fathered children by a slave named "Sally."

Thomas Jefferson as Music Teacher to His Slaves

Professor Gordon-Reed asserts: "The records show that all three of Hemings's sons played the same instrument associated with Thomas Jefferson, the violin."[76] From this, she reasons: "This raises the possibility that Jefferson may have stimulated their interest in the violin, given them their instruments, and provided lessons or taught them himself."[77] Speculation in the total absence of facts may be fun. Since many Monticello slaves played the fiddle, the same reasoning could be used to suggest that someone other than Thomas Jefferson must have written the Declaration of Independence, as Jefferson himself would have been far too busy fathering illegitimate children and then teaching them to play the fiddle, perhaps taking odd jobs to earn enough money to provide them with scores of musical instruments. (Then again, this might help explain his tremendous debt throughout his life.)

If one ventures back to reality for a moment, a major shortcoming in the "violin proof" surfaces. In his 2000 study, *Thomas Jefferson: Musician & Violinist*, Sandor Salgo, Professor of Music, Emeritus, at Stanford University, notes that in September 1786, Thomas Jefferson's ability to play the violin "was devastated by a crippling compound fracture of his right wrist," which "more or less permanently disabled his right wrist...."[78] After consultation with a violinist who was also a physician, Professor Salgo concludes that Jefferson probably "suffered significant discomfort from this injury for the rest of his life," and "had a much-restricted range of motion that almost certainly attenuated performance on his beloved instrument."[79] This injury occurred more than a decade before Sally's sons who would eventually play the violin were even born, and subsequently Thomas Jefferson did not often play his beloved violin.[80]

One need not totally abandon Professor Gordon-Reed's creative speculation. Perhaps it was *Uncle Randolph*, and not the President, who taught *his* (Randolph's) sons Beverly, Madison, and Eston to play the violin—as we know that Randolph was instructed by the same man (Francis Alberti) who taught his better known elder brother to play the instrument, and Randolph was *known* to have been fond of playing his fiddle among Monticello slaves.[81] Such farfetched, speculative arguments are not entitled to serious consideration, as there were many Monticello slaves as well as European craftsmen who might have taught Sally's children. Nor is the assertion that Thomas Jefferson and Eston Hemings each played the same piece of music probative of very much.[82]

---

76. Gordon-Reed, Thomas Jefferson and Sally Hemings 220.

77. *Id.*

78. Sandor Salgo, Thomas Jefferson: Musician & Violinist 29 (2000).

79. *Id.* at 30.

80. Helen Cripe, Thomas Jefferson and Music 27–31 (1974).

81. *See* Chapter Ten. It is, in reality, far more likely that Eston was taught by an older slave (perhaps Beverly?) or one of the European workers than by either Thomas Jefferson or brother Randolph (who died in 1815 when Eston was about seven years old). It is also possible that neither Madison nor Eston took up the violin until they were freed and lived in Charlottesville; we simply do not know.

82. Lucia Stanton, Free Some Day: The African-American Families of Monticello 13, 101 (2000).

Did Jefferson "Train" Sally's Children to Marry Whites?

Also in the "farfetched" category is Professor Gordon-Reed's suggestion that Thomas Jefferson may have trained Sally Hemings' children so that they would be able to marry white partners when they became adults:

> There is a lockstep quality to the progression of Hemings's sons through childhood that suggests that Jefferson singled them out for a particular reason.…
>
> Beverly and Harriet, Hemings's two oldest children, passed for white and married white people. The youngest married a black woman who was white enough to pass for white and, at a later point in life, changed his racial designation. Madison Hemings described the families that his two older siblings married into as being "in good standing," and "in good circumstances." Hemings was not necessarily saying that these families were rich or prominent, but clearly he meant that they were respectable people. The Hemings children's ability to deal with white spouses and in-laws suggests that they may have been prepared as young people to take on this role.[83]

If a Caucasian scholar had suggested that it was inconceivable that a former slave could marry a "respectable" white person without special, life-long training, they would most likely have difficulty finding employment in today's academic community. In addition to being offensive, the paragraph ignores the reality that, as Monticello house slaves, Sally's children would have had considerable exposure to the behavior of "respectable" white people day after day as friends and visitors journeyed to Monticello to experience the company of Thomas Jefferson. Finally, the suggestion that Sally's children were given such personal attention was expressly *denied* in the report attributed to Madison Hemings.[84]

In fairness to Professor Gordon-Reed, her bizarre arguments are often mirrored and even exceeded by Professor Brodie. For example, on page 435 of her book, Brodie quotes Madison Hemings' statement that Beverly married a white woman whose family "were people of good circumstances" and then adds: "All of which suggests that Beverly had schooling along with Jefferson's white grandchildren as well as training as a carpenter, and that he may also have had financial aid."[85]

The Alleged "Closeness" of Sally's Children

In an effort to prove that Sally Hemings was monogamous, the *Monticello Report* says: "Full-sibling relationships are further supported by the closeness of the family, as evidenced by documentation of siblings living together and naming children after each other."[86] One might, for convenience, group with this argument the assertion by Professor Gordon-Reed that both Sally Hemings and her son Madison named their children after Thomas Jefferson's relatives.[87]

---

83. Gordon-Reed, Thomas Jefferson and Sally Hemings 221.
84. *See* Chapter Four.
85. Brodie, Thomas Jefferson 435.
86. *Monticello Report* at 7.
87. Gordon-Reed, Thomas Jefferson and Sally Hemings 211, 220.

Since Cain and Abel, history is replete with examples of siblings who did not get along; and anyone with significant experience with broken homes knows of cases where the bonds of half-siblings equal or even exceed those of the children of more traditional families. For that matter, there is no evidence that Sally Hemings' children would have *known* with any certainty their full biological relationships. I am personally familiar with examples where children live for many years in a family without realizing that an older brother or sister had a different father.

Even if the underlying assumptions behind this argument were correct—that full siblings are more likely to bond closely than children with different fathers—there are serious questions about the alleged "closeness" of Sally Hemings' children. We know *very* little about them, just as we know almost nothing about Sally Hemings. But certainly Madison Hemings' 1873 account does not suggest unusual "closeness" among the Hemings children. As his recollections were reported by the newspaper editor who printed them, he had not had any contact with sister Harriet in ten years, he did not seem to know with certainty whether his brother Beverly was dead or alive, and he did not even seem to know quite when brother Eston had died.[88]

Nor, for that matter, is the choice of names for children very probative of issues of paternity. For example, my own seventeen-year-old son is named "Thomas"—specifically in honor of Thomas Jefferson—but neither he nor I would pretend that this makes him a direct descendant of our third President.

The Absence of Letters and References to Sally and the Great Coverup

There are remarkably few references to Sally or her children in Jefferson's *Farm Book* and *Memorandum Books* as compared with the more important members of her family at Monticello (see **Figure 7** on page 141). But rather than drawing the logical conclusions from this evidence—or, in an important sense, from this *lack* of evidence—Professor Brodie converts it into evidence of the affair. She attributes it to the "necessity for secrecy concerning Jefferson's liaison with Sally Hemings...."[89] Later, she added that the "extent to which Jefferson kept Sally Hemings and her children relatively anonymous in his *Farm Book* would seem to be symbolic of his entire relationship with her."[90] Perhaps. On the other hand, it may instead simply reflect the reality that there was no "relationship" beyond what was typical between Jefferson and any other slave who may have been less rather than more important in the scheme of things at Monticello.

Scholars like Professor Brodie and Gordon-Reed seem particularly frustrated at the lack of references to Sally Hemings in the tens of thousands of letters and other documents Thomas Jefferson left behind. Surely, if she were his true love, he must have written her often; or if she was illiterate he must have written to Martha or Maria and inquired about Sally's welfare or asked to be remembered to her. But the evidence is not there. Thus, there must be a cover up. Professor Gordon-Reed explains:

---

88. *See* Chapter Four.
89. GORDON-REED, THOMAS JEFFERSON AND SALLY HEMINGS 291.
90. *Id.* at 293.

If one considers Jefferson and his family's pattern of writing letters and the relationship that Sally Hemings bore to the Jeffersons, particularly in France, there
is something strange about the scarcity of references to her in their correspondence. It is not as though the Jeffersons did not mention their slaves in letters.
Such references, while not a matter of course, were not infrequent. Jefferson
wrote to those of his slaves who could read, and when the slaves could not read,
he wrote to them through individuals who could.... One might expect that once
during the twenty-six months that Sally Hemings was in France, he would have
let Elizabeth know about her youngest daughter.

The dispute about the meaning of the few references to Sally Hemings in Jefferson's correspondence boils down to what one thinks is most important. Do
actions and circumstances speak louder than words or the lack of words? The known
circumstances of Hemings's life and the Jeffersons' actions toward her and her
family are such that one would assume that, absent some reason not to, she
would have been mentioned more frequently....

Thomas Jefferson's only direct reference to Sally Hemings was in a letter that
he wrote in 1799 to his son-in-law John Wayles Eppes in which he mentioned
that she had given birth. He wrote two other letters that mentioned her indirectly....

The question whether Thomas Jefferson, while in Europe, went seven weeks
without writing a letter to his daughters remains. The notion that some of Jefferson's records from this period or from later periods were deliberately "lost" to
hide possible references to Sally Hemings is speculation that incites curiosity but
sheds little light on the matter. One could understand why it might have been done,
but there is no way to know that it was done.[91]

Might there be simpler explanations why there are no known letters written by Thomas
Jefferson for a brief period of time? Consider this account from William Howard Adams'
The Paris Years of Thomas Jefferson:

Jefferson discovered the "remains of Roman grandeur" at first hand the following winter, on his second and most extensive trip in Europe. The wrist he had
fractured the previous fall had not healed properly, so on February 28, 1787,
following his doctor's advice, he left Paris for the south of France. One object of
the trip, he explained to James Monroe, was "to try the mineral waters there for
the restoration of my hand".... [92]

Professor Brodie adds the following relevant information:

At age seventy-eight Jefferson fell from a broken step leading down from a ter-
race at Monticello and broke his left wrist and arm. As the bones healed this
wrist swelled and stiffened, as had his *right* wrist thirty-four years before. "Crip-
pled wrists and fingers make writing slow and laborious," he wrote to Adams on
October 12, 1823.[93]

---

91. GORDON-REED, THOMAS JEFFERSON AND SALLY HEMINGS 177–79 (1997). As discussed in
Chapter Two, in his 1799 letter to John Wayles Eppes, Jefferson did not refer to Sally by name, and
there is considerable reason to question whether "Maria's maid" at that time was Sally Hemings. See
discussion on pages 91–93.
92. WILLIAM HOWARD ADAMS, THE PARIS YEARS OF THOMAS JEFFERSON 108 (1997).
93. FAWN BRODIE, THOMAS JEFFERSON 459 (emphasis added).

Thomas Jefferson, it may be useful to emphasize, wrote with his right hand.

Using the Absence of Information as Evidence

The allegation that the absence of any letters from Thomas Jefferson to Sally Hemings is evidence of a cover up is but one of many examples of the bizarre efforts by advocates of Jefferson's paternity of Sally's children to use the total absence of information as "proof" of their claim.

To be sure (as Chapter Eleven will demonstrate), the absence of evidence may sometimes be quite probative of material facts. There are settings where circumstances are so likely to produce observable consequences that the absence of any record of those consequences constitutes credible evidence that the precursor activity may not have occurred. If a suspect accused of firing a high-powered rifle out of a window can show that several people in nearby rooms heard no noise, that might be highly significant. It might also be significant that a paraffin test of his hands and face produced no gunpowder residue.

If we seek to ascertain whether Thomas Jefferson injured his writing hand, the absence of any letters written by him during the weeks following the alleged injury may have probative value—at least in the absence of alternative explanations. But in the present case we have example after example where scholars simply "fill in the blanks" to convert innocent information—or lack of information—into incriminating evidence.

An example of this was mentioned in Chapter Two, which noted Professor Brodie's argument that Jefferson once recorded an expenditure of forty francs in 1788 for a "locket" and speculated that perhaps it was a gift for Sally.[94] Then there are the extensive French lessons for Sally's brother James, so that he could communicate with French chefs while learning that trade. There is not the slightest bit of evidence that Sally took French lessons, but Professor Brodie writes: "one could expect that Sally would likely have been included."[95] As was discussed in Chapter Two, while there is almost no record of Sally's activities in Paris, the better view is probably that she did not even live in the same building with James or Thomas Jefferson during most of her stay. She was, after all, the servant to Jefferson's daughters, so one might assume that she would have lived near them at the Abbaye de Panthemont convent. While the *Monticello Report* and other advocates of Jefferson's paternity of Sally Hemings' children find it convenient to assume that Sally must have lived with Jefferson at the Hôtel de Langeac, Monticello's Senior Research Historian, Lucia Stanton, acknowledges that "[I]t was not uncommon for the servants of boarding students to continue to attend their mistresses in the Abbaye," and that "some of the Jefferson sisters' schoolmates knew Sally well enough to send her greetings in their correspondence."[96] Admittedly, there are other possibilities and we know almost nothing about Sally Hemings' life in Paris. But logic would suggest that Martha and Maria would be accompanied by their maid, and there is not the slightest evidence Sally remained with Jefferson. The assumption seems founded entirely upon the presumption that Thomas Jefferson and Sally Hemings had to be together in Paris, away from the daughters, or otherwise how did Sally become pregnant with his son "Tom"? Now that the DNA tests have

---

94. BRODIE, 239.
95. *Id.* at 233.
96. STANTON, FREE SOME DAY 109.

demolished the "Tom" story,[97] it may be time to apply some more rational assumptions to Sally's experience in Paris.

Unlike many of her more important relatives at Monticello, there is no record that Sally received money from Jefferson after returning from France. Convinced that she was the love of his life, Professor Brodie reasoned there must be an explanation. After diligent research, she discovered that Jefferson made many entries in his *Memorandum Books* under the heading "charity," and he wrote of leaving "small money in my drawer at Monticello...."[98] Ignoring the fact that similar notations for "charity" were made by Jefferson long before Sally traveled to Paris,[99] Professor Brodie suggests that these must have been cryptic notations of the money he was actually giving to Sally. Similarly, when the *Memorandum Books* record Christmas gifts being sent for favorite Monticello slaves, but provide no record of gifts for Sally, Professor Brodie explains that the "special gifts" for Sally may have been concealed from his daughter Martha.[100] The idea that the absence of special attention to Sally Hemings might instead simply reflect her relative unimportance at Monticello seems to have eluded the good professor.

Does the Fact that Sally Hemings Apparently Did Not Bear Children by Other Slaves Imply Thomas Jefferson's Misconduct?

It has been suggested during the Scholars Commission deliberations that the fact that, given the reported light skin color of her children, Sally Hemings does not appear to have been sexually involved with black slaves — who might have been expected to take such a handsome woman by force in a plantation setting — is proof that Thomas Jefferson was either reserving her favors for himself or for some other designated individual. Whether he was sexually exploiting her himself, or reserving her for his brother, one of his Carr nephews, or perhaps different men at different times in her life — he nevertheless would be morally culpable for her exploitation.

We have so little reliable factual information about Sally Hemings' life that it is difficult to respond effectively to such an argument. There is considerable evidence that Thomas Jefferson was concerned with the treatment of his slaves, and prohibited rape and other acts of violence within the slave community. But it certainly does not follow that measures Jefferson may have established that had the effect of protecting Sally Hemings from being raped by other slaves are evidence of base motives on the part of the President. Indeed, from what we think we know about Jefferson's character, such a policy would be expected even if not widely enforced on other plantations.

We do know that if Sally Hemings was not sexually involved with other Monticello slaves, such conduct would have been consistent with the apparent behavior of her siblings. As Lucia Stanton has observed: "None of Betty Hemings's twelve children ... mar-

---

97. I am not suggesting that Thomas Woodson was not conceived in Paris by Sally Hemings. That may or may not be true. What has been proven is that his father was someone *other* than Thomas Jefferson. For the purposes of this inquiry, that is the only issue of relevance.

98. BRODIE 249.

99. *See, e.g.,* 1 JEFFERSON'S MEMORANDUM BOOKS 400, 424, 446–47, 494, 498, 506, 510, 512, 529–30, 537, 542, 545–56, 548.

100. BRODIE 249.

ried within the Monticello African-American community."[101] There are reports of re-sentment of the Hemingses by darker-skinned slaves, but it seems clear that it was understood throughout the plantation that the Hemings family was "special." If Sally was not abused by male slaves, that can be explained by something other than the assumption that Thomas Jefferson was "reserving" her for himself or a particular relative.

Related to this is the question (also raised during our deliberations) of whether other men could have had sexual access to Sally Hemings without the knowledge and blessing of Thomas Jefferson. Again, in the absence of evidence after nearly two centuries we can not be sure what he knew. But it is certainly easy to conceive how such a relationship might have gone on without his specific knowledge. Monticello was usually crowded with visitors, and Jefferson's practice of enchanting his guests with after-dinner conversation is well established. His far less cerebral brother, Randolph, is said to have preferred spending his evenings at Monticello playing his fiddle and dancing among the slaves. There is no reason to assume that, while Thomas Jefferson was occupied entertaining visitors, others—be they Randolph, one of his sons, or perhaps one of Jefferson's other nephews from the Carr family—could not have been exploiting the women in the slave quarters. This could have had aspects of mutual affection, violent rape, or simply acquiescence to the inevitable by a slave woman who felt powerless to resist—we just do not know. It may have occurred behind Thomas Jefferson's back or with his general knowledge. Given his well-established opposition to miscegenation[102] and the sexual exploitation of slave women,[103] not to mention his professed belief that slave holders had a moral duty to treat their slaves with dignity,[104] it is difficult to assume that it occurred at Monticello with his blessing. But we will likely never be certain.

French Law Governing Slaves

We also have the issue of the esoteric provision of French law that might have been used by Sally and James to claim freedom—a provision that not even Thomas Jefferson knew about until he researched the matter at the request of an American contemplating visiting France with a slave.[105] The only evidence that Sally or James was aware of this provision is the assertion by Madison Hemings in 1783, and he obviously had no first-hand knowledge of the matter and provides no source for his claim. And yet Professor Brodie writes that "Jefferson had under his roof in Paris two slaves who were learning to speak French, who counted themselves free, and were thinking of becoming expatriates."[106] This is fantasy, not history.

---

101. STANTON, FREE SOME DAY 106.

102. *See, e.g., Jefferson to George Buchanan,* Aug. 30, 1793, 26 PAPERS OF THOMAS JEFFERSON 788 (John Catanzariti, ed. 1995); *Jefferson to Edward Coles,* Aug. 25, 1814, 11 WORKS OF THOMAS JEFFERSON 416 (Fed. ed. 1905); and *Jefferson to William Short,* Jan. 18, 1826, 12 *id.* 434. THOMAS JEFFERSON, NOTES ON VIRGINIA, Query XIV, in 2 WRITINGS OF THOMAS JEFFERSON 201 (Mem. ed. 1903.)

103. THOMAS JEFFERSON, NOTES ON VIRGINIA, Query XVIII, in 2 WRITINGS OF THOMAS JEFFERSON 225–26. ("The whole commerce between master and slave is a perpetual exercise of the most boisterous passions, the most unremitting despotism on the one part, and degrading submissions on the other.... If a parent could find no motive either in his philanthropy or his self-love, for restraining the intemperance of passion towards his slave, it should always be a sufficient one that his child is present.")

104. *Jefferson to Edward Coles*, Aug. 25, 1814, 11 WORKS OF THOMAS JEFFERSON 416.

105. *See* Chapter Four.

106. BRODIE 235.

This is not to say that it is not possible that Sally and James knew of the relevant French law even when Thomas Jefferson did not. They certainly had contact with other servants, and perhaps some of them were cognizant of cases where slaves had achieved their freedom. Like almost everything else about Sally Hemings' life in Paris, we will likely never know the truth.

However, we do know a few things. The right of slaves to obtain freedom in France was not actually codified in French law until after the French Revolution, but there was a customary practice that did result in the freeing of some slaves who were brought to France. However, this was not an automatic process. James and Sally would have had to hire a lawyer and file a lawsuit. That would have cost money, quite possibly more money than either of them possessed.

Anyone who assumes that Sally and/or James could easily have obtained their freedom by walking into a French court must deal with both the problem of Jefferson's diplomatic immunity as America's chief diplomat in France and his obvious influence with the French government. One of the earliest principles of international law was that foreign diplomats are not subject to the jurisdiction of domestic courts in the country to which they are accredited,[107] and an eighteenth century French court might well have hesitated to even entertain a legal case against an important foreign diplomat. It is all the more unlikely that such a judge would have been enthusiastic about interfering with the American minister's household given Jefferson's favored position with the king.

International human rights law is largely a product of the post-UN Charter era, and the general rule in the late eighteenth-century was that how a state treated its own nationals was a matter of internal concern. It was not only improper, but a wrongful act for one state to interfere in the internal affairs of another by complaining about such treatment.

The most important issue is probably not what might have happened had James or Sally actually managed to hire a lawyer and brought suit to gain their freedom, but how confident they would have been that such an effort would be certain to succeed. Their master was a very powerful man, obviously far more influential than either of his slaves within the French government, and it is difficult to imagine that a teenaged Sally Hemings—particularly the frightened, immature child described by Abigail Adams—would elect to challenge Thomas Jefferson's authority even if she had heard rumors that some other slaves had been awarded their freedom by French courts.

Even if Sally Hemings had the sophistication and courage to bring a lawsuit against her master that would leave her free (and alone) in Paris, might she not have been deterred by the realization that her mother and other family members would be totally subject to the whim of the angry Jefferson after he returned home without her? And then there is the question of whether Thomas Jefferson would have continued a sexual relationship with a slave who had once blackmailed him. All things considered, like so much of the rest of the arguments considered in this chapter, the assertion that Sally Hemings compelled Thomas Jefferson to enter into a "treaty" while in Paris is highly unpersuasive.

---

107. The acts of diplomats are viewed as the acts of another sovereign state, and as such are generally immune from the host state's municipal laws and the jurisdiction of its courts.

10

Revisionist Arguments Reconsidered: Evidence Too Quickly Dismissed?

Having in the previous chapters addressed the major affirmative arguments supporting Thomas Jefferson's paternity of one or more children by Sally Hemings, it is now useful to reexamine some of the evidence in Jefferson's defense that was acknowledged, but then largely dismissed, by revisionist[1] historians and the Thomas Jefferson Memorial Foundation Research Committee in reaching their conclusion that Jefferson likely fathered Sally's children.

The Testimony of Edmund Bacon

Consider, for example, the testimony of former Monticello overseer Edmund Bacon, recounted in a manuscript[2] by the Reverend Hamilton W. Pierson and first published in book form in 1862. It was conveniently republished by the University Press of Virginia in 1967 as part of James A. Bear, Jr.'s, *Jefferson at Monticello*.

It is undisputed that Edmund Bacon served as Monticello overseer from September 29, 1806, until around October 1822.[3] It is clear that he was present at Monticello before assuming that position,[4] and Bacon asserted: "I went to live with him the 27th of the December before he was inaugurated as President; and if I had remained with him from the

---

1. I use this term for convenience only, and intend nothing pejorative by it. It refers to those who seek to "revise" the traditional view accepted by historians in the past, and in particular includes Professors Fawn Brodie, Annette Gordon-Reed, Peter Onuf, Jan Lewis, and Joseph Ellis. Professor Ellis seems to use the term in a similar manner. Joseph J. Ellis, *Jefferson: Post DNA*, 57 (1) WILLIAM & MARY Q. 131 (Jan. 2000).

2. Unfortunately, the location of the original copy of this document is unknown. This is "unfortunate" because it may have had several names that are rendered as blank lines in the published text—presumably to protect the privacy of individuals.

3. JEFFERSON AT MONTICELLO 130–31 n.2 (James A. Bear, Jr., ed. 1967). Bear asserts that Bacon left on October 15 (*id.*), while Bacon suggests it was either the 7th or 8th (*id.* at 40). There would seem to be no reason for Bacon to intentionally misstate this detail, and Bear's comment is almost certainly based upon the fact that Jefferson wrote in his *Memorandum Book* on October 15, 1822: "Had a final settlement with Edmund Bacon and paid him $41.90 the balance due him in full...." 2 JEFFERSON'S MEMORANDUM BOOKS 1390 (James A. Bear, Jr. & Lucia C. Stanton, eds. 1997). The two statements are not necessarily in conflict, as Bacon's final day of work might have been a few days before he received his final payment.

4. *See, e.g.,* 2 JEFFERSON'S MEMORANDUM BOOKS 1186. The Betts edition of Jefferson's *Garden Book* states that Edmund Bacon was "overseer since 1806 and before that working for him in various jobs...." THOMAS JEFFERSON'S GARDEN BOOK 601 (Edwin Morris Betts, ed., 1999).

8th of October to the 27th of December, the year that I left him, I should have been with him precisely twenty years."[5]

What little we know about Bacon's character is positive. Jefferson described him as "an honest, correct man in his conduct, and worthy of confidence in his engagements,"[6] and Reverend Pierson added: "Captain Bacon has now resided in Kentucky about forty years, and his neighbors, who have known him during all that time, would vouch as strongly for his character as Mr. Jefferson and his son-in-law, Governor Randolph, have done. He is a man of wealth and character."[7]

There is no reason to assume that Bacon misrepresented the length of his stay at Monticello, but his statement is nevertheless difficult to reconcile with the known facts. He seems to be asserting that he went to live at Monticello in late 1802, but Jefferson's two inaugurations were in March 1801 and 1805. It is not necessary to reconcile these details, but it is possible that Bacon lived at Monticello before formally assuming the position as overseer — a fact that could be significant in understanding his testimony.

During his conversations with Reverend Pierson, Bacon spoke highly of several members of the Hemings family. For example, he stated:

> Mr. Jefferson had a large number of favorite servants that were treated just as well as could be. Burwell was the main, principal servant on the place.... Mr. Jefferson had the most perfect confidence in him.... Mr. Jefferson gave him his freedom in his will, and it was right that he should do it.[8]

Similarly, carpenter John Hemings was described as a "first-rate workman"[9]; Joe Fossett was "a very fine workman ... [who] could do anything it was necessary to do with steel or iron"[10]; and "Burwell was a fine painter."[11] In contrast, he offered no praise for Sally Hemings, noting only that she "went to France with Maria Jefferson when she was a little girl.... They crossed the ocean alone. I have often heard her tell of it."[12]

But Edmund Bacon's most important comment of relevance to the present inquiry appears to concern Sally's daughter Harriet:

> Mr. Jefferson freed a number of his servants in his will. I think he would have freed all of them if his affairs had not been so much involved that he could not do it. He freed one girl some years before he died, and there was a great deal of talk about it. She was nearly as white as anybody and very beautiful. People said he freed her because she was his own daughter. *She was not his daughter; she was _____'s daughter. I know that. I have seen him come out of her mother's room many a morning when I went up to Monticello very early.* When she was nearly grown,

---

5. JEFFERSON AT MONTICELLO 39–40. Bacon's figures do not quite add up. Either he or Pierson may have erred in saying he began work "before" Jefferson's inauguration, and if he started in December of 1801 that would fit. There is a reference in Bacon's own memo book suggesting he may have returned to live with his father in 1803. If we subtract that year, the figures also work, and there would be no reason for Bacon to mention this relatively minor detail. For present purposes, we need not try to resolve this discrepancy beyond noting there are several possible explanations that do not require one to challenge the veracity of Edmund Bacon.

6. *Id.* at 34.

7. *Id.* at 34–35.

8. *Id.* at 99.

9. *Id.* at 101–02.

10. *Id.* at 102.

11. *Id.*

12. *Id.* at 100.

by Mr. Jefferson's direction I paid her stage fare to Philadelphia and gave her fifty dollars. I have never seen her since and don't know what became of her.[13]

This may be the most valuable single piece of evidence about the paternity of Sally Hemings' children. Bacon is a mature observer of established good character, who was clearly in a position to observe what was happening at Monticello for nearly two decades. He was testifying to facts he personally observed time and again, unlike virtually all of the sources being relied upon by the revisionists: a disreputable journalist who had never even been to Monticello reporting neighborhood gossip as part of a personal vendetta and effort to blackmail Jefferson into giving him a public job, Federalist politicians who admitted to having no firsthand knowledge of the facts, a New England schoolteacher who shared a stagecoach with one of Jefferson's bitter enemies and was reporting gossip from other Charlottesville critics with no apparent first-hand knowledge, and the unsourced allegations attributed to Madison Hemings and Israel Jefferson about matters which occurred years before they were born.

Indeed, one of the most troubling aspects of the January 2000 *Monticello Report* was its almost total dismissal of this important source. A photocopy of the excerpt is attached to the report in Appendix E,[14] and there are two other brief references to it. In the report itself, Bacon is dismissed with this language:

> 1862. The published account of former overseer Edmund Bacon—indicating but not naming another man as the father of Sally Hemings's daughter Harriet (born 1801)—has problems of chronology: Bacon was not employed at Monticello until five years after Harriet Hemings's birth.[15]

In Appendix F, we find this further reference in the *Monticello Report*:

VIEWS OF OTHER MONTICELLO RESIDENTS:

Edmund Bacon, Monticello overseer from 1806 to 1822, stated that Jefferson was not the father of Sally Hemings's children.

> Bacon told Hamilton Pierson in 1862 that "people said" Jefferson freed Sally Hemings's daughter Harriet "because she was his own daughter. She was not his daughter; she was _____'s daughter. I know that. I have seen him come out of her mother's room many a morning when I went up to Monticello very early." Pierson presumably deleted the name of the father for publication; the original manuscript has not been located. Harriet Hemings was born in 1801, five years before Bacon's arrival at Monticello (1862 Bacon recollections, p. 102).[16]

This superficial treatment of the only eyewitness account of Sally Hemings' apparent sexual behavior makes no sense at all if one is engaged in a serious search for the truth. It is akin to a police investigator finding an otherwise credible witness who can place the accused at the scene of the crime a week before it was committed. But then the officer discovers that his witness *erred*, and, instead of witnessing the accused perhaps "casing the joint" a week early, his observation actually occurred on the night of the crime. So the officer makes a small notation about the witness having "problems of chronology" and refuses to consider the testimony further.

---

13. *Id.* at 102 (emphasis added.). This was not the only name deleted in the original Pierson book in 1862. *See, e.g., id.* at 76, 77. Pierson sought to justify these deletions by explaining that he did "not like to publish facts that would give pain to any that might now be living." HAMILTON W. PIERSON, JEFFERSON AT MONTICELLO: THE PRIVATE LIFE OF THOMAS JEFFERSON 6 (1862).

14. *Monticello Report*, Appendix E at 22–23.

15. *Monticello Report* at 4.

16. *Id.*, Appendix F at 3.

Edmund Bacon's statement was not that he observed "_____" leaving Sally Hemings' room at the time that Harriet was conceived. His statement is perfectly consistent with a conclusion that, having witnessed a man other than Thomas Jefferson leaving Sally's room early in the morning on numerous occasions, that man was obviously Sally's "lover" and presumably fathered her children. Bacon was certainly aware of the Callender charges and resulting rumors that Thomas Jefferson began a relationship with Sally in Paris that produced several children, and upon observing a different man leaving her room time and again—irrespective of whether this was in 1800 or after 1806—it was *reasonable* for him to conclude the charge against Jefferson was unfounded. While there may be some temporal ambiguity in his remark (which, we should keep in mind, was recorded by another), there is not the slightest hint of intentional deception or other dishonesty.

Far more important, our inquiry is not primarily about *Harriet* Hemings. There is no compelling[17] evidence— DNA or otherwise—suggesting that Thomas Jefferson was the father of Harriet Hemings. The only Hemings child scientifically tied to a Jefferson father was Eston, who was conceived the year after everyone acknowledges that Edmund Bacon had assumed the duties of Monticello overseer. Edmund Bacon was born and grew up two or three miles from Monticello,[18] and his brother William was overseer during Jefferson's stay in Paris.[19] Edmund worked for Thomas Jefferson in other capacities before becoming overseer in 1806. It is certainly possible that he did visit Monticello about the time Harriet was conceived and saw another man leaving Sally's room. But it is also possible that his observations began in 1806 or 1807, and if so they are tremendously *more* valuable in the search for the father of Eston Hemings.

Finally, Edmund Bacon's testimony is critically important because, if true, it totally destroys a fundamental assumption upon which the revisionist case is premised. If Edmund Bacon personally witnessed a man other than Thomas Jefferson leaving Sally Hemings' room time and again in the early morning hours, it is a reasonable conclusion that his purpose was not to sell her encyclopedias or insurance, but to engage in sexual relations. And if that is so, either Sally Hemings was not monogamous, or she did not have a sexual relationship with Thomas Jefferson. This is obvious.

Before leaving the issue of Edmund Bacon's recollections, it may be worth noting that both Professor Gordon-Reed and Monticello historian Lucia Stanton appear to attempt to avoid the inconsistency between Bacon's comment that he put Harriet on a stage to Philadelphia and Madison's assertion that Harriet lived in Washington, D.C., by paraphrasing Bacon's account (making no reference to "Philadelphia") and asserting that Harriet was "put on a stagecoach to freedom *in the North* at her father's direction."[20]

If Sally was not sexually involved with Thomas Jefferson, then our inquiry is at an end. If we assume she may have been involved with Thomas Jefferson, then she could not have been monogamous—and without that assumption, the "evidence," such as it is, pointing to Thomas Jefferson as the father of Eston Hemings largely falls apart. As will be dis-

---

17. It is true that James Callender, assorted Federalist editors and politicians, and former slaves Madison Hemings and Israel Jefferson (according to anti-Jefferson partisan Samuel Wetmore) made the assertion; but none of them could possibly have had first-hand knowledge of the facts and they do not even give sources for where they heard the allegations.

18. JEFFERSON AT MONTICELLO 39.

19. *Id.*

20. Annette Gordon-Reed, *Engaging Jefferson: Blacks and the Founding Father*, 57 WILLIAM & MARY Q. 181–82 (Jan. 2000) (emphasis added). Ms. Stanton similarly writes: "Overseer Edmund Bacon remembered that, at Jefferson's request, he provided Harriet with travel funds and put her on the stage *to the north*." LUCIA STANTON, FREE SOME DAY 116–17 (2001) (emphasis added).

cussed, there is strong evidence that at least six other Jefferson males may have been present at Monticello when Eston was conceived. For a variety of reasons that will also be discussed, at least five of them would seem to be more likely suspects to have fathered Eston Hemings than President Thomas Jefferson.

Other than Madison Hemings' allegation (about facts that occurred prior to his birth that he obviously could not have known with certainty), there is no reason to believe that Sally Hemings was monogamous. Madison reportedly admits that Sally's mother had children by no fewer than four different men,[21] and it is not at all clear that slave women were given a great deal of *choice* about their sexual partners. Nor is the case made by the *Monticello Report* for Sally's monogamy persuasive:

> While the DNA results bear only on the paternity of Eston Hemings, the documents and birth patterns suggest a long-term relationship, which produced the children whose names appear in Jefferson's records. Even the statements of those who accounted for the paternity of Sally Hemings's children differently (Thomas Jefferson Randolph, Ellen Randolph Coolidge, and Edmund Bacon) never implied that Hemings's children had different fathers. Full-sibling relationships are further supported by the closeness of the family, as evidenced by documentation of siblings living together and naming children after each other.[22]

Some of the shortcomings of these strained arguments have already been addressed. Such unfounded suppositions hardly compare to the eyewitness account of Edmund Bacon. But they are necessary for the revisionist case, because without the assumption that Sally was monogamous the case against Thomas Jefferson quickly crumbles.

Professor Gordon-Reed attempts to discredit the Bacon testimony by asserting that he was motivated by an "interest in protecting his former employer's reputation...."[23] The only apparent basis for such an "interest" would be that Bacon genuinely admired and respected Thomas Jefferson, which presumably would be a consequence of evaluating everything he knew about the man. He said in 1862:

> I am now in my seventy-seventh year. I have seen a great many men in my day, but I have never seen the equal of Mr. Jefferson. He may have had the faults that he has been charged with, but if he had, I could never find it out. I don't believe that, from his arrival to maturity to the present time, the country has ever had another such a man.[24]

Bacon clearly appears to have respected Jefferson, but this does not establish a "bias" likely to affect his veracity. To suggest otherwise would be akin to saying that an individual who enjoyed a book or movie cannot be trusted to review it, as she or he will normally lie to others if asked if there were flawed passages. The kinds of biases that could undermine Bacon's credibility might result from things like his still being employed by Jefferson's family or having financial involvement with them. Edmund Bacon certainly may have lied, but there is no reason to assume that from what we know about the situation. He had less apparent reason to be biased than did Madison Hemings or any of Thomas Jefferson's relatives.

I raised this issue with Dr. Daniel Jordan, president of the Thomas Jefferson Memorial Foundation, and he provided a response by Lucia Stanton which stated in part:

---

21. *See* Chapter Four.
22. *Monticello Report* at 7.
23. Gordon-Reed, Thomas Jefferson and Sally Hemings 223.
24. Bear, Jefferson at Monticello 117.

> For many who have finally concluded that Thomas Jefferson was the most prob-
> able father of Sally Hemings's children, Bacon's account is the hardest bit of ev-
> idence to assimilate. So one needs to ponder what Bacon's motives for
> misrepresenting the situation might have been. He too can be viewed as having
> "a stake in the outcome," out of deep loyalty to Jefferson or pride in his associ-
> ation with the famous President. Then there are the circumstances of the inter-
> view to consider. Bacon was talking to a preacher in mid-Victorian 1860....
>
> For the Monticello committee, the issue boiled down to one lone voice against
> a chorus. A single dissenting opinion was not of sufficient weight to negate the
> preponderance of evidence on the other side.[25]

This sounds very much like the committee itself, having "finally concluded that Thomas
Jefferson was the most probable father of Sally Hemings's children," doubled back to speculate "what Bacon's motives for misrepresenting the situation might have been." A more
reasonable and objective starting point might have been to consider *whether* Bacon was
misrepresenting the facts. It may be true that Bacon was "talking to a preacher in mid-
Victorian 1860" — though it is also true that the minister in question was president of
Cumberland College in Kentucky — but that did not prevent Bacon from discussing the
young men who visited Monticello and became "too intimate with the Negro women" to
suit one young visitor.[26]

Where is this "chorus" of witnesses alleging that Sally Hemings and Thomas Jefferson
had a sexual relationship? As far as we know, there is not a *single* witness — among the
hundreds of Monticello residents and perhaps thousands of visitors — who has left behind
testimony that the two of them were seen alone together or in any kind of suggestive behavior. The "evidence" for the existence of the relationship consists of assertions attributed to Madison Hemings concerning events that occurred long before he was born,
surrounded by statements that are demonstrably untrue, and reportedly corroborated by
Israel Jefferson whose account is clearly false on numerous material points. More importantly, unlike Edmund Bacon, Madison is not testifying to facts he could have personally
observed. He is merely passing on assertions as they "came down to" him. Perhaps they
came from Sally Hemings, perhaps from James Callender, or perhaps from others. We
have no way of knowing.

Excluding Madison's problematic statement, there is no evidence that Sally Hemings
or any of her other children ever claimed that Thomas Jefferson was their father. When
former Monticello slave Isaac Jefferson told his memoirs, he made mention of Sally Hemings but said not a word about any alleged sexual relationship with Thomas Jefferson.
None of the other residents of Monticello claimed knowledge of this relationship, which
was consistently denied by the Jefferson family. Where is this "chorus of voices" or "preponderance of evidence" on the other side? Presumably it is James Callender, John Hartwell
Cocke, Thomas Gibbons, and Elijah P. Fletcher (as discussed in Chapter Nine) — none
of whom even alleged they had personally witnessed any behavior by Thomas Jefferson
or Sally Hemings that might support the allegation. Indeed, not one of them even alleges
he was *told* of the relationship by someone who had witnessed anything more suspicious
than the existence of light-skinned slaves at Monticello.

Finally, the statement that a "single dissenting opinion was not of sufficient weight to
negate the preponderance of evidence on the other side" misses the true significance of

---

25. Lucia Stanton, e-mail response to "Turner Questions," Dec. 8, 2000, response number 7.
26. JEFFERSON AT MONTICELLO 88.

the Bacon statement. To be sure, he does voice his *opinion* that Thomas Jefferson was not the father of Harriet Hemings. But that is not the critical part of his testimony. He states further that he frequently *witnessed*, with his own eyes, a man other than Thomas Jefferson coming out of Sally Hemings' room in the early hours of the morning. That is not "opinion," it is an assertion of *fact*—and it is probably the most reliable factual testimony we have to guide us.

Madison Hemings and others who allege that the relationship existed are *discussing* facts; but they are in reality merely voicing *opinions* about whether certain factual statements are true. Not one of them is testifying to material facts he personally saw, heard, or otherwise observed. It simply does not follow that a half dozen opinions by people with no personal knowledge of the key facts are of greater probative value than eyewitness testimony by one credible observer.

Nor, for that matter, is it close to being true that Edmund Bacon was "one lone voice" among Jefferson's contemporaries in this matter. While Ms. Stanton is correct in observing that the Jefferson family explanation that Sally Hemings' children were fathered by Peter and/or Samuel Carr has been shown by the DNA tests to have not been correct *in the case of Eston Hemings,* there is no reason to believe that they were wrong about some or all of Sally's earlier children. They all had far more contact with Thomas Jefferson than any of the advocates on the other side (many if not most of whom had never set foot on Jefferson's mountain); and while, as relatives, their testimony must be considered potentially biased, unless they were *all* lying their statements are probably of greater value than those of people who did not have an opportunity to witness events at Monticello over the decades.

As shown in Chapter Nine, even without removing the sources relied upon by Ms. Stanton and her colleagues who were clearly bitter enemies of Thomas Jefferson (like James Callender and Thomas Gibbons), and those who received their information on this matter from Jefferson's enemies (like Elijah Fletcher), Jefferson's contemporaries who voiced doubts about the accusations easily outnumber his critics. This list includes James Madison, Jefferson's physician Dr. Robley Dunglison, Elder John Leland, Thomas Paine, Jefferson's secretaries David Humphreys and William Burwell, and even prominent Federalist political opponents like John Adams, Alexander Hamilton, and General Light-Horse Harry Lee. Indeed, given the antipodal reputations of James Callender and Thomas Jefferson, it is likely that the overwhelming majority of Thomas Jefferson's friends found the charge so preposterous as to not even warrant comment. Sadly, from Ms. Stanton's response, it seems that the Monticello research committee began their inquiry having concluded that Thomas Jefferson was guilty.

The Accounts of Thomas Jefferson's Relatives

It is perhaps not surprising that Thomas Jefferson's children and grandchildren defended his innocence with respect to the paternity of Sally Hemings' children. This could easily be explained as nothing more than family loyalty, and from all accounts they loved him dearly. Professor Gordon-Reed tells us their views "must be taken with a grain of salt" because "[t]hey loved him."[27]

Nevertheless, their accounts ought not be lightly dismissed. For if this relationship had been going on regularly for decades, it is difficult to believe that they would not have

---

27. Gordon-Reed, Thomas Jefferson and Sally Hemings 126.

learned about it. This is particularly true in the early days, when Thomas Jefferson is alleged to have begun a sexual relationship with a fourteen- to sixteen-year-old Sally Hemings in Paris. Sally was the maid to Jefferson's two young daughters, and it seems unlikely that she would have had the discretion to keep such a relationship secret from them. Indeed, presumably it would have been in her interest for them to know that her status had been elevated from that of lowly "servant" to the beloved "partner"—to use the modern vernacular—of their powerful father. This point will be developed further in the next chapter.

Professor Joshua Rothman, who wrote his Ph.D. dissertation about race relations in antebellum Virginia, writes:

> In early national and antebellum Virginia, standing sexual affairs between white men and African American women were nearly always open secrets. Divorce petitions in Virginia involving accusations of interracial adultery, for example, amply demonstrate that neighbors, friends, and relatives ... always knew, sometimes for many years, about the illicit sexual conduct of both men and women in their families and communities.[28]

It is thus very difficult simply to assume that Jefferson's relatives would have been ignorant of a relationship that allegedly lasted for decades.

Martha Jefferson Randolph

Martha (Patsy) Jefferson was by all accounts an unusually bright and perceptive young woman, and in terms of her values an attractive person.[29] Shortly before Sally and Maria (Polly) arrived in Paris, Martha wrote to her father that "I wish with all my soul that the poor Negroes were all freed. It grieves my heart when I think that these our fellow creatures should be treated so terrible as they are by many of our country men."[30]

She later obviously became very much aware of the allegations made against her father, but she does not appear to have believed them. Professor Joseph Ellis, for example, clearly found it difficult to reconcile his study of Martha Jefferson's unpublished papers with his own newfound conviction that her father must have fathered children by Sally Hemings. Writing in the *William & Mary Quarterly*, he explains:

> My own reading of those [Martha Jefferson Randolph's] papers suggests that, much like her father, Martha Randolph possessed extraordinary powers of denial. She did not consciously cover up the ongoing sexual liaison so much as convince herself it did not exist. (How she managed this defies logic, but not in its new "Jeffersonian" version.)[31]

---

28. Joshua D. Rothman, *James Callender and Social Knowledge of Interracial Sex in Antebellum Virginia,* in SALLY HEMINGS & THOMAS JEFFERSON 96 (Jan Ellen Lewis & Peter Onuf, eds. 1999).

29. Monticello overseer Edmund Bacon writes of her: "I knew Mrs. Randolph as well as I ever knew any person out of my own family. Few such women ever lived. I never saw her equal. I was with Mr. Jefferson twenty years and saw her frequently every week. I never saw her at all out of temper. I can truly say that I never saw two such persons in this respect as she and her father.... Mrs. Randolph was more like her father than any lady I ever saw." JEFFERSON AT MONTICELLO 83.

30. *Martha Jefferson to Thomas Jefferson,* May 3, 1787, in THE FAMILY LETTERS OF THOMAS JEFFERSON 39 (Edwin Morris Betts & James Adam Bear, Jr., eds., 1966).

31. Joseph J. Ellis, *Jefferson: Post-DNA,* 57(1) WILLIAM & MARY Q. 135 (Jan. 2000).

Perhaps one need not invent a new theory of "Jeffersonian logic" to explain what has been observed. Occam's Razor would suggest that these same consequences might be explained by the conclusion that Thomas Jefferson and his daughter were not "in denial" at all, but rather they were simply aware that there was no truth behind the Callender allegations.

Consider also this account, from a letter from Jefferson biographer Henry S. Randall, to his colleague James Parton, written on June 1, 1868:

> Mr. Jefferson's oldest daughter, Mrs. Gov. Randolph, took the Dusky Sally stories much to heart. But she never spoke to her sons but once on the subject. Not long before her death she called two of them—the Colonel [Thomas Jefferson Randolph] and George Wythe Randolph—to her. She asked the Colonel if he remembered when ____ Henings [sic] (the slave who most resembled Mr. Jefferson) was born.... He said that he could answer by referring to the book containing the list of slaves. He turned to the book and found that the slave was born at the time supposed by Mrs. Randolph. She then directed her sons['] attention to the fact that Mr. Jefferson and Sally Henings [sic] could not have met—were far distant from each other—for fifteen months prior to such birth. She bade her sons (to) remember this fact, and always to defend the character of their grandfather. It so happened when I was afterwards examining an old account book of the Jeffersons I came *pop* on the original entry of this slave[']s birth; and I was then able (to know) from well known circumstances to prove the fifteen months separation ... but those circumstances have faded from my memory.[32]

Now this account goes from Jeff Randolph through Henry Randall to James Parton—triple hearsay—and is subject to all of the dangers characteristic of such evidence. Martha Randolph could have been mistaken or knowingly not telling the truth. Her son Jeff could have fabricated the story or confused the details after many years. Henry Randall could have created it from whole cloth. Even James Parton could theoretically have fabricated the incident.

But if the basic account is accurate, Martha Randolph's statement has some inherent credibility. If she believed her father guilty of the charges, and simply wanted to urge her sons to protect his memory, she would presumably not have asked Jeff Randolph to accept her account based upon his *own* recollection of certain facts. Because if Sally and President Jefferson had not been separated for fifteen months, Jeff Randolph would not be able to confirm her statement from his own knowledge. She could just as easily have fabricated some explanation that was not subject to confirmation (or, if she was lying, refutation) from his independent memory.

I am indebted to former Monticello Resident Director James Bear for a copy of an undated letter from Martha Randolph to her daughter Ellen—believed to have been written during the latter half of 1826, a few months after the death of her famous father—in which she discusses her father's character and concludes:

> [I]n the course of my life I can not call to mind one solitary action that I would censure.... What can I say my Dear Ellen that have so long basked in the sun shine of his affections, and been the witness to his private virtue, that will not look like partiality? But if I speak at all I must speak the truth, and so doing can utter nothing but praise.[33]

---

32. *Reprinted in* MILTON E. FLOWER, JAMES PARTON: THE FATHER OF MODERN BIOGRAPHY 237 (1951).

33. *Martha Jefferson Randolph to Ellen Randolph Coolidge* (undated), a copy of which is in the author's possession.

Jefferson's secretary William Short, who lived with him in Paris, perceived some jealousy on Patsy's (Martha's) part towards both Maria Cosway and Angelica Church, two of her father's lady friends in Paris.[34] Would she not have felt even more displeasure had she learned that he was sexually involved with a servant younger than herself? Would she have repeatedly brought her children to Monticello if she believed this alleged relationship was going on? To accept the story, we have to discard not only much of what we think we know about Thomas Jefferson's character,[35] but that of Martha Jefferson Randolph as well.

Thomas Jefferson Randolph, Ellen Randolph Coolidge, and the Carr Brothers

We have other statements attributed to Jeff Randolph that support Thomas Jefferson's innocence—at least with respect to *some* of Sally Hemings' children.[36] For example, in this same 1868 letter to James Parton, we find this account by Henry Randall:

> Colonel Randolph said that a visitor at Monticello dropped a newspaper from his pocket or accidentally left it. After he was gone, he (Colonel Randolph) opened the paper and found some very insulting remarks about Mr. Jefferson's mulatto children. The Colonel said he felt provoked. Peter and Samuel Carr were lying not far off under a shade tree. He took the paper and put it in Peter's hands, pointing out the article. Peter read it, tears coursing down his cheeks, and then handed it to Samuel. Samuel also shed tears. Peter exclaimed "Ar'nt you and I a couple of _____ pretty fellows to bring this disgrace on poor old uncle who has always fed us! We ought to be _____, by _____."[37]

Again, this is multiple hearsay, but Jeff Randolph's account does not read like a typical "coverup." Indeed, he is perhaps the primary source for one of the three strongest arguments usually made by revisionist scholars, that at least some of Sally Hemings' children bore a physical resemblance to the President. Consider Randall's account:

> Walking about mouldering Monticello one day with Col. T. J. Randolph (Mr. Jefferson's oldest grandson) he showed me a smoke blackened and sooty room in one of the colon[n]ades, and informed me it was Sally Hemings' room. He asked me if I knew how the story of Mr. Jefferson's connection with her originated. I told him I did not. "There was a better excuse for it,["] said he, ["]than you might think; she had children which resembled Mr. Jefferson so closely that it was plain that they had his blood in their veins." He said in one case the resemblance was so close, that at some distance or in the dusk the slave, dressed in the same way, might have been mistaken for Mr. Jefferson.[38]

This does not sound like the opening statement of Thomas Jefferson's lawyer in a paternity case, and other than James Callender's allegation that the slave child "Tom" resembled the President, there is little reason to believe that Jeff Randolph would have expected his audience to be aware of this physical resemblance. It is the kind of "admission against

---

34. Fawn Brodie, Thomas Jefferson 236 (1974).
35. *See* Chapter Eleven.
36. Obviously the DNA tests have ruled out either Peter or Samuel Carr as possible fathers for Eston Hemings. They tell us nothing about the paternity of Sally Hemings' other children, and thus the alleged confessions of Peter and Samuel Carr are still important to consider.
37. Brodie, Thomas Jefferson 238.
38. Flower, James Parton 236.

interest" that tends to make testimony credible, although clever liars sometimes include such statements to precisely that end.

Furthermore, the assertion that Jeff Randolph claimed that the Carr brothers had admitted paternity of at least some of Sally's children finds corroboration in a letter written by his sister, Ellen Randolph Coolidge, to her husband, Joseph, on October 24, 1858. The primary purpose of the letter (already discussed in my Introduction and Chapter Two) was to give her husband information on the subject to pass on to a Mr. Bulfinch. It was in this letter that she enumerated various reasons why the Callender charges could not be true, including the assertion that no female domestic servant was ever allowed in Jefferson's room when he was present, and none could have gone there without being visible to others in the house. This was one of the sentences that was altered in Professor Gordon-Reed's appendix with the result that its meaning was materially changed.[39]

Among the other arguments Ellen makes in the letter, which was first made public in full by Dumas Malone in 1974,[40] are these:

> The house at Monticello was a long time in building and was principally built by Irish workmen. These men were known to have had children of whom the mothers were black women. But these women were much better pleased to have it supposed that such children were their master's.... There were dissipated young men in the neighborhood who sought the society of the mulattresses and they in like manner were not anxious to establish any claim of paternity in the results of such associations.

> One woman known to Mr. J. Q. Adams and others as "dusky Sally" was pretty notoriously the mistress of a married man, a near relation of Mr. Jefferson's, and there can be small question that her children were his.[41]

After several pages of such arguments clearly designed to be shared with others, Ellen added the following comment, on a separate page, apparently intending that it *not* be communicated further:

> I have written thus far thinking you might chuse [*sic*] to communicate my letter to Mr. Bulfinch. Now I will tell you in confidence what Jefferson [her brother Thomas Jefferson Randolph] told me under the like condition. Mr. Southall and himself young men together, heard Mr. Peter Carr say with a laugh, that "the old gentleman has to bear the blame for his and Sam's (Col. Carr) misdeeds."

> There is a general impression that the four children of Sally Hemmings [*sic*] were *all* the children of Col. Carr, the most notorious good-natured Turk that every was master of a black seraglio kept at other men's expense.... [42]

The "like condition" in the second sentence presumably meant that the information was not to be communicated further. It was a confidential exchange between Ellen and her husband. And while the 1998 DNA tests clearly established that Samuel Carr was not the father of Sally's youngest child, Eston, they tell us nothing about his possible paternity of Beverly, either of the Harriets, or Madison (or Thenia if she was in fact Sally Hemings' child).

Of the Jefferson/Randolph family members, I have found Ellen to be among the most candid and credible in her comments. Professor Brodie notes that Margaret Bayard Smith

---

39. *See* Introduction, **Figure 4** on page 37.
40. Dumas Malone, *Jefferson's Private Life*, N.Y. Times, May 18, 1974 at 31.
41. *Id.* This letter is also *reprinted in Monticello Report*, Appendix E at 19.
42. *Id.*

described Ellen Randolph as "one of the finest and most intelligent children I have ever met"[43]; and of all of his children and grandchildren Ellen was probably the most intellectual.[44] She clearly loved her grandfather dearly, but she was willing to disclose "family secrets," including weaknesses of her own father.[45] This document has additional credibility because she was communicating to her own husband in the apparent expectation that he would keep the information confidential. So I am inclined to believe her account that Jeff Randolph told her this story; but, of course, that does *not* establish that her brother was telling the truth. We have two generally credible sources asserting that, on separate occasions, Jeff Randolph alleged that Peter Carr confessed that he and his brother Sam had fathered children by Sally Hemings. But note in one instance Jeff reportedly said Peter laughed and in the other that he cried during the confession.

There is another account attributed to Jeff Randolph that warrants our attention. In his 1868 letter to Parton, Henry Randall writes:

> I asked Col. [Jeff] Randolph why on earth Mr. Jefferson did [not[46]] put these slaves who looked like him out of the public sight by sending them to his Befond [*sic*—Bedford] estate or elsewhere,—He said Mr. Jefferson never betrayed the least consciousness of the resemblance—and although he (Col. Randolph) had no doubt his mother would have been very glad to have them thus removed, that both and all venerated Mr. Jefferson too deeply to broach such a topic to him. What suited him, satisfied them. Mr. Jefferson was deeply attached to the Carrs—especially to Peter. He was extremely indulgent to them and the idea of watching them for faults or vices probably never occurred to him.
>
> Do you ask why I did not state, or at least hint the above facts in my Life of Jefferson? I wanted to do so. But Colonel Randolph, in this solitary case alone, prohibited me from using at my discretion the information he furnished me with. When I rather pressed him on the point, he said, pointing to the family graveyard, "You are not bound to prove a negation. If I should allow you to take Peter Carr's corpse into Court and plead guilty over it to shelter Mr. Jefferson, I should not dare again to walk by his grave: he would rise and spurn me."[47]

So what are we to make of such "evidence"? Two respectable sources independently report that Jeff Randolph told them that one or both of the Carr brothers had confessed to fathering children by Sally Hemings, and *both* assert he pledged them to secrecy on the matter. We can easily understand why Jeff Randolph might fabricate such a story to protect his grandfather's reputation, but would he tell such a lie to his sister? Perhaps, but if

43. BRODIE, THOMAS JEFFERSON 364.

44. The Monticello web page describes Ellen as "in many ways the intellectual heir of her grandfather." *Available at* http://www.monticello.org/jefferson/breakfast/profile.html.

45. For example, in an 1856 letter to Henry Randall, Ellen discussed her "poor father's weaknesses" despite asserting "I loved him much." She explained: "If I speak at all I must speak the truth, and under the circumstances, can I refuse to speak? Would not my silence lead to wrong conclusions? You are preparatory to giving to the world, your Life of Jefferson, inquiring, as you are bound to do, most minutely and particularly, into all the details of his private life, and in order to understand him, you must understand those by whom he was surrounded." *Ellen Coolidge to Henry Randall,* Mar. 27, 1856, Accession #9090, University of Virginia. A few months later, she added in another letter: "I have been very frank, my dear Mr. Randall, in communicating to you family secrets, whenever they were of a nature to throw light upon character, leaving it to your discretion so to dispose of them that while they were of service to you they could be of disservice to none." *Ellen Coolidge to Henry Randall,* July 31, 1856, Accession #9090, University of Virginia.

46. The bracketed "[not]" is in Parton's book and seems clearly appropriate from the context.

47. FLOWER, JAMES PARTON 238.

he was prepared to deceive her why would he bar her from recounting the story to mislead people he presumably cared less about and who might have been able to use it to defend his grandfather's reputation?

Randall certainly could have fabricated his account, but had he been so inclined there is the question of why he did not include this information in his three-volume *Life of Thomas Jefferson* instead of in a private letter to a professional colleague? He told Parton that he had clearly made the correct decision in honoring Randolph's demand for secrecy, arguing that Jefferson's reputation did not need to be defended on this point. Implicit in this may be that Randall did not expect Parton to publish his letter, although that is not absolutely clear.

If Jefferson Randolph fabricated both stories about the Carr brothers admitting paternity for the purpose of defending his grandfather's reputation among the public, he behaved rather bizarrely in demanding that the information be kept *confidential*. Further, his apparent desire to protect the reputation of the Carr brothers (or at least *someone*) was manifested again in his letter to the *Pike County Republican* responding to the allegations of Israel Jefferson. It certainly would have been more persuasive to say "Samuel and Peter Carr admitted they were the fathers of Sally Hemings' children" than to write, as he did, that "To my own knowledge and that of others 60 years ago the paternity of these parties were admitted by others."[48] Even the reference to "others" knowing the truth is consistent with Ellen Coolidge's statement made more than fifteen years earlier that Jeff told her a Mr. Southall had also overheard the Carr confessions.

We cannot conclude with certainty that *any* of this is true. But the pieces "fit together" well; Jeff Randolph, while perhaps not a man of the highest intellect, does generally appear to have been an honorable man.[49] Furthermore, for the story to be a complete fabrication would require a conspiracy involving several apparently honorable people. Certainly the simplest explanation is that the Carr brothers (or perhaps only Peter, with Samuel remaining quiet) did confess to the belief[50] that they had fathered one or more of Sally Hemings' children.

Peter Carr was born on January 2, 1770, and thus was at least three years older than Sally Hemings. He began a Charlottesville law practice in 1793, and in 1801 began serving in the state legislature and simultaneously as an Albemarle magistrate. He appears to have been in Albemarle County and at least near Monticello around the conception periods for Harriet I, Beverly, Harriet II, Madison, and Eston Hemings (although DNA tests have established he could not have fathered Eston). However, we cannot place him at Monticello with certainty during these entire periods.[51] Visits by Jefferson's favorite nephews were presumably common enough so as not to warrant recording in most settings.

Samuel Carr was born October 9, 1771, and was largely raised by Thomas Jefferson at Monticello. He settled in the Charlottesville area permanently in mid-1802, and is known to have been in the vicinity of Monticello about the time Harriet I and Eston were conceived.[52] We have no information about his location when Sally Hemings' other children

---

48. *Reprinted in Monticello Report*, Appendix E at 38.

49. For example, following his grandfather's death he assumed the burden of paying all of Jefferson's more than $107,000 indebtedness, and was still paying Thomas Jefferson's creditors forty years after the former President's death. *See, e.g.,* STANTON, FREE SOME DAY 96, 141.

50. Again it is necessary to consider the monogamy question: Unless they were confident Sally Hemings had no other partners, it is unclear how they could have known with certainty that they were the father(s) of any of her children.

51. Cynthia Burton has researched the Carr brothers extensively and has provided valuable assistance in tracking their presence over the years. I am indebted to her for most of this information.

52. Like his brother Peter, Samuel Carr has been eliminated by DNA tests as a possible father for Eston.

were conceived. There are reports that he fathered children by a "mulatto concubine who lived next door to him" whose descendants are recognized as relatives by white descendants of Samuel Carr.[53] We can neither prove he was present nor rule him out as a suspect with respect to any child but Eston, who Dr. Foster's DNA tests proved could not have been fathered by a Carr.

Thomas Mann Randolph and the Rest of the Family

The *Monticello Report* asserts that "Jefferson's daughter Martha Randolph and two of her children denied the story to friends and family members."[54] The record strongly suggests that none of the Jefferson family members believed the charges. Thus, granddaughter Ellen Randolph Coolidge stated and pointedly asked:

> [Thomas Jefferson] had a large family of grandchildren of all ages, older & younger. Young men and young girls. He lived, whenever he was at Monticello, and entirely for the last seventeen years of his life, in the midst of these young people, surrounded by them, his intercourse with them of the freest and most affectionate kind. How comes it that his immoralities were never suspected by his own family — that his daughter and her children rejected with horror and contempt the charges brought against him[?][55]

We cannot know for certain that this statement is true, but there is not the slightest bit of evidence to contradict it. And if any of the grandchildren had believed the paternity story and mentioned that belief to others, it would seem to be significant enough news to have been recorded in some manner. Given Ellen Coolidge's remarkable candor in admitting family "secrets,"[56] I am inclined to believe her on this point.

Governor Thomas Mann Randolph,[57] Thomas Jefferson's son-in-law and husband to Martha, was a frequent presence at Monticello and thus, inevitably, an eyewitness to much that was going on. He has been largely ignored during this debate, but he did write at least one letter making it clear that he did not believe the allegations involving Sally Hemings against his father-in-law. About four months after Callender's original charge, in a December 24, 1802, letter to his attorney, he wrote:

> As I could not be with you to read to you what I had written I leave it for you. My conversation with gentlemen here has made me think lighter of those infamous stories than I did: Therefore, I have not sent it to the gazette as I intended: it being necessary to put my name to a paragraph such as it would be. I had no thought of any thing but demanding a certificate from Callender that I was not one he could prove believed the story until I spoke to you the day Mr. Hay beat him, which occurrence prevented for obvious reasons my going to him. Adieu.[58]

---

53. E-mail from Cynthia Burton to the author, dated 4 Mar 2001, 20:17:12 EST, a copy of which is in the author's possession.
54. *Monticello Report*, Appendix F at 3.
55. *Reprinted in id.*, Appendix E at 16.
56. *See* note 45 on page 210.
57. Thomas Mann Randolph served as Governor of Virginia from 1819–1822, and was also a Colonel. This has caused some confusion among historians between TMR and his eldest son, Colonel Thomas Jefferson Randolph.
58. *Thomas Mann Randolph to Peter Carr, Esq.*, Dec. 24, 1802, Carr-Cary Family Papers, Accession 1231, Box 1, University of Virginia. The reference to "Mr. Hay" is to an incident on December 20, 1802, in which George Hay, James Callender's attorney at the time, beat his client repeatedly on the forehead with a walking stick.

This note also challenges the popular allegation that "everyone" believed the Callender stories. Although it is somewhat ambiguous, Randolph seems to be referring to having concluded the charges were not doing serious harm to the President's reputation after talking with various "gentlemen" in Charlottesville or perhaps Richmond.

The Assessment of Sally Hemings by Abigail Adams and Andrew Ramsay

There is a remarkable difference between the "Sally Hemings" envisioned by Professors Brodie and Gordon-Reed—and still further embellished by Hollywood—and the only existing eyewitness accounts of her talents. Since there are no surviving descriptions of Sally's behavior in Paris, perhaps it is not surprising that both scholars and Hollywood writers have felt free to speculate and even fantasize about what her life *might* have been like. From Isaac Jefferson's account that Sally was "handsome,"[59] and Jeff Randolph's comment that she and her niece Betsy were "decidedly good looking," Sally is presented to us as a sophisticated temptress likely to turn the head of any virile male. *American Heritage* senior editor and author E. M. Halliday—a great admirer of Fawn Brodie—goes so far as to assure us that as a young teen Sally had "well-developed breasts."[60]

Conceivably some of this is true, but there is no basis for such speculation save from the pens of James Callender and Federalist editors who had never set eyes on the woman. The only eyewitness accounts we have about Sally Hemings beyond references to her "handsome" good looks came from the summer of 1787, when she was a child of thirteen or fourteen years.[61] The source for both observations—one repeated as hearsay—was the highly intelligent[62] and perceptive Abigail Adams, wife of the U.S. minister to Great Britain and later President, John Adams. Her first testimony simply relayed the observations of Captain Andrew Ramsay, on whose ship Maria (Polly) Jefferson and Sally Hemings had spent five weeks en route to London. We know little of Captain Ramsay beyond that Thomas Jefferson and Abigail Adams both seemed highly impressed with him and little Polly became so attached to him during the voyage that she had to be tricked into parting with him after arriving in England.[63] Professor Brodie tells us that Polly and Sally "must certainly have been treated like special pets, for Polly came to adore the captain. She clung desperately to him upon arrival and had to be decoyed away in order to effect separation."[64] When Abigail Adams tried to calm Polly with a promised trip to Sadler's Wells, Polly responded "I had rather … see Captain Rams[a]y one moment, than all the fun in the world."[65]

---

59. JEFFERSON AT MONTICELLO 4.

60. E. M. HALLIDAY, UNDERSTANDING THOMAS JEFFERSON 86 (2001). *See supra* p. 71 n.14.

61. Since we do not know on what day in 1773 Sally was born, and she arrived in London around the middle of the year, there is roughly a fifty-fifty chance that these observations were made before or after her fourteenth birthday.

62. This observation would appear to require no documentation, but if any is desired the point is conceded by Professor Brodie. BRODIE, THOMAS JEFFERSON 238.

63. *See, e.g., Jefferson to Ramsay,* July 2, 1787, in 15 PAPERS OF THOMAS JEFFERSON 637 (1958); *Abigail Adams to Jefferson,* 11 *id.* 501, 550 (1955). From his letter to Jefferson, Captain Ramsay comes across as being both honorable and educated. *Ramsay to Jefferson, id.* 556.

64. BRODIE, THOMAS JEFFERSON 217.

65. *Abigail Adams to Jefferson,* June 26, 1787, 11 PAPERS OF THOMAS JEFFERSON 502.

According to Ms. Adams in a letter to Thomas Jefferson in Paris: "Captain Ramsay is of [the] opinion [that Sally Hemings] will be of so little Service that he had better carry her back with him. But of this you will be a judge."[66] From this, Professor Gordon-Reed attempts to dismiss Captain Ramsay with what can only be called a stereotype:

> Captain Ramsey's [*sic*] remedy, that he just take Sally Hemings back to Virginia, suggests that he either was not very thoughtful or was not thinking in a totally disinterested manner about the situation. One wonders at his effrontery, thinking it proper that he decide who would be of no use in Jefferson's household and that, without consulting Jefferson, he would take Hemings back to Virginia. . . .

> As Fawn Brodie pointed out, it does not take much imagination to determine why Captain Ramsey [*sic*] might have been desirous of having the beautiful young girl make the voyage back to the United States with him. Think of "Dashing Sally" on a six-week ocean voyage with Captain Ramsey [*sic*] and his crew.[67]

Like so much of her book, this analysis is premised upon numerous assumptions for which there is not the slightest evidence. Abigail Adams did *not* say that the Captain was considering taking Sally Hemings back to Virginia without consulting Jefferson; the very purpose of her letter—or at least one of her purposes—seems to have been to convey the captain's judgment and offer and to seek Jefferson's wishes in the matter. (Indeed, in a letter to Jefferson dated July 6 Captain Ramsay declared that if Jefferson did not send someone to get Polly, and, presumably, Sally, in "another weeks time," he would be honored to escort them personally to Paris.[68])

Contrary to Professor Gordon-Reed's allegation, Captain Ramsay appears by all evidence to be a very "thoughtful" individual. In a May 1787 letter, Anne Blair Banister described Captain Andrew Ramsay as "a very worthy Man," adding "I am confident from my knowledge of him he will be perfectly attentive to [Polly]."[69] If one can get away from the bizarre stereotype that every sea captain was by nature a rapist at heart, every bit of evidence we know about Captain Ramsay is positive. His behavior around Polly seems to have been so loving and gentle that she clung to him as a father figure. Thomas Jefferson and Abigail Adams—two individuals of established good judgment—seemed very impressed with him.[70] Surely Abigail Adams was sophisticated enough to take measure of the man and consider alternative motives for his offer. But her eyewitness assessment after ten days of regular exposure to Sally Hemings is simply dismissed—presumably because it greatly undermines the popular mythology about the "dashing" Sally Hemings.

After leaving Captain Ramsay, Polly and Sally lived with the Adams family in London for three weeks. Ten days into their stay, Abigail Adams wrote to Jefferson again, this time providing her own eyewitness assessment of Sally Hemings: "The girl she [eight-year-old Polly] has with her, wants more care than the child, and is wholly incapable of looking properly after her, without some superiour to direct her."[71] Other than references to Sally being "handsome" or "good looking," and having "straight hair," these are the only sur-

---

66. *Id.* at 503.
67. Gordon-Reed, Thomas Jefferson and Sally Hemings 161.
68. *Andrew Ramsay to Jefferson,* 11 The Papers of Thomas Jefferson 556.
69. *Banister to Jefferson, id.* at 351.
70. *See, e.g., Jefferson to Ramsay,* 15 The Papers of Thomas Jefferson 638 ("Her distress at parting with you is a proof how good you have been to her.").
71. *Abigail Adams to Thomas Jefferson,* July 6, 1787, in 11 *id.* 551.

viving eyewitness evaluations of Sally Hemings.[72] Abigail Adams was one of the most remarkable individuals of her era and a dedicated opponent to slavery, and there is not the slightest reason to believe that her comments about Sally Hemings were designed to do anything more than inform her friend in Paris of the realities she had witnessed. The only apparent reason this highly credible testimony, supported as well by that of Captain Ramsay, has been largely ignored is that it undermines the revisionist image of fourteen- or fifteen-year-old Sally Hemings as a sophisticated, charming, and seductive woman whose remarkable charms Thomas Jefferson was simply incapable of resisting.

The Mysterious Thomas Hemings

We now come again to the very mysterious "Tom" upon whom James Callender largely based his 1802 allegations that Thomas Jefferson had fathered children by Sally Hemings. For generations, it has been widely assumed that "Tom" was in reality "Thomas Woodson," and a powerful oral tradition from various lines of Woodson's descendants supports this account.

As already discussed in Chapter One, Professor Gordon-Reed included a lengthy discussion of the pros and cons about "Tom" in the pre-DNA-tests version of her book, noting his critical importance to both sides of the argument and arguing—in my view quite persuasively—that had there been no "Tom," certainly Jefferson's friends and supporters would have mentioned that fact in their many responses to Callender. On the contrary, at least one Jefferson defender appears to have conceded the existence of Callender's "Tom."[73]

For years, the experts at Monticello have conceded that Thomas Woodson was probably the mysterious "Tom" born to Sally Hemings in 1790 after returning from Paris. They did not concede that he was fathered by Thomas Jefferson. There is no record of a slave named "Tom" being born to any of Jefferson's slaves in 1790 (however, there is a potentially interesting erasure in his *Farm Book* for that year[74]). Early that year, Jefferson assumed the post of Secretary of Foreign Affairs (later redesignated Secretary of State when the duties were expanded to include such things as keeping the national seal and issuing commissions to public officers), and he did not carefully maintain his *Farm Book* between 1783 and 1794 because of his frequent absences.[75] But had there been a "Tom," there should have been subsequent references in Jefferson's records. If there never was a "Tom" as described by Callender, the Callender allegations become even less credible. If Thomas Woodson was born to Sally Hemings in 1790, the DNA results show conclusively that his father was not a Jefferson. That means either that Sally was not sexually involved with Thomas Jefferson or that she was not monogamous. Again, the circum-

---

72. Sally Hemings is mentioned in the accounts attributed to her son Madison and to Israel Jefferson, but neither account comments upon her talents or abilities.

73. *Richmond Examiner*, Philadelphia Aurora, Oct. 1, 1802, at 2.

74. Thomas Jefferson: The Garden and Farm Books 247. I have not bothered to try to check the original, and it is quite possible that the erasure reveals enough information to establish that the removed name was not "Tom" or "Thomas." I doubt that it was. It does now seem clear from the DNA studies that, if there *was* a "Tom" as described by Callender at Monticello, he was not Thomas Jefferson's son.

75. *Monticello Report*, Appendix K at 2.

stantial case against Thomas Jefferson is largely founded upon the assumption that she was monogamous and gave birth to a son named "Tom" shortly after returning from Paris.

After the DNA reports, Thomas Woodson shifted from being the star witness for the prosecution to being a major impediment to a conviction of Thomas Jefferson. There was nothing in the DNA tests to cast doubt on Woodson's claim to be the son of Sally Hemings,[76] and scholars like Joseph Ellis have managed to reconcile their belief in a Jefferson-Hemings romance without questioning Thomas Woodson's status as Sally Hemings' presumptive son. Writing in a 2000 issue of the prestigious *William & Mary Quarterly*, Professor Ellis reasoned (after asserting that "Jefferson's paternity of several Hemings children is proven 'beyond a reasonable doubt'"):

> Whether Jefferson fathered all of Hemings's children is still unclear. Madison Hemings claimed he did. And since Eston Hemings was born in 1808, when Jefferson was sixty-five years old, it seems highly unlikely that the relationship began and ended at that time. On the other hand, the DNA study produced a nonmatch with Thomas Woodson, the first of Sally's surviving children. Either Madison Hemings was wrong about the origins of the relationship, or the nonmatch with Thomas Woodson is the result of a "false paternity," that is, a subsequent break in the genetic line that falsifies the results.[77]

This would seem to be a reasonable conclusion, except in this instance there is only the remotest, highly theoretical chance of a "false paternity" result. The initial study reported by Dr. Foster in *Nature* involved the testing of *five* male-line descendants of two different sons of Thomas Woodson. Four of these matched, and the fifth was judged a consequence of an illegitimate father somewhere in the line. Since then, yet another Woodson descendant—from a third son of Thomas Woodson—has been tested, with no match to Thomas Jefferson or any other Jefferson male. Occam would not favor concluding that the same illegitimate father, over a period of many years, produced three sons who were generally but wrongly believed to be Thomas Woodson's, over the simpler conclusion that Thomas Woodson was not fathered by any Jefferson. Even less likely would be the theory that the same man went from family to family fathering the sons of Thomas Woodson's three sons over a period of years. The "false paternity" option sounds reasonable, but it simply will not wash. Professor Ellis is factually mistaken when he postulates the option of "*a false paternity*"— there would have to be at minimum *three* "subsequent break[s] in the genetic line," and all of them would have to involve the same illegitimate father. Dr. Ellis is thus left with his first conclusion: that "Madison Hemings was wrong about the origins of the relationship."

The Monticello Research Committee seems to have simply decided to resolve the conflict between the Woodson oral history and Dr. Foster's DNA tests by summarily eliminating Thomas Woodson as one of Sally Hemings' possible children. After all of their years of interviewing Woodson family descendants in their "Getting Word" oral history project, their January 2000 "Research Findings and Implications" stated: "The DNA evidence indicates that, despite an enduring oral tradition in the Woodson family, Thomas Jefferson was not the father of Thomas C. Woodson. No documents have yet been found to support the belief that Woodson was Sally Hemings' first child, born soon after her re-

---

76. The DNA tests examined Y chromosomes seeking matches among male descendants of Sally's sons and those of descendants of Thomas Jefferson's paternal uncle and said nothing about Sally Hemings or any other possible mother.

77. Ellis, *Jefferson: Post-DNA* at 126–27.

turn from France."[78] They might have added that no "documents"[79] have been found to support the belief that Sally Hemings had *any* child in 1790.

It has gone almost unnoticed that Thomas Woodson's Y chromosome was not one characteristic of inhabitants of sub-Saharan Africa, but rather one common among European males.[80] This proves nothing, but it is consistent with a theory that Sally Hemings might have become pregnant in Paris by a man other than Thomas Jefferson, and that Thomas Woodson was born as claimed after she returned to the United States. This is possible, but there are many other equally plausible explanations. It is of no consequence to our inquiry.

Other Possible Fathers

Another problem with the *Monticello Report* and much of the other scholarship supporting a Jefferson-Hemings sexual relationship is the tendency to dismiss other potential fathers. To be sure, the *Report* admits that there were more than two dozen known[81] Jefferson males in Virginia when Eston was conceived who were old enough to father children and carried exactly the same DNA Y chromosome as Thomas Jefferson.[82] Since Thomas Jefferson inherited many of his slaves from his father, who in turn had inherited slaves from his father, there is at least some chance that a male Jefferson impregnated a slave and produced a son carrying this same Y chromosome, a slave who was later inherited by Thomas Jefferson. If so, that man (or those men) could also have produced children with Sally Hemings, who would pass on the same Y chromosome found in Eston's descendant.[83]

Peter and Samuel Carr

It is now clear that neither Peter nor Samuel Carr fathered Eston Hemings or Thomas Woodson. But that is all the DNA tests can tell us. They say *nothing* about who fathered Harriet I, Beverly, Harriet II, "Thenia" (if Sally Hemings had such a daughter[84]), or Madison Hemings. It is only when one ignores the eyewitness testimony of Edmund Bacon, the various references to confessions by the Carr brothers, and the new DNA evidence about Thomas Woodson, that it is possible to conclude that Sally Hemings possibly could have had a monogamous sexual relationship with Thomas Jefferson. But the assumption of monogamy is so critical to the revisionist case that they have found it desirable to por-

---

78. *Monticello Report* at 6.

79. The only "sources" for the contention that Sally Hemings conceived a child in Paris appear to be Callender's unsupported 1802 allegations and the statement attributed to Madison Hemings seventy-one years later.

80. It should be kept in mind that most Caucasian American men of the era came from European stock and thus would have carried the DNA of a "European male."

81. Obviously, Thomas Jefferson's great grandfather in England (or one of his male ancestors) might have produced a number of different lines of male descendants who were unknown to each other, and if any of these had emigrated to America and fathered sons, their male descendants would presumably have carried the same DNA Y chromosome as Thomas Jefferson.

82. *Monticello Report* at 9.

83. My own sense is that Eston was probably fathered by a member of the Jefferson family, but the possibility of a slave father must nevertheless be recognized as at least a theoretical possibility.

84. *See* the discussion of this issue on pp. 91–93.

tray the DNA evidence as having ruled out the Carrs as possible fathers for *any* of Sally Hemings' other children. That obviously is not true.

Professor Ellis, for example, asserts that the DNA evidence "exposes the Carr explanation as a contrivance,"[85] explaining: "The study shows no match between the Hemings *line* and the Carr family, thereby undermining the long-standing explanation offered by Jefferson's white descendants (that is, that Peter Carr or Samuel Carr is the culprit) and endorsed by several prominent Jefferson scholars...."[86] But this is factually in error. Unless Thomas Woodson was the son of Sally Hemings, the only member of the "Hemings line" tested was a descendant of Eston. As Dr. Foster has acknowledged,[87] the DNA tests said absolutely *nothing* about the paternity of Sally's other children.[88]

In the same issue of the *William & Mary Quarterly*, Monticello's Lucia Stanton writes:

> Now, because of the almost seismic effect of a scientific test, we will never again read the words of Jefferson and the members of his household in quite the same way. The core feature of the Jefferson family denial—that Peter Carr or Samuel Carr was the father of Hemings's children—has been discredited by chromosomes and haplotypes. Have the accounts of Jefferson's grandchildren Thomas Jefferson Randolph and Ellen Randolph Coolidge lost some of their credibility because, in this one area, they seem to have misrepresented the truth so materially?[89]

Ms. Stanton relies upon this alleged evidence of misrepresentation to question the reliability of Ellen Coolidge's descriptions of Jefferson's religious and other views.[90] This simply makes no sense. First, the Carrs remain viable suspects for the possible paternity of all of Sally Hemings' other children. Second, even were that not true, Ellen Coolidge was apparently basing her statement upon accounts provided by her brother Jeff. Even if we assume that every word he said to her was a lie, that does not make *her* repetition of the story in good faith an act of dishonesty on her part so as to call into question her own veracity.[91]

Randolph Jefferson and His Sons

Professor Gordon-Reed suggests in *Thomas Jefferson and Sally Hemings* that the only explanation for the physical similarities between Thomas Jefferson and Sally's children is either that one of the Carr brothers (sons of Jefferson's sister) was their father or that it was Thomas Jefferson himself. She writes:

> It is important to keep in mind the relationship between the two competing theories as to who fathered Sally Hemings's children. Members of the Jefferson family offered the Carr brothers as the likely fathers to explain why Sally Hemings's four children looked so much like Thomas Jefferson. Eliminating the Carr brothers does not erase the children's close resemblance to Jefferson. Some other as yet

---

85. Ellis, *Jefferson: Post-DNA* at 125.
86. *Id.* (Emphasis added).
87. *See* Chapter One.
88. Again, if one assumes that Thomas Woodson was Sally's child, he is ruled out by the DNA tests as being fathered by a Carr.
89. Stanton, *The Other End of the Telescope*, William & Mary Q. 139–40 (Jan. 2000).
90. *Id.* at 140.
91. Obviously, an element of the offense of "lying" or relating a falsehood is *knowledge* by the speaker that the information is untrue.

undesignated Jefferson relative must be substituted, or Thomas Jefferson remains the most likely father. In the absence of any contemporary source suggesting that another relative might have been the father or any present-day indication that it might have been someone else, such speculation seems a desperate attempt to absolve Jefferson at the cost of all reason.[92]

Professor Gordon-Reed does not even appear to have known of the *existence* of Thomas Jefferson's brother, Randolph, when she published her book in 1997. At least his name does not appear on her genealogical chart[93] or in her index,[94] and one hesitates to assume that she was intentionally trying to conceal his existence.[95] A relatively minor figure of little historic interest beyond being related to our third President, Thomas Jefferson's intellectually challenged[96] younger brother Randolph is ignored by many Jefferson scholars and is referred to as the President's "unknown brother" by the one scholar who has given him much attention.[97]

When it was determined by DNA testing that Eston Hemings was probably fathered by a member of the Jefferson family, some Jefferson defenders suggested that one of the most likely suspects among the more than two dozen male Jeffersons in Virginia at the time was Randolph, who was born on October 1, 1755, and thus was nearly twelve years younger than the President. Randolph and his twin sister Anna Scott were the youngest of the ten children known to have been born to Peter Jefferson and Jane Randolph.[98]

Professor Ellis (who makes no reference to Randolph in his own biography, *American Sphinx*, and reportedly admitted not knowing of Randolph's existence until his name surfaced following report of the DNA evidence[99]) provides this assessment of the suggestion that Randolph, rather than Thomas, might have fathered Eston Hemings:

---

92. Gordon-Reed, Thomas Jefferson and Sally Hemings at 217–18.

93. *Id.* at 22. (These citations are to the first edition of the Gordon-Reed volume.)

94. *Id.* At 285.

95. However, she does include in her bibliography the most extensive scholarly account of Randolph, *Thomas Jefferson and His Unknown Brother* (Bernard Mayo ed., 1981). See Gordon-Reed, Thomas Jefferson and Sally Hemings 278.

96. Randolph Jefferson has occasionally been referred to as being a "half-wit." Professor Brodie describes him at one point in her book as being "less than mediocre in talent and native intelligence," and at another as being "mentally ill." Brodie, Thomas Jefferson 264, 457. James Bear writes: "Randolph emerges, at best, as an unenlightened and simple dirt farmer...." Bear, *Preface*, Thomas Jefferson and His Unknown Brother vii (Bernard Mayo ed., 1981). In volume two of his 1951 biography, Nathan Schachner writes that Randolph's "mind was limited and his world circumscribed to the narrow confines of his daily routine. His elder brother treated him always with tenderness and respect, and helped him patiently in all the minutiae that troubled the younger man. Randolph would scrawl illiterate little notes to Thomas, in which the loan of a gig loomed larger than the deaths of his sisters.... Thomas would reply simply and kindly, speaking of small, everyday events that were within the scope of Randolph Jefferson's limited understanding." 2 Nathan Schachner, Thomas Jefferson 923 (1951). Yet Randolph briefly attended the College of William & Mary and managed his own plantation (with frequent advice from his older brother). Candidly, Randolph may have suffered somewhat from unfavorable comparisons to his truly brilliant elder brother. Having "half" the "wit" of Thomas Jefferson did not necessarily make him that far below the national norm. It does seem clear that he was not heavily focused upon *ideas*, and there is reason to believe he would not have especially enjoyed sitting around Monticello after dinner listening to Thomas expound upon the latest scientific theories or on political developments in Europe.

97. Thomas Jefferson and His Unknown Brother (Bernard Mayo, ed., 1981).

98. For general background on Randolph Jefferson, see *id.* at 1–6.

99. Conversation with Herbert Barger, who asserts that when he raised the possibility that Randolph or one of his sons might have fathered Eston, Professor Ellis acknowledged that he did not realize Thomas Jefferson had a brother.

To be sure, the DNA evidence establishes probability rather than certainty. A spirited rebuttal has been mounted by Jefferson genealogist Herbert Barger, suggesting that Randolph Jefferson or his son Isham (Jefferson's brother and nephew, respectively) is a more likely candidate. No one had mentioned Randolph Jefferson as a possible alternative before the DNA study. He is being brought forward now because he fits the genetic profile. This belated claim strikes me as a kind of last stand for the most dedicated Jefferson loyalists.... Historians of the Lost Cause syndrome will recognize the poignant fusion of sincerity and futility at work here.[100]

In a similar vein, the *Monticello Report* observed that "Randolph Jefferson and his sons are not known to have been at Monticello at the time of Eston Hemings's conception, nor has anyone, until 1998, ever before publicly suggested them as possible fathers."[101] In an attached memorandum on "The Possible Paternity of Other Jeffersons," the *Monticello Report* adds, "there are no known references (prior to the 1998 DNA results) to Randolph Jefferson as a possible father of Sally Hemings' children," and concludes without further explanation that Randolph's paternity is "very unlikely...."[102]

Prior Suggestions That Randolph Jefferson May Have Fathered Some of Sally's Children

It is true that most scholars who have addressed the Jefferson-Hemings story have not focused on Randolph Jefferson as the likely father of any of Sally's children. In terms of historical interest, he was a very minor figure. Most Jefferson biographers mention him only in passing, if at all. Their only concern with respect to Sally Hemings and her children was presumably whether the Callender allegations were true. Finding the story implausible, they tended simply to accept the stories attributed to Jeff Randolph that the Carr brothers had confessed to paternity and moved on to other issues. Once they were convinced that the allegations against the President were false, the details of Sally Hemings' life were of no greater interest to them than those of Randolph Jefferson's life.

Nevertheless, it is *not* true that Randolph's name has never come up in connection with Sally's children. To begin with, there are oral history accounts of families from the Monticello area asserting that Randolph fathered Sally Hemings' children. Rebecca Lee McMurry, whose ancestors grew up near Monticello and purchased pieces of china at the "great sale" following Jefferson's death that have been handed down through the generations, has sworn in an affidavit[103] that when Professor Brodie's book appeared in 1974, she (McMurry) was told by her mother that the "yellow people" at Monticello were the offspring of Randolph Jefferson. This, at least was the oral tradition of her family.

A similar account was reportedly provided by a caller named "Diane" on a February 23, 1999, radio call-in program. "Diane" asserted that she was "skeptical" about the DNA

---

100. Ellis, *Jefferson: Post-DNA* 126.
101. *Monticello Report* 6.
102. *Id.*, Appendix J at 3.
103. Ms. McMurry wrote: "Only after the publication of Fawn Brodie's book did my mother wax indignant and her statement was, 'Honey, that book is trash! Everyone knows it was his half-witted brother.'" Notarized statement, "Paternity of Sally Hemings' Children, Statement of Rebecca Lee McMurry," Apr. 1, 1999, a copy of which is in the writer's possession.

reports, because "my father is an amateur historian who grew up by Monticello, and my father told me right off the bat, that it was not Jefferson, it was his brother."[104]

Like all allegations based upon oral tradition, these statements do not come *close* to conclusively establishing the facts alleged. However, in one sense,[105] it can be argued that these accounts may be inherently more reliable than the oral traditions of families who have a vested interest in portraying their own ancestors in a positive light. At any rate, they are not offered here to "prove" that Randolph Jefferson fathered any of Sally Hemings' children, but to suggest that the allegation is not merely a desperate, last-minute, afterthought effort of Jefferson apologists to mislead the jury.

One of the most interesting discussions of Randolph's possible paternity is found in a 1958 letter from Pearl Graham to Professor Julian Boyd, at the time the editor of *The Papers of Thomas Jefferson* being published at Princeton University. Long before Professor Fawn Brodie's book was published, Ms. Graham was convinced that Thomas Jefferson was the father of Sally Hemings' children; and she had clearly done some serious research on the issue—including, allegedly, interviewing two granddaughters of Harriet Hemings. (Ms. Graham was instrumental in getting the Hemings family to donate a bell to Howard University that was allegedly given by Martha Wayles Jefferson, on her deathbed, to one of the Hemings girls.[106]) Noting the reported physical resemblance of Hemings' children to Thomas Jefferson, Graham discussed alternative theories that might explain this result:

> Among his paternal relatives, the possibilities could be narrowed down to three,— his brother, Randolph, and two nephews, Samuel and Dabney Carr. A study of the known facts about these three convinced me that, while some one of them <u>might</u> have fathered <u>one</u> of Sally's children, a liaison advering [*sic*] well over ten years was not in the realm of possibility,—and Jefferson's staunchest defenders have never charged that Sally was promiscuous. A further item would seem to eliminate Randolph Jefferson: one of Harriet's granddaughters had told me that Jefferson's younger brother "also" had colored children. Had it been the younger, instead of the elder, brother, who was her own ancestor, she would probably have known of some tradition to that effect. Moreover, if 'Tom' was not a figment of Callender's imagination, no one save Jefferson could possibly have been the father.[107]

I do not know how reliable this information is. At minimum, it clearly shows that Randolph Jefferson was being discussed as a serious alternative to Thomas Jefferson for the paternity of Sally Hemings' children four decades before the DNA tests were made public, even by a source who was clearly persuaded that the President was the father. It may be noteworthy that Randolph Jefferson was mentioned before two of the three Carr brothers (for some reason Peter Carr was not mentioned), and given a more extensive consideration in the process. One cannot help but note the irony in her suggestion that if [Uncle] Randolph were the father there would probably be "some tradition to that effect."

It is also unclear to me whether Pearl Graham's "source" for the allegation that Randolph Jefferson had "colored children" by his own slaves (a woman named "Kenny" who

---

104. WAVE (105.1 FM Radio), February 23, 1999, hosted by Janet Parshall.

105. While accounts passed down reflecting the opinions of third-party observers (whether eyewitness accounts or based merely on local gossip or speculation) may not be tarnished by a desire to further the image of a particular family, they may well suffer from other biases (including racial prejudice), and such observers may have less interest in carefully recording factual details than might a family member.

106. E-mail from Lucia Stanton to Bob Turner, Mar. 26, 2001, 4:09 PM, RE: Pearl Graham.

107. *Pearl M. Graham to Julian P. Boyd*, Jan. 11, 1958, a copy of which is on file with the writer.

claimed to be a descendant of Sally's daughter Harriet) was who she claimed to be; but Lucia Stanton of the Thomas Jefferson Foundation informs me that she finds Ms. Graham's "work on the Hemings descendants in the 1940s" to be "very very interesting," and concludes that "there seems no reason to doubt the Kenny sisters' connection somehow with Monticello, and probably to the Hemings family."[108] The charge—attributed to Hemings family descendants—that Randolph Jefferson had "colored children" of his own is noteworthy, as Ms. Graham and the Kenny sisters did seem to have a great deal of information about the matter, and one of their apparent goals was to convince people that Thomas Jefferson was the father of Sally Hemings' children. While certainly not "proven," the allegation that Randolph had "colored children" seems as strong as much if not most of the "evidence" being relied upon by the revisionists. It arguably makes Randolph Jefferson an even stronger candidate for Eston's paternity.

Monticello's Lucia Stanton asserts that the Kennys "were raised as part of the Charlottesville African-American community," and since Madison Hemings alleged that Harriet had settled into a white community, Ms. Graham may have erred in her conclusions about their ancestry. Ms. Stanton concluded this discussion by writing: "[M]y view is that Pearl Graham did some very good work, but sometimes got carried away by her enthusiasms. Her papers at Howard and at Alderman have been of great use to us in our work at Monticello."[109]

There is at least one other very interesting pre-DNA-test assertion that Randolph Jefferson might have been the father of Sally Hemings' children. Writing in *Sally Hemings and Thomas Jefferson,* Professor Gordon-Reed suggested that the truth about Thomas Jefferson would be more likely to emerge from artists than from scholars:

> In the end, it will probably be left to novelists, playwrights, and poets, unencumbered by the need for footnotes, to get at the ultimate meaning of this story. That effort, done in the right way, will yield universal truths as important and real as any to be found in history books.[110]

There is more than a little irony to this comment, as an award-winning playwright and producer in North Carolina addressed this issue in her play *Saturday's Children.*[111] Professor Karyn Traut (wife of Scholars Commission member Professor Thomas Traut) first became interested in writing a play about "Tom" Jefferson, the slave child made famous by James Callender, after reading and being deeply moved by Professor Fawn Brodie's 1974 book, *Thomas Jefferson: An Intimate History.* Assuming the story of a Jefferson-

---

108. E-mail from Lucia Stanton to Bob Turner, Mar. 26, 2001, 4:09 PM, RE: Pearl Graham.
109. *Id.*
110. Annette Gordon-Reed, *"The Memories of a Few Negroes,"* in SALLY HEMINGS AND THOMAS JEFFERSON 251 (Jan Ellen Lewis & Peter S. Onuf, eds. 1999). Professor Gordon-Reed's frustration with the burden of trying to support the claim of a Jefferson-Hemings sexual relationship with footnotes citing credible sources is understandable, but the implication that "novelists" and "poets" are preferable to sound scholarly writings in the search for the truth is a bit bizarre.
111. The clever title comes from the fact that when Thomas Jefferson moved his remarkable double-sided clock from Philadelphia to Monticello and installed it over the entranceway, the weighted chains that drove it were too long; so Jefferson cut holes in the floor to allow the weights to travel into the basement. As the weights moved downward during the week, Jefferson marked off lines on the wall indicating the current day of the week, but the "Saturday" mark is found in the basement (where slave children might have been found). It was the playwright's intent to symbolize that slavery itself, along with women's and minority rights, was left in the basement of the elegant American system.

Hemings relationship to be true, she spent seven years researching Jefferson in preparation for writing her play, which was first produced in 1988.[112]

As she explains in a narrative prepared at my request and (also at my urging) appended to the Individual Views of Professor Thomas Traut that appear later in this volume, Professor Karyn Traut concluded from her research that Professor Brodie had "thrown out the pieces of the puzzle that didn't fit her model...."[113] She concluded that Thomas Jefferson was *not* the father of Sally's children, and found the most likely suspect to be brother Randolph.

I would add only that Professor Traut—a Berkeley-educated transplant from California—is no "conservative" bent on upholding the image of Thomas Jefferson or other dead white males at all costs. She happily confesses to being a "liberal Democrat," and indeed attributes her ability to revise her initial judgment to her open-minded liberalism. I have not seen her play, but from the script and contemporary press clippings, it was clearly anything but "conservative" in its "four-dimensional" approach. Ms. Traut made use of sculpture, puppetry, and a musical mix combining African drums with harpsichord. One of the two actors portraying Thomas Jefferson was an African-American (which earned playwright Traut recognition in the 1992 *Aetna Calendar of Black History*).

Again, the point here is not that Karyn Traut's play was inevitably *correct* in its conclusions (although it has been praised by historians for its accuracy), but rather to demonstrate that the suggestion that Randolph Jefferson might have fathered one or more of Sally Hemings' children did *not* originate in response to the 1998 DNA studies.

Why Randolph Jefferson Is a Good Candidate for Paternity of Eston Hemings

It is not my position that Randolph Jefferson fathered Eston Hemings. We simply do not *know* who Eston's father was, and I suspect we never will with any certainty. But several pieces of evidence about Randolph make him highly relevant to our inquiry— and in my view make him a *much* stronger candidate for the paternity of Eston Hemings than President Thomas Jefferson from among the roughly two dozen other possible candidates.

First, we have the issue of *opportunity*. Was Randolph near Sally Hemings when Eston was likely conceived? While it is generally assumed that Randolph was a regular visitor to Monticello, such routine visits by close relatives were apparently not thought remarkable enough by Thomas Jefferson to make note of them in his various record books.[114] Indeed, throughout his life, although Randolph may well have made the twenty-mile trip to see his brother and other family members at Monticello several times each year,[115] there are only four visits actually documented in Thomas Jefferson's surviving records—each

---

112. For an excellent summary of this story, *see* Catherine House, *Which Jefferson?*, ENDEAVOURS ("Research and Creative Activity • The University of North Carolina at Chapel Hill"), Spring, 2002, at 18–20.

113. *See* Statement of Playwright Karyn Traut, *infra* at p.331.

114. For example, although nothing in Thomas Jefferson's surviving letters or memorandum books suggests that Randolph was at Monticello during the summer of 1802, in the fourth volume of his Pulitzer Prize-winning biography Jefferson scholar Dumas Malone documents that among the many visitors to Monticello that summer was the President's brother Randolph. DUMAS MALONE, JEFFERSON THE PRESIDENT: FIRST TERM 167 (1970).

115. In a letter to daughter Martha written from Monticello on January 22, 1795, Jefferson noted that he and Maria were "in hopes soon of a visit from my sister Anne." THE FAMILY LETTERS OF

of these because of some business that was transacted in connection with the visit.[116] This is not "proof" that Randolph and his family only visited every five or ten years, but rather an indication that his visits were considered so routine as to not be noteworthy.

In part because a fire at his Snowden home destroyed virtually all of Randolph Jefferson's papers, there are few surviving letters between Randolph and Thomas Jefferson. Indeed, for the period 1792 to 1808, during which Sally Hemings conceived all of her known children at Monticello,[117] there remain only *three* letters, all from the year 1807.[118] However, one of those letters is ironically of *great* importance to the present inquiry.

On Wednesday, August 12, 1807, Thomas Jefferson concluded a letter to Randolph (see **Figure 11** on the next page) by noting: "Our sister Marks arrived here last night and we shall be happy to see you also."[119] This was a reference to the arrival at Monticello of Randolph's twin sister, Anna Scott Marks. We know that Randolph was a frequent visitor to Monticello, that he was fond of his twin sister, and also that he tended to be very deferential to his famous brother and to follow his guidance on most matters.[120] August was also a good time for him to visit because the fields would have been plowed and the crops would have been planted, but it was not yet harvest time.[121]

We simply do not have surviving records to know with certainty whether or not Randolph made the trip in August 1807. Indeed, the language "we shall be happy to see you also" is sufficiently ambiguous to be either an invitation to visit or merely notice that his sister had arrived so that an already agreed-upon trip could be made. We do know that Randolph had promised to deliver grass seed to Monticello about this time.[122] Given Randolph's known love for his sister and his established deference to his older brother, in the absence of some reason to assume he did *not* make the trip, it would seem reasonable to treat the surviving letter as shifting the presumption in favor of such a visit—especially since there is no letter of "regret" informing Thomas Jefferson that for some reason Randolph could *not* make the short trip.

Let us speculate (in the absence of solid evidence) that it took two days for the letter to make the twenty-mile trip, and Randolph received it around Friday, August 14. Or perhaps it arrived on Monday, August 17. Perhaps Randolph (and, presumably, his family) departed immediately, or perhaps they needed a day or more to prepare for the trip—which took less than a day. Give or take ten days or so each way, it is estimated that Eston Hemings was conceived around August 27 or 28.[123] It was common for such visits to last weeks at a time, and thus, if Randolph made the trip, he (and his sons) would likely have been at Monticello during most and perhaps all of the "conception window" for Eston Hemings.

THOMAS JEFFERSON 133. Jefferson routinely used the word "sister" to refer as well to his "sister-in-law," and this may have thus been a reference to brother Randolph's wife Anne Lewis. We can only speculate about why she was mentioned, whether Randolph and the children would come with her (or were already at Monticello), and other details.

116. *Monticello Report*, Appendix J at 2. Cynthia Burton informs me that she has confirmed other visits on Jan. 15, 1790, in January 1795, on April 22, 1797, and on April 21, 1808.

117. If Thomas Woodson was Sally's child, he was apparently born in 1790.

118. THOMAS JEFFERSON AND HIS UNKNOWN BROTHER 19–21. *See also, Monticello Report*, Appendix J at 2.

119. THOMAS JEFFERSON AND HIS UNKNOWN BROTHER 21.

120. Deposition of Thomas Jefferson, Sept. 15, 1815, Jefferson Papers at University of Virginia.

121. I am indebted to Richard H. Crouch for this observation.

122. CYNTHIA HARRIS BURTON, JEFFERSON VINDICATED 57–58 (2005).

123. *See, e.g.,* Fraser D. Neiman, *Coincidence or Causal Connection?*, 57(1) WILLIAM & MARY Q. 205 (Jan. 2000).

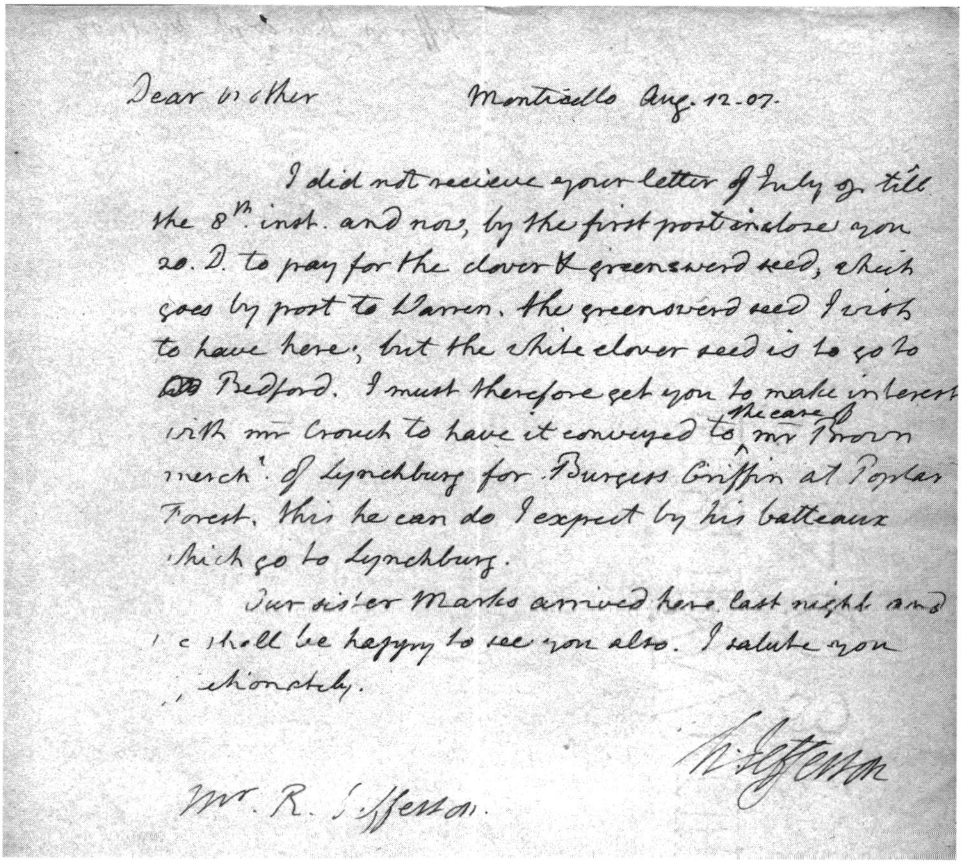
Dear Brother Monticello Aug. 12. 07.

I did not recieve your letter of July 29. till the 8th. inst. and now, by the first post inclose you 20. D. to pay for the clover & greensward seed, which goes by post to Warren. the greensward seed I wish to have here; but the white clover seed is to go to Bedford. I must therefore get you to make interest with mr Crouch to have it conveyed to the care of mr Brown merch^t. of Lynchburg for Burgess Griffin at Poplar Forest. this he can do I expect by his batteaux which go to Lynchburg.

Our sister Marks arrived here last night and we shall be happy to see you also. I salute you affectionately.

Th: Jefferson

Mr. R. Jefferson.

Figure 11. President Jefferson invited his younger brother Randolph to visit Monticello about ten days before the only Hemings child linked by DNA to a Jefferson father was conceived. Randolph and his five sons would havc carried the same Y chromosome detected in 1998 DNA tests of a descendant of Eston Hemings, and Randolph was documented by former Monticello slave Isaac Jefferson to have spent his evenings at Monticello dancing "half the night" with his brother's slaves. See page 228. Reproduced courtesy of Special Collections, University of Virginia Library.

Does this letter of invitation constitute "proof" that Randolph Jefferson was at Monticello when Eston Hemings was conceived? Certainly not. But Thomas Jefferson's other surviving letter to Randolph from 1807 expressed the hope of seeing his brother at Monticello during his spring visit,[124] and the *Monticello Report* concedes that similar invitations were presumably extended in previous years.[125] In this instance, Randolph had not only the enticement of being able to see his older brother but also his visiting twin sister. Again, given his known fondness for his sister and his propensity to follow his brother's advice, the existence of the letter ought to create a presumption that Randolph Jefferson probably was at Monticello during at least part of the time when Eston was likely conceived.

---

124. Thomas Jefferson and His Unknown Brother 19.
125. *Monticello Report*, Appendix J at 2.

The *Monticello Report* takes a different tack, noting (correctly) that "A search of visitors' accounts, memorandum books, and Jefferson's published and unpublished correspondence provided no indication that Randolph did, in fact, come at this time."[126] Of course, relying on this approach would lead us to believe that Thomas Jefferson's brother, who was clearly both fond of and highly dependent[127] upon the President, only made the twenty-mile trip from Snowden to Monticello four times in his entire life.

The *Monticello Report* adds that the correspondence between the Jefferson brothers "also suggests that Randolph Jefferson may not always have acted on these invitations."[128] That is *almost* correct. In June of 1810, Randolph explained that "I should of bin over before this but have bin very much put to it to git Iron to make an axiltree to my Gigg and have not got any yet[.]"[129] So Randolph clearly was explaining why he had *not* visited, but it is not at all clear this was in response to a specific *invitation* he had recently[130] received.

In September of 1811, Thomas Jefferson wrote to tell Randolph that their sister Martha, the widow of Dabney Carr and mother of Peter, Samuel, and Dabney, had passed away and had been buried beside her husband.[131] The letter made no specific reference to Randolph visiting. A month later, Randolph replied to express his extreme sorrow at the death of their sibling, and added "Would of bin over but it was not raly in My power," explaining "I have Just Got over a very severe tack of the Gravil"[132]—presumably referring to kidney stones.[133] Here again, this is presumably not really declining an invitation to visit Monticello, but rather a *sua sponte* explanation of why he had not visited in the recent past.

The final example occurred early in 1812, when, on January 14, Thomas Jefferson wrote to inform Randolph of the demise of their brother-in-law, Hastings Marks, and to let him know that his twin sister, Anna Scott Marks, was now living at Monticello, "but in very low health indeed, and scarcely able to walk about the house."[134] Unlike the 1807 letter referring to their sister, Jefferson made no specific reference to hoping Randolph would soon visit—quite possibly because January was the middle of winter. At any rate, on February 8, Randolph replied:

> As soon as the roads gits in good order we Will come over I expect it will be the last of next Month or the first of april, I am Very sorry to hear of My sister Marks low state of health, but hope she Will recover after a little time after the weather Gits a little Warmer, if My health should continue to keep as it is I will endeavour to come over next Month.[135]

So, in none of these examples did Randolph Jefferson clearly decline a specific invitation from Thomas Jefferson to visit Monticello in the immediate future. More im-

---

126. *Id.*
127. Consider, for example, the already mentioned sworn affidavit that Thomas Jefferson provided on September 15, 1815, in connection with a dispute over Randolph's will. He wrote: "That the testator [Randolph] was always in the habit of consulting this deponent [Thomas Jefferson] in all cases of importance respecting his interests, and he knows of no such case in which he did not consult him, except that of his last marriage...."
128. *Monticello Report*, Appendix J at 2.
129. Thomas Jefferson and His Unknown Brother 24.
130. Six months earlier, Jefferson had included a general invitation that Randolph "pay us a visit here with my sister" (the designation he used for his sister-in-law). *Id.* at 23.
131. Thomas Jefferson and His Unknown Brother 26.
132. *Id.* at 27.
133. *Id.* n.3.
134. *Id.* at 28.
135. *Id.* at 30.

portantly, not a single one of the surviving letters from Randolph Jefferson to his brother even arguably constitutes an "acceptance" of an invitation to visit. True, as Randolph got older, his health was bad, or winter weather made travel difficult, he did mention these things to explain why he had not recently visited and might not be able to do so for a while longer. This strongly suggests, among other things, that Randolph was normally a regular visitor to Monticello and that he may not have formally "accepted" invitations to visit in writing when he was able to make the trip without significant delay.

Note also Randolph's use of the plural *we* in the sentence that includes "we Will come over...." This suggests the (already logical) conclusion that when Randolph Jefferson visited Monticello, his normal practice was to bring his family. This is significant, because if he did so at the time Sally Hemings conceived Eston, it would likely have added another four Jefferson males to the scene who, if for no other reason than the fact they were in the prime of their sexuality, must be considered more likely to have fathered a child than the sixty-four-year-old Thomas Jefferson. This will be discussed in a moment.

How should we interpret the lack of a written response from Randolph following Thomas Jefferson's invitation to visit Monticello of August 12, 1807? Again, there is not a single example of Randolph ever writing when he was *coming* to Monticello in response to such an invitation.[136] There were no telephones, the mails could be slow, and the simplest response to such an invitation would have been to pack up the family and travel to Monticello. However, especially knowing that his sister was there and presumably hoping to see him, there would be far more logic in sending a "regrets" note if he could *not* make the August 1807 visit. Ultimately, the absence of information in this situation does not "prove" anything—especially since there may once have been a reply that has not been preserved. But the most probable explanation if Randolph did not write is that he packed up the family and traveled to Monticello—probably completing the short trip well before a posted letter would have arrived to announce his intentions.

We have as well in Randolph's letters to his brother suggestions that he may have had a drinking problem. For example, in a letter written on Thomas Jefferson's sixty-ninth birthday (although Randolph does not mention it) in 1812, Randolph adds "I have not put a drop of any kind of spirits in My Mouth since I saw you."[137] In a footnote to this sentence, editor Bernard Mayo observes that it might indicate that Randolph "may have had a drinking problem."[138]

Isaac Jefferson's Memoirs of a Monticello Slave

So it would seem at least "more likely than not" that Randolph Jefferson (and quite likely his sons, since this would be a family social visit) were present at Monticello in August 1807. What would he have done there? We have good reason to believe that he had little interest in science or world affairs,[139] and thus he probably would not have found great

---

136. In fairness, we certainly cannot rule out the possibility that such letters once existed.

137. THOMAS JEFFERSON AND HIS UNKNOWN BROTHER 32.

138. *Id.* n.1. Assuming that is correct, it does not prove that Randolph was the father of any of Sally Hemings' children. But the excessive use of alcohol has been linked to adventuristic or reckless sexual behavior.

139. *See, e.g.,* Thomas Jefferson's letter to Randolph of January 11, 1789—on the eve of the French Revolution—which began "The occurrences of this part of the globe are of a nature to interest you so little that I have never made them the subject of a letter to you." *Id.* at 13.

pleasure in sitting around the big house after dinner listening to his brilliant brother entertain other visitors with accounts of travels, government affairs, or new theories of science. Perhaps he would take his leave after dinner and seek pleasure elsewhere on the mountain?

Fortunately, we need not speculate on this point, as we have reliable eyewitness testimony. In 1847, Charles W. Campbell recorded a lengthy narrative from former Monticello blacksmith Isaac Jefferson. Later published under the title *Memoirs of a Monticello Slave*, this important document provides the following explanation of Randolph Jefferson's after-dinner behavior while visiting Monticello: "Old Master's brother, Mass Randall [*sic*], was a mighty simple man: used to come out among black people, play the fiddle and dance half the night; hadn't much more sense than Isaac."

Isaac Jefferson clearly thought very highly of Thomas Jefferson and had no apparent reason to fabricate this account. He confirms the prevailing wisdom that Randolph was a man of limited intellectual capacity, and his account is not that he *once* witnessed Randolph playing his fiddle for the slaves, but that this was apparently a common occurrence. Add to this the likelihood that Randolph was at Monticello when Sally Hemings conceived Eston; consider too the reports attributed to descendants of Harriet Hemings that Randolph had "colored children" of his own; and keep in mind as well that Randolph was a dozen years younger than the sixty-four-year-old President (who was presumably entertaining guests at the mansion while brother Randolph "fiddled" with the slaves); and the case for Randolph's paternity of Eston would seem to *strongly* outweigh that for the President's. This certainly does not *prove* that Randolph Jefferson was Eston Hemings' father. But when you add in the fact that Eston's descendants for generations passed down the story that Eston was the son of an "uncle" rather than Thomas Jefferson himself, the case that "Uncle Randolph" was Eston's father gets even stronger.

Given the outlandish speculation (discussed previously) that Sally's boys must have been fathered by Thomas Jefferson because some of them played the fiddle, it might be noted that Randolph Jefferson "took violin lessons from Francis Alberti, who had also instructed Thomas."[140] But, unlike President Jefferson's passion in his adult years for the *violin*, Randolph was apparently fond of the kind of "folk" *fiddle* music that was popular among Monticello slaves. Furthermore, as noted in Chapter Nine, Thomas Jefferson's ability to play the violin was seriously impaired by his 1786 wrist injury in Paris and subsequent rheumatism, and by the time Madison and Eston were old enough to learn to play, Jefferson seldom played.[141] Thus, all of these rather frivolous arguments about fiddle playing would apply with at least equal if not *greater* force to place paternity on brother Randolph. In reality, however, there were enough fiddle-playing slaves at Monticello that the fact that some of Sally's children developed similar skills is evidence of nothing remarkable.

How does the *Monticello Report* deal with the eyewitness account by former slave Isaac Jefferson that Randolph Jefferson was fond of socializing at night with Monticello slaves? With but a single sentence: "Since Isaac Jefferson left Monticello in 1797, his reference probably predates that year, and most likely refers to the 1780s, the period that is the subject of the majority of his recollections."[142] From this, we are told, "Isaac Jefferson's observation most likely relates to the period of Randolph Jefferson's youth."[143]

---

140. *Id.* at 3.
141. Helen Cripe, Thomas Jefferson and Music 27–31 (1974). *See also*, Sandor Salgo, Thomas Jefferson: Musician & Violinist 29–30 (2000).
142. *Monticello Report*, Appendix J at 2.
143. *Id.* at 3.

Randolph's *youth*? Even if one accepts the *Monticello Report's* assumptions, by the end of the 1780s Randolph Jefferson was a *thirty-four year old married man*. When Isaac left in 1797, Randolph would have been at least forty-six (and still married). The surviving records are so incomplete that we do not know when his first wife, Anne Jefferson Lewis, died; but it was between 1789 and 1808, and thus most probably before Eston Hemings was conceived in late 1807.[144] (To its credit, the *Monticello Report* acknowledges that "[t]he dates of Randolph's widowhood also may coincide with Sally Hemings's childbearing years...."[145]) So even if Randolph's practice of socializing with Monticello slaves was primarily witnessed by Isaac during his thirties when Randolph was married, by what logic should we assume that as a fifty-two-year-old widower in August 1807 he would behave differently? On the contrary, one might expect that the lack of a spouse might make him feel less constrained about partying with his older brother's slaves.

Nor is it at all clear that Isaac's observations were restricted to the 1780s. He clearly remained at Monticello until 1797, when Randolph was forty-two, and the fact that his *Memoirs* focused heavily upon events from an earlier time does not suggest that his observations of Uncle Randolph's behavior somehow ceased years before he left Monticello. One would normally assume the contrary.

Furthermore, there were several "Isaacs" at Monticello, and tracking them individually is not always a simple matter. Former Monticello Resident Director James A. Bear asserts that the Isaac whose *Memoirs* were later published was deeded to Jefferson's daughter Maria (Polly) in 1797, "but was soon returned to the Monticello family."[146] Add to this that Isaac himself claimed that he "left Monticello four years before Mr. Jefferson died,"[147] and it is quite possible that his observations of Randolph Jefferson's behavior extended through the birth of all of Sally's children.

It is not necessary to resolve this issue, because it strains credulity, in the absence of the slightest bit of evidence, to assume that a Randolph Jefferson who would frequently socialize with Monticello slaves "half the night" while a married man in his thirties and forties would cease doing so as a widower in his early fifties. And anyone attempting to argue that *age* might be a factor must address the reality that Thomas Jefferson, one of the alternative suspects, was a dozen years *older* and the record is totally devoid of the slightest hint from eyewitnesses that he enjoyed socializing at night with Monticello slaves.

The Eston Hemings Family Oral History

This issue has been addressed in Chapter Eight, but may warrant a brief mention here. Until Professor Brodie convinced them they were descendants of Thomas Jefferson, the descendants of Eston Hemings had been told by their parents and grandparents that they

---

144. The *Monticello Report* estimates that Randolph Jefferson's youngest son was born circa 1789 (*id.* at 3), and given the stress of childbirth in that era that may well have led to the death of Randolph's wife. All we really know is that she died sometime between giving birth to James and Randolph's remarriage in 1808 or 1809. *See* THOMAS JEFFERSON AND HIS UNKNOWN BROTHER 4. Randolph seems to have produced children about every second year until about 1789 (*Monticello Report*, Appendix J at 2–3), and the lack of any further children might suggest that his first wife either died around 1790 or perhaps was rendered incapable of producing children because of complications from childbirth. We are not likely ever to know the details.

145. *Monticello Report*, Appendix J at 3.

146. BEAR, JEFFERSON AT MONTICELLO, Genealogical Table A, following page 24.

147. *Id.* at 22.

were descendant from an "uncle" of Thomas Jefferson. Professor Brodie notes that nei-ther Madison nor Eston Hemings would have recalled any year at Monticello "without Martha Randolph in total charge."[148] While Thomas Jefferson's paternal uncles had been dead for decades before Eston was conceived, to Martha Randolph and her children the President's younger brother was "Uncle Randolph." Thus, the case for Randolph as opposed to Thomas Jefferson being the father of Eston Hemings is the most reasonable interpretation of Eston's own family oral history.

Randolph Jefferson's Sons

Finally, we also know that Randolph Jefferson had five sons living with him, at least four of whom were between the ages of nineteen and twenty-six when Eston Hemings was conceived,[149] and each of whom would have carried the same DNA Y-chromosome found in the descendants of Eston Hemings. According to the data in the *Monticello Report*, the fifth brother (James) was at least seventeen and probably eighteen at the time as well,[150] but other information suggests that Randolph's son James may have been younger than that[151] and thus I exclude him as a likely candidate for Eston's paternity (although the odds of a fifteen- or even fourteen-year-old boy fathering a child are probably greater than those of a man of sixty-four, especially in an era during which the average man did not even live to see forty).

Given their father's documented propensity for socializing with Monticello slaves, and other evidence we have that young men who visited Monticello were sometimes "inti-mate with the Negro women,"[152] Randolph's sons would also seem to be obvious candi-dates for the possible paternity of Eston. Yet none of the advocates of Thomas Jefferson's paternity of Eston have dealt seriously with the possibility that Randolph or one of his sons was Eston's father.

---

148. BRODIE, THOMAS JEFFERSON 440.

149. *Monticello Report*, Appendix J at 2–3.

150. *Id.* at 3. I say "probably," because they give his year of birth as "c. 1789," and Eston was not conceived until late August of 1807. Thus, if James was born between January and late August of 1789, he would have been eighteen when Eston was conceived.

151. I am aware of no reliable records giving a date of birth for James Lilburne Jefferson. How-ever, on February 18, 1816, he complained in a letter to his famous uncle that the court would not allow him to collect his inheritance until he chose a guardian. (Original letter in University of Vir-ginia Library.) Had he been born in the year the Monticello experts estimate, he would have been about twenty-six by 1816, when he alleges he needed a guardian to handle his legal affairs. This could still have been the case had he been mentally incompetent to handle his affairs, but there is no suggestion of that, and his penmanship is far superior to that of his father. Tax records suggest that he did not pay property taxes before 1818, which may also suggest (but certainly does not *prove*) that he was born after 1789. Genealogist Cynthia Harris Burton, who provided me with the above information, believes James was probably not born before 1796–97. On the other hand, his letter of February 18, 1816, makes references to a desire to get out of a rental agreement with a Mr. Thomas for a ferry—suggesting that he may have had legal capacity to enter into contracts at that time. The point is not critical to our inquiry but, given the uncertainty, I am inclined to exclude James as a se-rious candidate for Eston's paternity. If Ms. Burton is correct, this would presumably also undermine the argument that Sally Hemings began having children shortly after the death of Randolph's first wife. I am also indebted to Rebecca L. McMurry for providing me with a photocopy of the Febru-ary 18 letter.

152. BEAR, JEFFERSON AT MONTICELLO 88 (statement of Edmund Bacon, former Monticello over-seer).

One might think that, given Thomas Jefferson's advanced age, the much younger Randolph or his sons might be thought more likely to father a child. But, while noting that "Randolph Jefferson's sons Thomas, in 1800 [age 17], and Robert Lewis, in 1807 [age 20], may well have been at Monticello during the conception periods of Harriet and Eston Hemings,"[153] the *Monticello Report* simply dismisses them as possible candidates "because of their youth...."[154] Apparently, the Monticello Committee members believed that a sixty-four-year-old was physically more likely to father a child than a twenty-year-old.

Far more importantly, since Thomas Jefferson did not normally bother to record visits by Randolph or his family in the absence of some special purpose, there is no evidence that Randolph and his sons were *not* present when any or *all* of Sally's children (save perhaps "Tom"[155]) were conceived. We know Thomas Jefferson and his brother Randolph were close. We know that the primary reason Randolph would visit Monticello would be to see his brother (although there is one documented case of his going there briefly in Jefferson's absence[156]). Randolph would presumably be most likely to visit shortly after his brother returned from being away. Sally Hemings got pregnant—on those Jefferson visits when we know she *did* get pregnant—shortly after Thomas Jefferson arrived home. The distinguishing feature between those visits by Thomas Jefferson when Sally did not become pregnant, and those when she did so within a few weeks of his arrival, might well have been the presence of brother Randolph, who lived but twenty miles away—about a half day's ride by horseback.[157]

The Issue of the *Timing* of Sally's Conceptions

Much has been made of the fact that Thomas Jefferson may[158] have been at Monticello every time Sally Hemings conceived a child. But there are some other issues of timing we might want to consider:

---

153. *Monticello Report* at 9.

154. "[T]hey and their brothers are also unlikely fathers because of their youth and very intermittent presence." *Monticello Report*, Appendix J at 3. Once again, we are straying from Occam's Razor. The issue raised by the DNA tests is who was the father of *Eston* Hemings. Only one of Randolph's boys was even arguably too young to be a suspect in that matter, and compared with the sixty-four-year-old President, even a fourteen- or fifteen-year-old would have to be considered seriously. Assuming that there could only be a single father to all of Sally's children, in the absence of serious evidence to justify such an assumption, is precisely what Occam was cautioning us about. While it is true that Randolph's boys had an "intermittent presence" at Monticello, to impregnate Sally each time, one of them would only need to be at Monticello (or wherever Sally was) an hour or less for each child. Since we do not in most instances know whether or not they were present, we should not arbitrarily exclude them as possible suspects.

155. It is said that "Tom" was born in 1790. It is thus theoretically possible that this could have resulted from impregnation during the first three months of the year, as Sally returned to Monticello from Paris with Jefferson at the end of 1789.

156. *Monticello Report*, Appendix J at 3.

157. A few weeks before his sixty-seventh birthday, Jefferson wrote that he could still ride as far as forty miles in a single day. *Jefferson to Dr. Vine Utley*, Mar. 21, 1819, 15 WRITINGS OF THOMAS JEFFERSON 186 (Mem. ed. 1904).

158. Technically, in the case of Beverly, the statistical odds are that Thomas Jefferson was *not* present when the child was conceived. However, he arrived three days after the most probable conception date, and thus remains a serious candidate. Neiman, *Coincidence or Causal Connection?* 205.

- During the first decade of his first marriage, Randolph Jefferson managed to father a child by his wife approximately every second year. Assuming that she was pregnant for the normal nine months, and assuming a reasonable period during which she was lactating and thus unlikely to conceive, it appears that Randolph was very successful at quickly fathering children.

- A recent study reported in *Human Reproduction*[159] shows a statistically significant correlation between an increase in a man's chronological age and a decrease in his fecundity, or ability to father children within a given period of time. While this study dealt with younger men, there is no reason to believe the correlation does not continue—and indeed perhaps become more significant—with age. Thus, all other things being equal, a younger man like Randolph Jefferson would likely be able to more quickly impregnate a woman than his sixty-four-year-old brother. Give or take some number of days because of statistical variations in the length of the human gestation period, Sally conceived four out of five children within less than a month[160] after Thomas Jefferson returned home (an event that presumably triggered a flood of visits from friends and relatives).

- We do not know when Randolph's first wife died, but it could easily have been a year or two before Sally had her first child.[161] We do know that he remarried in 1808 or 1809,[162] and that his second wife was by most accounts a controlling, abusive, "shrew"[163]—quite possibly the kind of woman who would not tolerate having her husband wander down to the slave quarters for a night of socializing during family visits to Monticello.

The year 1809 is particularly important as a transition year:

---

159. W. C. L. Ford et al., *Increasing paternal age is associated with delayed conception in a large population of fertile couples: evidence for declining fecundity in older men.* 15 (8) HUMAN REPRODUCTION 1703 (2000). A more recent study in the same professional journal seems to confirm this conclusion: "Perhaps the most interesting result from our study is the observed decrease in fertility with male age, beginning in the late 30s." David B. Dunson, Bernardo Colombo & Donna D. Baird, *Changes with age in the level and duration of fertility in the menstrual cycle,* 17(5) HUMAN REPRODUCTION 1399–1403, May 2002.

160. W. C. L. Ford et al., *Increasing paternal age is associated with delayed conception in a large population of fertile couples: evidence for declining fecundity in older men.* 209 (8) HUMAN REPRODUCTION 1703 (2000).

161. Childbirth was one of the most common causes of death for women in this age group. While the *Monticello Report* speculates that James Lilbune Jefferson, Randolph's youngest son, was born "c. 1789," Cynthia Burton, who has studied the records carefully, believes he was born several years later. (*See* Chapter Two.) If Randolph's first wife Anne died from complications giving birth to James a few years later, Randolph might well have become a widower just in time to father Harriet I. Then again, Anne could have lived even longer (and perhaps died from some other cause or from the birth of a child who did not survive), and Harriet I could have been fathered by one of the Carr brothers. All we can do is speculate in the absence of serious evidence. The point is that there are lots of other possibilities without assuming that Thomas Jefferson had to have fathered all (or any) of Sally's children.

162. We know that Randolph was almost certainly not married when he wrote his May 28, 1808, will (since no mention is made of a wife), but he does mention his new wife's brother in a letter to Thomas Jefferson in December 1809.

163. *See, e.g.,* 2 SCHACHNER, THOMAS JEFFERSON 923. ("Randolph's second wife, whom he had married without consulting his brother, proved extravagant and a shrew. Poor Randolph fell under her domination, had to sell lands to pay her debts and finally, on his brother's advice, informed the local merchants that she was to receive merchandise only on his written order. Thereupon she forged the orders. Thus harassed, Randolph quietly died in 1815.")

- Thomas Jefferson retired from government and returned to Monticello full time, where he could presumably have access to Sally Hemings every single night if he so desired;

- Randolph Jefferson had recently remarried, and thus may have been either forced to adjust his social behavior or simply found less urge to seek companionship elsewhere now that he had a wife at home;

- Randolph's twenty-seven-year-old son, Thomas Jefferson, Jr.,[164] also married in 1808; and

- Sally Hemings had no more known children, even though she was only in her mid-thirties.

Is all of this a coincidence? Perhaps. But then again, perhaps not. As the *Monticello Report* acknowledges, "The dates of Randolph's widowhood also may coincide with Sally Hemings's childbearing years...."[165]

What about the Numerous Times When Thomas Jefferson Returned Home and Sally Hemings Did Not Become Pregnant?

There has been a great deal of speculation about the fact that Sally Hemings became pregnant four times within roughly a month of Thomas Jefferson's return to Monticello. But Thomas Jefferson made more than twenty trips to Monticello during the years 1794–1808, and there is information that Sally became pregnant within weeks four times and possibly a total of six times. (If one includes Thomas Woodson or another child born in 1790, then all of Jefferson's visits between 1790 and 1795 without Sally becoming pregnant must also be considered.)

Some of the non-productive visits can be explained by the fact that Sally was already pregnant or had recently given birth. But many cannot. This suggests that there may have been *two* variables involved in determining when Sally Hemings became pregnant. First, Thomas Jefferson had to come home, because that was the occasion when his friends and relatives were most likely to visit Monticello. (During his presidency, Monticello was kept shut up during his absence.) But that is not enough. And one very logical explanation for the fact that Sally became pregnant within weeks during some of Thomas Jefferson's visits, but on other occasions did not become pregnant even when he remained at Monticello for many months, is that the other variable—her actual lover[166]—was someone who visited Monticello often, but not every time that Thomas Jefferson returned home.

There is no proof that this is in fact what happened. But it has the virtue both of explaining Sally's pattern of pregnancies, while at the same time being fully consistent with the eyewitness testimony of Edmund Bacon that he often saw a man other than Thomas Jefferson leaving Sally Hemings' room early in the mornings.

---

164. Obviously, if he were Sally's sexual partner she could have told Madison that his father was "Thomas Jefferson" without making a false statement.

165. *Monticello Report*, Appendix J at 3.

166. By using the singular "lover" here I do not mean to exclude the possibility that her children had more than one father—a possibility whose likelihood is as difficult to quantify as is the monogamy possibility, given the scant evidence available.

Where Was Sally?

Finally, it should be noted that the revisionists simply assume that Sally Hemings must have been at Monticello every day between her return from Paris in 1789 and Thomas Jefferson's death in 1826. They do this because there is no clear evidence she was elsewhere at any given time. And they may be right. Certainly the safest assumption, given what little we know, is that she was at Monticello on any given day. But we have no clear evidence she was always there, and indeed there are years in which there are no references to her even existing.

This is an area where further research may well be warranted, although I am not at all optimistic that records exist to resolve the issue. We know that during periods of construction at Monticello, Jefferson's family members occasionally went elsewhere to live, taking slaves with them.[167] We know that Thomas Jefferson kept slaves at various different properties. And we know that historian Henry Randall claims to have independently confirmed the statement attributed to Martha Randolph that Thomas Jefferson and Sally Hemings could not have seen each other for fifteen months prior to the birth of one of her children. After his return from Paris, we have reliable information that Thomas Jefferson was never away from Monticello for fifteen straight months. *Ergo,* the most likely explanation—*if* the "fifteen months" statement was in fact made, and if it was *true*—is that during at least part of that period Sally Hemings had to have been elsewhere.

If someone could confirm Randall's alleged "finding," that would presumably make it clear that Thomas Jefferson could not have fathered all of Sally's children. Once the assumption of monogamy is disposed of, the case against Thomas Jefferson pretty much collapses to the very suspect allegations of James Callender, the problematic 1873 hearsay attributed to Madison Hemings, and the even more dubious account attributed to Israel Jefferson.

Candidly, I had tentatively concluded that the simplest explanation for this apparent discrepancy was that Henry Randall was simply not telling the truth. He wrote a quite good three-volume *Life of Jefferson*, but if he honestly believed that the Callender charges were false, one might envision him deciding to "recall" a nonexistent document to try to put the story to rest. But I no more like to assume that Henry Randall was intentionally misrepresenting the truth than I do Madison Hemings, Israel Jefferson, or anyone else. And there are some reasons to believe that Randall was telling the truth.

To begin with, the fact that Randall did not include the story allegedly told to him by Jeff Randolph in his own book (assuming, of course, that Randall did not simply fabricate the story years later for his letter to Parton) suggests that he could have made a far stronger defense of Jefferson than he did were that his goal. The story told to Parton is in turn supported by Ellen Coolidge's earlier letter asserting that her brother (Jeff) had told *her* the Carr boys had admitted paternity and also asked her to keep it confidential. I was not comfortable with merely assuming that Henry Randall was not truthful, so I looked a little more carefully at some of the dates.

---

167. Cynthia Burton informs me that she has found evidence Sally left Monticello by April 1790 with Martha and/or Maria, who spent the summer visiting relatives at various Virginia locations in the Richmond area before returning to Monticello. An October 1790 letter from Maria to Thomas Mann Randolph suggests that she and Sally were still in Cumberland County.

Eston Hemings was reportedly born on May 21, 1808. Fifteen months prior to that would have been in February of 1807. Thomas Jefferson left Monticello on October 11, 1806, and returned for about a month from April 11 to May 13, 1807. He returned again on August 5 of that year, and Eston was probably conceived towards the end of that month. He returned again on May 12, 1808, and presumably was still there on the date Eston was born.

One does not have to assume that Sally was away from Monticello for fifteen months. Had she been away for any reason for as much as four to six months, if those absences happened to coincide with Jefferson's two visits, they might not have seen each other — but it would have been for more like *eighteen* months, not fifteen. That cannot be the answer if Randall's statement is correct. If Jefferson's records of his own visits to Monticello are accurate (and there is no reason to doubt them), it is difficult to reconcile Henry Randall's statement with facts that seem to be reliable.

I even considered whether the passage of years might have confused Randall, and perhaps the statement was really that Jefferson and Hemings had been separated for fifteen months prior to the *conception* of Eston. That works better, because if Sally had been present at Monticello when Jefferson left on May 13, 1807, and then had gone elsewhere and remained away through Eston's conception, the period would round out to about fifteen months. We have virtually no information about Sally Hemings during this period, and just as one can thus argue "there is no evidence she was not at Monticello" it could also be said "there is no evidence she *was* at Monticello" during those two critical visits. But there is, in fact, neither reason to assume Sally was not at Monticello nor to assume that Henry Randall misstated Martha Randolph's alleged comment about a fifteen-month separation. Occam would presumably tell us it is simpler to assume that Randall was not telling the truth in this instance.

There is yet a third possibility (aside from the possibility that the child in question was not Eston at all), and that is that at some point Sally Hemings was sent away for a fifteen-month or longer period. Maria (Polly) died long before Eston was born, and Martha normally returned to Monticello with her father, so we cannot simply assume Sally was sent to serve one of the daughters. However, it is possible that Sally went to live at Edgehill for a year or two during Jefferson's presidency, and Martha did not bring her back when she returned with the children during her father's occasional visits to Monticello.

One original member of the Scholars Commission expressed an interest in doing further research at Jefferson's Poplar Forest retreat; however, we know that Jefferson visited "Bedford" in September 1807 — presumably shortly after Eston was conceived, but overlapping the projected conception window. So if Eston was the child who most resembled Thomas Jefferson, discovering evidence at Poplar Forest that Sally Hemings was there for an extended period would not solve the puzzle.

I am not optimistic that detailed evidence of Sally's whereabouts during these relevant years, if it ever was recorded, will be found. It may be an issue worthy of further inquiry by a patient scholar, since if Sally was indeed absent from Monticello for a fifteen-month period prior to the birth of any of her children, that could prove to be very important information in bringing this controversy to an end. The circumstantial case is largely premised upon the assumption of monogamy.[168] But until such evidence is found, my

---

168. It is a fairly simple matter to posit any of a number of Jefferson's visitors as having possibly fathered any one or two of Sally Hemings' children. Once we insist (without the slightest bit of evidence other than a statement attributed to one of her sons, who could not possibly have known that his mother was, in fact, monogamous) that every one of her children had to have a common father, suspicion obviously is directed at potential fathers who were regularly at Monticello year after year.

own inclination is to discount the double-hearsay account Henry Randall attributes to Martha Randolph through her son Jeff—or at least to give it little probative weight. Perhaps the statement was made and the facts were confirmed by Henry Randall. Perhaps someone was lying in an effort to protect Jefferson's reputation. It is not in my view necessary to resolve the matter, because there is a wealth of other, more credible, data that make it easy for me to reach the conclusion that it is *highly unlikely* that Thomas Jefferson fathered Eston or any other Hemings child.

Ergo, Thomas Jefferson becomes the most likely suspect. By similar reasoning, if a police officer investigating a series of robberies at a convenience store over a number of years were to note that none of the witnesses speculated about whether the robber they observed might have been different from the perpetrator(s) of previous robberies (when the same witnesses were not present), and from that information *ruled out the possibility* of multiple robbers, the odds are good that he would soon arrest the store proprietor as the only individual known to have been present during every crime. To use another example, over the years we have had several pens, purses, and even a few laptop computers stolen from the University of Virginia law library. It is doubtful that many of the victims speculated that the unknown individual who took their property was responsible for specific other thefts as well. But if we *assume* that there can be only one thief for all of the stolen property, over a period of a decade, that would pretty much rule out students (who graduate after three years) and point suspicion to long-term library employees or administrators. The assumption that Sally Hemings could not have had more than one father to her children is precisely the kind of unwarranted assumption that Occam cautioned us against.

11

The "Silent Dogs" and Other Issues Ignored by Most Revisionist Scholars

<hr>

INSPECTOR GREGORY: "Is there any point to which you would wish to draw my attention?"
SHERLOCK HOLMES: "To the curious incident of the dog in the night-time."
INSPECTOR GREGORY: "The dog did nothing in the night-time."
SHERLOCK HOLMES: "That was the curious incident."

> —Sir Arthur Conan Doyle, *Silver Blaze*, in
> THE COMPLETE SHERLOCK HOLMES 347 (1992).

In the first nine chapters, I have sought to identify and analyze all of the key arguments offered by revisionist historians in support of their conclusion that Thomas Jefferson fathered one or more children by Sally Hemings. Chapter Ten looked in greater detail at evidence they acknowledge to exist, but may have dismissed a bit prematurely. This chapter will briefly consider two other issues:

- the absence of evidence that *ought to exist* if the allegations against Thomas Jefferson were true; and

- the improbable assumptions one must accept in order to conclude that the allegations are true.

The Missing Evidence that Ought to Exist

First is the issue of what I call the "silent dogs." Just as Sherlock Holmes found it "curious" that the stable dog did not bark in the night when a stranger allegedly caused a great commotion, if a Jefferson-Hemings sexual relationship lasted for decades, as we are asked to believe, we ought to find evidence from at least one of the hundreds if not thousands of visitors who were in a position over the years to observe happenings in Paris and at Monticello. The Callender accusations first published on September 1, 1802, spread quickly around much of the United States and eventually to Europe as well. Surely, many of the visitors to Monticello had heard the charges and would be alert to any evidence of such a relationship. Anyone who had observed suggestive behavior in Paris might also have been prompted by the Callender stories to record it.

There Is Not a Single Credible Eyewitness Account from Paris or Monticello of a Jefferson-Hemings Sexual Relationship

University of Alabama Professor Joshua Rothman, a believer in the Jefferson-Hemings story, writes:

> [T]he evidence of racial mixing at Monticello must have been quite obvious, and no matter how discreet he was, Jefferson could not have hidden it from guests. The children of his relationship with Sally Hemings also would be visible to visitors. As a member of the Virginia gentry, Jefferson knew of similar affairs carried out in supposed secrecy and likely understood that he could never hide every clue or quash every rumor.[1]

Professor Rothman, who wrote his Ph.D. on race relations in antebellum Virginia, is certainly right. It is extremely unlikely that Thomas Jefferson and Sally Hemings could have carried on a love affair for decades without anyone being suspicious. Both in Paris and when Thomas Jefferson was home at Monticello, he normally was surrounded by visitors. And yet, beyond fantasies about the intended recipient of an inexpensive locket[2] and comparable silliness, there is no contemporary evidence from the period 1787 through Jefferson's death in 1826 recording a single witness alleging having observed so much as a suggestive glance, a passing caress, or even close proximity at an unusual hour, between Thomas Jefferson and Sally Hemings.

Is It Reasonable to Assume that Thomas Jefferson Could Have Carried on a Decades-Long Sexual Relationship with Sally Hemings without Leaving a *Single* Witness or Piece of Contemporary Evidence?

Given the circumstances of his life, it is very difficult to reconcile this total absence of such evidence with the allegations of a long-term sexual relationship. Both in Paris and at Monticello, Jefferson was usually surrounded by very intelligent people—many of them virtual strangers, who had no apparent reason to cover up things they might have seen that might otherwise be considered newsworthy gossip—and it is inconceivable that this relationship occurred without a single one of them witnessing a single thing to suggest that it was going on.

Thomas Jefferson Had Little Privacy in Paris, and Sally Was Probably Not Living with Him

In *The Paris Years of Thomas Jefferson,* historian William Howard Adams tells us that Thomas Jefferson's residence in Paris had "a steady but unpredictable stream of guests," and "served as a boardinghouse for visiting Americans."[3]

---

1. Joshua D. Rothman, *James Callender and Social Knowledge of Interracial Sex in Antebellum Virginia,* in SALLY HEMINGS & THOMAS JEFFERSON 88 (Jan Ellen Lewis & Peter Onuf, eds. 1999).
2. *See* Chapter Nine.
3. WILLIAM HOWARD ADAMS, THE PARIS YEARS OF THOMAS JEFFERSON 47 (1997).

Professor Adams discusses the Sally Hemings story and his own assessment of the like-lihood of the affair:

> Despite the attention she has received from historians, Sally Hemings remains a shadowy presence in the envoy's life.... Apart from nine notations in Jefferson's *Memorandum Book* recording purchases of clothing, her servant's pay, and a fee for smallpox vaccination, Sally Hemings is completely absent from the Paris record. We know nothing of her living arrangements or duties at the rue de Berri.... Given her lack of training and education, it is difficult to imagine how Sally fitted into the arcane hierarchy of French servants, although she did manage to learn some French. She was known to at least one of Polly Jefferson's class-mates at the convent, and there has been reasonable speculation that she acted as maid for Jefferson's girls while they were in school....
>
> On purely practical grounds, it is difficult to see how Jefferson could have kept an affair with Sally Hemings secret. The Hôtel de Langeac was a relatively small, semipublic establishment always open to visitors: the second floor had only two bedrooms in addition to the large oval room where the minister worked and slept. William Short was a full-time resident, houseguests regularly put up, and Patsy and Polly also lived at the rue de Berri during their last six months in Paris. The daily traffic of visitors, tutors, guests, and servants has not left a single shred of evidence of the putative liaison.[4]

Like Sherlock Holmes' silent dog, if Thomas Jefferson and an immature teenaged servant were in fact regularly engaging in a sexual liaison in the fishbowl existence of his life, there ought to be at least some eyewitness evidence. There is none.

There is also a serious issue of *opportunity* here. Revisionists from Brodie to Gordon-Reed simply *assume* that when Sally came to Paris she remained at the Hôtel de Langeac with Thomas Jefferson when the two young girls she was supposed to be waiting upon went off to the convent. Other than the fact that classmates at the convent *knew* Sally, there is no clear evidence one way or the other. But that does not mean the odds become fifty-fifty. Is it logical that Patsy's and Polly's maid would not bother to accompany them to a boarding school that was well equipped to house servants? The presumption would nor-mally be that the maid would follow her mistresses, but that makes it much more difficult to support Madison Hemings' and James Callender's allegations against Thomas Jefferson.

When Thomas Jefferson Was Home Monticello Was Usually Crawling with Potential Witnesses

As noted in Chapter Ten, when Randolph Jefferson visited Monticello he was fond of spending his evenings among the slaves, playing his fiddle and dancing half the night. That presumably gave him considerable opportunity for sexual encounters as well.

In contrast, as has already been noted in Chapter Five, "It was his [Jefferson's] wont throughout his life to entertain large numbers of guests, and a constant stream of visi-tors made its way to Albemarle County to call whenever he was at Monticello."[5] The ques-tion necessarily arises, if this relationship continued over a period of decades at Monticello,

---

4. *Id.* at 221–22.
5. Joshua D. Rothman, *James Callender and Social Knowledge of Interracial Sex in Antebellum Vir-ginia*, in SALLY HEMINGS AND THOMAS JEFFERSON 87.

why did not a *single* person leave behind so much as a scrap of paper recording some observation supporting the relationship?

Grandson Thomas Jefferson Randolph wrote that at Monticello Jefferson was "surrounded" by his family, "who saw him in all the unguarded privacy of private life" and "believed him to be the purest of men."[6] Edmund Bacon's account of the "swarms of visitors that well-nigh ate up all his substance and consumed his life"[7] at Monticello led James Bear to wonder whether Jefferson "ever dined alone."[8] Slave Isaac Jefferson, in *Memoirs of a Monticello Slave,* speaks of the "great many carriages at Monticello at a time...."[9] Professor Gordon-Reed acknowledges that Jefferson "entertained lavishly" at Monticello, "receiving, housing, and feeding dozens of guests at a time" in a "home that was being run like a hotel."[10]

Jefferson's personal physician wrote, "I had the curiosity to ask Mrs. Randolph what was the largest number of persons for whom she had been called upon unexpectedly to prepare accommodations for the night, and she replied *fifty!*"[11] Ellen Randolph Coolidge complained to her famous grandfather about "how much you are harassed and oppressed by the crowd of strangers who think themselves privileged to waste and misuse your time, intruding upon you at all hours, and sacrificing your comfort, and even health without reflection and without remorse...."[12]

The Reverend Peter Fossett, son of freed Monticello slave Joe Fossett, told a writer from the *New York World* in 1898 that at "Monticello, we always had the house full of company. Not only did Jefferson's own countrymen visit him, but people from all parts of Europe came to see his wonderful home."[13]

Jefferson was a conscientious host, and he would have been unlikely to leave dinner companions to fend for themselves while he slipped down to Sally's room for a little after-dinner romance. While brother Randolph was fiddling and dancing with slaves, Thomas Jefferson would be entertaining his numerous visitors with stories of political intrigue in Washington or perhaps stories from his years in Paris. Could he have slipped out after others had gone to bed, or had Sally sneak into his room? That is certainly possible, but, given the lack of privacy at Monticello, it is highly unlikely this could have gone on night after night, year after year, decade after decade, without a single person discovering one of them sneaking through the corridors at an odd hour.

There were occasions when Jefferson demanded privacy, and nearly every day he retreated to his study to read, think, and keep up his immense correspondence. Isaac recalled: "When he was a-writin' he wouldn't suffer nobody to come in his room."[14] But there were reportedly exceptions, as Edmund Bacon writes:

> All the time I was with him I had full permission to visit his room whenever I thought it necessary to see him on any business. I knew how to get into his room

---

6. 3 HENRY S. RANDALL, THE LIFE OF THOMAS JEFFERSON 672 (1858).

7. JEFFERSON AT MONTICELLO 28 (James A. Bear, Jr., ed. 1967). *See also, id.* at 111. ("Mr. Jefferson always had a great deal of company.")

8. *Id.* at 126 n.48.

9. *Id.* at 23.

10. ANNETTE GORDON-REED, THOMAS JEFFERSON AND SALLY HEMINGS 131 (1997).

11. *Quoted in* SARAH N. RANDOLPH, THE DOMESTIC LIFE OF THOMAS JEFFERSON 403 (1871).

12. THE FAMILY LETTERS OF THOMAS JEFFERSON 458.

13. *Once the Slave of Thomas Jefferson: The Rev. Mr. Fossett, of Cincinnati, Recalls the Sage of Monticello—Reminiscences of Jefferson, Lafayette, Madison and Monroe,* THE WORLD (New York), Jan. 30, 1898, at 33.

14. JEFFERSON AT MONTICELLO 12. Isaac added that he had personally visited Jefferson's library "a thousand times" over the years. *Id.* at 18.

at any time of day or night. I have sometimes gone into his room when he was in bed....

Mrs. Randolph.... was always busy.... She used to sit in Mr. Jefferson's room a great deal and sew, or read, or talk, as he would be busy about something else.[15]

Thomas Jefferson Randolph wrote of his grandfather: "His private apartments were open to me at all times. I saw him under all circumstances."[16] Describing a conversation with Jeff Randolph, Henry Randall wrote to James Parton:

He said Mr. Jefferson never locked the door of his room by day: and that he (Col. Randolph) slept within sound of his breathing at night. He said he had never seen a motion, or a look, or a circumstance which led him to suspect for an instant that there was a particle more of familiarity between Mr. Jefferson and Sally Hemmings [sic] than between him and the most repulsive servant in the establishment—and that no person ever living at Monticello dreamed of such a thing.[17]

Consider also the more recent assessment of Dr. Daniel Jordan, president of the Thomas Jefferson Memorial Foundation, in an interview for the Ken Burns film on Jefferson that aired on Public Broadcasting in 1997:

He was also totally devoted to his family and he had eleven grandchildren living with him. And one of the granddaughters lived essentially directly above him. She heard everything. She heard him when he got up in the morning and sang Scottish airs and the like.... There are no secrets on a plantation, certainly not at Monticello. And his family, to whom he was totally devoted, completely discounted this possibility [that he was sexually involved with Sally Hemings].[18]

One cannot rule out the possibility that all of these people were lying, but that is not the simplest or most reasonable explanation. Given the very little privacy that Thomas Jefferson had during most of his adult life, it is noteworthy that not a single friend or visitor left any hint of having seen anything to support the Callender allegations. Were they true, we should have a wealth of eyewitness accounts at least hinting at the relationship from the thousands of people who passed through Jefferson's home in Paris and at Monticello over the decades. The absence of such evidence is not conclusive of anything, but it does provide support for the proposition that James Callender was not telling the truth and that the "relationship" between Thomas Jefferson and Sally Hemings was nothing more than master and slave.

Problems with Some Implicit Assumptions of Revisionist Scholars

To accept the revisionist argument that Thomas Jefferson had a decades-long sexual relationship with Sally Hemings that began in Paris and produced one or more children, we

---

15. *Id.* at 84.

16. 3 RANDALL, THE LIFE OF THOMAS JEFFERSON 671.

17. MILTON E. FLOWER, JAMES PARTON: THE FATHER OF MODERN BIOGRAPHY 237 (1951).

18. The full text of this insightful interview can be found on the PBS web page at http://www.pbs.org/jefferson/archives/interviews/Jordan.htm. Dr. Jordan has more recently confirmed to me that he and other Monticello scholars agreed that "it was certainly possible for individuals on the second floor to have overheard voices or singing below." E-mail from Dan Jordan to Robert F. Turner, Feb. 18, 2002, 8:59 AM, Subject: "Three Requests," a copy of which is in the writer's possession.

must make certain assumptions about Thomas Jefferson—assumptions that are in many cases very much at odds with the information we do have about our third President.

Jefferson's Character

Foremost among these, in the eyes of many Jefferson scholars over the years, has been the belief that Thomas Jefferson was a man of remarkably high character.[19] He was a human being, and like all human beings he was imperfect and prone to error—a reality he readily acknowledged.[20] But many have long believed that he was far better than most of us in living up to the strong moral standards he repeatedly expressed to his daughters and others.

For example, when Dr. Jordan was interviewed for the Ken Burns video, he asserted that the alleged sexual relationship between Thomas Jefferson and Sally Hemings would be "totally out of character" for Jefferson,[21] and concluded that it was "morally impossible for that relationship to have occurred."

Similarly, Professor Winthrop Jordan, in his landmark 1968 volume, *White Over Black*—winner of the 1969 National Book Award, the Francis Parkman Prize from the Society of American Historians, and the Bancroft Prize from Columbia University—provided this assessment of Jefferson's character and the Callender charges:

> In 1802 James T. Callender charged in the *Richmond Recorder* that it was "well known" that Jefferson kept Sally, one of his slaves, as concubine and had fathered children by her. The features of "Tom," the eldest offspring, were "said to bear a striking although sable resemblance to those of the president himself." Callender was a notorious professional scandalmonger who had turned upon Jefferson when the president had disappointed his hope for federal office. Despite the utter disreputability of the source, the charge has been dragged after Jefferson like a dead cat through the pages of formal and informal history, tied to him by its attractiveness to a wide variety of interested persons and by the apparent impossibility of utterly refuting it. Ever since Callender's day it has served the varied purposes of those seeking to degrade Jefferson for political or ideological reasons, of abolitionists, defamers of Virginia, the South, and even America in gen-

---

19. To mention but one example, Jefferson inherited debts to English creditors from his mother and his father-in-law. Under the Virginia sequestration law passed during the Revolution, many prominent Virginians—including the Lees, the Marshalls, Patrick Henry, and Edmund Pendleton—elected to discharge sterling debts with greatly depreciated paper currency. Writing to one of his father-in-law's creditors, Jefferson said: "What the laws of Virginia are, or may be, will in no wise influence my conduct. Substantial justice is my object, as decided by reason, and not by authority or compulsions." As a matter of principle, Jefferson refused to take advantage of legal loopholes that would have permitted him to significantly reduce the indebtedness that haunted him all of his life. *See The Debt to Farell & Jones,* in 15 Papers of Thomas Jefferson 642 (Julian P. Boyd, ed. 1958).

20. "I shall often go wrong through defect of judgment. When right, I shall often be thought wrong by those whose positions will not command a view of the whole ground. I ask your indulgence for my own errors, which will never be intentional; and your support against the errors of others, who may condemn what they would not if seen in all its parts." Thomas Jefferson, *First Inaugural Address,* Mar. 4, 1801, *reprinted in,* 3 Writings of Thomas Jefferson 323 (Mem. Ed.1903).

21. This is not to suggest that such a relationship would have not also been "out of character" for Sally Hemings, as the reality is we know virtually nothing about her character. Nor, for that matter, is there any reason to assume she would have believed she had any voice in the decision had Thomas Jefferson actually made sexual advances towards her.

eral, and both defenders and opponents of racial segregation. Jefferson's conduct has been attacked from several angles, for in fact the charge of concubinage with Sally Hemings constitutes not one accusation but three, simultaneously accusing Jefferson of fathering bastards, of miscegenation, and of crassly taking advantage of a helpless young slave (for Sally was probably twenty-two when she first conceived). The last of these, insofar as it implies forced attentions on an unwilling girl, may be summarily dismissed.... Jefferson was simply not capable of violating every rule of honor and kindness, to say nothing of his convictions concerning the master-slave relationship.[22]

Consider also the account attributed to Jefferson's personal physician, Dr. Robley Dunglison, by historian Henry Randall in 1856:

You ask me what where [*sic*] his private virtues that appeared conspicuous to all acquaintances?.... He was kind, courteous, hospitable to all; sincerely attached to the excellent family that were clustered around him; sympathizing with them in their pleasures, deeply distressed in their afflictions. I mentioned to you the scene I witnessed on the approaching death of a grand-daughter, Mrs. Bankhead. I knew nothing of any private vice of any kind, and never heard from him a loose or indecorous speech. I would say in your own language, that he was always in my observation "peculiarly decorous, modest, and decent in all things."...

In sum, I had the most exalted opinion of him. I believed him essentially a philanthropist, anxious for the greatest good to the greatest number; a distinguished patriot, whose love of country was not limited by any considerations of self; who was eminently virtuous, with fixed and honorable principles of action not to be trammeled by any unworthy considerations; and whose reputation must shine brighter and brighter, as he is more and more justly judged and estimated.[23]

Writing in 1995, Andrew Burstein adds:

Knowing what we do about Jefferson's Heart and Head, that the first made him generous and the second ruled his actions, it seems highly unlikely that because light-skinned Sally Hemings bore light-skinned children at Monticello, they necessarily were fathered by Monticello's master. Moreover, Jefferson would have been uncharacteristically imprudent to be responsible for giving Sally Hemings the two children that she bore in the years after the charges surfaced, while he remained President.[24]

With the release of the DNA evidence, Burstein became a revisionist. But even then, he acknowledged that "[t]o today's historian, Jefferson's writings and action are irreconcilable...."[25]

The most prominent post-DNA convert to revisionism was Professor Joseph Ellis, who had previously noted that "the alleged relationship with Sally Hemings ... defies the dominant patterns of his personality."[26] He wrote that Jefferson's "idealization of domestic

---

22. WINTHROP D. JORDAN, WHITE OVER BLACK 465 (1968).

23. *Dunglison to Randall*, June 1, 1856, in 3 HENRY S. RANDALL, THE LIFE OF THOMAS JEFFERSON 670–71 (1858).

24. ANDREW BURSTEIN, THE INNER JEFFERSON 231 (1995).

25. Andrew Burstein, *Jefferson's Rationalizations*, 57(1) WILLIAM & MARY QUARTERLY 196 (Jan. 2000).

26. JOSEPH ELLIS, AMERICAN SPHINX 367 (1996).

bliss as the ultimate source of his personal happiness was certainly sincere,"[27] and that after the death of his wife he would "rather be lonely than vulnerable."[28] In Professor Ellis' view, "[i]n the long run the head prevails"[29] for Thomas Jefferson.

Even after the DNA evidence had been released and Professor Ellis had shifted to a leadership position of the revisionist movement, he acknowledged that the Hemings story could not easily be reconciled with the known information about Jefferson's character. He found an explanation by drawing a comparison between Thomas Jefferson and William Jefferson Clinton. As reported by the *New York Times*:

> "I thought it would have been unduly reckless of Jefferson to have continued the relationship when under scrutiny," Dr. Ellis said, "but we recently have had reason to recognize that Presidents of the United States are perfectly capable of that degree of recklessness."

> Dr. Ellis also noted that the character of Jefferson as it emerges from his voluminous correspondence makes it extremely hard for readers to believe he would have had an illicit relationship of any kind.

> "The more you immerse yourself in the Jefferson papers," Dr. Ellis said, "the more difficult it becomes to imagine a liaison between Jefferson and Sally Hemings. It's ironic, the more grounded you are, the more likely you are to get this wrong."[30]

Professor Brodie also acknowledges Jefferson's remarkable self-control and his apparent unwillingness or inability to display emotions he thought coarse. She wrote:

> Callender's praise had an intellectual quality that Jefferson must particularly have enjoyed when it was directed toward himself, but his vituperation had a kind of demonic brilliance that may have attracted Jefferson even more. So rigorous was his own self-discipline, he probably found in Callender's explosions of hate vicarious relief from the rages he could not himself express. Callender printed about his enemies that which he could not himself say even in private and which he may not have permitted himself even to think.[31]

Indeed, a reading of Jefferson's "love letters" from some of the several women he clearly found attractive in Paris and thereafter strongly suggests that his "self-discipline" was a source of occasional frustration to them, as his gentlemanly manners may have precluded more intimate relationships they would have welcomed. Many have speculated about the nature of Thomas Jefferson's relationship with Maria Cosway, Angelica Church, and others following the death of his wife Martha; but there is no persuasive evidence that any of them went beyond warm friendship, mutual affection, and elaborate flirtation.[32] Discussing Jefferson's views on extramarital sex as of 1789 (the year that Sally Hemings is alleged to have conceived "Tom"), William Howard Adams writes in *The Paris Years of Thomas Jefferson*:

> To Jefferson, such extramarital affairs were a sign of moral decay, a blot on the otherwise near-perfect *vertu* of French society. Like a frontier preacher from the Piedmont, he was constantly taking the higher ground in letters to Amer-

---

27. *Id.* at 109.
28. *Id.* at 79.
29. *Id.* at 113.
30. Nicholas Wade, *Defenders of Jefferson Renew Criticism of DNA Analysis Linking Him to Slave's Child*, N.Y. TIMES, Jan. 7, 1999.
31. FAWN BRODIE, THOMAS JEFFERSON: AN INTIMATE HISTORY 319 (1974).
32. This is not to say that Thomas Jefferson did *not* have a sexual relationship with one or more of these women. We simply do not know.

ican friends. "Intrigues of love occupy the young, and those of ambition, the elder part of the great," he wrote disapprovingly to Carlo Bellini, professor of modern languages at William & Mary College. "Conjugal love having no existence among them, domestic happiness of which that is the basis, is utterly unknown."[33]

Returning to this theme again in a later chapter, Adams writes that:

> Temptation was an inescapable part of the glamorous, libidinous society of Paris. For the French in the late eighteenth century, adultery was a class issue, hardly a political or social problem. To Jefferson, however, such moral lapses reflected the corruptions of despotism and privilege; even marital infidelity could be traced to France's odious system of government rather than to any innate human flaw.... Lacking what a later age would call firm family values, Parisians cultivated "pursuits which nourish and invigorate our bad passions, and which offer only moments of ecstasy amidst days and months of restlessness and torment."[34]

Consider also this account by Monticello President Daniel Jordan, from his interview for the 1997 Ken Burns film:

> I think ultimately with Maria Cosway and in so many other instances, the Head prevails [with Jefferson]. There's a rationality and a kind of a controlled reason with Jefferson that, more times than not, would win out over raw emotion. He was a man of great discipline and great self-control."[35]

It might be added that Jefferson was a remarkably forgiving man. Discussing Jefferson's final years, grandson Thomas Jefferson Randolph asserted:

> In speaking of the calumnies which his enemies had uttered against his public and private character with such unmitigated and untiring bitterness, he said that he had not considered them as abusing him; that they had never known him. They had created an imaginary being clothed with odious attributes, to whom they had given his name; and it was against that creature of their imaginations they had leveled their anathemas.[36]

Perhaps Thomas Jefferson's character and self-restraint were not nearly so strong as most contemporary accounts, and the assessments of most Jefferson scholars until very recently, would have us believe. Sadly, it is no longer difficult for Americans to believe that an American President could succumb to the temptations of the flesh with a much younger woman. But even if we assume that was the case, and that Thomas Jefferson, like so many other men, could not resist sexual temptation, as the intriguing and popular American minister to France he was clearly in great demand socially; and, equally obviously, he could have had his pick of some of the most beautiful and talented women in France. As a bachelor, little obvious approbation would have attached had Thomas Jefferson been seen in the company of almost any unmarried adult woman in Paris. To find sexual release, Jefferson did not have to violate his strongly held principles against the sexual exploitation of slave women or to place at risk his reputation with his daughters and friends. And that raises a related but also distinct issue.

---

33. William Howard Adams, The Paris Years of Thomas Jefferson 21 (1997).
34. *Id.* at 207.
35. The full text of this interview can be found on the PBS web page at http://www.pbs.org/jefferson/ archives/interviews/Jordan.htm.
36. *Quoted in* Sarah N. Randolph, The Domestic Life of Thomas Jefferson 428 (1871).

Jefferson's Investment in His Reputation

The revisionists not only ask us to accept the Callender charges, but also to recognize that Thomas Jefferson was not nearly so special as we have long liked to believe. He was, they tell us, not only a hypocrite, but "just a typical southern slave owner" in the words of Professor Gordon-Reed.[37]

So let us assume, for the sake of discussion, that Thomas Jefferson was essentially an evil, self-centered, hypocrite. Whether that is true or not, it cannot be denied that, apparently unlike some of his contemporaries,[38] he was incredibly invested in promoting and preserving a *reputation* as being among the most honorable of men. My distinguished Scholars Commission colleague Professor Paul Rahe, who is far more critical of Thomas Jefferson than are some of us, writes in his Dissenting Views that Thomas Jefferson "cared far more about his future reputation than about anything else...."[39] I suspect this may overstate the case slightly, and that Jefferson's love of his family and his country may have exceeded his desire to be remembered fondly by future generations. But one cannot doubt that his concern for his public image was immense—to the point that modern psychiatrists might well label it a serious character flaw if not a personality disorder.[40]

In January 1793, while serving as Secretary of State in Washington's cabinet, Jefferson wrote to his daughter Martha that he had planned on retiring and returning to Monticello, but that he had come under some public criticism and several friends had urged him not to leave. He wrote:

> Among these [arguments] it was urged that my return just when I had been attacked in the public papers, would injure me in the eyes of the public, who would suppose I either withdrew from investigation, or because I had not tone of mind sufficient to meet slander. The only reward I ever wished on my retirement was to carry with me nothing like a disapprobation of the public.[41]

In a letter to Henry Randall, Thomas Jefferson Randolph made it clear that his grandfather was aware of the consequences that his desire to uphold his public reputation might have for his family:

> He [Jefferson] returned to [Monticello] in his old age to be hunted down by the reputation he had won in the service of his country. Twelve years before his death, he remarked to me, in conversation, that if he lived long enough he would beggar his family—that the number of persons he was compelled to entertain would devour his estate; many bringing letters from his ancient friends, and all coming with respectful feelings, he could not shut his door in their faces.[42]

---

37. GORDON-REED, THOMAS JEFFERSON AND SALLY HEMINGS 148.

38. John Adams, for example, told Jefferson that he cared "not a farthing" for his reputation. 2 NATHAN SCHACHNER, THOMAS JEFFERSON 924 (1951). I have my doubts about whether the statement was true.

39. *See* Professor Rahe's Dissenting Opinion, page 351.

40. I claim no expertise in psychiatry, but a very strong case can be made that Jefferson's unusually strong investment in his reputation kept him from turning away hundreds and perhaps thousands of strangers who arrived at his door expecting to be housed, fed, and entertained for in some cases weeks at a time; and rather than conserving his diminishing resources—or, more accurately, avoiding further unnecessary indebtedness that would later produce immense suffering for family members he deeply loved—he squandered his assets in his desire to avoid being thought poorly of by strangers.

41. *Jefferson to Martha Randolph*, 9 THE WRITINGS OF THOMAS JEFFERSON 15–16 (Mem. ed., 1904).

42. 3 RANDALL, THE LIFE OF THOMAS JEFFERSON 676. This statement, of course, suggests that I may be mistaken in my earlier judgment that his love for his family exceeded his investment in his reputation.

Jefferson biographer Samuel Schmucker wrote in 1857 that "[t]he chief fault of this illustrious man was a pusillanimous and morbid terror of popular censure, and an insatiable thirsting after popular praise."[43] In 1903, Henry Adams added that Jefferson "yearned for love and praise as no other great American ever did."[44]

This is not a point of dispute by most revisionists. Professor Brodie notes that, as Jefferson's increasing indebtedness drove him closer and closer to bankruptcy, "[t]here were certain expenditures Jefferson would not reduce, especially the costs of hospitality." She adds that:

> Even in Paris, when he had written diffidently to Madison about asking Congress to provide him more money so that he could properly meet the social duties of a minister, he would not let Madison press the matter to the point of angering the congressmen. "I had rather be ruined in fortune," he wrote, "than in their esteem."[45]

Professor Ellis, among the most distinguished of the modern revisionists, notes that "Jefferson felt every criticism personally,"[46] and indeed had a "hypersensitivity to criticism."[47] Or in the words of Thomas Jefferson himself—writing from Paris in 1789, when he was allegedly in the early stages of a decades-long affair that would have been almost certain to place at risk his reputation among the public and his own family—"I find the pain of a little censure, even when it is unfounded, is more acute than the pleasure of much praise."[48]

Accepting Thomas Jefferson's tremendous investment in his reputation—even if we assume, for the sake of argument, that his true character was deeply flawed—we must ask whether such a man would jeopardize that *reputation* by commencing a sexual relationship with an immature slave child?

The concern expressed here is not about "race." To begin with, by all accounts, Sally Hemings was almost white in appearance, and legally was as close to being white as she could be without actually being classifiable as white. Indeed, after she was "given her time" and began living free in Charlottesville, the census taker classified Sally Hemings as a white woman.

The concern rather is the inherently coercive nature of the master-slave relationship, plus the fact that Sally was (again by all surviving accounts) very much a "child" when she went to Paris, while Thomas Jefferson was well into his forties. It is true that females married younger on average in that era than today, and the age of consent was twelve, but—keeping in mind that days before Sally Hemings arrived in Paris, the highly respected Abigail Adams remarked that Sally Hemings was incapable of caring even for herself and wanted more "care" than Jefferson's eight-year-old daughter—is it *reasonable* to assume that a man so deeply invested in his public image would entrust that reputation to the discretion of such a child? Is there a *single* other incident in Jefferson's widowhood that suggests he was prone to reckless sexual indiscretions? Not to my knowledge.

---

43. Samuel M. Schmucker, The Life and Times of Thomas Jefferson ix (1857).

44. 1 Henry Adams, History of the United States of America During the First Administration of Thomas Jefferson 324 (1903).

45. Brodie, Thomas Jefferson 455.

46. Joseph J. Ellis, American Sphinx: The Character of Thomas Jefferson 142 (1996). *See also, id.* at 41, 50, 51, 73, 74, 90.

47. *Id.* at 71.

48. *Jefferson to Francis Hopkinson*, Mar. 13, 1789, in 7 Writings of Thomas Jefferson 302 (1904).

Assuming that the relationship did begin in Paris as alleged, and was exposed to the world by Callender, would a man so invested in his reputation have continued the affair thereafter — essentially flouting the public and broadcasting his indiscretion to every Monticello resident and visitor? Consider the assessment by Professor Ellis, offered just two years before the DNA evidence led him to reverse his position. After concluding that the truth of the scandal could not likely be proven by either side in a court of law, and noting "the flimsy and wholly circumstantial character of the evidence," Professor Ellis concludes that "after five years mulling over the huge cache of evidence that does exist on the thought and character of the historical Jefferson, I have concluded that the likelihood of a liaison with Sally Hemings is remote." He explains:

> Two pieces of circumstantial evidence strike me as telling: First, Sally's last two children, Madison and Eston, were born after Callender's charges created the public scandal in 1802, and it is difficult to believe that Jefferson would have persisted in producing progeny with Sally once the secret had been exposed and the Federalist press was poised to report it; second, among Jefferson's contemporaries neither Alexander Hamilton nor John Adams, both of whom were political enemies who undoubtedly enjoyed the sight of their chief adversary being stigmatized by the kind of innuendo he had spread against them, found it possible to believe that Callender's accusations were true. Nor, for that matter, did Henry Adams, whose critical appraisal of Jefferson's character established the scholarly standard for ironic dissection.[49]

It is very difficult to accept the Callender story, in any of its subsequent versions, without first having to reject everything we know about Thomas Jefferson's remarkable craving for public approval.

Jefferson's Love for His Daughters

In a similar vein, in order to accept the story that Thomas Jefferson became sexually involved with Sally Hemings in Paris, we must either abandon the abundant evidence we have that he was a man of remarkable intellect, or question the very evident love he had for his daughters and his desire to maintain their love and respect. After all, if the Callender story is to be believed, one of the most offensive aspects of Jefferson's conduct in Paris was his carrying on with Sally Hemings "before the eyes of two young ladies."[50] Even had he wished to keep such a relationship discreet, was he foolish enough to assume that such an immature child would, or could, resist the temptation to disclose her special new role to Patsy or Polly?

Thomas Jefferson's letters are filled with expressions of love for his family. In 1788, allegedly in the early stages of his sexual liaison with Sally Hemings, Jefferson wrote: "I had rather be shut up in a very modest cottage with my books, my family, and a few old friends, dining on simple bacon, and letting the world roll on as it liked, than to occupy the most splendid post that any human power can give."[51] And early the following year, still from Paris, he wrote his brother Randolph that "no society is so precious as that of one's own family."[52]

---

49. ELLIS, AMERICAN SPHINX 366.
50. [James Thomson Callender], *The President Again*, RICHMOND RECORDER, Sept 1, 1802.
51. S.N. RANDOLPH, THE DOMESTIC LIFE OF THOMAS JEFFERSON 133 (1978).
52. *Id.* at 137.

The classic statement of this dilemma is that of Ellen Randolph Coolidge, who asked:

> [I]s it likely that so fond, so anxious a father, whose letters to his daughters are replete with tenderness and with good counsels for their conduct, should (when there were so many other objects upon whom to fix his illicit attentions) have selected the female attendant of his own pure children to become his paramour? The thing will not bear telling. There are such things, after all, as moral impossibilities.[53]

If such a relationship had taken place in Jefferson's "cabinet" (bedroom/study), Ellen would likely have learned of it as a child, as her bedroom at Monticello was immediately above his. She wrote of hearing him frequently singing in the morning hours. Dr. White McKenzie Wallenborn, who served for many years as a Monticello guide, has told me that when in the room (now an office) immediately above Jefferson's chamber he could easily hear the voice of a tour guide in the room below. Thomas Jefferson Foundation President Daniel Jordan has confirmed this point to me as well.[54] And these observations were made after Monticello was air conditioned and the windows kept closed.

We know that Thomas Jefferson was philosophically strongly *opposed* to sexual commerce (intercourse) between master and slave—*especially* when carried out in a setting where children might be exposed to it. Among his passionate denunciations of the institution of slavery in his *Notes on the State of Virginia*, written on the eve of his travels to Paris, Jefferson wrote:

> The whole [sexual[55]] commerce between master and slave is a perpetual exercise of the most boisterous passions, the most unremitting despotism on the one part, and degrading submissions on the other. Our children see this, and learn to imitate it; for man is an imitative animal.... If a parent could find no motive either in his philanthropy or his self-love, for restraining the intemperance of passion towards his slave, it should always be a sufficient one that his child is present.[56]

It is virtually inconceivable that Thomas Jefferson would have *intentionally* exposed his children and grandchildren to such a relationship, as it would reveal the hypocrisy of all of his moral teachings to them throughout their lives. Certainly, if he found himself for some reason unable to resist the charms of young Sally, he would have sought to insulate their relationship from his family. But he did not. On the ship back from Paris, he insisted that Sally's room be convenient to that of his daughters—a reasonable choice if his purpose was to provide a nearby servant for his daughters, but a horrible choice if he hoped to sneak into her cabin after dark and make passionate love with her, or simply rape her.

As president, even before Callender first wrote of her, Thomas Jefferson did not take Sally Hemings to Washington. He did visit Monticello once and usually twice every year, and during some of these visits, Sally Hemings promptly became pregnant. But for each visit he asked his daughter Martha to bring her family—including nearly a dozen curious grandchildren—to Monticello to be with him.

---

53. *Ellen Randolph Coolidge to Joseph Coolidge*, Oct. 24, 1858, in *Monticello Report*, Appendix E, at 18.

54. *See supra*, note 18.

55. Like its synonym 'intercourse,' the word 'commerce' was commonly used during Jefferson's era to describe sexual relations.

56. Thomas Jefferson, Notes on the State of Virginia, *Query XVIII*, *reprinted in* 2 Writings of Thomas Jefferson 225–26 (Mem. Ed. 1903).

Writing in *Jefferson: A Revealing Biography,* historian Page Smith (at the time one of the relatively rare historians to accept the Sally Hemings story) alleged that, because of his relationship with Sally, Jefferson was relieved when his daughter Martha got married and moved away from Monticello:

> Jefferson's enthusiasm for Martha's marriage was certainly not unrelated to the role of Sally Hemings in his life. He doubtless felt the weight of Martha's silent disapproval and was glad to have her out of the house, especially in view of the birth of Sally Hemings's son not long after the return to Monticello.[57]

If the story of a sexual relationship were true, this reaction would seem so intuitive as to not even warrant comment. But, as with many other parts of this volume, Professor Smith has totally missed his mark. Not only has the DNA evidence disproved the legend that Thomas Woodson was the son of Thomas Jefferson and Sally Hemings, but Professor Smith's assumption that Jefferson did not want his daughter Martha around Monticello reflects a remarkable ignorance of well-established facts to the contrary.

Indeed, Thomas Jefferson Randolph wrote:

> If he [President Jefferson] visited home for a week, he came to my father's to breakfast and would not leave untill [*sic*] every member of the family accompanied him. When he left home my father preferring to reside on his own farm carried his family back. Previous to the close of his presidency he wrote to my mother to say he had never lived at home without her and never could and she must prepare for a final removal.[58]

We know from numerous other documents that Martha did return to Monticello virtually every time her father ventured home, and that upon his retirement she did move back to the mountain to be with him. If Sally Hemings were the secret passion of his life, why would Thomas Jefferson on every occasion insist that his daughter and grandchildren accompany him to Monticello?

We must also consider the moral character of Martha Jefferson Randolph, whose reputation by all accounts rivaled that of her father. If she knew or believed that her father was bedding a servant woman, would she have *wanted* to accompany him back to Monticello on every visit? Would she have brought her own children and exposed them to such an environment? None of this makes any sense.

Speaking of the grandchildren, Edmund Bacon tells us that "Mr. Jefferson was perfectly devoted to his grandchildren, and they to him."[59] All of the evidence supports that conclusion. Perhaps Thomas Jefferson could have counted on Martha to respect his privacy by not venturing into certain parts of the mansion and knocking before entering, but few men engaged in an illicit sexual relationship would make special efforts to voluntarily fill their home with inquisitive children. It makes no sense at all—*if* one believes the Callender allegations.

Was it possible that such a relationship could have lasted for decades without Martha or anyone else being suspicious? That's really the wrong question, as we must ask whether a man of Thomas Jefferson's intellect and judgment—a man constantly concerned about preserving his reputation—would have believed that the relationship definitely *would* (not just "might") remain secret; and that is a much higher standard.

---

57. Page Smith, Jefferson: A Revealing Biography 229 (1976).
58. Memoirs of Thomas Jefferson Randolph, transcribed by James Bear, Alderman Library, University of Virginia, Accession 5454-c.
59. Jefferson at Monticello 85 (James A. Bear, Jr., ed. 1967).

On this topic, Professor Brodie is certainly correct when she writes: "only the most naïve of men could have believed that he could continue to keep a liaison with the slave girl secret, especially from his daughters."[60] And given his investment in his own reputation, and his deep love for his daughters and grandchildren, I believe it is inconceivable that Thomas Jefferson would have engaged in such a relationship.

Professor Gordon-Reed appears to recognize that Jefferson's love for his family is an impediment to her theory of a romance with Sally Hemings. She deals with this, in essence, by saying that the fact that Jefferson was bright does not mean he loved his family any more than any other slave owner, and there were other slave owners who had sex with slaves. *Ergo*, she implies, this issue is irrelevant. She writes:

> The third prong of the character defense purports to debunk the Jefferson-Hemings liaison by citing Jefferson's love for his children and grandchildren as having been too great to have allowed for such involvement. The first thing to observe about this assertion is that it is not a fact in the sense that Thomas Jefferson was the third president of the United States or that he was the founder of the University of Virginia could be considered facts. It is a value judgment. A person making this assertion is revealing his or her own values more than Thomas Jefferson's.[61]

Is this really true? It may be easier to establish the realities of Thomas Jefferson's election as President or his role in the establishment of the university, but whether he was telling the truth or lying when he professed his love to his family is a factual issue rather than one involving the values of observers.[62] If we asked whether it was a good thing that Thomas Jefferson loved his family, *that* would be a value judgment. But Professor Gordon-Reed continues:

> One need not have a detailed knowledge of the character of every master who ever owned a slave to know that there were slave masters who had slave mistresses and who at the same time loved their white children deeply. One could argue that Thomas Jefferson was not every slave master. But are we to consider Jefferson's capacity to love as greater than what we would expect from an average person just because he had the ability to express his love through his many elegantly written letters to his family? Thomas Jefferson was a genius, but there is no reason to believe that his genius made the character, depth, and nature of his love for his family any greater than those of a person of more modest capabilities.[63]

Put simply, the reason we recognize Thomas Jefferson's immense love for his children and grandchildren is not because we have taken measure of his intelligence, but because we have numerous accounts of not merely his expressions of love but his physical *demonstrations* of that feeling. This has nothing to do with assuming that, simply because he was intelligent and articulate, Thomas Jefferson must have loved his grandchildren. The hard evidence of that love is abundant, and for most of us it is compelling. It comes from numerous sources in addition to the letters of Thomas Jefferson. It is extremely difficult to

60. BRODIE, THOMAS JEFFERSON 239.
61. ANNETTE GORDON-REED, THOMAS JEFFERSON AND SALLY HEMINGS 127 (1997).
62. There may well be some subjective elements in ascertaining or agreeing upon the truth in this issue, as different observers may have different senses of what "family love" is or ought to mean. It may also be much more difficult to ascertain the truth about someone's emotions. But even if not easily quantifiable, the basic issue of whether Thomas Jefferson actually felt certain emotions he expressed is a question of fact.
63. *Id.* at 127–28.

reconcile Jefferson's love for his children and his belief that the sexual exploitation of slaves was particularly harmful to the master's children with the idea that he pressured Martha to bring her family to Monticello while he carried on a sexual relationship with Sally Hemings.

Jefferson's Treatment of Madison and Eston Hemings

Every account of Jefferson and his children and grandchildren emphasizes his deep love and open affection showed towards all of them. And yet, all of the available evidence—including Madison Hemings' alleged statements printed in the *Pike County Republican,* and Jefferson's extensive *Memorandum Books* (which include only a single reference to Madison and Eston out of many thousands of entries)—suggests that he showed *no affection at all* towards his alleged "colored children." His only son by his wife Martha died in infancy, all of Sally's children were apparently seven-eighths (88%) white by blood, and all but one or two were reportedly white enough in their physical appearance to pass for white; so it is difficult to understand why Jefferson almost totally ignored Madison and Eston if they were, in fact, his own sons. Was he so ashamed of his relationship with Sally over all the decades that he could not bear to look at his own children? He clearly had a very close relationship with several members of the Hemings family. Was the Sally Hemings who allegedly confronted and dominated Thomas Jefferson in Paris so timid once she returned to Monticello that she would tolerate her children being *ignored* by their father? None of this makes any sense.

To be sure, one might understand Jefferson's being discreet in showing affection to Madison and Eston in front of visitors to Monticello, but surely there would have been occasions, even if only in the privacy of Sally's room, that he could hold them on his knee and show them the love he exhibited to his other relatives and allegedly felt for their mother. While not conclusive, Thomas Jefferson's lack of visible affection for Sally's children must be considered yet another strong piece of evidence for the proposition that he was not their father. Indeed, there does not appear to be another explanation that can easily be reconciled with what we know about Thomas Jefferson and his love for his children.

Jefferson's Age and Health

Although reliable data are difficult to find, the best estimate is that the life expectancy for an American male during the years Sally Hemings was producing children was about thirty-five or thirty-six years.[64] Modern medical marvels that prolong quality of life for added decades did not exist, and life was generally harsh. Viagra did not become available until 1998. Thomas Jefferson lived a better life than most, and for the era he was a remarkably healthy man.

But even Jefferson suffered from a variety of medical problems as he grew older, including both debilitating rheumatism and intense migraine headaches that often lasted for weeks. Professor Ellis notes that in April 1776, Jefferson was prevented from return-

---

64. I am indebted to Stephen Coles (MD, Ph.D.) of the Los Angeles Gerontology Research Group for this information, which is based upon a 35.5 year estimated life-expectancy-at-birth for males born in 1789 in Massachusetts and New Hampshire. He references: L. I. Dublin, A. J. Lotka, & M. Spiegelman, Length of Life (1936). Former Monticello guide Dr. Michael Moffitt brought this source to my attention.

ing to Philadelphia for more than a month because of incapacitating headaches, and that this was "a lifelong affliction that flared up whenever he felt unduly pressured."[65]

On January 1, 1784, Jefferson wrote to James Madison from Annapolis that he had been in "very ill health since I have been here and am getting rather lower than otherwise."[66] Two months later, he came down with an attack of migraine headaches that lasted six weeks and limited his ability to read or write.[67]

Shortly after arriving in Paris in 1784, Jefferson came down with a severe cold that he wrote James Monroe had kept him "confined" for nearly six months.[68] Another bout with "very violent"[69] migraines struck him shortly after he returned to America, on May 1, 1790, and lasted more than two months.[70] On May 28, 1790, Dr. George Buchanan wrote to Jefferson:

> Mr. Sterett has just arrived from New York, and upon enquiring after your health, he informed me that you had been confined for some weeks past with a periodical headache, which would not yield to Bark, and that you had declined the use of that remedy for some time, in hopes that it would have a better effect when again repeated.—It frequently happens, Sir in periodical affections that the Bark fails, and the disease requires something more powerfully antispasmodick to prevent its return.[71]

The following year, Jefferson complained of "the almost constant headache with which I had been persecuted thro the whole winter and spring."[72] This problem, which plagued him the rest of his life, was "very painful and sometimes rendered him almost immobile."[73]

About four months before Sally Hemings is estimated to have conceived her daughter Harriet I,[74] Jefferson began a letter to Secretary of State Edmund Randolph: "Your favor of Aug. 28 finds me in bed, under a paroxysm of the Rheumatism which has now kept me for ten days in constant torment, and presents no hope of abatement."[75]

Three weeks later, Jefferson added in a letter to Thomas Divers: "I have no prospect of getting on a horse for a month to come."[76] Jefferson's health was so poor that it contributed to a three-month period during which "little ploughing was done" at Monticello, despite "fine" weather.[77]

Three months after the predicted date of conception of Harriet I, Jefferson wrote to James Madison: "My health is entirely broken down within the last eight months; my age requires that I should place my affairs in a clear state...."[78]

---

65. Ellis, American Sphinx 52.

66. *Jefferson to Madison,* 6 Papers of Thomas Jefferson 438.

67. The Family Letters of Thomas Jefferson 23 n.3.

68. *Jefferson to Monroe,* Mar. 18, 1784, 8 Papers of Thomas Jefferson 43.

69. The Family Letters of Thomas Jefferson 58.

70. *Id.* at 56 n.1.

71. 16 The Papers of Thomas Jefferson 487 n. (Julian P. Boyd, ed. 1961). For another reference to suffering from "violent" headaches, *see Jefferson to Monroe,* June 20, 1790, *id.* 536.

72. The Family Letters of Thomas Jefferson 85.

73. *Id.* at 145 n.1.

74. This child died at the age of two and the same name was given to Sally's second daughter. *See* Chapter Two.

75. *Jefferson to Edmund Randolph,* Sept. 7, 1794, *in* 8 Works of Thomas Jefferson 152 (Fed. ed. 1904).

76. *Jefferson to Thomas Divers,* Sept. 28, 1794, in 28 Papers of Thomas Jefferson 168 (2000).

77. The Garden and Farm Books of Thomas Jefferson 275 (Robert C. Baron, ed. 1987).

78. *Jefferson to Madison,* Apr. 27, 1895, *in* 9 Writings of Thomas Jefferson 302–03.

On October 7, 1802, he complained in a letter to Martha of "an excessive soreness all over, and a deafness and ringing in the head."[79] Eleven days later he wrote to Martha and Maria about his "rheumatic," noting that it had "confined me to the house some days...."[80]

Five months before Eston Hemings is estimated to have been conceived by Sally Hemings and an unidentified male carrying the Jefferson Y chromosome, President Jefferson wrote Treasury Secretary Albert Gallatin that his migraines were so painful that he was "shut up in a dark room from early in the forenoon til night."[81] He complained to Martha that "neither Calomel nor bark have as yet made the least impression" on the headaches.[82] Professor Malone tells us the headaches "lasted from nine to five everyday at first, and he was not wholly recovered for about three weeks."[83] Malone attributes the headaches in part to the "great stress of mind" under which the President was suffering during that period.[84]

Three months later, the pain from rheumatism in the President's leg was so intense that he again sought medical assistance. A letter from Doctor Thomas Patterson, received by Jefferson on July 14, 1807 — about six weeks before Eston's estimated conception date — recommended the use of a vinegar-soaked bandage as "a proper remedy for your leg, as it would support the vessels & promote absorption."[85]

Former Monticello slave Isaac Jefferson provided this account:

> About the time when my Old Master begun to wear spectacles, he was took with a swellin' in his legs; used to bathe 'em and bandage 'em; said it was settin' too much. When he'd git up and walk it wouldn't [sic?[86]] hurt him. Isaac and John Hemings nursed him two months; had to car[t] him about on a han'barrow.[87]

Jefferson described an attack of rheumatism the following year as being so painful that he could "scarcely walk, and that with pain."[88]

None of this proves that Thomas Jefferson could not have fathered one or more of Sally Hemings' children. But it is relevant to our inquiry, and along with the other data we have, it greatly reduces the probability that Thomas Jefferson was more likely than his much younger brother or nephews (or someone else) to have fathered Eston Hemings.

---

79. THE FAMILY LETTERS OF THOMAS JEFFERSON 236.

80. *Id.* at 237.

81. *Id.* at 302 n.1.

82. *Id.* at 304.

83. DUMAS MALONE, JEFFERSON THE PRESIDENT: SECOND TERM 1805–1809 at 143 (1974).

84. *Id.*

85. *Patterson to Jefferson,* July 14, 1807, original at the Massachusetts Historical Society. *See also,* 2 JEFFERSON'S MEMORANDUM BOOKS 1207 n.16.

86. Dr. Bear has correctly copied the original book, but the context suggests to me that Jefferson was probably in pain when he walked. The subsequent references to his being "nursed" and transported by wheelbarrow are more consistent with the interpretation that he was in substantial pain.

87. *Quoted in* BEAR, JEFFERSON AT MONTICELLO 19. Jefferson bought his first pair of spectacles at the age of fifty near the end of 1793. *Id.* at 128 n.73. *See also,* ISAAC JEFFERSON, MEMOIRS OF A MONTICELLO SLAVE 44–45 (1951). Mr. Bear seems to believe Isaac was referring to the 1793 period, but my physician friend Dr. White McKenzie Wallenborn has examined Jefferson's health far more closely than I have and believes Isaac's remark related instead to Jefferson's health problems of 1807. If he is correct, then the incident is even more significant as it relates to the period shortly before Eston Hemings was conceived.

88. *Jefferson to Ellen Wayles Randolph,* Oct. 25, 1808, in THE FAMILY LETTERS OF THOMAS JEFFERSON 354 (Edwin Morris Betts & James Adam Bear, Jr., eds. 1966).

Would Thomas Jefferson Have Entrusted His Reputation to the Discretion of Sally Hemings?

The only accounts we have of Sally Hemings as she traveled to Paris tell us she was exceptionally immature and lacked the judgment of an eight-year-old child. As the servant to Jefferson's daughters, she was presumably in their presence for hours at a time, day after day. Again, the issue is not whether Thomas Jefferson would have believed that such a child might be able to preserve his confidences, but whether he would be *certain* that he could entrust his cherished reputation to her discretion.

Imagine for a moment life at the Abbaye Royale de Panthemont. Sally Hemings is a young slave girl, far from home, required to wait hand and foot on Jefferson's daughters as they and their wealthy schoolmates enjoy the finer things of life. If she was wise enough (and *bold* enough) to confront the U.S. Minister to France and demand a "treaty," surely she would realize that by raising her status from lowly servant to "Daddy's mistress" in the eyes of Patsy and Polly, her social standing would improve. *De facto* "stepmother" is a much more powerful position than slave or servant.

Thomas Jefferson had a very close relationship with some of the Hemings men who served as his slaves. He clearly trusted them, gave them considerable discretion, and on occasion even borrowed money from at least one of them. But he was also cognizant that servants who overheard his conversations could be sources of rumors and gossip. William Howard Adams writes in *The Paris Years of Thomas Jefferson*:

> One of the new Parisian fashions that Jefferson immediately adopted—and later introduced at Monticello and in Washington—was the use of small, individual serving tables placed between guests in dining rooms, eliminating the need for servants in the room during the meal. Years later in Washington, Margaret Bayard Smith recalled Jefferson's remark "that much of the domestic and even public discord was produced by the mutilated and misconstructed repetition of free conversations at dinner tables, by these mute but not inattentive listeners."[89]

Was Sally Hemings Thomas Jefferson's "Type"?

About the only thing we know about Sally Hemings is that she was "handsome" and "mighty near white." Certainly she might have been sexually attractive even at age fourteen or fifteen to many adult men. At one point, both Jefferson's secretary William Short and his close friend James Madison had romantic interests in teenaged girls much younger than themselves.[90] But there is no evidence that Thomas Jefferson's tastes in women were in that direction.

---

89. ADAMS, THE PARIS YEARS OF THOMAS JEFFERSON 19. Obviously, the problem Jefferson identifies here has nothing to do with race. Indeed, only two of his servants in Paris were of African heritage (James and Sally). But given Sally's reported immaturity, it is virtually inconceivable that Jefferson would not have perceived that any confidence he shared with her might be disclosed both to other servants in the house and from them to his guests, visitors, and even strangers. This, plus the obvious risk that Sally would disclose an intimate relationship to Patsy and Polly, would obviously have been *major* impediments to such a relationship, even if he found Sally otherwise irresistible.

90. On thirty-one-year-old James Madison's interest in a girl less than half his age, *see* GORDON-REED, THOMAS JEFFERSON AND SALLY HEMINGS 112.

Indeed, *all* of the women that we know Jefferson as an adult found sexually appealing were married or widowed, mature, and—above all else—highly accomplished and talented.[91] In an era filled with impediments to the serious education of women, Jefferson was drawn to urbane, sophisticated, and above all *talented* women. His wife Martha, a mature widow, was an accomplished musician.[92] Maria Cosway had been elected to the Florence Academy of Fine Arts at the age of nineteen, and had exhibited nearly two dozen paintings at London's Royal Academy. She was accomplished on the pianoforte and harp, had a beautiful singing voice, and was a music composer—as well as being an accomplished linguist.[93] Angelica Church was also worldly, witty, and likely far more talented than had been Martha Wayles. Even Elizabeth Walker, the wife of Jefferson's friend John Walker, towards whom Jefferson later admitted having made inappropriate advances while a young bachelor, was a mature married woman.

Andrew Burstein notes that Jefferson had an "intellectual approach" to sexual behavior.[94] Professor Ellis refers to his "romantic innocence"[95] and "conspicuous gallantry"[96] towards women. Assessing Jefferson's lengthy correspondence with the beautiful and talented Maria Cosway, Ellis finds it "abundantly clear that Jefferson preferred to meet his lovers in the rarefied region of his mind rather than the physical world of his bedchamber,"[97] and concludes "his deepest urges were more self-protective and sentimental than sexual."[98]

Since we have almost no information about Sally in Paris, we cannot say much about her with certainty. But the description attributed to Captain Ramsay, and echoed through the experienced eye of Abigail Adams, is so far from the kind of woman Thomas Jefferson was ever known to find attractive that the Callender allegations are yet further problematic. As a slave, there is little reason to believe that young Sally had any formal education or was especially accomplished as an artist, musician, or the like. Indeed, it is noteworthy that witnesses like Edmund Bacon and Isaac Jefferson, who described Sally's relatives by praising their talents, made not a single suggestion that Sally Hemings had any special talents and focused instead on her "handsome" appearance and the fact that she had once traveled to Paris. The most reasonable reading of Madison Hemings' 1873 statement strongly suggests that, even as an adult, Sally Hemings could neither read nor write English, much less other languages.[99] And unlike the paternity statements attributed to Madison, his words bearing on Sally's attainments could have stemmed from direct, first-hand knowledge.

I have never researched the issue, but Benjamin Franklin is alleged to have had a very active sex life during his years as Jefferson's predecessor in Paris. William Howard Adams writes:

---

91. *See, e.g.,* Ellis, American Sphinx 110.
92. *See, e.g.,* Jack McLaughlin, Jefferson and Monticello 183 (1998).
93. Virginius Dabney, The Jefferson Scandals 41 (1981).
94. Burstein, *Jefferson's Rationalizations* 184.
95. Ellis, American Sphinx 62.
96. *Id.* at 110.
97. *Id.* at 115.
98. *Id.* at 261.
99. Had Sally been literate, one might have expected her to take the lead in educating her children. But Madison said he learned to read by persuading the white children at Monticello to teach him. This of course does not *prove* anything, and conceivably Sally was so busy looking after the personal needs of the President that she did not have time to help educate her children. But there is not a single scrap of paper in existence known to contain her writing or other evidence that she could read or write.

If Henry Adams was right in judging Jefferson's Paris years his happiest, it had little connection with the cynical, often risqué era of Franklin's triumphs. The fact that the Virginian is rarely mentioned in contemporary French letters and memoirs, while Franklin turns up regularly, attests to his private, diffident manner. By temperament and by choice, Jefferson distanced himself from the shallow, sarcastic wit that defined *mondain* society. Rather, he took pleasure in exchanging ideas with the extraordinary array of talented individuals in that talented age—writers, scientists, artists, philosophers—who thrived in the urban setting.[100]

Revisionist scholars seem to acknowledge Jefferson's obvious preference for women of talent and intellect, and some attempt to identify such attributes in Sally Hemings. Princeton history professor Sean Wilentz, for example, wrote in *The New Republic*: "It is said that Hemings spoke French and, it seems, could interest her lover from the neck up, too."[101] The problems with this reasoning include: (1) the only suggestion we have that Sally had any significant proficiency with the French language comes from the very problematic 1873 assertions attributed to Madison Hemings, who had no apparent ability to judge the matter; and (2) assuming a superficial[102] ability to communicate in French in addition to Sally Hemings' other known attributes does not come close to placing her in the league of any of the women Jefferson is known to have found sexually attractive.

Again, as far as we know, Sally could neither read nor write in English, much less communicate seriously in any other language, draw, paint, sing, or play a musical instrument. We have good reason to believe she was "handsome," and she *may* have been drop-dead beautiful, as Hollywood likes to suggest. But Paris was filled with beautiful women, and even if Sally had not been in daily contact with Jefferson's daughters (and, most likely, not even *near* Thomas Jefferson during most of her Paris stay), yet another reason for doubting the Callender allegations is that Sally Hemings clearly was not Thomas Jefferson's "type."

Why Did Sally Not Confirm the Relationship after Jefferson's Death?

If Sally Hemings was in fact Thomas Jefferson's lover and confidante, one might expect that she would take some pride in that relationship. During his life she might conceivably have had the self-restraint not to brag about it, but it is more difficult to accept that she could live as a free woman in Charlottesville for many years after Jefferson's death and not bother to mention this remarkable distinction to anyone.

---

100. ADAMS, THE PARIS YEARS OF THOMAS JEFFERSON 76–77.

101. Sean Wilentz, *What Tom and Sally Teach Us*, NEW REPUBLIC, Nov. 30, 1998 at 15.

102. We know from Jefferson's letters that even after living eighteen months in Paris and with the aid of a tutor James Hemings was unable to communicate in French. Jefferson remarked in a letter to Anthony Giannini that James "has forgot how to speak English, and has not learnt to speak French." *Jefferson to Giannini*, 5 Feb. 1786, 9 PAPERS OF THOMAS JEFFERSON 252, 254 (Julian P. Boyd, ed. 1954). *See also*, 14 *id.* 426 (1958). If Sally had developed a proficiency with the language, it is reasonable to assume she would have shown off such a talent at Monticello on occasion and someone like Isaac Jefferson or Edmund Bacon (both of whom recorded talents by other members of the Hemings family) might have made note of it.

Of course, perhaps she did. We do not have records of statements she may have made during those years, and it is possible that she bragged about her famous lover to everyone she met. But this would be rather newsworthy stuff, and even if some did not believe her, one might expect that at least someone who heard her story would put it down on paper. The "Black Sal" story had been spread across the country, and had Sally confirmed it, she would presumably have been taken seriously. The absence of any clear record that she ever confirmed the rumors does not *prove* anything, and possibly can be explained by other causes; but it is another "silent dog" that supports the conclusion that the relationship never existed.

Why Did None of Sally's Children Confirm the Relationship During the Four Decades after Jefferson's Death?

As discussed in Chapter Four, we know that in 1873 an anti-Jefferson newspaper editor in Ohio published an article alleging that Madison Hemings had told him that Sally Hemings was his mother and that Thomas Jefferson had fathered all of her children. The factual errors and other problems with this account have already been discussed.

Madison could not personally have known the identity of his own father or that of the father of any of his siblings, as he was but two years old when Sally's last known child was conceived. Most scholars have assumed that, if he or Samuel Wetmore (the journalist who actually wrote the story) did not simply fabricate the entire matter from the well-known Callender charges, Madison's source must have been his mother.

But if Sally Hemings told her children they were President Thomas Jefferson's children—which many revisionist scholars assume[103]—why did none of them mention it to anyone else until Jefferson had been dead nearly fifty years? (Obviously, we cannot be certain that they did not all discuss it regularly, but given the nature of the claim and the context of the Callender charges, it would seem likely that if they did discuss this regularly, someone would have mentioned it in a letter or other writing and someone else would have realized this document was of sufficient historical value to preserve.) Professor Gordon-Reed admits that Madison Hemings' statement "is the only known recitation of the details of this controversial story by any of the parties involved...."[104]

It is unkind to the "intelligent"[105] Madison to suggest that he was not bright enough to realize that being known as the son of the famous Thomas Jefferson might benefit him. His friend Israel Gillette—who was the subject of a similar Wetmore article later that year—readily admitted that his decision to drop the name of his real father and assume the surname "Jefferson" was done because "it would give me more dignity to be called after so eminent a man."[106]

Brother Eston Hemings went so far as to change his last name to "Jefferson" when he moved from Ohio to Wisconsin, but, as far as we can tell, he never openly claimed to be

---

103. Jan Ellen Lewis & Peter S. Onuf, *Introduction*, SALLY HEMINGS & THOMAS JEFFERSON 9 (1999).

104. GORDON-REED, THOMAS JEFFERSON AND SALLY HEMINGS 7.

105. *Monticello Report*, Appendix H at 12 (quoting Samuel Wetmore).

106. [Samuel Wetmore,] *Life Among the Lowly, No. 3*, Pike County [Ohio] REPUBLICAN, Dec. 25, 1873, at 4.

the son of Thomas Jefferson.[107] Nor, again, as far as we can tell, did any of the other children of Sally Hemings. And this appears to have been true not only in the decades after Jefferson's death, but also when they lived at Monticello. The simplest explanation for this would seem to be that they did not believe they were Thomas Jefferson's children.

With One Problematic Exception, Other Monticello Slaves Did Not Confirm the Allegation

Joshua Rothman wrote his doctoral dissertation on interracial sex in antebellum Virginia. In *Sally Hemings and Thomas Jefferson,* he asserts: "Slaves at Monticello knew of the association between Hemings and Jefferson and had greater access to details of the relationship than nearly anyone else."[108] Rothman's comment is probably valid. But had the relationship been of a *sexual* character, one would expect that, following his death, at least some of Thomas Jefferson's former slaves would have passed on this remarkable story and ultimately it would have found its way into written form and been preserved for posterity.

It is thus noteworthy that, with the exception of Israel [Gillette] Jefferson, as an old man in 1873 and in an account so filled with errors as to suggest either that his memory had failed him or he was intentionally fabricating his story to support his friend Madison, of the hundreds of people owned by Jefferson over the years, not a single account survives in which a slave confirms Madison Hemings' story. Surely this long-lasting affair, had it existed, would have been widely known within the slave community. After Jefferson's death, most of his slaves were sold and spread across the south. Yet—again, except for the story attributed to an aging Israel Jefferson—there is not a scrap of paper suggesting that any of them ever said a word to anyone, even to acknowledge the rumor.

Some might reason that slaves feared they would be severely punished if they spread rumors about the sex lives of their masters. Or perhaps they thought it improper to discuss inter-racial sex with strangers—a social taboo that was not to be mentioned. But Isaac Jefferson, in his *Memoirs of a Monticello Slave,* did not hesitate to note rumors within the Monticello slave community that Sally and some of Betty Hemings' other children were the offspring of John Wayles, Thomas Jefferson's father-in-law.

Again, these "silent dogs" are not conclusive proof of anything. But one would expect that a decades-long romance between an American President and one of his slave women, producing numerous children over many years, would be known to other Monticello slaves. If so, it is reasonable to assume that they would find it noteworthy and, upon moving to new plantations and making new acquaintances, they would share the rumors with others, who would find it interesting and pass it along themselves. Somewhere along the line, someone would put the account down in writing. And the absence of such accounts

---

107. On one occasion he may at least have encouraged speculation on the subject, but there is no known instance in which he actually asserted that Thomas Jefferson was his father. *See, e.g., Monticello Report*, Appendix F at 3; and Lucia Stanton & Dianne Swann-Wright, *Bonds of Memory*, SALLY HEMINGS AND THOMAS JEFFERSON 173. ("Although it was widely 'rumored' in southern Ohio that he was Jefferson's son, he is not known to have made an unequivocal statement of his parentage, as did his brother Madison.") But *cf.,* Gordon-Reed, THOMAS JEFFERSON AND SALLY HEMINGS 211 ("Not only did Madison Hemings claim to be Jefferson's son; his brother Eston did as well.").

108. Joshua D. Rothman, *James Callender and Social Knowledge of Interracial Sex in Antebellum Virginia*, SALLY HEMINGS AND THOMAS JEFFERSON 98.

(again, with the exception of Israel Jefferson's problematic story) is yet another bit of "non-evidence" that *ought* to exist were the story true.

To Accept This Story, We Must Dismiss the Oral Tradition of Eston Hemings' Family and Accept Instead the Unsupported Allegations of Vile Racists Like James Callender and Thomas Gibbons

One of the greatest ironies in the desire of some to accept the allegations of the revisionists in the name of "political correctness" is that, in so doing, they must dismiss the oral history of Eston Hemings' descendants (passing down that Eston's father was not Thomas Jefferson, but "an uncle")—which points most likely to "Uncle Randolph," Thomas Jefferson's younger brother—and instead accept as truth the allegations of blatant racists like James Callender and Thomas Gibbons, neither of whom had ever even been to Monticello and both of whom had strong personal grievances against Thomas Jefferson.

As discussed in Chapter Eight, at its core, "oral tradition" refers to multiple hearsay testimony passed down over many generations, often with decades elapsing between retellings by individuals who have an obvious incentive to embellish the achievements of their ancestors. It is hardly the most reliable form of evidence, but it can be very useful as a means of identifying leads to investigate further—and sometimes it is simply all we have with which to work.

The oral tradition of the Eston Hemings family would appear to be more reliable than most on the issue of Eston's paternity, as there would be no clear benefit to the family in acknowledging that Eston's father was not the famous historical figure who wrote the Declaration of Independence and served two terms as President, but rather merely "an uncle" of that famous man. The current efforts of some of Eston Hemings' descendants to discredit the accounts they repeatedly admit they were told by their parents and grandparents so they can claim lineage from the famous President is an excellent example of the dangers of relying upon such accounts as evidence of the truth.

But surely the family traditions passed from one generation of Eston Hemings' descendants to another for a century and a half ought not be rejected simply because they are at odds with the rantings of James Callender (who, it should be recalled, without the slightest apparent knowledge of the facts referred to Eston's mother as a "slut"), or Thomas Gibbons (who described Sally Hemings' children, whom he had never laid eyes upon, as "flat nosed" and "thick lipped," and called Sally herself a "prostitute"). Particularly given how well their oral traditions fit with the other information we have about Randolph Jefferson, the oral traditions of Eston's family deserve greater respect than this.

Why Did Thomas Jefferson Not Free Sally in His Will?

There is an erroneous perception by many that Thomas Jefferson freed Sally Hemings and all of her children in his will. This was one of the many false statements made by Israel Jefferson in 1873, and perhaps he is the source for some of the modern misinformation. In reality, although she was eventually allowed to leave the plantation and apparently spent the final years of her life living with her freed sons Madison and Eston in Charlottesville, Sally Hemings was never legally freed from her status as a slave.

Given what we know about Thomas Jefferson, is it credible that—if Sally Hemings were, in fact, his lover for decades and the mother of most of his children—he would neglect to provide for her future in any way in his will? Would he have allowed her to become subject to being sold at auction—perhaps to an abusive master who would whip or sexually abuse her, or perhaps to a political enemy who would take her from town to town and force her to recount the details of her romance with the once beloved President? No reasonable person can assume that.

So perhaps it was his intention to leave Sally to the care of his beloved daughter, Martha Randolph—whom he could count upon to treat her lovingly and to protect her dignity as she grew older? The problem with this theory is that, if there had been a sexual relationship, Martha would certainly have known of it. While she might have played the role of dutiful daughter while her father was still alive, Jefferson would almost certainly have realized that Martha would also likely blame Sally for the relationship that had harmed his reputation and so clearly upset her. Could he be certain that Martha would on her own provide Sally with the love and comfort any honorable man would wish at the time of his death for the love of his life?

Even if Martha had promised to provide a safe and comfortable living environment for Sally Hemings, if she believed the stories were true and wanted to protect her father's reputation, is it likely that she would have allowed Sally to move to Charlottesville to live with her sons—in an environment where she could tell her story to the entire world? The answer to all of these questions, presumably, is "We don't know." Conceivably, the answer is "yes." But from what we believe we know about Thomas Jefferson and his daughter Martha, the more likely response is "no." It is very difficult to reconcile Sally's treatment (being totally ignored) in Thomas Jefferson's will with any theory that she was the love of his life and the mother of most of his children.

The argument on the other side, presumably, is that Jefferson still cared deeply about his future reputation (certainly true), and that he knew if he freed the infamous Sally Hemings, it could be seen as an admission of guilt by many Americans. But if that were his concern, why did he give freedom to Madison and Eston—two of his alleged children by Sally Hemings who could be expected to produce the same kinds of rumors?

We are told that Sally was the love of his life, the woman who "knew Thomas Jefferson at least as well as did any of his white friends and relatives,"[109] whereas by Madison Hemings' own account, he and his brother were shown no affection by Jefferson, and Jefferson's records treat them as almost nonentities at Monticello.

Perhaps (as some of the revisionists would apparently wish us to believe), everything we thought we knew about Thomas Jefferson's character for the past two centuries is wrong, and he was truly a "monstrous"[110] figure. A far simpler and more rational conclusion, from the totality of the evidence before us, is that Sally Hemings was *not* Thomas Jefferson's lover, and her children were *not* his children.

---

109. David Brion Davis, *Preface*, in Lucia Stanton, Free Some Day 11 (2000).

110. Joseph Ellis, American Sphinx 23 (quoting University of Virginia history professor Peter Onuf as characterizing "the emerging scholarly portrait of Jefferson as 'a monster of self-deception.'").

Individual Views of
Professor Jean M. Yarborough
joined by
Professor Charles Kessler
and
Professor Harvey C. Mansfield

12

Individual Views of Jean M. Yarborough, Charles Kessler, and Harvey C. Mansfield

After reviewing the report of the Thomas Jefferson Memorial Foundation and the materials presented in this report, we do not believe the evidence that Jefferson fathered one or more of Sally Hemings' children is compelling.

The case for Jefferson's paternity rests on three principal arguments: recent DNA evidence, greater weight to the oral tradition of Madison Hemings, and Jefferson's presence at Monticello during each of the periods when Sally Hemings conceived her children. But as even the authors of the article analyzing the DNA results make clear, the DNA evidence does not "prove" that Jefferson was the father of Sally's children. Moreover, there is not one oral tradition, but three in play, and these contradict each other on key points. The Thomas Woodson tradition was conclusively refuted by the DNA evidence. Until recently, the descendents of Eston Hemings asserted that a relative of Jefferson's was the father of Eston, a claim not inconsistent with the DNA findings.

Only Madison Hemings claimed that Thomas Jefferson was the father of all the Hemings children, and, significantly, this was not until 1873, in an interview given to a newspaper editor in Ohio. If Jefferson were the father, it seems likely that all the Hemings children would have known it, and not just one. Further, it seems plausible that the story would have surfaced earlier, and that there would be some contemporaneous evidence somewhere that would corroborate the charge. There is not.

Equally troublesome is the assumption that Sally Hemings was monogamous and that all her children were fathered by the same man. It is true that earlier historians had also been quick to assume that only one man (Jefferson's nephew Peter Carr) was the father of all of Sally's children. But a serious reconsideration of the question in light of the DNA evidence requires that this assumption also be scrutinized, especially in light of contemporary accounts that suggest several possible fathers. None of this is inconsistent with the fact that Sally's conceptions took place when Jefferson was in residence. When else would Jefferson's relatives come to visit?

Although we do not believe that the case against Jefferson's paternity is air tight, and there remain legitimate questions that cry out for better answers than we can give, we think that a fair and impartial review of all of the evidence suggests that Thomas Jefferson was not the father of any of Sally's children.

Individual Views of
Professor Lance Banning

13

Thomas Jefferson and Sally Hemings: Case Closed?

Whether Thomas Jefferson fathered children by Sally Hemings is a harder question for me than it seems to be for many. The DNA results, in combination with the data concerning Sally Hemings' conceptions, have persuaded many able scholars that Thomas Jefferson fathered Eston Hemings and may have fathered some or all of Eston's siblings. But there is powerful evidence to the contrary, as creditable as reported statements by Madison Hemings and often too lightly dismissed. The conclusion that Jefferson fathered these children, moreover, cannot be accepted unless we are also able to give credence to a much longer list of radical implausibilities than I have been able to swallow. Thus, I continue to doubt that Jefferson fathered any of the Hemings children, have signed the commission's report, and find Robert Turner's individual statement generally convincing.

The informal essay which follows was prepared as all of the commission members were grappling with the issue late last year [2000]. It continues to reflect my thinking.*

Within the last three years, the old story that Thomas Jefferson fathered several children by his slave Sally Hemings—a claim that most Jefferson scholars had earlier considered so implausible that nearly all of them rejected it without a truly rigorous investigation—has gained new credibility and extensive national publicity. In 1997, Annette Gordon-Reed offered a powerful argument that the case for Jefferson's paternity was notably stronger than the leading Jefferson scholars had been willing to admit, while the case that Hemings' children were fathered by one of Jefferson's Carr nephews, which was widely accepted by those scholars, was markedly weaker than they had supposed. In the aftermath of Gordon-Reed's book, several former skeptics moved to a neutral position and Joseph Ellis, who still thought Jefferson's paternity unlikely, insisted in his *American Sphinx*, which won the National Book Award, that neither side had a clearly convincing case. Then, in 1999, DNA testing proved compatible with the possibility that Thomas Jefferson fathered Eston Hemings, Sally's youngest son, but incompatible with the possibility that one of the Carr brothers did. At that point, numerous former skeptics or neutrals, led by Ellis himself, moved firmly to the other side. A few have even suggested that no reasonable person can continue to doubt it. The DNA report (very misleadingly titled), a conference held at the University of Virginia, a volume of essays resulting from that conference, a forum in the *William & Mary Quarterly*, a bad movie, a dreadful TV miniseries, and a report by the staff of the Thomas Jefferson Memorial Foundation, which manages Mon-

---

* Editor's Note: Sadly, Professor Banning passed away January 31, 2006, at the age of sixty-four. The world lost an outstanding human being and an exceptionally able scholar at that time. He was a mainstay of our inquiry and a man of remarkable insight and intellectual courage. We shall miss him.

ticello—all accepting the likelihood of Jefferson's paternity—publicized the accusation far and wide. A good bit of politics, some of it racial and some of it prompted by the close conjunction of the release of some of the reports with Bill Clinton's impeachment, erupted on both sides.

Political considerations continue, as they always will, to affect the ongoing dispute over whether the story is true. Thomas Jefferson is an icon: more closely identified than any other individual with the foundational principles of the American regime. Logic may tell us that his personal character has little to do with whether his principles were sound or his public contributions useful, but it still has symbolic importance for many. People, moreover, are strongly inclined, for the most part, to believe what they want to believe, to give more weight to evidence that supports their position than to evidence that disputes it, and, regrettably often, to impugn the motives of those who disagree. Professional historians and other scholars are not immune to these weaknesses, but the discipline of history does insist that we make our best effort to recognize our biases and control for them. Even when we do, we may not get the history right, but if no historical "truth" is ever discoverable at all, if we don't at least aim at that, whether the result seems politically helpful or not—in short, if it is never really possible for us to learn something from the past, if our encounters with the records are little more than occasions for symbolic battles and incidents in current cultural conflicts—it's hard to see why we bother with history at all. There are other, perhaps more forthright, grounds to fight those battles on. Let's start, at least, by getting the history as straight as discipline allows. Only then, as I conceive it, are we ready to ask if the history holds any lessons. Is the story true? This, at least, is an interesting question for historical detectives—and one that any student or citizen can pursue quite seriously on his own, since so many of the original sources are readily available, courtesy of Monticello's website and websites on the other side.[1] Politically, the subject is a landmine. Rightly handled, though, it has some useful things to teach about the method of sound historical inquiry and the uses or abuses of the past. That's what attracted my interest, and this paper is meant to share my own reasoning and conclusions. I've studied most of the relevant primary and secondary sources on the subject, and although I haven't given it years or even months of study, I think I do see pathways through the thicket.

I start by recognizing clearly that the case *for* Jefferson's paternity of the Hemings children is strong enough that we can readily understand why so many able scholars have come to think it likely. Their argument stands basically on five substantial pillars:

> (1) The mountaintop at Monticello was populated by numerous mixed-race slaves, some of whom resembled Jefferson and one of whom (probably Eston Hemings) was said by Jefferson's grandson to bear him such a striking resemblance that, at a distance, in the dusk, they might have been mistaken for one another. Jefferson, moreover, was privately and publicly accused during his lifetime of being the father of Sally Hemings' children and sometimes of other slaves as well, most famously, perhaps, in an 1802 blurb in the *Richmond Recorder* by the notorious scandal-monger James Thomson Callender. President Jefferson, Callender wrote, "keeps and for many years has kept as his concubine, one of his own slaves. Her name is SALLY. The name of her eldest son is TOM. His features are said to bear a striking although sable resemblance to those of the President himself. The boy is ten or twelve years of age.";

---

1. See www.monticello.org, www.tjheritage.org, and www.angelfire.com/va/TJTruth.

(2) In an interview with an Ohio newspaper reporter in 1873, Madison Hemings, another of Sally's sons, said that he and his siblings were Jefferson's children (and his only slave children) in a report which accords in much of its substance with what we know from other sources. According to this interview, Thomas and Sally initiated an affair while they were together in Paris from 1787 to 1789. Sally became pregnant and agreed to return to the United States after they entered into a "treaty" in which Jefferson promised "extraordinary privileges" for Sally and freedom for her children when they reached age 21;

(3) Sally Hemings conceived all her children when Jefferson was at Monticello and no children when he was not;

(4) DNA tests show that a descendent of Eston Hemings carries a Jefferson gene; and

(5) DNA tests are incompatible with the possibility that Eston Hemings was fathered by Peter or Samuel Carr, the sons of Dabney Carr and Jefferson's sister Martha and the most often mentioned and most plausible alternatives to Jefferson himself as a father.

The case for Jefferson's paternity, in brief, is strong enough that the burden of persuasion has shifted to the skeptics. This may be true if we apply the test of Occam's razor: the logical standard that tells us that the simplest of workable, competing explanations of a set of facts should be preferred. It certainly seems true in a political sense: in an atmosphere inflamed by suggestions that to doubt this story is somehow to denigrate African Americans and deny them their rightful place in American history.

Nevertheless, it is by no means true that no reasonable person can continue to doubt—not, at least, for this occasional participant in modern life, who, in any case, confesses a great deal of puzzlement over the implications some have found in the story. It seems to me quite evident that unconscious bias and, in some cases, professed political objectives are as plainly at work on one side of this issue as the other. For example, the Thomas Jefferson Memorial Foundation staff report, which is presented in a tone of dispassionate historical inquiry, is nevertheless, to my mind, markedly one-sided: it makes a strong case for Jefferson's paternity, on much the lines I've just sketched out, but barely touches on serious grounds for doubt; and it is nearly as biased in its differential weighting of evidence as some of the earlier discussions condemned by Gordon-Reed and others. Thus, despite the genuine strength of the contrary case, there remains, I think, ample reason for continuing skepticism about a claim which, if false, gravely libels a great American founder and, if true, compels a serious reconsideration of his moral character, though a claim which, either way, does not strike me, as it strikes so many others, as greatly affecting either our understanding of this founder's public contributions or our understanding of African American history.

Space and time will not permit a thoroughly detailed discussion of every instance of biased treatment of evidence or slips of logic in the case for Jefferson's paternity. That would be work for an article or even a book. But there should be room, at least, to stress that there are remarkably few uncontested or uncontestable facts in this matter. It is very much a problem of weighing and interpreting the thin and disputable evidence we have—and, ideally, of being wary of our own predispositions and examining this record with as much dispassion as we can possibly muster.

Critics have advanced stronger or weaker responses to virtually every element in the pro-paternity case in rebuttals already in circulation, some of which are powerful if by no means temperate. Briefly, though, let me run again through those five main pillars as a way of getting a bit more deeply into the subject:

(1) A supposed resemblance between Thomas Jefferson and some of Sally Hemings's children (or other Monticello slaves) is certainly evidence of his possible paternity, but it is hardly evidence of a very substantial kind. A resemblance between one person and another is seen by some people and denied by others. It may not even be the best of evidence that some of Sally's children had *a* Jefferson (or a Carr) for a father, which was generally conceded long before the DNA results.

(2) Madison Hemings' "Memoir," which is actually a reporter's account of an interview with him, first published in an Ohio newspaper in 1873, is entitled to the same respect and should be considered with the same skepticism and the same concern for corroborating evidence—no more, no less—as similar reports of conversations with others. Like virtually all those others, it is an "as told to" account in which we cannot tell with certainty which words and statements came from Madison Hemings and which may have been changed by the reporter—a report, moreover, in which both the interviewee and the reporter might or might not have been telling the truth. In this case, many of its details can be corroborated from other sources. Some can be disproved.[2] And some suggest that Madison Hemings or the interviewer was leaning on previously published accusations by Callender or others.[3] I am strongly inclined, for my own part, to believe that Hemings was telling the truth as he understood it. But, obviously, he could not have known first-hand who was the father of Sally's children or whether all of them were fathered by the same man. It is not even certain (although it seems likely) that he had the story of the affair and the "treaty" from Sally herself, who left no reported statement that it was true. That Madison Hemings' descendents also believed the story is not surprising and adds nothing that Madison did not say himself. This "Memoir," in brief, is a valuable historical resource and was dismissed too easily, sometimes with prejudice, by earlier historians. But it is not inherently racist to question its details, nor does the memoir, in my judgment, unquestionably outweigh the countervailing testimony of Edmund Bacon, a former overseer at Monticello, and of several members of the family of Thomas Mann and Martha Jefferson Randolph, Thomas Jefferson's daughter. Neither is Madison's story consistent as I understand it with the oral tradition in the family of Madison's brother Eston, who apparently passed down a claim that he was the son of a close relative of Jefferson, not of Jefferson himself. We can well doubt that Sally Hemings became pregnant in France and would have had any reason to enter into the improbable "treaty" that Madison described. No one has solved the mystery of the baby that Madison said was born in 1790 but lived only a short time, the baby that may have become the twelve-year-old "Tom" of James Thomson Callender's public accusation against Jefferson in 1802. It is not clear that Thomas Woodson, said to be that baby in another oral tradition, was Sally

---

2. For example, it does not seem true that Dolley Madison was present at Madison's birth, and it would seem highly unlikely in the aftermath of Callender's accusations that she would have begged to name the baby after her husband. All of Sally's children were not freed at age 21. Sally did not receive "extraordinary privileges" at Monticello. There is great room to doubt that Sally became pregnant in Paris. Etc.

3. The use of the word "concubine" to describe Sally's relationship with Jefferson, together with other language in the "Memoir," strongly suggests that Hemings or the reporter, Samuel Wetmore, had read James Thomson Callender's original 1802 accusation. Both accounts misspell "Wayles" as "Wales."

Hemings' son, and it now seems certain that, if he was, he was not the son of Thomas Jefferson too.[4]

(3) The facts about Sally Hemings' conceptions — at least about the conceptions after 1789 — are certainly among the strongest elements in the case for Thomas Jefferson's paternity. They do strongly suggest that Jefferson (or someone who was at Monticello only when Jefferson was there, or someone whose sleeping arrangements were altered by his presence) fathered her several children.[5] Occam's razor would point to Jefferson himself as the simplest of the workable answers. But it is curious that Jefferson's grandson, Thomas Jefferson Randolph, and the historian Henry Randall both believed that they had independently confirmed Martha Randolph's insistence that the child who most resembled Jefferson (presumably Eston) could not have been his, since he and Sally were "far distant" from one another for fifteen months before the baby's birth. We know that Jefferson was at Monticello during those fifteen months and, indeed, for most of the specific period during which Eston would have been conceived. We have no documentary evidence that Sally was ever away. But we have no reason either to believe that all these other people were simply lying.

(4) The DNA results certainly do *not* prove Thomas Jefferson's paternity of any of the Hemings children. They were widely misreported as having done that, and this misperception may well have spread indelibly among the public. But every knowledgeable authority, including the scientists who conducted the tests, has denied that this is what was found and even that it was possible to make such findings from the sort of tests that were done. These tests compared 19 markers on the y chromosomes of 14 individuals: 5 living male-line descendents of 2 sons of Thomas Jefferson's paternal uncle, who was assumed to have the same y chromosome as Jefferson's father and thus of Jefferson himself; 3 male-line descendents of 3 sons of the paternal grandfather of Peter and Samuel Carr; 5 male-line descendents of 2 sons of Thomas Woodson; and one male-line descendent of Eston Hemings. The results showed a match between the haplotypes of the Jefferson descendents and the Hemings descendent, but no other matches. In plain words, they showed that a descendent of one of Sally Hemings' children carries a Jefferson gene, not a Carr one, and that neither the Carrs nor the Jeffersons are related to the Woodsons.

(5) Although they implicate a Jefferson, not a Carr, as Eston Hemings' father, the DNA results cannot exclude the Carrs as possible fathers of Sally Hemings' earlier children. Neither can they show, in and of themselves, that Thomas Jefferson was any more likely to have been Eston's father than any of Thomas's male-line relatives who might have had relations with Sally Hemings at the relevant times. To me, the absence of a wholly plausible alternative to Jefferson as a father is another of the strongest elements in the pro-paternity case. Thomas's younger brother, Randolph Jefferson, or one of Randolph's sons, might possibly have fathered Eston. Randolph was probably at Monticello at the right time, perhaps with some of his sons; and Randolph, unlike Thomas, was known to dance

---

4. Joe Fosset, whose descendents apparently preserve an equally strong oral tradition of descent from TJ, was clearly not the son of either.

5. They do not, however, suggest this as strongly as is argued in Fraser Neiman's Monte-Carlo study, which is severely flawed by the assumption that the presence of other potential fathers at Monticello would have been random.

and play his fiddle with the slaves. But Randolph or one of his sons seems so unlikely to have fathered all of Sally Hemings' children that respondents will continue to protest that this is a grasping at straws by Jefferson's defenders. Peter or Samuel Carr, the nephews who were believed to be Sally's lovers by Jefferson's grandchildren and who were reported to have confessed it to him and another witness by Thomas Jefferson Randolph, might still, to be sure, have fathered all of Sally's children except Eston. But this would not explain why Sally became pregnant only when Thomas was at home. So far as we know, one or both of the Carr brothers was usually at Monticello or quite nearby from 1794 to 1808.

Given greater space and time, I might continue at greater length to review the chinks in the case for Jefferson's paternity. But rebuttals are widely available as is, and others will be forthcoming. Moreover, even if I were to fill in the heads of this sort of critique, the case for Jefferson's paternity might still seem stronger, in terms of Occam's test, than the arguments against it.

On the other hand, Occam's razor tells us to prefer the simplest theory *only* when the simplest theory seems equally true. And here, it seems to me, the simplest explanation of most of the salient facts—that Jefferson fathered all the children born between 1795 and 1808—seems sound only when we focus so intently on the points I have reviewed thus far. I remain a skeptic, and I remain one principally because of a long list of highly implausible things we have to believe in order to accept the Jefferson-Hemings story in anything like the terms advanced by Madison Hemings and assumed to be likely in much recent work—a good part of which dismisses countervailing evidence too easily and passes very lightly over these implausibilities when they are mentioned at all.

Thomas Jefferson was not a saint. He was capable, on demonstrable occasions, of mendacity, hypocrisy, and even, when young and single, an untoward advance toward a married woman. (This, he said, was the only one of the Federalist charges against him in which there was any truth.) But neither was Thomas Jefferson a moral monster—unless, of course, we think that everyone who was born and died a slaveholder deserves that epithet. Rather, the Jefferson we know from the records was profoundly concerned with personal morality and religiously convinced that conduct would be punished or rewarded after death. He was deeply affectionate toward his family and intensely jealous of his public and private reputation. He was fastidious about feminine delicacy, cleanliness, and such, no sort of womanizer, perhaps even celibate after the death of his wife. He was invariably attracted in the few cases we know of for sure to accomplished, mature women. But in 1788 or 1789, we are asked to believe, this U.S. minister to France, a man with ready access to some of the most beautiful and accomplished women in Europe, living in a society (as he put it) where "beauty goes begging on every street," initiated an affair with a 15- or 16-year-old slave girl, whom Abigail Adams had recently described as more in need of care than the 8-year-old she had attended across the ocean. This girl was the personal servant (and likely something of a confidant) of Jefferson's two daughters—he would refer to her years later as "Maria's maid" [1799]—an individual, that is, whose discretion the accomplished politician and diplomat could not possibly have trusted. Although it may well be that Sally lived, during much of her time in Paris, in the cross-town convent where Patsy and Polly were being schooled, we are to assume that Thomas and Sally carried on their affair in the crowded two-bedroom townhouse where Jefferson lived—and did so without arousing the suspicion of David Humphreys, who slept in one of the bedrooms, or of anyone else who was there. She became pregnant with Jefferson's child, the story continues, entered into an agreement with him, and (with Jefferson taking care that she would have a berth convenient *to his daughters*) sailed back to the

U.S. in this condition with him, his two girls, and her brother James.[6] (The baby, if it existed, either died soon after birth, without leaving a trace other than Madison Hemings' statement, or became the elusive, unrecorded 12-year-old of Callender's 1802 accusation, who, if he later took the name Tom Woodson, was not Thomas Jefferson's child.)

Well, in any event, infatuated enough to make this improbable "treaty" with his slave, Jefferson would continue in a monogamous and fertile relationship with Sally for nearly 20 years, according to this story, ultimately fathering five or six more children (the first of whom, however, was not born until 1795). During these twenty years, he was content, as was she, to confine the relationship to the times when he was at Monticello, although he took other slaves with him wherever he went and as many as a dozen to the White House. Both he and Sally were so extraordinarily cautious as never to arouse the suspicions of anyone around them. On these terms, he continued in the relationship until at least age 64, when Eston Hemings was conceived, five years after he had been publicly accused of a relationship with Sally and while he was completing his second presidential term. He carried it on, all this while, while constantly surrounded by visitors and by a large white family, none of whom—and least of all the daughters who would have known Sally best—ever had the least suspicion that he was involved with any of his slaves or ever saw the slightest indication that he was closer to Sally than to any other servant. Indeed, the grandchildren who grew up at Monticello and managed it during Jefferson's last years did not just say that any such relationship was wholly unsuspected—never a touch or a word or a glance—they said it was simply impossible in this particular house. I slept within sound of his breathing, his grandson said, in a room across the hall. "His apartment," his granddaughter told her husband, "had no private entrance not perfectly accessible and visible to all the household. No female domestic ever entered his chambers except at hours when he was known not to be there and none could have entered without being exposed to the public gaze." In fact, apart from Madison Hemings, no one who ever lived at Monticello and none of the uncounted visitors who stayed there overnight ever said that he was involved with Sally—not Sally herself, though she lived in practical freedom in Charlottesville for 10 years after his death, and not Eston Hemings, whose only known statement on the subject neither affirmed nor denied that Jefferson was his father.[7] It is possible, of course, that everyone except Madison Hemings was lying or covering up or engaged in psychological "denial." Jefferson's family had an interest in protecting his reputation, much as Madison Hemings had an interest in claiming descent from a famous man. But, again, I see no reason to think that any of these people were deliberately making things up. And what of the only two witnesses who had no obvious interest in the matter either way? Isaac Jefferson, a former household slave, mentioned Sally Hemings in a "memoir"

---

6. French historians tell me that (leaving diplomatic immunity aside) it is by no means certain that contemporary French law would have freed SH, who, if she thought it would, could more certainly have secured freedom for herself as well as any future children by staying in France. It seems rather hard, in any case, to envision the 45-year-old diplomat pleading with an illiterate slave girl to return to America with him and the 16-year-old girl contracting a bargain with her master.

7. In the latter, some citizens of Chillicothe who knew Eston had seen a statue of Jefferson that looked very like him. They asked him if Jefferson was his father. Eston might have had an interest in saying yes. He replied, however, that his mother was single and had belonged to TJ. The only corroboration of Madison Hemings' account came in an interview with the same Ohio newspaper of former slave Israel Jefferson, which is so replete with provable misrepresentations as to be the only relevant source that I consider completely untrustworthy. Contrast this with the recorded memories of Isaac Jefferson, who, unlike Israel, actually did have duties around the house. Isaac mentioned and described Sally Hemings, but did not so much as hint that there was any special relationship between her and TJ.

of his own; he was the one who described her as attractive and "mighty near white." But there is not a hint in Isaac's reminiscences that Sally stood out otherwise from the rest of her mother's family. And Edmund Bacon, who was overseer at Monticello when Eston was conceived and may have worked there for years before that, poses an even larger problem for the pro-paternity story. In an interview of his own, Bacon raised the subject of the accusations against his employer[8]:

> He freed one girl some years before he died, and there was a great deal of talk about it. She was nearly as white as anybody, and very beautiful. People said he freed her because she was his own daughter. She was not his daughter; she was _____'s daughter. I know that. I have seen him come out of her mother's room many a morning, when I went up to Monticello very early. When she was nearly grown, by Mr. Jefferson's direction I paid her stage fare to Philadelphia and gave her fifty dollars.

The girl was certainly Harriet Hemings, Sally's daughter. The father was named by Bacon but protected by the reporter, a preacher in Kentucky.

All of Sally Hemings' children who lived to adulthood did achieve their freedom, either de facto or de jure, and it is often said that they were the only nuclear family of Monticello who did. What, finally, of that? Well, contrary to the terms of the "treaty" as Madison Hemings described it, Sally Hemings did not receive extraordinary privileges at Monticello. There may be few uncontestable facts in this matter. But it *is* quite clear that Jefferson fed, clothed, housed, and treated Sally Hemings pretty much indistinguishably from his other household servants, recorded her life and childbirths in much the same way, and left her as part of his estate. There is nothing in Jefferson's records that would identify Sally as especially significant among the household servants, nothing that makes her distinguishable in her treatment or duties from her sister or her Hemings cousins. By Madison Hemings' own account, moreover, Jefferson showed no particular affection for her children and reared them much as he did other household slaves. Beverley ran away, probably at age 24, and Jefferson did not attempt to catch him. Harriet fled into white society, probably with Jefferson's assistance to the amount of fifty dollars and a stagecoach ticket. And Madison and Eston received the *least* favored treatment of the 5 skilled slaves— all members of the broader family of Sally's mother, Betty, who were freed in Jefferson's will. By the terms of this document, Burwell Colbert, Joe Fosset, and John Hemings were granted their freedom, various amounts of money, tools, cabins, and land. A codicil to the will, written less than three months before his death, also gave John Hemings the services of his apprentices, his two nephews, until age 21, when they would also receive their freedom, though none of the other gifts granted to the older servants. But until then, if we are to believe this story, another statement by Thomas Jefferson Randolph would suggest that his thin-skinned grandfather, always concerned for contemporary and historical regard, would not only have continued the affair with Sally long after it became a public scandal—and still without arousing the suspicion of his family—he would have been so brazen about it as to have a slave whose resemblance to him was absolutely startling serve his foreign guests at dinner.

Strange things happen where sex is concerned, not to mention slavery and race. Racial mixing between masters and servants happened all the time in the Old South. It does not tax us highly to imagine how perfectly ordinary it was, or what a range of conduct it en-

---

8. Similarly, the strongest statements we have about the physical resemblance between Jefferson and some of his slaves, are those made to historian Henry Randall by Jefferson's grandson, Thomas Jefferson Randolph.

compassed: from boys and girls coming into adolescence together in the familiarity of a plantation and playing games more adult, to deep affection, to the tyranny in which it was as easy for a master so inclined to order a woman to his bed as it was to order her to do the laundry or tend the crop. As Jefferson himself told us, "the man must be a prodigy who can retain his manners and morals undepraved" within such a system.

Was Jefferson such a man? Did he, though a slaveholder, retain his morals relatively undepraved? The honest answer, to my mind, is that we simply do not know and may never possess the evidence that could answer the question absolutely. Parts of the argument *for* his paternity of Sally Hemings' children are hard to overcome. But this does not seem any harder, to my mind, than swallowing the lengthy list of radical implausibilities we have to swallow to accept that the story is true. It's a close call: a hard case, as the lawyers would say. But there are surely grounds for strong, continuing doubts. Count me, then, in the minority who seem to think that the proper verdict, at this moment, has to be "not proven."

Individual Views of
Professor Robert H. Ferrell

14

Individual Views of
Professor Robert H. Ferrell

512 South Hawthorne
Bloomington, IN 47401
March 25, 2001

Dear Professor Turner:

You asked if I might have any further observations to add to your commentaries on the Hemings controversy. I do want to say, again, my complete support of your committee's position, the unalloyed support of the president. It does seem to me so ridiculous that the accusations of Callender of so long ago should have such a recent public airing.

And let me add a few recent experiences of my own, to illustrate what seems to be a virtual climate of accusation that is flourishing in our own time. A few years ago, seeking to investigate the illness and death of President Warren G. Harding—this after having published a general book about presidential illness from Grover Cleveland through the administration of the first President Bush, I began to see, as my research developed, that in the case of Harding there had occurred a virtual smearing of his reputation, this after his death in 1923. And so I undertook a book with the title of *The Strange Deaths of President Harding*, a play on the title of the old Gaston B. Means book of 1930, in which I wrote of Harding's physical death and the subsequent death of his reputation through slander and innuendo. In the course of it I wrote at length of the accusations of the late Nan Britton (d. 1991), which were without foundation but widely believed.

A year or two ago I undertook a long taping here in Bloomington for a CBS hour-long account of "sex in the White House," in which I spoke unrestrainedly of the way that Harding had been maligned and made the point, I thought, that the same thing had happened to President Franklin D. Roosevelt. Someone at CBS, who, so far as I know, has no standing as an historian, interpreted what I said—interpreted it into the exact opposite of what I said. I of course protested to the CBS studio, after viewing the resultant film, and had a smart-aleck letter back from some vice president relating how helpful I had been to the production.

Lastly an experience of very recent date. *The Journal of American History*, published at my university for the generality of American historians across the country, ran a lead article in its December issue entitled "What Happened to Sex Scandals: Political Peccadilloes from Jefferson to Kennedy." Its author is a graduate student in American history at the University of Rochester presently teaching at Harvard. Quite apart from the smarty title the article was a compendium of innuendo and surmise, and the author wrote flat-out that President Harding's mistress was Nan Britton and that President Roosevelt's mistresses were Mrs. Rutherfurd and Ms. LeHand. I asked the editor of the journal to print an apology, and in response to her suggestion that I instead write a letter to the editor I did so, in collaboration with Warren G. Harding III of Cincinnati. The letter has not yet been printed, awaiting a response by the offending author.

Sincerely,

Robert H. Ferrell

Individual Views of
Professor David N. Mayer

15

The Thomas Jefferson-Sally Hemings Myth and the Politicization of American History*

Introduction

I concur in the Scholars Commission's conclusion that the allegation that Thomas Jefferson fathered one or more children by his slave Sally Hemings is "by no means proven." My own view is that the allegation is not at all plausible. Moreover, I unreservedly join Robert F. Turner in his Individual Views, which I regard as the most complete and objective analysis yet written of all the evidence relevant to the Jefferson-Hemings allegation. I write my own separate report to state my views on the matter and to discuss the Jefferson-Hemings controversy in a broader context. As I see it, belief in the paternity allegation—which, to me, is quite literally a myth—is a symptom of a disturbing trend in the history profession in recent years, discussed below.

It is primarily out of my concern for the history profession, and far less so out of my concern for Jefferson's legacy, that I agreed to serve on the Commission and that I am writing this essay. Let me make clear from the outset what has motivated me, and what has *not* motivated me, in this endeavor.

I freely admit that I am an admirer of Thomas Jefferson; but my admiration for Jefferson always has focused on his ideas, principally his ideas about government, and not on Jefferson as a man. For over 25 years—since I first began my formal studies of Jefferson's political and constitutional thought as an undergraduate student at the University of Michigan—I have been fascinated with Jefferson's philosophy. My own studies have focused particularly on Jefferson's ideas about limits on governmental power, the subject of my book *The Constitutional Thought of Thomas Jefferson*.[1] While I necessarily learned a great deal about Jefferson's life and times while doing the research for this book and my other writings on Jefferson's thought, I always have found the substance of his ideas far more interesting than the circumstances of his life. Moreover, I believe that Jefferson's place in American history—his central role in our nation's founding and the evolution of its system of government—justly derives from his ideas. As I see it, genealogy is irrelevant: the true "children" of Jefferson today are those who understand his ideas and work to keep them alive. His true legacy is the body of ideas he has given us, ideas still quite relevant today, to the perennial problems of protecting individual rights and limiting the

---

1. David N. Mayer, *The Constitutional Thought of Thomas Jefferson* (Charlottesville: University Press of Virginia, 1994).

powers of government. The attributes of Jefferson the man—his character and the circumstances of his life—are essentially irrelevant to that legacy. Indeed, as I noted in my comments at the University of Virginia on the 250th anniversary of his birth (April 13, 1993), it saddens me that Americans today seem to have done a better job preserving Jefferson's legacy in bricks and mortar (having in mind the splendid restorations of Jefferson's "academical village" in the University as well as his two homes, Monticello and Poplar Forest) than we have in preserving his legacy of ideas.

Frankly, I regard Jefferson's personal life as neither interesting nor important. What troubles me most about the controversy over Jefferson's alleged relationship with Sally Hemings is that this matter unjustifiably has overshadowed Jefferson's true significance. I do not join with those who regard the Hemings paternity allegation as a *per se* libel of Jefferson's character; as discussed below, belief in that allegation has served to advance the interests of a number of partisans, some of them detractors of Jefferson but others genuine admirers of Jefferson, who use the story of a relationship with Sally Hemings to transform Jefferson into either a villain or a hero to advance their own agendas.

I agreed to serve on the Scholars Commission because I became increasingly concerned about the way *both* the admirers and the detractors of Jefferson were willing to use the Hemings story for their own purposes without regard to historical truth or to objective, well-recognized standards of good historical scholarship. I was particularly troubled by the fact that many eminent scholars have so readily abandoned professional standards in seizing upon the 1998 DNA study—and, in the process, either blithely ignoring or deliberately misrepresenting the findings of that study—as so-called "proof" of the paternity allegation, again to advance their own partisan agendas.

Evolution of the Myth

Throughout American history, the Jefferson-Hemings paternity allegation has been used for partisan purposes. That certainly was the case with the allegation's early history, during Jefferson's own lifetime. It originated in an 1802 Richmond, Virginia newspaper story by the hatchet journalist James Thomson Callender, a disappointed job-seeker who felt he had been betrayed by the new President and whose bitterness toward Jefferson was quite evident throughout the piece. The allegation was nothing more than unsubstantiated rumor, for there is no evidence that Callender had any first-hand knowledge of Monticello. The allegation then was spread by Jefferson's political enemies in the bitterly partisan Federalist press, particularly in the fall of 1802. Significantly, however, after Americans gave President Jefferson and his party an overwhelming vote of confidence by bolstering Republican majorities in both the House and Senate in the mid-term Congressional elections, the Hemings allegation seemed to die. "Little was said about Hemings, for example, in the months before [Jefferson's] 1804 landslide re-election, and only infrequently during the remainder of Jefferson's lifetime did references to the alleged affair appear in print," concluded the scholar who has most thoroughly studied the Hemings story in the context of Jefferson's reputation during his lifetime.[2] The Hemings paternity allegation resurfaced again in New England—the last bastion of the Federalist party—in 1805, occasioning Jefferson's letter to friends denying the "charges" made

---

2. Robert M.S. McDonald, "Race, Sex, and Reputation: Thomas Jefferson and the Sally Hemings Story," *Southern Cultures* 4: 46–63 (Summer 1998), p. 47.

against him, except for the truthful allegation of his youthful affair with the wife of his neighbor John Walker, an allegation which at the time probably was taken far more seriously than the Hemings story.[3]

In the decades following Jefferson's death, both before and after the Civil War, the Hemings paternity allegation—together with other miscegenation stories linked to Jefferson—surfaced from time to time as partisans of North and South, Whigs (or Republicans) and Democrats, and anti-slavery political activists and pro-slavery Southern apologists, all used the "Jefferson image" to help further their own cause. As Merrill D. Peterson has noted, the story was revived and retold especially by abolitionists in the antebellum period. "The most common version of the story in anti-slavery circles was the one related in 1838 by Dr. Levi Gaylord, of New York. He had heard, he said, from the lips of a Southern gentleman: 'I saw for myself, the DAUGHTER OF THOMAS JEFFERSON sold in New Orleans, for one thousand dollars.' Gaylord wanted this 'sounded longer and louder through the length and breadth of the land' until a virtuous indignation should wipe out slavery. Goodell's *Friend of Man* printed Gaylord's story, whence it spread to other newspapers."[4] After the anonymous poem "Jefferson's Daughter" appeared in the abolitionist newspaper *Liberator*, other anti-slavery activists—principally the black writer and abolitionist William Wells Brown—popularized the story. "Upon the flimsy basis of oral tradition, anecdote, and satire, the most intelligent and upright abolitionists avowed their belief in Jefferson's miscegenation," Peterson reports.[5]

Although the underlying motives changed, 19th-century exponents of the Hemings story and other Jefferson miscegenation legends continued to use the allegations for partisan purposes. "Unlike the Federalists, the abolitionists were smearing the South's peculiar institution, not Jefferson or democracy. They dwelled less on Jefferson's 'African brothel' than on his alleged mulatto offspring."[6] Peterson also notes that one other group contributed to the revival of the legend in the second quarter of the 19th century: British aristocrats who, in their commentary on America found Jefferson—the symbol of American democracy   "a convenient target for their criticism."[7] After the Civil War, the legend continued to be used for partisan purposes, by Republican Party activists (many of them former abolitionists) who took Jefferson as a symbol for both the defeated Confederate cause and for the Democratic Party.

It is in the context of this 19th-century manipulation of the "Jefferson image" that we must place the so-called "memoirs" of Madison Hemings, published on March 13, 1873 as the first of a series of interviews with former slaves entitled "Life Among the Lowly," in the Pike County (Ohio) *Republican*, a partisan newspaper edited by Samuel F. Wetmore, a Republican Party activist. As Professor Turner notes in his individual views, there are many good reasons to be highly skeptical of this 1873 newspaper article. One reason is that we are not sure the statements attributed to Madison Hemings really were his and not the words of the editor, Wetmore. Even if the statements were indeed Hemings', they are clearly hearsay, for Madison Hemings had no first-hand knowledge of a relationship between Jefferson and his mother. Indeed, given that there is no evidence that Sally Hemings herself claimed Jefferson as the father of any of her children, as well as the fact that Madison Hemings' statements so closely resemble the Callender allegations from 1802, it

---

3. *Ibid.*, pp. 55–59.
4. Merrill D. Peterson, *The Jefferson Image in the American Mind* (New York: Oxford University Press, 1960, 1962), p. 182.
5. *Ibid.*, p. 183.
6. *Ibid.*, p. 182.
7. *Ibid.*, pp. 183–84.

is possible that Hemings based his story on Callender's.[8] Whatever the source of the words attributed to Madison Hemings, they clearly reflect a deep bitterness toward Jefferson—a bitterness that is fully understandable if Madison Hemings genuinely believed he was Thomas Jefferson's son, for all the available evidence indicates Jefferson essentially ignored him. (The significance of the lack of any evidence showing Jefferson's affection toward Madison Hemings, or any of Sally Hemings' other children, in refuting the paternity allegation is discussed more fully below.)

The unreliability of Madison Hemings' story as reported in the 1873 Pike County *Republican* is further highlighted by Wetmore's follow-up interview in his "Life Among the Lowly" series with another former Monticello slave, Israel Jefferson, which Samuel Wetmore published in his newspaper several months later (on December 25, 1873) in an effort to corroborate Hemings' story. As Professor Turner notes in his individual views, Israel Jefferson's statements are even less credible than Madison Hemings'. Shortly after Israel's story was published, Jefferson's grandson, Thomas Jefferson Randolph, wrote a scathing six-page letter to the editor in response, pointing out many factual errors in Israel's account and, of course, denying the "calumny" of the Hemings paternity allegation. Randolph added, "To my knowledge and that of others 60 years ago the paternity of these parties were admitted by others."[9]

The "others" to whom Randolph referred were Peter and Samuel Carr, nephews of Thomas Jefferson (the sons of his sister Martha and his childhood friend Dabney Carr, whom he raised as if they were his own sons). James Parton, in his 1874 biography of Jefferson, quoted Jefferson's grandson Thomas Jefferson Randolph as telling fellow Jefferson biographer Henry S. Randall that "there was not the shadow of suspicion that Mr. Jefferson in this or any other instance had commerce with female slaves." T. J. (Jeff) Randolph alleged that Sally Hemings was the mistress of Peter Carr, while Sally's sister Betsey Hemings was the mistress of Peter's brother, Samuel.[10] Jeff Randolph also told Randall that he once confronted Peter and Samuel Carr over the matter (after a visitor at Monticello had left a newspaper with "insulting remarks about Mr. Jefferson's mulatto children"), and that the Carr brothers tearfully confessed their guilt, with Peter saying, "Ar'nt you and I a couple of _____ pretty fellows to bring this disgrace on poor old uncle who has always fed us! We ought to be _____, by _____."[11]

Randall explained that he did not include the allegation against the Carr brothers in his *Life of Jefferson* because Jeff Randolph prohibited him from doing so, saying "You are not bound to prove a negative. If I should allow you to take Peter Carr's corpse into Court and plead guilty over it to shelter Mr. Jefferson, I should not dare again to walk by his grave: he would rise and spurn me." Randall added, again citing Jeff Randolph, that Jefferson was "deeply attached to the Carrs—especially to Peter. He was extremely indulgent to them and the idea of watching them for faults or vices probably never occurred to him."[12]

---

8. Madison Hemings' account, as printed in the *Pike County* [Ohio] *Republican* in 1873, also misspells the last name of Jefferson's father-in-law, John Wayles, as "Wales"—the same misspelling found in 1805 newspaper articles in Boston and Washington, D.C., which were the first allegations in print that John Wayles was the father of Sally Hemings. On the 1805 articles, see my discussion of Jefferson's 1805 denial, below. This coincidence suggests that the 1805 articles also may have been the source of the Madison Hemings story as written by Samuel Wetmore.

9. Thomas Jefferson Randolph letter, circa 1874, University of Virginia Library.

10. Letter from Henry S. Randall to James Parton, June 1, 1868, *printed in* Milton E. Flower, *James Parton: The Father of Modern Biography* (Durham, N.C.: Duke University Press, 1951), pp. 236–37.

11. *Ibid.*, p. 238.

12. *Ibid.*

Randolph's sister, Ellen Randolph Coolidge, claimed that the father of Sally Hemings' children rather was Samuel Carr, "the most good-natured Turk that ever was master of a black seraglio kept at other men's expense."[13] Ellen Coolidge further claimed that her brother had overheard Peter Carr "say with a laugh, that 'the old gentleman had to bear the blame of his and Sam's (Col. Carr) misdeeds.'"[14]

One other direct observer of happenings at Monticello offered his testimony denying the Hemings paternity allegation against Jefferson. Edmund Bacon, who was Jefferson's slave overseer for many years, in a reminiscence first recorded in 1862, denied that Sally Hemings' daughter (presumably Harriet) was Jefferson's daughter. "She was not his daughter, she was _____'s daughter. I know that. I have seen him come out of her mother's room many a morning when I went up to Monticello very early."[15]

Notwithstanding the denial of the Hemings paternity allegation by members of Jefferson's family and eyewitnesses to life at Monticello, the allegation survived in the oral traditions of several American families who claimed descent from Thomas Jefferson and Sally Hemings, including the descendants of Madison Hemings as well as the descendants of Thomas Woodson, who claimed to be the child Callender had identified as "Tom." (These oral traditions are discussed more fully in the next section, below.) The Hemings allegation also remained alive in the writings of many black American political activists and scholars, including W. E. B. DuBois.[16] But the allegation was given new life when the claims made in Madison Hemings' "memoir" were resurrected in a bestselling biography of Jefferson published in the 1970s.

In her book *Thomas Jefferson: An Intimate History*, the late Fawn M. Brodie resurrected the story attributed to Madison Hemings, as well as the original 1802 Callender allegation, that while in France, Jefferson took as his "concubine" the teenaged Sally Hemings.[17] Jefferson scholars have long rejected Ms. Brodie's flimsy "psychological evidence" of a Jefferson-Hemings affair in France—and with good reason, for Brodie's "psycho-history" was not only implausible but also failed to fit the facts. As Jefferson biographer Willard Sterne Randall writes:[18]

> [Brodie] suggested that, when Jefferson traveled through France and Germany and eight times described soil as mulatto in his twenty-five sheets of notes, he was not referring, as he labeled the appropriate column of his charts, to yellowish soil in the hills and valleys he traveled through but was really thinking of the contours of Sally's body. And when he was taking notes on a new kind of moldboard plow that he invented shortly after the journey, he was really thinking of plowing the fertile Sally as soon as he returned to Paris. But *mulatto* is a precise term describing yellowish-brown soil. And when Jefferson used the term *mulatto* to describe soil during his French travels, Sally was still on a ship with Polly, accompanying her to France. If he had ever noticed her or remembered her at all, Sally had been only ten years old when Jefferson last visited Monticello hur-

---

13. Ellen Randolph Coolidge to Joseph Coolidge, October 24, 1858, Coolidge Family Papers, University of Virginia Library.

14. *Ibid.*

15. Rev. Hamilton Wilcox Pierson, "Jefferson at Monticello: The Private Life of Thomas Jefferson," manuscript of the recollections of Edmund Bacon, *printed in* James A. Bear, ed., *Jefferson at Monticello* (Charlottesville: University Press of Virginia, 1967), p. 102.

16. See Peterson, *Jefferson Image in the American Mind*, p. 184.

17. Fawn M. Brodie, *Thomas Jefferson: An Intimate History* (New York: W.W. Norton & Co., 1974), pp. 294–300.

18. Willard Sterne Randall, *Thomas Jefferson: A Life* (New York: Henry Holt and Co., 1993), p. 476.

riedly in 1784 to pack [Sally's brother] James Hemings off to France with him. She was only eight when Jefferson last resided at Monticello and was mourning his wife's death. Unless Brodie was suggesting that Jefferson consoled himself by having an affair with an eight-year-old child, the whole chain of suppositions is preposterous.

Despite its obvious shortcomings, Fawn Brodie's account of a sexual liaison between Jefferson and Sally Hemings, beginning in France and continuing at Monticello following their return to the United States, captured the imagination of many people and became a part of American popular culture in the last quarter of the 20th century. From scholarly treatments such as Winthrop Jordan's book *Black over White* (1968) to imaginative recreations such as Barbara Chase-Riboud's novel *Sally Hemings* (1979) or the Merchant-Ivory film *Jefferson in Paris* (1995), the story of a Jefferson-Hemings relationship became widely accepted by many Americans. Thus, when Annette Gordon-Reed, an African-American associate professor of law at New York Law School, sought to vindicate Madison Hemings' claims in her book *Thomas Jefferson and Sally Hemings: An American Controversy* (1997), she found a ready audience. (The flawed case for Jefferson's paternity of Hemings' children presented in Professor Gordon-Reed's book is further discussed below.) Although historian Joseph J. Ellis, in his book *American Sphinx: The Character of Thomas Jefferson* (1997), had joined other Jefferson biographers in doubting the story of a sexual liaison with Sally Hemings, he had read the manuscript of Gordon-Reed's book—which was going to print just as his own book was published—and declared in a blurb for its inside cover, "Short of digging up Jefferson and doing DNA testing on him and Hemings' descendants, Gordon-Reed's account gets us as close to the truth as the available evidence allows."

Without having to disturb Jefferson's corpse, Dr. Eugene A. Foster was able to conduct DNA tests, which compared the Y chromosome haplotypes of 14 individuals: five living male-line descendants of two sons of Field Jefferson (Thomas Jefferson's paternal uncle), five living male-line descendants of two sons of Thomas Woodson, three living male-line descendants of three sons of John Carr (paternal grandfather of Samuel and Peter Carr), and one living male-line descendant of Eston Hemings. The results showed a match between Eston Hemings' descendant and the descendants of Field Jefferson. The tests found no match, however, between the Jefferson male DNA and that of Thomas Woodson's descendants. Nor did the tests find a match between the Eston Hemings descendant and the Carr descendants. As historian (and fellow Scholars Commission member) Lance Banning succinctly puts it in his paper "Thomas Jefferson and Sally Hemings: Case Closed?": "Although they implicate a Jefferson, not a Carr, as Eston Hemings' father, the DNA results cannot exclude the Carrs as possible fathers of Sally Hemings' earlier children. Neither can they show, in and of themselves, that Thomas Jefferson was any more likely to have been Eston's father than any of Thomas's male-line relatives who might have had relations with Sally Hemings at the relevant times."[19] In fact, Jefferson was one of at least 25 adult male Jeffersons (male-line descendants of his paternal uncle, Field Jefferson) who might have fathered Eston Hemings, passing on to him the Y chromosome with the distinctive Jeffersonian characteristics. Indeed, eight of these 25 Jefferson males lived within 20 miles (a half-day's ride) of Monticello—including Thomas Jefferson's younger brother, Randolph Jefferson, and Randolph's five sons, who ranged in age from about 17 to 26 at the time of Eston's birth.

The results of Dr. Foster's DNA tests were reported in the November 5, 1998 issue of the British journal *Nature*, in an article bearing the misleading headline, "Jefferson fa-

---

19. Professor Banning's paper, p. 290.

thered slave's last child." (A more accurate headline, of course, would have been "*A Jefferson—not necessarily Thomas Jefferson—fathered*" Sally Hemings' youngest child.) The article on the DNA test results was accompanied by an article "Founding father," co-authored by Professor Ellis, which proclaimed that the DNA analysis "confirms that Jefferson was indeed the father of at least one of Hemings' children."

Thus began the "spin" on the DNA test results—and the most recent telling of the Jefferson-Hemings story. No doubt referring to his own book which portrayed Jefferson as an enigmatic "sphinx," Professor Ellis wrote, "Recent work has also emphasized his massive personal contradictions and his dexterity at playing hide-and-seek within himself. The new evidence only deepens the paradoxes." And, further evidencing new uses for the Jefferson image in modern American politics, Professor Ellis concluded, "Our heroes—and especially presidents—are not gods or saints, but flesh-and-blood humans, with all the frailties and imperfections that this entails."[20]

The timing of the *Nature* article's publication—on the eve of the November 1998 Congressional elections and just weeks before the U.S. House of Representatives' vote to impeach President Bill Clinton—was not purely coincidental. Professor Ellis' accompanying article also noted, quite frankly, "Politically, the Thomas Jefferson verdict is likely to figure in upcoming impeachment hearings on William Jefferson Clinton's sexual indiscretions, in which DNA testing has also played a role." In television interviews following release of the article, Professor Ellis elaborated on this theme; and Clinton's apologists made part of their defense the notion that every President—even Jefferson—had his "sexual indiscretions." (It should be added that Ellis was among the so-called "Historians in Defense of the Constitution" who signed an October 1998 ad in the *New York Times* opposing Clinton's impeachment.)

Others besides Clinton apologists seized upon the alleged DNA "proof" of Jefferson paternity to advance their own ideological agendas. British journalists and commentators used the story much as they had in the 19th century, to denigrate American Revolutionaries by associating them with slaveholding. Thus, for example, Christopher Hitchens suggested in *The Nation* that Jefferson henceforth be described as "the slave-owning serial flogger, sex addict, and kinsman to ax murderers." (One is reminded of reviews in the British press of the Mel Gibson movie, "The Patriot," last summer. *The Express* noted that the real Francis Marion, the "Swamp Fox" on whom Gibson's Benjamin Martin character was based, "raped his slaves and hunted Red Indians for sport.") And for many scholars of race and race relations in America, the Jefferson-Hemings story and reactions to it (particularly by those who continued to be skeptics) provided further evidence of the racism they say permeates American society. Indeed, for many, acceptance of the paternity thesis has become a kind of litmus test for "politically correct" views: those of us who continue to question it have been denounced as racially insensitive, if not racist. (For more on this, see the discussion of Annette Gordon-Reed's views, below.)

The Jefferson-Hemings story is useful symbolism for people of various political persuasions today: to those on the left, for example, it can serve as a metaphor for racism in America; to those on the right, a metaphor for immorality. Not just leftists, but conservatives too, have used the Hemings story to denigrate Jefferson and, with him, two of the cardinal values of his life, reason and individualism. As Timothy Sandefur notes in his essay "Anti-Jefferson, Left and Right," "What damns Thomas Jefferson in conservative and multiculturalist eyes alike is his appeal 'to all men and at all times,' and not to the consider-

---

20. Joseph J. Ellis, with Eric S. Lander, "Founding Father," in *Nature*, November 5, 1998, pp. 13–14.

ations of race, class, and sex, of which the left approves, or to the 'whispers of dead men' that the conservative hears."[21] The Hemings story permits some to see Jefferson's whole political philosophy as "bound up in the sexual exploitation of a slave," Sandefur adds. "Jefferson's position as *the* Enlightenment figure in America can thus be seen as inseparable from his ownership and exploitation of slaves, and the Enlightenment can be dismissed accordingly. Conservative writer Dinesh D'Souza describes a conversation he had with some thoroughly indoctrinated college students: 'On Jefferson, the three were agreed: he was, in various descriptions, a 'hypocrite,' a 'rapist'..., and a 'total racist.' Jeffersonian principles of individualism, reason, science, and private property, all become tainted."[22]

It is not just the enemies of the Enlightenment in America today who find symbolism in the Hemings story. Libertarians, too, find the story a useful vehicle for advancing their agendas, whether they are detractors or admirers of Jefferson. Some want to believe the story because they are anxious to pull him off his pedestal, to show in Jefferson's hypocrisy "the need to be a nation of laws and not of men," as an editor of *Reason* magazine put it.[23] Others, who genuinely admire Jefferson, hope that "this new, racially-conflicted Jefferson," who some now imagine as having had a long-term monogamous relationship with a mulatto woman, might be "more authentically libertarian" than "the old, much more 'racist' Jefferson," as one libertarian scholar suggested to me in private correspondence. This last comment suggests that some admirers of Jefferson, whatever their political persuasion, find in the Hemings story a new way to "humanize" Jefferson, to make him less aloof. Indeed, for some who idolize Jefferson, the Hemings story provides proof that Jefferson was able to transcend the racial attitudes of his time. They are, frankly, engaged in wishful thinking, idealizing Jefferson into a 20th- (or even 21st-) century individualist comfortable with interracial relationships—which, sadly, he was not (as his retirement-years writings on race matters show).

The lesson is obvious: today, as throughout American history since the inception of the story nearly 200 ago, many Americans for various reasons want passionately to believe that Thomas Jefferson fathered some or all of Sally Hemings' children, whether or not the evidence supports the charge.

Myth vs. History: Oral Tradition as Unreliable Evidence

Traditionally, historians long have recognized the unreliability of oral tradition as evidence. Family "oral history" or "family tradition" particularly is unreliable, for many reasons, as Professor Turner points out in his report. These include the high probability of errors creeping into stories that are told and retold from one generation to the next, as well as the tendency "to embellish the family legacy to instill pride and confidence in the next generation." The problem is not peculiar to American history or modern times: notables in ancient Rome frequently claimed descent from the gods—Julius Caesar, from the goddess Venus, for example—to make them even more patrician.

Indeed, family oral traditions really ought not to be called "history" at all, for they are rather, quite literally, *myth*. That realization hit home with me last summer when I was at-

---

21. Timothy Sandefur, "Anti-Jefferson, Left and Right," *Liberty*, October 1999, p. 52.
22. *Ibid.*, p. 34.
23. Nick Gillespie, in reply to the author's and other readers' letters "In Defense of Jefferson," *Reason*, April 1999, p. 11.

tending a conference at the University of British Columbia in Vancouver and visited the Museum of Archeology, which is famous for its collection of totem poles and other artifacts relating to Pacific Northwest Indians (or "First Peoples," as they are called in Canada). Totem poles, of course, were used by the native peoples to memorialize their own myths. Here's how the guidebook I purchased at the Museum explained their mythology[24]:

> There were two kinds of myths on the Northwest Coast—those which were known to and could be told by everyone and those which were the private property of particular families and could only be told by their members. Both kinds tell of a primordial age before the world became as it is now, a time when finite divisions between humans, animals, and spirits had not yet been created and beings could transform themselves from one form into another.... It was a time now lost but remembered. It was a world now gone, but one that people recreated in art and ritual. Through ceremonial and artistic re-enactment of their heritage, through dance, song, and ritual acting, people maintained continuity with their genesis. So, even though mythological time belonged to long ago, before mankind became separated and distinguished from animals and nature, the memory of it could be kept alive.

> The myths which everyone could tell concerned the change of that other world into this one.... The family myths, on the other hand, told of family origins, of ancestors who came down from the sky as birds or who married mythical animals and shining celestial beings; they told of the wanderings of the ancestors, their settlement in their present locations, and their acquisition of the privileges and powers which defined the greatness of the family line. Paramount among these were those rights whose representations the family could display on totem poles and ceremonial objects to broadcast their heritage to others.

As noted below, the Monticello Committee report essentially takes the "family myths" of the Madison Hemings descendants and treats them as history. It would be like a historian today saying that a famous tribal leader among the Pacific Northwest First Peoples really was descended from a raven bird, because his family myth says so—it must be true because it's a story people "continued to tell their children and grandchildren..., often at significant times in their lives"![25]

There are many reasons to doubt the reliability of the oral tradition handed down by Madison Hemings' descendants. Significantly, there is no evidence of an oral tradition corroborating the assertions attributed to Madison Hemings which antedates the publication of the 1873 Pike County *Republican* story. Thus, rather than being an oral history handed down to her descendants by Sally Hemings herself—or by any contemporaries of hers with first-hand knowledge of happenings at Monticello, or even by Madison Hemings himself, who presumably had only second-hand knowledge of his paternity—the allegation of Jefferson's paternity of Sally Hemings' children appears to have originated with these 1873 newspaper stories. And, like the oral tradition handed down to Thomas Woodson's descendants, it is quite likely that the Madison Hemings oral tradition ultimately owes its origin to the original 1802 Callender allegation.

Yet, as discussed below, the Monticello Committee report treats the Madison Hemings story as key evidence linking Jefferson to Sally Hemings. Indeed, apart from the so-

---

24. Marjorie M. Halpin, *Totem Poles: An Illustrated Guide* (Vancouver: University of British Columbia Press, 1981), pp. 9–10.
25. See discussion in the section on the Monticello Committee report, below.

called "Monte Carlo" simulation (the problems of which are also discussed below), it is literally the only evidence cited by the Committee report in support of its conclusion that Jefferson likely fathered *all* the children of Sally Hemings—that is, the children other than Eston.

Among other families of Hemings descendants, a quite different oral tradition—attributing the paternity of Sally Hemings' children to an "uncle" of Jefferson's—appears to have been handed down from generation to generation. The Monticello Report's effort to discount that tradition, while accepting the Madison Hemings story, is quite unconvincing, as noted below.

Broader Context of the Myth Today: The Assault on Standards

The rise of three related phenomena in higher education generally—the "political correctness" movement, multiculturalism, and post-modernism—helps explain why the Jefferson-Hemings myth has become so readily accepted today, not only by the American general public but also by scholars who should know better.

The term *political correctness* was coined in the early 1990s, in the midst of a controversy over perceived threats to academic freedom on America's college and university campuses. Originally an approving phrase used by those on the Leninist left to denote someone who steadfastly toed the party line, "politically correct" or "P.C." began to be used ironically by critics of the left—first by conservatives (such as Dinesh D'Souza, author of the best-selling book *Illiberal Education: The Politics of Race and Sex on Campus* (1991)) and later by liberals and many old-school leftists—who sought to defend campus freedoms against "P.C." censors. The debate encompasses many issues, among them official campus speech codes, designed to protect certain groups of students from "oppressive" or even merely "insensitive" racist or sexist speech, as well as new curriculums emphasizing race and ethnic distinctions.[26]

Perhaps the most important attribute of the "politically correct" movement has been its emphasis on "race/class/gender-ism," which pictures culture and language as giant hidden structures that permeate life and which assumes that American culture (or Western culture generally) has been dominated by the culture and language of European white males.[27] In its opposition to this perceived hegemony, the P.C. movement overlaps with the other two modern movements in higher education, multiculturalism and postmodernism.

Multiculturalism began as a well-intentioned movement to diversify education—and the teaching of history, in particular—by calling attention to the experiences of women, blacks, American Indians, immigrants, and members of other groups whose stories largely had been neglected in textbooks. What began as a movement on behalf of diversity and cultural pluralism, however, devolved into a "particularist" movement that, in its overreaction to perceived "Eurocentrism," fostered even more extremely distorted views of

---

26. Paul Berman, Introduction to *Debating P.C.: The Controversy over Political Correctness on College Campuses* (New York: Dell Publishing, 1992), pp. 1–6. On the threats to campus speech generally, see Alan Charles Kors and Harvey A. Silverglate, *The Shadow University: The Betrayal of Liberty on America's Campuses* (New York: The Free Press, 1998).

27. Berman, Introduction to *Debating P.C.*, pp. 14–15.

American history, such as Afrocentrism.[28] Particularists "have no interest in extending or revising American culture; indeed, they deny that a common culture exists. Particularists reject any accommodation among groups, any interactions that blur the distinct lines between them. The brand of history that they espouse is one in which everyone is either a descendant of victims or oppressors."[29]

When advocates of political correctness or extreme multiculturalism challenge the culture of rationalism and humanism, they also ally themselves with an even more pervasive movement among American intellectuals in recent decades, the so-called "post-modern" movement. Postmodernist theory attempts to "deconstruct," or expose, the underlying subjectivity and indeterminacy of everything we assume we know. Among historians, postmodernism has meant an assault on objectivity: a rejection of traditional standards for discovering facts, weighing evidence, and interpreting events. Traditional analytic and empirical methods are rejected in favor of history as mere "narrative." As one theorist put it, "The past is not discovered or found; it is created or represented by the historian as text." History, to the postmodernists, is no more factual or objective than any other discipline; "there are no grounds to be found in the historical record itself for preferring one way of construing its meaning over another," for interpretation is inevitably "socially constructed."[30]

Postmodernists and radical multiculturalists frequently argue that white male culture has achieved domination over other cultures through values such as rationalism, humanism, universality, and literary merit—values which the multiculturalists claim are not objective but rather are tools for oppressing other people by persuading them of their own inferiority.[31] These views lead to "disturbing distortions in scholarship and public discourse," argue law professors Daniel Farber and Suzanna Sherry. (It should be noted that Professors Farber and Sherry are not conservatives; they are mainstream liberal law professors who are alarmed at the threats posed to law and legal scholarship by radical multiculturalist movements in the legal academy such as Critical Legal Studies, radical feminism, and Critical Race Theory.) "Because they reject objectivity as a norm, the radicals are content to rely on personal stories as a basis for formulating views of social problems. These stories are often atypical or distorted by self-interest, yet any criticism of the stories is inevitably seen as a personal attack on the storyteller," they observe. Indeed, "because radical multiculturalists refuse to separate the speaker from the message, they can become sidetracked from discussing the merits of the message itself into bitter disputes about the speaker's authenticity and her right to speak on behalf of an oppressed group. Criticisms of radical multiculturalism are seen as pandering to the power structure if they come from women or minorities, or as sexist and racist if they come from white men."[32] Thus, not only objectivity, but also civility—the basic prerequisite for genuine dialogue—has been jeopardized.

In recent years, many American historians have become concerned at the degree to which radical multiculturalism and postmodernism have apparently dominated the nation's two leading organizations of historians, the American History Association (AHA) and the Organization of American Historians (OAH). Many historians consequently have resigned their membership in one or both of these groups. A politically diverse coalition

---

28. See generally Diane Ravitch, "Multiculturalism: E Pluribus Plures," in Berman, ed., *Debating P.C.*, pp. 271–98.

29. *Ibid.*, p. 278.

30. See Daniel A. Farber and Suzanna Sherry, *Beyond All Reason: The Radical Assault on Truth in American Law* (New York: Oxford University Press, 1997), pp. 15, 108–10.

31. Berman, in *Debating P.C.*, p. 14.

32. Farber and Sherry, *Beyond All Reason*, p. 12.

of historians, ranging in their political views from conservative and libertarian to left-liberal—all who share a concern for how radical multiculturalism and "identity politics" have been destroying the profession—even have formed a new organization to compete with the AHA and the OAH, called The Historical Society (THS).[33]

Sadly, the historical profession today has lost much of the standards by which evidence can be objectively weighed and evaluated in the search for historical truth. History, in effect, has become politicized in America today, as illustrated by the widespread acceptance of the Jefferson-Hemings myth as historical fact.

Taken together, political correctness, multiculturalism, and post-modernism have created an environment in the academic world today in which scholars feel pressured to accept the Jefferson-Hemings myth as historical truth. White male scholars in particular fear that by questioning the myth—by challenging the validity of the oral tradition "evidence" cited by some of the Hemings descendants—they will be called racially "insensitive," if not racist. As discussed more fully below in my critique of Annette Gordon-Reed's book, among many proponents of the Jefferson paternity claim there has emerged a truly disturbing McCarthyist-like inquisition that has cast its pall over Jefferson scholarship today. Questioning the validity of the claim has been equated with the denigration of African Americans and the denial of their rightful place in American history. In this climate of scholarly and public opinion, it requires great personal courage for scholars to question the Jefferson paternity thesis and to point out the dubious historical record on which it rests.

The Flawed Case for the Jefferson-Hemings Story

The two most significant briefs on behalf of the Jefferson-Hemings paternity claim that have appeared thus far in print are Annette Gordon-Reed's book, *Thomas Jefferson and Sally Hemings: An American Controversy*,[34] and the Thomas Jefferson Memorial Foundation (TJMF) *Ad Hoc* Research Committee Report (referred to below as the Monticello Report), released in 2000.[35] I refer to both these works as *briefs* on behalf of the paternity claim, for both share this essential weakness: rather than objectively weighing all the relevant evidence according to established standards of historical scholarship, they both are markedly one-sided, based on a highly selective reading of the evidence, presenting the case for Jefferson's paternity as if it were accepted as an article of faith. And for both Professor Gordon-Reed and for the staff at Monticello, it apparently is.

Annette Gordon-Reed's Book

Annette Gordon-Reed is a law professor, not trained as a historian; her book is a classic example of what historians call "lawyer's history"—an advocacy brief which marshals

---

33. See, for example, William R. Keylor, "Clio on the Campus: The Historical Society at Boston University," in *Bostonia*, Summer 1999, pp. 20–23.

34. Annette Gordon-Reed, *Thomas Jefferson and Sally Hemings: An American Controversy*, (Charlottesville: University Press of Virginia, 1997).

35. Thomas Jefferson Memorial Foundation Research Committee, *Report on Thomas Jefferson and Sally Hemings* [hereafter, "Monticello report"], released January 2000 and available on the Monticello website, <www.monticello.org>.

the evidence in favor of a predetermined thesis rather than objectively weighs the evidence in the search for historical truth.

In both the preface and conclusion to her book, Professor Gordon-Reed quite directly admits that her mission is to expose the "troubling"—i.e., racist—assumptions made by historians who have denied "the truth of a liaison between Thomas Jefferson and Sally Hemings." To sustain the denial, she argues, historians must "make Thomas Jefferson so high as to have been something more than human" and "make Sally Hemings so low as to have been something less than human." Historians have engaged in "the systematic dismissal of the words of the black people who spoke on this matter—Madison Hemings, the son of Sally Hemings, and Israel Jefferson, a former slave who also resided at Monticello—as though their testimony was worth some fraction as that of whites." Indeed, she regards Madison Hemings as "a metaphor for the condition of blacks in American society." He was, she notes, "a black man who watched his three siblings voluntarily disappear into the white world" and yet who "chose to remain black and to speak for himself," only to be "vilified and ridiculed in a vicious manner" and then be "forgotten." To vindicate him, she wrote the book.[36]

Throughout her book, Professor Gordon-Reed vilifies as racist—without ever directly using that term—virtually every historian who has ever written about Jefferson and Sally Hemings: these include established Jefferson scholars such as Merrill Peterson, Douglass Adair, Dumas Malone, and John Chester Miller, as well as younger scholars such as Andrew Burstein. Her treatment of Burstein is illustrative of her technique. In his 1995 book *The Inner Jefferson: Portrait of a Grieving Optimist*, Burstein briefly addressed Madison Hemings' 1873 newspaper interview, noting that it was "possible that his claim was contrived—by his mother or himself—to provide an otherwise undistinguished biracial carpenter a measure of social respect." Burstein added, "Would not his life have been made more charmed by being known as the son of Thomas Jefferson than the more obscure Peter or Samuel Carr?" Professor Gordon-Reed answers this rhetorical question with an emphatic "no," in the process ridiculing Burstein's choice of words, particularly his reference to a "charmed" life.[37] Burstein has since reversed his position of skepticism and now argues that the DNA test results "have convincingly linked [Jefferson] to Sally Hemings sexually."[38]

In addition to rhetorical arguments designed to ridicule the white male historians who have written about the Jefferson-Hemings matter—suggesting not so subtly that their writings have been infused with racist assumptions—Professor Gordon-Reed also carefully selects the evidence and presents it in the light most favorable to her cause, exposing what she regards as "double standards" in historical scholarship. In the process, however, she breaks down most accepted standards for weighing evidence, particularly for weighing oral tradition evidence, creating a new double standard which gives preference to the oral tradition supporting the Jefferson paternity thesis. Legitimate doubts about the veracity of the 1873 newspaper "memoir" attributed to Hemings—doubts based not only on the many problems found in the account itself but also in its broader political context, as noted above—are swept aside, as Professor Gordon-Reed focuses on such matters as scholars' questioning whether a word like *enciente* would have been used by a black man at that time period.[39] Her aim, again, is to vindicate Madison Hemings and his story, "to present the strongest case to be made that the story might be true."[40]

---

36. Gordon-Reed, *Thomas Jefferson and Sally Hemings*, pp. xiv, 234–35.

37. *Ibid.*, p. 18.

38. Andrew Burstein, "Jefferson's Rationalizations," *William & Mary Quarterly*, 3rd ser. 57 (Jan. 2000): 183.

39. Gordon-Reed, *Jefferson and Hemings*, p. 20.

40. *Ibid.*, p. 210.

More broadly, Professor Gordon-Reed's agenda is to use the Jefferson-Hemings story as a metaphor for American race relations. In a letter to the editor published soon after the DNA test results went public, Professor Gordon-Reed admitted quite directly the "silver lining" she found in this controversy, what it shows about "the history of racism in America": "If people had accepted this story, he would never have become an icon. All these historians did him a favor until we could get past our primitive racism. I don't think he would have been on Mount Rushmore or on the nickel. The personification of America can't live 38 years with a black woman."[41]

Because her mission was to rebut the case made by Jefferson scholars—virtually all of whom have accepted at face value the paternity allegations made against Peter and Samuel Carr by Jefferson's grandchildren T.J. Randolph and Ellen Coolidge Randolph—Professor Gordon-Reed ignores entirely the possibility that Jefferson's brother Randolph or one of Randolph Jefferson's five sons could have fathered one or more of Sally Hemings' children. Although she lists in her bibliography Bernard Mayo's *Thomas Jefferson and His Unknown Brother Randolph* (1942), she excludes Randolph and his sons from her genealogical table of "The Jeffersons and Randolphs (Relevant Connections Only)," as well as from the nearly 50 "Important Names" listed in Appendix A to her book. Nor is Randolph Jefferson or any of his children even referenced in her index.

The flawed scholarship of the book is further epitomized by a significant transcription error which appears in Appendix E, the text of Ellen Randolph Coolidge's 1858 letter to Joseph Coolidge. In relevant part, the original letter as found in the Coolidge Letterbook, University of Virginia Library[42]—in clear handwriting—states the following about Jefferson's rooms at Monticello:

> His apartments had no private entrance not perfectly accessible and visible to all the household. No female domestic ever entered his chambers except at hours when he was known not to be there and none could have entered without being exposed to the public gaze.

As printed in the appendix to Professor Gordon-Reed's book,[43] however, the passage reads:

> His apartments had no private entrance not perfectly accessible and visible to all the household. No female domestic ever entered his chambers except at hours when he was known not to be in the public gaze.

Even if we give Professor Gordon-Reed the benefit of the doubt and assume that omission of the crucial words—which obviously changes significantly the meaning of the sentence—was not a deliberate distortion of the evidence but rather an innocent transcription mistake, so critical an error casts doubt on the reliability of her work.

The TJMF (Monticello) Committee Report

Following release of the DNA study in the fall of 1998, Daniel P. Jordan, the president [1985–2008] of the Thomas Jefferson Memorial Foundation (TJMF)[44]—the insti-

---

41. "The All-Too-Human Jefferson," Letter to the editor, *Wall Street Journal*, November 24, 1998.

42. Letter of Ellen Coolidge to Joseph Coolidge, October 24, 1858, in Ellen Coolidge letterbook, University of Virginia Library.

43. Gordon-Reed, *Jefferson and Hemings*, p. 259.

44. The Thomas Jefferson Memorial Foundation subsequently changed its name to "The Thomas Jefferson Foundation." *Thomas Jefferson Memorial Foundation*, or *TJMF*, as used in this report, of course refers to the organization now known as *Thomas Jefferson Foundation*, or *TJF*.

tution that owns and operates Jefferson's home Monticello—appointed a nine-person in-house research committee which was charged, in Jordan's words, to "review, comprehensively and critically, all the evidence, scientific and otherwise," including Dr. Foster's DNA study, "relating to the relationship of Thomas Jefferson and Sally Hemings." The Committee was chaired by Dianne Swann-Wright, Director of Special Programs at Monticello (including its Getting Word Oral History Project described below), and its members—described in its report as "including four Ph.D.'s and one medical doctor"— were all Monticello staff members. Although the Committee consulted with members of two other Monticello committees—the Advisory Committee for the International Center for Jefferson Studies and the Advisory Committee on African-American Interpretation—it is worth emphasizing that no scholar independent of Monticello had any input in the report.

Although the Committee had concluded its work by spring 1999, its report was not released until January 27, 2000. The report was immediately posted on the Internet, and Dan Jordan noted that within a week the Monticello website received nearly 60,000 "hits" a day, with some 3000 different individuals downloading the report. Two weeks later, after the television airing of the CBS miniseries *Sally Hemings: An American Scandal*, Jordan noted that the hits "maxed out" Monticello's system, with as many as 900,000 in one day. Although he dismissed the CBS miniseries as "ridiculous as history," "a soap opera," and "strictly Hollywood," Jordan acknowledged that "it certainly did encourage an interest in the story." He added, "Anything that encourages and raises the consciousness of the American people about history and race is a good thing."[45]

What was not mentioned in the TJMF's press conference and not acknowledged on its website until about three months later, on March 23, 2000, was that one of the members of the Monticello Committee—White McKenzie (Ken) Wallenborn, M.D. (the "medical doctor" identified in the committee's description)—had dissented stridently from the Committee's report. Noting several areas of disagreement with the majority's report, Dr. Wallenborn in his minority report (dated April 12, 1999) concluded that "[t]here is historical evidence of more or less equal statu[r]e on both sides of this issue that prevent a definitive answer as to Thomas Jefferson's paternity of Sally Hemings' son Eston Hemings or for that matter the other four of her children." He urged the TJMF to continue to regard the paternity question as an open one. In an essay published subsequent to the release of his minority report, Dr. Wallenborn has charged that the Monticello Committee—and particularly its chair, Dianne Swann-Wright, and Lucia (Cinder) Stanton (Shannon Senior Research Historian at Monticello), whom he identified as the principal author of the Committee's final report—"had already reached their conclusions" at the start of their deliberations. According to Dr. Wallenborn's account, the Committee followed "the same tactic" that Professor Annette Gordon-Reed employed in her book, of ignoring or dismissing as problematic "most of the evidence that would exonerate Mr. Jefferson."[46] Equally troubling is Dr. Wallenborn's statement that Dianne Swann-Wright failed to share his dissenting report with other members of the committee. Indeed, he notes that it was not shared with the interpretive staff at Monticello nor with the TJMF Board of Trustees until he began circulating it after the January 26, 2000 press conference.[47]

---

45. Dan Jordan, interviewed in Shannon Lanier and Jane Feldman, *Jefferson's Children: The Story of One American Family* (New York: Random House, 2000), p. 113.

46. White McKenzie Wallenborn, "A Committee Insider's Viewpoint," *in The Jefferson-Hemings Myth: An American Travesty* (ed. Eyler Robert Coates, Sr., Charlottesville, Va.: Thomas Jefferson Heritage Society, 2001, special advance ed.), pp. 57–58.

47. *Ibid.*, p. 64.

Dr. Wallenborn's criticisms of the Monticello Committee appear to be well-founded. Upon close reading, its final report is far from being the "scholarly, meticulous, and thorough" analysis Dan Jordan claims it is. Its general conclusion, that Thomas Jefferson fathered one, if not all, of Sally Hemings' children, fails to be adequately supported by the evidence gathered by the Committee and summarized in its findings.

Indeed, a fundamental problem with the Committee report is the apparent absence of any methodology for evaluating or weighing evidence. When the report concludes, specifically, that the "currently available documentary and statistical evidence, indicates a high probability that Thomas Jefferson fathered Eston Hemings, and that he was most likely the father of all six of Sally Hemings children," it offers no standard by which the conclusory terms *high probability* or *most likely* can be objectively measured. Generally speaking, the Committee report seems to rest this conclusion on just a few pieces of evidence — the results of Dr. Foster's DNA tests, Madison Hemings' 1873 "memoir," and the "Monte Carlo" statistical study conducted by Committee member Fraser Nieman — plus one critical, but unsupported, assumption: that all of Sally Hemings' children were fathered by just one man. This single father postulate rests on the flimsiest of evidence: the naming of the Hemings siblings' children after one another, which supposedly demonstrates the "closeness" of the family (and thus, it is assumed, Sally Hemings' monogamy), and the claim of an absence of evidence that Sally Hemings was not monogamous (a false claim in light of the Edmund Bacon evidence, which the Committee discounts, as noted below). The only documentary evidence which the Committee can cite in support of its conclusion that Jefferson "most likely" fathered Sally Hemings' children other than Eston is the Madison Hemings 1873 interview.[48]

Another fundamental flaw in the Committee's report is the problem of bias and conflict of interest. Since 1993 the TJMF has been conducting an oral history research project called "Getting Word," to locate the descendants of Monticello's African-American community and to record and preserve their stories and histories. The project has interviewed over 100 people, including 22 descendants of Madison Hemings and four descendants of Eston Hemings. The very fact that Monticello staff members have been involved in this project makes it difficult for an in-house research committee to objectively evaluate oral history evidence. The problems of bias in favor of oral history evidence generally — and selective bias in favor of those particular families interviewed through the Getting Word project — were compounded by the fact that the chair of the *ad hoc* research committee was Dianne Swann-Wright, director of Special Programs at Monticello, who had been employed to work on the project since its inception (and her arrival at Monticello) in 1993. Given the intimate involvement of Dr. Swann-Wright and other Committee members with the people interviewed for the Getting Word project, it is not surprising that the Committee report heavily relies on the 1873 Madison Hemings story and the oral tradition among his descendants as the key evidence in support of the Jefferson paternity thesis.

As noted above, oral tradition evidence has a general problem of unreliability. The Committee report is flawed not only because it relies heavily on oral tradition evidence, but that it relies on it *selectively*, taking seriously only that oral tradition that fits with the story of Jefferson's paternity. The bias is evident in the report, where it infers from the seriousness of the Madison Hemings' descendants' "history" that it is true and therefore ought to be treated on par with documentary and other evidence. "In a climate of disbelief

---

48. Monticello report, Appendix H, "Sally Hemings and Her Children: Information from Documentary Sources," pp. 8, 10, 12.

and hostility," the report notes, "they continued to tell their children and grandchildren of their descent from Thomas Jefferson, often at significant times in their lives...."[49] On the same page of the report, however, the Committee notes that the oral history of the Eston Hemings descendants claimed descent from Jefferson's "uncle"—an oral tradition which apparently was taken just as seriously by this line of the family, until publication of Fawn Brodie's *Intimate History* prompted family members to change the story—but the Committee dismisses the earlier tradition among Eston Hemings' descendants as "altered to protect their passing into the white world."[50] The change of the Eston Hemings family oral tradition following publication of the Brodie book is acknowledged by family members. "We're just learning—from some of our cousins—stories we weren't able to hear," one family member said.[51]

Significantly, the Committee report also concluded that Thomas Woodson was not the son of Thomas Jefferson, and indeed that there was no documentary evidence linking him even to Monticello and Sally Hemings.[52] The significance of this is twofold. First, it acknowledges the falsity of a core allegation of both the original 1802 Callender story and the 1873 story attributed to Madison Hemings: the notion that Jefferson's sexual relationship with Sally Hemings began in France, and that she bore him a son soon after their return to the United States. As the Committee report finds, there is no evidence of any child being born to Sally Hemings prior to 1795. Second, the findings regarding Thomas Woodson starkly reveal the inherent unreliability of oral tradition as evidence. The Woodson descendants just as fervently believed that their ancestor was the son of Thomas Jefferson, and the Committee found that "the longstanding oral history warrants inclusion of information" about Woodson despite the absence of documentation to connect him to Sally Hemings and Monticello, let alone to Thomas Jefferson.[53]

There is one other oral tradition, of course, which was summarily rejected by the Committee. Beginning with the direct testimony of Jefferson's grandchildren, Thomas Jefferson Randolph and Ellen Randolph Coolidge, the oral tradition in the family descended from Jefferson's daughter Martha Jefferson Randolph has identified one of the Carr brothers, Peter or Samuel (Jefferson's nephews by his sister Martha) as the father of Sally Hemings' children. Although that tradition apparently too was taken just as seriously as the tradition of Hemings descendants—and although it is arguably far more reliable, for it was based on the testimony of eyewitnesses to the events in question—the report essentially dismisses Carr paternity by pointing to the DNA test results on Eston Hemings' descendant and assuming that Sally Hemings' children were all fathered by the same man.

The Committee's bias is evident also in the double standard it employs in weighing evidence. For example, the published account of Monticello overseer Edmund Bacon, which identified another, unnamed man as the father of Harriet Hemings, is dismissed as having "problems of chronology," noting that Bacon was not employed at Monticello until five years after Harriet's birth.[54] But this ignores the real possibility that Bacon resided at Monticello as early as 1800 and also assumes that Bacon was describing an event he witnessed prior to Harriet's birth when indeed he might have concluded that the man he saw some years later was the father of her children. However, immediately following this

---

49. Monticello report, Appendix G, "Oral History in the Hemings Family."
50. *Ibid.*
51. See Julia Westerinen, interview in Lanier and Feldman, *Jefferson's Children*, p. 56.
52. Monticello report, Appendix K, "Assessment of Thomas C. Woodson's Connection to Sally Hemings."
53. Monticello report, Appendix H, "Sally Hemings and Her Children," p. 6.
54. Monticello report, Part III, "Review of Documentary Sources," p. 4.

curt dismissal of Bacon's account, the Committee report states that Israel Jefferson's 1873 interview "corroborated Madison Hemings's claim of Jefferson paternity"—even though Israel Jefferson's account, besides the many problems noted above, also has a real "chronology problem" of its own: Israel was only *eight* years old at the time of the birth of Sally Hemings' youngest child, Eston![55]

Important pieces of evidence that question the Jefferson paternity thesis are either ignored or blithely dismissed by the Committee's report. For example, Jefferson's own denial of the Callender allegations, in an 1805 letter written to a member of his administration, is dismissed as "ambiguous"[56]—an assessment that fails to take into account its clear historical context (as discussed below). The account of former household slave Isaac Jefferson, who mentioned and described Sally Hemings in his memoir, is omitted from the Committee report, even though the fact that Isaac did not so much as hint that there was any special relationship between Jefferson and Sally Hemings is powerful evidence questioning the paternity thesis.[57]

Other problems, though relatively minor, in the Committee's report reveal that it was far less meticulously written than one would expect it to be. For example, although the report does include a facsimile of the 1858 Ellen Randolph Coolidge letter, it follows it with the flawed transcription as found in Appendix E of Professor Gordon-Reed's book. The draft of Committee member Fraser Neiman's article, "Coincidence or Causal Connection? The Relationship between Thomas Jefferson's Visits to Monticello and Sally Hemings's Conceptions"—which was going to print in *The William & Mary Quarterly* in January 2000, just as the Committee report was released—contains a typographical error which distorts the DNA study in a significant way. The molecular geneticists tested "male-line descendants of *Thomas* Jefferson" (emphasis added), the article states, when of course it was not Thomas but Field Jefferson, Thomas Jefferson's paternal uncle, whose descendants were tested.

The article by Mr. Nieman, who is director of archeology at Monticello, has far more serious problems than this embarrassing typographical error. As the Scholars Commission report notes, none of us was impressed by this so-called "Monte Carlo" statistical study. The Monte Carlo approach estimates the probability of a given outcome by comparing it to a very large number of random outcomes generated by a simulation model. Nieman's study rested on two unsupported postulates: that there could only be a single father for all of Sally Hemings' children, and that rival candidates to Thomas Jefferson would have had to arrive and depart on the exact same days he did. Here, the assumption of random behavior makes little sense, because the visits to Monticello of the other candidates for paternity—Jefferson's friends and relatives (including his brother Randolph, Randolph Jefferson's sons, and the Carr brothers)—were not random occurrences; they certainly would have been far more likely to occur after Jefferson's return to Monticello from extended absences in Washington or elsewhere. The final impression one gets of the Nieman study is of a simulation whose parameters were deliberately set to "get" Thomas Jefferson as the father of Sally Hemings' children.[58]

---

55. *Ibid.*, p. 4.

56. Monticello report, Appendix F, "Review of the Documentary Evidence," p. 2.

57. *Memoirs of a Monticello Slave*, Isaac Jefferson as interviewed by Charles W. Campbell in 1847, *printed in* James A. Bear, ed., *Jefferson at Monticello* (Charlottesville: University Press of Virginia, 1967).

58. Ken Wallenborn reports that when Neiman presented his study to the Committee, he stated: "I've got him!" Wallenborn, "A Committee Insider's Viewpoint," in *The Jefferson-Hemings Myth: An American Travesty*, p. 53.

As Dr. Wallenborn has noted, Neiman's statistical study "cries out for valid comparative studies of the other Jefferson males who might have fathered Eston, and in the absence of these comparisons, the results are inconclusive."[59] As the Scholars Commission report notes, the circumstantial case that Eston Hemings was fathered by Randolph Jefferson, Thomas Jefferson's younger brother, is "many times stronger" than the case against Jefferson himself. Significantly, even the Monticello Committee report notes documentary evidence that Randolph Jefferson visited Monticello in August 1807, a probable conception time for Eston Hemings (this evidence consisting of a letter from Jefferson to his brother, inviting him to visit Monticello while Randolph's twin sister, Anna Marks, was then visiting) — but the Committee rejects this evidence because no corroborating evidence has been found to indicate that Randolph did in fact visit at this time.[60] The Committee report also notes that Randolph Jefferson's sons Thomas, in 1800, and Robert Lewis, in 1807, "may well have been at Monticello during the conception periods of Harriet and Eston Hemings."[61]

One final, critical assumption made both in the Neiman study and in the Monticello Committee report as a whole is the assumption that Sally Hemings was continuously present at Monticello. As the Scholars Commission concludes, however, that assumption may be problematic. Sadly, we simply do not know enough about Sally Hemings — even her duties at Monticello — to conclude that she would have remained at Monticello rather than travel to, say, Poplar Forest, at some of the probable times of her conceptions. The question is particularly important given biographer Henry Randall's intriguing reference to "well known circumstances" that prove Martha Jefferson Randolph's denial of the charge that Jefferson fathered Sally Hemings' children. As documented by Randall, Jefferson's daughter "directed her sons' attention to the fact that Mr. Jefferson and Sally Hemings could not have met — were far distant from each other — for fifteen months prior to the birth" of the child who supposedly most resembled Jefferson. Almost everyone has assumed that Mrs. Randolph was referring to *Jefferson's* absence from Monticello at that time, but she may very well have been referring to *Sally Hemings'*.[62] This intriguing possibility is yet another matter that cries out for additional research.

The Implausibility of the Story

Some people have suggested that the logical principle of Occam's razor, which states essentially that the simplest of competing theories be preferred to the more complex, when applied to this controversy would make Thomas Jefferson the father of Sally Hemings' children, or at least of Eston Hemings. But this is a gross misapplication of the principle. Indeed, as Professor Banning points out in his paper, "Occam's Razor tells us to prefer the simplest theory *only* when the simplest theory seems equally true."[63] Here, the simple theory advanced by proponents of the Jefferson-Hemings story — that Sally Hemings' children all had the same father, and that he was Thomas Jefferson — seems plausi-

---

59. *Ibid.*, p. 51.
60. Monticello report, Appendix J, "Summary of research on the possible paternity of other Jeffersons."
61. Monticello report, Part V, "Assessment of Possible Paternity of Other Jeffersons."
62. *Henry S. Randall to James Parton*, June 1, 1868, in Flower, *James Parton*, pp. 237–38.
63. Professor Banning, "Thomas Jefferson and Sally Hemings: Case Closed?", p. 274.

ble only if one ignores all the many facts that strongly suggest against Jefferson's paternity. Both Professor Banning and Professor Turner have identified a large number of relevant facts, either ignored or unjustifiably downplayed by Professor Gordon-Reed and the Monticello Report, which raises serious questions about the Jefferson paternity thesis. I agree fully with these points and would like here to emphasize two additional matters which, to me, make the thesis extremely implausible.

Denials by Jefferson Himself and Virtually All His Contemporaries

Jefferson refused to dignify Callender's charges by denying them publicly, but in private correspondence stated generally that there was "not a truth existing which I fear or would wish unknown to the whole world."[64] And on one occasion in private correspondence he denied the Hemings paternity charge, among other allegations.

In a cover letter dated July 1, 1805 and written to Secretary of the Navy Robert Smith, Thomas Jefferson denied the "charges" made against him, admitting that he was guilty only of one — "that when young and single [he] offered love to a handsome lady" — which he maintained was "the only one founded in truth among all their allegations against me." Jefferson's letter to Smith referenced an enclosed letter written to Attorney General Levi Lincoln which fully responded to the charges but which, unfortunately, has not survived. From Jefferson's cover letter it is clear that he desired both Smith and Lincoln to read the enclosed letter, as "particular friends" of Jefferson with whom he "wish[ed] to stand ... on the ground of truth."[65]

Both the Thomas Jefferson Memorial Foundation majority report[66] and Professor Annette Gordon-Reed[67] dismiss Jefferson's letter as "ambiguous" and referring directly only to the charge of Jefferson's affair with Mrs. John Walker. Although it is true that the cover letter on its face does not identify either the "charges" or those who were asserting them, nevertheless it is reasonably clear from the full context of Jefferson's letter itself and its historical circumstances that Jefferson was denying all the charges made against him by his political enemies, including the Hemings paternity allegation.

Jefferson wrote the letter ten days after the Washington, D.C. newspaper *The Washington Federalist* reprinted a letter from a "Thomas Turner, Esq.," declared to be a Virginia gentleman, which had been first published in the Boston newspaper *The Repertory* on May 31, 1805. The newspaper articles raised virtually the same charges Callender had made in the *Richmond Recorder* in 1802, including the affair with Mrs. Walker, "Mr. Jefferson's disgraceful concubinage" with Sally Hemings, and Jefferson's "timidity" as Governor of Virginia when it was invaded by British troops during the Revolutionary War.[68] Indeed, Jefferson referred directly to the latter accusation ("transactions during the invasion

---

64. Jefferson to Henry Lee, May 15, 1826; see also Jefferson to William Duane, March 22, 1806.

65. Thomas Jefferson to Robert Smith, July 1, 1805, quoted in Dumas Malone, *Jefferson the President: First Term, 1801–1805* (Boston: Little, Brown and Co., 1970), p. 222.

66. Monticello report, Appendix F, "Review of the Documentary Evidence," p. 2.

67. Gordon-Reed, *Thomas Jefferson and Sally Hemings: An American Controversy*, p. 146.

68. Text of the June 19, 1805 *Washington Federalist* article as reproduced in Rebecca L. McMurry and James F. McMurry, *Jefferson, Callender, and the Sally Story: The Scandalmonger and the Newspaper War of 1802* (Toms Brook, Va.: Old Virginia Books, 2000), pp. 107–110.

of Virginia") in his cover letter to Smith, in the sentence immediately following his admission of the Walker affair.

The *Washington Federalist* and *Boston Repertory* articles also alleged, according to "opinion," that Sally Hemings was "the natural daughter" of John Wayles, misspelled "Wales"— the first time this allegation appeared in print.

The fuller context of the reappearance of the Callender allegations in Boston newspapers—including the debates on Jefferson's character in the Massachusetts legislature in January 1805—has been discussed by Dumas Malone.[69] Given the political climate in Massachusetts, it is not surprising that Jefferson wrote this letter to Levi Lincoln, who served as Jefferson's political adviser on matters concerning New England, and Massachusetts in particular.

The significance of Jefferson's denial in this letter to a friend, who was also a member of his administration and a political confidant, should be obvious: it is the only direct evidence left by Jefferson in his own words and handwriting that bears on the question.

The Monticello Committee report also notes, without any analysis, the only known account of the paternity allegation being raised in Jefferson's presence: biographer Henry S. Randall's report that when confronted by his indignant daughter Martha with an offending poem (a couplet by Irish poet Thomas Moore linking Jefferson with a slave), his only response was a "hearty, clear laugh."[70] This was hardly the response of a man with a guilty conscience.

Taken together, Jefferson's denials are consistent with the testimony of many family members, friends, and acquaintances who similarly denied the Sally Hemings paternity allegation. With the exception of those few cited in the Monticello Committee report, there is little evidence that the Jefferson paternity allegation survived, even among Jefferson's political enemies, much past the 1802 elections, but for the brief resurrection of the Callender allegations in Massachusetts in 1805. Jefferson's 19th-century biographer Henry Randall reported that Dr. Robley Dunglison, Jefferson's doctor in 1825 and 1826, did not believe the story and that both Dr. Dunglison and Professor Tucker, "who lived years near Mr. Jefferson in the University, and were often at Monticello," never heard the subject mentioned in Virginia.[71] Significantly, after his retirement from the presidency, not even Jefferson's political enemies took the allegation seriously enough to press it.

Jefferson's Character

Historians and biographers who have spent their lives studying Thomas Jefferson have found the notion of an "affair" with Sally Hemings highly implausible, given various aspects of Jefferson's character. Indeed, before his recent turnabout resulting from the TJMF Report, TJMF president Dan Jordan once described a Jefferson-Hemings liaison as "morally impossible," echoing the very words used by Jefferson's granddaughter, Ellen Randolph Coolidge, in her 1858 letter.[72]

---

69. Malone, *Jefferson the President: First Term, 1801–1805*, pp. 218–223.

70. Monticello report, Appendix F, "Review of the Documentary Evidence," p. 2.

71. Randall to Parton, in Flower, *James Parton*, p. 239.

72. "There are such things, after all, as moral impossibilities." Ellen Randolph Coolidge to Joseph Coolidge, October 24, 1858, Coolidge Collection, University of Virginia Library.

Annette Gordon-Reed deals with this issue by presenting superficial "character" arguments—Jefferson as "gentleman," Jefferson as "cold-blooded," Jefferson as "family man," and Jefferson as "racist"—and then dealing with each of these straw man arguments.[73] But the character questions are far deeper and more complex than Professor Gordon-Reed's caricatures suggest.

What Ellen Coolidge meant by "moral impossibility" is rather clear from the context of the statement in her letter: that it is highly unlikely that Jefferson would begin a sexual relationship with Sally Hemings in France, where she was "lady's maid" to his daughters, for this would require us to imagine "so fond, so anxious a father, whose letters to his daughters were so replete with tenderness, and with good counsels for their conduct, should ... have selected the female attendant of his own pure children to become his paramour."[74] Similarly, the likelihood of such a relationship existing at Monticello during Jefferson's presidency—given not only Jefferson's undoubted love for his children and grandchildren but also the logistic difficulties entailed in keeping secret a sexual liaison—suggest a high improbability of such an affair.

Another sense in which a sexual relationship with Sally Hemings would have been "morally impossible" to Jefferson focuses on his own personal moral code—his self-described "Epicurean" philosophy—and the abundant evidence suggesting the seriousness of his adherence to it.[75] This aspect of Jefferson's character, and its relevance to his personal life and particularly the Hemings paternity thesis, has yet to be fully explored by scholars. One obvious question is whether Jefferson's professed beliefs that "[t]he *summum bonum* is not to be pained in body, nor troubled in mind" and that "the indulgence which prevents a greater pleasure, or produces a greater pain is to be avoided"[76] might have given Jefferson reason to remain celibate.

Virtually all the evidence we have about Jefferson himself suggests that he was celibate following the death of his wife, Martha, in 1782. The closest he came to a sexual relationship with any woman after 1782 was his "affair" with Maria Cosway in France, but that relationship might be more accurately described as a non-sexual romantic friendship. The very passion with which Jefferson expressed his feelings for Mrs. Cosway—illustrated by his effusive correspondence with her, particularly his famous "Head and Heart" letter—makes even more striking the complete absence of evidence of any similar romantic feelings toward any woman after Jefferson's return to the United States. The intensity with which Jefferson involved himself in politics during the period 1789–1809 fits the pattern of other celibate persons throughout history who obsessively pursue their careers as a substitute for a fulfilling sexual relationship.[77] And after his retirement from the presidency, Jefferson just as passionately pursued the three admitted obsessions of his life—his "family, farm, and books"—and thus to all appearances kept his deathbed promise of fidelity to his wife, Martha.

Finally, there is the matter of Jefferson's unquestioned love and devotion for his children and grandchildren—amply evidenced in his correspondence with them and in various other documentary evidence of life at Monticello and Poplar Forest—in contrast to

---

73. Gordon-Reed, *Thomas Jefferson and Sally Hemings: An American Controversy*, pp. 107ff.

74. Ellen Coolidge to Joseph Coolidge, October 24, 1858, U.Va. Library.

75. On this generally, see Jean M. Yarbrough, *American Virtues: Thomas Jefferson on the Character of a Free People* (Lawrence: University Press of Kansas, 1998), and also Andrew Burstein, *The Inner Jefferson: Portrait of a Grieving Optimist* (Charlottesville: University Press of Virginia, 1995).

76. Jefferson to William Short, October 31, 1819, in *Jefferson: Writings* (ed. Merrill D. Peterson, New York: Library of America, 1984), pp. 1432–33.

77. See generally Elizabeth Abbott, *A History of Celibacy* (New York: Scribner, 2000).

the complete absence of any evidence, direct or circumstantial, showing that Jefferson displayed any signs of affection toward either Sally Hemings or any of her children. Given this great contrast, one would have to assume Jefferson had a Dr. Jekyll/Mr. Hyde type of split personality in order to maintain these two very different families. Jefferson was a very private man and in many respects a complicated man (and some would say a man of many contradictions), but not even he would have been able so successfully to lead the double life that some proponents of the Hemings paternity thesis would have us believe he led.

Conclusion

Obviously a large number of people, for various reasons, passionately want to believe that Thomas Jefferson fathered Sally Hemings' children. These include some of the descendants of two of Sally Hemings' children who passionately want their families' oral traditions—and for many of them and their supporters, their places in American history—somehow validated by widespread acceptance of the Jefferson paternity thesis as historical fact. But it is not the role of historians to make people feel good about themselves or their family stories; "feel-good" history is not good history. It is, rather, the role of historians to explain the past as best they can, by following objective methodology and the evidence. However upsetting this conclusion may be to many people, again for a wide variety of reasons, it is simply the case that no credible evidence has proven that Thomas Jefferson fathered any of Sally Hemings' children.

Individual Views of
Professor Forrest McDonald

Individual Views of Professor Forrest McDonald

I have read the drafts of the Jefferson-Hemings Scholars Commission report and want to go on record as endorsing it without reservation.

I should like, however, to make an addendum to be included with the final report if possible. Lest anyone think I have acted out of preconceived ideas favoring Jefferson, let it be known that I am an unreconstructed Hamiltonian Federalist, and out of my admiration for Alexander Hamilton I have long been disposed to believe the worst about Thomas Jefferson. Indeed, for nearly four decades I assumed, without thinking much about it, that the allegations regarding a Thomas Jefferson-Sally Hemings relationship were founded in fact. Since the kindling of the current controversy over the DNA evidence and Eston Hemings, however, I have studied the subject as thoroughly as I could, have read the evidence produced by Herbert Barger, and have of course followed the work of the Scholars Commission—the result being that I have entirely abandoned my earlier assumption. Thomas Jefferson was simply not guilty of the charge.

Forrest McDonald
Distinguished University Research Professor
University of Alabama

Individual Views of
Professor Thomas Traut

17

Does the DNA Analysis Establish Thomas Jefferson's Paternity of Sally Hemings' Children?*

Because of his remarkable contributions to both the discussions about, and the actual writing of the original documents encoding the American concepts and principles for liberty and justice in a new democratic society, Thomas Jefferson remains an icon of liberal thinking and of democratic ideals. This lofty stature, however, continues to make him a tempting target for those hoping to expose some flaw in his character.

A long-standing hypothesis, with little historical foundation, claims that Jefferson is the father of one or more children born by his slave, Sally Hemings. Because DNA analysis has become a powerful tool for identifying any individual, and because parents pass on their DNA to their descendants, it would appear that such a scientific test might help to accurately test the paternity hypothesis, if living descendants of the original characters in this historic drama could provide DNA samples.

A team of eight scientists, led by Dr. Eugene A. Foster, a retired pathologist in Charlottesville, Virginia, undertook to perform such a DNA analysis.[1] They had obtained blood samples from the descendants of two putative sons of Sally Hemings (Thomas Woodson and Eston Hemings), though there is debate as to whether Thomas Woodson was actually a child of Sally Hemings. They also had blood samples from five descendants of Field Jefferson, the uncle of Thomas Jefferson, and samples from three descendants of John Carr, the father-in-law of Thomas Jefferson's sister.

Background on DNA Analysis

Most of the DNA that encodes the human genome is located in the nucleus of cells, and is distributed among twenty-three different chromosomes. All such chromosomes exist in pairs, with one member of each pair coming from each parent. For twenty-two of these chromosomes it is very difficult to distinguish which member of the pair is the paternal chromosome. Only with the XY chromosome pair is it obvious and therefore easy to make this distinction, because the Y chromosome determines maleness and is passed from father to son. An additional benefit is that the Y chromosome is the smallest of all the chromosomes. It has only a small amount of genetic information; it does not undergo as much variation with time in different generations, so that the Y chromosome

---

* Notes for this chapter begin on page 324.

in a modern descendant should still greatly resemble the ancestral Y chromosome of 200 years ago.[2,3,4] Thus, the clear benefit of using only the Y chromosome is that it specifically and reliably follows the paternal line of descent.

The DNA in human chromosomes consists of a duplex of two DNA strands. Each strand is a linear molecule, composed of only four types of nucleotides, designated by the letters A, C, G, and T.[5] DNA is organized as informational units, genes, and each gene has the information to define the amino acid sequence of a specific protein, which are the functional agents in cellular biochemistry. Because it requires three consecutive nucleotides, defined as a codon, to designate a specific amino acid, there are actually sixty-four codons to define the twenty different amino acids found in our proteins. That is, for each amino acid there are usually three possible codons, and sometimes five or six codons. An important benefit of this is that frequently a codon in a gene can undergo a change at one nucleotide, and this altered codon will have the same identity for the amino acid that was originally specified. Therefore many alterations in our DNA have absolutely no effect, because they cause no change in the protein that is coded by that gene.

Like our DNA, proteins are also linear molecules, containing the twenty different types of amino acids in a string, or sequence, that is again unique for each protein. Alterations in our DNA are also tolerated because of the twenty types of amino acids that make up proteins; often several different amino acids can be placed at some specific position in the protein sequence without changing the shape of the protein, and therefore without changing the function of the protein. Again, this feature makes it permissible for certain DNA alterations (mutations) to occur, because by substitution of a single amino acid they cause a change in the protein that has no harmful consequences.

Types of Changes in DNA

When cells divide, the entire DNA content in the nucleus must first be duplicated to yield two complete sets of DNA that are in theory identical. The actual duplication of the parental DNA is performed by enzymes which are remarkably efficient, but which are not perfect. Occasionally they will make an error, so that the newly copied DNA may now include some small alteration. Such alterations are of two types:

1. nucleotide substitution

2. insertion or deletion of nucleotide(s)

If a typist were to simply type all the text in some book, occasionally the typist might strike the wrong letter key in a particular word. This would be comparable to a nucleotide substitution. If the typist becomes distracted and types the same sentence three times in succession, this would be an insertion because there is now extra text. Or, the typist could miss several sentences in the original text, and produce a slightly abbreviated copy. This is a deletion.

The above changes are not always harmful, and therefore are retained in the copied DNA. In the same way that we can often still understand a word even though it contains a typographical error, substitutions in DNA are often tolerated. And while insertions of duplicated text are unattractive, they again may not change the meaning. Deletions are more likely to be serious.

Through time many such changes, or mutations, may occur in our DNA when they cause no harm to the person(s) carrying these slightly altered genes. Even harmful mutations may continue in the twenty-two autosomes, because these come in pairs and the matching chromosome may still have a normal gene. Therefore, in our population all people have inherited comparable, but often unique changes in their DNA. These changes are very specific to a family line, though some of them have naturally spread more widely into our population, depending on how far back in time a particular change first occurred. The result of this continuing alteration of our DNA is that among living humans, for any two individuals more than 99% of their DNA will be identical when compared position by position along the DNA sequence. At the same time, enough variation has arisen in the human lineage that each individual probably has at least one truly unique feature.

Strategy of the DNA Analysis

Because variations or changes in DNA are caused by one or more specific alterations in a very large sequence, how do we detect such changes? Three major experimental approaches exist, which differ in their complexity and expense, and also in their resolution or accuracy:

Method 1. Sequencing a complete segment of DNA.

Method 2. Restriction fragment length polymorphism (RFLP).

Method 3. Identifying unique sites by amplifying the DNA with the polymerase chain reaction (PCR).

Method 1 is the most accurate, but also the most difficult. Clearly, one could completely sequence the entire Y chromosome from two or more men. Then, by carefully comparing these linear sequences, we could detect any position at which the nucleotide in the separate sequences was not identical—thereby implying that one or more had undergone a change. While this procedure would be very accurate, the sheer size of a single chromosome, in terms of the number of total nucleotides to be sequenced, makes this an enormously complex and therefore exceedingly expensive effort. Even the human Y chromosome, the smallest of all twenty-four human chromosomes, contains an estimated 35,000,000 bases in its sequence.[6]

Scientists have therefore devised two simpler procedures that are likely to give us a meaningful test. Method 2 depends on the ability of a select group of DNA-cutting enzymes to accurately recognize a short string of nucleotides, like a short string of letters in a sentence, and chemically cut the DNA at this position, thereby producing two smaller DNA molecules. These DNA-cutting enzymes are called *restriction enzymes*. Because it is very simple to measure the physical size of a DNA molecule, then by using several such restriction enzymes one can easily test how many cuts are made (by the number of smaller DNA restriction fragments produced), and estimate where the cuts are made (by the variable size of the DNA fragments).

As more changes have occurred between two DNA molecules that are being compared, the likelihood increases that at least one such change will alter a recognition site for a restriction enzyme. This will be directly visible in the number of DNA fragments produced, and by changes in the size of such DNA fragments. Thus, when cut by a single restriction enzyme, the DNA fragments will vary as to the number and size when DNA from very different human groups are compared. That is, one DNA molecule may contain four sites at which it is cut by a single enzyme while a different DNA molecule may contain six sites for cutting. If the two DNA molecules are initially the same size, then the number and sizes of fragments will be different when the sample molecules are cut four times or six times. Such variations are referred to as "restriction fragment length polymorphism," or simply by the initials RFLP. Note that large segments of DNA need not be accurately sequenced by this procedure. Instead it helps to determine if two or more different DNA molecules have the same few, small identical sites. The observed variation in such RFLPs was an early method for a DNA identification test.

Method 3 uses a different approach, based on identifying by sequence small sites in the DNA at which change occurs more frequently. Clearly this is only possible if the sites being changed are not essential for our normal health and function, and therefore are maintained over generations. Imagine that one wanted to find where, in older automobiles driving down a street, damage was likely to exist. Clearly damage would not be likely in the engine or carburetor if the cars are actually running. But one might readily observe dents in door panels, sagging bumpers, or rust on the fenders. This is the type of damage that an automobile may accumulate with age, while otherwise running normally. Now, if different car models were constructed with different quality sheet metal or different construction standards, then it might happen that Fords had problems with door panels, while Hondas were more likely to have rusty fenders, and so forth. This analogy is intended to suggest why specific changes may occur and be maintained within a family line, and that they are likely to be observed only at specific sites in the DNA. Such positions where various changes in the DNA are observed are then the *sites of polymorphism*.

Helpful to such comparative studies is the fact that some regions in a DNA molecule are more susceptible to change. Currently studies of the human Y chromosome have led to a series of defined sites for restriction enzymes or PCR probes that are both readily detectable and also shown to have varying frequencies of occurrence among different groups of people.[7,8,9,10,11,12,13] Such established DNA sites are therefore useful in efforts to compare separate DNA samples without an inordinate amount of work. For the work by Foster *et al.* on the Y chromosomal DNA, nineteen separate sites had been identified as useful because variations frequently were observed there. As shown in **Figures 12–16**, these include seven bi-allelic markers, eleven microsatellite short tandem repeats (STRs), and the minisatellite MSY1. The latter is considered one site, though it contains various arrangements of four different DNA patterns, whose type or identity is identified in parentheses.[14]

Once the exact sequence of such individual sites is known, it is possible to detect their existence by using a small DNA probe (synthesized chemically) designed for that specific site, and then using the polymerase chain reaction (PCR) technique to make very many copies of this DNA segment, if in fact the Y chromosome being tested contains this segment. This highly amplified set of DNA molecules will all be small and identical, and therefore very easy to measure. This method clearly depends on knowing in advance the sequence of sites that are likely to show variation in a population (polymorphism). Only in the last ten years have enough such polymorphic sites become identified for the Y chromosome to make Method 3 more applicable.[15]

All our chromosomes come in pairs. The set of chromosomes inherited from one parent is half the total, and is referred to as a *haploid* set, while the combination of these two haploid sets from our two parents equals a *diploid* set. When only one member of a chromosome pair (the Y chromosome from the XY pair) is analyzed for its DNA, the DNA pattern is then designated a *haplotype*.

For the work by Foster *et al.* both Methods 2 and 3 were used in an analysis that included nineteen distinct sites in the DNA haplotype at which changes have been observed in the general population.

It is important to appreciate that many changes may have occurred that would be undetected by this analytic procedure, because only nineteen small sites within a very large amount of DNA are being examined. However, any observed change would be a true and positive result. As an illustration of this, consider that one wished to verify if a typist had correctly typed the entire text of an encyclopedia, and could examine only nineteen pages of the newly typed text. Clearly many errors could have occurred on the unexamined pages, and these would not be detected. But, any error that was observed on the nineteen pages being examined would be direct proof that a change had occurred.

Results of the DNA Analysis by Foster *et al.*

While Dr. Eugene Foster, the lead author of the *Nature* paper, organized this DNA project, it appears that most of the specific scientific work was done by the seven co-authors, who were scientists working in England or in Holland. Because these scientists had recently published papers on examining Y chromosome polymorphisms in humans,[16] they appear to be well qualified for the scientific work involved.

Normally Y chromosomes are carried by males who are designated as XY, for this chromosome pair, in contrast to females who are designated as XX. Because Thomas Jefferson had no sons that lived to adulthood, it was not possible to get a Y chromosome sample from a direct descendant of Thomas Jefferson. Foster and associates therefore relied on samples derived from descendants of Field Jefferson. As the paternal uncle of Thomas Jefferson, this individual and his direct male descendants would be expected to share the same Y chromosome inherited by both Thomas Jefferson and Field Jefferson from their common ancestor, Thomas Jefferson II — the grandfather of Thomas Jefferson (see **Figure 12**).

Of the five direct descendants expected to carry the original Jefferson haplotype, four had identical patterns, and the fifth had evidence of a single change at one position out of the nineteen specific positions in the DNA being examined (as shown in **Figure 12**).

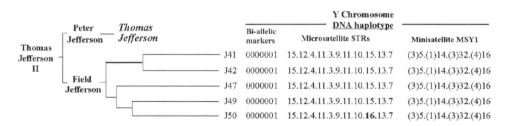

Figure 12. **The Jefferson Family Line.** Five living descendants of Field Jefferson, designated by code (J##) have the DNA haplotypes shown, as determined by Foster *et al.* The haplotypes are also by a numerical code, where the number represents how often that microsatellite or minisatellite sequence segment was repeated. One needs only compare the numbers, at a given position from left to right, to see if they are the same or different. It can then be seen that the first four men have identical haplotypes, while J50 has an extra STR segment at one position, an insertion, indicated in bold. All five men would be considered to have the Jefferson haplotype. This is the family tree presented in the DNA study by Foster *et al.* that omitted Randolph Jefferson and his sons, who have been added in **Figure 16**.

| | | Bi-allelic markers | Y Chromosome DNA haplotype | |
			Microsatellite STRs	Minisatellite MSY1
John Carr — Thomas	— C27	0000011	14.12.5.12.3.10.11.10.13.13.7	(1)17.(3)36.(4)21
Dabney	— C29	0000011	14.12.5.**11**.3.10.11.10.13.13.7	(1)17.(3)**37**.(4)21
Overton	— C31	0000011	14.12.5.12.3.10.11.10.13.13.7	(1)17.(3)36.(4)21

Figure 13. The Carr Family Line. Two of the men have an identical haplotype, while C29 has a change at two positions. All three men would be considered to have the Carr haplotype.

These results give some assurance about the constancy of the DNA being examined, because it spans more than 200 years and up to eight generations.

DNA from the three descendants of John Carr had a very different haplotype from that of the Jeffersons (**Figure 13**), varying at almost half the sites in comparison to the Jeffersons (see **Figure 16**). Because the Carrs were related to Thomas Jefferson by his sister, and they had no known common ancestor, they would of course have a different Y chromosome. This result is therefore quite normal. Again, the three Carr descendants have a haplotype pattern that is very similar to each other, consistent with the general constancy of the Y chromosome.

Five descendants of Thomas Woodson had a haplotype pattern that was significantly different from the Jefferson haplotype (**Figure 14**). Of these five, four had a haplotype pattern that was almost the same, while W70 had a completely different haplotype. This latter finding strongly supports that for this individual the original Woodson Y chromosome was replaced at some time in the past seven generations by an outside Y chromosome. Thus, the current Woodson descendants are completely unrelated to the Jefferson male line. By extension, their ancestor Thomas Woodson cannot be descended from Thomas Jefferson.

Because there are reports that Peter and Samuel Carr had made claims about fathering Sally Hemings' children, we can compare the Woodson and Carr haplotypes. If Thomas

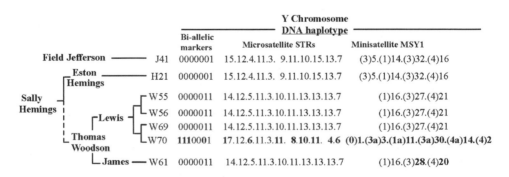

Figure 14. The Woodson/Hemings Family Line. The dashed line from Sally Hemings to Thomas Woodson reflects a lack of consensus as to whether he was her son. Three of the Woodson men (W55, W56, W69) have an identical haplotype, while W61 has a change at two positions. These four men would be considered to have the Woodson haplotype. W70 has a completely different haplotype. H21, descended from Eston Hemings, has the Jefferson haplotype which is shown by J41.

		Y Chromosome DNA haplotype	
	Bi-allelic markers	Microsatellite STRs	Minisatellite MSY1
Field Jefferson —— J41	0000001	15.12.4.11.3. 9.11.10.15.13.7	(3)5.(1)14.(3)32.(4)16
Lewis Woodson —— W55	0000011	14.12.5.11.3.10.11.13.13.7	(1)16.(3)27.(4)21
Thomas Carr —— C27	0000011	14.12.5.12.3.10.11.10.13.7	(1)17.(3)36.(4)21

Figure 15. Comparison of the three family haplotypes, using three individuals from **Figure 16**. Positions where the Jefferson haplotype differs from the other two are marked by a solid circle. Where the Woodson and Carr haplotypes differ is marked by an open circle.

Woodson was indeed conceived while Sally Hemings was in Paris, then no relationship is expected between the Carrs and Thomas Woodson. The comparison in **Figure 15** was done by taking one member from the Carr family (C27) plus a descendant of Thomas Woodson (W55), plus one member from the Jefferson family (J41) for comparison. This directly emphasizes how different the Jefferson haplotype is from the other two. And, while there are only four differences between C27 and W55, the probability of that occurring in a few generations from a common ancestor is highly unlikely, as will be described later. Therefore, it is not credible that a Carr brother was the father of Thomas Woodson.

The two more significant results of the DNA study are the DNA correspondence between the Jefferson haplotype and the Eston Hemings haplotype, and the complete lack of such a correspondence with the Woodson haplotype. That Thomas Woodson, who is presumed to have been conceived while Sally Hemings was with Thomas Jefferson in Paris, did not have the Jefferson haplotype is very significant, because this indicates that Sally Hemings conceived by another male at a time (in Paris) when Thomas Jefferson was the only member of his clan in that city.

The finding that one current descendant of Eston Hemings has a haplotype that is exactly the same as the Jefferson haplotype (**Figure 16**) strongly implies that some ancestor of this person was sired by a man carrying the Jefferson Y chromosome. Most probably this occurred with the conception of Eston Hemings at Monticello, because Eston Hemings himself moved as an adult out of Virginia, thereby physically separating his descendants from the Jefferson family.

What Is the Likelihood for Changes Within a Haplotype?

Clearly, the benefit of using the Y chromosome for this analysis was the expectation, based on current knowledge, that overall changes in this chromosome are not common. However, a few specific sites have been identified in recent years where variability is sufficiently frequent that changes at these sites may now help to identify individuals. We see clear support for this, because after 6–8 generations, for the three family haplotypes shown in **Figures 12–14**, only one person in each set has shown changes from the pattern of the others in that family. (W70, in the Woodson family, is excluded from this analysis, because he clearly was not a member of the Woodson haplotype.)

Within the three family haplotypes (all summarized in **Figure 16**) two current males have a change at one position (J50 and W61) and one has changes at two positions (C29). The frequency for a single change at the MSY1 site has been determined at 2–11%,[17] so

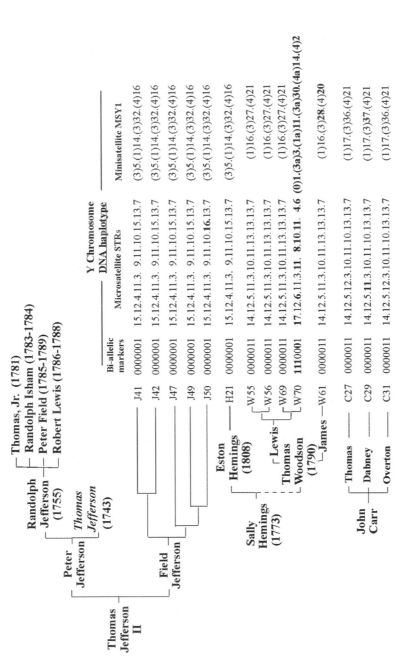

Figure 16. Family lines of descent for the Jeffersons, the Carrs, and two possible children of Sally Hemings. The figure is adapted from Foster *et al.*, 1998. Also included are Randolph Jefferson and four of his sons, for whom the best estimate for their birth year is shown. For some other individuals the year of their birth is shown in parentheses. The dashed line between Sally Hemings and Thomas Woodson indicates the uncertainty as to her being his mother.

that having two out of fourteen men (in **Figure 16**) show a change at this site is quite normal. The frequency for change in the microsatellite STRs is about 2.1×10^{-3} (about one in 500).[18] Therefore, seeing two of fourteeen men in **Figure 16** (J50 and C29) with one STR change is unexpected for such a small sample. However, these probabilities almost completely exclude a relationship between the Carrs and Thomas Woodson. To change the Carr haplotype to the Woodson haplotype requires two changes in the STRs for a single person, with a combined probability of 4.4×10^{-6} (about one in 227,000). While the Carr brothers may have fathered children by Sally Hemings, the current DNA samples do not support this in regard to Thomas Woodson.

Interpretation of the DNA Analysis by Foster *et al.*

The title of the article published by Foster *et al.* to report their results was: "Jefferson fathered slave's last child." This title is not a statement of fact. It therefore represents an unfortunate lapse, because Foster *et al.* omitted any presentation of the number of adult male Jeffersons living in 1807 in that region of Virginia (**Figure 12**). This has been corrected (**Figure 16**) to include Thomas Jefferson's younger brother Randolph, and Randolph's five sons, who all lived nearby. Four of Randolph Jefferson's sons would have been old enough to beget a child. This would have been possible at their age in 1807, which can be determined from their birth year (**Figure 16**), obtained from family records.[19] A title that would have been more correct, given the available data, would be: "A member of the Jefferson clan fathered slave's last child." Even this would not be an absolute statement of fact, but simply a more reasonable interpretation.

The above article in *Nature* was preceded by an opinion piece which was meant to focus attention on the DNA article, and to emphasize its dramatic conclusion.[20] This opinion piece was written by two American professors: Eric S. Lander, a molecular biologist and geneticist, and Joseph J. Ellis, a historian. In their article these two authors state: "DNA analysis by Foster *et al.* shows that he [Thomas Jefferson] fathered at least one child by his slave, Sally Hemings." Again, this statement misrepresents the actual results.

What was actually demonstrated by the DNA analysis is that a male with the Jefferson Y chromosome was the father of Eston Hemings. Even the DNA results do not absolutely establish this connection with a Jefferson male because the statistical probability that a non-family member near Monticello would have this haplotype is less than 1%, but it is not zero. Therefore, while the probability that a member of the Jefferson clan fathered Eston Hemings is very high, greater than 99%, it is not 100%. However, for most people these results confirm that a Jefferson male sired Eston Hemings.

It is of interest that *Nature*, a very prestigious journal that carefully limits the size (page space) of accepted research articles, gave slightly more space to the opinion piece by Lander and Ellis than was used for the actual DNA paper itself,[21] because Foster *et al.* in a later commentary claimed "Space constraints prevented us from expanding on alternative interpretations."[22]

Clearly, the journal was willing to give extra page space to promote an exciting interpretation of the DNA results, and this was helped by the actions of Foster *et al.* in omitting to mention that Jefferson had a brother and nephews living nearby. As shown in **Figure 16**, little extra space is required to include Randolph Jefferson and his sons in the family tree. In responding to criticisms of his paper, Foster stated: "we hoped to obtain some objective data that would tilt the weight of evidence in one direction or another."[23] However, one should not "tilt" the evidence by omitting important facts.

Two final possibilities need to be considered:

1. While it is normal to assume that Thomas Jefferson shares the Jefferson DNA haplotype, there is a small chance that he in fact had some other DNA, in the same way that we see in **Figure 14** that one of the current Woodsons has a Y chromosome different from the rest of his family. This is an unlikely scenario, and there is no historical support for this.

2. An ancestor of Thomas Jefferson may have produced male children by a slave woman. Such a male slave on the estate would then have had the same Y chromosome DNA haplotype as the Jefferson family. If such a slave produced a son by Sally Hemings, this would also lead to this child's descendants having the Jefferson Y haplotype.

Conclusion

The DNA test has several important results:

1. Thomas Woodson could not have been related to Thomas Jefferson. Then if Thomas Woodson was conceived in Paris, it had to be by a different father. This in turn argues for Sally Hemings conceiving children by more than one partner, because the Woodson descendants have a different haplotype from the descendant of Eston Hemings.

2. The Carr brothers could not have been related to Thomas Woodson. Also, the Carr brothers have a haplotype significantly different from the Jefferson haplotype found in a descendant of Eston Hemings. These results show that they could not have sired the first or last child of Sally Hemings. The DNA gives no evidence regarding the paternity by either Carr brother of the remaining children born to Sally Hemings.

3. One current descendant of Eston Hemings had the Jefferson DNA haplotype. This strongly supports that Eston Hemings, the last child of Sally Hemings, also had the Jefferson Y DNA haplotype. People who could have been responsible for this child's paternity include Thomas Jefferson, Randolph Jefferson and four of Randolph's sons, other Jefferson males in the Field Jefferson family, or even male slaves sired by ancestors of Thomas Jefferson. It will require some careful documentation by historians (if appropriate records exist) to determine which of these males could have been at Monticello during the few weeks in 1807 when Eston Hemings could have been conceived.

Notes

1. E. A. Foster, M. A. Jobling, P. G. Taylor, P. Donnelly, P. de Knijff, R. Mieremet, T. Zerjal and C. Tyler-Smith, "Jefferson fathered slave's last child," *Nature*, 396 (1998), 27–28.

2. S. Jakubiczka, J. Arnemann, H. Cooke, M. Krawczak and J. Schmidtke, "A search for restriction fragment length polymorphism on the human Y chromosome," *Human Genetics*, 84 (1989), 86–88.

3. P. Malaspina, F. Perischetti, A. Novelletto, C. Iodice, L. Terrenato, L. Wolfe, M. Ferraro and G. Prantera, "The human Y chromosome shows a low level of DNA polymorphism," *Annals of Human Genetics*, 54 (1990), 297–305.

4. A. Spurdle and T. Jenkins, "The search for Y chromosome polymorphism is extended to negroids," *Human Molecular Genetics*, 1 (1992), 169–170.

5. Because nucleotides contain, and are defined by, one of the four bases, the term *base* is as frequently used in describing a DNA sequence.

6. In 1998 this represented an enormous amount of DNA sequence, and at that time not a single human Y chromosome had been completely sequenced.

7. N. Mathias, M. Bayés and C. Tyler-Smith, "Highly informative compound haplotypes for the human Y chromosome," *Human Molecular Genetics*, 3 (1994), 115–123.

8. M. T. Seielstad, J. M. Hebert, A. A. Lin, P. A. Underhill, M. Ibrahim, D. Vollrath and L. L. Cavalli-Sforza, "Construction of human Y-chromosomal haplotypes using a new polymorphic A to G transition," *Human Molecular Genetics*, 3 (1994), 2159–2161.

9. L. S. Whitfield, J. E. Sulston and P. N. Goodfellow, "Sequence variation of the human Y chromosome," *Nature*, 378 (1995), 379–380.

10. C. Kwok, C. Tyler-Smith, B. B. Mendonca, I. Hughes, G. D. Berkovitz, P. N. Goodfellow and J. R. Hawkins, "Mutation analysis of the 2 kb 5' to SRY in XY females and XY intersex subjects," *Journal of Medical Genetics*, 33 (1996), 465–468.

11. M. Kayser, Caglia, M., Corach, D., Fretwell, N., Gehrig, C., Graziosi, G., Heidorn, F., Herrmann, S., Herzog, B., Hidding, M., Honda, K., Jobling, M., Krawczak, M., Leim, K., Meuser, S., Meyer, E., Oesterreich, W., Pandya, A., Parson, W., Penacino, G., Perez-Lezaun, A., Piccini, A., Prinz, M., Schmitt, C., Schneider, P. M., Szibor, R., Teifel-Greding, J., Weichhold, G., de Knijff, P., Roewer, L., "Evaluation of Y-chromosomal STRs: a multicenter study," *International Journal of Legal Medicine*, 110 (1997), 125–133.

12. T. Zerjal, B. Dashnyam, A. Pandya, M. Kayser, L. Roewer, F. R. Santos, W. Schiefenhövel, N. Fretwell, M. A. Jobling, S. Harihara, K. Shimizu, D. Semjidmaa, A. Sajantila, P. Salo, M. H. Crawford, E. K. Ginter, O. E. Evgrafov and C. Tyler-Smith, "Genetic relationships of Asians and Northern Europeans, revealed by Y-chromosomal DNA analysis," *American Journal of Human Genetics*, 60 (1997), 1174–1183.

13. M. A. Jobling, E. Heyer, P. Dieltjes and P. de Knijff, "Y-chromosome-specific microsatellite mutation rates reexamined using a minisatellite, MSY1," *Human Molecular Genetics*, 8 (1999), 2117–2120.

14. Because interesting results occur in the microsatellite STRs and the minisatellite MSY1, only these will be defined here. Microsatellite short tandem repeats (STRs) are sequences of 2–6 bases that are repeated in tandem many times along a DNA sequence. The eleven STRs examined, by position from left to right, were: 19-388-389A-389B-389C-389D-390-391-392-dxys156y. The number at each position defines how many repeats of that STR occur. The minisatellite MSY1 is considered one site, because it contains four patterns or types of DNA sequences in one continuous sequence. In the figures these pattern types (1–4) are designated in parentheses, and the number following the parenthesis indicates how often that pattern type was repeated.

15. *Supra*, notes 4 and 11.

16. *Supra*, notes 8, 9, 10, and 11. C. A. Tilford, T. Kuroda-Kawaguchi, H. Skaletsky, S. Rozen, L. G. Brown, M. Rosenberg, J. D. McPherson, K. Wylie, M. Sekhon, T. A. Kucaba, R. H. Waterston and D. C. Page, "A physical map of the human Y chromosome," *Nature*, 409 (2001), 943–945.

17. *Supra*, note 11.

18. E. Heyer, J. Puymirat, P. Dieltjes, E. Bakker and P. de Knijff, "Estimating Y chromosome specific microsatellite mutation frequencies using deep rooting pedigrees," *Human Molecular Genetics*, 6 (1997), 799–803.

19. Cynthia H. Burton, *Jefferson Vindicated*, 2005, Keswick, VA: Cynthia H. Burton, p. 51.

20. E. S. Lander and J. J. Ellis, "Founding Father," *Nature*, 396 (1998), 13–14.

21. *Id.*

22. E. A. Foster, M. A. Jobling, P. G. Taylor, P. Donnelly, P. de Knijff, R. Mieremet, T. Zerjal and C. Tyler-Smith, "The Thomas Jefferson paternity case," *Nature*, 397 (1999), 32.

23. *Id.*

Statement of
Playwright Karyn Traut

18

Thomas Jefferson: Brother's Keeper[*]

A Playwright's Progress

I first began researching Thomas Jefferson and Sally Hemings in connection with writing a play more than three decades ago. Because my process of exploration and research into the topic was different from academic or legal conventions, I thought it best to write of my experiences in this subject matter as it evolved from a playwright's perspective.

A playwright's task when writing of either historical or fictional characters is to understand them so thoroughly that they come to life within the mind of the playwright. At that point the characters seemingly begin to "talk" for themselves. With an historical figure, especially one as pivotal to the very nature of the American consciousness as Thomas Jefferson, a playwright must work hard at the research, checking many sides and angles of point of view. Not every playwright sees his/her task this way. Shakespeare himself worried little about historical accuracy and his plays have not suffered for the lack. However, for myself as an American playwright who is concerned that our history and mythology are too often commingled, I felt it imperative to present an accurate portrait of this crucial American figure.

The second quality I bring to my research, which is perhaps different from a typically scholarly or legal approach to a subject, is a proficiency at working jigsaw puzzles. There are many trials and errors in the working of a jigsaw puzzle, not to mention frustration and hair pulling over near attempts at fit. Not all pieces slip perfectly into alignment. Two sides to a piece can fit yet the piece can be erroneous because a third or fourth does not. If the piece is the wrong fit, the puzzle won't coalesce until the wrong piece is removed. When a piece does fit it is like music. Every other piece in the puzzle can now find its place in the resulting unified whole. This is what happened when I found the "piece" of the Jefferson "puzzle" that was Randolph, Thomas Jefferson's brother.

In the late 1970s, I read the Book of the Month club selection, *Thomas Jefferson, An Intimate History*, by Fawn M. Brodie.[1] It was enormously popular at the time and much was written about it. Important to our discussion, Brodie was said to have presented a unique

---

 * Editor's Note: Upon learning that Scholars Commission member Professor Thomas Traut's playwright spouse had researched Thomas Jefferson and Sally Hemings in preparation for a play she produced in the 1980s, we urged him to bring her with him to our December 2000 meetings near Dulles Airport. We found her account of her own efforts to find the truth in this matter fascinating, and urged her to prepare the following essay for inclusion as an annex to her husband's Individual Views in our final report. I commend it to anyone interested in the search for the truth in this matter, and especially to those who believe that Randolph Jefferson was never considered a paternity suspect until after the 1998 DNA tests ruled out the Carr brothers as possible fathers of Eston Hemings.

 1. *Thomas Jefferson, An Intimate History*; Fawn M. Brodie; Bantam Books, New York, 1974.

picture of Thomas Jefferson's relationship with Sally Hemings as a love story rather than as sexual abuse of a slave. It was a compelling theory, which the nation took to heart. It appeared to be a successful attempt to soften the anger that many African Americans held against Thomas Jefferson for this purported relationship. Brodie was said also to have defended her interpretation by saying that the All White Male establishment of American historians simply could not believe that Thomas Jefferson could have had an affair with a slave and so dismissed it out of hand. Thus, she dismissed their dismissal with an *ad homonym* argument.

Being inclined to believe Brodie's story, I read the book, embraced it and became fascinated with the character of "Tom Hemings." Tom Hemings, Brodie claimed, was conceived in France and born to Sally Hemings shortly after her return to Virginia. Brodie further suggests that "Tom" grew to adulthood and passed into white society, disappearing from historical records.

> When her [Sally Hemings'] son Tom left Monticello is unknown. It is likely, as we have said, that he was one of the four "yellow" children" at Monticello, described by Jefferson's granddaughter Ellen Randolph Coolidge as "white enough to pass for white" who were permitted to leave under the euphemism of "running away." [2]

This "Tom" also supposedly looked like Thomas Jefferson. Brodie leads the reader to believe "Tom" was an actual person and that we have a possible image of him:

> We do not know if it was Tom or Madison or Eston Hemings that Jefferson's grandson was describing when he talked to Henry Randall: " ... in one case the resemblance was so close that at some distance ... the slave, dressed in the same way, might have been mistaken for Mr. Jefferson."[3]

Note here that Thomas Jefferson Randolph is describing a resemblance from a distance. This would imply that the resemblance [of most possibly Eston, Sally Hemings' last son who is linked with the male Jefferson line by the DNA study] to Thomas Jefferson was one of skin tone, height and weight, not necessarily facial features. This would explain the difference in contemporary points of view between African Americans who say that Eston looked like Thomas Jefferson and Euro-Americans who say he did not. Many African Americans distinguish looks on the basis of skin tone whereas Euro Americans tend to distinguish looks on the basis of facial features, hair color and texture.

Here was my character for a play. A son born to the most compelling American Founding Father, who in a fully free country would have been an obvious candidate for president (as was John Adams' son John Quincy Adams), but because of slavery and the law against miscegenation (which was struck down in Virginia only in 1967 by the Supreme Court ruling in *Loving v. Virginia*),[4] could only at best "pass" into oblivion.

I began work. I mulled the play and talked it over with my colleagues, among whom were many African Americans. There was much fascination and excitement. The conversations were deep and poignant.

In 1978, actively imaging the play about "Thomas Hemings," I moved with my husband and two teenage sons from Los Angeles to Chapel Hill, North Carolina. I joined a

---

2. Ibid. p. 479; Brodie's reference is: *Ellen Randolph Coolidge to Joseph Coolidge, Jr.* October 24, 1858, manuscript owned by Harold Jefferson Coolidge.

3. Ibid.; Quoting Randall quoting Thomas Jefferson's grandson, Thomas Jefferson Randolph; p. 322.

4. Supreme Court of the United States, Loving et Ux. V. Virginia, 1967.

book reading group and again read Fawn Brodie's *Thomas Jefferson* for their selection. One of the women in the group was a social worker married to an historian. She said her husband said the book was complete "nonsense" (I'm not sure of the exact word, but it was along this line) and more of an historical novel than a work of history. I asked her what she herself thought. She said that she loved it. All in the group loved it. My project continued.

In this same year, 1978, the permanent residents of Chapel Hill, as contrasted with the student population, were largely faculty or connected to the University in some way. Our neighborhood held several historians who became our friends. When I told the idea of my project to one of them he gently informed me that "no one" in the historical community believed the Jefferson-Hemings liaison. I couldn't dismiss his statement with Brodie's defense that white men alone opposed her theory because his wife was also an historian.

My undergraduate education in English at the University of California at Berkeley was rigorous regarding the importance of checking sources. From my early years there I'd adhered to the belief that it was imperative to let the research determine the model rather than the model determine the research. To honor my neighbors' expertise, and also to be able to hold my play up to them, I decided to check Brodie's sources.

It was a sunny day when I took my work outside to read through the footnotes and appendages from *Thomas Jefferson: An Intimate History*. As I read Madison Hemings' account, a storm brewed in my mind despite the luxuriant weather. Madison's account tells of the child supposedly conceived by Sally Hemings in France to be one who died in infancy. Further, Madison's account gives the child no name.

> ... She [Sally Hemings] returned with him [Thomas Jefferson] to Virginia. Soon after their arrival, she gave birth to a child, of whom Thomas Jefferson was the father. It lived but a short time.[5]

Fawn Brodie had thrown out the pieces of the puzzle that didn't fit her model. Where she then left holes, she simply filled in with conjecture using often the word "innuendo" to defend her position. Even further, there was no evidence that the historical character I had centered my play upon had ever existed. There was no record of such a birth in the Monticello ledger. If he had existed, he wasn't necessarily named Tom and he might have died in infancy. I suddenly had no play.

By this time Thomas Jefferson himself had taken hold of me. I began to entertain the idea of his being a central character, but wondered how I could take on such a huge symbol. I wanted my play to be historically accurate, but if Thomas Jefferson himself were to be the central character I would have to do much more research than I'd originally planned. Fortunately I was in an academic community with an excellent library. I decided to take six months off from my day job to do the research, not knowing at this point where it would lead.

I spent months in the stacks and at the card catalogue of the Wilson Library at the University of North Carolina at Chapel Hill. I found sections on early Charlottesville records which enabled me to get a sense of the "feeling" of the times; I read not only personal materials on Thomas Jefferson, looking always for the person behind the figure, but writings of others at the times in order to flesh out the 18th and early 19th centuries

---

5. Madison Hemings, "Life Among the Lowly, No. 1," Pike County Ohio *Republican*, March 13, 1873 ("*Reminiscences of Madison Hemings*" Appendix I, Part I; *Thomas Jefferson: An Intimate History*, Brodie, p. 639.).

in Virginia and Paris. I visited Monticello. I took on several "Jefferson" activities to "get inside," as theater people say, "the character." I concentrated on long letter writing, long walks, idealistic government, innovations in the home, and discovered for the first time blessings of the 20th century not known in the 18th and 19th: We didn't have to deal with plagues such as yellow fever that could sweep through a city while one was visiting. We also expected each child to live to adulthood. The grief that the wealthiest people suffered as common occurrences in the 18th and 19th centuries is known only among the poorest of today's population. Thomas Jefferson and his wife lost, including her son from her first marriage, five children in infancy. Mrs. Jefferson herself died in her early 30s. The burden of these losses was so great that, when their daughter, Lucy, died while he was in France, Jefferson became profoundly intent on bringing his last surviving daughter in America, Polly, to join him in Paris. An ocean voyage for his daughter, with all its dangers, was apparently less ominous to him than the possibility of death by disease during separation. A 'servant' who was in attendance to Polly would have been less significant to him than the presence of Polly herself, the third in his family now reduced to three: Himself, his daughter Martha, and she. His concern for Polly's health would also make it most likely that the servant would have continued to attend Polly in the convent where Polly spent most of her time in France. As Jefferson reported two weeks after Polly arrived in Paris: "She [Polly] is now established in the convent, perfectly happy."[6]

Polly's character was a delight for a playwright to encounter. From her letters she appears to have been more independent than her older sister Martha. An expressive child, she did not want to go to France and told her father of these wishes succinctly in several letters. Mrs. Eppes, with whom Polly was staying while Jefferson and his daughter Martha were in France, wrote to Jefferson in March, 1787, regarding the difficulty of persuading Polly to join them in Paris:

> We have made use of every stratagem to prevail on her to consent to visit you without effect. She is more averse to it than I could have supposed; either of my children would with pleasure take her place for the number of good things she is promised.[7]

It is my acknowledged conjecture—based on my knowledge of children, having both raised and taught them—that Polly is the one who did not want to leave for France unless her young companion (perhaps even friend) Sally went with her. In her own letters, as well as the above from Mrs. Eppes, Polly resisted the trip:

> [ca. 22 May 1786?]
>
> Dear Papa – I long to see you, and hope that you and sister Patsy are well ... and hope that you and she will come very soon to see us.... I am very sorry that you have sent for me. I don't want to go to France. I had rather stay with Aunt Eppes.... Your most happy and dutiful daughter. Polly Jefferson[8]

My six months of planned research had stretched into seven years. I realized I could spend my life researching Jefferson. I'd also discovered, as Brodie before me, an intense dislike of Thomas Jefferson among African American colleagues. This dislike was curious to me because I'd been riveted by his lifelong attempts to end slavery. Even though unable to end

---

6. Letter from Thomas Jefferson to Mrs. Eppes, Paris, July 28, 1787 in *The Domestic Life of Thomas Jefferson* by S. N. Randolph, Thomas Jefferson Memorial Foundation; The University Press of Virginia, 1978; p.127.

7. *The Domestic Life of Thomas Jefferson*; S.N. Randolph; p. 124.

8. *The Family Letters of Thomas Jefferson*; Edited by Edwin Morris Betts and James Adam Bear, Jr.; University of Missouri Press; Columbia, MO, 1986; p. 31.

it himself, his hopes for its eventual end never ceased. For example: When the Missouri compromise was reached his anguish was articulated in a letter to John Holmes:

Monticello, April 22, 1820

This momentous question, like a fire-bell in the night, awakened and filled me with terror. I considered it at once as the knell of the Union. It is hushed, indeed, for the moment. But this is a reprieve only, not a final sentence. A geographical line coinciding with a marked principle, moral and political, once conceived and held up to the angry passions of men, will never be obliterated; and every new irritation will mark it deeper and deeper ... there is not a man on earth who would sacrifice more than I would to relieve us from this heavy reproach, in any practicable way. The cession of that kind of property, for so it is misnamed, is a bagatelle which would not cost me a second thought, if, in that way, a general emancipation and expatriation could be effected; and, gradually, and with due sacrifices, I think it might be....

I regret that I am now to die in the belief, that the useless sacrifice of themselves of the generation of 1776, to acquire self-government and happiness to their country, is to be thrown away by unwise and unworthy passions of their sons and that my only consolation is to be, that I live not to weep over it. If they would but dispassionately weigh the blessings they will throw away, against an abstract principle more likely to be effected by union than by scission, they would pause before they would perpetrate this act of suicide on themselves, and of treason against the hopes of the world.[9]

It became clear to me that slave owners were as enslaved in the slave system as were the slaves themselves. (Albeit in a materially preferred life, but a life morally repugnant to any who could not blind themselves to their condition.) Thus I found the central conflict for my character: The man who wrote the text of the Declaration of Independence struggling throughout his life to free himself and his country of slavery. I did not have a fitting answer to the puzzle of the paternity of Sally Hemings' children until late in my research.

Regarding Sally Hemings and the children of unnamed paternity, I went back and forth for years. Clearly there was no evidence of a child conceived by Sally in France. No listing in the Monticello register, no first hand stories of this child as seen or witnessed at Monticello by anyone who lived or worked on the premises.

The Woodson family oral history claims were not public in the early 80s when I was doing the research for my play, which became *Saturday's Children*. The DNA now proves there is no connection between the Woodson male line and the Jefferson male line. If the Woodson oral history had been available to me at the time I would have discounted it because I was looking only at reports by witnesses of Thomas Jefferson and Sally Hemings. Second and third hand stories were too easily embellished. For this reason I dismissed the Carr brothers as possible fathers of Sally Hemings' children. The only stories of the Carr brothers available to me at the time were second and third hand.

The Woodson family bibles are compelling family treasures but could not have been recorded by witnesses because Thomas Woodson himself could not have witnessed events and people during the time of his own conception. After his twelfth year Thomas Wood-

9. Letter to John Holmes from Thomas Jefferson; *The Life and Selected Writings of Thomas Jefferson*; edited by Adrienne Koch and William Peden, The Modern Library, Random House, Inc., New York, 1944, pp. 698–99.

son would have lived only among non-relatives. Finally, Madison Hemings' account makes no reference to a Thomas who was sent to another plantation:

> According to the Woodson family descendants, who now hold regular reunions, Thomas Woodson was secretly ushered from Monticello at the age of 12 after rumors began spreading about a relationship between Jefferson and Sally Hemings. Angered that his father would disown him, he took the surname of the family he lived with after leaving Monticello.

> Woodson wound up in southern Ohio, living 20 miles east of his brothers Madison and Eston. All of Woodson's children became educators, ministers or both.[10]

If Woodson knew Madison and Eston were his brothers and only 20 miles east of him in Ohio, why did Madison not seem to know of his existence? Even if there had been a child conceived in France, why a child of obviously white paternity would be proof of Thomas Jefferson's seed eluded me. Most of the men living in France at the time were white—including the servants.

The "fit" just wasn't there. There were thirty years difference in age between Thomas Jefferson and Sally Hemings. It was inconsistent with his character to be attracted to maidens. His wife was a widow, Maria Cosway. The recipient of the famed letter from Thomas Jefferson known as 'Dialogue between my Head and my Heart' was married, and the flirtation he admitted to having had in his bachelor days was also to a married woman, Mrs. Walker. [11]

Then again Sally Hemings was possibly his wife's half sister. Could he have seen the features of his wife in her face? If so, how could he have remained a racist to the end of his life?

Could he have found similar character traits of one he loved intensely beyond the grave? But if so, why would it not soften the intensity of his feelings for his deceased wife? Sarah N. Randolph records:

> Years afterwards (after Mrs. Jefferson's death) he wrote the following epitaph for his wife's tomb: "Torn from him by death/Sept. 6, 1782:/This Monument of his Love is inscribed.

>> If in the melancholy shades below
>> The flames of friends and lovers cease to glow,
>> Yet mine shall sacred last; mine undecayed
>> Burn on through death and animate my shade*

> *These four lines Mr. Jefferson left in the Greek in the original epitaph.[12]

It was clear that he was against slavery but for separation of the races—"Beyond the reach of mixture...."[13] How could he have fathered children into both slavery which he found abominable and dark skin which he found inferior? If they were his children, why did he not dote on them as he did his grandchildren? In Madison's account—he was uniformly

---

10. "Researchers focus on descendants of Jefferson's slaves" by Ian Zack; *Daily Progress*, (date unknown), photocopy provided to me by relative of historian at the University of Southern California, circa mid-1990s.

11. *The Wolf by the Ears; Thomas Jefferson and Slavery*; John Chester Miller; The Free Press, Macmillan Publishing Co, Inc.; New York, 1977; p. 197.

12. *The Domestic Life of Thomas Jefferson*; S.N. Randolph; p. 64.

13. *The Life and Selected Writings of Thomas Jefferson*; edited by Adrienne Koch and William Peden; p. 262.

kind to all. "He was not in the habit of showing partiality or fatherly affection to us children.... He was affectionate toward his white grandchildren...."[14] Surely if he were the father of Sally Hemings' children, he was in no way behaving as her lover.

Could it have been that Fawn Brodie was right about the sexual aspect of the relationship, if not the romantic? Was it possible that a human physical need was so strong that he went against all his beliefs and inclinations, taking advantage of a slave for purely physical reasons? Surely other slave owners did. But few other slave owners had the same convictions against slavery as Thomas Jefferson.

When I came across his calculations of how much intermarriage with whites it would take to "clear" the black blood,[15] I asked myself: Could it have been that he actually saw himself as doing a favor to Sally Hemings and her children by infusing her offspring with "white blood?" It was an appalling thought, but I entertained it so as to cover all possibilities.

The witnesses deny any sexual relationship between Thomas Jefferson and Sally Hemings. His grandson, T.J. Randolph, told the biographer Henry S. Randall that he himself slept within hearing of his grandfather's breathing and never heard a disturbance in his sleep.[16] Captain Bacon, the overseer at Monticello, said that he'd seen someone, whose name the editor blanked out, come out of Sally Hemings' room "many a morning"[17]:

> He freed one girl some years before he died, and there was a great deal of talk about it. She was nearly as white as anybody and very beautiful. People said he freed her because she was his own daughter. She was not his daughter; she was ____'s daughter. I know that. I have seen him come out of her mother's room many a morning when I went up to Monticello very early.[18]

Three aspects of the above comment convinced me it was likely to be true: 1) That he'd seen an obvious lover of Sally's leaving her room on "many a morning," which implied that she had this particular lover for some time (suggesting a monogamous relationship) and therefore this person was likely the father of Harriet Hemings and Sally's other children as well ... even if Harriet had been born before Capt. Bacon's time as overseer. 2) It is also likely that a lover would stay until morning. A morning departure suggests a welcome and not particularly hidden visitor. An abuser would more likely have used the cover of night for comings and goings. 3) That the editor blanked out the name given by Capt. Bacon indicated to me that the man named was being protected or hidden. Because the Carr brothers were often named at the time as possible fathers for both Sally and Betty Hemings' children, the editor's act suggested to me that there was someone other than a Carr brother.

The coincidence of the residencies of Thomas Jefferson and the conceptions of Sally Hemings is not extraordinary when one realizes that Jefferson stayed for several weeks at a time and there were abundant visitors whenever he was in residence. By residency alone, it was as likely that a visitor was parenting Sally Hemings' children as Thomas Jefferson himself. Referring to 1809 and times after, Sara Randolph writes:

---

14. Reminiscences of Madison Hemings; "Life Among the Lowly, No. 1." *Thomas Jefferson: An Intimate History,* Brodie; p. 642.

15. Jefferson to Francis C. Gray, March 4, 1815, Volume XIV p. 267, *The Writings of Thomas Jefferson;* definitive edition, Albert Ellery Bergh, Editor, The Thomas Jefferson Memorial Association, 1907.

16. *James Parton: The Father of Modern Biography,* Milton E. Flower, Durham, N.C. 1951, pp. 236–39.

17. *Jefferson at Monticello: The Private Life of Thomas Jefferson* by Rev. Hamilton Wilcox Pierson. Edited by James A. Bear, Jr.; University Press of Virginia, 1971; p.102.

18. Ibid.

No one could have been more hospitable than he was, and no one ever gave a
more heartfelt or more cordial welcome to friends than he did: but the visits of
those who were led by curiosity to Monticello was an annoyance which at times
was almost painful to one of as retiring a disposition as he was. These visitors came
at all hours and all season, and when unable to catch a glimpse of him in any way,
they not unfrequently begged to be allowed to sit in the hall.... On one occasion
a female visitor, who was peering around the house, punched her parasol through
a window pane to get a better view of him.[19]

The crowds at Monticello increased after his retirement, but visitors were the norm
throughout his years in public office. A guide to Boone Farm outside Charleston, S.C.
remarked on tour in 1999 that when visitors came in the 19th century, they didn't stay
for a day or a week, they stayed for a month or two.

Even if visitors made shorter stays, the time required to father a child is registered in
minutes, not months. I spent time making charts with the births of Sally and Betty Hemings' children. I wondered why, if Sally's sister Betty Hemings (called Bett) was also having light-skinned children, Sally alone is rumored to have had a liaison with Thomas
Jefferson.

Although Cyndi Burton has suggested what I too saw at the time of my initial research,
that Sally was elevated in the eyes of her peers by having gone to France,[20] I saw another
possibility. Sally had one daughter who lived to maturity. When Jefferson freed Harriet
was when, as Capt. Bacon says: "People said he freed her because she was his own daughter."[21] Jefferson and his times were sexist beyond our imagination today. A woman of any
race had no right to property once she married. Any or all inheritance became her husband's to do with as he willed. (Note in the codicil to Jefferson's will he requests that an
exception be made for his daughter Martha, rather than her husband, Thomas Mann
Randolph, to inherit his estate.)[22] I imagined that the neighbors would have been stunned
when Thomas Jefferson freed a girl, as he did Harriet Hemings, Sally's daughter. Neither
Sally nor Bett were freed in his will, as were their brothers. In my opinion, the neighbors
imputed paternity where generosity stood.

Madison's account is not a witness account, but rather an "as told to" account. Further,
because the story that "comes down to me" as reported in the document[23] happened before he was born, he himself is not a witness but rather the recipient of possible first generation oral history, which can be embellished by the individual teller. Nor does he in the
"as told to" account say that his mother herself told him the story, but again that it is the
story that "comes down to me." Such a phrase could mean that he read about it in the
James Callendar account. What he *was* witness to is consistent with what others wrote
about Thomas Jefferson:

> [Jefferson] was uniformly kind to all about him. He was not in the habit of show-
> ing partiality or fatherly affection to us children. [Himself and his brother Eston

---

19. *The Domestic Life of Thomas Jefferson*; S.N. Randolph; pp. 400–01.

20. E-mail correspondence with Cynthia H. Burton, July 2007, author of *Jefferson Vindicated; Fallacies, Omissions, and Contradictions in the Hemings Genealogical Search,* 2005, Keswick, Virginia,
Cynthia H. Burton.

21. *The Private Life of Thomas Jefferson* by Rev. Hamilton Wilcox Pierson. Ed. J.A. Bear, Jr.; pp
102–03.

22. Jefferson's Will, Facsimile of the Original Document in the Circuit Court, Albemarle, Va., *The
Writings of Thomas Jefferson, Volume* XIX, TJ Memorial Association, 1903; p. x.

23. Madison Hemings; "Life Among the Lowly, No. 1," Brodie; p. 638.

implied.] He was affectionate toward his white grandchildren, of whom he had fourteen.[24]

There is no indication of a special relationship between Madison Hemings as a child and Thomas Jefferson, contrasted with the special relationship Madison himself observed between Thomas Jefferson and his grandchildren.

If not Thomas Jefferson, I asked myself, then who? At Monticello I purchased a book titled *Thomas Jefferson and Music,*[25] as well as a record and booklet of sheet music used by Thomas Jefferson.[26] I wanted music in my play, but also felt the way to know a man's heart was through music he loved. In the book I discovered a comment about his brother. Until that time I had not known that he had a brother. Thomas paid for Randolph's violin lessons, but Randolph used his skill to play not the art music that Jefferson loved, but folk music with the "servants":

> Thomas, assuming guardianship of Randolph and the other younger children after their father's death, sent Randolph to the College of William and Mary from 1771 to 1773, and noted at least one payment of slightly over six pounds to the violin teacher Alberti for Randolph's violin lessons. It is quite obvious, however, from later letters, that Randolph was not inclined to be scholarly. He settled near Scottsville, Virginia, married "a Jade of genuine bottom," and seems to have used his musical experience only for country fiddling—"Used to come out among the black people, play the fiddle and dance half the night."[27]

What would it have been like to have been Thomas Jefferson's brother, twelve years his junior, and married to a "jade of genuine bottom"[28] as the family thought of his wife? I was fascinated. I began to see Randolph as possibly a rebel to his older more famous and authoritative brother.[29]

Turning the piece around in my hand one more time I decided to try another angle. What if everyone was telling the truth? What if Thomas Jefferson's family, Capt. Bacon, and Madison Hemings were all telling the truth? What if Madison Hemings truly believed Thomas Jefferson was his father? What if perhaps Sally Hemings had herself told Madison? She most likely wouldn't have referred him as "Thomas Jefferson," but as the more widely used appellation: "Mr. Jefferson." There were two Mr. Jeffersons. Suddenly it bubbled up from within me ... it was the brother.

Randolph Jefferson lived within visiting range and had his own estate at Snowdon. With his own estate, he would also have been a "Mr. Jefferson." Randolph, by dancing with the "servants," seemed to be living within the times rather than, as his brother was, trying to change them. Randolph was uninterested in political matters. "Paris, January 11th, 1789," Jefferson wrote: "Dear Brother - The occurrences of this part of the globe are of a nature to interest you so little that I have never made them the subject of a let-

---

24. Ibid.

25. *Thomas Jefferson and Music*; Helen Cripe; University Press of Virginia, 1979.

26. *Mr. Jefferson's Favorite Tunes*; selected and compiled by Sarah L. Yancey; copyright 1978 by Sarah L. Yancey.

27. *Thomas Jefferson and Music*; Helen Cripe; p. 13 cites: Bernard Mayo, *Memoirs of a Monticello Slave, in Jefferson at Monticello,* James A. Bear, Jr.; p. 22.

28. Ibid.

29. Cynthia Burton suggests recently that 'the jade' was most likely Randolph's second wife. I had no knowledge of which wife that might have been in my early research. The important thing to me was that the family depiction of Randolph's choices of music, social activity and wife, clearly presented a character very different from his older brother, Thomas.

ter to you." [30] Given the date, the occurrences he refers to are the events leading up to the French Revolution. Imagine, I thought, a brother of Thomas Jefferson's not being interested in the French Revolution.

Randolph was twelve years younger than Thomas, closer to Sally's age and therefore a more likely candidate for sexual attraction. He married twice, so was not as compelled to be true to a love beyond death as was Thomas Jefferson. (Thomas may have had a love affair with Maria Cosway in Paris, but of course, never married her even after she was, years later, widowed.) Randolph, as a piece to the Jefferson puzzle, slipped into place, a perfect fit for the possible father of Sally Hemings' children. My effort to get the facts right, to my surprise, had given me an original answer to an historical question.

When my play, *Saturday's Children,* was produced in 1988, one historian who came said to a member of the company that it was the first historically accurate play about Jefferson he'd ever seen. I was highly complimented that my efforts to write a play that would hold up to the scrutiny of historians had paid off. Partially funded by the North Carolina Arts Council, it gained, to my surprise, an additional honor by being listed in the 1992 *Aetna Calendar of Black History* for having cast a black actor in the role of Thomas Jefferson in Chapel Hill, North Carolina in 1988. (The actor who plays the character of Thomas Jefferson is scripted as: African American, while the "Real Jefferson" is to be played by a white actor. "The "Real Jefferson" reads only from Jefferson's writings on another platform of the "spiral" that is history. The character who plays Jefferson within the play acts out conjectures on the part of the contemporary characters.) Writing a play about Thomas Jefferson had become a larger experience than I'd ever imagined. We had made history.

When news of the DNA study hit the press in 1998, I was surprised at the distortion in several articles and astonished that the existence of Randolph Jefferson was left off the Jefferson family tree in the Foster *et al.* article in the journal, *Nature.*[31]

However, before the *Nature* article was available (the American press had scooped the story) I wrote a letter to the *News and Observer* of Raleigh, N.C. in which I pointed out that there were *two* Mr. Jeffersons. That letter found its way through the Internet to Mr. Herbert Barger, a Jefferson family historian who contacted me by phone. Barger, I learned, also held Randolph to be the possible father of Sally Hemings' children. His source was the Jefferson family oral tradition. He had additional information on Randolph, which also fit the puzzle. Randolph, he informed me, was widowed before Sally's first child was born and then married after her last child was born. All her children conceived in America were born between Randolph's marriages.

Cynthia H. Burton, in her book *Jefferson Vindicated,* corrects this. In personal correspondence with me she wrote: "Randolph Jefferson's first wife had to have died after giving birth to a son around 1797. Whether she died during childbirth or years later, I don't really know. I do know that Randolph was single in 1807–08. However, he was married when Sally Hemings conceived Harriet I and also possibly when Beverly was conceived."[32]

Based on Burton's research, if Randolph Jefferson was the father of all Sally's children, he was promiscuous in the early years of their relationship. If he was the father of Madison and Eston when he was a widower, and was not promiscuous earlier, then Sally had

---

30. *The Domestic Life of Thomas Jefferson*; S.N. Randolph; Thomas Jefferson Memorial Foundation; The University Press of Virginia, 1978 pp. 136–37.
31. "Jefferson Fathered Slave's Last Child"; Foster, E., *et al.*; *Nature* 396, 27–28, 1998.
32. E-mail correspondence with Cynthia H. Burton.

more than one lover. In either event, Sally stopped having children after Randolph re-married and Thomas Jefferson retired, remaining in residence most of the time at Monticello, even though Sally Hemings was then only thirty-five years of age.

The other piece of information that Mr. Barger brought to me was that there were several male Jeffersons in and around Monticello of age to parent Sally Hemings' children conceived in America. I had not known earlier of Randolph's sons and other Jeffersons except George Jefferson, a cousin, who was a correspondent of Thomas Jefferson's and did not appear to be in the vicinity of Monticello on a regular basis.

Per Mr. Barger's request, I spent most of a week in April of 2000 perusing the Nicholas Trist Collection at the University of North Carolina. Because I also held an appointment as an adjunct assistant professor in the Department of Social Medicine, in which I taught in the courses Theater and Medicine and Performance, Culture, Art and Healing, I had access to the Wilson Library's reserved collection on the UNC-CH campus. The collection consists of original letters, notes and occasional drawings in Nicholas Trist's possession during his life. Though not able to read every item registered during the pertinent years of Jefferson's life and the lives of his children and grandchildren, I was able to read over a hundred letters of the tiny flawless handwriting of Jefferson family members (all writing with quill pens!) and peruse a hundred more. I did not find a letter, which Barger thought might be in the collection, referencing a "Sally" who possibly went to work with Ellen Coolidge (Jefferson's granddaughter) in Boston during Jefferson's lifetime. Such a letter would have disproved a life-long romance between Sally Hemings and Thomas Jefferson. I did however find rich material on the character of these people and their times. They were a deeply feeling people. The letters are rich with emotional expression and none of it angry in any way at their "beloved grandpapa." It is hard to believe that a "grandpapa" raising his own blood in slavery would have been referred to consistently without "innuendo" as Brodie would have it.

The most scandalous activity I found in the Trist collection alluded to Thomas Jefferson's desire to visit Charlottesville to hear a Unitarian minister. Thomas Jefferson's granddaughter, Virginia, writing her husband, Nicholas Trist, says that the Unitarian outing will depend upon "Grandpapa's" wishes. "Mama" (Martha Jefferson Randolph) objected to hearing the Unitarian minister "because she thinks it will scandalize our neighbors with whom we already stand suspected." [33]

An interesting note suggests that John Hemings, Sally's brother, was almost a "free" agent. "Sept. 4, 1825: The carriage is broken and cannot be repaired until John Hemmings [sic] returns from Bedford."[34]

Cynthia Burton wrote by e-mail July 2007: "The Trist letter concerning John Hemings' return from Bedford refers to when Jefferson sent Hemings to Bedford with his two aids [sic] (prob. Eston and Madison) to make repairs caused by a fire at Poplar Forest."[35]

By "free agent" I intended to suggest John Hemings was able to come and go on his own, not that he could choose whether or not to come or go. Although on a mission of business for Thomas Jefferson, John Hemings does not appear to have had a chaperone. Such would indicate that Jefferson treated him as he would a trusted employee.

33. Nicholas Trist Papers; Trist Family Collection; Special Collections, University of North Carolina; Wilson Library, Chapel Hill, NC, 27599. Virginia to Nicholas Trist, Jan. 9th, 1824, Monticello.
34. Ibid. (Virginia (at Monticello) to Nicholas Trist, who was at the Springs for his health.)
35. E-mail correspondence with Cynthia H. Burton.

The letters were not private because at that time the mail was not secure. Martha Jefferson Randolph was careful to have, whenever possible, letters that were not for others' eyes hand delivered. The feelings she secreted however were not regarding her father but rather her husband, whom she would like to have divorced. In a letter from Cambridge, August 2, 1827, from Martha J. Randolph to Nicholas Trist she writes: "As soon as you have read this, burn this."[36] She writes of the torment of her travails, mostly economic, with her husband and her fear that if she separated from him legally he would keep her from ever seeing her two youngest children again.

Surely if there was a sexual liaison with Sally Hemings, Nicholas Trist—who spent so much time at Monticello in his youth, who married Thomas Jefferson's granddaughter Virginia, and became executor of Thomas Jefferson's will—would have mentioned something in some letter. Since he didn't burn the letter about Thomas Mann Randolph as requested, it's not likely that he feared historical exposure of family secrets.

In December of 2000, I found a note I made while researching the Trist collection:

> Is that the way of human nature? That those we call "great," those who have the vision to drive us toward needed changes and magnificence are surrounded by those who are embarrassed by those very acts and others who are encouraged by them so much that 200 years later people still want to destroy the passion of their memory?

I leave this quotation unedited as it stands, a surprise to me having forgotten that I wrote it on an unseasonably cold Spring morning of the kind that can surprise us in central North Carolina. There is no evidence that Thomas Jefferson had any relationship with Sally Hemings other than in his way of treating slaves with a kind of respect as if they were, in the European tradition, old family servants rather than bonded and vulnerable to sale. His writings throughout indicate a fervent hope that the future would find a way out of the slave system he both loathed but lived within his entire life. There is no evidence that Thomas Jefferson himself abused this system, even though others clearly did. The system itself was abuse enough. Yet it can be argued that Jefferson's forward thinking, as evidenced in his writings, laid down a moral foundation for slavery's eventual demise.

The DNA study confirms that the descendants of Sally Hemings' last son Eston are cousins of the descendants of Thomas Jefferson's uncle, Field Jefferson. The descendants of Sally Hemings' son Eston are also cousins of the descendants of her son Madison. Black and White are cousins. Whether Thomas Jefferson was a great, great, … grandfather, uncle, or cousin can be disputed as long as people are inclined, but the family connection is clear. By his character, Randolph is the most likely paternal possibility for Sally Hemings' last child. Thomas Jefferson is most likely an innocent member of this family doing the best he knew how in an unjust system, to free a relative's, possibly even his brother's, children. Regardless, it is time to embrace the familial relationship of these two lines and in so doing embrace the bi-racial nature of our American Heritage.

Additional Sources

In researching my play I made use of the following:

Early Charlottesville; Recollections of James Alexander 1828–1874; Albemarle County Historical Society; edited by Mary Rawlings.

---

36. Nicholas Trist Papers; Wilson Library, UNC-Chapel Hill, NC.

Jefferson Himself; Edited by Bernard Mayo; University Press of Virginia, 1970.

Jefferson and Monticello; by Paul Wilstach; Doubleday, Page and Co.; New York, 1925.

Green Mountain Boy at Monticello: A talk with Jefferson in 1822 by Daniel Pierce Thompson; The Book Cellar; Brattleboro, VT, 1962.

The Virginia Almanac "For the year of our lord 1800/ being the fourth after Leap Year:"

Democracy in America, Alexis de Tocqueville; edited and abridged by Richard D. Heffner; A Mentor Book, The New American Library; New York and Toronto, 1956.

Thomas Jefferson and American Democracy; Max Beloff; Collier Books, New York, 1962.

The Promise of American Life; Herbert Croly; Capricorn Books, New York, 1964.

The Writings of Thomas Jefferson, The Definitive Edition; 20 Volumes; The Thomas Jefferson Memorial Association; Washington D.C., 1907.

Thomas Jefferson's Paris, Howard Rice, Jr.; Princeton University Press, Princeton, New Jersey, 1976, 3rd printing 1991.

Up From Slavery; Booker T. Washington, Introduction by Louis Lomax; Laurel Leaf Library; 1966

In addition to the above books that I studied, there were numerous magazine articles, trips to the Natural Bridge, Monticello, and even Paris in which I walked the old quarters, imagining the carriages coming in and out of the mammoth doors to the courtyards of the dwellings.

Minority Views of
Professor Paul A. Rahe

19

Minority Views of
Professor Paul A. Rahe

Regarding the relations that existed between Thomas Jefferson and his slave Sally Hemings, lies were told long ago, and today, some two centuries after it was first suggested in print that the author of the Declaration of Independence fathered children with one of his slaves, we still cannot be certain as to who told the truth. On 1 September 1802, James T. Callender, an investigative journalist with a taste for scandal, a gift for invective, and a grudge against Jefferson, published an article in a Richmond paper called *The Recorder; or Lady's and Gentleman's Miscellany,* charging that it was "well known" that the man then holding office as President of the United States "for many years past has kept, as his concubine, one of his own slaves." He identified this slave as "Sally" and "her eldest son" as "Tom," and he reported that the latter was "ten or twelve years of age" and that "his features are said to bear a striking although sable resemblance to those of the president himself." "By this wench Sally," he added, "our president has had several children. There is not an individual in the neighborhood of Charlottesville who does not believe the story."[1]

It was not Jefferson's practice to countenance charges of this sort by responding directly to them, but in a letter of July, 1805, now lost, directed to "particular friends," he appears to have denied "all" of the various "allegations" directed against him in the press apart from one referring to a youthful indiscretion involving indelicate behavior on his part towards a married woman. His friends tended to regard the story told by Callender as preposterous. James Madison told its author "that he had known Mr. Jefferson for the greater part of his life; and that he knew so much about the excellence of his heart, as to make this allegation incredible."[2] But there were those tolerably well-acquainted with Jefferson who came to think otherwise. His friend John Hartwell Cocke referred in his diary in late January, 1853 to "Mr. Jeffersons notorious example" in a context in which he was discussing the fact that it was commonplace for slave owners to father children with their slaves. "In Virginia," he wrote more than six years thereafter, "this damnable practice prevails as much as anywhere — and probably more — as Mr. Jefferson's example can be [cited?] for its defence."

On her deathbed, Jefferson's daughter Martha Jefferson Randolph, who had long resided with her father at Monticello, is said fiercely to have denied the charge and to have drawn the attention of her two sons to the fact that one of Sally Hemings's children — "the slave," her elder son later noted, "who most resembled" her father in appearance — was born at a time when her father and Sally Hemings had been "far distant

---

1. Unless otherwise specified, here and hereafter, I quote from the documentary evidence collected in the appendices to Thomas Jefferson Memorial Foundation Research Committee, *Report on Thomas Jefferson and Sally Hemings,* January, 2000, which can be accessed on the Internet.
2. *The Recorder* (Richmond), 29 September 1802.

from each other" for some "fifteen months." Years later, Henry S. Randall, the historian to whom Martha's son Thomas Jefferson Randolph related this story, reported to a correspondent that he was able "from well known circumstances to prove the fifteen months separation" when he came across the pertinent slave's date of birth in "an old account book" belonging to Thomas Jefferson.

Thomas Jefferson Randolph, who had charge of Monticello at the time that a number of Sally Hemings's children were born, acknowledged to Randall that "she had children which resembled" his grandfather "so closely that it was plain that they had his blood in their veins." Their paternity, however, he attributed not to Jefferson himself but to Peter Carr, one of the sons of Jefferson's sister and his close friend, her late husband Dabney Carr. Peter Carr's connection with Sally Hemings was, he averred, "perfectly notorious at Monticello," "scarcely disguised," "never disavowed," and on one occasion in his presence openly confessed.

There need be no doubt that Jefferson's grandson told Randall that one of the two Carr brothers was responsible.[3] In October, 1858, when his younger sister Ellen Randolph Coolidge came to visit, he told her much the same tale. "There is a general impression," she wrote her husband, "that the four children of Sally Hemmings were *all* the children of Col. [Samuel] Carr, the most notorious good-natured Turk that ever was master of a black seraglio kept at other men's expense." To believe the calumnies spread concerning her grandfather, she observed, one must be willing to suppose that "he must have been carrying on his intrigues in the midst of his daughters family and insulting the sanctity of the home by his profligacy. But he had a large family of grandchildren of all ages, older & younger. Young men and young girls. He lived, whenever he was at Monticello, and entirely for the last fifteen years of his life, in the midst of these young people, surrounded by them, his intercourse with them of the freest and most affectionate kind. How comes it that his immoralities were never suspected by his own family—that his daughter and her children rejected with horror and contempt the charges brought against him. That my brother, then a young man certain to know all that was going on behind the scenes, positively declares his indignant belief in the imputation and solemnly affirms that he never saw or heard the smallest thing which could lead him to suspect that his grandfather's life was other than perfectly pure. His apartments had no private entrance not perfectly accessible and visible to all the household. No female domestic ever entered his chambers except at hours when he was known not to be there and none could have entered without being exposed to the public gaze. But again I put it to any fair mind to decide if a man so admirable to his domestic character as Mr. Jefferson, so devoted to his daughters and their children, so fond of their society, so tender, considerate, refined in his intercourse with them, so watchful over them in all respects, would be likely to rear a race of half-breeds under their eyes and carry on his low amours in the circle of his family."[4]

The claims advanced by Thomas Jefferson Randolph and his sister are confirmed in part by the testimony of Edmund Bacon, who served Jefferson for a time as overseer. Years after his departure from Monticello, he told a minister of the Gospel in Kentucky that Jefferson was not the father of Harriet Hemings, whom he himself had put on a stage-coach for Philadelphia "when she was nearly grown" and to whom he had given, on Jef-

---

3. As will become clear, there is some confusion in the record as to which of the two brothers— Peter or Samuel—Jefferson's grandson implicated.

4. Using the facisimile copy of this letter provided in the Thomas Jefferson Memorial Foundation Research Committee's *Report on Thomas Jefferson and Sally Hemings*, I have corrected the committee's transcription of it.

ferson's instructions, fifty dollars to start her on her way. "She was as white as anybody," he reported, "and very beautiful. People said he freed her because she was his own daughter. She was not his daughter; she was ___ ___'s daughter. I know that. I have seen him come out of her mother's room many a morning when I went up to Monticello very early."

In 1873, however, Sally Hemings's penultimate son Madison, then a man of advanced age, told the editor of the *Pike County Republican* in Ohio that his mother had become "Mr. Jefferson's concubine" in Paris where, for eighteen months, she served as "body servant" to his daughter Maria. When Jefferson was summoned home, Madison Hemings reported, his mother was already pregnant by him. "He desired to bring my mother back to Virginia with him but she demurred. She was just beginning to understand the French language well, and in France she was free, while if she returned to Virginia she would be re-enslaved. So she refused to return with him. To induce her to do so he promised her extraordinary privileges, and made a solemn pledge that her children should be freed at the age of twenty-one years. In consequence of his promise, on which she implicitly relied, she returned with him to Virginia. Soon after their arrival, she gave birth to a child of whom Thomas Jefferson was the father. It lived but a short time. She gave birth to four others, and Jefferson was the father of all of them. Their names were Beverly, Harriet, Madison (myself), and Eston—three sons and one daughter. We all became free agreeably to the treaty entered into by our parents before we were born."

Madison Hemings's fellow former Monticello slave Israel (Gillette) Jefferson later gave an interview to the editor of the same newspaper and confirmed, in part, his friend's story—that Madison Hemings's mother was Jefferson's "concubine" and that Jefferson was the father of Beverly, Harriet, Madison, and Eston Hemings. The former claim he knew as a house servant from his "intimacy with both parties"; the latter he could "as conscientiously confirm ... as any other fact which I believe from circumstances but do not positively know."

Until quite recently, historians were inclined to dismiss the allegations of James Callender as irresponsible journalism, to discount the story told by Madison Hemings and confirmed in part by Israel Jefferson as self-serving, and to credit Thomas Jefferson Randolph's assertion that one of the Carr brothers fathered the children of Sally Hemings.[5] It seemed inconceivable that a man of Thomas Jefferson's character would have been guilty as charged.

In 1968, in his book *White Over Black*, Winthrop Jordan did observe, if only in passing, that Jefferson's account books failed to bear out the testimony of Martha Jefferson Randolph, her son Thomas Jefferson Randolph, and Herman S. Randall. In fact, he noted, Thomas Jefferson was present at Monticello on each and every occasion when Sally Hemings is known to have conceived, and he could therefore have been the father of all her known children, as Madison Hemings alleged.[6] Apart, however, from psycho-biographer Fawn Brodie, no one seems until quite recently to have reflected in print on the implica-

---

5. The best statement of this case was made in an essay written in 1960 by Douglass Adair. See Adair, "The Jefferson Scandals," *Fame and the Founding Fathers*, ed. Trevor Colbourn (New York: Norton, 1974) 160–91.

6. See Winthrop D. Jordan, *White Over Black: American Attitudes Towards the Negro, 1550–1812* (Chapel Hill: University of North Carolina Press, 1968) 465–68. See, now, Jordan, "Hemings and Jefferson: Redux," in *Sally Hemings & Thomas Jefferson: History, Memory, and Civic Culture*, ed. Jan Ellen Lewis and Peter S. Onuf (Charlottesville: University Press of Virginia, 1999) 35–51.

tions of Jordan's discovery, and her highly speculative approach to Jefferson's psychology did not recommend her book to academic historians.[7]

It was only in 1997, when law professor Annette Gordon-Reed published her *Thomas Jefferson and Sally Hemings: An American Controversy*, that the tide began to turn. By that time, students of slavery were almost all inclined to acknowledge that slave concubinage was as common as John Hartwell Cocke had supposed and that public silence regarding one's follies in this regard was part of the unwritten social code of the slaveholding class. Only those who lived openly with their concubines were subject to stern disapproval.[8] It also helped a great deal that Gordon-Reed's reassessment of the evidence was careful, thorough, and, for the most part, dispassionate.[9]

In consequence, when the storm broke in 1998 with the publication of a DNA study by a Charlottesville physician showing that Eston Hemings was a direct male descendant of Thomas Jefferson's grandfather, the great majority of historians were quick to conclude that Madison Hemings's testimony was largely true. I know whereof I speak, for I was one such — inclined, like most of my brethren, to suppose Callender's charges improbable; stunned by the DNA data, and more than willing, in the immediate aftermath, to believe Madison Hemings's claims. Only since consenting to review the evidence for the Jefferson-Hemings Scholars Commission have I begun to wonder whether the indictment against Thomas Jefferson is really true. I am still inclined, on balance, to think it more likely than not that he was the father of Eston Hemings, but I can now understand why honest and reasonable human beings can be deeply skeptical. On the available evidence, the charge remains unproven. The question of the relations of Thomas Jefferson and Sally Hemings is an historical puzzle of considerable complexity, and in the end we are forced to resort to educated guesswork.

Before resorting to such guesswork, I want to acknowledge a very considerable debt to Annette Gordon-Reed, whose book makes for compelling reading; to Dan Jordan and the staff of the Thomas Jefferson Memorial Foundation who have gathered and analyzed the available evidence in a manner that is highly professional, generally cautious, and exceedingly helpful to anyone wanting to review it for the purpose of making up his own mind; and to Professor Robert F. Turner of the Center for National Security Law at the University of Virginia School of Law, who organized the Jefferson-Hemings Scholars Commission and led its members in a reassessment of the available evidence item by item.

As should be clear from the material presented above, virtually every piece of available testimony on this subject can be impeached; virtually everyone who commented had an interest in saying what he or she said. James Callender believed that Jefferson had betrayed him and wanted revenge. Madison Hemings wanted to make himself more important by tracing his paternity to a famous man, and Israel Jefferson came to the support of a friend. Such are the charges that can be made. By the same token, it could be said that Martha Jefferson Randolph and her children were eager to protect the reputation of her father. They certainly had a personal stake in doing so, and it was not uncommon for members of their class to try to cover up the sort of misdeed with which Thomas Jefferson was charged. Something of the sort can be said concerning Jefferson's onetime overseer Edmund Bacon,

---

7. See Fawn Brodie, *Thomas Jefferson: An Intimate History* (New York: Norton, 1974).

8. In this connection, see Philip D. Morgan, "Interracial Sex in the Chesapeake and the British Atlantic World, c. 1700–1820," and Joshua D. Rothman, "James Callender and Social Knowledge of Interracial Sex in Antebellum Virginia," in *Sally Hemings & Thomas Jefferson* 52–84, 87–113.

9. See Annette Gordon-Reed, *Thomas Jefferson and Sally Hemings: An American Controversy* (Charlottesville: University Press of Virginia, 1997).

who could and did dine out on his connection with the great man. As for Herman S. Randall, he was among the initiators of the Jefferson cult. The value of his biography of the statesman depended on his compatriots' estimation of Thomas Jefferson's accomplishments and character. In the aftermath of the Civil War, southerners were looking for a useable history, and it made more sense to dwell on Jefferson's apparently unimpeachable example than to credit the charges once made against him. Monticello, as visitors are wont to comment, is a very small place. To believe that Thomas Jefferson carried on an extended affair with one of his slaves under the noses of his grandchildren would require that we rethink from the ground up our inherited image of the man.

I find two pieces of evidence impressive—first, the fact that the beginning of Sally Hemings's pregnancies coincided with Thomas Jefferson's sojourns at Monticello, and, second, the fact that at least one of her children was fathered by a direct male descendant of Jefferson's grandfather.

It is, of course, possible that Hemings was elsewhere during one or more of the pertinent visits by her master, but, in the absence of contrary evidence, it is unreasonable to think her anywhere other than her home. In a recent article in *The William & Mary Quarterly*, Monticello archaeologist Fraser D. Neiman has sought to demonstrate statistically, on the basis of Jefferson's presence each time she conceived, that he must have been the father.[10] This he has failed to achieve. What he has accomplished, however, is to show the very high likelihood that Sally Hemings's pregnancies are somehow due to Jefferson's presence. One can go even further. Given that she tended to get pregnant in the first month after his arrival, Neiman has established a correlation between Jefferson's homecomings and her pregnancies.

The most economical explanation would be that Jefferson himself sought her out on such occasions, but we must keep in mind that there is no good reason to believe that she had only one sexual partner. For what it is worth, the gossip reported by James Callender suggests the contrary.[11] On this question, in any case, we must keep an open mind. Slaves were generally not in a position to refuse when approached by white men. There is, then, a real possibility that some, if not all of Sally Hemings's pregnancies were a consequence of social calls made on Jefferson by his friends and relatives on the occasions of these homecomings. We know that visits to Monticello were rare in his absence and frequent when he was present. Among those whom Jefferson could expect to make such a social call shortly after he came home was his brother Randolph, who lived twenty miles away and had four or five sons. At the time of Eston Hemings's birth, Thomas Jefferson was 64; his brother Randolph was 52; and Randolph's sons ranged in age from about 17 to 26. All carried the tell-tale Y chromosome. Any one of them could have been Eston Hemings's father.

As it happens, we know that, at the very time that Sally Hemings became pregnant with her son Eston, Thomas Jefferson's brother Randolph was expressly invited to come to Monticello on the occasion of a visit by his twin sister. The surviving correspondence, limited as it is, suggests that he was a frequent visitor to Monticello and that ordinarily he did not come alone: we can, in fact, presume that he was usually accompanied by one or more of his sons. Furthermore, we have reason to suspect that his son Thomas may

---

10. Fraser D. Neiman, "Coincidence or Causal Connection? The Relationship between Thomas Jefferson's Visits to Monticello and Sally Hemings's Conceptions," *The William & Mary Quarterly* 57 (January, 2000): 198–210.

11. See *The Recorder*, 22 and 29 September, 5 November, and 1 December 1802. In this connection, see Gordon-Reed, *Thomas Jefferson and Sally Hemings* 61–62.

have been in residence at Monticello when Harriet Hemings was conceived and that his son Robert Lewis may have been present when Eston Hemings was conceived. We know also, from the testimony of Isaac Jefferson, a slave at Monticello, that, when he did visit, Randolph Jefferson "used to come out among black people, play the fiddle and dance half the night." We know that Thomas Jefferson's children and grandchildren referred to Randolph Jefferson as "Uncle Randolph"; we know that there was a somewhat confused tradition in the family that traced its descent back to Eston Hemings that they were descended from Thomas Jefferson's uncle or cousin;[12] and there is evidence of the existence of an oral tradition in more than one Albemarle County family that Randolph Jefferson had African-American offspring.[13] None of this proves that either Randolph Jefferson or one of his sons was Eston Hemings's father, but it does give one pause. And nothing in the available evidence rules out our wondering whether the charge lodged by Thomas Jefferson Randolph against the Carr brothers was not at least partially true. Despite what can be learned from the DNA evidence and what can be inferred from the apparent connection between Thomas Jefferson's sojourns at Monticello and Sally Hemings's pregnancies, the mystery remains unsolved.

Further light may one day be shed on this question. Sally Hemings's eldest son Beverly Hemings ran away from Monticello when he was in his early twenties and was never found. He apparently made his way to Washington, D. C., married, and started a family, and there is reason to believe that he passed as white. Someday one of his direct male descendants may turn up and may be willing to undergo a DNA test. Furthermore, in the U. S. Military Cemetery at Fort Leavenworth, in Kansas, lie the remains of Madison Hemings's son William Beverly Hemings, who has no known descendants. It may be possible to exhume his body and collect a DNA sample. If it could be shown that the son of Madison Hemings or a descendant of his elder brother Beverly was a Jefferson, we could be more confident that Thomas Jefferson Randolph had lied to Herman S. Randall and to his sister concerning the brothers Carr, and the only plausible explanation for lying on his part would be the knowledge that his grandfather was, in fact, the father of Sally Hemings's children.

There is also the mysterious "Tom" mentioned by James Callender. Madison Hemings knew nothing of him: he was told of a child born to his mother at about the time that this Tom would have been born, but this child supposedly died in early infancy. In the records at Monticello, no such Tom appears.[14] These records are scanty in the period stretching from 1783 to 1794, when Callender's "Tom" would have been born, but they are more fulsome thereafter when Thomas Jefferson resumed his earlier practice of making notations in his *Farm Book*. The absence of any mention of the pertinent Tom therein suggests that Callender may have, in this particular, been misinformed. It is, nonetheless, true that none of Jefferson's defenders rose to Callender's challenge by denying the existence of his "Tom"; and when the Federalist editor of Virginia's *Frederick-Town Herald* looked into the matter, he claims to have discovered what he termed "circumstances of confirmation," reporting that there was a "Sally" and that she worked as a "seamstress" within

---

12. See Lucia Stanton and Dianne Swann-Wright, "Bonds of Memory: Identity and the Hemings Family," in *Sally Hemings & Thomas Jefferson* 161–83 (at 174). Stanton and Swann-Wright are, I think, too quick to discount this evidence.

13. See Chapter Eleven of Professor Turner's Individual View.

14. For a thorough discussion of what can be gleaned from these records and from the other evidence with regard to Sally's mother Elizabeth Hemings and her many descendants, see Lucia Stanton, *Free Some Day: The African-American Families of Monticello* (Monticello: The Thomas Jefferson Memorial Foundation, 2000) 102–40.

the Jefferson household; observing that "she is an industrious and orderly creature"; and noting that "her son, whom Callender calls President Tom," did, indeed, bear "a strong likeness to Mr. Jefferson."[15]

There is, moreover, a family which traces its ancestry to a freedman named Thomas C. Woodson, and in its various branches the members of this family have preserved an oral tradition that this Tom Woodson was the son of Sally Hemings and Thomas Jefferson. In this case, the DNA evidence rules out paternity on the part of any Jefferson (or, for that matter, any Carr).[16] If Thomas C. Woodson was, nonetheless, a son of Sally Hemings, the "Tom" mentioned by Callender, she had more than one lover in the course of her life, and Callender was wrong about the paternity of the slave who looked so much like the President. It is also possible that further investigation will turn up another candidate more likely to have been Callender's "Tom" and that he has direct male descendants whose DNA can be compared with the samples already collected.

As things stand, however, it all comes down to what we think of Thomas Jefferson. Was he capable of doing what Ellen Randolph Coolidge considered unthinkable — of "carrying on his intrigues in the midst of his daughters family and insulting the sanctity of the home by his profligacy?" As professional historians, Douglass Adair once noted, we have been "taught to be extremely skeptical of any purported episode in a man's career that completely contradicts the whole tenor of his life and that requires belief in a total reversal of character."[17] As human beings, however, we are nonetheless acutely, even painfully aware of our own capacity for self-deception, hypocrisy, and outright deceit. If in one part of his life, Thomas Jefferson behaved in a manner at odds with the dictates of respectability that, almost without exception, he faithfully honored in the rest of his life, would it be terribly surprising?

I have long been persuaded that we do not know Thomas Jefferson at all well; that virtually all of the surviving letters written after he had entered on the public stage were composed not only for their particular correspondents but for posterity; that he donned a mask at a very early age and very rarely let it slip; that he cared far more about his future reputation than about anything else; that his conduct in public life was less than honest and forthcoming; that he was more prone to vanity and hypocrisy than figures such as George Washington, Alexander Hamilton, and James Madison; and that, in contrast with John Adams, introspection was decidedly his short suit.[18] I do not find it particularly hard to imagine that a lonely widower, who had sworn to his dying wife that he would not remarry and subject their daughters to a stepmother, should have found a beautiful young woman such as his deceased wife's slave half-sister a temptation more

---

15. *Frederick-Town Herald*, reprinted in *The Recorder*, 8 December 1802. See Gordon-Reed, *Thomas Jefferson and Sally Hemings* 63–64.

16. Any attempt to salvage the Woodson family claim to Jeffersonian descent on the presumption that at some point there was an unacknowledged interruption in the line of paternity founders on the fact that three such lines of descent from Thomas C. Woodson have now been tested. To think the Woodson family claim plausible in this particular, one would have to presume that Thomas C. Woodson was cuckolded thrice. Cf. Joseph J. Ellis, "Jefferson: Post-DNA," *William & Mary Quarterly* 57 (2000): 125–38 (126–27).

17. Adair, "The Jefferson Scandals," 181.

18. See Paul A. Rahe, *Republics Ancient and Modern: Classical Republicanism and the American Revolution* (Chapel Hill: University of North Carolina Press, 1992) 617–772. In this last connection, consider what Joseph J. Ellis, *Founding Brothers: The Revolutionary Generation* (New York: Knopf, 2000) and Joanne B. Freeman, *Affairs of Honor: National Politics in the New Republic* (forthcoming in October, 2001), have to say about Jefferson's political *modus operandi*. Note also Andrew Burstein, "Jefferson's Rationalizations," *William & Mary Quarterly* 57 (2000): 183–97.

than he could bear. And once he had given way to lust, what was there to prevent him, even if he sought to exercise an iron self-control, from slipping again? He was, after all, a man subject to temptation like other men, and he must have known that his family would do what it could to hide whatever dark secrets he may have harbored.

In 1781–82, prior to his extended sojourn in Paris, Thomas Jefferson remarked in his *Notes on the State of Virginia* that "the whole commerce between master and slave is a perpetual exercise of the most boisterous passions, the most unremitting despotism on the one part, and degrading submissions on the other," and he then added that "the man must be a prodigy who can retain his manners and morals undepraved by such circumstances."[19] Was the proprietor of Monticello such a prodigy? There were, we know, others within the slaveholding class who were, and they were more numerous than we might be inclined to think. In the end, one's judgment really does depend on what one thinks of the man who drafted the Declaration of Independence, wrote the Virginia Statute of Religious Liberty, founded the University of Virginia, denounced slavery in unequivocal terms, and yet gave sanction in his *Notes on the State of Virginia* to the pseudo-scientific racial doctrines that were later used to justify slavery as a positive good.[20] To be frank, I know not what to think. Regarding the relations that existed between Thomas Jefferson and his slave Sally Hemings, lies were told long ago, and today, even with the help of DNA analysis, we still cannot be certain as to who told the truth.

What we do know, however, is damning enough. Despite the distaste that he expressed for the propensity of slaveholders to abuse their power, Jefferson either engaged in such abuse himself or tolerated it on the part of one or more members of his extended family. In his private, as in his public, life, there was, for all his brilliance and sagacity, something dishonest, something self-serving and self-indulgent about the man.

---

19. Thomas Jefferson, *Notes on the State of Virginia*, ed. William Peden (Chapel Hill: University of North Carolina Press, 1954) Query XVIII.

20. Jean Yarbrough, "Race and the Moral Foundations of the American Republic: Another Look at the Declaration and the *Notes on Virginia*," *The Journal of Politics* 53 (1991): 90–105.

Editor's Postscript:
Reactions to the Scholars Commission Report
Professor Robert F. Turner

20

Editor's Postscript: Reactions to the Scholars Commission Report

The comments that follow are not a part of the formal report of the Scholars Commission and represent only the views of the editor. They are included in this volume with the thought that some readers may find them of interest. However, they have not been shared in advance with all members of the Commission, and responsibility for the accuracy of facts and judgments expressed in this chapter is the editor's alone.

Ten years have passed since the Scholars Commission Report was released. As the revised and expanded book version is finally going to press[1] it seems useful to note some of the initial reactions and subsequent developments, and to respond to some of the criticisms of our report that have come to my attention. I cannot justify the delay, which is my fault alone. But perhaps I should try to explain it.

I had promised the final version of the Scholars Commission Report to Carolina Academic Press by November 2001. But my "day job" involves legal scholarship about terrorism and related national security issues, and the terrorist attacks of September 11, 2001, left me no choice but to set this project aside. The demands of my work simply left me with no spare time.

At the same time, the events of that historic date made it all the more important that the record be set straight, because—perhaps more than any other human being in history—Thomas Jefferson is the antithesis to the bigotry and intolerance of Osama bin Laden and his terrorist followers. Indeed, in a letter to the editor of the *New York Times* published in late 2001, science writer Steven T. Corneliussen argued: "History may well remember Osama bin Laden as the anti-Jefferson, the benighted opponent of inalienable human rights, religion-respecting secular democracy and progress based on reason.... Jefferson's vision of history is now more vital than ever."[2] As we seek to deal with these

---

1. Our report was available for anyone in the world with Internet access to download and read for several years, first at www.mindspring.com/~tjshcommission and then, after demand for the report exceeded the permissible bandwidth of that site, at http://www.geocities.com/tjshcommission/. Not being knowledgeable about managing Web pages, I prevailed upon the late Eyler Coates, Jr., to establish this free account and maintain the site on our behalf. Unfortunately, I did not think to ask for the password to access the site prior to Eyler's untimely passing in January 2002; so through 2002 and most of 2003 it existed without being maintained and then disappeared. Since the book version was expected to be published soon, when the second site stopped working I did not attempt to establish a third site.

2. Steven T. Corneliussen, *Black and White in a New America*, Dec. 24, 2001 at A16.

new threats from abroad, all Americans should cherish the traditions of human freedom Thomas Jefferson and his contemporaries bequeathed to us.

I would add that, as with so many other areas, Jefferson's contribution in America's earliest struggle against terrorists was tremendous. He argued over many years with his friend John Adams about the need for a navy so the new nation could protect its commerce from the Barbary Pirates; but Adams' more pragmatic approach—that it was cheaper to pay tribute than to raise a navy, and that the states of Europe would not think less of America for doing precisely what the Europeans were already doing—prevailed during our nation's first dozen years.

But, at his first cabinet meeting after being elected President, Jefferson (with the unanimous support of his cabinet) decided to order two-thirds of the new American navy to sail to the Mediterranean with orders to sink and burn pirate ships at will if they learned that the Bey of Tripoli had, as expected, declared war against America for not increasing its annual tribute. For two centuries the European powers had been paying tribute, but Jefferson's successful defense of American rights on the high seas led ultimately to an assertion by European states of their own rights and to an end to the reign of terror of the Barbary Pirates.[3]

Thomas Jefferson has indeed left us a great legacy for which all Americans should be in his debt. I believe the work of the Scholars Commission in helping to establish the truth in the Jefferson-Hemings controversy is all the more important in the wake of the terrorist attacks of September 11, 2001.

The Press Conference

Several members of the Scholars Commission gathered at the National Press Club in Washington, D.C., on April 12, 2001—the day before Thomas Jefferson's 258th birthday—to distribute copies of our report and answer questions from media representatives. Attendance at the press conference exceeded our expectations, especially after we learned that a few blocks away at the White House President George W. Bush was hosting an event for descendants of Thomas Jefferson and Sally Hemings. There were allegations that people in the White House had confirmed that the last-minute event was arranged at the suggestion of the Thomas Jefferson Foundation (Monticello), and speculation that the timing (celebrating Jefferson's birthday a day early[4]) had been planned to draw attention away from the release of our report.[5]

---

3. *See, e.g.,* Robert F. Turner, *State Responsibility and the War on Terror: The Legacy of Thomas Jefferson and the Barbary Pirates*, 4 CHICAGO J. INT'L L. 121 (2003); and Robert F. Turner, *President Jefferson and the Barbary Pirates*, in PIRACY AND MARITIME CRIME: HISTORICAL AND MODERN CASE STUDIES 157 (Bruce A. Elleman, Andrew Forbes & David Rosenberg, eds., 2010).

4. When it became clear that our report would be finished in early April, I proposed that we schedule our press conference the day before Jefferson's birthday with the thought that it might increase press interest in our report and perhaps lead to some additional editorial coverage in connection with Jefferson's birthday on Friday.

5. Thomas Jefferson Heritage Society President John Works, whom I first met just prior to our Washington press conference, was reported to have claimed that the President had been "duped" by those who scheduled the White House event. (*See, e.g., The Wrong Jefferson?*, WASH. POST, Apr. 15, 2001.) Given the reports that the event had been orchestrated on short notice and at the same time as our press conference, I initially found the circumstantial case troubling, but I was assured by the Chairman of the Board of the Thomas Jefferson Foundation that the White House had initiated the discussions and the Foundation had merely sought to be cooperative—which, given the reputation of the indi-

Whatever the explanation, as it turned out the White House event almost certainly increased the attention paid to our report. Many journalists could not resist the temptation to combine the stories, often complete with a photograph of a smiling President Bush meeting with descendants of Sally Hemings, and noting that just as this was taking place a group of prominent scholars a few blocks away was casting serious doubt upon the Hemingses' claim.[6]

It may also have been a slow news day, for the following day the story was covered in almost every major American daily newspaper[7]—several with page-one coverage—and in countless local papers as well based upon AP, UPI, or other news service accounts. As we had hoped, several editorials making reference to our report also appeared.[8] And like the original 1802 allegations, the Scholars Commission report crossed the Atlantic and was publicized in prominent European newspapers.[9]

The report also received extensive coverage on CNN, beginning Thursday evening and continuing through much of Friday. National Public Radio (NPR) ran the story, Bryant Gumbel mentioned it on Friday morning's CBS News Early Show, and stories were carried as well on ABC, NBC, MSNBC, and Fox News.

In the months that followed, there were other encouraging signs that our efforts had produced positive results. Just before our report was released, *American Heritage* ran a story suggesting that the DNA tests had ended the debate over a Jefferson-Hemings affair. But early the following year, the editors noted the conclusions of our report and asserted: "it's important for the public to realize that the purported Jefferson-Hemings liaison remains a disputed possibility, not an established fact."[10]

---

viduals involved, I am confident was a truthful statement. Whether individual employees at Monticello may have independently encouraged such contact is less clear.

6. *See, e.g.,* William Branigin, *Pruning Thomas Jefferson's Family Tree: Historians' Report Attacks Theory That 3rd President Fathered Slave's Children,* WASH. POST, April 13, 2001 ("The release of the 550-page report by a panel of 13 scholars from across the country came as President Bush hosted a gathering in honor of Jefferson's birthday that a White House spokesman said included 'both family members from [Jefferson's] marriage with Martha Wayles Jefferson and his descendants from Sally Hemings.'"); Michael Killan, *Panel Rebuts Jefferson-Hemings Theory,* CHICAGO TRIB., Apr. 13, 2001 ("the report was issued as President Bush played host to Jefferson and Hemings family descendants for a White House celebration of Jefferson's birthday"); *Report Says Jefferson Didn't Do It,* DES MOINES REGISTER, Apr. 13, 2001 ("The 258th anniversary of Thomas Jefferson's birth was marked Thursday with a visit to the White House by descendants of Sally Hemings, a Jefferson slave, and the revival of a 200-year-old debate over whether the third president fathered the children of his servant. A new study ... contradicts previous theories...."); Jeffrey T. Kuhner, *Bush Recognizes Black Jefferson Kin: Scholars Doubt Slave Child Story,* WASH. TIMES, Apr. 13, 2001; *Study Finds Jefferson Unlikely Slave Father,* PLAIN DEALER, Apr. 13, 2001 ("As President Bush was welcoming a multiracial group of descendants of Thomas Jefferson to a White House ceremony yesterday commemorating the birthday, a panel of scholars released a 500-page report concluding that Jefferson probably did not father any children by his slave Sally Hemings.").

7. The only exceptions that came to my attention at the time were the *Wall Street Journal* and the *Los Angeles Times.* However, a few weeks later the *Journal* printed a lengthy op-ed I had written summarizing our conclusions. *See* Robert F. Turner, *The Truth About Jefferson,* WALL STREET JOURNAL, July 3, 2001.

8. *See, e.g., A Happy Occasion for Jeffersonians,* OMAHA WORLD-HERALD, Apr. 16, 2001 ("So the question is still open. Those of us who thought it had ended with the last report were guilty of judging prematurely."); *Jefferson and Hemings redux,* WASH. TIMES, July 11, 2001; *It Seems to Us...,* BUFFALO NEWS, Apr. 14, 2001, at C10; and Robert L. Bartley, *Thinking Things Over: Accountability for Anderson, Also the High-Minded,* WALL STREET JOURNAL, Mar. 18, 2002.

9. *See, e.g.,* Laura Peek, *Jefferson Child Theory Disputed,* TIMES (London), Apr. 14, 2001; *Jefferson "did not father slave boy,"* THE INDEPENDENT (London), Apr. 13, 2001.

10. *Doubts About Jefferson and Hemings: The Debate Goes On,* AMERICAN HERITAGE, March 2002.

The influence of the Scholars Commission report was also evident on several Web sites identified by searching "Jefferson Hemings." A biography of Sally Hemings on u-s-history.com, for example, noted:

> An article in *Nature* (November 5, 1998) reported that DNA samples taken from Jefferson descendants was [*sic*] compared with Hemings' descendants and concluded that Jefferson may have fathered one of Sally Hemings' sons.

> Later research casts doubt on the earlier findings and notes that other Jefferson relatives lived in close proximity to the Monticello household and one could have been the father of the child or children in question.

> Perhaps a more accurately state [*sic*] question is, "Which Jefferson fathered the Hemings children?"[11]

A 2002 *Google* search of the Internet for "Jefferson Hemings" produced forty-five pages of Web listings, beginning with the primary link to the Scholars Commission report. Ignoring links that pre-dated the release of our report, fewer than one-third of the first two-dozen sites presented the allegation of a Jefferson-Hemings sexual relationship as established fact, and most ranged from doubtful to very doubtful.

Not everyone learned of our study, and not all who did found it persuasive. Indeed, some groups that should have known better still seemed ignorant of the basic findings of the 1998 DNA tests, which proved beyond any reasonable doubt that Thomas Woodson could not have been the child of Thomas Jefferson.[12] For example, the American Library Association in 2001 listed Byron W. Woodson's *A President in the Family* as an "Editor's Choice," and the following year listed it as among the top-ten African-American *nonfiction* books.[13] After appearing on a public television program with Mr. Woodson, I politely asked him how he dealt with the DNA evidence pointing against his claim. He explained (correctly) that there was no known DNA sample from *Thomas* Jefferson, and reasoned: "perhaps he was illegitimate." The one thing that he seemed certain about was that his family oral tradition was more probative of the truth than any DNA tests.

I have not seen any scientific polling of public perceptions on the Jefferson-Hemings issue following our report. A month after the report was released, however, I attended portions of a reunion of my law school class, and one of the attorneys at my dinner table remarked that he had seen my name in his local paper in connection with our inquiry. Most of the people at the table—working in various locations across the United States— were at least aware that the story had recently been called into serious question by some new report or evidence. It was hardly a sufficient sample to draw scientific conclusions, but I was nevertheless encouraged by the response.

---

11. *See* http://www.u-s-history.com/pages/h665.html.

12. *See* Chapter One of my Individual Views.

13. Dr. Douglas Day, Director of the Albemarle Charlottesville Historical Society, press release dated July 1, 2003, distributed by e-mail. In the press release, Dr. Day adds: "Wherever one falls in the on-going debate about Jefferson's relationship with Sally Hemings, an objective reader must acknowledge that *A President in the Family* is masterfully written, and a thoroughly compelling story,...." The Woodson family's history is inextricably entwined with that of the Jeffersons." *Id.* In fact, the only evidence that "the Woodson family's history is inextricably entwined with that of the Jeffersons" is Thomas Woodson's allegation that he was the famous son of Sally Hemings named "Tom" and mentioned in the Callender allegations. He may or may not have been the child of Sally Hemings. While Byron Woodson's book may well be "masterfully written, and a thoroughly compelling story," one would expect an historian familiar with the facts to at least observe that overwhelming scientific tests have now established that the story is *fiction*.

The Monticello Association Vote

In 1913, descendants of Thomas Jefferson's daughters Martha and Maria created a family organization known as the "Monticello Association" (MA) to celebrate their heritage, promote the reputation and fame of Thomas Jefferson, and provide for the maintenance of the family graveyard at Monticello, which was deeded to the descendants of Jefferson's daughters. Even before the DNA tests became public, descendants of Thomas Woodson had sought admission to the group and permission to be buried in the graveyard. Publication of the *Nature*[14] report on the DNA tests led to demands by not only Woodson descendants, but also those of Madison and Eston Hemings, for admission to the family group; and the family's failure to immediately grant admission was criticized by many—including some family members—as evidence of racial bigotry.

At its 1999 annual meeting, the MA welcomed fifty-five Hemings family members to their annual meeting in Charlottesville as "guests," while appointing a Membership Advisory Committee (MAC) to examine the facts and make a recommendation on granting them full membership. Dr. Eugene Foster, who had organized the DNA tests and co-authored one of the *Nature* articles, addressed the group. Based upon conversations with MA members, there was media speculation that the Hemingses would soon be admitted.[15] Many MA members were shocked by the new DNA evidence, but most seemed anxious to "do the right thing" and the relatively small faction that openly refused to accept the Hemingses' claim was treated coolly by most of the family. At the 2000 annual meeting, Dianne Swann-Wright and Lucia Stanton—the principal authors of the *Monticello Report* released earlier that year—addressed the group, as did the Monticello committee's sole dissenting voice, Dr. White McKenzie Wallenborn. Many observers expected the family to vote formally to accept Hemings applicants into membership at the meeting scheduled for May 2001.

Word that the Scholars Commission would be releasing a report on the subject in April 2001 led to a decision to delay the vote on admitting the Hemingses until the 2002 annual MA meeting. Knowing that the MA (along with the Thomas Jefferson Foundation and the Thomas Jefferson Heritage Society) had a special interest in the issue, when our summary report (pages 3–21 of this volume) was completed I e-mailed copies simultaneously to the heads of all three organizations at the end of the first week in April. I was invited to make a presentation to the Monticello Association annual meeting the following month, at which time I received a courteous reception. Based upon the questions from the audience—including several from Hemings family members present as guests—and comments made to me before I left the hotel, I had no idea how the family would vote on the issue. Early the following year, the MAC recommended that the Hemings descendants not be admitted to full membership but that an umbrella organization be created to promote further interaction between the Jeffersons and Hemingses/Woodsons. The issue of full membership in the MA could be revisited if additional evidence was found in the future supporting their claim.

---

14. *See* Chapter One of my Individual Views.

15. *See, e.g.,* Patrick Rogers Glenn Garelik & Amanda Crawford, *Out of the Past: All Tom's Children—A President's presumed affair with a slave gives new meaning to the term Jeffersonian*, PEOPLE, Nov. 23, 1998. ("Now even such stalwart Jefferson defenders as the members of the Monticello Association, who trace their pedigrees back to Jefferson's two daughters with Martha, seem to have backed down in the face of the DNA tests.... 'Who knows,' says the group's secretary, Gerald Morgan, 75, who had once discounted the President's affair as a 'moral impossibility.' 'It was probably [Thomas] Jefferson who was the father.'")

I was invited to attend portions of the May 2002 MA annual meeting as a guest, in part on the theory that questions about our report or the facts of the case might arise on which I might be able to shed some light. To provide for a full exchange of views, a large meeting hall away from the hotel where the group was meeting was reserved for a public discussion of the issue. There was a good deal of back and forth by both sides, although most of the speakers seemed to come from what might be described as the "paternity-belief" camp.

What struck me the most about the comments, however, was that the nature of the argument had dramatically changed. Rather than alleging that the DNA tests had resolved the issue, that Jefferson had freed all of Sally's children at the age of twenty-one and otherwise given her special treatment unlike that given to any other slaves, and the like, there was very little substantive rhetoric in favor of admission. As the meeting progressed, the emotions increased. Several members of the Woodson family announced that their strong "oral history" was more persuasive than the DNA tests, and a common theme was that anyone who opposed their admission was a racist. This, in turn, understandably offended some of the descendants of Martha and Maria Jefferson (who, I sensed, felt they had been very civil to the Hemingses for the previous two years), and the debate became even more rancorous. When one MA member made reference to the Scholars Commission report, an angry Woodson family member shouted that it was "funded by the KKK." Someone else said that it had been "refuted" by a recent issue of the *National Genealogical Society Quarterly* (which will be discussed below), but there was little substantive debate on the merits and I heard no specific attempt to challenge a single one of our factual conclusions. However, several Hemings family members and supporters made it clear that if the family voted against admission they would immediately rush to tell the assembled media that the vote was motivated by racial bigotry—an approach that did little to calm the growing anger on both sides of the debate.

I was surprised by the margin of the subsequent 67-to-5 vote against admitting the Hemings and Woodson applicants to membership. Ironically, this 93% margin was within one percent of the 12-to-1 (92.3%) margin by which the Scholars Commission concluded that the story of a sexual relationship between Thomas Jefferson and Sally Hemings was probably not true. Even more surprising was the nearly four-to-one margin by which the proposal for an umbrella organization was rejected—which I attributed largely to the strong emotions obviously felt by many Jefferson descendants in response to the allegation that they were motivated by racism. Immediately following the first vote, many of the Woodsons, Hemingses, and their supporters within the MA rushed out of the room to announce the decision to the media and denounce those who voted with the majority as bigots. The obvious anger apparent in the remarks of several Jefferson descendants who tried to counter the charges in front of the TV cameras certainly contributed further to the perception by many in the media that the vote was founded in racism. From my perspective, however, it appeared to be motivated instead by an understandable displeasure that, after years of welcoming the Hemings descendants as guests and examining the facts in great detail, they were being repaid by what appeared to be almost a blackmail scheme. The clear message of many of the Woodson and Hemings guests was, whatever the facts, vote to admit us now or you will be denounced as racists. I could not help but note the irony that the original allegation published two hundred years earlier by James Callender had also been part of a blackmail scheme.[16]

---

16. *See* Chapter Three of my Individual Views.

The Thomas Jefferson Foundation (Monticello)

Perhaps the most difficult group to understand in this controversy has been the Thomas Jefferson Foundation (TJF, known as the Thomas Jefferson *Memorial* Foundation [TJMF] until 2000), which following the DNA studies became one of the strongest champions of the paternity story. As discussed in the original chapters to my Individual Views in this report, the Foundation's in-house "Research Committee" produced a seriously flawed report in January 2000 that one of its members asserted seemed to have been written to support a position already arrived at by Monticello leaders. Many of the errors found in Professor Annette Gordon-Reed's *Thomas Jefferson and Sally Hemings* are repeated in the *Monticello Report*, including a quotation from the altered transcription of a letter from Jefferson's granddaughter, Ellen Randolph Coolidge.[17]

When I first met with TJF President Daniel Jordan after being appointed chairman of the Scholars Commission in mid-2000, he seemed anxious to cooperate fully with our inquiry and expressed high praise for the scholars who had agreed to take part in the inquiry—with a single exception, who subsequently withdrew from the project before the report was completed.[18] I was more than fully satisfied with the cooperation I received throughout our inquiry both from Dr. Jordan and his senior research staff. But in taking groups of visitors on Monticello tours in 2000 and early 2001, I sensed a dramatic shift in focus and indeed a *hostility* by some guides towards Jefferson that I had never seen before during numerous visits over several decades to Thomas Jefferson's Monticello.

My impressions were reinforced by several current and former Monticello guides who contacted me and reported that guides who questioned the official TJF position affirming the high probability that Jefferson fathered Sally Hemings' children were being threatened with dismissal. The dropping of the name "Memorial" from the Foundation's name was reinforced by reports that guides were told that the Foundation was "no longer in the business of *memorializing* Thomas Jefferson."

I was also confused and surprised when I was told that, shortly after being notified of the date and time of our press conference, TJF officials had reportedly contacted the White House and promoted an "early" birthday celebration bringing Jefferson and Hemings descendants together for a photo opportunity with the President.[19] The allegation made no sense to me. Even if Monticello scholars had found the DNA evidence persuasive, surely they would welcome a new scholarly inquiry—all the more so after they

---

17. Errors in the *Monticello Report* are discussed extensively in my Individual Views. The Coolidge transcript alterations are illustrated in **Figures 3** and **4** on pages 36 and 37.

18. The individual in question did not withdraw over a difference with the group's majority over substantive conclusions, but rather because he was heavily committed in trying to finish another book and felt that he needed many more months before he would be able to do justice to this issue. Without dissent, the rest of the group agreed to postpone our report for several months, but when at that time he reported that he still had not found time to begin his research and the rest of the group decided that further delays for the research he had in mind would be unlikely to produce new evidence that would alter anyone's view, he elected to withdraw.

19. I have no way of knowing with certainty whether these reports were true, or not. There was ample evidence that Jefferson descendants were invited on short notice subsequent to the announcement of our press conference, and I was told that some invitees had been informed that the program had been suggested by the Thomas Jefferson Foundation. My accounts were at least third-hand, so I cannot be certain of the details. But I am not inclined to question to words of the Chairman of the Board and President of the Thomas Jefferson Foundation, and thus am confident that any such suggestion was not approved by the Monticello board.

learned that our findings might be expected to restore some of the luster to Thomas Jefferson's public image.

In addition to simultaneously e-mailing an advance copy of our summary report to the leaders of the TJF, the MA, and the TJHS, I offered all three groups an advance copy of our full report as soon as it could be reproduced.[20] Dr. Jordan courteously thanked me for the offer, but explained that the TJF Board of Directors would be meeting during the week of our press conference and planning for the annual commemoration of Jefferson's birthday would leave no time for anyone to review our report in advance.[21] Four days after the Washington press conference, I arranged for a copy of our full report to be hand-delivered to Monticello for Dr. Jordan. The following day, April 17, 2001, I received an e-mail from Dr. Jordan confirming receipt of the report and saying "we look forward to giving it a close reading."[22] Two days later, Dr. Jordan requested additional copies of the report in a message that began: "The press of daily business has kept us from reviewing your large report in detail...."[23]

Since no one at Monticello would have even *seen* our full report until the week following our press conference, I assumed that any press inquiries to Monticello in connection with the initial release of our report would be met with a general statement—perhaps noting that TJF scholars had not yet had an opportunity to read the full report, but that they welcomed new scholarship on the issue and looked forward to reading it. Instead, press accounts published the day after our press conference (several days before the first copy of the full report was delivered to Monticello) produced a dismissive response.

A UPI story filed a few hours after our press conference on April 12 reported:

> Daniel Jordan, president of the Thomas Jefferson Foundation in Charlottesville, Va., said the study does not offer any new information, but simply reexamines the existing data from another perspective.

> The Foundation has concluded, based on its own research, that Jefferson and Hemings were the parents of at least one child.

> "We're confident about our own findings, but always welcome new evidence which we will take seriously," Jordan told United Press International. "But there is no new evidence here, no original evidence." ...

> Jordan told UPI, "We never said that DNA proved it. We said that the science and the history, especially the oral history, suggest a high probability that Thomas Jefferson fathered all of Sally Hemings' children."[24]

A Cox News reporter wrote: "The findings were questioned by Daniel P. Jordan, president of the Thomas Jefferson Foundation. 'Their scholars disagree with our scholars,' he said. 'We are confident about our findings....'"[25] A *Chicago Tribune* writer reported: "Daniel

---

20. Turner e-mail to John Works, Dan Jordan, and James Truscott, dated April 6, 2001, subject: DRAFT of Scholar's [*sic*] Commission Report. The e-mail noted that there were several hundred pages of "individual views" that were still being finalized and would not be available until the press conference on April 12.

21. "With our Board meeting just ahead, I'll not likely have a chance to review your report until much later. Thanks again for sharing a copy, and all the best. Dan." Dan Jordan e-mail to Bob Turner dated April 10, 2001.

22. Dan Jordan e-mail to Bob Turner dated Tue, 17 April 2001.

23. *Id.,* Thursday, 19 April 2001.

24. Kurt Samson, *Slave Children Not Jefferson's,* UPI wire, Thursday, 12 April 2001.

25. Bob Dart, *New Jefferson study rejects theories that he fathered children by his slave,* Austin American-Statesman, Apr. 13, 2001.

Jordan, president of the Thomas Jefferson Foundation, said his organization would stand by its conclusions."[26] A *Washington Times* account concluded:

> The commission's findings were in turn disputed by those at Monticello who argue that the evidence shows that Jefferson had an affair with Miss Hemings and fathered children with her. "The scientific, historical and documentary evidence indicates that Jefferson fathered Eston Hemings and was most likely the father of all six of her children," said Wayne Mogielnicki, spokesman for the Thomas Jefferson Foundation.
>
> "At first glance they did little or no original research and we have seen nothing that would cause us to alter our opinion on the matter," Mr. Mogielnicki said.[27]

Since Mr. Mogielnicki and his colleagues at Monticello had not yet *seen* a copy of our full report at the time of these comments,[28] his statement that "we have seen nothing" may have been factually accurate, if misleading. But, under the circumstances, such statements are difficult for me to understand. Furthermore, ignoring the fact that they had not yet even seen the report, given the large number of errors that we pointed out in their *own* internal report on the issue, if our report contained no "new information," one must ask why Monticello had not previously corrected such errors as:

- Relying upon the altered transcription of Ellen Randolph Coolidge's letter from Professor Gordon-Reed's book *Thomas Jefferson and Sally Hemings*, that totally reversed the clear intent of the original document;[29]

- Asserting that all of Sally Hemings' children were freed at the age of 21;[30]

- Relying upon the 1873 story attributed to Madison Hemings without acknowledging its clear factual errors—such as the allegation that Dolley Madison was present at the birth of Madison Hemings;[31]

- Relying upon obviously biased "witnesses" like John Kelly and Thomas Gibbons as evidence of a widely held belief that Thomas Jefferson fathered children by Sally Hemings;[32]

- Contending that no one had ever suggested Randolph Jefferson was the likely father of some of Sally's children, and failing to point out the obvious correlation between the Eston Hemings family oral history—that Eston was the child of Thomas Jefferson's "uncle"—and the fact that Randolph Jefferson was widely known as "Uncle Randolph" at Monticello;[33] and

- Asserting that the "oral histories" of all of Sally Hemings' descendants confirmed that Thomas Jefferson fathered her children, whereas—if one excludes the obvi-

---

26. Michael Killian, *Panel rebuts Jefferson-Hemings theory*, CHICAGO TRIBUNE, April 13, 2001.

27. Jeffrey T. Kuhner, *Bush recognizes black Jefferson kin: Scholars doubt slave child story*, WASH. TIMES, April 13, 2001.

28. An earlier draft of my own Individual Views had been provided in confidence to the chairman of the Monticello Association's MAC at his request and it is certainly theoretically possible that this was shared with someone at Monticello prior to our press conference. But the final version of the full report was not even printed off of my computer until the day before our press conference, and as soon as photocopies were bound and placed in boxes at the copy center they were moved to my car, where they remained until a few minutes before our Washington press conference the next morning.

29. *See* **Figures 3** and **4** on pages 36 and 37.

30. *See* Chapter Six of my Individual Views.

31. *See* Chapter Four of my Individual Views.

32. *See* Chapter Nine of my Individual Views

33. *See* Chapter Ten of my Individual Views.

ously *false* stories passed down (and presumably accepted and repeated in good faith) among Woodson descendants (by far the strongest of the oral traditions)— only the descendants of Madison Hemings passed down a consistent story that they were descendants of Thomas Jefferson, and their accounts add little to the published account attributed to Madison in 1873. If Madison Hemings, like Thomas Woodson, either knowingly misrepresented the facts or was simply misinformed about his paternity, the entire oral history project adds nothing to the search for the truth in this matter. And, as discussed in Chapter Four, we *know* that many of the facts attributed to Madison Hemings are clearly not true.

It is simply not accurate to say there is "nothing new" in terms of factual information of relevance to the Jefferson-Hemings issue in the Scholars Commission report. But it probably is true that our greatest contribution has not been in uncovering a wealth of new documents or historical facts relevant to the debate, but rather in pointing out major factual and logical *errors* in the arguments being used by champions of the Hemingses' claim. It is, after all, very difficult to find compelling evidence to prove a negative.

Another troubling aspect of the *Monticello Report* is that some of their factual findings contradict positions they held prior to the DNA tests that had nothing to do with those tests. A Monticello visitors guide prepared in the late 1980s, for example, noted that Thomas Jefferson "privately denied" Callender's charge that he fathered children by Sally Hemings.[34] That is a factually correct statement: in 1805 the Federalist press had just renewed a series of allegations, including the Sally Hemings story, and Jefferson wrote to a friend that the "only" one of "all their allegations against me" that was "founded in truth" was the one involving Mrs. Walker.[35] It is certainly possible that Jefferson was not telling the truth, but the use of "only" and "all" in that context *excludes* the reasonable interpretation that—because Jefferson did not specifically mention Sally Hemings in his comment—that Federalist charge was not encompassed by his statement. But in the *Monticello Report,* we are told: "An ambiguous private letter of 1805 has been interpreted by some historians as a denial."[36]

Perhaps nothing better illustrates the "problem" with Monticello's handling of this issue than their treatment of "oral history," or what is more accurately called "oral tradition." For years, Monticello interviewed descendants of Thomas Woodson, accepting their claim that he was the child of Sally Hemings even when they were not prepared to acknowledge the truth of his claim that Thomas Jefferson was his father. By far the strongest oral tradition alleging a Jefferson-Hemings sexual relationship came from Woodson descendants, and most of the interviews related to Sally Hemings in Monticello's "Getting Word" program of recording slave descendant family traditions reportedly involved individuals claiming Thomas Woodson as their ancestor.

When six DNA tests proved beyond any reasonable doubt that Thomas Woodson could not have been Thomas Jefferson's child—but said *nothing* about Woodson's possible connection with Sally Hemings—one might have expected Monticello to respect their extensive collection of oral traditions except to the degree they had been proven inaccurate by science. But this would have meant acknowledging that Sally Hemings could not have been both monogamous and a sexual partner of Thomas Jefferson (or for that matter any Jef-

---

34. Thomas Sheehan, *Thomas Jefferson/Sally Hemings: Two Hundred Years of Controversy* 16 (1999).
35. This letter is discussed in Chapter Nine of my Individual Views and reprinted as **Figure 10** on page 187.
36. *Monticello Report,* Appendix F at 2.

ferson male[37]), and that, in turn, would undermine the strongest circumstantial case pointing to Thomas Jefferson as opposed to one of the two dozen or more other candidates as the father of Eston Hemings. So—while Monticello continued to host the Woodson descendants as part of the Hemings family for purposes of a family reunion[38] —they *assumed* for the purposes of their paternity investigation that Woodson could not have been Sally Hemings' child.[39]

Nor were they any more considerate of the oral traditions passed down by descendants of Eston Hemings. It is understandable that some of those individuals, after having been told by Fawn Brodie that they were in reality descendants of perhaps America's brightest President, would look for ways to dismiss the stories they had been told by parents and grandparents that Eston's father was not President Jefferson but merely an "uncle." But it is more difficult to understand why Monticello scholars would dismiss this oral tradition—unless, without it or the strong traditions passed down through the Woodson family, they realized that all they really had were reports that descendants of Madison Hemings had passed down the story published by Samuel Wetmore in 1873, with all of its obvious shortcomings.

When the Scholars Commission report was released and it became obvious to most that the DNA tests had been misrepresented and did not come close to *proving* that Thomas Jefferson fathered any children by Sally Hemings (indeed, by disproving the Woodson predicate to the Callender allegation, the DNA tests actually *undermined* Callender's original story), Dr. Jordan explained to the media that it did not really matter, because "We never said that DNA proved it. We said that the science and the history, especially the *oral* history,"[40] made Thomas Jefferson the most likely father of Sally Hemings' children. But, on the contrary, the DNA test exposed the Woodson oral history claims to be *false*, and the story passed down by descendants of Eston Hemings (prior to their corruption in the mid-1970s through the intervention of Fawn Brodie) that Eston's father was a Jefferson "uncle," could most easily be reconciled with the DNA tests by concluding that "Uncle" Randolph Jefferson was Eston's father. Monticello *knew* Randolph had been invited to Monticello shortly before Eston was conceived and had a documented propensity to socialize at night with his brother's slaves.

Until *Nature* misreported the significance of the DNA tests, few serious scholars took Fawn Brodie's "psycho-history" of Thomas Jefferson seriously. Over the years, scholarly reviewers from across the political spectrum have panned it as silliness, and quite rightly.[41] But the Monticello Research Committee alleged that Brodie's scholarship "has stood the test of time."[42]

Throughout our entire inquiry, and extending to his retirement in 2008,[43] Dr. Jordan and his staff at Monticello were totally cooperative and more than gracious in their deal-

---

37. The DNA tests exclude the possibility that Thomas Woodson and Eston Hemings were fathered by the same man, so if both were in fact children of Sally Hemings she could not have been monogamous.

38. *See, e.g.,* http://www.woodson.org/reunion2003_news.asp.

39. *See Monticello Report*, Appendix K at 2.

40. *See* page 161 (emphasis added).

41. *See, e.g.,* the excerpts from Garry Wills' 1974 review from the *New York Review of Books*, quoted in the Introduction to my Individual Views on page 175–76.

42. *Monticello Report* at 5.

43. I am genuinely fond of Dr. Daniel Jordan, who has graciously invited me to take part in a variety of special events at Monticello over the years, and for that reason I have agonized over whether I should even mention these concerns in this Postscript. But they are a part of the story, and—while I still have no idea how to explain them—to conceal them out of concern that they might offend a friend would be inconsistent with my commitment to pursue the truth.

ings with me. Not once, in my presence or in their written communications to me, have I heard any criticism of the material facts or conclusions contained in the Scholars Commission report. Yet, from other sources, including current and former guides and financial contributors to Monticello, I hear very different reports. Guides speak of having to move away from the mansion even to *discuss* the report among themselves, for fear that they may lose their jobs, and tell stories of other guides being reprimanded for mentioning during a tour that some prominent Jefferson scholars do not agree with the Foundation's conclusion that Thomas Jefferson probably fathered Sally Hemings' children. One substantial contributor reports that a senior Monticello fundraiser told her that the Scholars Commission report was "full of inaccuracies," mentioning as an example our observation that Thomas Jefferson wrote that Monticello was kept locked while he was away in Washington. This, she said, was a "foolish" argument, because no one "could lock up a whole plantation." This is absurd. As documented above at page 132, in a 1797 letter Jefferson wrote: "our house is shut up one half the year."[44] Monticello employees are certainly aware that, to prevent theft, Jefferson installed locks on many interior and all exterior doors, and the exterior doors were routinely kept locked when the family was away during his service in the White House. Although the word "Monticello" (Italian for "little mountain") denotes Thomas Jefferson's plantation near Charlottesville, Virginia, it is also used to describe the mansion he built on top of the mountain.[45] Our obvious point was not that there were barbed-wire-capped chain-link fences all around the mountain, but that Jefferson's home—where friends and relatives would routinely gather during his presence—was kept locked or "shut up" during his absence and thus visitors would be uncommon.

At about the same time, I received a fax (from an unidentified sender) of a copy of a letter signed by a senior Monticello official to a New York attorney, who had written to a mutual friend asking why, following the release of the Scholars Commission report, the Thomas Jefferson Foundation did not at least take a more neutral position on the Sally Hemings issue. I sought the consent of both parties to reprint this letter, and the recipient gave his consent but suggested that I avoid mentioning names. The sender indicated it was a "private" letter which should not be shared beyond the original recipient and anyone copied on the original.

I have agonized about how to handle this letter since it first came into my possession. Were I convinced that it was, in fact, a "private" communication between two friends, the case against publication would be extremely powerful and could only be overcome by the strongest considerations of public good. But on its face it appears to be an official explanation of Thomas Jefferson Foundation views—written to an apparent stranger on Monticello letterhead—and it may contribute to an explanation of the Foundation's position.

Rather than reprinting the letter in its entirety, however, I have decided to make only two brief references. The letter asserts that the Scholars Commission report "offered no surprises and very little in the way of new insights or evidence"—essentially the position taken publicly by the Foundation's President and press spokesman the day our report was issued—

44. *Jefferson to Van Hasselt*, Aug. 27, 1797, reprinted in THE GARDEN BOOK 257 (Edwin Morris Betts, ed. 1974).

45. *See, e.g.*, this definition from Encyclopedia.com:

> MONTICELLO (constructed between 1769 and 1809) was designed and built by Thomas Jefferson to be his home, farm, and plantation. Construction progressed through two stages.... Altered throughout most of Jefferson's life, the brick house embodies the ideals of the American Enlightenment, as well as the moral, aesthetic, political, and scientific motives of its designer.

Available at http://www.encyclopedia.com/doc/1G2-3401802737.html.

and it informed the recipient that the "only truly third-party, objective, and independent assessment[s]" of the debate were "a recent article in the *William & Mary Quarterly*" and a "special issue of the *National Genealogical Society Quarterly*." These articles have also been referenced by other supporters of the revisionist viewpoint, and they will be discussed below.

About a year later, however, a significant change appears to have taken place at Monticello. I received several reports from individuals who had recently taken tours of Jefferson's home saying that the guides were now taking a more balanced view, noting both the initial conclusions of the Foundation's Research Committee and the fact that a group of scholars later reached a different conclusion—leaving visitors to make up their own minds on the issue. During much of 2001 and all of 2002, the Monticello Web site had included a section entitled "Thomas Jefferson and Sally Hemings: A Brief Account."[46] Perhaps most importantly, this Web page concluded:

> It likely will take newly uncovered historical evidence or scientific methods still unknown to determine beyond doubt the truth about Thomas Jefferson and Sally Hemings, and the complete story may never be known. The Thomas Jefferson Foundation stands by its original findings—that the weight of evidence suggests that Jefferson probably was the father of Eston Hemings and perhaps the father of all of Sally Hemings' children—but is ready to review new evidence at any time and to reassess its understanding of this matter in the light of new information.[47]

However, in February 2003, Monticello altered this Web page, inserting the following new conclusion:

> Although the relationship between Jefferson and Sally Hemings has been for many years, and will surely continue to be, a subject of intense interest to historians and the public, the evidence is not definitive, and the complete story may never be known. The Foundation encourages its visitors and patrons, based on what evidence does exist, to make up their own minds as to the true nature of the relationship.[48]

This is a far more defensible position.

In early 2008 the TJF announced that the number of visitors to Monticello had continued to decline since 2002—reaching a twenty-eight-year low in 2007. This was despite the fact that the Foundation had "offered discounts and worked with cultural and historic organizations to get Monticello on people's minds."[49] Monticello spokesmen explained the decline in part as a result of "[h]igher gas prices and the lackluster fall foliage," but the primary explanation was a "nationwide trend at similar places."[50]

---

46. The account is of mixed quality. It acknowledges, for example, that "[t]here is no evidence in Jefferson's records of any special privileges accorded to Sally Hemings that would distinguish her from other members of her family," and that "in his records, Jefferson made no mention of Sally Hemings that would distinguish her from other members of the enslaved community at Monticello." But it also alleges that the oral history of Eston Hemings' descendants asserted that he was Thomas Jefferson's son until the 1940s—a claim for which there appears to be no compelling evidence.

47. This language was included at *http://www.monticello.org/plantation/hemingscontro/hemings-jefferson_contro.html* as late as February 18, 2003, but within the next nine days was changed to the language below.

48. *http://www.monticello.org/plantation/hemingscontro/hemings-jefferson_contro.html* (last checked on August 24, 2009).

49. Jeremy Borden, *Fewer Tourists See Monticello: Visits at 28-Year Low*, DAILY PROGRESS (Charlottesville, VA), Jan. 8, 2008.

50. *Id.*

However, in covering the story, the Charlottesville *Daily Progress* did some independent research and reported:

> Two similar historic sites in Virginia didn't see the same attendance pattern last year. Mount Vernon, the home of George Washington outside Alexandria, had 1.08 million visitors in 2007, the first time since the 9/11 tragedy that the site had more than 1 million visitors, a spokesman said. James Madison's Montpelier in Orange County [located within thirty miles of Monticello] saw an increase in visitation in 2007 of about 25 percent from 2006.... [51]

While there may be many variables at play here, some consideration might be given to the possibility that many Americans bring their families to places like Monticello, Mount Vernon, and Montpelier to celebrate the lives and pay respect to the memories of the nation's founders. The Thomas Jefferson Foundation's decision to stop "memoralizing" Thomas Jefferson clearly alienated many visitors, and might well have been a factor in the downward trend of Monticello visitors.

Reaction of Scholars

One of the greatest surprises (and, from my perspective, disappointments) was the reaction of the leading revisionist scholars to our report. I had anticipated that they would vigorously challenge us, and that the public would benefit from the scholarly exchanges that might follow. When Scholars Commission member Professor Paul Rahe (our sole dissenter) asked whether I would be willing to take part in a debate on the Jefferson-Hemings issue at the 2002 annual meeting of the American Political Science Association, I enthusiastically accepted. But, in the end, the planned program had to be cancelled when Professor Rahe proved unable to find a prominent revisionist scholar willing to debate the issue. Others have contacted me about possibly taking part in debates as well, only to report later that the leading revisionists had said they had "moved on" to other issues.

It is perhaps understandable that the two most prominent scholars supporting the Hemingses' claim withdrew a bit from the limelight on this issue, as both came under fire about the time our report was released. While the first case was addressed in our original report, it has largely been ignored (despite several front-page stories about similar behavior from other scholars[52]). The second received major press coverage shortly after our report was released, but because the scholar was so respected and so critical to the widespread misunderstanding of the DNA stories it probably warrants further mention here. I will take them in order and discuss them before considering the views of other scholars and writers.

Professor Annette Gordon-Reed

Although the Scholars Commission was not the first[53] to point out the alterations[54] in historical documents transcribed by Professor Gordon-Reed and included in her 1997

---

51. *Id.*

52. *See* the Introduction to my Individual Views at page 31.

53. The late Eyler R. Coates first discovered the alteration in the Ellen Randolph Coolidge letter in 2000 and brought it to my attention by e-mail.

54. *See* Introduction to my Individual Views, **Figures 1-4**, on pages 33, 35, 36, and 37.

book *Thomas Jefferson and Sally Hemings*, the release of our report probably did bring them to the attention of a larger audience. When she was asked by the media about the "incorrect transcription of a key letter from one of Jefferson's granddaughters," Professor Gordon-Reed "acknowledged her mistake ... but said it was a 'non-issue,' because she would have used the letter regardless."[55] (One has to wonder *why*, since when transcribed correctly the letter would be the only document in her appendices that clearly undermines the case she is advocating.)

Troubled that there were no apparent consequences for what he viewed as a serious act of professional misconduct, TJHS President John Works wrote to the Dean and President of New York Law School and asked whether the school was looking into the matter. On July 16, Professor Gordon-Reed responded to this letter directly to Mr. Works. She denied intentionally altering the text of the Ellen Randolph Coolidge letter, declaring: "Any mistake that appears in my work is just that—a mistake."[56]

The following month, Mr. Works received a brief letter dated August 14, 2001, from New York Law School Dean Richard Matasar stating in its entirety:

> Dear Mr. Works:
>
> I know Professor Gordon-Reed very well. I find the tone of your letter extremely offensive. She has told you she mistakenly transcribed the letter and that she will correct the error in future editions of her book.
>
> As a scholar—and a careful one at that—I have made similar mistakes in my own work. I fully support Professor Gordon-Reed.
>
> Sincerely,
> Richard A. Matasar
> Dean and President

This would make more sense if "the mistakes" had involved transcribing "that" as "the" or "1873" as "1973"—most prolific scholars do occasionally make such mistakes—but, in order to make the Coolidge letter useful to her case, Professor Gordon-Reed had to make nearly a *dozen* alterations to a single sentence. The "mistakes" do not appear random, but rather remarkably transformed the original sentence into a grammatically correct new sentence with a very different meaning. There was another little "mistake" in the same letter, involving transcribing "disbelief" as "belief"—resulting in an implication that Thomas Jefferson's favorite grandson believed the allegations against the President. One might add that virtually all of the "mistakes" in her transcription of the 1873 story about Madison Hemings also appear to have corrected obvious inaccuracies in the original that might have decreased the document's credibility. Thus, Professor Gordon-Reed dropped a dozen words in a sentence so that it falsely appeared that Madison Hemings described not five-year-old Maria but nearly twelve-year-old Martha as "just budding into womanhood"[57] when Thomas Jefferson went to live in Paris. The original document was very legible, and the words deleted could not be explained on the basis of mistakenly skipping a line while transcribing. As with other alterations in her book, the deletion of a dozen words from the sentence removes a passage that if not altered would have raised doubts about the credibility of the document being transcribed.

---

55. Sam Hodges, *Scholars: No Proof Jefferson Fathered Slave's Children*, Mobile Register, Apr. 13, 2001.

56. *Gordon-Reed to Works,* July 16, 2001, copy on file with author.

57. *See* the Introduction to my Individual Views at page 35.

I must admit that I had never heard of Dean Matasar before I read Professor Gordon-Reed's book and then read the letter he wrote to Mr. Works, and I have not to my knowledge read any of his scholarly writings. But I would be interested in seeing even *one* example of his published works that includes "similar mistakes" to altering even *half*-a-dozen words in a key sentence so as to reverse its original meaning. Excluding situations of obvious fraud, I do not believe I have ever encountered such "errors" before from any serious scholar, much less a former member of *Harvard Law Review* like Professor Gordon-Reed.

Interestingly, Mr. Works had the same reaction and wrote back to Dean Matasar asking for an example of comparable "mistakes" in his own published writings. That was more than nine years ago. To the best of my knowledge, he has not yet received either the requested example (much less "examples"), or for that matter any other response to his letter.

Although other historians in the interim have been sanctioned, had awards withdrawn, and in some cases lost their jobs for the lesser offense[58] of plagiarism, Professor Gordon-Reed has apparently suffered no adverse consequences. Indeed, she has gone on to be named a tenured professor at Harvard Law School and to win the National Book Award, the Pulitzer Prize in history, the George Washington Prize, a $500,000 "genius" award from the McArthur Foundation, and numerous other distinguished literary prizes for her latest book.[59]

After the DNA tests were made public, Professor Gordon-Reed issued a new edition of her 1997 book *Thomas Jefferson and Sally Hemings*, addressing the DNA findings in an "Author's Note" before the Preface. She reasoned: "'Passionless' science has stepped in to help solve a controversy that history and politics—driven by human passion—would not allow to be resolved by normal means. Let me be clear. There is currently no reasonable basis for doubting Madison Hemings's story about his life at Monticello."[60] Although she refers to "the Carr brothers story"[61]—not in the possessive, but rather the story told by Jefferson family members that Sally Hemings' children were fathered by Peter and Samuel Carr (a story she inaccurately alleges has been destroyed by the DNA tests[62])—and noted that "Jefferson's relatives" had "named two of their relatives as the fathers,"[63] she nevertheless asserts in this Note that "[t]he suggestions about multiple fathers—in a way that is very telling and depressing—comes from current-day commentators."[64]

Indeed, Professor Gordon-Reed seems to find no possible explanation but racism to explain why white historians had ever challenged Madison Hemings' account:

---

58. Plagiarism is obviously dishonest and constitutes intellectual "theft," but in the field of history it does not necessarily mislead the reader in the search for the truth. To alter historic documents that, at the time, were not readily available to readers in order to conceal obvious factual errors and make the original document appear more credible—or to present a credible witness as having said something she clearly did not say—undermines the search for the truth itself and thus is in my view a far more serious offense.

59. *See* the Introduction to my Individual Views at p. 30.

60. ANNETTE GORDON-REED, THOMAS JEFFERSON AND SALLY HEMINGS xi (1998). The issue, in reality, is not so much Madison Hemings' account of "his life at Monticello," but rather his alleged account of events in Paris and elsewhere that occurred years before his own life began.

61. *Id.* at x.

62. *Id.* at xi. This ignores the reality that the DNA tests only addressed the paternity of Thomas Woodson and Eston Hemings, and said nothing about whether one or both Carr brothers—or anyone else—fathered Sally Hemings' older children.

63. *Id.*

64. *Id.* at xii. As noted in Chapter Three of my Individual Views, James Thomson Callender, the originator of the story of a Jefferson-Hemings sexual relationship, alleged that Sally Hemings had as many as "thirty different lovers...."

We should also ask whether stereotypes about black women have any useful role to play in considering this issue. The casual implication that Sally Hemings's children may have been fathered by different men is not based upon anything we presently know about the social situation at Monticello. It is more likely a product of long-held beliefs about black women's natural licentiousness and the looseness of the black family structure.[65]

While noting that some progress was evident from the positive reviews of her book even before the DNA tests were announced, she laments: "very few reviewers grappled with the role that the doctrine of white supremacy played in all of this."[66] I can assure readers that the fear that anyone who disagreed with Professor Gordon-Reed might be attacked as a "racist" or "white supremacist" deterred several able Jefferson scholars who were approached about joining the Scholars Commission in 2000. Professor Merrill Peterson did not give a reason for his decision to decline the invitation to join our group, and now that he has passed on I want to be careful about speculating as to his motives. At the age of seventy-nine he certainly needed no excuse to avoid additional burdens on his time. But he had openly and proudly supported the Civil Rights movement in the South, had played a prominent leadership role in the struggle to integrate the University of Virginia, and, as well, had worked hard to recruit African-American professors and students.[67] I know that he was deeply hurt by patently false suggestions that he was some sort of white supremacist for being skeptical about the story attributed to Madison Hemings, and I have good reason to believe that he was pleased with the conclusions of our group.[68]

I have only encountered one instance where Professor Gordon-Reed specifically discussed the Scholars Commission (although there may well be many others). On September 24, 2008, she took part in an online discussion of her latest book sponsored by the *Washington Post*, from which the following exchange with an unidentified individual from Virginia is excerpted:

> **VA:** I have read most of the scholars commission report. It has convinced me that Jefferson did not father Sally's children. What is your opinion of the report?

---

65. *Id.* As discussed in Chapter Two of my Individual Views, the statement attributed to Madison Hemings and relied upon so heavily by Professor Gordon-Reed alleged that Sally's mother Betty Hemings had children by at least four different men.

66. *Id.* at xiii. *See also, id.* at viii ("The treatment of the story well into modern times is evidence of the continuing grip that the doctrine of white supremacy has on American society.")

67. Bruce Weber, *Merrill D. Peterson, Jefferson Scholar, Dies at 88*, N.Y. TIMES, Oct. 2, 2009 ("At Virginia, Mr. Peterson was known for his liberal views. Outspoken on the subject of integration, he had arrived on campus before blacks were recruited either for the student body or for the faculty. In March 1965, shortly after civil rights marchers in Selma, Ala., were attacked by the state and local police, he delivered a fervent and eloquent speech at the campus rotunda. 'We are concerned with what is happening in Selma because what is happening there involves what is taught here—truth, honesty, justice, compassion, the rights and freedom of all men in a democratic society,' Mr. Peterson said. 'Today Selma is a vital link in the heritage of American liberty. No university in America or in the world has a clearer title to speak for that heritage in the present crisis than the University of Virginia. And it's high time, long past time, we were heard from. Selma is a symbol, but as President Johnson told us the other night, it has become a turning point, like Lexington and Concord and Appomattox, of America's unending search for freedom.'")

68. I was told by a Monticello guide that on July 4, 2001, Dr. Peterson had posted on the bulletin board in the break room used by the guides a copy of a short summary of our work I had written for the *Wall Street Journal*. For the article in question, *see* Robert F. Turner, *The Truth About Jefferson*, WALL STREET JOURNAL, July 3, 2001, available online at http://www.opinionjournal.com/extra/?id=95000747.

Annette Gordon-Reed: I have problems with the Scholars Commission Report—by the way—anytime a group has to call itself a "Scholar's [*sic*] Commission" you know something is up. Sort of like an establishment calling itself a "Gentleman's Club." In any event, as I recall there was not one scholar of slavery in the group. It would be as if someone were claiming to be an expert on France in the 18th century, and they didn't know how to speak or read French. That would not pass muster. The lives of French people would be taken too seriously for that. That some think it should pass muster when dealing with the lives of enslaved African Americans speaks volumes about blacks' position in this country. The scholarship about slavery in America is really the crown jewel in American historiography. It is a subject worthy of study and mastery (if I may use that ironic term) and that anyone could purport to seriously talk about an issue involving slavery without having input from people who spend their lives studying the institution—and I mean multiple people—is beyond mysterious.[69]

After more than nine years, I honestly don't recall who coined the term "Scholars Commission." I am pretty sure it was not me or another member of our group, and I suspect it was someone affiliated with the Thomas Jefferson Heritage Society. But I don't find the term offensive or inappropriate. Among the Merriam-Webster definitions for the term "commission" is "a group of persons directed to perform some duty...."[70] While "directed" may be a bit strong—we were "requested" and all served as uncompensated volunteers— I think the title fairly accurately describes the group. While I don't disagree that the study of American slavery is important, our task was not to do a broad study of interracial sex in Virginia during the era of Thomas Jefferson, but rather the far more specific mission of assessing whether charges that Jefferson fathered one or more children with Sally Hemings were true. There were a variety of allegations and arguments to be assessed, and it is not clear to me that having spent decades studying the behavior of other individuals on other plantations would have been of tremendous value in our more specific inquiry. Certainly, though, everyone on the Scholars Commission was very much aware that interracial sex on southern plantations in that era was not uncommon, and that it represented yet another dimension of the injustice of slavery.

Lest I be misunderstood, my concerns about Professor Gordon-Reed's scholarship go well beyond the apparent "evidence tampering" documented in **Figures 1–4**. Because racism is such an evil prejudice, I find highly offensive her false allegations that scholars like Merrill Peterson who reached conclusions that differed from her own were "racists" or "white supremacists." It has been an effective tactic for intimidating some scholars who might otherwise have been tempted to challenge her, but it is as irresponsible as falsely accusing an innocent man of rape. She is obviously a very bright and knowledgeable person on these issues—too bright and knowledgeable to believe that Thomas Jefferson was "just a typical southern slave owner...."[71] Her obvious talents and expertise make it difficult for me to dismiss as mere incompetence her exclusion of Randolph Jefferson and his family from her book (she included a book specifically about Randolph in her bibliography), or to ignore on similar grounds her clearly false assertions that the DNA tests

---

69. Annette Gordon-Reed, *The Root: Sally Hemings and Me*, Wednesday, Sept. 24, 2008; 12:00 PM, *available at* http://www.washingtonpost.com/wp-dyn/content/discussion/2008/09/18/DI2008091 802348.html.

70. Merriam-Webster OnLine Dictionary, *available at* http://www.merriam-webster.com/ dictionary/Commission.

71. GORDON-REED, THOMAS JEFFERSON AND SALLY HEMINGS 148.

disproved the Jefferson family's oral traditions that the Carr brothers fathered children by Sally Hemings.

Other than her rather snide "gentlemen's club" remark and denying that the alterations in transcriptions in her first book were anything but "mistakes," Professor Gordon-Reed does not appear to have addressed our report on the merits. When invited to debate the Jefferson-Hemings issue at the 2002 annual meeting of the American Political Science Association—where she could have defended her past writings and pointed out any flaws in our research or conclusions—she declined. For the record, the offer to debate her is still open.

Professor Joseph Ellis

Professor Joseph Ellis, who had co-authored one of the original *Nature* stories on the DNA tests and was certainly the most distinguished champion of the Hemingses' cause, received the Pulitzer Prize in History in 2001 for his best-selling *Founding Brothers*. His shift in positions—from characterizing the possibility that Thomas Jefferson was sexually involved with Sally Hemings as being "remote" and based upon "flimsy and wholly circumstantial" evidence in his highly acclaimed 1996 biography, *American Sphinx*,[72] to asserting the Hemingses' case had been proven "beyond a reasonable doubt"[73] by the DNA study—was difficult for me to reconcile with my conviction that he was an exceptionally able scholar and my assumption that he was an honorable man. His overstatement (and *Nature*'s) of the DNA evidence was so great that Dr. Eugene Foster, who organized and oversaw the DNA tests, found it necessary to publish letters in both *Nature* and *The New York Times* seeking to correct the record.[74]

As noted in the Introduction to my Individual Views, during our inquiry I exchanged letters with Professor Ellis and found him to be most gracious and candid in his comments. I liked him. But in his letters to me—bracketed before and after by scholarly articles repeating the "beyond reasonable doubt" assessment[75]—he took the view that the DNA results had changed his view from it being somewhat more likely that the story was false to somewhat more likely that it was true. That was a perfectly reasonable position, but it hardly explained his much stronger assessment in the *Nature* story or in subsequent public statements. I could not escape the suspicion that either Professor Ellis was not the outstanding historian that his record suggested or he was not the honorable individual his letter to me strongly suggested. I was unwilling to believe that he would intentionally misrepresent the truth, and yet I could not reconcile his obviously false and exaggerated scholarship with my perception of his skills as a professional historian.

Both Joseph Ellis and the leadership at Monticello were enigmas to me. Every indicator told me they were honorable and able people. Yet their revisionist scholarship on this issue was so terribly flawed that it made no sense to me. And between them, their influence in shifting public and professional thinking on the Sally Hemings issue had been extraordinary. Widely recognized as among the most outstanding members of his profession, when Joseph Ellis changed positions and announced the case was proven "beyond reasonable doubt," there was little reason for other scholars, who had not taken the time to examine

---

72. JOSEPH J. ELLIS, AMERICAN SPHINX: THE CHARACTER OF THOMAS JEFFERSON 366 (Vintage ed. 1998).

73. Joseph J. Ellis, *Jefferson: Post-DNA*, 57 WILLIAM & MARY QUARTERLY 126 (Jan. 2000).

74. *See* Chapter One of my Individual Views.

75. *Id.*

all of the evidence in detail, to question the Hemingses' story. And when the Thomas Jefferson Foundation quickly conceded the point, and the public was told that DNA tests had "seal[ed] the case,"[76] the debate indeed seemed over.

Two months after the Scholars Commission report was made public, a highly respected journalist dropped a bombshell, disclosing on page one of the *Boston Globe* that Professor Ellis had a long history of telling untrue stories to students, colleagues, and the media about such things as having served in the Vietnam War, having been a civil rights and anti-war activist, and having scored the winning touchdown in his high school homecoming football game.[77] Careful research had revealed that Ellis was at Yale earning two master's degrees and a Ph.D. in history during the years he claimed to have been in Vietnam as an infantry platoon leader with the elite 101st Airborne Division and later on the personal staff of General William Westmoreland. His high school yearbook revealed that he played no sports (but may have been on the football field at half-time as a member of the band), and his Yale friends and advisers had no recollections of any summer spent with the civil rights movement in Mississippi or anti-war activism on campus.[78]

Mount Holyoke President Joanne V. Creighton initially defended Professor Ellis, issuing a statement that said in part "We at the College do not know what public interest the *Globe* is trying to serve through a story of this nature."[79] But, as pressure grew, she acknowledged what Ellis had done was wrong and finally was forced on August 17 to suspend her college's most distinguished faculty member for one year without pay.[80] On the same day, Professor Ellis—who had initially simply issued a statement through the college saying he "would not discuss any of the issues"[81] raised in the *Globe* article—released a statement through his lawyer saying in part: "By misrepresenting my military service to students in the course on the Vietnam War, I did something both stupid and wrong. I apologize to the students, as well as to the faculty of this institution, for violating the implicit covenant of trust that must exist in the classroom."[82]

The *Boston Globe* revelations made it easy for some who were struggling to decide whether Professor Ellis was a poor historian or was simply willing to misrepresent the truth when it served his interests. It was already known that he had been actively involved in the campaign to prevent the impeachment of President Clinton at the time he wrote that the DNA tests had proven Thomas Jefferson was also guilty of sexual misconduct while in office. Indeed, Ellis made frequent reference to the similarities between Jefferson and Clinton in several of his articles and public statements at the time.[83] But the conventional wisdom was that his misrepresentation of his own biography had not infected

---

76. Eric S. Lander & Joseph J. Ellis, *DNA Analysis: Founding Father,* NATURE, Nov. 5, 1998, vol. 395, issue 6706 at 13, *reprinted in Monticello Report,* Appendix A.

77. Walter V. Robinson, *Professor's past in doubt: Discrepancies surface in claim of Vietnam duty,* BOSTON GLOBE, June 18, 2001 at A1.

78. *Id.*

79. Patrick Healy & Walter V. Robinson, *Professor Apologizes for Fabrications,* BOSTON GLOBE, June 19, 2001 at A1; Walter V. Robinson, *Professor Faces Investigation at Mount Holyoke,* BOSTON GLOBE, June 21, 2001 at B3. ("Creighton also retreated from her Monday criticism of the Globe for disclosing Ellis's misrepresentations.")

80. Statement of President Joanne V. Creighton, August 17, 2001, *available at* http://www.mtholyoke.edu/offices/comm/news/ellisdecision.shtml.

81. Robinson, *Professor's past in doubt.*

82. "Further Statement of Joseph J. Ellis," Aug. 17, 2001, *available at* http://www.mtholyoke.edu/offices/comm/news/ellisstatement.html.

83. *See* Chapter One of my Individual Views.

his professional scholarship. For example, his editor at Alfred A. Knopf asserted: "no one has questioned his scholarship in any of the books he has written."[84]

In retrospect, I guess it is not necessary for me to attempt to resolve the issue. Whatever the explanation, it is clear that Professor Ellis seriously misstated the facts about the DNA test results, and in so doing he misled large numbers of people both within the community of professional historians and among the general public. And, like Professor Gordon-Reed, since the Scholars Commission report was released he has turned down invitations to defend his position on the Jefferson-Hemings issue in public debate. Readers tempted to rely upon his assessments of this issue should keep these realities in mind as they seek to weigh the value of his contributions.

Historian Henry Wiencek

Perhaps the most helpful criticism I received while working to finalize this volume came from Henry Wiencek, whose books on slavery and the Founding Fathers include the 2003 prize-winning volume, *An Imperfect God: George Washington, His Slaves, and the Creation of America.* He contacted me in late 2007 in connection with some research he was doing on Jefferson and slavery, and in the process argued (in my view quite persuasively) that Jefferson's notation that Harriet II and her brother Beverly had "run" in 1822 must be interpreted in the light of other existing evidence to mean he allowed them to leave Monticello in search of a better life. He noted (as I had as well) that Monticello overseer Edmund Bacon later spoke of having put Harriet on a stage to Philadelphia with fifty dollars from Mr. Jefferson, but also reminded me that granddaughter Ellen Randolph Coolidge later stated: "It was his principle (I know that of my own knowledge) to allow such of his slaves as were sufficiently white to pass for white men, to withdraw quietly from the plantation; it was called running away...."[85] Although I quoted that sentence in Chapter Six of my original Individual Views, in retrospect I clearly failed to give it the weight I now believe it warrants. I have thus made appropriate changes to my Individual Views, and am most grateful to Mr. Wiencek for pointing this out.

To be sure, Ellen referred specifically to slaves who were white enough to pass "for white *men*," but that would cover Beverly—and the perhaps more elaborate measures of having Bacon put Harriet on a stage with a significant amount of cash could reflect a greater concern for her physical safety because she was a woman (and, in any event, that incident is already persuasively documented by Bacon himself). So, thanks in large part to Mr. Wiencek, I am now persuaded that Jefferson's notations about Beverly and Harriet having "run" in 1822 are not reliable evidence that either of them left Monticello without Thomas Jefferson's consent. This, in turn, suggests that Jefferson may well have informally "freed" Harriet within a few months of her twenty-first birthday, which occurred in May 1822.

But by the time Harriet turned twenty-one, Beverly would have been twenty-four. So allowing a twenty-three- or twenty-four-year-old Beverly to "withdraw quietly" from Monticello, and having Bacon put a twenty- or twenty-one-year-old Harriet on a stagecoach, is still hardly serious evidence that this was the result of some sort of "treaty" in which Thomas Jefferson promised an adolescent Sally Hemings he would free all of their

---

84. Josh Tyrangiel, A History of His Own Making: Author Joseph Ellis Invented a Vietnam tour of duty. But Why?, TIME online edition, June 24, 2001, *available at* http://www.time.com/ time/education/article/0,8599,165156,00.html.

85. Henry Wiencek e-mail to Bob Turner, Sept. 11, 2007.

children when they turned twenty-one if she would return to Monticello with him from Paris. Ellen's use of the plural "men" suggests that Beverly was not the only light-skinned slave to be thus permitted to withdraw quietly, and her language suggests that this was a consistent policy. We do not have sufficient evidence to determine with authority how often this occurred, but from Ellen's statement the motivating factor was that slaves had to be "sufficiently white to pass for white men...." Assuming this was true, and that Beverly was as light-skinned as Harriet or Eston, then this would explain his departure without any need for a "treaty" commitment made in Paris to persuade a reluctant Sally to return to Virginia.

Science Writer Steven T. Corneliussen

Subsequent to the release of our April 2001 report I have benefited greatly from the assistance of Steven Corneliussen,[86] a science writer at the Thomas Jefferson National Accelerator Facility (Jefferson Laboratories) in Newport News, Virginia. Among his other activities, Mr. Corneliussen is a media advisor for the American Institute of Physics and a leader of the effort to preserve Virginia's Fort Monroe, where the Civil War's first self-emancipators helped push slavery toward collapse. Corneliussen is an agnostic on the paternity question but a student and critic of what he calls "Hemings-Jefferson science abuse," by which he means misuse of the special authority of science in the paternity controversy. He charges that this abuse began when *Nature*'s editors confused the public worldwide concerning the DNA evidence by conflating molecular findings and historical interpretation of molecular findings. He charges that the abuse worsened when Dr. Fraser D. Neiman's statistical study confused both the public and "credulous historians" concerning the correlation between Hemings' conceptions and Jefferson's visits to Monticello. Corneliussen believes that, irrespective of whether or not Jefferson and Hemings were parents together, this abuse discredits science itself and requires scrutiny because of science's special authority on matters in public discourse.

After the 2000 Neiman study confidently claimed that statistical science proved that Jefferson fathered Hemings' children, Corneliussen—skeptical that statistical science can be usefully applied in a two-century-old paternity mystery—began inquiring whether experts would be vetting the study independently. Only later did I come to know him. After we had exchanged a number of e-mails, I asked him to review Chapter Five of my Individual Views, concerning Dr. Neiman's study. Most of the members of the Scholars Commission were not professional scientists, and I wanted to get another opinion on my very critical assessment of Dr. Neiman's scholarship to make sure I was not being unfair. Corneliussen is not a scientist either, but on his own initiative—having long since realized that no one in science was going to review a scientific study sequestered in a humanities journal—he informally sought the scientific judgments of two of his colleagues concerning the statistical study. He called on Dr. William C. Blackwelder, a biostatistician and Fellow of the American Statistical Association, and Dr. David R. Douglas, a Fellow of the American Physical Society whose particle-accelerator work involves computer simulations akin to those on which Dr. Neiman built his statistical study.

---

86. In order to make certain that I was doing justice to his views and to the technical issues of science involved, at my request Mr. Corneliussen drafted much of this portion of my Postscript, which I have only lightly edited.

Later Corneliussen published an excellent op-ed article in the *Richmond Times-Dispatch* summarizing his view that the paternity controversy has involved abuse of science's special authority. In part, he elaborated on Dr. Blackwelder's and Dr. Douglas's judgment that, even setting aside the statistical study's questionable assumptions and other problems, "two failings in particular fatally undermine" it. First, correlation or association cannot prove causation. Corneliussen reported that Dr. Blackwelder "emphasized that at most statistical science can only investigate whether Jefferson was present more often" at times of conceptions "than would be expected by chance alone." Second, the study failed to account for the varying probabilities with which conception can take place on one of the days during a window of time approximately nine months before birth. Dr. Blackwelder had criticized this failing for the case of Sally Hemings' son Beverly by noting, as Corneliussen put it, that "Jefferson's presence for less than 50 percent of the window in [Beverly's] case means an overall probability of less than 50 percent for Jefferson's presence in all six. So just by itself, this one absence upends the entire study." (As I have explained elsewhere,[87] Sally Hemings likely had five children, not six. Corneliussen engaged Dr. Neiman's claims as he found them.)

Corneliussen notes that the statistical study merely "awarded itself a fudge factor" of sorts concerning Beverly's case, and that the failure to account for a distribution of conception-window probabilities mattered notably in three more cases as well. Using historical data recorded in Dr. Neiman's article and in Cynthia H. Burton's *Jefferson Vindicated*, and building on observations by Burton and in my Individual Views, Corneliussen wrote, "Depending on biological assumptions, Jefferson missed a week of [Hemings'] unnamed third child's conception window. He missed a day or more of Madison Hemings'. A Lynchburg trip caused the same for Eston's. That means Jefferson could have been absent when the only child linked to [a Jefferson father] by DNA was conceived." Corneliussen charges that the "statistical study called itself a 'probabilistic evaluation,' but didn't even try to compute" the four absences' statistical implications. He asserts that this point is crucial in that it shows that whatever may be the qualitative significance of the conceptions-coincidences evidence, the Neiman study is not merely weak as a scientific, quantitative claim, but is completely useless.

Professor Gordon-Reed, in a letter to the editor of the *Times-Dispatch* accusing Corneliussen of "smoke and mirrors,"[88] apparently completely missed this qualitative-vs.-quantitative distinction. According to Dr. Douglas, in a letter of his own,[89] her letter showed no awareness that Corneliussen was condemning not the qualitative argument about the conceptions' coincidences, but what purported to be a quantitative proof backed by the authority of statistical science. Dr. Douglas re-asserted that distinction and challenged as well Professor Gordon-Reed's charge that in this matter and also in the DNA matter Corneliussen was attacking historians, when in fact he was criticizing scientists.

Corneliussen points out something else that's crucial as well. I mentioned at the start of Chapter Five that the statistical study has been hailed by believers in the paternity allegations as likely to persuade those who disbelieve. He notes that R. B. Bernstein's *Thomas Jefferson*, which the eminent scholar of the Jefferson era Professor Gordon S. Wood has called "the best short biography of Jefferson ever written,"[90] declares the Neiman study one of "three pillars"[91] of parenthood proof, along with historical evidence and

87. *See* Chapter Two of my Individual Views, pages 91–93.
88. Annette Gordon-Reed, *Let's Not Muddle Historical Fact*, Richmond Times-Dispatch, Jan. 28, 2007, at E5.
89. David R. Douglas, *Rebuttal Muddled Scientific Fact*, Richmond Times-Dispatch, Feb. 10, 2007, at A10.
90. Gordon S. Wood, *Slaves in the Family*, N.Y. Times Book Review, Dec. 14, 2003 at 10.
91. R. B. Bernstein, Thomas Jefferson 196 (2003).

the DNA evidence. Corneliussen and I have both noted that historian Jan Lewis has argued similarly.

Corneliussen remains agnostic about what the historical evidence and the DNA evidence together may show, but his commentary piece concludes: "[T]hanks to DNA confusion and the bogus statistical study, many today believe that science itself has proven the paternity. It hasn't."[92] Anyone interested in a full airing of Corneliussen's criticisms of Hemings-Jefferson science abuse will want to see his essay at TJscience.org, "Sally Hemings, Thomas Jefferson, and the Authority of Science." The essay's thumbnail summary says, "Whether or not Hemings and Jefferson had children together, misreported DNA and misused statistics have skewed the paternity debate, discrediting science itself."[93]

The *National Genealogical Society Quarterly* Special Issue

In September 2001 the National Genealogical Society issued a "Special Issue" of its quarterly journal entitled, *Jefferson-Hemings: A Special Issue of the National Genealogical Society Quarterly*. A sense of what is to come appears in the one-page "Editor's Corner" in which we are told "Monticello—ruled by the Jeffersons and populated by the Hemingses—is the symbol, if not the seat, of the world known as American slavery."[94] It is unclear whether the editor believes Jefferson created American slavery, or just that slave life at Monticello was typical of the evil institution throughout the south. Either way, her assessment is far from accurate, as slave life at Monticello was far better than at most plantations in eighteenth- and early nineteenth-century America.

The lead article in this special issue is entitled "Sally Hemings's Children: A Genealogical Analysis of the Evidence," and was written by Helen F. M. Leary. This article has already been dissected brilliantly by a genealogist who has spent decades studying the Jefferson family and other families in the Monticello area, and little purpose would be served by my attempting to duplicate that exhaustive, nearly two-hundred page effort.[95] But a few comments may be in order. For example, Ms. Leary asserts that "the conception of each Hemings child coincided precisely and exclusively with Jefferson's visits to Monticello."[96] Again, one wonders what she is trying to say. Is she telling us that Jefferson arrived "precisely" on the day Sally conceived each of her children and left the following morning, that Sally always became pregnant when Jefferson visited Monticello, and that Jefferson was the "exclusive" potential father present on that day? Whatever she is trying to say, we have no evidence that any of these possible interpretations is true.

In reality, there is very little—"precise" and "exclusive" or otherwise—that we really know about Sally Hemings. We do not even know with any certainty where Sally was when she became pregnant with her various children. The silliness of Leary's assertion that "pre-

---

92. Steven T. Corneliussen, *Have Scientific Data Proved Hemings-Jefferson Link?*, RICHMOND TIMES-DISPATCH, Jan. 14, 2007 at E1.

93. Steven T. Corneliussen, "Sally Hemings, Thomas Jefferson, and the Authority of Science: Whether or not Hemings and Jefferson had children together, misreported DNA and misused statistics have skewed the paternity debate, discrediting science itself," May 6, 2008, *available at* http://www.tj-science.org/.

94. Elizabeth Shown Mills, Editor's Corner: *The Past Is a Foreign Country*, 89(3) NATIONAL GENEALOGICAL SOCIETY QUARTERLY 163 (Sept. 2001).

95. CYNTHIA H. BURTON, JEFFERSON VINDICATED (2005).

96. Helen F. M. Leary, *Sally Hemings's Children: A Genealogical Analysis of the Evidence*, 89 (3) NATIONAL GENEALOGICAL SOCIETY QUARTERLY 165–66 (Sept. 2001).

cise" evidence exists in this matter is apparent when we look at what we believe we know about the conception of Sally's son Beverly. As discussed in Chapter Five of my Individual Views, Monticello scholar Dr. Fraser Neiman calculates that Beverly was conceived on July 8, 1797.[97] From Jefferson's records, it appears that he had been away from Monticello for more than two months prior to the estimated conception date and did not return until July 11—three days *after* the estimated conception. Now it is certainly possible that Dr. Neiman erred in his calculations or that Sally gave birth later than the "norm"; but, to mention just one example, we have no idea "precisely" where Randolph Jefferson was on July 8 or any other day in July 1797. Without knowing Randolph's location—or that of his sons—how can anyone pretend to "know" that Thomas Jefferson's presence was "exclusive"?

In a footnote on page 174 of her article, Ms. Leary seems to suggest that I attempted to mislead readers. She quotes me as saying in Chapter Ten of my Individual Views that "There was nothing in the DNA tests to cast doubt on Woodson's status as the son of Sally Hemings," and asserts this is "a statement that is correct but misleading to those unfamiliar with the nature of DNA evidence. Because Y-chromosomes exist only in males, a Y-chromosome test cannot provide any evidence on maternity."[98] I will submit to the reader the judgment of whether I attempted to "mislead" anyone with this statement. In reality, I had already carefully made her point in Chapter One, and the point I was making in the clause she quotes[99] was that the shift in position by some advocates of the Hemingses' story in suddenly assuming that Thomas Woodson was *not* Sally's child was not warranted by anything in the DNA tests. I remain agnostic about the maternity of Thomas Woodson, but I find it noteworthy that many who once seemed certain he was conceived in Paris by Thomas Jefferson and Sally Hemings, and others who had doubts about Thomas Jefferson's paternity but accepted Woodson's claim to be the son of Sally Hemings, suddenly found it convenient to "assume" he was *not* Sally's child either once the DNA excluded Thomas Jefferson as a possible father.

Leary also asserts without the slightest explanation that all of Sally's children "were likely offspring of the same man."[100] Indeed, unwarranted assumption seems to be Ms. Leary's favorite analytical tool. She notes Jefferson's long and close friendship with George Wythe—noting Jefferson called Wythe "my earliest & best friend"—and then notes rumors that Wythe may have fathered a son by a "free mulatto who kept his home." From this she concludes: "Obviously convinced by Jefferson's stoicism in the face of Federalist pressures concerning the Hemings children, Wythe named Jefferson as executor and entrusted to him the responsibility for overseeing Brown's property and education."[101] Is this really all that "obvious," or might the choice of Jefferson as executor have been influenced by the fact that the two men had been best of friends since Jefferson's days as Wythe's student at William & Mary?

---

97. Fraser D. Neiman, *Coincidence or Causal Connection: The Relationship between Thomas Jefferson's Visits to Monticello and Sally Hemings's Conceptions,* 57 WILLIAM & MARY QUARTERLY 198 (Jan. 2000).

98. Leary, *Sally Hemings's Children* 174 n. 48.

99. See page 216.

100. *Id.* at 187. Ironically, later in her article Leary argues that "mother-to-daughter lifestyle transmission" is a common phenomenon, and that "girls raised in a particular environment tend to grow up accepting that familiar lifestyle as both the norm and their fate." *Id.* at 197 and n.143. And since Madison allegedly told Wetmore that Betty Hemings had at least four different fathers for her children (*see* JAMES A. BEAR, JR., JEFFERSON AT MONTICELLO 26 n.1 (1967)), it makes even *less* sense for Leary to *assume* that Sally's children all had but a single common father.

101. *Id.* at 182.

Ms. Leary repeats the common canard that the DNA test of Eston Hemings disproved "the family claim that Sally's children greatly resembled Jefferson because they were fathered by a Carr nephew…."[102] On the contrary, the test showing Eston Hemings was likely fathered by a Jefferson male said *nothing* about the paternity of any of Sally's other children. This is so obvious that it is difficult to understand why apparently serious people keep repeating the claim.

It is clear that, like many genealogists, Ms. Leary places little stock in "oral traditions" passed down through generations about their ancestry. But it is a bit bizarre for her to say, without the slightest bit of hard evidence, that "[l]ike many 'family traditions,' the 'Jefferson's uncle' story" passed down by Eston Hemings' descendants "was a whitewashing of the truth, made necessary by the circumstances."

Ms. Leary seeks to rebut our observation that Sally appears to have stopped having children about the time Randolph Jefferson remarried and Thomas Jefferson retired from the presidency and returned full-time to Monticello by arguing:

> A more logical explanation for the end of Sally's pregnancies is the fact that Jefferson's daughter Martha and her family came back to live at Monticello in that year 1809 — a long-cherished goal for Jefferson. The Randolphs made the move in March, bringing children aged one to seventeen, and, presumably, some of their own servants. With the house now filled to capacity and Martha installed as chatelaine, continuing the liaison would have been problematic and dangerous, lest its discovery cause Martha to return to her own plantation, Edgehill.[103]

Unlike other parts of her article, this reasoning is, indeed, "logical." But it raises yet another problem Ms. Leary fails to address. Reasonable people can agree that it would be "problematic and dangerous" for Thomas Jefferson to carry on a sexual liaison with Sally Hemings with his beloved daughter and a house full of grandchildren at Monticello. But at Jefferson's insistence, Martha and her family returned to Monticello virtually every time Thomas Jefferson did during the entire period of his presidency. So the same "logical explanation" that persuades reasonable people that he would not have carried on the relationship after 1809 would have applied with equal force during the years when Sally was having children.

Leary argues that the reason Madison Hemings did not claim to be Thomas Jefferson's child until more than four decades after Jefferson's death was because, prior to ratification of the Thirteenth Amendment in "1870" (*sic* — the Thirteenth Amendment was ratified on December 6, 1865), Beverly and Harriet and all of their children would have been "at risk of capture and re-enslavement had their identity been discovered. That possibility, however remote, was fearsome."[104] This speculation is neither scholarship nor genealogy, it is supposition and fantasy. According to Wetmore, Madison had not been in touch with Harriet in a decade and did not know whether she was alive or dead. All he revealed about Beverly was that he went to Washington and then "married a white woman in Maryland" and they had a daughter. For "prudential reasons" he did not give the name of Harriet's husband. Had Madison actually been seriously concerned for their welfare,

---

102. *Id.* at 189. Nor was the family claim that Sally's children were fathered by *a* Carr nephew. Both accounts attributed indirectly to Thomas Jefferson Randolph report that he said *two* Carr nephews confessed in his presence to fathering children by Sally Hemings. *See* Chapter Ten of my Individual Views on pages 208–12. So much for the assertion that no one ever questioned Sally's monogamy.

103. *Id.* at 191.

104. *Id.* at 185.

all he needed to do was omit their names and even the geographic areas in which they lived from his alleged account of his family background.

She notes census taker William Weaver's 1870 marginal notation next to Madison Hemings' name that "This man is the son of Thomas Jefferson!" and declares that this is "primary information from an original source." One wonders what on Earth she is talking about. Presumably, while Weaver was speaking with Madison Hemings to obtain his name, age, and other information necessary for the census, Madison declared that he was Thomas Jefferson's child. Recording this hearsay adds little to the *Pike County Republican* story published three years later that made the same claim. The sole basis for both claims is Madison Hemings, who could not have known with certainty the facts involved because they occurred before his birth.

As noted in Chapter Four of my Individual Views, both Fawn Brodie and Annette Gordon-Reed acknowledged that the polished prose of Wetmore's 1873 article was likely that of the editor and not a former slave with minimum formal education. In contrast, Leary asserts that "the language is commensurate with Madison's background and training," reasoning: "He was undoubtedly brought up to enter the white world, as his brother and sister had done. His conversational model had been the discourse of an articulate orator and one of the most literate men this nation has produced."[105] In reality, Thomas Jefferson was *not* "an articulate orator"[106] and Madison reportedly admitted to Wetmore that Jefferson had never shown him "partiality or fatherly affection" and that he had learned to read by "inducing the white children to teach me the letters." One may speculate that perhaps Madison was "trained" to "enter the white world," but given the facts we know it is unreasonable to allege that this assumption is "undoubtedly" true.

Ms. Leary asserts that "[l]arge portions of Madison's statement represent primary data based on his own experience," noting that he claimed to have been "measurably happy" — a statement that "was not hearsay; it was his own direct experience."[107] That's true. But, more significantly, for our purposes, Madison's unsourced allegations — assuming for the moment that Madison was indeed the source for Wetmore's rhetoric — about what occurred in Paris before he was born or his own paternity and that of his older siblings is clearly hearsay, at best. It was not testimony based on "his own direct experience."

Consider also this bit of fantasy from Leary's article:

> Sally's part of the bargain, clearly, was her availability when he wanted her and her pledge to have no other sexual partner. This mutual agreement, scrupulously observed, is the only reasonable explanation for the subsequent behavior of both Jefferson and Hemings. He assisted the departure of Beverly and Harriet and provided for manumission of Madison and Eston, thereby freeing all her children.[108]

Again, this is not "genealogy" and it is not history. And Leary's conclusions certainly are not "clear" based upon the evidence she offers. Thomas Jefferson already legally *owned* Sally Hemings. He did not need her "consent" to demand sex from her or control her sexual involvement with other men. Even if one assumed that Beverly was se-

---

105. *Id.* at 195.

106. Jefferson was uncomfortable in the role of a public speaker and much preferred the pen to the spoken word. Indeed, as President he departed from the precedents set by Washington and Adams of making his annual report to Congress in person and elected instead to submit written reports.

107. Leary, *Sally Hemings's Children* at 196.

108. *Id.* at 197.

cretly allowed to withdraw from Monticello in 1822 (at the age of 23 or more likely 24), this was hardly scrupulous observance of an alleged promise to "free" him at the age of 21. And if the "only reasonable explanation" for freeing Madison and Eston in his will was that he was having sex with their mother, how do we explain the fact that all but two of Betty Hemings' sons and grandsons known to be alive and in Jefferson's possession in 1826 were also freed—most of them under considerably more favorable terms than those given Madison and Eston? Was Thomas Jefferson having sex with *their* mothers too?

There is more than a little irony in Ms. Leary's suggestion that *I* attempted to "mislead" readers in making the observation (which she concedes is correct) that the DNA tests of descendants of Thomas Woodson provided no evidence on his maternity. Consider Ms. Leary's own effort to discredit the 1858 letter from Ellen Randolph Coolidge by noting Ellen's denial of a Jefferson-Hemings sexual relationship was contained in a letter "intended to influence a publication."[109] What she fails to reveal is that, while the first part of the letter was indeed provided to assist with a publication, the portion discussing her brother Jefferson Randolph's comment on the Carr brothers' admission was prefaced with this language: "I have written thus far thinking you might chuse [*sic*] to communicate my letter to Mr. Bulfinch. Now I will tell you *in confidence* what Jefferson told me under the like condition."[110] We often do not know the full purpose for which historic letters were written. But in this case it appears clear that Ellen Coolidge did *not* intend to have her discussion of the Carr brothers' admission disclosed to any third party. Ms. Leary does her subscribers a disservice by misrepresenting this fact.

Speaking of Ellen Randolph Coolidge, Ms. Leary's attempts to defend Professor Gordon-Reed's "inadvertent" alteration in Ellen's October 24, 1858, letter to her brother in a footnote, asserting: "Gordon-Reed dropped a short part of this quotation from her transcription (*Thomas Jefferson and Sally Hemings*, 259), probably inadvertently; but the omission is viewed with dark suspicion at the Thomas Jefferson Heritage Society website...."[111] As a factual matter, this statement is untrue. Professor Gordon-Reed did not merely "drop" a "short part of this quotation"—she altered nearly a dozen words by either deletion, insertion, or moving words around in the sentence to materially change its original meaning. And this "inadvertent" alteration just happened to be on the most critical sentence in the letter for our purposes.

This is important, because intentionally altering historical evidence to mislead readers is a far greater sin than merely plagiarizing another scholar's work. Plagiarism merely converts the intellectual property of another, whereas doctoring an historical document that most readers cannot readily check intentionally misleads everyone who reads the book. As Thomas Jefferson observed, "he who knows nothing is nearer to truth than he whose mind is filled with falsehoods and errors."[112]

Consider the evidence. In the original letter, Ellen Randolph Coolidge wrote—and I have here kept her lines as they appeared in the original hand-written letter (see **Figure 4** on page 37) so readers can consider the possibility that Professor Gordon-Reed merely "skipped a line" in making her transcription:

---

109. *Id* at 199.

110. *Id.* (emphasis added.) *See* the introduction and Chapter Ten of my Individual Views for a more detailed discussion of this letter.

111. *Id.* at 206 n.178.

112. *Jefferson to John Norvell*, June 11, 1807, in 11 Writings of Thomas Jefferson 225 (Mem. Ed. 1903).

No female domestic ever entered his chambers except
at hours when he was known not to be there and none
could have entered without being exposed to the public gaze.[113]

Professor Gordon-Reed transcribed this as:

No female domestic ever entered his chambers except at hours when he was
known not to be in the public gaze.[114]

This is the most critical sentence in the altered letter, and it was transformed from a piece of evidence for the defense into an "admission against interest" by a defense witness confirming that Sally was allowed to go to Jefferson's bedroom when no one was thought to be looking. The other key "error" in Professor Gordon-Reed's transcription of this document involved replacing the word "disbelief" with the word "belief" in a sentence asserting that Ellen's brother Thomas Jefferson Randolph had "positively declared his indignant disbelief in the imputations" that President Jefferson had fathered Sally Hemings' children.[115] Then we have the alterations to the *Pike County Republican* story attributed to Madison Hemings to consider.[116] I will leave to the reader the task of deciding whether Ms. Leary was justified in her assumption that this first alteration of key evidence was "probably inadvertent."

Consider also Leary's treatment of the statement by Monticello overseer Edmund Bacon that Harriet Hemings was not Thomas Jefferson's daughter but the child of a man whose name was omitted from the published version of Pierson's account and replaced with _____. Bacon is quoted as explaining: "I know that. I have seen him [the man other than Thomas Jefferson whose name is replaced with _____] come out of her mother's room many a morning, when I went up to Monticello very early."[117] Of this statement, Ms. Leary writes:

- Harriet was conceived in August 1801, Madison in April 1804. Unless the teenaged Bacon was hanging around Monticello for reasons of his own "on many a morning … very early," his account cannot relate to any of the conceptions prior to Eston's.

- Eston is proved to have been a Y-line Jefferson descendant. If there is any truth at all in Bacon's account, the man he saw leaving the room of Harriet's mother would have to be a Jefferson. Bacon's "many a morning" phrase implies not only that he, Bacon, was a Monticello inhabitant but that the Jefferson male was also in residence—and the only Jefferson living at Monticello was Thomas.[118]

On the contrary, the statement that Bacon "went up to Monticello very early" on "many a morning" suggests not that he "was a Monticello inhabitant" at the time, but instead that he was going from his residence to Monticello very early in the morning—presumably on the way to work. Bacon later told the Reverend Hamilton W. Pierson "I went to live with him [Jefferson] the 27th of the December before he was inaugurated as President,"[119] it seems clear from Jefferson's records that Bacon lived at Monticello from at least 1806 to 1822, and he claimed that had he stayed until December 27, 1822, "I should have been with him [Jefferson] precisely twenty years,"[120] or since 1802.

---

113. *Monticello Report,* Appendix E at 17.
114. Annette Gordon-Reed, Thomas Jefferson and Sally Hemings 259. Readers can examine excerpts of the original and transcription in **Figure 4** on page 137.
115. *Id.* at 258–59. See **Figure 3** on page 36.
116. *See* the Introduction to my Individual Views, **Figures 1** and **2** on pages 33 and 35.
117. *Quoted in* Leary, *Sally Hemings's Children* at 203.
118. *Id.* at 204.
119. Jefferson at Monticello 39.
120. *Id.* at 39–40.

It is also clear that Bacon worked for Thomas Jefferson in various capacities prior to becoming overseer.[121] And it would seem logical that his statement "I have seen him [an unidentified man other than Thomas Jefferson] come out of her [Harriet Hemings'] mother's room many a morning when I went up to Monticello very early"[122] might well have occurred *prior* to Bacon's going to live at Monticello. He presumably "went up to Monticello very early" during a period or periods when he was working for Mr. Jefferson but residing elsewhere — so he would have had to make the trip up the mountain "very early" in the morning. However, we cannot completely dismiss the possibility that as overseer he might have traveled off the mountain for any of a number of reasons and then returned "very early" — so these observations of another man leaving Sally Hemings' room could have been made while he was overseer or many years earlier (or both).

While it is true that Eston's father was almost certainly a Jefferson, he did not have to be "in residence" on a full-time basis as Ms. Leary contends, but merely present at Monticello on the mornings (and, presumably, through part of the previous night) that Bacon observed him. Jefferson did not keep a record of routine visits by brother Randolph or his family members (unless their visit pertained to some business matter that on that basis warranted an entry in his records), and if Randolph and his sons only made the twenty-mile trip twice a year and stayed only a week or two each visit it is perfectly possible that Bacon could have observed one of them leaving Sally's room a half dozen times over a period of two or three years and thus made the statement to Pierson. Leary's attempt to persuade her readers that Sally's lover for some unexplained reason had to be a full-time resident at Monticello (versus an overnight visitor who came to Monticello from time to time over a period of time), and thus Bacon *had* to be talking about Thomas Jefferson, is obviously *absurd*. The clear content of Bacon's statement was that Harriet Hemings was *not* Thomas Jefferson's child because Bacon had frequently observed *another* man leaving Sally's room early in the morning. It is obtuse to fill in the blank line with the name "Thomas Jefferson," pretending that Bacon might have said, essentially, "I know Tom Jefferson was not Sally's lover, because I often saw him slipping out of her room early in the morning."

Ms. Leary also assures her readers that Thomas Jefferson Randolph and his sister Ellen Randolph Coolidge could not have been telling the truth when they separately described hearing President Jefferson snoring or singing in his bedroom at night or early in the morning. "[B]oth implied that they would have heard any midnight visits by Sally because their rooms were either above or beside their grandfather's. There was no bedroom within sound of Jefferson's bedchamber (unless he was a thunderous snorer) and there was no room above it."[123] One must wonder if Ms. Leary has ever been permitted to visit the upper floors of Monticello, which are generally closed to the public because the very narrow staircases are viewed by the fire marshal as a safety hazard. There is indeed a room above Jefferson's chamber where one can readily hear the voices of tour guides below as they point out the unusual features of Jefferson's bed.[124] And in Jefferson's day, before modern air conditioning — when windows were normally kept open during the hot summer months, it would presumably have been even easier for the grandchildren sleeping in the "Appendix" above his chamber to hear any unusual noises coming from his bed during the night.

Albemarle County genealogist Cynthia Burton has written nearly 200 pages (65,000 words) with hundreds of footnotes meticulously rebutting Ms. Leary's article, and I have

---

121. THOMAS JEFFERSON'S GARDEN BOOK 601 (Edwin Morris Betts, ed., 1999).
122. JEFFERSON AT MONTICELLO 102.
123. *Id.* at 205.
124. *See* Chapter Eleven of my Individual Views on page 241.

no interest in duplicating that effort here.[125] I highly commend it for anyone who views the Leary article as a serious piece of scholarship.

Dr. Thomas Jones' "Review Essay"

The Leary article actually made few references to the Scholars Commission report. But the special issue of the *Quarterly* also included an eleven-page "review essay" entitled, "The 'Scholars Commission' Report on the Jefferson-Hemings Matter: An Evaluation by Genealogical Proof Standards," written by Professor Thomas W. Jones, which seems to constitute the Society's primary attempt to challenge our report.

According to the Gallaudet University Web site,[126] Thomas W. Jones holds a B.A. in "Mental Retardation," an M.A. in "Education of the Multihandicapped and Deaf-Blind," and a Ph.D. in "Early Childhood Special Education." Although he apparently had no specific past interest in Thomas Jefferson, he clearly has had an active extra-curricular interest in genealogy and was serving as the *Quarterly*'s review editor at the time his review was published.

When I learned of the special issue I immediately ordered a copy, and when it arrived I looked eagerly to see what errors they had found in our report—knowing that errors could still be corrected prior to submitting the manuscript to the publisher. Candidly, I came away from reading Professor Jones' "review" more than a little disappointed—as he did not engage a single one of the key substantive arguments of our report. Instead, he criticized us for not including a genealogist on the Commission and complained that we failed to clarify the "genealogical question" of "*Who fathered Sally Hemings's children.*"[127] Again and again, he tells his readers, "the scholars applied an inappropriate paradigm,"[128] and "[i]gnoring the genealogical paradigm has caused the report to fall short of genealogical standards in crucial ways. It does not specify an appropriate objective."[129] Jones explains:

> For genealogical research to be efficient and effective, it must begin with an appropriate objective. Typically, the objective is to identify the parent of a given ancestor. Such a goal frames the scope of the research, enabling the scholar to seek relevant sources; and it provides a context for evaluating the findings.

> Although established "for the purpose of reexamining the entire issue" (p. 8), the Scholars Commission explicitly eschewed the essential genealogical objective, stating: "We were not tasked with the job of identifying the father(s) of Sally Hemings' children, and that has not been a primary focus of our inquiry. Our mandate was to examine the case against Thomas Jefferson" (p. 31), a mission the panelists viewed as "trying to prove a negative" (p. 31).

> This arbitrary limit on the Commission's purpose guaranteed a failed effort. In narrowly focusing their inquiry, the panelists touched on—but ignored the significance of—subsidiary genealogical questions, where additional research might

---

125. CYNTHIA H. BURTON, JEFFERSON VINDICATED (2005).

126. http://academic.gallaudet.edu/cce/extonline.nsf/0/EF734C8CC4CF59738525672D000C5BEA?Open Document.

127. Thomas W. Jones, *The "Scholars Commission" Report on the Jefferson-Hemings Matter: An Evaluation by Genealogical Proof Standards*, NATIONAL GENEALOGICAL SOCIETY QUARTERLY 218 (Sept. 2001).

128. *Id.* at 209.

129. *Id.* at 210.

have helped to solve the problem they were considering. These include tracing the descendants of Beverly and Harriet Hemings.... [130]

Mea culpa. It is true that we did not spend a lot of time trying to establish who fathered Sally's children, nor did we spend time speculating about whether John Wayles was Sally's father. Both issues may be of great interest to genealogists, but our task was to examine the evidence pro and con about whether *Thomas Jefferson* fathered one or more children by Sally Hemings. While I personally did work closely with one genealogist and received helpful information from others, I did not—and do not—view this as primarily a matter of genealogy, which I understand to involve the tracing of generations of ancestors or descendants of a specific individual or family. Much of Jones' critique sounds to me like a critique of a soccer game because the players failed to abide by the standard rules of rugby or American football. Professor Jones is interested in genealogy, and he apparently wishes we had spent our year doing genealogy instead of what we were commissioned to do.

To be sure, some of the factual questions we did address might be of interest to anyone trying to trace the genealogy of the Hemings or Woodson families and presumably the Jefferson family as well. But our primary inquiry was confined to examining a single alleged relationship: Did Thomas Jefferson father one or more children by Sally Hemings? And for that inquiry the tools of the historian were of primary concern to us. This is not to say that we might not have benefited from having a senior Professor of Genealogy on our panel; but, in all candor, nothing in Professor Jones' review left me believing he would have contributed much of value to our efforts.

Jones does concede that the Scholars Commission consisted of "an impressive panel of distinguished academics,"[131] and that "thirteen eminent scholars signed the final report."[132] But rather than challenging our conclusions on the merits, his review consists largely of procedural comments that often are misleading if not clearly false. He tells his readers, for example, that:

> Although the Commission's title and the credentials of its members imply that conventional standards of scholarship have been applied, the "Final Report" offers no source citations.... The Commission grants liberal reproduction rights for the "Final Report," whose lack of documentation will prevent the public from testing its assertions; but it restricts dissemination or quoting from the documented portions of the report."[133]

There are two things Jones does not mention to his readers. First, in our individual views we discuss every issue in great detail and include more than 1,400 footnotes citing our sources so that other scholars, as well as "the public," may "test" our assertions. As should be apparent to anyone who has read this far in this volume, the implication that we refused to provide "source citations" and sought to compel readers simply to take our word for the facts is not even close to a fair or accurate statement. But, of course, most of Professor Jones' readers will not have seen our full report.

The second terribly misleading aspect of this quotation is Jones' suggestion that we sought to *restrict* "dissemination or quoting from the documented portions of the report." For the record, as Jones well knew, we put the *entire report* on the Internet for

---

130. *Id.* at 211.
131. *Id.* at 208.
132. *Id.*
133. *Id.* at 209.

anyone in the world to download, print, and read at their leisure. And we certainly did not attempt to prohibit *anyone* from "quoting from the documented portions of the report." What Jones is really talking about is that we did make a distinction between the official Final Report, which summarized the majority and minority conclusions and is printed at the beginning this volume, and the more detailed and heavily documented "individual views" that followed. We allowed anyone to reprint the entire "Final Report" for any non-profit purpose without even bothering to ask permission. The entire volume is copyrighted, but to promote wider distribution of the summary Report (pages 3–21) we gave advance consent to reprint that part for any non-profit purpose without any need to seek permission. The explanation for this was that we intended to eventually publish the entire collection as a book—this book—for future reference in libraries and for scholars and interested members of the public, and we knew that few publishers would want to invest the resources involved in publishing a book if the entire product was already in the public domain and could be published at will by any competitor at any time.

It is the overwhelming practice for scholarly books to be copyrighted, and doing so does not in the *least* prevent fair use "quoting" for purposes of scholarly review or rebuttal. Professor Jones clearly understood this, as he included quotations from our individual views in his published review. But his language misled his readers into believing we had somehow tried to conceal our documented analysis from other scholars and the public and sought to prevent anyone from quoting us. Both implications are absolutely false. We strongly favor a public debate—it is our critics who have refused to debate.

Yet another absurdity in Professor Jones' essay is his assertion that individual views are "disavowed." This is premised upon a disclaimer I included explaining that I had made several changes to my own Individual Views after four other members of the Scholars Commission had agreed to add their names as generally concurring with those views. Thus, I wrote that they should not be held accountable for specific facts or arguments in my final chapters. However, rather than "disavowing" responsibility, I emphasized: *the words are mine and responsibility for the specific arguments and the accuracy of facts is mine alone.*[134] The "disclaimer" is not intended to disavow responsibility, but to make it clear to the readers that if they find errors or believe a particular argument is fallacious they should blame any such problems on me individually and not on other scholars who agreed generally with my overall views but had not even seen all of the final changes in my lengthy statement. There is nothing even arguably evasive or improper in that statement—it was a clarification of precisely who is responsible for the words that I had written. As Harry Truman put it: "The buck stops here!"

Professor Jones complains: "the Commission appears to have conducted very little original investigation. It cites virtually none of the mainstays of quality genealogical research, such as deeds, court records, and tax rolls from which direct, indirect, and negative evidence can be gleaned."[135] Jones does not explain how he envisions "deeds, court records, and tax rolls" will disclose whether Thomas Jefferson fathered children by Sally Hemings. In the early nineteenth century the births of slave children were not recorded at the county courthouse, nor were slaves permitted to own real property or required to pay taxes. We did take note of the fact that an 1870 census taker in Ohio made a marginal notation that Madison Hemings was Thomas Jefferson's son, but there is no evidence he

---

134. The slightly edited disclaimer appears on page 44 of this volume (emphasis in original).
135. *Id.* at 212–13.

was doing more than recording hearsay from Madison. We did, of course, discuss Thomas Jefferson's will at some length and make frequent use of his farm, garden, and memorandum books.

Professor Jones does not appear to have even read some of the sources he discusses. For example, he notes that we dismissed the probative value of the "Monte Carlo" study contained in an article in the *William & Mary Quarterly,* asserting that "'the Monte Carlo study' is a nickname that the Commission itself gave to the article in the course of its meeting."[136] This is absurd. The use of Monte Carlo simulations has been well established in science and other fields for a half-century.[137] Indeed, Dr. Fraser Neiman described his methodology as a "Monte Carlo study"[138] and used the term more than *two dozen times* in the article in question. It is difficult to understand how Professor Jones could have made such an error if he had bothered to even glance through the piece.

Like Ms. Leary, Professor Jones notes that the letter Ellen Randolph Coolidge sent her husband in 1858 was "a letter Ellen explicitly penned so her husband could convince a Boston writer that an interracial liaison was 'morally impossible' for her grandsire."[139] And, like Leary, he fails to point out that the specific reference to an admission by the Carr brothers of paternity for Sally's children was contained not in the main body of the letter but in a separate attachment which she expressly prefaced by saying it was to be held in confidence by her husband. Obviously, there is always a possibility that an historical letter was penned to mislead future historians, and that is certainly a possibility in this instance. But it is *dishonest* to portray Ellen's reference to the Carr brothers as having been explicitly provided for the purpose of convincing a third party of a fact when that part of the letter is instead prefaced by instructions that the information should *not* be disseminated further.

Professor Jones concludes his short essay by saying: "The Commission's eminent scholars could have applied decades of genealogical scholarship in their approach to a genealogical question. Instead, their report—rather than clarifying the question '*Who fathered Sally Hemings's children'*—contributes to the plague of confusion."

After reading his "review" of our report, I concluded that the easiest way to deal with it would be to reprint it on our Web site (and as an annex to the book version of our report) and allow each reader to examine both documents and draw their own conclusions. This would be in keeping with Jefferson's vision of the University of Virginia, where I have been employed for more than two decades:

> This institution will be based on the illimitable freedom of the human mind. For here we are not afraid to follow truth wherever it may lead, nor to tolerate any error so long as reason is left free to combat it.[140]

Given what I felt was the weakness of his case, I also thought it might be worthwhile to debate Professor Jones on our points of disagreement and raised both possibilities with him in an e-mail. His reply is instructive:

Dear Professor Turner:

---

136. *Id.* at 213.

137. A Google search of "Monte Carlo simulation" produced more than one million hits.

138. Fraser D. Neiman, *Coincidence or Causal Connection: The Relationship between Thomas Jefferson's Visits to Monticello and Sally Hemings's Conceptions,* 57 WILLIAM & MARY QUARTERLY 198, 208 (Jan. 2000).

139. Jones, *The "Scholars Commission" Report* at 218.

140. *Jefferson to William Roscoe*, Dec. 27, 1820, in 15 WRITINGS OF THOMAS JEFFERSON 303 (Mem. Ed., 1904).

Thank you for your interest in publishing on the Scholars Commission web site my NGSQ review essay on the "Scholars Commission Final Report." As with any scholarly publication, I am happy for anyone to refer to it and to quote from it. If the review is to be re-published in the future, however, my feeling at this time is that I should do so myself in a suitable context....

You also referred to the position that I "seem to embrace," asking whether I would "be willing to take on the role of advocating the position that Thomas Jefferson fathered one or more children by Sally Hemings in a public debate." The answer is unequivocally negative.[141]

I am tempted to make a comment about "restrictive dissemination" policies; but, in retrospect, given the quality of his work, and his refusal to defend it in public debate, perhaps Professor Jones is wiser than I had originally assumed.

The *William & Mary Quarterly* Review

In October 2001 the *William & Mary Quarterly* published an eight-page review of three books[142]—not including the Scholars Commission report—that nevertheless included some references to our work. It was written by Alexander O. Boulton, an assistant professor at Villa Julie College in Maryland.

After discussing the Thomas Jefferson Heritage Society's *The Jefferson-Hemings Myth* and noting the subsequent report of the Scholars Commission, Professor Boulton writes: "Together, the two publications offer a strong corrective to the early enthusiasm over a new consensus."[143]

There is very little substantive discussion of the Scholars Commission report in this review (appropriately so, since it was not included among the volumes being examined), but Professor Boulton makes several statements that probably nevertheless warrant comment. For example, he finds Edmund Bacon's statement that Jefferson could not have been the father of Harriet II because he (Bacon) often saw another man leaving her room early in the morning "implausible"[144] because, Boulton believes, Bacon was not at Monticello during the period about which he made the statement. That may, or may not, be true—we really do not know if Bacon was visiting or doing odd jobs at Monticello around the time Harriet II was conceived—but even if we assume his observations were made several years later, when we know with certainty that Bacon was the Monticello overseer, his statement is inherently among the least obviously biased[145] and is the only clearly eye-witness account pertaining to the question of Sally's monogamy.

---

141. *E-mail from Tom Jones to Bob Turner*, 2/20/02.

142. The three books reviewed were Eyler Robert Coates, Sr. (ed.), *The Jefferson-Hemings Myth*; Byron W. Woodson, Sr., *A President in the Family*; and Lucia Stanton, *Free Some Day*.

143. Alexander O. Boulton, *The Monticello Mystery—Case Continued*, 58(4) WILLIAM & MARY Q. 1039, 1040, Oct. 2001.

144. *Id.* at 1041 n.8.

145. Presumably the Jefferson and Hemings family members all had a "self-interest" in either portraying Jefferson as saintly or confirming the Hemings family claim to famous ancestry. Bacon clearly admired Jefferson, but he had no obvious benefit in misrepresenting the facts as he understood them. He was independently wealthy, living far away from Jefferson's impoverished relatives, clearly unfriendly to the southern cause, and also clearly respected as a man of honor. Whether his story is true or false, objectively he appears to be among the most credible sources and the only actual "witness" to specific activity that was likely directly related to Sally's sexual behavior pattern.

And it really does not matter whether Bacon's observations took place about the time Harriet II was conceived or closer to Eston's conception. For if the story is true, the account strongly suggests that Sally either was not sexually involved with Thomas Jefferson or else was not monogamous in such a relationship. If she was monogamous with a man other than Thomas Jefferson, then it follows the President was not the father of any of her children. If she was not monogamous, the foundation for much of the case against Jefferson — which is expressly premised upon a presumption of monogamy — crumbles.

Professor Boulton also repeats the argument that "Randolph Jefferson ... had never seriously been considered as a possible partner of Sally Hemings until the DNA evidence indicated that a Jefferson was unquestionably the father of Eston."[146] That argument has already been addressed and shown to be false (although, in fairness, there is no reason Professor Boulton should have known that).[147]

Similarly, he asserts "all previous testimony has agreed that Sally Hemings was faithful to the one father of all her children."[148] Unless by this he means only the highly problematic statements attributed to Madison Hemings by Samuel Wetmore in 1873,[149] and the clearly *false* claims of Israel Jefferson published by the same source,[150] this also is inaccurate. At best, scholars have assumed this to be true without examining the issue in detail or making any serious finding on the issue. (If one assumes that Bacon's statement about the paternity of Harriet II was based upon observations he made years later, then he may be counted among those at least assuming monogamy — but we really do not know with any certainty when his observations were made.) Historically, most serious Jefferson scholars seem to have dismissed the Callender allegations on the basis of what they knew about Callender and Jefferson, and then accepted the accounts attributed to Jeff Randolph that the Carr brothers fathered her children. But since those accounts indicated that *two* brothers were fathers to Sally's children,[151] one cannot reasonably conclude that they "agreed" only a single father was involved. And this doesn't even consider the original Callender charge that Sally was a prostitute.

Again, we read "there was never a suggestion from any source close to Monticello that Sally was anything other than faithful to the father of her children (whoever he may have been)."[152] First of all, it would be equally accurate to note that (save for the factual allegations attributed to Madison Hemings decades after Jefferson's death, the truth of which he could not possibly have personally known because they occurred years before his birth) "there was never a suggestion from any source close to Monticello that Sally was not the 'slut as common as the pavement,' who had 'fifteen, or thirty' different lovers 'of all colours,'" as James Callender alleged.[153] I mention this not because I place the slightest credence in anything Callender wrote, but because so much of the paternity-belief scholarship is premised upon the assumption that Callender was, at root, an honest journalist who may have stretched the truth a bit at the edges.[154]

---

146. Boulton, *The Monticello Mystery* 1042.
147. *See* Chapter Ten of my Individual Views.
148. Boulton, *The Monticello Mystery* 1042.
149. *See* Chapter Four of my Individual Views.
150. *Id.*
151. *See* Chapter Ten of my Individual Views.
152. Boulton, *The Monticello Mystery* 1046.
153. *See* page 101.
154. For example, in another article in the special issue of the *National Genealogical Society Quarterly* discussed above, Professor Joshua D. Rothman writes: "Jefferson scholars have routinely dis-

Furthermore, unless one is prepared to exclude the possibility that Sally bore children by Thomas Jefferson, there certainly was "a suggestion from any source close to Monticello that Sally was other than faithful to the father of her children," as overseer Edmund Bacon—the senior employee at the plantation—very clearly asserted that he had frequently witnessed a man other than Thomas Jefferson leaving Sally's room early in the morning. One simply cannot seriously contend that there is no "evidence" from the Monticello community that Sally Hemings was not "faithful" to the father of her children if one believes that Thomas Jefferson was that father.

Then we have Professor Boulton's allegation that "[a]ll defenders and critics of Jefferson agree that Sally Hemings bore a child, perhaps named Tom, around 1790."[155] One wonders where he gets such an idea. There is no record of a child being born to Sally Hemings in 1790 in any of Jefferson's records, and the only apparent sources for such an allegation were Callender's 1802 assertion and the Woodson claim (both now apparently refuted by DNA testing) and the story attributed to Madison Hemings more than seven decades later. While one cannot say with certainty that no such child was born, credible evidence is slight and the point is certainly not accepted by "all defenders ... of Thomas Jefferson."

Professor Joyce Appleby

While the immediate press reaction to the issuance of our report in April 2001 was encouraging, the academic community response has been somewhat less so. Scholars have not criticized our report on the merits for the most part; they have simply continued to embrace the revisionist mythology. This is not the time to examine all of the many books on Jefferson that have been published since 2001, but a few examples may be useful.

In 2003, UCLA Professor Joyce Appleby—former president of both the Organization of American Historians and the American Historical Association—wrote a volume on *Thomas Jefferson* for the American Presidents Series being edited by Arthur M. Schlesinger, Jr., for Times Books. At first I thought she had made a brief reference to the Scholars Commission, writing: "A dissenting group of scholars has challenged the idea that the DNA findings established Jefferson as the father of Eston Hemings."[156] But the sentence was mysteriously footnoted to a 1999 collection of essays (*Sally Hemings and Thomas Jefferson*) by scholars who accept or assume Thomas Jefferson's paternity.[157]

The short Appleby volume is well written and in many ways more respectful of Jefferson than many other modern biographies. She identifies shortcomings in Jefferson's writings and beliefs, but then adds: "If they appall us, they should also provoke our wonder

---

missed Callender's allegations out of hand, arguing that his motives and character made him and anything he wrote entirely unbelievable. Gordon-Reed points out that his personal repugnancy and malicious motivations—both valid reasons to view his articles with a skeptical eye—do not necessarily make him a liar or absolve historians of a responsibility to examine his claims. Indeed, Callender's biographer notes that over the course of the man's career he sometimes misinterpreted information, but there 'is little, if any, evidence of his purposeful invention of stories or falsification of facts.'" Joshua D. Rothman, *Can the "Character Defense" Survive?*, 89(3) JEFFERSON-HEMINGS: A SPECIAL ISSUE OF THE NATIONAL GENEALOGICAL SOCIETY Q. 219, 221 (Sept. 2001). I would submit that there is not the slightest evidence to support Callender's libelous attacks on Sally Hemings, a woman he had probably never even seen and about whom he seemed to know very little.

155. Boulton, *The Monticello Mystery* 1044.
156. JOYCE APPLEBY, THOMAS JEFFERSON 75 (2003).
157. *Id.* at 162 n.2 (citing *Sally Hemings and Thomas Jefferson* [Peter Onuf and Jan Lewis, eds. 1999]).

than anyone born in the bosom of a misogynist, slave-holding aristocracy could have dreamed of a society of equals."[158] To me, that was among many things that were truly exceptional about Thomas Jefferson, and I commend Professor Appleby for acknowledging it at a time when it is not fashionable within the professional historical community to praise him.

Nevertheless, the Appleby volume includes numerous troubling factual errors. For example, she writes that some people in the past "suggested that the white father of Sally Hemings's children was more likely one of Jefferson's nephews, a possibility that has since been disproved."[159] In reality, the DNA tests said nothing about the paternity of any of Sally Hemings' children except Eston (and Thomas Woodson if he was, in fact, Sally Hemings' child). The Jefferson DNA for the tests came from descendants of Thomas Jefferson's cousins, but Professor Appleby asserts it was "taken from a living descendant of Jefferson's brother."[160] She adds that "there were eighteen Jefferson men in Virginia" at the time (in fact there were more than two dozen), and claims that "only Jefferson lived in close proximity to her"[161] (ignoring Randolph and his five sons less than twenty miles away).

It is surprising that such a distinguished scholar would make so many careless errors, even referring at one point to Jefferson's "apt ... depiction of slave owners as having the wolf by the tail!"[162] Surely she has in mind Jefferson's famous April 22, 1820, letter to John Holmes, in which the former President describes the dilemma of slave-holders: "[W]e have the wolf by the ears, and we can neither hold him, nor safely let him go."[163] (A copy of the original handwritten letter can be found on the Library of Congress Web site, and it is clear that Jefferson actually wrote "ear" rather than "ears"—but the point is not material to our discussion.[164]) One does not get the sense that Professor Appleby was "out to get" Jefferson or has in any way altered her facts to make him look bad— most of her errors are essentially benign (e.g., it is immaterial whether the DNA samples used by Dr. Foster were taken from descendants of Randolph Jefferson or other male members of the Jefferson family). Nevertheless, they are disturbingly careless, particularly given the ease with which these facts could have been checked.

Christopher Hitchens

Another relatively short volume on Jefferson was published in 2005 as part of the Eminent Lives series by HarperCollins. Written by Christopher Hitchens, it devotes about six pages to Sally Hemings at the end of Chapter Three. As is now common, Hitchens assures his readers that, while in Paris, Jefferson "began an affair" with Sally that was to "produce many children...."[165] Indeed, he confidently asserts that it began in 1788.[166]

158. APPLEBY, THOMAS JEFFERSON 3.

159. *Id.* at 74.

160. *Id.* at 75.

161. *Id.*

162. *Id.* at 79.

163. *Jefferson to Holmes*, Apr. 22, 1820, 15 WRITINGS OF THOMAS JEFFERSON 248, 249 (Mem. ed. 1903).

164. A copy of the original page is *available at* http://memory.loc.gov/master/mss/mtj/mtj1/051/1200/1238.jpg.

165. CHRISTOPHER HITCHENS, THOMAS JEFFERSON: AUTHOR OF AMERICA 59 (2005).

166. *Id.* at 64.

Some of his reasoning is in the finest traditions of Fawn Brodie and Annette Gordon-Reed (whose 1997 book he describes as "brilliant" and "dispositive"[167]):

> The first clue to the relationship may lie in the simple fact that Jefferson, having met Sally and received his daughter from her in good condition, did not send her home again (as he had planned to do with the original escort). He did not require an extra servant at the Hotel de Langeac, his well-appointed residence, where Sally's brother James was already on the staff, being trained as a French chef. Possibly the latter consideration influenced him, in inviting Sally to stay on. But nor did he exactly need a governess, since both his daughters were destined for boarding school. Thus the beautiful Sally became a part of the ministerial household, with no specific duties.[168]

Given Abigail Adams' description of a teenage Sally as requiring "more care" than eight-year-old Polly, and the fact that the "boarding school" had quarters for servants, it is hardly remarkable that Thomas Jefferson did not send Sally back to Monticello alone.[169] There is no contemporary evidence that Sally lived with Thomas Jefferson and significant evidence that she lived instead across town with the daughters at the Abbaye Royale de Panthemont. Why else would classmates from the Abbaye years later make reference to Sally in letters to Jefferson's daughter Martha?[170]

Mr. Hitchens notes that "[m]ost historians until recently took the view that a sexual liaison was literally unthinkable" because of the "revulsion that it is simply assumed that Jefferson must have felt, either for any carnal knowledge of a slave or ... any carnal knowledge of a black woman."[171] Jefferson's belief that blacks were less attractive than whites was well-documented in his *Notes on the State of Virginia* written shortly before Sally came to Paris, as was his outrage over the sexual exploitation of slave women by their masters.[172]

At another point Hitchens informs his readers that it is "probable" that Sally Hemings was literate, even though there is no evidence to support that belief and her son is alleged to have claimed that he learned to read and write by persuading Jefferson's grandchildren to teach him.[173] Hitchens acknowledges that "[a]ll we have is the testimony of her son Madison Hemings that she had while in Paris exacted a promise from Jefferson to free any children she had with him as soon as they achieved adulthood. And the 'only' evidence for that promise is that he did indeed free them, all of them, and *no other slaves*, ever."[174]

This is obviously not true. There is credible but not conclusive evidence that favored slaves Great George and his wife Ursula (both unrelated to the Hemings) were given their freedom in 1781,[175] and it is clearly established that Sally's brothers Robert and

---

167. *Id.* at 62.

168. *Id.* at 60.

169. *See* page 74.

170. James A. Bear, Jr., *The Hemings Family of Monticello,* Virginia Cavalcade, (Autumn 1979), 85. *See also* 16 Papers of Thomas Jefferson xxxi (1961).

171. Hitchens, Thomas Jefferson 61.

172. Thomas Jefferson, Notes on the State of Virginia Query XIV, *reprinted in* 2 The Writings of Thomas Jefferson 193–94 (Mem. ed. 1903).

173. Hitchens, Thomas Jefferson 62. *See* Chapter Two of my Individual Views at pages 78, 116.

174. Hitchens, Thomas Jefferson 62 (emphasis added).

175. Their son Isaac, a Monticello blacksmith whose statement forms the basis for the book *Memoirs of a Monticello Slave,* asserted that was a result of extraordinary services rendered Governor Jef-

James were legally manumitted by Jefferson in 1794 and 1796, respectively. Further, only two of the five slaves given their freedom in Jefferson's will were children of Sally Hemings.[176]

Then we find this language:

> When they left for America, with Jefferson insisting that she [Sally] be berthed next to him on shipboard, it has been suggested by some historians that Sally was pregnant though the child, if there was a child, did not survive. But all her subsequent children, duly entered into the log of Jefferson's "farm book" at Monticello, were born exactly nine months after one of his much-punctuated sojourns at the house. No other possible father was present at all such times, which would seem to take care of the disgusting and unwarranted suggestion, made by several eminent historians, that Sally Hemings might have been giving or even selling herself to any male member of the Jefferson family.[177]

One wonders where to start in responding to this. Thomas Jefferson did not insist that Sally Hemings be berthed next to *him* on the ship back to Virginia—he asked for a berth for a woman servant "convenient to that of my daughters...."[178] Since Sally's job was to be their maid, that request made considerable sense. But since Martha and Maria were also likely to be located near their father's cabin, had Jefferson wanted to have passionate sex with Sally on the cruise home one might have expected him to ask instead that Sally's room be located *away* from that of his daughters—ideally in a secluded part of the ship where he could find privacy. The sole source for the report that Sally may have been pregnant during the trip home is the very problematic 1873 *Pike County Republican* article discussed in Chapter 4. I have seen no historical work making reference to the possibility that Sally was pregnant when she returned to Monticello in 1789 that did not appear to be based, directly or indirectly, upon the problematic 1873 newspaper article.[179]

Whatever Hitchens means by "exactly," he is wrong. As discussed in Chapter Five of my Individual Views, to take the example of Sally's first son, Beverly, nine months before his birth would have been July 1, 1797. Jefferson's records clearly establish that he did not arrive at Monticello for another ten days.[180] That doesn't mean he could not have fathered Beverly Hemings, but it does demonstrate the silliness—and factual inaccuracy—of using the word "exactly" in this context.

---

ferson when he had to flee Richmond to evade the oncoming British, and Jefferson's records of his "taxable property" for the following year records "129 slaves, 2 free." *See* Chapter Two at p. 81.

176. John Hemings was Sally's brother, and Joe Fossett and Burwell Colbert were the sons of Sally's sisters Mary and Bett. *See* Chapter Two at pp. 142–46.

177. HITCHENS, THOMAS JEFFERSON 64.

178. *Jefferson to James Maurice*, Sept. 16, 1789, in 15 PAPERS OF THOMAS JEFFERSON 433 (1958). This letter is discussed in Chapter Six of my Individual Views at p. 149.

179. By this I mean I am unaware of any independent historical source for such speculation other than the *Pike County Republican* article. Callender argued in September 1802 that Jefferson's alleged son "Tom" was "ten or twelve years of age," but he did not specifically allege Sally was pregnant in Paris.

180. *See* Chapter Five of my Individual Views at pp. 126–27. In reality, "nine months" is but a rough approximation of the human gestation period, which is usually closer to 266 days. Jefferson's records reveal that Beverly was born on April 1, 1798. Sally's most likely conception date for Beverly would thus have been July 9 of the previous year. The four-week conception window would have begun about June 25, 1797, and Jefferson's records clearly establish that he did not return to Monticello unti July 11. Thus, for more than sixteen of Sally's twenty-eight-day conception window (roughly three-fifths), Thomas Jefferson was *not* present at Monticello.

Nor can anyone say with full confidence that "[n]o other possible father was present at all such times" (as we simply don't know the whereabouts of many of the theoretically possible fathers in this drama) — and, far more importantly, there is no reason to *assume* that there could have been but a single father. (Madison Hemings, after all, is said to have testified that Sally's mother gave birth to children by no fewer than four different fathers.[181]) As for the "disgusting and unwarranted suggestion" allegedly "made by several eminent historians," that "Sally Hemings might have been giving or even selling herself" — Mr. Hitchens seems ignorant of the fact that the "suggestion" that Sally Hemings was "a slut as common as the pavement," who had "fifteen, or thirty" different lovers, was not a creation of "eminent historians" at all. It originated with James Thomson Callender — the author of the 1802 newspaper article that started the rumor that President Jefferson had fathered children with Sally Hemings. I'm unaware of a single serious Jefferson scholar who has alleged that Sally was a prostitute. As far as I could tell, the common belief shared by everyone on the Scholars Commission was that Sally Hemings was most likely a totally innocent *victim* of Callender's virulent racism.

Speaking of Callender, to Mr. Hitchens' credit he observed that Callender was "a scandal-mongering journalistic hack" who had "become a propagandist for Federalism." He added: "Callender was an alcoholic thug with a foul mind, obsessed with race and sex," and "a contemptible bigot who had a political agenda."[182] He got that part right, unlike much of his discussion of the Hemings matter.

Like too many post-DNA writers, Hitchens asserts that "a detailed DNA analysis ... showed an excellent match between blood drawn from Jefferson's and Hemings's descendants," and concludes:

> [T]his precise genetic compatibility entirely excludes Peter and Samuel Carr, Jefferson's nephews, upon whom his white descendants, white society more generally, and "damage-control" historians like Douglass Adair had been willing to place such circumstantial blame or suspicion as might accrue. Circumstances, remarked Emerson, are often persuasive as evidence — "as when you find a trout in the milk." But the evidence we now possess, which is to trout and milk what cream is to coffee, and something rather beyond that, leaves no space for any reasonable doubt.[183]

The only issue about which there can be little serious doubt is that Eston Hemings was fathered by one of the more than two dozen Jefferson men in Virginia in 1807. Only a single Hemings descendant was linked by DNA to a Jefferson father, and if — as long believed by his own descendants and Monticello experts — Thomas Woodson was Sally Hemings' child, the tests proved her "1790" child could not have been fathered by any Jefferson. As discussed in Chapter One of my Individual Views — and readily acknowledged by the scientists involved — the DNA tests said *nothing* about the paternity of Sally's other children. The story passed down by Thomas Jefferson's grandchildren that the Carr brothers had admitted fathering children by Sally Hemings is not at all incompatible with the 1998 DNA tests, which only addressed the paternity of Thomas Woodson and Sally's youngest child Eston.

* * *

On balance, while the report of the Scholars Commission released nine years ago has certainly not ended the debate, criticism of the report on its merits has been rare and

---

181. *See* Chapter Four of my Individual Views, at 87.
182. HITCHENS, THOMAS JEFFERSON 65–66.
183. *Id.* at 64–65.

there seems to be a growing recognition that the case that Thomas Jefferson fathered one or more children by Sally Hemings is far from established fact. It is not insignificant, in my view, that during this period not one of the senior scholars who once championed the Hemings cause has been willing to engage us in public debate on the merits of the controversy.

The mandate of the Scholars Commission was not to examine Thomas Jefferson's attitudes towards slavery, but merely to examine the issue of whether he fathered one or more children by Sally Hemings. Yet, even if one accepts the view that the Callender accusations were unfounded, it will be difficult for many to accept Jefferson as someone worthy of our respect and admiration unless we come to terms with the slavery issue. Why did he own human beings as slaves? Why didn't he grant them their freedom? Why did he not at least free them in his will, as George Washington had done? These are critically important questions that I believe can readily be explained. Indeed, I am working on a short monograph designed for just that purpose. But the task of searching for the truth on this topic is made more difficult by some prevailing social and political trends in the academic community. Scholars who might otherwise wish to counter the new conventional wisdom realize that doing so could come at considerable professional risk.

Multiculturalism and Thought Reform in America

Much of the recent debate about the Jefferson-Hemings controversy has been perceived as having racial overtones. Professor Gordon-Reed and some other scholars have been quite open in their allegation that white historians who did not accept as gospel the 1873 *Pike County Republican* story attributed to Madison Hemings were fundamentally "white supremacists" and are unworthy of the respect of decent people. And since Jefferson himself owned slaves and—with the qualification that his tentative conclusions might easily be explained by the conditions of slavery in which they lived,[184] and that he hoped his concerns would be proven wrong over time[185]—recorded some unfavorable observations about the intellectual capacity and work ethic of his slaves,[186] the very idea of honoring or "memorializing" him is now offensive to many honorable people. Indeed, in recent years it has been suggested by some that Jefferson's image ought to be removed from Mount Rushmore.[187]

As my colleague David Mayer has observed in his own Individual Views,[188] the legacy of Thomas Jefferson has been caught up as well in a cultural war that is going on across the nation and around much of the world. This reality is readily conceded by many who have played an active role in promoting the story that Thomas Jefferson fathered children by Sally Hemings. Discussing a 1993 conference of Jefferson scholars at the Univer-

---

184. JEFFERSON, NOTES ON THE STATE OF VIRGINIA, in 2 WRITINGS OF THOMAS JEFFERSON 200–01 (Mem. ed. 1903).

185. *Jefferson to Rutledge,* July 14, 1787, in 6 WRITINGS OF THOMAS JEFFERSON 173 (Mem. ed. 1903); *Jefferson to Benjamin Banneker,* Aug. 30, 1791. 22 *id.* 97–98. *See also,* MILLER, WOLF BY THE EARS at 76.

186. JEFFERSON, NOTES ON THE STATE OF VIRGINIA, reprinted in 2 WRITINGS OF THOMAS JEFFERSON 194–95, 208.

187. Joseph J. Ellis, *Jefferson: Post-DNA,* 57 WILLIAM & MARY QUARTERLY 129–30 (Jan. 2000).

188. Professor Mayer's views appear on pages 285–307.

sity of Virginia on the occasion of Jefferson's 250th birthday, Professor Joseph Ellis writes: "the conference assumed the character of a public trial, with Jefferson cast in the role of defendant." Ellis continues:

> The chief argument for the prosecution came from Paul Finkelman, a historian then teaching at Virginia Tech, and the chief charge was hypocrisy.... Finkelman thought it was misguided—worse, it was positively sickening—to celebrate Jefferson as the father of freedom.

> If Finkelman was the chief prosecutor, the star witness for the prosecution was Robert Cooley, a middle-aged black man who claimed to be a direct descendant of Jefferson and Sally Hemings [through their alleged first son, Thomas Woodson]. Cooley stood up in the audience during a question-and-answer session to offer himself as "living proof" that the story of Jefferson's liaison with Sally Hemings was true. No matter what the scholarly experts had concluded, there were several generations of African-Americans living in Ohio and Illinois who *knew* they had Jefferson's blood in their veins.... His version of history might not have had the hard evidence on its side, but it clearly had the political leverage. When he sat down, the applause from the audience rang throughout the auditorium. The *Washington Post* reporter covering the conference caught the mood: "Jefferson's defenders are on the defensive. What tough times these are for icons."[189]

Pulitzer Prize-winning historian Professor Gordon Wood, of Brown University, told the 1993 conference that "It's been coming for a long time. Public culture is demanding this change.... We should accept it and even celebrate it."[190]

For many decades, the Thomas Jefferson Memorial Foundation Chair of History at the University of Virginia was held first by the legendary Dumas Malone, whose six-volume biography of Jefferson, *Jefferson and His Time*, won the Pulitzer Prize for History in 1975, and then by Merrill Peterson, who until his death in 2009 was widely regarded as the greatest living scholar of Jefferson's life. After Peterson retired in 1989, the chair was filled by Peter Onuf, whom no one would call a great admirer of America's third President. Onuf organized the 1993 conference. Professor Ellis writes:

> Onuf suggested that Jefferson's stock was definitely going down but that only a few historians were willing to follow Finkelman all the way and transform Jefferson from the ultimate American hero to the ultimate American villain. Scholars were not quite ready to raze the Jefferson Memorial or chip his face off Mount Rushmore. On the other hand, the mindless devotion to the mythical Jefferson that still dominated the popular culture clearly drove serious students of Jefferson to the edge of sanity. And the filio-pietistic tradition represented by Malone and Peterson was certainly dead in the scholarly world.[191]

Again summarizing Onuf, Professor Ellis writes:

> [Jefferson was] a large and obvious target for those ideologically inspired historians and political pundits who went charging back into the American past in search of monstrous examples of racism, sexism and patriarchy to slay, then drag back into the present as trophies emblematic of how bad it was back then. And he was the perfect target for such raiding parties precisely because so

---

189. ELLIS, AMERICAN SPHINX 20–21.
190. Santos, *Scholars Accept DNA Tests*, RICHMOND TIMES-DISPATCH, Mar. 7, 1993 at C1.
191. *Id.* at 22.

many ordinary Americans had so much invested in him. He was a contested prize in the ongoing culture wars. If history was any kind of reliable guide, the more wild-eyed critics were unlikely to win the war, but the growing emphasis on Jefferson as a slave-owning white racist had the potential to erode his heroic reputation, as the critical judgment of scholars seeped into popular culture.[192]

Professor Ellis reports: "Onuf described the emerging scholarly portrait of Jefferson as 'a monster of self-deception'.... For Onuf, the multiple personalities of Jefferson were looking less like different facets of a Renaissance man and more like the artful disguises of a confidence man."[193]

According to Dr. White McKenzie Wallenborn, Professor Onuf was present at a meeting of the Research Committee of the Thomas Jefferson Memorial Foundation during which a draft report was being considered. Dr. Wallenborn pointed to a particular assertion and remarked to the effect that they did not have reliable evidence to prove it was true. At this point Professor Onuf reportedly interjected: "We don't need proof. We are historians. We write history the way we want to."[194]

In an interview with filmmaker Ken Burns, Onuf explained: "Jefferson ... was not a multiculturalist or somebody who celebrated diversity. He believed that diversity would give way in the face of enlightened discourse to a common enlightened understanding."[195] But with the Sally Hemings story, historians have been able to solve the dilemma that one of America's most respected icons was not "politically correct" by the newest standards. Professor Gordon Wood writes:

> [Jefferson] remains a touchstone, a measure of what we Americans are or where we are going. No figure in our history has embodied so much of our heritage and so many of our hopes. It is not surprising therefore that he should not have become a new symbol of our multicultural and multiracial society.[196]

To achieve the goals of "multiculturalism" and "diversity," traditional rules of scholarship are clearly being "relaxed"[197] and a commitment to seeking the truth is now in conflict with the goal of telling the people that which will make them most receptive to supposedly socially desirable outcomes. Professor Annette Gordon-Reed, whose *Thomas Jefferson and Sally Hemings* began the most recent debate on this issue, asserts that "Anything you don't want to believe you don't have to believe."[198]

Writing in the *Washington Post* in early 2001, historian John Ferling observed that "the study of the stereotypical 'dead white male' has gone out of fashion in academe...."[199] A 2002 *New York Times* article about a "radical course" by the operators of George Washington's home at Mount Vernon to "reposition" the first President "for a new era" explained:

---

192. *Id.* at 22–23.

193. *Id.* at 23.

194. White McKenzie Wallenborn, *A Committee Insider's Viewpoint*, in THE JEFFERSON-HEMINGS MYTH 62 (Eyler Robert Coates, Sr., ed. 2001).

195. Peter Onuf Interview with Ken Burns, *available at* http://www.pbs.org/jefferson/archives/interviews/Onuf.htm.

196. Gordon S. Wood, *The Ghosts of Monticello*, in SALLY HEMINGS AND THOMAS JEFFERSON 19, 29 (Jan Ellen Lewis & Peter S. Onuf, eds. 1999).

197. John Ferling, *Sage and Sinner*, WASH. POST. Mar. 4, 2001, Book World 06.

198. Carlos Santos, *Scholars Accept DNA Tests: Jefferson-Hemings Story Echoes in Race Relations Today, They Say*, RICHMOND TIMES-DISPATCH, Mar. 7, 1999 at C1.

199. John Ferling, *Sage and Sinner*, WASH. POST. Mar. 4, 2001, Book World 06.

"When teachers and curriculum planners and textbook authors look at the founding fathers today, they see too many white males," said David W. Saxe, a professor of education at Pennsylvania State University who studies American history textbooks. "George Washington is dissipating from the textbooks. He's still mentioned, but you don't spend a week in February talking about him, doing plays and reciting the farewell address. In the interest of being inclusive, material about women and minorities is taking the place of material about the founders of our country."[200]

Sean Wilentz, the Dayton-Stockon Professor of History and Director of the American Studies Program at Princeton University, wrote in *The New Republic*:

> What, exactly, is stoking the contemporary rage against Jefferson? An anachronistic political correctness, certainly, in which early twenty-first-century personal is the early nineteenth-century political; and an ideological disquietude about the greatest articulator of American democracy, the burden of whose principles might be lifted off certain shoulders if he could be shown to have been a mountebank. Jefferson embodies the Enlightenment, which infuriates both the religious right and the postmodernist left. Trashing Jefferson is also a sure path to attention and fame. Until now, partisans from across the American political spectrum sought to use Jefferson for their own purposes. Today it is fashionable on the left and on the right to debase Jefferson, and score contemporary political points, and pray for the best-seller lists....
>
> At the most recent meeting of the American Historical Association, for example, an audience of academics roared its approval when Joseph Ellis pronounced Jefferson 'the deadest white male in American history'.[201]

If I react more negatively than some to these new trends in scholarship, it may be because for many years my academic focus was on Leninism and the Communist world.[202] I was thus very familiar with campaigns to impose social consciousness in arts, science, and education. I recall reading (and writing) about artists being selected for distinction not on the basis of their virtue and artistic talent but on how well they portrayed the ruling Party's political objectives. Ho Chi Minh once wrote: "Truth is what is beneficial to the Fatherland and to the people. What is detrimental to the interests of the Fatherland and people is not truth."[203] (Of course, it was the Communist Party's responsibility to determine what was "beneficial" to the "Fatherland" and the "people.") During Stalin's reign in the Soviet Union, artists and photographic technicians would be tasked with copying or altering paintings or photographs to remove individuals who had fallen out of favor with Stalin and/or insert images of newly favored Party mem-

---

200. Stephen Kinzer, *Mount Vernon, Alarmed by Fading Knowledge, Seeks to Pep Up Washington's Image*, N.Y. TIMES, July 29, 2002 at E1.

201. Sean Wilentz, *The Details of Greatness: American Historians Versus American Founders*, THE NEW REPUBLIC, Mar. 29, 2004, at 27, 29.

202. In addition to studying Leninism and its implementation in Indochina in preparation for my undergraduate honors thesis in the mid-1960s, and studying North Vietnam and its front organization in South Vietnam while an army officer assigned to the American Embassy in Saigon, I spent several years at Stanford's Hoover Institution on War, Revolution and Peace researching various aspects of international Communism. In addition to writing *Vietnamese Communism: Its Origins and Development* (1975), I served for two years as Associate Editor of the Hoover Institution's *Yearbook on International Communist Affairs*.

203. 4 HO CHI MINH, SELECTED WORKS 175–76 (1962), *quoted in* TURNER, VIETNAMESE COMMUNISM: ITS ORIGINS AND DEVELOPMENT 114 (1975).

bers.[204] Such behavior is not conducive to democratic governance, or a respect for historical truth.

When in 2000 I read stories about University of Wisconsin officials altering a photograph of students watching a football game to insert the image of an African-American student (who had never attended a football game at the school), so the photograph could be used on the cover of an undergraduate application document and reflect the "diversity" the officials wished to portray,[205] it troubled me. I am all for having diverse student bodies and faculties at our colleges and universities and also for efforts to make minority students feel welcome and comfortable in this process. But when universities or other institutions conclude it is appropriate to alter photographs or other documents to deceive their prospective students into believing something that may not be true, where do we draw the line at other forms of dishonesty—and what message are we giving our students when such duplicity becomes known? If we teach our historians that it is acceptable to rewrite or invent history to promote a desirable social attitude, who is to be empowered to determine *which* social attitudes it is permissible to deceive our students and the public about? One does not have to be so naïve as to believe that all "facts" taught as history over the years accurately reflect reality in order to be troubled by a pedagogy that permits the intentional falsification of truth within our universities to promote some political end. Certainly such an approach undermines Jefferson's belief that our universities should be premised upon "the illimitable freedom of the human mind," that the goal of education is "to follow truth wherever it may lead," and that error may be tolerated "so long as reason is left free to combat it."[206] In my view, the use of universities to deceive the people is incompatible with the concept of a free people associated in a democratic government dedicated to human freedom and decision by the will of the people.

Conclusion

The allegation that Thomas Jefferson fathered children by Sally Hemings began as part of a blackmail threat by a disreputable journalist with no apparent first-hand knowledge of the facts. His case was premised upon the theory that while U.S. Minister to France Jefferson had begun a sexual relationship with Sally Hemings that produced a son named "Tom," and the story gained some credibility when Thomas Woodson claimed after Jefferson's death that he was in fact that child. But six DNA tests of descendants of three sons of Thomas Woodson have established that Thomas Woodson could not have been the son of any man carrying the Jefferson Y chromosome.

Most of Thomas Jefferson's friends and many of his political enemies rejected the charge, in part because it was so out of character for Jefferson and in part because the author of the charge was well known for defaming popular political figures. Throughout most of the past two centuries, serious Jefferson scholars have either ignored the charge altogether or dismissed it as false. It received new life in 1974 with the publication of Fawn Brodie's biography, but few scholars found her speculative arguments persuasive at the time.

---

204. *See, e.g.,* DAVID KING, THE COMMISSAR VANISHES: THE FALSIFICATION OF PHOTOGRAPHS AND ART IN STALIN'S RUSSIA (1997).

205. *See, e.g., Ethical Issues on Campus: University of Wisconsin Officials Doctor Photograph,* JOURNAL OF COLLEGE AND CHARACTER, *available at* http://www.collegevalues.org/ethics.cfm?id=288&a=1.

206. *Jefferson to William Roscoe,* Dec. 27, 1820, in 15 WRITINGS OF THOMAS JEFFERSON 303 (Mem. ed. 1904).

The pendulum began to shift with the 1997 publication of Professor Annette Gordon-Reed's *Thomas Jefferson and Sally Hemings*, which the following year was reinforced by misleading reports about DNA tests that showed Sally Hemings' youngest son, Eston, was probably fathered by one of the more than two dozen Jefferson males in Virginia at the time of his conception. As discussed in my Individual Views, there are numerous inaccuracies in the Gordon-Reed volume, and there were at least six other Jefferson males who were likely at Monticello when Eston was conceived. For various reasons, all but one of them may have been a more likely candidate for Eston's paternity than the elderly President. The most likely candidate is probably Thomas Jefferson's younger brother Randolph, who is documented by a slave memoir to have spent his nights at Monticello socializing and dancing with his brother's slaves, is reported to have fathered children by other slaves, and is the only "suspect" who is consistent with the oral traditions passed down by Eston's descendants prior to the mid-1970s. For generations the story was told that Eston was not the President's child, but rather the child of a Jefferson "uncle" — and the President's brother was widely known at Monticello as "Uncle Randolph" because of his relationship to Jefferson's daughters.

It is my hope that our report will at minimum help to correct some of the mythology that has grown up around this issue in recent years. The ninety-two-percent margin by which the members of the Scholars Commission concluded that the allegation is probably false should at least give those otherwise inclined to accept the charge reason to pause, as should the fact that the leading scholars who embraced the argument that Thomas Jefferson fathered children by Sally Hemings prior to the release of our report have been unwilling to defend that position in public debate.

Clearly, the legend of Sally Hemings has experienced major setbacks since the start of the new millennium. Professor Gordon-Reed's account has suffered from the disclosure that key historical evidence she relied upon was altered to materially change its meaning. The dilemma we encountered in trying to reconcile Professor Joseph Ellis' distinguished reputation as a scholar with his misstatement that the DNA tests had proven the case against President Jefferson "beyond a reasonable doubt"[207] became a bit easier for some when, two months after our report was released, the *Boston Globe* disclosed that Professor Ellis had a long history of telling falsehoods to his students, colleagues, and others.

As someone who has long admired Professor Ellis, but at the same time is persuaded that his conclusions on the Sally Hemings issue are profoundly wrong, I take some satisfaction from a prediction he made in an article published in the *William & Mary Quarterly* in January 2000 — perhaps the zenith of what I perceive to be the Sally Hemings myth. He wrote: "If the American past were a gambling casino, everyone who has bet against Jefferson has eventually lost. There is no reason to believe it will be different this time."[208]

---

207. Ellis, *Jefferson: Post-DNA*, p. 126.
208. *Id.* at 129.

Index